Architect's Legal Handbook
The Law for Architects

Sixth edition

Edited by

Anthony Speaight QC
Gregory Stone QC

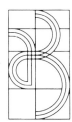

Butterworth Architecture

Butterworth Architecture
An imprint of Butterworth-Heinemann
Linacre House, Jordan Hill, Oxford OX2 8DP
A division of Reed Educational & Professional Publishing Ltd

ℛ A member of the Reed Elsevier plc group

OXFORD   BOSTON   JOHANNESBURG
MELBOURNE   NEW DELHI   SINGAPORE

First published in 1973 by the Architectural Press Ltd
Second edition 1978
Third edition 1982
Fourth edition 1985
Reprinted 1987
Reprinted 1989 by Butterworth Architecture
Fifth edition 1990
Sixth edition 1996

British Library Cataloguing in Publication Data
Architect's Legal Handbook: Law for
Architects – 6 Rev. ed
  I. Speaight, Anthony   II. Stone, Gregory
  344.1037872

ISBN 0 7506 2161 3

Library of Congress Cataloguing in Publication Data
Architect's legal handbook: the law for architects/[edited by]
  Anthony Speaight, Gregory Stone – 6th ed.
  p.   cm.
  Includes bibliographical references and index.
  ISBN 0 7506 2161 3
  1. Architects – Legal status, laws, etc. – Great Britain.
  2. Building laws – Great Britain.   I. Speaight, Anthony.   II. Stone,
  Gregory, MA.
  KD2978.A35
  343.41′07869–dc20   95–37724
  [344.1037869]   CIP

Printed in Great Britain

Architect's Legal Handbook

Contents

Editors' Preface

The aim of this book is to set out within the compass of a single volume a summary of the law relevant to the work of architects. In this new edition, as in its predecessors, the route towards that aim has been to assemble chapters contributed by different authors, each of whom is a specialist in his or her field.

Our contributors are drawn from a wide range of backgrounds. On this occasion the English contributors comprise two Queen's Counsel, four other barristers, four solicitors, two architects, one academic lawyer, one building control officer, one insurance consultant and one judge. The Scottish contributors are one Queen's Counsel, three solicitors and one building consultant. It would be invidious to single out any of them for special mention. For their patience, for their enthusiasm for the project of this book, and for their skills, we are deeply grateful to them all.

In the case of past contributors, however, we can feel a little less constricted from making special mentions. Therefore, we should not like the occasion to pass without an acknowledgment of the contribution to this book in its early editions from Donald Keating QC, who died very recently. Not only was he the leading construction lawyer of his day, but he transformed the study of the law of building contracts from a despised backwater to the place of respect which it now occupies. An acknowledgment is also appropriate to the loyal service to this work of Charles Harpum, whose appointment as a Law Commissioner precludes his continued participation. We hope our younger contributors will in due course proceed to equivalent distinctions.

The material in this edition has been grouped in what we hope will be found to be a more logical arrangement. The chapters are now organized in the following four sections. The first deals with general principles of the law. The second is a study of the area of the law with which architects are, perhaps, more concerned than any other, namely, the law of building contracts. The third covers statutory regulations – planning, building, and health and safety – and the statutory authorities who administer them, together with European directives. The fourth is concerned with the architect in practice – how he organizes his office and employs his staff, his own contracts of appointment and his own liabilities, and his standards of professional conduct. We are indebted to Dr David Chappell RIBA for the germ of this idea, but any readers who dislike it must blame us alone for our implementation of it.

There are two wholly new chapters, both at the suggestion of architect readers. They are on health and safety law, and the use by architects of direct access to the Bar for legal advice. The chapter on tort is totally rewritten, and fully reflects the recent

upheaval in the law of negligence. Chapter 11 contains a new section on Alternative Dispute Resolution.

The last five years has seen many developments. Amongst many new cases discussed in the book are the House of Lords' decisions *Murphy* v *Brentwood DC* (1991) and *Henderson* v *Merrett* (1994) on the law of negligence and *Linden Gardens* v *Lenesta Sludge* (1993) on assigning contractual rights of action. The book also discusses the impact of the Court of Appeal's decision in *Crown Estates* v *Mowlem* (1994) which would win any prizes offered for either the decade's worst decision in law or the decade's worst news for architects. Recent statutes covered include the Sale and Supply of Goods Act 1994, the Building (Amendment) Regulations 1994 and the Clean Air Act 1993. The new regulations with which we have done our best to cope include the new CDM regime for health and safety, the Unfair Terms in Consumer Contracts Regulations 1994 and the European public procurement regulations. Last, but far from least in impact on the text of this book, have been the changes to standard forms of contract, including the Standard Form of Agreement for the Appointment of an Architect (SFA 92), the British Property Federation's forms of collateral warranty and many new building contract forms. It would be impossible to furnish a commentary on all the building contracts, but we have a full discussion of the JCT's 1991 method of nominated sub-contracting, and, for the first time, a section on how to select the contract best suited to a particular situation.

None of this is intended to turn architects into fully fledged legal advisers. But we hope that the book will serve to identify for architects the legal issues affecting their work, and to alert them to the circumstances in which professional legal advice is necessary. Nothing less would be good enough for the architect in practice today. Unrealistic as some of us may consider the law's standard to be, the hard fact is that judges expect architects either to know the law themselves or to advise their clients that legal advice is necessary. In *West Faulkner Associates* v *London Borough of Newham* (1994) an architect's interpretation of 'regularly and diligently' in clause 25 of JCT 1963 was different to the judges'. The Court of Appeal said he would have been 'fireproof' if he had taken legal advice; but he had not, so he was not, and a heavy judgment against him for professional negligence was the result.

Anthony Speaight
Gregory Stone

1995

Acknowledgements

Acknowledgement is given to the following bodies for permission
to use sample documents and statutory publications:

Architects' Registration Council of the United Kingdom
British Property Federation
Building Employers' Confederation
Her Majesty's Stationery Office
Office for Official Publications of the European Communities
Royal Incorporation of Architects in Scotland
Royal Institute of British Architects
Scottish Building Contracts Committee

The editors would also like to thank Anthony Lavers, Professor of
Law at Oxford Brookes University for compiling the Bibliography,
and Michael Ginn, barrister for compiling the Table of Statutes
and Statutory Instruments, and the Table of Cases.

Contributors

Consultant Editors

Anthony Speaight, QC – Barrister, of 12 Kings Bench Walk, Temple; co-author of *The Law of Defective Premises*; contributor to *Construction Disputes: Liability and the Expert Witness*; contributor of articles on legal topics to the *Architects' Journal*; Chairman of the Editorial Board of *Counsel*, journal of the Bar of England and Wales (1990–94); member of the Bar Council's Direct Professional Access Committee

Gregory Stone, QC – Barrister, of 4–5 Gray's Inn Square, Gray's Inn; co-author of *The Law of Defective Premises*; contributor of articles on legal topics to the *Architects' Journal*; educated in England and France; did postgraduate work in Economics, and worked as Chief Economist to a merchant bank before coming to the Bar; now specializes in planning, administrative and local government work

---

Peter Anderson – Senior Litigation Partner, Simpson & Marwick W.S.; Honorary Legal Adviser, Royal Incorporation of Architects in Scotland; Solicitor Advocate; Past-time Senior Lecturer, University of Edinburgh, Faculty of Law; Solicitor, Supreme Court of Scotland (1975). Extensive experience acting for architects for the past 15 years. Extensive experience in other commercial litigation over the past 20 years

Stephen Bickford-Smith – Barrister. Editor of *Emden's Construction Law*. Consultant editor of *Building Law Monthly*. Practises at 4 Breams Buildings, specializing in construction, property and planning law

Graham Brown, RIBA – Architect and consultant at the Graham Brown Consultancy; Principal Lecturer at University of Portsmouth School of Architecture; Visiting Lecturer at various schools of architecture in UK and overseas; professional practice experience at ARCUK and Architectural Association; founder member of College of Professional Practice and Management and Association of Professional Training Advisers in Architecture

George Burnet – Writer to the Signet. Former secretary of the Scottish Building Contracts Committee from 1964–1987. Previously legal adviser to the Royal Incorporation of Architects in Scotland

Lawrence Davis, MBE, PPIBC – A practising building control officer for 34 years. He served on the Building Regulations Advisory Committee from 1982 to 1991. He is Technical Adviser to, and former President of, the Institute of Building Control, was Editor of the Institute's publication *Building Control* for 7 years and a member of the Council of the British Board of Agrément from 1987–91. Author of *Guide to the Building Regulations*

Martin Dixon – Fellow in Law, Robinson College, Cambridge and University Lecturer in Land Law, Department of Land Economy, University of Cambridge. Sometime Legal Officer to the United Nations in Vienna. He has written extensively on Land Law, including casenotes, comments, articles and two student texts

Richard Dyton, LLB, MSc, AKC – Solicitor; specialist advice to architects and engineers; negotiation and conclusion of international commercial agreements; author of *Eurolegislation in Building Maintenance and Preservation* (2nd edn) and *EC Legislation affecting the Practice of UK Architects and Engineers*; Contributor to SEPIA Newsletter; Series Editor: Butterworth-Heinemann Architects Legal Series

Patrick Elias, QC – Fellow of Pembroke College, Cambridge; lecturer in law at the University of Cambridge; author of *Trade Disputes*; joint author of *Labour Law: Cases and Materials*; editor of the unfair dismissal section of *Harvey on Labour Relations and Employment Law*

Michael Flint – A consultant to Denton Hall, having been the Chairman of that firm and a partner since 1960 except for a period of five years which he spent as an executive in the film industry. He is the author of *The User's Guide to Copyright*, the part author of *Intellectual Property – The New Law* by Flint, Thorne and Williams and of *Television by Satellite – Legal Aspects* edited by Stephen de Bate. He is also Chairman of the Council of the Intellectual Property Institute

Kim Franklin, ACI Arb – Barrister, was called to the Bar in 1984 and practises in the field of construction disputes from the Middle Temple. She is a joint editor of *Construction Law Journal*, a contributing author of *Construction Disputes – Liability and the Expert Witness* and *The Legal Obligations of the Architect*, and an occasional contributor to the *Architects' Journal*

Peter Franklin – Building Control and Fire Safety Consultant. Formerly Senior Building Adviser at the Scottish Office and involved with building control legislation since 1966 as well as active involvement with many BSI committees. He lectures regularly to universities, colleges and professional institutions and has specialist knowledge of the safety in sports grounds and prison and health buildings

Andrew Geddes, MA (Oxon) – Called to the Bar in 1972; while at the Bar he specialized in EEC law writing extensively on that topic in the specialist press. Publications include: *Product and Service Liability in the EEC*, *Protection of Individual Rights under EC Law* and *Public and Utility Procurement*. He was appointed a circuit judge in March 1994 and authorized to sit as a High Court judge in August 1995

Sir Desmond Heap, LLM, Hon LLD, PPRTPI – Solicitor; formerly Comptroller and City Solicitor to the Corporation of London; author of *An Outline of Planning Law* (10th edn); consultant editor of *Encyclopaedia of Planning Law and Practice*; member of the editorial board of *Journal of Planning and Environmental Law*; past President of the Law Society and of the Royal Town Planning Institute; associate of the Royal Institute of Chartered Surveyors; Gold Medalist, RTPI, 1983; Gold Medal Award, Lincoln Institute of Law Policy, Cambridge, MA, USA, 1983

Alan D. Mackay, LLB WS – Solicitor; Partner of Lindsays WS, Edinburgh specializing in Building and Construction Law; accredited by the Law Society of Scotland as a specialist in Construction; considerable experience in arbitration and has lectured on arbitration topics at courses of the Law Society of Scotland, Chartered Institute of Arbitrators and others

Peter Madge, LLM, FIRM, ACII, FCI Arb – Has spent all his career in the insurance and risk management fields; Principal of Peter Madge Risk Consultancies, prior to which he was a Director of Willis Faber where he was Managing Director of Corporate Liability and Managing Director of Willis Wrightson Risk

Management Services Limited; author of many books dealing with liability and construction insurance including *The Indemnity and Insurance Aspects of Building Contracts* and *A Concise Guide to the 1986 Insurance Clauses*; acts as insurance consultant to the Royal Institute of British Architects and the Joint Contracts Tribunal

A. Roderick Males, MA, CIM, RIBA, FRSA – Architect and practice consultant; lecturer and author on professional practice matters; member of various institutional groups and committees

M.S. Matheou, LLB (Hons) – A partner in Lovell White Durrant in the firm's London office where he is dealing with major construction and engineering projects in the UK, in Europe, the Indian sub-continent and the Middle East; previously in Hong Kong; presently working in London, has written one of the standard student text books on civil litigation in Hong Kong, and has recently produced one of the modules in the *Construction Law, Litigation and Regulation* distance learning course

E. Ann Minogue – Having qualified as a solicitor in 1980, Ann Minogue joined the construction department at McKenna & Co specializing principally in non-contentious matters. She was responsible for drafting a number of standard forms of contract including the ACA Form of Building Agreement 1982 and a BPF Edition 1984. She drafted standard forms of BPF collateral warranty as

well as forms for some of the major projects of the 1980s including Canary Wharf and Broadgate

Vincent Moran, MA (Cantab) – Barrister and member of Gray's Inn. He specializes in professional negligence, including architects' and surveyors' negligence. He went to the Bar after studying History at Clare College, Cambridge and working for an American Bank

Dr A.R. Mowbray, LLB (Warw.), PhD (Edin) – Lecturer in Law at Nottingham University; editor of the 5th and 6th editions of *Garner's Rights of Way* and author (with S.H. Bailey and B.L. Jones) of *Cases and Materials on Administrative Law*; author of numerous articles on public law

Angus Stewart, QC, BA (Oxon), LLB (Edin) – 1975 called to Scottish Bar; 1983–88 Standing Junior Counsel to the Department of the Environment in Scotland; Keeper of the Advocates Library

Nicholas Vineall, MA (Cantab and Pittsburgh), Dip L – Barrister and member of the Middle Temple. He specializes in employment, landlord and tenant and contract/commercial work. He went to the Bar after reading Natural Science at Cambridge University and holding a Harkness Fellowship at the University of Pittsburgh

Lana Wood, BA (Cantab), BCL (Oxon) – Barrister and member of Gray's Inn

Part One

General principles of law

1

Introduction to English law

ANTHONY SPEAIGHT QC

1 The importance of law

Ignorantia juris non excusat

1.01 The well-worn maxim that ignorance of the law is no excuse applies with equal force to everyone, including architects. Everyone who offers a service to others and claims expertise to do what he offers has a responsibility to society in general and to his clients in particular to know the law.

Architects and the law

1.02 Architects and other professional people are under a special obligation to have a sound working knowledge of the law in every aspect of the services they give. The responsibility is a heavy one. In matters such as building law and regulations, planning legislation and building contracts, clients seem to expect near infallibility. Architects should always be capable of advising what action should be taken, when and in what circumstances, but readers must realize that architects must never assume the role of barristers or solicitors in offering advice in purely legal matters. At most they should do no more than express their considered opinions, which should be reinforced by knowledge and enlightened judgement. All architects should tell their clients to seek their own legal advice on matters that exceed the knowledge an architect can reasonably be expected to have. Alternatively, architects should suggest that their clients instruct them to obtain legal advice through architects' direct access to the Bar (see Chapter 27).

The legal system – rules of society

1.03 People living in all types of community have one thing in common: mutually agreed rules of conduct appropriate to their way of life, with explicit consequences for failure to observe the rules. This is what law is about. The more varied the activities and the more complex the social structure, the greater is the need for everyone to be aware of the part he or she must play in formulating and observing the rules. In highly developed communities these rules have grown into a complex body of law. In Britain the law is continually developing and being modified as personal rights and social responsibilities are re-interpreted.

The English system of law

1.04 There is no single code of English law such as exists in many countries, though there is an increasing tendency towards codification, and the statute books already contain codes covering many areas of law. Roman law, on which most of the continental codes were based, failed to make a lasting impression in England; Roman laws, like their architecture, disappeared with the legions. Roman influence has survived to a much greater degree in Scotland, where, by the Act of Union of 1707, a largely independent system has been preserved. This accounts for many differences between English and Scottish law (see Scottish sections of this book, particularly Chapter 4).

2 Sources of law

2.01 English law may be conveniently divided into two main parts – unwritten and written – and there are several branches of these.

Common law

2.02 Common law – the unwritten law – includes the early customary laws assembled and formulated by judges, with modifications of the old law of equity (paragraph 3.09). Common law therefore means all other than enacted law (paragraph 2.06), and rules derived solely from custom and precedent are rules of common law. It is the unwritten law of the land because there is no official codification of it.

Judicial precedent

2.03 The basis of all legal argument and decision in the English courts is founded upon the application of rules announced in earlier decisions and is called *stare decisis* (let the decision stand). From this has evolved the doctrine of judicial precedent, now a fundamental characteristic of common law.

2.04 Two factors contributed to the important position that the doctrine of judicial precedent holds today: the Judicature Acts (paragraph 3.12) and the creation of the Council of Law Reporting, which is responsible for issuing authoritative reports which are scrutinized and revised by judges and which contain a summary of arguments by counsel and of the judgments given. It is essential for the operation of a system of law based on previous cases that well-authenticated records of arguments and decisions be available to all courts and everyone required to advise on the law.

Authority of a judgment

2.05 Legally, the most important part of a judgment is that where the judge explains the principles on which he has based his decision. A judgment is an authoritative lecture on a branch of the law; it includes a *ratio decidendi* (the statement of facts or grounds for the decision) and one or more *obiter dicta* (things said by the way, often not directly relevant to the matters at issue). It is the *ratio decidendi* which creates precedents for the future. Such precedents are binding on every court with jurisdiction inferior to the court which gave the decision; even courts of equal or superior jurisdiction seldom fail to follow an earlier decision. Until recently both the Court of Appeal and the House of Lords regarded themselves as bound by their own decisions. The House of Lords has to some extent freed itself from this limitation but took the opportunity in *Davis* v *Johnson* [1978] 1 All ER 84 of stating that the Court of Appeal remains strictly bound by its own decisions.

Legislation

2.06 Legislation – the written or enacted law – comprises the statutes, acts and edicts of the sovereign and his advisers. Although historically enacted law is more recent than common law because Parliament has been in existence only since the thirteenth century, legislation by Acts of Parliament takes precedence over all other sources of law and is absolutely binding on all courts while it remains on the statute books. If an Act of Parliament conflicts with a common law rule, it is presumed that Parliament was aware of the fact and that there was a deliberate intention that it should do so.

2.07 All legislation must berive its authority directly or indirectly from Parliament; the only exception being that in cases of national emergency the Crown can still legislate by Royal Proclamation. In its statutes, Parliament usually lays down general principles, and in most legislation Parliament delegates authority for carrying out the provisions of statutes to non-parliamentary bodies. Subordinate legislation is required which may take the form of Orders in Council (made by the government of the day – in theory by the sovereign in Council), regulations, statutory instruments or orders made by government departments, and the by-laws of statutory undertakings and local authorities.

2.08 The courts are required to interpret Acts in accord with the wording employed. They may not question or even discuss the validity of the enactment. Rules have been established to help them interpret ambiguities: there is a presumption that Parliament in legislative matters does not make mistakes, but in general this principle does not apply to statutory instruments unless the governing Act says anything to the contrary. The courts may decide whether rules or orders are made within the powers delegated to the authorized body ordered to make them, or whether they are *ultra vires* (outside the body's power). By-laws must not only be *intra vires* but also reasonable.

Branches

2.09 Of the branches of the law, those with the greatest general effect are civil law and criminal law; others are ecclesiastical (canon), military and naval, and administrative laws. These latter derive more than most from Roman law.

Civil law

2.10 Civil law is related to the rights, duties, and obligations of individual members of the community to each other, and it embraces all the law to do with family, property, contract, commerce, partnerships, insurance, copyright and the law of torts. The latter governs all actionable wrongs against persons and property – actions for damages, such as defamation, trespass, nuisance, negligence and a wide variety of other matters.

Criminal law

2.11 Criminal law deals with wrongful acts harmful to the community and punishable by the State. Except when wrongful action may fall within the scope of both civil and criminal wrong, architects are usually concerned with civil law.

European Community law

2.12 Since 1 January 1973 there has been an additional source of law: that is the law of the European Community. By our accession treaty Her Majesty's Government undertook that the United Kingdom would accept the obligations of membership of the three original European Communities, that is the Coal and Steel Community, the Economic Community and the Atomic Energy Com-

munity. That commitment was honoured by the enactment of the European Communities Act 1972. Section 2(1) of the 1972 Act provided that all directly applicable provisions of the treaties establishing the European Communities should become part of English law; so, too, would all existing and future Community secondary legislation. Since the terms of the treaties are in the main in very general terms, most detailed Community policy is embodied in secondary legislation. Most major decisions are taken in the form of 'directives', which require member states to achieve stated results but leave it to the member state to choose the form and method of implementation. Other Community decisions, known as 'regulations', have direct effect.

In consequence, there is today an ever growing corpus of European Community decisions incorporated into English law. This topic is discussed more fully in Chapter 18.

3 Legal history
Origins of English law

3.01 The roots of English law lie deep in the foundations of English history. The seeds of custom and rules planted in Anglo-Saxon and earlier times have developed and grown gradually into a modern system of law. The Normans interfered little with common practices they found, and almost imperceptibly integrated them with their own mode of life. William I did not regard himself as a conqueror, but claimed to have come by invitation as the lawful successor of Edward the Confessor – whose laws he promised to re-establish and enforce.

Feudal system and land law

3.02 The Domesday Book (1086), assembled mainly by itinerant judges for taxation purposes, provided William I with a comprehensive social and economic survey of his newly acquired lands. The feudal system in England was more universally applied than it was on the Continent – a result perhaps of the thoroughness of the Domesday survey. Consequently, in England feudal law was not solely a law for the knights and bishops of the realm, nor of some parts of the country alone: it affected every person and every holding of land. It became part of the common law of England.

3.03 To the knowledge acquired from Domesday, the Normans applied their administrative skills; they established within the framework of the feudal system new rules for ownership of land, new obligations of loyalty to the adminstration under the Crown, and reorganized arrangements for control of the people and for hearing and judgement of their disputes. These were the true origins of our modern legal system.

3.04 Ultimate ownership of land in England is still, in theory, in the Crown. The lord as 'landowner' merely held an 'estate' or 'interest' in the land, directly or indirectly, as tenant from the king. A person holding an estate of the Crown could, in turn, grant it to another person, but the ownership still remained in the Crown. The tenant's 'interest' may have been of long or short duration and as varied as the kinds of services that might be given in return for the 'estate'. In other words, many different estates and interests in land existed. Tenure and estate are distinct. 'Tenure' refers to the relation of the landlord to his overlord, at its highest level to the king. 'Estate' refers to the duration of his interest in the land, and has nothing whatever to do with the common use of the word.

Possession not ownership

3.05 English law as a result has never used the concept of ownership of land but instead has concentrated on the fact of 'possession', mainly because ownership can refer to so many things and is ill-fitted to anything so permanent and immovable as a piece of land. A man's title to land in England is based on his being able to prove that he has a better right to possession of it than anyone else who claims it.

Real and personal property

3.06 Law makes a distinction between 'real' and 'personal' property. The former are interests in land other than leasehold interests; the latter includes leasehold interests and applies to movable property (personal property and chattels). A leasehold interest in land is classed as 'personal' rather than 'real' property because in early times it was not possible to recover a leasehold interest by 'real' actions for the return of the thing (*res*). In common law a dispossessed owner of freehold land could bring an action for recovery of possession, and an order would be made for the return to him of his land. For the recovery of personal (tangible or movable) articles his remedy was limited to a personal action in which the defendant had the option of either returning the property or paying its value.

Beginnings of common law

3.07 Foundations of both the common law and the courts of justice were laid by Henry II (1154–1189). In his reign the 'king's justice' began to be administered not only in the King's Court – the *Curia Regis* – where the sovereign usually sat in person and which accompanied him on his travels about the country, but also by justices given commissions of assize directing them to administer the royal justice systematically in local courts throughout the whole kingdom. In these courts it was their duty to hear civil actions which previously had been referred to the central administration at Westminster. It was the judges of assize who created the common law. On completion of their circuits and their return to Westminster they discussed their experiences and judgments given in the light of local customs and systems of law. Thus a single system common to all was evolved; judge-made in the sense that it was brought together and stated authoritatively by judges, but it grew from the people in that it was drawn directly from their ancient customs and practices.

3.08 Under the able guidance of Edward I (1272–1307) many reforms were made, notably in procedures and mainly in the interest of the subject as against the royal officials and the law began to take its characteristic shape. Three great common law courts became established at Westminster:

1. The King's Bench, broadly for cases in which the Crown had interest.
2. Common pleas, for cases between subject and subject.
3. Exchequer, for those having a fiscal or financial aspect.

However, as adminstered in these courts, the common law was limited in its ability to meet every case. This led to the establishment of the principles of equity.

Equity

3.09 In the Middle Ages the common law courts failed to give redress in certain types of cases where redress was needed, either because the remedy the common law provided (i.e. damages) was unsuitable or because the law was defective in that no remedy existed. For instance, the common law did not recognize trusts and at that time there was no way of compelling a trustee to carry out his obligations. Therefore disappointed and disgruntled litigants exercised their rights of appeal to the king – the 'fountain of all justice'. In due course, the king, through his Chancellor (keeper of his conscience, because he was also a bishop and his confessor), set up a social Court of Chancery to deal with them.

Rules of equity

3.10 During the early history of the Court of Chancery, equity had no binding rules. A Chancellor approached his task in a different manner to the common law judges; he gave judgment when he was satisfied in his own mind that a wrong had been done, and he would order that the wrong be made good. Thus the defendant could clear his own conscience at the same time. The remedy for refusal was invariably to be imprisoned until he came to see the error of his ways and agree with the court's ruling. It was not long before a set of general rules emerged in the Chancery Courts which hardened into law and became a regular part of the law of the land. There is, however, another and even more fundamental aspect of equity. Though it developed in the Court of Chancery as a body of law with defined rules, its ideal from earliest times was the simple belief in moral justice, fairness, and equality of treatment for all, based on the idea of natural justice as opposed to the strict letter of the law. Equity in that sense has remained to this day a basic principle of English justice.

Common law and equity in the nineteenth century

3.11 Up to the end of the fifteenth century the Chancellor had generally been a bishop, but after the Reformation the position came to be held by professional lawyers (of whom the first was Sir Thomas More) under whom the rules of equity became almost as rigid as those of common law; and the existence of separate courts administering the two different sets of rules led to serious delays and conflicts. By the end of the eighteenth century the courts and their procedures had reached an almost unbelievable state of confusion, mainly due to lack of coordination of the highly technical processes and overlapping jurisdiction. Charles Dickens describes without much exaggeration something of the troubles of a litigant in Chancery in the case of '*Jarndyce* v *Jarndyce*' (*Bleak House*).

Judicature Acts 1873–1875

3.12 Nineteenth century England was dominated by a spirit of reform, which extended from slavery to local government. The law and the courts did not escape reform, and the climax came with the passing of the Judicature Acts of 1873 (and much additional and amending legislation in the years that followed) whereby the whole court system was thoroughly reorganized and simplified, by the establishment of a single Supreme court. The Act also brought to an end the separation of common law and equity; they were not amalgamated and their rules remained the same, but henceforth the rules of both systems were to be applied by all courts. If they were in conflict, equity was to prevail.

The Supreme Court 1875–1971

3.13 The main object of the Judicature Act 1873 was an attempt to solve the problems of delay and procedural confusion in the existing court system by setting up a Supreme Court. This consisted of two main parts:

1. The High Court of Justice, with three Divisions, all courts of Common Law and Equity. As a matter of convenience cases concerned primarily with common law questions being heard in the Queen's Bench Division; those dealing with equitable problems in the Chancery Division; and the Probate, Divorce, and Admiralty Division with the three classes indicated by its title.
2. The Court of Appeal – hearing appeals from decisions of the High Court and most appeals from County Courts.

Modern reforms

3.14 In 1970, mainly as the result of recommendations by a Royal Commission on Assizes and Quarter Sessions under the chairmanship of Lord Beeching, Parliament made further reforms among the Chancery Division, the Queen's Bench Division, Commercial court, Admiralty Court, and the newly formed Family Division – the latter for dealing with guardianship, adoption, divorce and other matrimonial matters.

Courts Act 1971

3.15 The Courts Act 1971 then followed, with effect from January 1972, and the object of separating civil from criminal proceedings throughout the country and of promoting speedier trials. The Act established the Crown Court in all cities and main towns for hearing criminal cases in continuous session, leaving the High Court to deal with civil actions. The County Courts, Magistrates' Courts, and the Coroners' Courts remain unaffected by the new changes; but the Act abolished all Courts of Assize and Quarter Session and various other long-established courts of special jurisdiction, such as the Liverpool Court of Passage and the Tolzey and Pie Poudre Courts of Bristol and others whose usefulness had long been in decline.

Courts and Legal Services Act 1990

3.16 Following the Civil Justice Review of 1988 the jurisdiction of the lowest tier of civil courts, the County Courts, was greatly increased. Previously the maximum judgment which they had been able to give was for £5 000. By the 1990 Act an unlimited jurisdiction was conferred on them at the same time that slightly complicated provisions were enacted with a view to securing that claims for over £50 000 would remain in the High Court, claims for under £25 000 would be dealt with in the County Court and claims for between £25 000 and £50 000 could be heard in either court. The result is that building cases and other cases involving architects, are now more likely to be heard in the County Court.

4 Construction cases within the present system

4.01 Most construction industry claims today are heard by Official Referees. Official Referees are judges nominated by the Lord Chancellor to hear 'Official Referees' business'. The definition of such business is a High Court case,

(a) which involves a prolonged examination of documents or accounts, or a technical scientific or local investigation such as could more conveniently be conducted by an official referee; or
(b) for which trial by an official referee is desirable in the interests of one or more of the parties on grounds of expedition, economy or convenience or otherwise. (Rules of the Supreme Court, Order 36, Rule 1)

In practice, however, any substantial building or engineering case is regarded as 'Official Referees' business', and little else figures as such. Therefore, for most practical purposes one can consider there to be a specialist construction division of the High Court. At present there are six full-time Official Referees in London; in addition a number of circuit judges based at important provincial centres have been nominated to handle Official Referees' business in their localities. An anomalous feature of the situation is that Official Referees have a lower status and lower pay than High Court judges, and yet they handle cases of a greater complexity than most High Court work. If their status were to be differentiated from that of ordinary High Court judges, it would be more logical to confer an elevated status upon them. In general Official Referees are extremely popular with court users: the heavy workload brought to their courts at the choice of litigants is the best possible testimony to the skill with which the present Official Referees conduct their work.

4.02 Another tribute to the work of the Official Referees is the fact that a number of innovations in procedure which they pioneered have been copied throughout the remainder of the civil court system. One such innovation was the requirement for prior disclosure of statements of witnesses of fact. Another innovation was a procedure whereby experts would meet to discuss the issues in the case at an 'off the record' meeting with a view to narrowing dispute and identifying the real issues. A third feature of the practice of Official Referee courts recently has been a far greater use of written submissions by advocates. A new chapter in civil procedure is being written by the introduction of a video camera and visual display units into the courtroom of one Official Referee: there seems little doubt that over the next few years they will lead to the introduction of information technology into the daily life of the courts.

4.03 An alternative method of dispute resolution, which is often used in construction cases, is arbitration. This topic is more fully discussed in Chapter 11. An arbitrator has jurisdiction to determine a dispute only if the parties agree. But such agreement is commonly included in contracts. Indeed, almost all standard forms of building or engineering contracts contain arbitration clauses. So, too, does the Memorandum of Agreement between architect and client published by the RIBA for use with the RIBA Architects Appointment (see Chapter 5). The importance of arbitration in the construction field became even greater with the Court of Appeal's decision in *Northern Health Authority* v *Crouch* [1984] 1 QB 644: it was held that where a contract defined parties' obligations with reference to certificates, and conferred on an arbitrator power to 'open up, review and revise' such certificates, only an arbitrator and not a judge could so modify certificates. The *Crouch* decision has created a number of difficulties. It is proposed in the Courts and Legal Services Bill that, if the parties consent, such powers may once again be exercised by a judge.

5 The scheme of this book

5.01 In this edition the chapters have been re-arranged into what it is hoped is a more logical order. The book deals with Scots law as well as English law: so far as possible, we endeavour to identify all respects in which Scots law is different, and not infrequently this involves entirely separate chapters. There are now four main sections of the book:

1. In the first section the reader is offered the general principles of the law. This introductory chapter is immediately followed by chapters setting out the principles of the two areas of English law of the greatest importance to architects, namely contract (Chapter 2) and tort (Chapter 3). A third area of basic English law of relevance to architects, namely land law, is also covered in an early chapter (Chapter 5). There are separate chapters dealing with Scots law, here and later in the book.
2. The next main section of the book deals with what is almost certainly the legal subject of greatest day to day importance to architects, namely building contracts. This section begins with a general introduction. There is a full commentary on the most important of all standard forms, namely the JCT standard form 1980 edition, in which the text of every single clause is reproduced. In the next chapter there is a full discussion of nominated sub-contracting under the current JCT documents, and a briefer discussion of some of the other principal standard forms used on building contracts. When arbitration concerns architects it is usually as an unhappy end consequence of a building contract, and so the arbitration chapter is also in this section.
3. The third section is concerned with statutory authorities (Chapters 16 and 17) and statutory regulations. The latter involves planning, construction regulations, and health and safety regulations. The chapter on European Community law as it affects architects is also included in this section.
4. The final section of the book concerns the architect in practice. It begins with the law affecting the legal organization of an architect's office. It covers the contracts which architects make with their own clients for the provision of their professional services, and contracts which architects enter with non-clients to provide them with a cause of action against the architect if his professional work was faulty (Chapter 21). The next chapter deals with the liability of architects when faulty professional services are alleged (Chapter 22). That is followed by the chapter on professional indemnity insurance to cover architects against such risks. An architect's copyright of his own drawings is dealt with in the chapter on the distinct area of the law of copyright. The ever-changing field of employment law, which affects every architect who employs staff, is the subject of a separate chapter (Chapter 25). The chapter on international work does not, by its very nature, deal with English or Scots law, and so in one sense ought not to be part of this book at all: but the information on the practices in other jurisdictions is invaluable to architects who undertake work abroad, and fits more logically here than anywhere else in this book. The architect in practice is increasingly obtaining legal advice direct from the Bar, which, at the suggestion of architect readers, is now the subject of its own chapter. Finally, this section deals with architects' registration and professional conduct.

2

The English law of contract

NICHOLAS VINEALL

1 Introduction

1.01 The purpose of this chapter is to give an overview of the law of contract: to show both how it relates to other areas of the law, and to describe the general principles on which the English law of contract operates. Although most of the examples are from areas with which architects will be familiar, the principles they illustrate are for the most part general. Other sections of this book deal in detail with specific areas of the law of contract and their own special rules. The general rules described in this chapter may on occasion seem trite and hardly worth stating. Yet it is often with the most fundamental – and apparently simple – principles of law that the most difficult problems arise, and without understanding the framework of contract law, detailed knowledge of any particular standard form of contract is of little use. This chapter condenses into a few pages material which if fully discussed would fill many long books. The treatment is necessarily selective and condensed.

2 Scope of the law of contract

2.01 The criminal law sets out limitations on people's behaviour, and punishes them when they do not conform to those rules. A criminal legal action is between the State (the Crown) and an individual. The civil law is quite different. It determines the liabilities which exist between parties in particular circumstances. The sanctions of the civil law are not (save in most unusual circumstances) punishments, but rather remedies – the law tries to put things 'back to rights'.

2.02 Two of the biggest areas of the civil law are contract and tort. In certain factual contexts they can overlap, and in recent years their overlap has caused the courts great problems, but they are conceptually quite distinct, and it is important to understand the distinction.

2.03 A plaintiff will sue a defendant in contract or tort when he objects to something the defendant has done or failed to do. Sometimes the plaintiff will not have spared a thought for the defendant – indeed may very well not know the defendant – before the objectionable act or omission occurs. For example: the defendant carelessly runs the plaintiff over; the defendant's bonfire smoke ruins the plaintiff's washing; the defendant tramples across the plaintiff's field; the defendant writes a scurrilous article about the plaintiff in the local paper. All these wrongs are torts (respectively negligence, nuisance, trespass and defamation), and the law of torts may impose a liability on the defendant. The law of torts is considered in Chapter 3.

2.04 On other occasions the plaintiff and defendant are parties to a contract, so that before the objectionable event occurs the parties have agreed what their legal obligations to one another shall be in certain defined circumstances. So, for instance, if the plaintiff gets the defendant plumber to install a new sink, and it leaks, or gets the defendant architect to design a house which falls down, or gets the defendant builder to build a house and it is not ready on time, the extent – if any – of the defendant's liability in contract will depend on the contract between them – and on nothing else. Of course, there may be liability in tort as well for the two are not mutually exclusive. But the conceptual distinction is quite clear.

3 What is a contract?

3.01 A contract is a promise or a set of promises which the law will enforce: it is the legal relationship between the parties. Although one often talks of a 'written contract' it is not really the piece of paper which itself is the contract – the piece of paper merely records what the terms of the contract are.

Contracts under seal

3.02 Some contracts have to be made or evidenced in writing, and some contracts have to be made under seal. Either there is literally a wax seal at the end of the document where the parties sign, or there is some mark representing a seal. Any contract may be made under seal, and the seal provides the consideration for the contract (see below). The most important consequence is that the limitation period for contracts under seal is twelve years instead of the usual six (see paragraph 13.01).

Ingredients and recipe

3.03 There are basically three essential ingredients of any contract: intention to create legal relations, consideration, and agreement. The recipe is simple: offer and acceptance. Each of these aspects requires further consideration.

4 Intention to create legal relations

4.01 'If you save me my seat I'll buy you a drink.' 'OK.' Such a casual exchange has all the appearances of a contract, but if the thirsty seat saver tried to claim his dues through a court he would probably be disappointed, for the law will not enforce a promise if the parties did not intend their promises to be legally binding. A moral obligation is not enough.

5 Consideration

5.01 A one-way promise – 'I'll paint your ceiling' – is not a contract, because there is no element of bargain. With the exception of contracts under seal, English contract law demands that there must be consideration to support any contract. Consideration in layman's terms is the other half of the bargain or the quid pro quo: in legal terms it has been defined like this:

> 'An act or forbearance of one party, or the promise thereof, is the price for which the promise of the other is bought, and the promise thus given for value is enforceable.' (*Dunlop* v *Selfridge* [1951] AC 847 at 855.)

There are a number of important rules about consideration.

1. Adequacy of consideration irrelevant

The value of the consideration can be quite disproportionate to the other half of the bargain which it supports. In *Midland Bank Trust Company* v *Green* [1980] Ch 590, a farm worth £40 000 was sold by a husband to his wife for just £500. £500 was good consideration.

2. Consideration must move from the promisee

If A promises B he will build a wall in B's garden, and C agrees to pay A £1 000 for building the wall, there is no contract, for the consideration of £1 000 has not come from the person who benefited from the promise to build the wall. This doctrine is similar in some ways to the notion of privity of contract discussed below.

3. Consideration need not move to the promisor

On the other hand, if A, the builder of the wall, says to B that he wants him to pay £1 000 to the Battersea Dogs Home, then B's promise to do so is good consideration.

4. Consideration must not be past

The general rule (there are some ways round it) is that an act which has already been performed cannot provide consideration to support a contract subsequently entered into. Suppose A gives B £1 000 at Christmas, and at Easter B agrees to build a wall for B 'in consideration of the £1 000'. A cannot sue B if he does not build the wall, for there is no element of bargain, and no consideration supports the promise to build the wall.

5.02 Consideration rarely causes problems in contract law, because it is usually abundantly clear what the consideration is: very often in the contracts architects deal with the consideration for providing works or services will be the fee to be paid for them. But on the rare occasions when consideration is lacking the consequences can be fatal for the aggrieved party, who has no contract on which he can sue.

6 'Agreement'

6.01 The existence of agreement between the parties to a contract is in practice the most troublesome of the three essential ingredients.

6.02 The inverted commas around 'agreement' are intentional. The law of contract does not peer into the minds of contracting parties to see what they really intended to contract to do; it contents itself with taking an objective view and, on the basis of what the parties have said and done, and the surrounding context in which they did so, the courts decide what the parties should be taken to have intended. The court asks whether, in the eyes of the law, they should be considered to have been in agreement.

6.03 To perform this somewhat artificial task the courts use a set formula or analytical framework which can be thought of as the recipe which must be followed by parties to a contract. The recipe is simple: offer and acceptance.

George Cruikshank.

Offer

6.04 An offer is a promise, made by the offeror, to be bound by a contract if the offeree accepts the terms of the offer. The offer matures into a contract when it is accepted by the other party.

6.05 The offer can be made to just one person (the usual case) or it can be made to a group of people, or even to the world at large. The case of *Carlill* v *Carbolic Smoke Ball Company* [1892] 2 QB 484, [1893] 1 QB 256, is an example of an offer to all the world. The defendant company manufactured a device called a carbolic smoke ball, which was intended to prevent its users from catching flu. They advertised it with the promise that they would pay £100 to anybody who used the smoke ball three times a day as directed and still caught flu. The unfortunate plaintiff caught flu despite using the smoke ball, and not unnaturally felt she was entitled to the £100 offered. The Court of Appeal held that the company's advertisement constituted an offer to contract, and by purchasing the smoke ball the plaintiff had accepted the offer, so that a contract was created. Accordingly the plaintiff successfully extracted her £100 from the company.

6.06 Not all pre-contractual negotiations are offers to contract. In deals of any complexity there will often be a lot of exploratory negotiation before the shape of the final contract begins to emerge, and it is not until a late stage that there will be a formal offer to contract by one party to the other.

6.07 Easy to confuse with an offer to contract is an invitation to treat. An invitation to treat is an offer to consider accepting an offer to contract from the other party. Most advertisements 'offering' goods for sale, and also the goods lying on a supermarket shelf with their price labels, are merely invitations to treat. When the prospective purchaser proffers the appropriate sum to the cashier at the desk it is the customer who is making the offer, which can be accepted or rejected by the cashier. It will by now be obvious that the dividing line between an invitation to treat and an offer to contract can be very thin, but the distinction is important.

Acceptance

6.08 The acceptance of the offer can be by word – written or oral – or by conduct.

6.09 An acceptance must be unequivocal and it must be a complete acceptance of every term of the offer. 'I accept your terms but only if I can have 42 days to pay instead of 28' will not be an acceptance, for it purports to vary the terms of the offer. It is a counter-offer, which itself will have to be accepted by the seller. And such a counter-offer will destroy the original offer which it rejects, and which can therefore no longer be accepted. In the old case of *Hyde* v *Wrench* (1840) 3 Beav 334, the defendant Wrench offered to sell some land to the plaintiff for £1 000. On 8 June Hyde said he would pay £950. On 27 June Wrench refused to sell for £950 and on 29 June Hyde said he would pay £1 000 after all. Wrench refused to sell. It was held that there was no contract. Hyde's counter-offer on 8 June had destroyed the initial offer of £1 000 and by 29 June it was too late for Hyde to change his mind.

Revocation and the postal rules

6.10 An offer can be withdrawn or revoked up until such time as it is accepted. An acceptance is of course final – otherwise people would constantly be pulling out of contracts because they had had afterthoughts. Since an offer can be both revoked by its maker and destroyed by a counter-offer, yet matures into a contract when it is accepted, it can be crucial to decide when these events occur.

6.11 An acceptance is generally effective when it is received by the offeror. But if the acceptance is made by posting a letter then the acceptance takes effect when the letter is posted. But revocation by post takes effect when the letter is received by the offeree. The working of these rules is neatly exemplified by the case of *Byrne* v *Van Tienhoven* (1880) 5 CPD 344. There the defendants made an offer to the plaintiffs by letter on 1 October. The letter was received on 11 October and immediately accepted by telegram. Meanwhile, on 8 October the defendants had thought better of their offer and sent a letter revoking it. The second letter did not reach the plaintiffs until 20 October. There was a binding contract because the acceptance took effect before the revocation. The result would have been the same even if the acceptance had been by letter and the letter had arrived with the defendants after 20 October.

Battle of the forms

6.12 These mostly Victorian rules about offer and acceptance may seem rather irrelevant to modern commercial transactions. But there is one context in which they regularly appear: the so-called 'battle of the forms' which takes place when two contracting parties both deal on their own standard terms of business, typically appearing on the reverse of their estimates, orders, invoices and other business stationery.

6.13 A vendor sends an estimate on his usual business form, with his standard terms and conditions on the reverse, and a note saying that all business is done on his standard terms. The purchaser sends back an order purporting to accept the estimate, but on the back of his acceptance are his standard terms, which are doubtless more favourable to him than the vendor's. The vendor sends the goods, and the purchaser pays for them. Is there a contract, and if there is, whose standard terms is it on?

6.14 The purchaser's 'acceptance' and order is not a true acceptance, because it does not accept all the terms of the vendor's offer, since it purports to substitute the pruchaser's standard terms. So the purchaser's order is in legal terms a counter-offer, and this is accepted – in this example – by the vendor's action in sending the goods.

6.15 If there are long drawn-out negotiations as to quantities, prices and so on, all on business stationery containing standard terms, the problems are compounded, and the result, best found by working backwards and identifying the last communication on standard terms, is rather artificial and is rather a matter of luck.

6.16 The courts have tried on occasion to substitute a rather less mechanical analysis of offer and acceptance, looking at the negotiations as a whole (see especially Lord Denning in *Butler Machine Tool Co Ltd* v *Ex-Cell-O Corporation (England) Ltd* [1979] 1 WLR 401 at 405) but this approach has not found widespread judicial acceptance, and it seems that whatever the artificiality of a strict analysis in terms of offer and acceptance it is difficult to find an alternative approach which is workable.

6.17 This topic leads on naturally to the next. Once it is established that a contract exists, what are its terms?

7 Terms of a contract

Express terms

7.01 The most obvious terms of a contract are those which the parties expressly agreed. In cases where there is an oral contract there may be conflicting evidence as to what actually was said and agreed, but with the written contracts with which architects will most often deal, construing the express terms is usually less problematic: just read the document evidencing the contract. The 'four corners rule' restricts attention to within the four corners of the document, and even if the written terms mis-state the intention of one of the parties – perhaps that party had not read the document carefully before signing it – he will be bound by what is recorded save in exceptional circumstances. This is another manifestation of the objective approach of English contract law discussed above.

7.02 It should be noted at this stage that things said or written prior to making a contract may affect the parties' legal obligations to one another even though they are not terms of the contract. This matter is discussed in the section on misrepresentation.

Implied terms

7.03 Implied terms are likely to catch out the unwary. There are three types of implied term: those implied by statute, those implied by custom, and those implied by the court.

Terms implied by the court

7.04 With unfortunate frequency contracting parties discover too late that their contract has failed to provide for the events which have happened. One party will wish that the contract had included a term imposing liability on the other in the circumstances that have turned out, and will try to persuade the court that such a term in his favour should be implied into the contract, saying, in effect, that the court ought to read between the lines of the contract and find the term there.

7.05 There are some particular terms in particular types of contract which the courts will, as a matter of course, imply into contracts of a particular kind. For instance, a contract for the lease of a furnished property will be taken to include a term that it will be reasonably fit for habitation at the commencement of the tenancy.

7.06 More frequently there will be no authority on the particular type of term which is sought to imply. The courts have developed an approach to these problems, based on an early formulation in the case of *The Moorcock* (1889) 14 PD 64. There the owner of the ship *The Moorcock* had contracted with the defendants to discharge his ship at their jetty on the Thames. Both parties must have realized that the ship would ground at low tide; in the event it not only grounded but, settling on a ridge of hard ground, it was damaged. The plaintiff owners said that the defendants should be taken to have given a warranty that they would take reasonable care to ensure that the river bottom was safe for the vessel – and the Court of Appeal agreed. Bowen LJ explained:

'the law [raises] an implication from the presumed intention of the parties, with the object of giving to the transaction such efficacy as both parties must have intended it should have'.

This is called the 'business efficacy' test; but it is clear that the term must be *necessary* for business efficacy, rather than be simply a term which makes better sense of the contract if it is included than if it is not. In *Shirlow* v *Southern Foundries* [1939] 2 KB 206 at 227, Mackinnon LJ expressed the test in terms of the 'officious bystander' which provides a readily memorable – if not always easy applicable – formulation of the rule:

'Prima facie, that which in any contract is left to be implied and need not be expressed is something which is so obvious it goes without saying; so that, if while the parties were making their bargain an officious bystander were to suggest some express provision for it in their agreement, they would testily suppress him with a common, "Oh, of course".'

The officious bystander test is obviously difficult to pass. *Both* parties must have taken the term as 'obvious'. The ploy of trying to persuade a court that a term should be read into the contract in favour of one party is tried much more often than it succeeds. The moral for architects as for any other contracting party, is that the proper time to define contractual terms is before the contract is made, not after things have gone wrong.

Terms implied by custom

7.07 The custom of a particular type of business is relevant in construing the express terms of a contract and may on occasion be sufficient to imply into a contract a term which apparently is not there at all. In *Hutton* v *Warren* (1836) 1 M & W 466, a lease was held to include a term effecting the local custom that when the tenant's tenancy came to an end he would be entitled to a sum representing the seed and labour put into the arable land. There are other examples from the law of marine insurance, many of which are now crystallized in statute law, but

'An alleged custom can be incorporated into a contract only if there is nothing in the express or necessarily implied terms of the contract to prevent such inclusion and, further, that a custom will only be imported into a contract where it can be so imported consistently with the tenor of the document as a whole.' (*London Export* v *Jubilee Coffee* [1958] 2 All ER 411, at 420)

The place of terms implied by custom in the modern law is small; but custom as a guide in construing terms of a contract continues to be of some importance.

Terms implied by statute

7.08 For architects there are two very important statutes which may automatically incorporate terms into their contracts: the Sale of Goods Act 1979 and the Supply of Goods and Services Act 1982. The principal relevant sections of those Acts are fairly straightforward, but of course they have to be read in their context to see their precise effect (see Extracts 2.1 and 2.2).

Extract 2.1 Sale of Goods Act 1979, as amended by Sale and Supply of Goods Act 1994

14.(1) Except as provided in this section and section 15 below and subject to any other enactment, there is no implied condition or warranty about the quality or fitness for purpose of goods supplied under a contract of sale.
(2) Where the seller sells goods in the course of a business, there is an implied term that the goods supplied under the contract are of satisfactory quality.
(2A) For the purposes of this Act, goods are of satisfactory quality if they meet the standard that a reasonable person would regard as satisfactory, taking account of any description of the goods, the price (if relevant) and all the other relevant circumstances.
(2B) For the purposes of this Act, the quality of goods includes their state and condition and the following (among others) are in appropriate cases aspects of the quality of goods –
(a) fitness for all the purposes for which goods of the kind in question are commonly supplied,
(b) appearance and finish,
(c) freedom from minor defects,
(d) safety, and
(e) durability.

(2C) The term implied by subsection (2) above does not extend to any matter making the quality of goods unsatisfactory –
(a) which is specifically drawn to the buyer's attention before the contract is made,
(b) where the buyer examines the goods before the contract is made, which that examination ought to reveal, or
(c) in the case of a contract for sale by sample, which would have been apparent on a reasonable examination of the sample.
(3) Where the seller sells goods in the course of a business and the buyer, expressly or by implication, makes known –
(a) to the seller, or
(b) where the purchase price or part of it is payable by instalments and the goods were previously sold by a credit-broker to the seller, to that credit-broker,
any particular purpose for which the goods supplied under the contract are reasonably fit for that purpose, whether or not that is a purpose for which such goods are commonly supplied, except where the circumstances show that the buyer does not rely, or that it is unreasonable for him to rely, on the skill or judgement of the seller or credit-broker.

Extract 2.2 Supply of Goods and Services Act 1982

12.(1) In this Act a 'contract for the supply of a service' means, subject to subsection (2) below, a contract under which a person 'the supplier' agrees to carry out a service.
(2) For the purposes of this Act, a contract of service or apprenticeship is not a contract for the supply of a service.

13. In a contract for the supply of a service where the supplier is acting in the course of a business, there is an implied term that the supplier will carry out the service with reasonable care and skill.

14.(1) Where, under a contract for the supply of a service by a supplier acting in the course of a business, the time for the service to be carried out is not fixed by the contract, left to be fixed in a manner agreed by the contract or determined by the course of dealing between the parties, there is an implied term that the supplier will carry out the service within a reasonable time.
(2) What is a reasonable time is a question of fact.

15.(1) Where, under a contract for the supply of a service, the consideration for the supply of a service is not determined by the contract, but left to be determined in a manner agreed by the contract or determined by the course of dealing between the parties, there is an implied term that the party contracting with the supplier will pay a reasonable charge.
(2) What is a reasonable charge is a question of fact.

7.09 The terms implied by SOGA and SOGASA can be excluded by express provision in the contract (SOGA, Section 55 and SOGASA, Section 16), although in both cases this is subject to the provisions of the Unfair Contract Terms Act 1977.

8 Exclusion clauses, UCTA, and the Unfair Terms in Consumer Contracts Regulations 1994

8.01 A contracting party, particularly a contracting party with a dominant position relative to the other, may try to include in the contract terms which are extremely advantageous to him in the event that he is in breach of some principal obligation under the contract. The commonest way to do this is to exclude or limit his liability in certain circumstances. A carrier might, for example, offer to carry goods on terms including a clause that in the event of loss or damage to the goods being carried his liability should be limited to £100 per each kilo weight of the goods carried. The consignor of a parcel of expensive jewellery would be little assisted by a finding that the carrier was liable for their loss if the damages he could recover were limited to £100 per kilo.

UCTA

8.02 The Unfair Contracts Terms Act 1977 has an ambit more narrow than its title suggests, but it does impose a series of restrictions on the ability of contracting parties to exclude or limit their liability in cases of breach.

8.03 Section 2(1) of the Act precludes anybody from excluding or restricting their liability for death or personal injury arising from negligence by reference to any contract term or notice, and Section 2(2) precludes any such limitation of liability for loss or damage of any kind resulting from negligence, save where the exclusion satisfies the requirement of reasonableness. The test of reasonableness is basically that the term should be fair and reasonable having regard to the circumstances which were known to the parties when the contract was made (Section 11).

8.04 The Act also affects the ability of parties to exclude their liability for straightforward breach of contract whether or not negligence is involved, although the circumstances are more limited. One section from this important Act will serve to exemplify its operation.

'**3.**(1) This section applies as between contracting parties where one of them deals as consumer or on the other's written standard terms of business.
(2) As against that party, the other cannot by reference to any contract term –
　(a) when himself in breach of contract, exclude or restrict any liability of his in respect of the breach; or
　(b) claim to be entitled –
　　(i) to render a contractual performance substantially different from that which was reasonably expected of him, or
　　(ii) in respect of the whole or any part of his contractual obligation, to render no performance at all,
except in so far as (in any of the cases mentioned above in this subsection) the contract term satisfies the test of reasonableness.'

Even on a cursory inspection of this section its importance will be appreciated as will some of its limitations. As between two large commercial enterprises drawing up a tailor-made contract the section will have no effect since a party does not 'deal as a consumer' if he makes the contract in the course of a business (Section 12). On the other hand, it is important to realize when dealing near the bottom of a contractual chain which ends up with the final consumer, that it may be impossible to transfer to the ultimate consumer the burden of exclusion clauses which the superior members of the contractual chain have been able to impose on the middlemen.

Unfair Terms in Consumer Contracts

8.05 The Unfair Terms in Consumer Contracts Regulations 1994 were made to give effect to an EC directive on unfair terms in consumer contracts.

8.06 These new regulations take effect from 1 July 1995. It is unclear whether they apply retrospectively, but certainly they are of potential significance to contracts made after that date. As is commonly the case with domestic legislation required by European law, the regulations use expressions and ideas which are not well established in English law, and it is too early to be confident about the way in which the courts will interpret this new legislation.

8.07 The regulations apply to contracts where:
　(a) one party is a consumer and
　(b) the other is a seller or supplier,
and can only affect a term which has not been individually negotiated. Employment contracts, and various other types of contract, are excluded from the regulations. A term in a printed contract document will be the most common type of term to be attacked under the regulations.

8.08 A term as to price, or which defines the main subject matter of the contract, cannot be challenged so long as it is in plain, intelligible language.

8.09 But any other type of term can be challenged as being unfair. 'Unfair' means, for the purposes of the regulations, 'a term which, contrary to the requirement of good faith, causes a significant imbalance in the parties' rights and obligations under the contract to the detriment of the consumer'. In determining whether a term satisfies the requirement of good faith, the court must have regard in particular to the strength of the parties' bargaining positions, whether the consumer had an inducement to agree to the term, whether the goods or services were a special order, and the extent to which the seller or supplier has dealt fairly and equitably with the consumer.

8.10 If a contract term is found to be unfair, then it will not be binding on the consumer. The contract is otherwise unaffected.

8.11 The impact of these regulations remains to be seen. It may well be that most terms which are unfair under UCTA will be unfair under the regulations, and vice versa. But the draftsman of a contract, especially a standard form contract, will now have to consider whether the terms he incorporates will satisfy both these regulations and the 1977 Act.

9 Standard term contracts

9.01 Many of the contracts with which architects are involved are standard form contracts. Chapter 8 deals at length with one such contract, the JCT Standard Form of Building Contract, and in other areas other standard form contracts are available. The use of such contracts has a number of advantages. A great deal of experience has gone into drafting these contracts so that many pitfalls of fuzzy or uncertain wording can be avoided. And where the words used are open to different interpretations it may well be that case law has definitively settled their meaning. In effect the user of a standard term contract enjoys the benefit of other people's earlier litigation in sorting out exactly what obligations the standard terms impose. The effects of well litigated and well-established terms and conditions also have an impact on third parties. Insurers in particular will know where they stand in relation to a contract on familiar terms and therefore the extra premiums inevitable on uncertain risks can be avoided.

9.02 One potential problem with STCs can be minimized if it is appreciated. Just as tinkering with a well-tuned engine can have catastrophic consequences, so 'home-made' modifications of STCs can have far-reaching effects. Many of the provisions and definitions used in STCs interlink, and modifying one clause may have unforeseen and far-reaching ramifications. If parties to an STC want to modify it because it does not seem to achieve exactly the cross-obligations they want to undertake, it is highly advisable to take specialist advice.

10 Misrepresentation

10.01 Pre-contractual negotiations often cover many subjects which are not dealt with by the terms (express or implied) of the eventual contract. In some circumstances things said or done before the contract is made can lead to liability.

Representations and misrepresentations

10.02 A representation is a statement of existing fact made by one party to the eventual contract (the misrepresentor) to the other (the misrepresentee) which induces the representee to enter into the contract. A misrepresentation is a representation which is false. Two elements of the definition need elaboration.

Statement of existing fact

10.03 The easiest way to grasp what is meant by a statement of existing fact is to see what is not included in the expression.

A promise to do something in the future is not a representation – such a statement is essentially the stuff of which contracts are made, and the place for promises is therefore in the contract itself.

An opinion which is honestly held and honestly expressed will not constitute an actionable misrepresentation. This is sometimes said to be because it is not a statement of fact and it is perhaps simplest to see this by realizing that it does not make sense to talk of an opinion being false or untrue, so that in any event it cannot be a misrepresentation. But a statement of opinion 'I believe such and such . . .' *can* be a representation and can therefore be a misrepresentation if the representor does not actually hold the belief, because, as Bowen LJ explained:

> 'The state of a man's mind is as much a fact as the state of his digestion. It is true that it is very difficult to prove what the state of a man's mind at a particular time is, but if it can be ascertained it is as much a fact as anything else. A misrepresentation as to the state of a man's mind is, therefore, a statement of fact.' (*Edgington* v *Fitzmaurice* (1885) 29 ChD 459 at 483.)

10.04 A somewhat more surprising line of authority holds that 'mere puff' does not constitute a representation: 'simplex commendatio non obligat'. Hence describing land as 'uncommonly rich water meadow' was held not to constitute a representation in *Scott* v *Hanson* (1829) 1 Russ & M 128. But the courts today are rather less indulgent to exaggerated sales talk and if it can be established that effusive description of a vendor's product is actually untrue it seems that the courts would today be more likely to hold that to be a misrepresentation than would their nineteenth century predecessors.

10.05 Silence generally does not constitute a representation. A vendor is generally under no obligation to draw to the attention of his purchaser the defects in that which he is selling, and even tacit acquiescence in the purchaser's self-deception will not usually create any liability. However, there are cases in which silence can constitute a misrepresentation. If the representor makes some representation about a certain matter he must not leave out other aspects of the story so that what he says is misleading in toto: so although a total non-disclosure may not be a misrepresentation, partial non-disclosure may be.

Reliance

10.06 To create any liability the representee must show that the misrepresentation induced him to enter into the contract – the misrepresentation must have been material. Therefore if the misrepresentee knew that the representation was false, or if he was not aware of the representation at all, or if he knew of it but it did not affect his judgement, then he will have no grounds for relief. But the misrepresentation need not be the only, nor even indeed the principal, reason why the misrepresentee entered into the contract.

The three types of misrepresentation

10.07 If the representor making the misrepresentation made it knowing it was untrue, or without believing it was true, or recklessly, not caring whether it was true or false, then it is termed a fraudulent misrepresentation.

If, however, the representor made the false statement believing that it was true but had taken insufficient care to ensure that it was true, then it will be a negligent misstatement.

Finally, if the misrepresentor had taken reasonable care to ensure that it was true, and did believe that it was true, then it is merely an innocent misrepresentation.

Remedies for misrepresentation

10.08 This is a very difficult area of the law, and the finer details of the effects of the Misrepresentation Act 1967 are still not entirely clear. The summary which follows is extremely brief.

Principal remedy: rescission

10.9 The basic remedy for misrepresentation is rescission. The misrepresentee can in many circumstances oblige the misrepresentor to restore him to the position he would have been in had the contract never been made.

10.10 Rescission is not available if the misrepresentee has, with knowledge of the misrepresentation, affirmed the contract. A long lapse of time before the misrepresentee opts to rescind is often taken as affirmation. Rescission is not available if a third party has, since the contract was made, himself acquired for value an interest in the subject matter of the contract. Nor is it available, almost by definition, if it is impossible to restore the parties to the status quo before the contract was made.

10.11 The court now has a general power to grant damages in lieu of rescission (Misrepresentation Act 1967, Section 2(2)), and may award damages to the victim of a negligent or innocent representation even where the misrepresentee would rather have the contract rescinded instead.

Damages

10.12 The victim of a fraudulent misrepresentation may sue for damages as well as claim rescission, and the measure of damages will be tortious.

10.13 The victim of a negligent misrepresentation may also recover damages (Section 1) as well as rescission. It is not entirely clear how damages should be calculated.

10.14 In the case of an innocent misrepresentation there is no right to damages, but, as already explained, the court may in its discretion award damages in lieu of rescission.

The law of negligent misstatement

10.15 Misrepresentation alone is complicated. The matter is compounded by the availability of damages for the tort of negligent misstatement (rather than misrepresentation), which is discussed in Chapter 3. There will be many instances in which an actionable misrepresentation is also an actionable misstatement.

11 Performance and breach

11.01 All the topics considered so far have been concerned with matters up to and including the creation of a contract – matters generally of greater interest to lawyers than to men of business or to architects. But both lawyers and architects have a close interest in whether or not a party fulfils its obligations under a contract and, if it does not, what can be done about it.

The right to sue on partial performance of a complete contract

11.02 Many contracts take the general form of A paying B to perform some work or to provide some service. It is unusual for the party performing the work or providing the service to do nothing at all; the usual case will be that much of the work is done according to the contract, but some part of the work remains incomplete, undone, or improperly performed. This situation needs to be considered from both sides. We begin with examining whether the incomplete performer can sue his paymaster if no money is forthcoming.

11.03 The general rule of contract law is that a party must perform precisely what he contracted to do. The consequence is that in order to make the other liable in any way under the contract all of that party's obligations must be performed. If the contract is divided up into clearly severable parts each will be treated for these purposes as a separate contract, and virtually all building contracts will of course make provision for stage payments. Nevertheless it is important to be aware of the general rule which applies to a contract where one lump sum is provided for all the works. Non-performance (as opposed to misperformance) of some part will disentitle the partial performer from payment.

11.04 An example is *Bolton* v *Mahadeva* [1972] 1 WLR 1009. There the plaintiff agreed to install a hot water system for the defendant for a lump sum payment of £560. The radiators emitted fumes and the system did not heat the house properly. Curing the defects would cost £174. The defendant was held not liable to pay the plaintiff anything.

11.05 There is an important exception to this rule, even for entire contracts. If the party performing the works has 'substantially performed' his obligations then he is entitled to the contract sum subject only to a counter-claim for those parts remaining unperformed. In *Hoenig* v *Isaacs* [1952] 2 All ER 176, there was a lump-sum contract for the decoration and furnishing of the defendant's flat for the price of £750. When the plaintiff left, one wardrobe door needed replacing and one shelf was too short, and would have to be remade. The Court of Appeal held that although 'near the border-line' on the facts, the plaintiff had substantially performed his contractual obligations and was therefore able to recover his £750, subject only to the deduction of £56, being the cost of the necessary repairs.

Remedies against the incomplete performer

11.06 The flip-side of the situation of suing on an incompletely performed contract is suing the incomplete performer. Obviously incomplete performance or misperformance gives to the other party, who has so far performed his obligations as they fall due, a right to damages to put him in the position he would have been in had the contract been performed. But in some circumstances another remedy will be available to the aggrieved party, for he will be able to hold himself absolved from any further performance of his obligations under the contract.

11.07 This right to treat the contract as at an end arises in three situations.

Breach of a contractual condition

11.08 The first situation is if the term which the non or misperforming party has breached is a contractual condition rather then merely a warranty. It used to be thought that all contractual terms were either conditions or warranties. Whether a term was one or the other might be determined by statute, by precedent, or might have to be decided by the court by looking at the contract in the light of the surrounding circumstances. If the term was a condition then any breach of it, however minor, would allow the aggrieved party to treat the contract as at an end. The modern tendency is to adopt a more realistic approach and to escape from the straitjacket dichotomy of conditions and warranties. In *Hong Kong Fir Shipping Co Ltd* v *Kawasaki Kisen Kaisha Ltd* [1962] 2 QB 26, at 70 Lord Diplock explained that

> 'There are, however, many contractual terms of a more complex character which cannot be categorised as being "conditions" or "warranties" . . . Of such undertakings all that can be predicated is that some breaches will and others will not give rise to an event which will deprive the party in default of substantially the whole benefit which it was intended he should obtain from the contract; and the legal consequences of the breach of any such undertaking, unless provided for expressly in the contract, depend on the nature of the event to which the breach gives rise and do not follow automatically from a prior classification of the undertaking as a "condition" or "warranty".'

These terms which are neither conditions nor warranties have been unhelpfully named 'innominate terms' and although their existence decreases the importance of this first type of circumstance in which an aggrieved party can treat its contractual obligations as at an end, it is nevertheless still open for the contracting parties expressly to make a contractual term a condition, in which case any breach of it allows this remedy in addition to a claim for damages.

Repudiatory breach

11.09 If the breach 'goes to the root of the contract' or deprives the party of substantially the whole benefit the contract was intended to confer on him, then he will be entitled to treat the contract as at an end.

Renunciation

11.10 If one party evinces an intention not to continue to perform his side of the contract then the other party may again treat the contract as at an end.

Election

11.11 In all three of the circumstances described above the innocent party has a choice as to whether or not to treat himself as discharged. He may prefer to press for performance of the contract so far as the other party is able to perform it, and to restrict himself to his remedy in damages. But once made the election cannot unilaterally be changed, unless the matter which gave rise to it is a continuing state of affairs which therefore continues to provide the remedy afresh.

11.12 The rule that the innocent party may, if he prefers, elect to press for performance following (for instance) a renunciation can have a bizarre result. In *White and Carter (Councils)* v *McGregor* [1962] AC 413 the plaintiff company supplied litter bins to local councils. The councils did not pay for the bins, but they allowed them to carry advertising, and the plaintiffs made their money from the companies whose advertisements their bins carried. The defendant company agreed to hire space on the plaintiffs' bins for three years. Later the same day they changed their mind and said that they were not going to be bound by the contract. The plaintiffs could have accepted that renunciation, but, perhaps short of work and wanting to keep busy, opted to carry on with the contract, which they proceeded to do for the next three years. They sued successfully for the full contract price: there was no obligation on them to treat the contract as at an end and they were not obliged to sue for damages only.

12 Privity of contract and agency
Privity of contract

12.02 As was explained in the opening section of this chapter, the distinguishing feature of contract law is that it defines the rights and obligations of two parties between whom there is a contract. A person who is not a party to a contract cannot gain any benefit by suing on it, nor can he suffer any detriment by being sued on it. This principle – which is simplicity itself – is all that is meant by the expression 'privity of contract'. But although the basic notion is straightforward, its application is not always so simple, for it is not always obvious who the parties to a contract are. The law of agency provides the framework within which that question is decided.

The two aspects of agency in contract law

12.02 For A to act as an agent for P his principal, is for A to act as P's representative. A's words or actions will create legal rights and liabilities for A who is therefore bound by what A does. It is just as if P had said or done those things himself. The agent's actions might have consequences for P in contract, or tort, or some other area of the law, but in this chapter it is naturally only with contractual liabilities that we are concerned. In general, if A, as P's agent, properly contracts with C, then the resulting contract is a contract between P and C. A is not privy to the contract, and can neither sue or be sued upon it.

12.03 There are two sets of legal obligations which are of interest. The first is those between the principal and his agent. That relationship of agency may, but need not, itself be the subject of a contract – the contract of agency. For instance, A may be rewarded by a percentage commission on any of P's business which he places with C. If A does not receive his commission he may wish to sue P, and he will do so under their contract of agency. That is a matter between P and A, and of no interest to C. It is governed by the rules for contracts of agency. These rules, just a specialized subset of the rules of contract generally, will not be further discussed here.

12.04 The second set of legal questions raised by an agency concerns how the relationship is created, whether and how it is that A's actions bind his principal, and whether A is ever left with any personal liability of his own. We begin by considering the first of these issues.

Creation of agency

12.05 There are three important ways in which an agency may be created.

1. By express appointment

This is of course the commonest way to create an agency. Generally no formalities are necessary: the appointment may be oral or in writing. To take an example, the employees of a trading company are frequently expressly appointed by their contract of employment to act as the agents of the company and to place and receive orders on its behalf.

2. By estoppel

If P by his words or conduct leads C to believe that A is his agent, and C deals with A on that basis, A cannot escape the contract by saying that, in fact, A was not his agent. In these circumstances P will be stopped, or 'estopped', from making that assertion.

3. By ratification

If A, not in fact being P's agent, purports to contract with C on P's behalf, and P then discovers the contract, likes the look of it and ratifies and adopts it, then, ex post facto, A is P's agent for the purposes of that contract. The precise working of the rules of ratification are rather involved.

Authorization

12.06 The effect of an agent's words or actions will depend crucially on whether or not he was authorized by his principal to say or do them. The agent's authority will usually be an actual authority, that is to say an authority which he has expressly or impliedly been granted by his principal. But the scope of the agent's authority may, most importantly, be enlarged by the addition of his ostensible authority.

12.07 Ostensible authority is another manifestation of the operation of estoppel. If P represents to C that his agent A has an authority wider than, in fact, has been expressly or impliedly granted by P to A, and in reliance on that representation C contracts with P through A, then P will be stopped ('estopped') from denying that the scope of A's authority was wide enough to include the contract that has been made.

The liabilities of principal and agent

12.08 We now consider the liabilities of both principal and agent with the contracting third party C, and the discussion is divided into those cases in which the agent is authorized to enter into the transaction, and those in which he is not so authorized.

The agent acts within the scope of his authority

12.09 This division has three subdivisions, depending on how much the contracting party C knows about the principal. The agent may tell C that P exists, and name him. Or he may tell C that he has a principal, but not name him. Or – still less communicative – he may not tell C that he has a principal at all, so that as far as C is concerned he is contracting with A direct.

1. Principal is named

This is in a sense the paradigm example of agency in action. A drops out of the picture altogether, the contract is between P and C and A can neither sue nor be sued on the P–C contract.

2. Existence of principal disclosed, but not his identity

The general rule is the same as in case 1.

3. Neither name nor existence of principal disclosed to C

This case is described as the case of the undisclosed principal. The rule here is somewhat counter-intuitive: both the agent and the principal may sue on the contract, and C may sue the agent, and, if and when he discovers his identity, the principal.

The agent acts outside the scope of his authority

12.10 The position as regards the principal is clear. The principal is not party to any contract, and can neither sue nor be sued upon it. This of course would have to be the case, for really in these circumstances there is no agency operating at all. But it is important to remember that ostensible authority may fix a principal with liability when the agent is acting outside his express or implied authority.

12.11 The position of the agent is more complex. We first consider the position of the agent as far as benefits under the contract are concerned - whether the agent can sue upon the contract. If the agent purported to contract as agent for a named principal, then the agent cannot sue on the contract. On the other hand, if the name of the principal is not disclosed the agent can sue upon the contract as if it were his own.

12.12 Turning now to the liability of an unauthorized agent to be sued by C, the position depends on what the agent thought was the true position between himself and P. If A knows all along that he does not have P's authority to enter into the contract, then C can sue A, although for the tort of deceit, rather than under the contract.

12.13 If on the other hand A genuinely thought that he was authorized by P to enter into the contract, he cannot be sued by P for deceit – after all, he has not been deceitful, merely mistaken. But C has an alternative means of enforcing his contract. A court will infer the existence of a collateral contract by A (as principal) with C, under which A warranted that he had P's authority to contract. This is a quite separate contract to the non-existent contract which C thought he was entering into with P, but from C's point of view it is just as good, for now C can sue A instead.

13 Limitation under the Limitation Act 1980

13.01 Armed with the information derived from this chapter a prospective plaintiff should have some idea of what his contract is, whether it has been breached, what he can do about it, and who he should sue. There is one more point to consider.

13.02 An action for breach of contract must generally be commenced within six years. Time begins to run – the six years starts – when the contract is breached. This may mean that the plaintiff can sue before any real physical damage has been experienced.

Suppose the defendant is an architect who has, in breach of contract, designed foundations for a building which are inadequate, and it is clear that in ten to twenty years' time the building will fall down if remedial works are not carried out. The plaintiff can sue straight away. Of course, although no physical damage has yet occurred there has been economic loss because the defendant has got out of the contract a building worth much less than what he paid for it, and it is obviously right that he should be able to sue straight away.

13.03 The exception to this rule is that a plaintiff may sue on a contract contained in a deed up to twelve years after the contract was breached. It is for this reason that building contracts – which may take more than six years from inception to completion – are frequently made under deed.

13.04 The law on limitation periods is to be found in the Limitation Act 1980. The law on limitation periods for suing on a tort is different and more complicated, and is explained in Chapter 3.

3

The English law of tort

VINCENT MORAN

1 Introduction

1.01 The law of tort is concerned with conduct which causes harm to the interests of other people. It is the law of wrongdoing. Its aim is to define obligations that should be imposed on members of society for the benefit of all. Its purpose is to compensate (or sometimes to prevent in the first place) interference with personal, proprietary, or, sometimes, non-physical interests (such as a person's reputation or financial position). It therefore provides a system of loss distribution and regulates behaviour within society.

1.02 A general definition is difficult because it is impossible to fit the various separate torts that have been recognized by the common law into a single system of classification. The best that one can say is that torts are legally wrongful acts or omissions. However, to be actionable it is not enough that an act or omission as a matter of fact harms another person's interests in some way. The wrong must also interfere with some legal right of the complaining party.

1.03 The various categories of tortious rights provide the basis for assessing when actionable interference has occurred and when a legal remedy is available. But the law does not go so far as to protect parties against all forms of morally reprehensible behaviour, as Lord Atkin described in *Donoghue* v *Stevenson* [1932] AC 562 at 580:

> 'Acts or omissions which any moral code would censure cannot in a practical world be treated so as to give a right to every person injured by them to demand relief. In this way rules of law arise which limit the range of complaints and the extent of their remedy.'

1.04 A factual situation may give rise to actions in a variety of overlapping torts. Further, the same circumstances may give rise to concurrent claims both in tort and contract (see generally Chapter 2). However, in contrast to the law of contract which effectively seeks to enforce promises, the interests protected by tort are more diverse. Contractual duties are agreed by the parties themselves, whereas tortious duties are imposed automatically. Contractual duties are therefore said to be owed *in personam* (i.e. to the other contracting party only), whereas tortious duties are owed *in rem* (to persons in general).

2 Negligence

2.01 The tort of negligence is concerned with the careless infliction of harm or damage. It has three essential elements, namely (a) the existence of a legal duty of care, (b) a breach of that duty, and (c) consequential damage.

The legal duty to take care

2.02 The concept of the duty of care defines those persons to which another may be liable for his negligent acts or omissions. The traditional approach to defining the situations that give rise to a duty of care was based upon a process of piecemeal extension by analogy with existing cases, rather than on the basis of a general principle. The first notable attempt to elicit a more principled approach occurred in the landmark case of *Donoghue* v *Stevenson* [1932] AC 562. There, the plaintiff, who was given a bottle of ginger beer by a friend, alleged that she had become ill after drinking it due to the presence of a decomposed snail in the bottle. As the plaintiff had no contractual relationship with the seller, since it was her friend who had purchased it from the shop, she attempted to sue the manufacturer in tort.

2.03 The House of Lords held that a manufacturer of bottled ginger beer (or other articles) did owe the ultimate purchaser or consumer a legal duty to take reasonable care to ensure that it was free from a defect likely to cause injury to health. Therefore in principle the plaintiff had a cause of action against the ginger beer's manufacturer. However, the main significance of the case is contained in Lord Atkin's description of the general concept of the duty of care:

> 'The rule that you are to love your neighbour becomes in law, you must not injure your neighbour: and the lawyer's question, who is my neighbour? receives a restricted reply. You must take reasonable care to avoid acts or omissions which you can reasonably foresee would be likely to injure your neighbour. Who, then, in law is my neighbour? The answer seems to be – persons who are so closely affected by my act that I ought reasonably to have them in contemplation as being so affected when I am directing my mind to the acts or omissions which are called in question.'

2.04 What became known as Lords Atkin's 'neighbour principle' was initially criticised as being too broad, but in time it became accepted and remains today the central concept to an understanding of the tort of negligence. In the 1970s there was a more ambitious development of a general principle of liability in negligence. This was based on a 'two-stage test' derived from the decisions of the House of Lords in *Dorset Yacht Co. Limited* v *Home Office* [1970] AC 1004 and *Anns* v *Merton London Borough Council* [1978] AC 728. The first stage involved a consideration of whether there was a reasonable foreseeability of harm to the plaintiff. If so, there would be liability unless, under the second stage, there was some public policy reason to negate it. The piecemeal approach to the recognition of duty of care relationships was now very much in decline.

2.05 The 'two-stage test' was a very wide application of Lord Atkin's dicta and it was at first applied with enthusiasm. However, increasingly it appeared to many judicial eyes to herald an unwarranted potential extension of liability into situations previously not covered by the tort of negligence. As a result there has been a steady retreat from the acceptance of a general principle of liability back to the traditional emphasis on existing case analogy and the incremental approach to the extension of liability situations. This has manifested itself in the development of a 'three-stage test' involving a consideration of (a) foreseeability of damage, (b) the relationship of neighbourhood or proximity between the parties and (c) an assessment of whether the situation is one which in all the circumstances the court considers it fair and reasonable for the imposition of a legal duty.

2.06 Thus, in *Caparo Industries* v *Dickman* [1990] 2 AC 605 Lord Bridge described the judicial rejection since *Anns* of the ability of a general single principle to provide a practical test as follows:

> '... the concepts of proximity and fairness ... are not susceptible of any such precise definition as would be necessary to give them utility as practical tests, but amount in effect to little more than convenient labels to attach to the features of different specific situations which, on a detailed examination of all the circumstances, the law recognises pragmatically as giving rise to a duty of care of a given scope. Whilst recognising, of course, the importance of the underlying general principles common to the whole field of negligence, I think the law has now moved in the direction of attaching greater significance to the more traditional categorisation of distinct and recognisable situations as guides to the existence, the scope and the limits of the varied duties of care which the law imposes.'

2.07 The *Anns* 'two-stage test' was further undermined by Lord Keith in the important recent decision of the House of Lords in *Murphy* v *Brentwood District Council* [1991] AC 398. In relation to the consideration of the duty of care in novel situations Lord Keith commented at p. 461:

> 'As regards the ingredients necessary to establish such a duty in novel situations, I consider that an incremental approach ... is to be preferred to the two-stage test.'

2.08 However, *Murphy* v *Brentwood* and most of the cases connected with this retreat from the recognition of a general principle of liability in negligence have been mainly concerned with the duty of care to avoid causing economic loss (for which see Section 2.16 below). In respect of non-economic loss situations, that the *Anns* approach still provides a useful framework for the consideration of the existence of a legal duty of care. There should be little difficulty in considering whether such a duty exists where either damage to the person or property has been occasioned.

Breach of duty

2.09 In general a person acts in breach of a duty of care when behaving carelessly. As Alderson J stated in *Blyth* v *Birmingham Waterworks Company* [1856] 11 Ex 781:

> 'Negligence is the omission to do something which a reasonable man, guided upon those considerations which ordinarily regulate the conduct of human affairs, would do, or doing something which a prudent and reasonable man would not do.'

2.10 The standard of care required, then, is that of the reasonable and prudent man; the elusive 'man on the Clapham omnibus'. It is not a counsel of perfection and mere error does not necessarily amount to negligence. The standard applied is objective in that it does not take account of an individual's particular weaknesses. However, where a person holds himself out as having a special skill or being a professional (such as an architect), the standard of care expected of him is higher than one would expect of a layman. He is under a duty to exercise the standard of care in his activities which could reasonably be expected from a competent member of that trade or profession, whatever his actual level of experience or qualification. In contrast, however, there are also circumstances where the law accepts a lower standard of care from people, such as at times of emergency or dilemma, or generally in the level of care expected from children.

2.11 The value of the concept of 'reasonable care' lies in its flexibility. What will be considered by a court as 'reasonable' depends on the specific facts of a particular case and the attitude of the judge. Precedent is seldom cited or useful in this respect. However, in general the assessment of reasonableness involves a consideration of three main factors: (a) the degree of likelihood of harm, (b) the cost and practicability of measures to avoid it, and (c) the seriousness of the possible consequences. The application and balancing of these factors is best illustrated by reference to actual cases.

2.12 In *Brewer* v *Delo* [1967] 1 LIR 488, a case which involved a golfer hitting another player with a golf ball, it was held that the risk was so slight as to be unforeseeable and therefore the golfer had not acted negligently. Similarly in *Bolton* v *Stone* [1951] AC 850 the occupiers of a cricket ground were held not to be liable for a cricket ball that had left the pitch and struck the plaintiff because of the improbability of such an incident occurring. Finally, in *The Wagon Mound* (No 2) [1967] 1 AC 617, crude oil escaped from a ship onto the surface of the water in the Sydney Harbour. It subsequently caught fire and caused substantial damage to a wharf and two ships. However, notwithstanding expert evidence that the risk of the oil catching fire had been very small, it was held that the defendants were negligent in not taking steps to abate what was nevertheless a real risk and one which, if it occurred, was very likely to cause substantial damage.

Damage must be caused by the breach

2.13 In order to establish liability in negligence it is necessary to prove that the careless conduct has caused actual damage. There are two requirements in this process. The first is that, on the balance of probabilities, there must as a matter of fact be a connection between the negligent conduct and the damage (causation in fact). The second is that the harm or damage caused is of a kind that was a foreseeable consequence of such conduct (causation in law).

2.14 Foreseeability of harm therefore plays a role in all three constituents of the tort of negligence: duty of care, breach and damage. In certain respects this makes a separate consideration of these factors artificial. However, foreseeability of damage has a slightly different application when considering the causation of actionable damage. In assessing the existence and breach of a duty of care, it is the reasonable foreseeability of a risk of *some* damage that is being considered. Foreseeability of the occurrence of a particular *kind* of damage does not affect the existence of this duty or the assessment of carelessness, but it does dictate whether the damage that has been caused is actionable in law.

2.15 If the *kind* of damage actually caused was not foreseeable, there is no liability in negligence. However as long as the kind of damage *is* reasonably foreseeable there will be potential liability even if the factual manner in which it was caused was extremely unusual and unforeseeable in itself. In *Hughes* v *Lord Advocate* [1963] AC 837 workmen left a manhole overnight covered by a tent and surrounded by paraffin lamps, but otherwise unguarded. The eight year old plaintiff ventured into the tent, fell down the manhole, dragged some of the lamps down with him and thereby caused an explosion which caused him to be severely burned. The House of Lords held that although the manner of the explosion was highly unusual, the source of the danger and kind of damage that materialised (i.e. burns from the lit paraffin) were reasonably foreseeable and therefore the workmen were liable.

Economic loss

2.16 Economic loss is a category of non-physical damage. It consists of financial losses (such as lost profits), as opposed to personal injury or physical damage to property. Unfortunately, as well as being an area of the utmost practical importance for architects, the concept of a duty of care to prevent economic loss is also one of the more demanding aspects of the law of tort.

2.17 The tort of negligence originally developed in the late nineteenth and early twentieth centuries as a cause of action for a person who had been physically injured by the careless acts of another. It also quickly developed into a remedy for careless damage to property. However, the attempt from about the 1960s (associated with the developing concept of a general principle of liability in negligence described above) to extend its ambit to economic loss generally has been largely unsuccessful. Today, economic loss is not always irrecoverable, but it requires a plaintiff to prove the exceptional circumstances necessary in order to establish that a defendant owed him a duty not to cause such damage. This long-standing reluctance to recognize a duty of care to prevent economic loss has been largely based on what is referred to as the 'flood gates' argument – the concern that it would widen the potential scale of liability in tort to an indeterminable extent.

2.18 Although there is no general liability for economic loss which is disassociated from physical damage, economic loss consequential to damage to property is treated separately and is recoverable. The distinction between such 'consequential' economic loss and 'pure' economic loss is not always clear. Perhaps the best illustration is provided by the case of *Spartan Steel and Alloys Ltd v Martin & Co (Contractors Ltd)* [1973] 1 QB 27. In this case the defendants negligently cut off an electricity cable which supplied the plaintiff's factory. As a result some of the plaintiff's molten metal that was being worked upon at the factory was damaged, causing the defendants to make a smaller profit on its eventual sale. Production was also delayed generally at the factory and the plaintiff lost the opportunity to make profits on this lost production. It was held that although the economic loss caused by the general delay in production was not recoverable (being pure economic loss), the lost profit from the molten metal actually in production at the time of the power cut was recoverable as it was immediately consequential to the physical damage to the molten metal itself. Thus, economic loss immediately consequential to damage to property is recoverable in negligence.

2.19 The first exception to the general rule of there being no duty to avoid causing *pure* economic loss was provided in the area of negligent mis-statement and the line of cases following *Hedley Byrne & Co Ltd v Heller & Partners* [1963] AC 465. In this important case, the defendants gave a favourable financial reference to the plaintiff's bankers in respect of one of the plaintiff's clients. The plaintiff relied on this incorrect reference and as a result suffered financial losses when the client became insolvent. The House of Lords held that a defendant would be liable for such negligent mis-statements if: (a) there was a 'special relationship' between the parties, (b) the defendant knew or ought to have known that the plaintiff was likely to rely upon his statement, and (c) in all the circumstances it was reasonable for the plaintiff to so rely on the defendant's statement.

2.20 In accordance with the general retreat from an acceptance of a general principle of liability in negligence and, in particular, its extension to economic loss generally, the circumstances where the courts will now recognize the required 'special relationship' have narrowed since the 1970s. In *Caparo v Dickman* [1990] 2 AC 605 the House of Lords held that auditors of a company's financial reports did not owe a duty of care to prospective share purchasers to avoid negligent mis-statements because, unlike a company's existing shareholders, the parties were not in a relationship of sufficient proximity. Liability for economic loss caused by negligent mis-statement was to be restricted to situations where the statement was given to a known recipient for a specific purpose of which the maker of the statement was aware.

2.21 This represented a narrow interpretation of the *Hedley Byrne* principle consistent with the revival of the incremental approach

to liability discussed above in paragraph 2.06. Although there is now authority for a more relaxed basis for liability based on the voluntary assumption of responsibility (see paragraph 2.33 below), it is submitted that these restrictive criteria will probably continue to be applied by the courts.

2.22 Liability for negligent mis-statement may be of relevance to architects when giving their clients advice, for example in relation to cost estimates or which builders to use. For example, in *Nye Saunders v Bristow* [1987] 37 BLR 92 although there was no allegation of defective work, the architect was found to be in breach of a *Hedley Byrne* duty by not advising his client as to the possible effect of inflation on his estimate for the cost of proposed works.

2.23 In contrast to the position with negligent statements, the attempt in a number of leading cases since the 1970s to extend liability for pure economic loss to negligent conduct has largely failed. The initial momentum for such an extension was provided by *Anns v Merton* which concerned structural damage in a building that had been caused by defective foundations. The House of Lords allowed the recovery in tort of the pure economic loss caused by the need to carry out repairs so that the property was no longer a threat to health and safety.

2.24 However, in its recent decisions in *Murphy v Brentwood District Council* [1991] 1AC 398 and *Department of the Environment v Thomas Bates & Sons Ltd* [1991] 1AC 499 the House of Lords has overruled *Anns v Merton*. The facts of *Murphy v Brentwood* also concerned a house which had been built on improper foundations allegedly due to the Council's negligence in passing the building plans. It was held that the Council (and anyone else involved in the construction of a building) did not owe a duty in tort to the owner or purchaser of property in respect of the costs of remedying such defects in the property. The repair costs were held to be pure economic loss and irrecoverable, whether or not the defects amounted to a threat to health or safety.

2.25 There were two main reasons for the decision in *Murphy v Brentwood*. Firstly, it was considered established law that in tort the manufacturer of a chattel owed no duty in respect of defects that did not cause personal injury or damage to other property. Thus, in *Donoghue v Stevenson* (see paragraphs 2.02 and 2.03 above) the defendant was not liable for the diminution in value of the bottle of ginger beer by reason of the presence of a decomposed snail in it. Mrs Donoghue could only recover damages against the manufacturer in respect of the physical harm caused to her by drinking it. The defective house in *Murphy v Brentwood* was effectively considered analogous to the bottle of ginger beer in *Donoghue v Stevenson*. Their Lordships held that it would be anomalous in principle if someone involved in the construction of a building should be in any different position from the manufacturer of bottled ginger beer or any other chattel. The second main justification was that innovation in the law of consumer protection against defects in the quality of products should be left to Parliament, especially in the light of the remedies provided by the Defective Premises Act 1972 in the case of residential dwellings (for which see Section 3 below).

2.26 This latter justification is not very convincing since most decisions in this field, including *Donoghue v Stevenson* itself, can be viewed as essentially judicially-created consumer-protection law in any case. However, it does illustrate the influence of judicial policy in the 'incremental' approach to the recognition of a duty of care in novel situations. Further, although *Murphy v Brentwood* has certainly simplified the law in this area, there remain recognized exceptions to the general rule against the existence of a duty of care to prevent economic loss in negligence.

2.27 Firstly, the position in respect of economic loss consequential to physical damage and negligent mis-statements remains unaffected by the decision.

2.28 In addition, in *Murphy* v *Brentwood* their Lordships recognized that damage to a building caused by defects in a part of it could in certain circumstances be recoverable in tort. Under the pre-*Murphy* v *Brentwood* 'complex structure theory' the individual parts of a building (such as the foundations, walls or roof) could be treated as distinct items of property. Therefore liability for damage caused to, say, the roof by a defect in the foundations could be justified by treating the building as a complex structure and depicting the damaged roof as a separate piece of damaged property. This analysis was proposed as a means of reconciling the post-*Anns* v *Merton* recognition of liability in negligence for defective premises with the established principle that there is no tortious liability for defective products.

2.29 In *Murphy* v *Brentwood* their Lordships rejected the complex structure theory and viewed the damaged house as a single piece of property (i.e. not a complex structure). However, they have left open the possibility of liability in the normal way where the item within a building that causes the damage is a distinct one (perhaps a faulty electrical fuse box which causes a fire) and is built or installed by a separate party from the builder. If damage is caused by such a 'non-integral' part of the building, it may be considered as damage caused to separate property (which under normal principles would be actionable damage in negligence). Therefore, in place of the complex structure analysis, their Lordships appear to have left a more restrictive 'non-integral piece of property' theory as a possible basis for continuing liability in tort for defective premises.

2.30 This concept is illustrated by the case of *Nitrigin Eireann Teoranta* v *Inco Alloys* [1992] 1 All ER 854. The defendants had manufactured and supplied the plaintiff's factory with some alloy tubing in 1981 which had developed cracks by 1983. It was held that although the cracked tubing in 1983 constituted pure economic loss (because at this time there was no damage to other property), damage to the factory caused by an explosion in 1984 (itself caused by the continuing weakness in the tubing) did give rise to a cause of action in negligence. The structure of the factory surrounding the tubing was considered to be separate property and therefore this damage was not pure economic loss.

2.31 Two other bases for liability in negligence for defective premises have, in theory, survived the decision in *Murphy* v *Brentwood*, although their application in practice is extremely unlikely. Firstly, Lord Bridge suggested that there may be a duty to prevent economic loss where the defective building is so close to its boundary that by reason of its defects the building might cause physical damage or injury to persons on neighbouring land or the highway. However, finding liability in these circumstances would appear to contradict the reasoning in the rest of their Lordships' judgments in *Murphy* v *Brentwood*. It is submitted that the better view is that the cost of repairing such defects would still be irrecoverable in negligence as it amounts to pure economic loss. However, until this point is clarified by future decisions it will remain a possible, if unlikely, basis for liability.

2.32 Secondly, there is the anomalous case of *Junior Books* v *Veitchi & Co* [1983] 1 AC 520 which the House of Lords could not bring itself to overrule in addition to *Anns* v *Merton*. In *Junior Books* the defendants were specialist floor sub-contractors who were engaged by main contractors to lay a floor in the factory of the plaintiff, with whom they had no formal contract. The floor subsequently cracked up and the plaintiff sued for the cost of relaying it. The House of Lords held that on the particular facts of the case, there was such a close relationship between the parties that the defendants' duty to take care to the plaintiff extended to preventing economic loss due to defects in their laying of the floor. This decision at first appears completely contradictory to the reasoning in *Murphy* v *Brentwood*, although some of their Lordships sought to explain it as a special application of the *Hedley Byrne* principle. One view is that *Junior Books* will continue to be considered as an anomalous case decided very much on its own facts, and not one that establishes as a matter of principle a further

category of exceptions from the main decision in *Murphy* v *Brentwood*.

2.33 However, an alternative interpretation is now possible in the light of Lord Goff's seminal judgment in the recent decision of the House of Lords in *Henderson* v *Merrett Syndicates Limited* [1994] 3WLR 761. Here their Lordships unanimously held that a concurrent duty of care was owed in tort by managing agents to Lloyd's names notwithstanding the existence of a contractual relationship between them. However of more significance in the present context are Lord Goff's comments on the ambit of the duty of care in tort under the *Hedley Byrne* principle.

2.34 In addition to characterizing the basis of such liability as being the voluntary assumption of responsibility, Lord Goff also interpreted the *Hedley Byrne* principle as applying to the provision of professional services generally, whether by words or actions. Thus at p. 776 of his judgment he concludes:

'. . . the concept provides its own explanation why there is no problem in cases of this kind about liability for pure economic loss: for if a person assumes responsibility to another in respect of certain services, there is no reason why he should not be liable in damages for that other in respect of economic loss which flows from the negligent performance of those services. It follows that, once the case is identified as falling within the *Hedley Byrne* principle, there should be no need to embark upon any further enquiry whether it is "fair, just and reasonable" to impose liability for economic loss – a point which is, I consider, of some importance in the present case.'

2.35 This represents a major conceptual extension of the category of conduct in which the courts may recognize a duty to prevent causing economic loss. Although it is not as yet clear how the courts will apply Lord Goff's judgment in this respect, it is submitted that they will probably expressly recognize from now on liability for economic losses caused by the negligent actions of professionals if there is a *Hedley Byrne* special relationship with the party suffering damage. Invariably, of course, this will be the case where there is a contractual relationship between an architect and his client.

2.36 Finally, in the light of *Henderson* v *Merrett* it should be emphasized that *Murphy* v *Brentwood* does not shut off the possible recognition of new categories of relationships in which a non-contractual duty to avoid causing economic loss will be recognized. For example, in *Punjab National Bank* v *de Boinville* [1992] 1 WLR 1138 the Court of Appeal held that (a) the relationship between an insurance broker and his client was a recognized exceptional category of case where such a duty existed, and (b) it was, on the facts of the case, a justified extension of this category to hold that a broker owed a like duty to a non-client where the broker knew that the insurance policy was to be assigned to this person and that he had been involved in instructing the broker in the first place.

2.37 In summary, as far as the particular position of professional architects is concerned the consequences of the landmark decisions in *Murphy* v *Brentwood* and *Henderson* v *Merrett* are probably as follows:

1. Liability for economic loss claims by third parties (i.e. those not in a contractual relationship with the architect) for defective work (subject to the existence of a Hedley Byrne relationship as described in 4–6 below) has been eliminated.
2. However, potential *Donoghue* v *Stevenson* type liability for damage caused to other property or the person as a result of such work remains, for example, if a piece of roofing falls off a building due to an architect's negligent design and breaks a person's leg or dents their car (whether or not that person is the owner of the building or a client).
3. There will be a revival of interest in potential liability pursuant to the Defective Premises Act 1972 (see below).
4. Otherwise there will be a re-focusing of attention on possible

Hedley Byrne relationships as the only other effective basis for liability in tort for defective work to buildings.

5. It is submitted that in practice the existence of a sufficiently proximate relationship to attract such liability between an architect and a client will rarely occur outside contractual relationships.

6. Where there is a relationship of proximity between an architect and his client or third party, the architect will owe a duty of care to prevent causing purely economic losses as a result of careless statements (via negligent designs, certification or advice) and, probably, his conduct and provision of his services in general.

3 The Defective Premises Act 1972

3.01 Section 1 of the Act provides:

'(1) A person taking on work for the provision of a dwelling (whether the dwelling is provided by the erection or by the conversion or enlargement of a building) owes a duty –

(a) if the dwelling is provided to the order of any person, to that person; and

(b) without prejudice to paragraph (a) above, to every person who acquires an interest (whether legal or equitable) in the dwelling;

to see that the work which he takes on is done in a workmanlike or, as the case may be, professional manner, with proper materials and so that as regards that work the dwelling will be fit for habitation when completed.'

3.02 All building professionals, including architects, can be 'persons taking on work' pursuant to the Act if the work undertaken is concerned with a dwelling. The person undertaking the work is liable not only for his own work, but also for the work of independent sub-contractors employed by him if they are engaged in the course of his business. The reference to a 'dwelling' implies that the Act is limited to property capable of being used as a residence. Further, liability under the Act is limited to a period of six years after the completion of the work concerned. This special limitation period provides a major restriction on the potential significance of the Act.

3.03 The Act appears to impose a dual statutory duty to ensure that (a) work is done in a workmanlike manner, and (b) as regards that work the dwelling will be fit for human habitation. It is unclear to what extent the latter requirement restricts liability under the Act for defective work. In *Thompson* v *Clive Alexander & Partners* [1993] 59 BLR 77 it was held that allegations of defective work alone on the part of an architect were not capable of amounting to a breach of the Act. It was held that the provision regarding fitness for habitation was the measure of the standard required in performance of the duty pursuant to section 1(1) and that trivial defects were not intended to be covered by the statute. There is authority to the contrary that suggests that the unfitness for habitation requirement adds nothing to the main one that the work is to be done properly. However, on its proper construction the Act probably does not cover every defective piece of work and something more than trivial defects are required to be in breach of it, although the precise ambit of the duty will have to await further litigation.

3.04 However, notwithstanding these restrictions it is likely that liability under the Act will be of greater significance for architects and other building professionals in the future than it has been to date. There are two main reasons for this. Firstly, although the decision in *Murphy* v *Brentwood* eliminated liability in negligence for pure economic loss caused to third parties by defective property, such pure economic loss is still recoverable under the Defective Premises Act 1972. Typically claims against architects involve a large proportion of purely economic losses, therefore attention is likely to concentrate in the future on potential liability under the Act.

3.05 Secondly, the exception to liability created by Section 2 of the Act which excludes certain approved building schemes from its provisions is likely to be of less significance in the future. This is because the last NHBC Vendor–Purchaser Insurance scheme to be approved by the Secretary of State as an 'approved scheme' under Section 2 was in 1979. However, sometime before 1988 the NHBC and the Secretary of State agreed that due to changes in the 1979 approved scheme it was no longer effective. No further scheme has been approved. Thus, there is potentially a large amount of post-1979 building work that will no longer be caught by Section 2 and will now be subject to the Act's duties.

4 Nuisance

4.01 The tort of nuisance is concerned with the unjustified interference with a person's use of land. Whether activity which may as a matter of fact be a considerable nuisance to an individual is actionable in law depends, as in the case of the tort of negligence, on a consideration of all the circumstances of the case and the proof of consequential damage. Although most nuisances arise out of a continuing state of affairs, an isolated occurrence can be sufficient if physical damage is caused.

4.02 There are two varieties of actionable nuisance; public and private. A public nuisance is one that inflicts damage, annoyance or inconvenience on a class of persons or persons generally. It is a criminal offence and only actionable in tort if an individual member of the public has suffered some particular kind of foreseeable damage to a greater extent than the public at large, or where some private right has also been interfered with. Examples of public nuisances can include selling food unfit for human consumption, causing dangerous obstructions to the highway, and (by way of statutory nuisances) water and atmospheric pollution.

4.03 A private nuisance is an unlawful act which interferes with a person's use or enjoyment of land or of some right connected with it. Traditionally interference with enjoyment of land in which the plaintiff had some kind of proprietary interest was one of the defining characteristics of a private nuisance. However, in *Khorasandjian* v *Bush* [1993] QB 727 a majority of the Court of Appeal granted an injunction against the defendant to prevent him telephoning the plaintiff at her mother's home (in which she was staying as a mere licensee with no proprietary interest). This decision may in time be seen as the precursor of a wider concept of actionable nuisance amounting to a general tort of harassment, and possibly the beginning of a tort of invasion of privacy. At present, however, it is submitted that the decision is best seen as a narrow extension of the availability of an action in private nuisance to interference with the enjoyment of premises at which the plaintiff *lives*, whether or not pursuant to a proprietary interest in the property itself.

4.04 A private nuisance consists of a person doing some act which is not limited to his own land but affects another person's occupation of land, by either: (a) causing an encroachment onto the neighbouring land (for example when trees overhang it or tree roots grow into the neighbouring land), (b) causing physical damage to the land or buildings (such as when there is an emission of smoke or other fumes which damage his neighbour's crops or property), or (c) causing an unreasonable interference with a neighbour's enjoyment of his land (such as causing too much noise or obnoxious smells to pass over it).

4.05 The actual or prospective infliction of damage is a necessary ingredient of an actionable nuisance. In a nuisance of the kind at (a) damage is presumed once the encroachment is proved. In (b) there must be proof of actual or prospective physical damage. Therefore in both these cases the requirement of damage is an objective test which does not involve a further examination of the surrounding circumstances. In nuisances of the kind at (c), however, there is no objective standard applied by the courts. Whether the acts complained of amount to the unreasonable use of land is a question of degree. The nuisance needs to amount to a material interference with the use of other land that an average man (with no particular susceptibilities or special interests) would consider unreasonable in all the circumstances of the particular case.

4.06 The duration and timing of the acts complained of is a relevant factor in this balancing of neighbours' interests. So too is the character of the locality. In *Sturges* v *Bridgman* [1879] 11 ChD 852 at 856 Thesiger LJ put it as follows:

'. . . whether anything is a nuisance or not is a question to be determined, not merely by an abstract consideration of the thing itself, but in reference to its circumstances: what would be a nuisance in Belgrave Square would not necessarily be so in Bermondsey; and where a locality is devoted to a particular trade or manufacture carried on by the traders or manufacturers in a particular and established manner not constituting a public nuisance, judges . . . would be justified in finding . . . that the trade or manufacture so carried on in that locality is not a private or actionable wrong.'

4.07 The conduct of the defendant may also be a relevant factor. In *Hollywood Silver Fox Farm Ltd* v *Emmett* [1936] 2KB 468 the defendant maliciously encouraged his son to fire shotguns on his own land but as near as possible to the plaintiff's adjoining property in order to disrupt his business of breeding silver foxes. Although entitled to shoot on his own land, the Court held that the defendant was nevertheless creating a nuisance. The Court held that the defendant's intention to alarm the plaintiff's foxes was a relevant factor in reaching this conclusion and specifically limited the injunction granted against the defendant to prevent the making of loud noises 'so as to alarm' the plaintiff's foxes. Similarly, it is a nuisance if a person deliberately uses his land in a manner which he knows will cause an unreasonable interference with another's, whether or not he believes that he is entitled to do the act or has taken all reasonable steps (short of not doing the act itself) to prevent it amounting to a nuisance.

4.08 Traditionally it was accepted that outside this kind of conduct nuisance had an uncertain overlap with the tort of negligence. There were some situations in which it involved negligent behaviour and others where this was not considered a requirement for liability. As Lord Reid rather confusingly put it in *The Wagon Mound (No 2)*:

'It is quite true that negligence is not an essential element in nuisance. Nuisance is a term used to cover a wide variety of tortious acts or omissions and in many negligence in the narrow sense is not essential . . . although negligence may not be necessary, fault of some kind is almost always necessary and fault generally involves foreseeability.'

4.09 Not surprisingly, a degree of confusion has been introduced by this distinction between negligence on the one hand and the requirement of some kind of fault, incorporating the concept of foreseeability, on the other. It is now established that liability in nuisance is not strict and that foreseeability of damage is a necessary ingredient (see *Leaky* v *National Trust* [1980] QB 485). However, the requirement of foreseeability of damage does not necessarily imply the need for negligent conduct, but may sometimes only be relevant to what kind of damage will be actionable. Further, the concept of 'fault' in nuisance is better viewed as unreasonable conduct (which is the essence of the tort) and may not always amount to negligent conduct (in the sense used in the tort of negligence).

4.10 Although increasingly the distinction between negligence and nuisance has become blurred (and in practice they have to a large extent become assimilated) they are not synonymous in principle. The following points should be emphasized: (a) where the nuisance is the interference with a natural right incidental to land ownership (such as the right to obtain water from a well) then liability is strict, (b) the act complained of may constitute the required 'unreasonable user' of land to constitute a nuisance without necessarily amounting to 'negligent' behaviour, (c) economic loss is generally recoverable in nuisance, (d) some kinds of damage recognized and protected in nuisance (such as creating an unreasonable noise or smell, or harassment such as in *Khorasandjian* v *Bush* above) would not amount to actionable damage in the tort of negligence, and (e) the remedy of an injunction is available to prevent an anticipated or continuing nuisance, but not to prevent someone acting negligently.

5 The rule in *Rylands* v *Fletcher*

5.01 An example of strict liability in tort (which does not require the proof of negligence or intent on the part of the wrongdoer) is the rule as stated by Blackburn J in *Rylands* v *Fletcher* [1866] LR 1 Ex 265 at 279:

'We think that the true rule of law is, that the person who for his own purposes brings on his land and collects and keeps there anything likely to do mischief if it escapes must keep it in at his peril, and, if he does not do so, is prima facie answerable for all the damage which is the natural consequence of its escape.'

5.02 In the House of Lords the rule was limited to apply only to the 'non-natural user' of land. The courts have failed to clarify precisely what non-natural user of land consists of and in what particular circumstances the rule should apply. However, it has been applied to water, fire, explosives, poison, and, in *Hale* v *Jennings Brothers* [1938] 1 All ER 579, to a seat becoming detached from a high speed fairground roundabout. In general, the rule is applicable where a person brings onto his land something that is 'dangerous', in the sense that if the thing escapes from the land it would be likely to cause either personal or physical damage.

5.03 There are various specific defences available to *Rylands* v *Fletcher* liability, namely (a) that the escape of the dangerous thing was caused by an Act of God, (b) that it was caused by the independent act of a stranger (though not an independent contractor), or the plaintiff himself, (c) that the plaintiff has consented to the dangerous thing being kept on the defendant's land, and (d) that the dangerous thing has been stored pursuant to some statutory duty (in which case negligence must be established on the part of the defendant).

5.04 The tendency of the courts to adopt a very restrictive interpretation of what was considered as 'non-natural use' of land and therefore a limited application of *Rylands* v *Fletcher* was recently considered in *Cambridge Water Co. Ltd* v *Eastern Counties Leather Plc* [1994] 1 All ER 53. In its first consideration of the rule for over half a century, the House of Lords took the view that the rule should be seen as no more than an extension of the law of nuisance to cases of isolated escapes from land.

5.05 Although the House of Lords considered that the concept of non-natural user had been unjustifiably extended by the courts, a restrictive interpretation of the rule was nevertheless confirmed as it found that foreseeability of harm of the relevant type was a prerequisite to liability under the rule (as in the case of nuisance). In an approach reminiscent of the House of Lords' attitude in *Murphy* v *Brentwood* to economic loss, the imposition of no-fault liability for all damage caused by operations of high risk was considered a more appropriate role for parliamentary, not judicial, intervention.

6 Trespass

6.01 Trespass to the person involves an interference, however slight, with a person's right to the security of his body. It can be of three varieties: (a) a 'battery' which is caused by unlawful physical contact, (b) an 'assault' which is where the innocent party is caused to fear the immediate infliction of such contact, and (c) 'false imprisonment' which involves the complete deprivation of liberty without proper cause for any period of time.

6.02 The tort of trespass to land involves any unjustifiable entry upon land in possession of another, however temporary or minor the intrusion. It is also a trespass to leave, place or throw anything onto another person's land, although if the material passes onto that person's land pursuant to the defendant exercising his own proprietary rights it is a nuisance. Unlike nuisance or negligence trespass is actionable without proof of damage, although if consequential harm or losses are thereby caused damages are recoverable. Ignorance of the law or the fact of trespass provides no defence for a trespasser.

6.03 As far as architects and building professionals are concerned, even the smallest infringements may be actionable. Thus setting foot without permission on land adjoining the property where work is being conducted will constitute a trespass, as will allowing equipment or other material to rest against, hang over, fall upon or be thrown over adjoining land. However, it should be emphasized that trespass is only a civil wrong which involves no automatic criminal liability in the absence of aggravating circumstances (such as criminal damage).

7 Breach of statutory duty

7.01 Breach of a duty imposed by statute may lead to civil liability in tort. There is a vast array of statutory duties covering a wide variety of activities. In any particular case, however, in order to establish civil liability for breach of the statutory duty the plaintiff must prove: (a) that he is part of the class of persons intended to be protected by the statute, (b) that the loss or damage he has suffered is of a kind intended to be prevented under the statute, (c) that there is no express provision in the statute that civil liability is not created by a breach of its provisions, (d) that on the balance of probabilities his injury, loss or damage was caused by the breach of statutory duty, and (e) that there has been a breach of the relevant statutory duty by the defendant.

7.02 Some statutory duties are akin to the duty of care in the tort of negligence and are based upon what is considered to be reasonable behaviour in all the circumstances of the case. Others, notably in the field of health and safety in the workplace, impose strict liability for damage caused in certain circumstances. The Consumer Protection Act 1987, in response to an EEC directive, even extended statutory strict liability in certain circumstances into the field of defective domestic consumer products (the very area which gave birth to Lord Atkin's 'neighbour principle' in *Donoghue* v *Stevenson*).

7.03 As far as architects are concerned, the most important statutory duties are those imposed by the Defective Premises Act 1972 (which has been discussed above) and the Occupier's Liability Acts of 1957 and 1984. These impose duties on the occupiers of land (which an architect could be considered as if supervising a building project) in respect of consensual and non-consensual visitors to the land not unlike those owed at common law in the tort of negligence. There is probably no civil liability, however, for breaches of the Building Act 1984 and its associated Building Regulations.

8 Limitation periods

8.01 The law imposes time limits within which causes of action must be commenced if they are to remain actionable. The law aims to give plaintiffs a reasonable opportunity to bring claims and defendants the assurance that the threat of liability will not be eternal and that any claim that they may have to face will not be so old as to prejudice the fairness of any proceedings. The two statutes that govern these time limits are The Limitation Act 1980 and The Latent Damage Act 1986.

8.02 Section 2 of the Limitation Act 1980 provides for tortious actions a prima facie limitation period of six years from the accrual of the cause of action. However, in personal injury cases the period is three years. Therefore when damage is an essential ingredient in liability (such as in negligence), time begins to run from the date that damage occurs. If further damage occurs subsequently, then in respect of the additional damage time will run from this later date. If there is a trespass, libel or other act which in itself amounts to an actionable tort, time begins to run from the date of the act itself. In the cases of continuing torts therefore (such as nuisance or trespass) the limitation period begins on each repetition of the wrong. In calculating whether the limitation period has expired, the date on which the cause of action accrues is normally excluded and the date on which the action is commenced is included.

8.03 However, these prima facie limitation periods may not be applicable in certain exceptional circumstances. In relation to personal injuries cases, Section 33 of the Limitation Act 1980 provides the court with a general discretion to disapply the primary limitation period of three years if it considers it reasonable to do so. Further, Section 32 provides that in a case where either: (a) there has been fraud by the defendant, or (b) any fact relevant to the plaintiff's cause of action has been deliberately concealed from him by the defendant, or (c) the action is for relief from the consequences of mistake, the limitation period shall not begin to run until the plaintiff has discovered this fraud, concealment or mistake, or until he could with reasonable diligence have done so. In building cases Section 32 may become relevant where a party deliberately conceals negligent design or construction work by building over and hiding defects.

8.04 The common law rule that the cause of action in negligence accrues when damage is caused creates serious difficulties in construction cases. Often damage which is caused in the process of building works is not discovered until some time after the building is completed. However, in *Pirelli General Cable Works* v *Oscar Faber* [1983] 2 AC 1 the House of Lords held that a cause of action for negligent advice by an engineer in connection with the design of a chimney accrued when damage, in the form of cracks in the chimney, occurred. The fact that they may only become reasonably discoverable some time later was held not to be relevant. This approach left open the possibility of plaintiffs becoming statute barred before they had a means of knowing that a cause of action actually existed.

8.05 The perceived injustice of this rule was addressed in the Latent Damage Act 1986. The Act modifies the limitation period for claims other than for personal injuries in the tort of negligence. The period should either be six years from the date that the cause of action accrued (on the basis of the *Pirelli* test for the time of damage), or, if this expires later, three years from the time the plaintiff knew certain material facts about the damage. This latter period is subject to a long stop provision expiring 15 years from the date of the negligent act or omission.

8.06 Regrettably, this has not entirely clarified matters. There remains the question of what constitutes damage in the first place.

In *Pirelli* the House of Lords decided that there was actionable damage only when there were actual cracks in the chimney. The difficulty with this proposition is reconciling it with the House of Lords' recent decision in *Murphy* v *Brentwood*. As we have seen, there it was held that damage of the kind which occurred in *Pirelli* was really economic loss, not physical damage, and therefore no longer recoverable. However, their Lordships also rather confusingly approved the previous decision in *Pirelli* which suggests that if there is liability in negligence for defectively constructed buildings (which could now probably only be pursuant to a *Hedley Byrne* relationship or one where damage is caused by a 'non-integral' item in the building) the time for the accrual of the cause of action for limitation purposes starts at the time physical damage first occurs.

8.07 In practice, in defective building cases the courts have continued to apply this 'manifestation of physical damage' test for deciding when a cause of action in tort accrues. However, it is submitted that the post-*Murphy* v *Brentwood* characterization of defective building work as economic loss (which logically may be present before there is any physical manifestation of it) is irreconcilable with the *Pirelli* test. Either such economic loss is suffered at the date on which the negligent service which caused it was relied upon (which would probably be an earlier date than the date of its physical manifestation) or it occurs at the date that the 'market' is able objectively to recognize and measure the financial scale of the loss suffered (which would suggest a later date for the accrual of the cause of action, namely the date of discoverability of the physical manifestation of defects by the 'market'). It is submitted that the earlier 'date of reliance' test will probably in due course be adopted as the most consistent position.

9 Remedies

9.01 The principal remedies in tort are the provision of damages and the granting of an injunction. The general aim of an award of damages is to compensate the plaintiff for the damage and losses sustained as a result of the tort. In principle damages are intended to put the plaintiff into the same position as he would have been in if the tort had not occurred. This restitutionary principle is inappropriate where personal injury has been caused, and so in these cases the courts apply a more general principle of what is fair and reasonable in all the circumstances. However, damages are only recoverable in respect of losses actually sustained and the plaintiff is under a duty to mitigate his losses by taking all reasonable steps to limit them.

9.02 In addition a plaintiff may only recover damages in respect of losses that are reasonably foreseeable consequences of the defendant's tort (reasonable foreseeability has already been discussed in relation to the existence and breach of duty). Further, as also referred to above, the law does not always recognize a duty of care to prevent certain kinds of loss (such as pure economic loss or nervous shock or embarrassment caused by an invasion of privacy). Thus, for all of these reasons it is not unusual for a plaintiff's actual losses suffered as a result of a tort to be greater than those that are recoverable in law.

9.03 The remedy by way of injunction is aimed at preventing loss and damage rather than compensating for it. It operates to prevent an anticipated tort or restrain the continuance of one (such as in the case of 'continuing' torts like nuisance or trespass). An injunction will be available where the threatened tort is such that the plaintiff could not be compensated adequately in damages for its occurrence. Injunctions are of two varieties. Firstly, 'prohibitive injunctions' which order a party not to do certain things that would otherwise constitute a legal wrong. Secondly, 'mandatory injunctions' in which the court directs a defendant positively to do certain things to prevent a tort being committed or continued.

10 Apportionment of liability

10.01 More than one person can be responsible for the same damage. The plaintiff is under a duty in tort to take reasonable care of his own safety. If the plaintiff is the only cause of the damage, then he will not succeed in a tortious action against another person. If the plaintiff and one or more other persons are at fault, then damages are apportioned pursuant to the Law Reform (Contributory Negligence) Act 1945 according to the court's assessment of the relative degree of fault of the parties.

10.02 In assessing this relative responsibility the court considers both the causative potency of the parties' actions (i.e. how important was each party's role as a matter of fact to the ensuing damage) and their relative moral blameworthiness (for example, if one party to a road traffic accident is drunk at the time, he is likely to be apportioned more of the blame). Contributory negligence applies in negligence, nuisance, the rule in *Rylands* v *Fletcher*, trespass, under the Occupier's Liability Acts and other breaches of statutory duty.

10.03 Further, Section 1 of the Civil Liability (Contribution) Act 1978 provides:

'Subject to the following provisions of this section, any person liable in respect of any damage suffered by another person may recover contribution from any other person liable in respect of the same damage (whether jointly with him or otherwise).'

10.04 Thus, between themselves, defendants are also able to apportion blame and restrict their relative contribution to the plaintiff's damages. This may take the form of an apportionment of blame at the trial of the matter or the commencement of separate proceedings (called third party proceedings) by a defendant against another party who is said to be jointly or wholly to blame. Of course if two or more persons are responsible for the plaintiff's damage, he may seek a remedy against either or both of them under the doctrine of joint and several liability.

11 Conclusion

The above has, no doubt, given some indication of the complex ever changing nature of the law of tort and its relevance to the everyday activities of professional architects. Unfortunately, given the restrictions on space, this chapter is unavoidably limited in its scope and introductory by nature.

The above purports to reflect the law as at January 1995.

4

Introduction to Scots law

ALAN D. MACKAY*

1 Law and Scotland

1.01 To many Scots, their legal system is an institution which expresses their individuality as a nation and is at least the equal of the more widespread English system of law. Despite the union of the Scottish and English legislative bodies in 1707 into the Parliament of Great Britain, the Treaty of Union preserved Scottish law and courts. As a result, Scots law is still in many respects entirely different from English, particularly in branches such as the law of property, constitutional and administrative law, and criminal law. But since 1707 much legislation has been enacted for the whole of the UK, and appeals have been permitted from the Scottish civil courts to the House of Lords, which since 1876 has always had at least one Scottish Law Lord and now, customarily, at least two. The current Lord Chancellor, Lord Mackay of Clashfern, is a former Scottish judge. Thus, much English law has been superimposed, sometimes unhappily, on what had previously been an entirely Scottish system.

2 Sources

2.01 Legislation, or enacted law, is still one of the principal sources of Scottish law. Considerations applicable to it are the same as for English law. Many of the Acts of the Scottish Parliament prior to 1707 are still in force, applying only to Scotland. Some UK legislation is not applicable to Scotland, while some is applicable there alone. In addition, membership of the European Economic Community binds the UK to give effect to European Community law properly made under the treaties.

2.02 The two other principal sources of modern Scottish law are to be found in judicial decisions and in the work of 'institutional' writers (paragraph 2.09). Together these sources make up the common law, and form a body of law which has grown up over almost as long a period as has English law and has been changed and added to by statute.

Feudal system

2.03 While primitive customary law has traces of Scots law, the first recognizable organized system of law derived from Norman feudalism, which was fully accepted in Scotland by the mid twelfth century. This system, embracing most aspects of organized society, was pyramidal. Theoretically all land belonged to the king, who granted areas to barons (his vassals) in return for military and other services when required. Each baron was able to grant smaller areas of his land to his own vassals on a similar basis and so on down the scale. In time military service was replaced by a money

payment called feu-duty, and although the feudal system still forms a theoretical basis of land tenure in Scotland, the owner being the vassal 'of a superior', it has been substantially reformed in the last twenty years. In 1970 provision was made enabling unreasonable, inappropriate, or unduly burdensome feudal conditions imposed by the superior to be varied or discharged. In 1974 machinery was created for redeeming existing feu-duties and prohibiting the creation of new feu-duties.

Sheriffs

2.04 At about the same time as the feudal system became accepted in Scotland, another institution was introduced which was to become of great importance in the administration of law: the office of sheriff. The sheriff was, and remains, an important administrative and judicial officer, and today the Sheriff Courts conduct the greatest part, by volume, of litigation. Actions for debt and damages can be raised there irrespective of the sums involved. Action for sums of up to £1 500 may only be raised in the Sheriff Court.

Dean of Guild Court

2.05 Another ancient legal institution, once familiar to architects, was the Dean of Guild Court, which exercised various functions in relation to buildings in burghs. The Dean of Guild Court has been abolished and its building control functions transferred to a local authority committee.

Fundamental institutions

2.06 The period prior to 1532 is of interest here only because by that date most of the fundamental institutions of Scottish law had come into existence. Lack of documentation in Scotland is the reason for much uncertainty; fewer records were kept there than in England, because Scotland was in a relatively backward and troubled state. The thirteenth and fourteenth centuries, however, saw the development of an early form of trial by jury, and the establishment of Sheriff Courts and the circuit courts.

2.07 In 1532 the College of Justice was founded with a court of 15 judges, the direct predecessors of the judges of the present Court of Session (paragraph 3.01) which today comprises 26 judges. This was a major step towards establishing the present Scottish legal institutions.

Influence of Roman law

2.08 It is often said that Scots law is based on Roman law. While not immediately apparent today, this is still partly true, and is one of the principal causes of difference between Scottish and English private law. There are two reasons for this influence. First, prior

---

* This chapter is based on the chapter written for the first edition by Donald MacFadyen QC and William Nimmo Smith QC.

to the reformation, much jurisdiction of private law was in the hands of ecclesiastical courts, which administered canon law with an ultimate appeal to the Papal Court at Rome; this formed the basis of matrimonial law and influenced other branches, such as the law of succession and the law of contract. Second, for many years Scotland was more in touch with other European countries than with England. Many Scots lawyers underwent part of the legal education abroad, particularly in Holland and, as a result, were influenced by study of Roman law in Continental universities.

Institutional writings

2.09 The year 1681 marked a turning-point in Scots law with the publication of Stair's *Institutions*, a book which is the foundation of modern Scots private law. It is a systematic treatise, drawing together all the influences mentioned above. It was followed by a few other books by different authors, notably Eskine and Bell, which are together referred to as 'institutional writings'. They are highly regarded by the courts, and in some branches of law they may carry as much weight as previous judicial decisions.

2.10 Today's Scots lawyers in practice use for everyday reference statutes and statutory instruments, law reports (which are found in the official series of Session Cases, started in 1820, or in the *Scots Law Times* and other series of reports), and number of standard textbooks.

Equity in Scots law

2.11 The dichotomy in English law between common law and equity, which were administered by separate courts, was never a feature of Scots law. Scottish courts have long taken equitable principles into consideration, and equity is regarded as a principle which forms part of the law rather than as a force acting in opposition to it.

3 Courts and the legal profession

3.01 Apart from certain matters referred to the EC Court, in civil matters the House of Lords is the ultimate resort for appeals from the Court of Session, which is the supreme court of Scotland in civil matters. The Court of Session is made up of the Inner House and the Outer House (paragraph 3.03). In the Inner House there are two Divisions, equal in authority, each with four judges. The First Division is presided over by the Lord President and the Second Division by the Lord Justice-Clerk. The work of each Division is to hear appeals from decisions of lower courts, including single judge decisions of a Court of Session judge or Sheriff Court decisions, and to deal, as the court of first instance, with certain special cases and stated cases, e.g. in arbitrations, and some types of petition (they do not hear cases where evidence must be taken).

3.02 Architects are more likely to be concerned, as a party or a witness, in two types of action: those arising from contract and those from delict (paragraph 4.06), the name given in Scotland to what in England is called the law of torts. The hearing of evidence in such actions is either by way of a proof before a single judge, or by way of jury trial before a judge and jury. A jury trial is principally limited to actions for damages for personal injuries.

3.03 Actions may be commenced in the Outer House of the Court of Session or in the Sheriff Court. Court of Session judges who sit in the Outer House are called the Lords Ordinary i.e. as single judges in non-appellate work. The decision of a Lord Ordinary may be appealed to one of the Divisions of the Inner House and from there to the House of Lords. The Court of Session sits only in Edinburgh. Sheriffs sit in local Sheriff Courts throughout Scotland. A Sheriff's decision may be appealed to either the Sheriff Principal of the Sheriffdom, and from him to one of the Divisions of the Inner House of the Court of Session and so on, or direct from the Sheriff to one of the Divisions of the Inner House. The decision as to where an action is raised is that of the pursuer, subject to the Court having jurisdiction. In general terms any action where the value of the case does not exceed £1 500 must be raised in the Sheriff Court. Disputes may also be resolved by arbitration which is often used in contractual matters or by various forms of Alternative Dispute Resolution.

Court procedure

3.04 Before a case comes to proof or jury trial there is a system of written pleading designed to make the parties – pursuer and defender (in England the plaintiff and defendant) – state the facts and principles of law on which they base their cases as clearly as possible, and points of difference between them are narrowed down. An action is started or raised by service on the defender of a summons (in the Court of Session) or an initial writ (in the Sheriff Court), setting out the pursuer's claim. Then follow various steps which must be taken within fixed periods. Defences are lodged on behalf of the defender, and for a time the parties are allowed to adjust their pleadings to meet what is said for the other side. Thereafter, a document called a 'closed record' is printed, containing the final version of the pleadings.

3.05 Before there is any proof or jury trial, there may be legal debate about the closed record, at which the sufficiency in law of the parties' pleadings may be called in question, with the result that some parts may be struck out, or even the whole action dismissed. At the proof or jury trial which follows, parties are restricted in the evidence to proving facts stated in the closed record. After the hearing of evidence for both parties, the speeches by their counsel or solicitors, the judge may, at a proof, give an immediate decision but more commonly makes avizandum (takes time to think and gives his decision later). At a jury trial, the jury, after being instructed or charged by the judge, retire to consider what they have heard and give their verdict unanimously or by a majority. Court procedures have been the subject of much reform in the last few years both in the Court of Session and Sheriff Court with a view to expediting litigation and avoiding unnecessary legal procedures.

Legal profession

3.06 There have been many reforms in the legal profession both in Scotland and England in recent years partly as a result of Government pressures. These reforms are wide ranging and in many areas the effect will only be measurable once they have become established practice. The most significant change for the profession is the granting of rights of audience in the higher courts to solicitors. These rights of audience apply both to civil work in the Court of Session and criminal work in the High Court of Justiciary. The solicitors who have been granted these rights are called 'Solicitor Advocater'. Until now the profession has been divided into two branches. By far the more numerous are solicitors, who deal directly with clients and see to all their legal affairs. All solicitors are members of the Law Society of Scotland, which is their statutory regulatory body. They may also belong to a professional society, such as the Writers to the Signet or the Solicitors in the Supreme Courts, and put the letters 'WS' or 'SSC' after their names. Whether they do or do not makes no practical difference to the work they undertake for clients.

3.07 The other branch of the profession consists of advocates divided into senior counsel (QCs) and junior counsel, who belong to the Faculty of Advocates, a collegiate professional body. They undertake work of broadly the same sort as that done by barristers in England, and specialize in arguing cases before courts and other tribunals and in giving opinions on matters of law. Until recently an advocate could only receive instructions indirectly from clients through their solicitors, however, again this aspect of the system is under review and instruction may be accepted in particular circumstances directly from professional bodies.

4 Branches of law

4.01 Differences among branches of English and Scottish law of interest to architects will be mentioned when particular topics are discussed later in this book. At this stage, only some of the more important differences are noted.

Contract

4.02 In Scots law the element of consideration essential to the formation of a binding contract in England is unnecessary. A contract is an agreement between parties which is intended to have legal effect. It is therefore perfectly possible to have a gratuitous contract, i.e. one in which all obligations rest on one side.

4.03 Sealed contracts have no place in Scots Law but some contracts must normally be in writing to be properly constituted, the most important examples of these being contracts relating to heritable property, i.e. land and buildings, and leases. The Requirements of Writing (Scotland) Act 1995 introduced changes for executing legal documents in Scots Law. For example, documents which used to require two witnesses now require only one. The provisions of the Act are complex and care needs to be taken to avoid becoming unwittingly committed to a legally enforceable contract by informal documentation or actings. In case of any doubt legal advice should be sought.

Jus quaesitum tertio

4.04 In Scots law, parties to a contract may confer an enforceable right on a third party, but take no part in the formation of the contract. Provided appropriate circumstances obtain, a right known as a *jus quaesitum tertio* can be conferred on the third party, which enables the third party to enforce provisions in their favour agreed upon by the contracting parties. This is particularly important in relation to enforcement of building conditions. Where several feuars (vassals, paragraph 2.03) hold land from the same superior, building conditions imposed in the feu contract may, in appropriate circumstances, be enforceable by one feuar against another; for example, alterations of particular kinds may be prevented.

Partnership

4.05 In contrast to the English position, a Scottish partnership is not in law simply a collection of individuals. The firm has a legal personality – i.e. an existence of its own – separate from those persons who compose it, and it can, for example, sue for debts owed to it in its own name. The separate existence of the firm does not, however, prevent the personal liability of the partners from being unlimited. Partnership law is dealt with in detail in Chapter 20.

Delict

4.06 The law of delict is that part of the law which deals with righting of legal wrongs, in the civil, as opposed to the criminal, sense. Broadly it is the Scottish equivalent of the English law of tort. The background and details of the Scots law of delict and the

English law of torts are different in too many respects to mention here. They cover broadly the same ground, with the Scottish law concentrating more on general principle and less on specific wrongs than the corresponding English law. Although the wrong complained of may arise out of deliberate conduct, most actions based in delict arise out of negligence.

Property

4.07 Property law is perhaps the field in which Scots and English law diverge most widely, particularly in relation to the law of land ownership. Differences are so great and so fundamental that consideration of them is deferred to Chapter 6.

Limitation periods

4.08 Limitation periods also differ in some respects between Scots and English Law. Legal advice should always be sought in any question of when proceedings should be issued. In general terms actions for personal injuries require to be raised within three years of the date of the incident giving rise to the right of action (or from death arising if in a fatal accident case). Actions for enforcements of civil obligations, e.g. contracts or debt, must generally be raised within five years from when the right of action comes into existence. There are various other periods which should be considered, e.g. in relation to obligations relating to land. Legislation regarding statutory periods is principally to be found in the Prescription and Limitation (Scotland) Act 1973.

5

English land law

MARTIN DIXON*

1 Conveyancing

1.01 This study is intended to give an impression of those aspects of land law that are relevant to architects, either in their professional capacity as they design buildings for clients, or in their personal capacity as tenants of their offices. It is necessary to distinguish land law as such from conveyancing. Land law is concerned with the rights of a landowner in or over his land and the rights which others have over that land. The law of conveyancing is concerned with the creation and transfer of rights in and over land, usually, but not necessarily, pursuant to a contract. An architect need not concern himself with the intricacies of conveyancing. A certain amount must, however, be said about title to land in England and Wales and the methods that exist to protect rights in and over land.

* This chapter draws heavily on the chapter in the previous edition by Charles Harpum, now a Law Commissioner.

1.02 Many of the concepts that underlie English land law are ancient, and this is reflected in much of the curious terminology which is associated with the subject. The law was greatly simplified and restructured in 1925 by a series of important statutes. These form the foundation of the modern law.

1.03 Title to land in England and Wales is either unregistered or registered. Since 1 December 1990, all land in England and Wales must be registered following a transfer of ownership, and, in time, unregistered conveyancing will disappear. In unregistered conveyancing the landowner will be either a freeholder or a leaseholder. On the sale of the freehold, or upon an assignment of a lease, the vendor's proof of title is found in the title deeds to the property, and the purchaser's solicitor will investigate these title deeds to satisfy himself that the vendor does indeed have title to the land. Until 1969, it was necessary for the purchaser's solicitor to peruse all dealings with the land back to the first conveyance of it more than 30 years old. That conveyance is known as 'the root of title'.

Since 1969 it has been necessary to go back only to the first root of title that is more than 15 years old (Law of Property Act 1969, Section 23). Following a successful sale of the freehold or leasehold, the purchaser's solicitor will then apply for first registration of title.

1.04 Rights over unregistered land are either 'legal' or 'equitable'. It is unnecessary to explain why some rights are legal and some equitable. The distinction is historical in origin, but now as a result of statutory intervention, the dichotomy is relevant largely for conveyancing purposes. Legal estates and rights are binding on all the world, regardless of whether a purchaser of land knows of them or not. The only legal *estates* that can now exist are freeholds and leaseholds. Most easements and many mortgages are legal rights. Equitable rights, by contrast, are good against all the world except a purchaser in good faith of a legal estate or interest in land for value and without notice of the right. Notice is actual, constructive, or imputed and will exist in most cases through registration of the equitable interest as a 'land charge' (see paragraph 1.05):

1. A purchaser has *actual notice* of those encumbrances of which he is aware, and automatically of what are called 'land charges' (see paragraph 1.05).
2. A purchaser has *constructive notice* of those matters which would have come to his attention if he had made those enquiries which a reasonable purchaser would have made. A reasonable purchaser will do two things: (a) inspect the title deeds back to a good root of title, and (b) inspect the land itself, making enquiries, for example, of any person whom he finds in occupation of it.
3. A purchaser has *imputed notice* of all those matters which his agent (such as his solicitor) knows or discovers while acting as agent in that transaction, or which the agent ought reasonably to have discovered.

1.05 Many equitable encumbrances on land are registrable at the Land Registry as land charges under the Land Charges Act 1972 (replacing the Land Charges Act 1925). This has nothing to do with registered land. Some of the most important from an architect's point of view are:

1. Estate contracts, i.e. contracts for the sale of land or of any interest in land, including contracts to grant leases, options to purchase (i.e. a standing offer by a landowner to sell), and rights of pre-emption (i.e. rights of first refusal).
2. Restrictive covenants (fully explained in paragraph 4.01), except those found in a lease and those entered into before 1926.
3. Certain types of easement, such as those not granted by deed or those which endure only for the life of a given person.

Registration of such an encumbrance constitutes actual notice of it to all persons for all purposes. If the encumbrance is registrable but not registered, it will be void against a purchaser of the land regardless of whether he knows of it. This will be so even if the sum paid by the purchaser is only a fraction of the true value of the property (*Midland Bank Trust Co Ltd v Green* [1981] AC 513). Land Charge registration suffers from a serious defect: registration of the charge is not made against the land itself, but against the name of the landowner for the time being. In order to search the Land Charges Register, it is therefore necessary to discover the names of the persons who have owned the land from time to time. This is done by looking at the title deeds. However, it is only possible to examine the deeds back to a good root of title, which may now be only 15 years old. Land charges have been registrable since 1925. It is often impossible, therefore, to discover the names of all the landowners back to 1925. Because registration of the land charge constitutes actual notice, a purchaser will still be bound by it, even though he could not discover the name of the landowner against whom it was registered and could not therefore search the Register. Under the Law of Property Act 1969, compensation is payable for any loss suffered because of land charges registered against landowners whose names lie behind the root of

title. It should be noted that any person may search the Land Charges Register, and that an Official Certificate of Search is conclusive in favour of a purchaser, actual or intending. Thus, if for any reason, a Certificate of Search fails to reveal a registered land charge, the purchaser will take free of it, provided that he searched against the correct name.

1.06 Registered land is quite different:

1. The actual title to the land is itself registered, eliminating the need for title deeds. Details of many encumbrances will also appear on the Register, and such encumbrances are registered against the land and *not* against the name of the landowner at the time the encumbrance was created. Transfer of the land is effected by registering the purchaser as the new proprietor. Freeholds and many but not all leaseholds may be registered.
2. The Register is, subject to certain exceptions, conclusive as to the state of the title to the land, and the doctrine of notice has no application to registered land. If for any reason the Register is not a true reflection of the title, it may, in certain circumstances, be rectified. Any person suffering loss as a result may be entitled to compensation out of public funds. Because the Register is conclusive, if an erroneous Certificate of Search is issued which omits a registered encumbrance, a purchaser will still be bound by it, but will be entitled to compensation.
3. A purchaser of registered land will take the following steps: (a) Inspect the Register. The Land Register is now a public document (Land Registration Act 1988) and may be inspected by any person on payment of the appropriate fee.
   (b) Inspect the land itself, because the Register is not conclusive on all matters. Certain rights – called overriding interests – may not appear on the Register. These include many easements, leases of 21 years or less, squatters' rights, local land charges (paragraph 1.08), and the rights of persons in actual occupation. This last category can be a trap for the unwary. A person may protect any right of a proprietary nature simply by virtue of his actual occupation of the land over which it exists, even though such a right is in fact capable of protection by an entry on the Register: *Williams & Glyn's Bank Ltd v Boland* [1981] AC 487.

1.07 It will be clear from this that the registered land system considerably facilitates and expedites conveyancing and provides a more efficient method of protecting encumbrances than is found in unregistered conveyancing. Now that first registration of title is compulsory throughout England and Wales, unregistered conveyancing and all its anomalies will gradually disappear.

1.08 Whether the land is registered or unregistered, there are certain rights which are registrable quite separately at a register kept by all local authorities. These are called local land charges, and they are regulated by the Local Land Charges Act 1975, which came into force in 1977. These charges are registered by reference to the land which they affect and not against the name of the landowner. Registration of such charges constitutes actual notice of it to all persons for all purposes. A charge is, however, enforceable even if not registered, but a purchaser of land burdened by an unregistered charge will be entitled to compensation from the local authority. Local land charges are numerous and of considerable importance. They include:

1. Preservation instructions as to ancient monuments.
2. Lists of buildings of special architectural or historic interest.
3. Planning restrictions.
4. Drainage schemes.
5. Charges under the Public Health and Highway Acts.

1.09 An architect will be well advised to find out from the client what encumbrances if any affect the client's property. It is particularly important that he discovers the existence of any easements, restrictive covenants, and, local land charges, because these may constrict the architect in his plans.

2 The extent of land

2.01 'Land' in English law includes not only the soil but also:

1. Any buildings, parts of buildings, or similar structures.
2. Anything permanently attached to the soil ('fixtures', see paragraph 5.03).
3. Rights under the land. It has never been definitely settled how far down the rights of a landowner extend, though it is commonly said that they extend down to the centre of the earth. Certainly they go down as far as the limits of economic exploitation. A landowner is therefore entitled to the minerals under his land, though all gold, silver, coal and petroleum are vested in the Crown.
4. Rights above the land 'to such height as is necessary for the ordinary use and enjoyment of [a landowner's] land and the structures upon it' (*Baron Bernstein* v *Skyviews & General Ltd* [1978] QB 479, 488).
5. Easements (such as rights of way or rights to light) and profits (such as a right to fish on another's land).

2.02 Any unjustifiable intrusion by one person upon land in the possession of another is a trespass – a tort. It is likewise a trespass to place anything on or in the land in the possession of another (for example, by driving a nail into his wall, or propping a ladder against his house). It is a popular misconception that to be actionable as a tort, the trespass must involve damage to the plaintiff's property. Even if no damage is done, the court may restrain the trespass by injunction. It was once thought that the court must suspend the injunction if no harm was suffered, but the better view is that an injunction will be binding immediately (*Anchor Brewhouse Developments Ltd* v *Berkley House (Dockland Developments) Ltd* [1987] 2 EGLR 173, not following *Woollerton and Wilson Ltd* v *Richard Costain Ltd* [1970] 1 WLR 411). In both those cases, the trespass arose out of building works on land adjacent to that of the plaintiff. If construction work is likely to necessitate an incursion on to neighbouring land in some way – for example, to erect scaffolding, or because a crane jib will swing over that land – then the client must come to an arrangement with the landowner. This will usually take the form of a contractual licence (paragraph 2.03). But if a permanent incursion is contemplated – for example, by the eaves of a building – it may be better to negotiate an easement (see paragraph 3.01).

2.03 Something can conveniently be said at this point about licences. A licence is permission to do something which would otherwise be unlawful. A licence to enter upon land therefore makes lawful what would otherwise be a trespass. There are several types of licence, of which only two need be considered here. First, there is a bare licence, that is, permission to enter land, given quite gratuitously without any consideration. It is revocable at any time by the licensor, and on such revocation, the licensee becomes a trespasser, though he is entitled to a reasonable time to enable him to leave the land. The second type of licence is the contractual licence. This is a licence that is granted for some consideration, usually a fee. Often a residential contractual licence closely resembles a lease. If the arrangement confers exclusive possession on the grantee for a fixed period, it will create a lease and not a licence: *Street* v *Mountford* [1985] AC 809. The typical hallmark of a contractual licence is the provision of services (such as cleaning) by the licensor. Whether a contractual licence can be revoked depends upon the construction of the contract in question. If a licence is either expressly or by necessary implication irrevocable during its agreed duration the licensor will be unable to prevent the licensee from going on to the land, because a court will prevent any purported revocation of the licence either by the grant of an injunction or in appropriate circumstances, by a decree of specific performance (*Verrall* v *Great Yarmouth Borough Council* [1981] QB 202).

2.04 If a landowner has an easement over adjacent land – such as a right of way – any interference with it will not constitute a trespass but a nuisance. Not every interference will amount to a nuisance. If the easement is a positive one (e.g. a right of way), the interference will constitute a nuisance only if it prevents the practical and substantial enjoyment of the easement. If the easement is negative (e.g. a right of light), the interference will be actionable only if it substantially interferes with the enjoyment of the right. (On positive and negative easements, see paragraph 3.03.)

Boundaries

2.05 A boundary has been defined as 'an imaginary line which marks the confines or line of division of two contiguous parcels of land' (*Halsbury's Laws of England* (4th edn) vol 4, paragraph 831). Boundaries are fixed in one of three ways: (1) by proved acts of the respective owners; (2) by statutes or by orders of the authorities having jurisdiction; or (3) in the absence of either of these, by legal presumption.

Proved acts of the parties

1. The parties may expressly agree on the boundaries.
2. The boundaries may be defined by the title deeds. These may in turn refer to a plan or to an Ordnance Survey map. Ordnance Survey maps do not purport to fix private boundaries, and it is the practice of the Survey to draw the boundary line down the middle of a boundary feature (e.g. down the middle of a ditch) regardless of where the boundary line actually runs. If the title deeds do refer to an Ordnance Survey map, however, then that map *will* be conclusive (*Fisher* v *Winch* [1939] 1 KB 666). In the case of registered land, the plans used by the Land Registry are based on the Ordnance Survey maps, but the boundaries on them are regarded as general and are not intended to be fixed precisely by the plan. A little used procedure exists by which the boundary may be defined exactly, and where this has been done the plan on the Register is definitive.
3. A boundary may be proved by showing twelve or more years' undisturbed possession.

Orders

Establishment of boundaries by orders of authorities is now largely historical. Under the Enclosure Acts, the Tithe Acts, and certain Agricultural Acts, awards were made, defining boundaries precisely. In rural areas such an award may help in determining a boundary. A boundary may be fixed by judicial decision, for example, in an action for trespass or for the recovery of land.

Legal presumption

In the absence of clear definition by either of the above methods, certain rebuttable presumptions apply:

Hedges and ditches

It is presumed that a man excavating a ditch will not di : into his neighbour's land, but that he will dig it at the very edge of his own property, making a bank on his side of the ditch with the soil that he removes. On top of that bank a hedge is usually planted. He is, therefore, owner of both the hedge and the ditch. This presumption applies only where the ditch is known to be artificial.

Fences

It is said that there is a presumption that a wooden fence belongs to the owner of the land on whose side the posts are placed, on the basis that a landowner will use his land to the fullest extent. Likewise, it is often said that nails are 'driven home'. These presumptions are, however, unsupported by authority and must be regarded as uncertain.

Highways

The boundary between lands separated by a highway or a private right of way is presumed to be the middle line of the highway or private right of way. There is no such presumption with railways. The bed of a railway will be the property of Railtrack, or its successors.

The seashore

The boundary line between the seashore and the adjoining land is (unless usage to the contrary is proved) the line of the median high tide between the ordinary spring and neap tide (*Attorney General* v *Chambers* (1854) 4 De GM & G 206 at 218). Prima facie the seashore belongs to the Crown.

Rivers and streams

If a river or stream is tidal, the soil of the bed of the river or stream belongs to the Crown, or the Duchies of Cornwall or Lancaster, where appropriate. As a general rule, the boundary between the bed of a tidal stream and adjoining land is the line of medium high water mark. If the river or stream is non-tidal, it is assumed that adjoining owners own land to the middle of the watercourse, the 'thalweg'.

Walls

If the division between two properties is a wall and the exact line of the boundary is not known, in determining the ownership of the wall, certain presumptions apply. Party walls outside London and Bristol (for the situation in London and Bristol, see Chapter 14) are subject to rights at common law. The usual, but by no means necessary, presumption is that the party wall is divided longitudinally into two strips, one belonging to each of the neighbouring owners, but where each half is subject to a right of support in favour of the other. If one owner removes his building, he is obliged to waterproof the exposed party wall. (See Chapter 14 for the complicated procedures necessary when changes to party walls are contemplated in London.) Extensions can bear only on the half of the wall belonging to the owner of the building being extended, unless the consent of the adjoining owner is obtained; this cannot be enforced as it can in London (Chapter 14).

3 Easements

3.01 Easements are rights which one owner of land may acquire over the land of another. They should be distinguished from profits, i.e. rights to take something off another's land, for example, to cut grass or peat, or to shoot or fish; natural rights, for example, rights of support of land (but not of buildings; a right of support for a building is an easement); public rights, for example, rights of way over a highway; restrictive covenants (paragraph 4.01); and licences (paragraph 2.03).

3.02 The essentials of an easement are:

1. There must be a dominant and a servient tenement (a tenement being a plot of land held by a freeholder or leaseholder).
2. The easement must benefit the dominant tenement to which it will become attached. The servient tenement is subjected to the burden of the easement. Although the two plots need not be contiguous, they must be sufficiently close for the dominant tenement to be benefited by the easement.
3. The two tenements must not be owned and occupied by the same person.
4. The easement claimed must be capable of forming the subject matter of a grant, that is, of being created by deed. Although there are well-defined categories of easements – rights of way, rights to light, rights of support – the list is not closed. Within the last 30 years, the following rights have been held to be capable of existing as easements: to use a neighbour's lavatory; to use an airfield; to use a letter-box; to park on adjoining land, though not in designated bays; to use paths in a park for pleasure and not simply for getting from one place to another. Against this, certain rights cannot exist as easements; a right to

a view; to privacy; to a general flow of air; to have a property protected from the weather; an exclusive right to use boats on a canal.

3.03 Easements may be either positive or negative. A positive easement is one which enables the dominant owner to do some act upon the servient tenement, for example, a right of way. A negative easement merely allows the dominant owner to prevent the servient owner from doing something on his land, for example, a right to light, which restricts the servient owner's ability to build on the servient tenement. Some easements do not readily fall into either category, for example, a right of support for a building.

3.04 Easements may be acquired in one of four ways:

1. By express grant or reservation. A landowner may by deed expressly grant an easement over his land in favour of a neighbouring landowner. Equally, if a landowner is selling off part of his land, he may expressly reserve in his favour in the conveyance an easement over the part that he is selling, for the benefit of the part he retains.
2. By implied reservation or grant. A landowner sells off part of his land and retains the rest. He fails to reserve expressly any easements over the part sold. The only easements that will be implied in his favour over the part sold will be easements of necessity and easements necessary to give effect to the common intentions of the parties. An easement of necessity in this context means an easement without which the vendor's retained land cannot be used at all. For example, if he retains land to which there is no access (often called a land-locked close), an easement of necessity will be impliedly reserved over the land that he has sold. Likewise, if a purchaser buys land from a vendor (the vendor again retaining certain land), the following easements will be implied in the purchaser's favour against the land retained by the vendor:
   (a) Easements of necessity, which in this context mean easements without which the grantee cannot enjoy the land *for the purposes for which it was intended*.
   (b) Easements necessary to give effect to the common intentions of the parties.
   (c) Easements within the rule in *Wheeldon* v *Burrows* (1879) 12 ChD 31. This is best explained by an example. A landowner owns two adjacent plots, A and B. He does certain acts over B for the benefit of A which would be an easement if A and B were separately owned. This is called a 'quasi-easement'. When he sells off plot A, retaining plot B, the purchaser of plot A will acquire an easement to do those acts over plot B which the common owner had hitherto done providing the quasi-easement was 'continuous and apparent', that is, discernible on a careful inspection of the land; necessary for the reasonable enjoyment of plot A; and had been and was at the time of the grant used by the grantor for the benefit of plot A.
3. Under the statutory 'general words'. By Section 62 of the Law of Property Act 1925, there will pass on every conveyance (unless a contrary intention is shown) all 'liberties, privileges, easements, rights and advantages whatsoever appertaining to or reputed to appertain to the land'.

   It has been held by the House of Lords that this section will not pass quasi-easements. This is because a landowner does not have 'rights' or 'easements' over his own land. What he does on his own land, he does as owner (*Sovmots* v *The Secretary of State* [1979] AC 144).
   Therefore the section will convert merely permissive user into a full easement. For example, A, a freeholder, permits B, a tenant of part of A's land to drive over A's land. A then sells and conveys to B the land, of which he has hitherto been only a leaseholder. On the conveyance B acquires a full easement to drive over A's land (*International Tea Stores Co* v *Hobbs* [1903] 2 Ch 165). It is imperative for the successful creation of easements by Section 62 that the plots of land involved were in different occupation prior to the conveyance, even if they were owned by the same freeholder.

4. By prescription. Long user *nec vi, nec clam, nec precario* – without force, secrecy, or permission – can give rise to easements. An easement by prescription can only be claimed by one freehold owner against another, and, with certain exceptions, user must be shown to have been continuous. There are three methods of acquiring easements by prescription:

(a) at common law;
(b) under the doctrine of lost modern grant; and
(c) under the Prescription Act 1832.

At common law an easement could be acquired by prescription only if it could be proved to have been used from time immemorial (i.e. from 1189). In fact, user for 20 years before the claim was made would normally be accepted, but a claim could always be defeated by showing, for example, that a right of light claimed for a building could not have existed since 1189 if the building had been constructed in 1500.

The doctrine of lost modern grant was invented because of the ease with which it was possible to defeat a claim to prescription at common law. Where the origin of an alleged easement cannot otherwise be accounted for, then provided that there has been upwards of 20 years' user of the right, the court will presume that the right was lawfully granted and that the document making the grant has been lost. Of course, this is a fiction. This presumption can be rebutted only by evidence that the existence of such a grant was impossible. The evidence necessary to persuade a court to infer a lost modern grant must be stronger than that required to prove common law prescription. A claim to an easement by lost modern grant will not be precluded just because the party claiming the right exercised it under the mistaken belief that he had permission to do so: *Bridle* v *Ruby* [1989] QB 169. The doctrine of lost modern grant can be invoked only if common law prescription is for some reason excluded.

The Prescription Act 1832 laid down prescriptive time periods in general and for rights of light in particular (the latter are discussed in paragraph 3.08). The Act provides that uninterrupted user for 20 years before some action by the dominant owner for confirmation of a right of easement or by the servient owner for a declaration that a right does not exist, means that the claim cannot be defeated merely by showing that it cannot have existed since 1189. The Act further provides that user without interruption for 40 years before a court action confirms an absolute and indefeasible easement. In both cases user must be of right, i.e. *nec vi, nec clam, nec precario*. 'Interruption' is important because if a person wishes to establish an easement by prescription, he must not acquiesce in interruption of his right for one year by the owner of the property on which he wishes to establish the easement. Acquiescence to interruption does not necessarily imply agreement; the owner who wishes to establish the easement may simply not notice an interruption. Any period during which the owner of the land on which the easement is claimed could not give consent to establishing an easement (e.g. because he was an infant or a lunatic) must be added to the 20-year period. Any period in excess of three years during which the servient tenement is leased must be added to the 40-year period.

Extinguishment of easements

3.05 Apart from an express release by deed, the most important method of extinguishing an easement is by the dominant and servient tenements coming into the same ownership and possession.

Types of easement

Rights of way

3.06 A right of way, whether acquired expressly, impliedly, or by prescription, may be limited as to both frequency and type of use, e.g. a right obtained for passage by horse and cart in the nineteenth century will not extend to passage for many caravans if the dominant tenement has become a caravan site.

Rights of support

3.07 Although the natural right of support for land by other land has been distinguished from an easement (paragraph 3.01), it is possible for one building to acquire an easement of support against another after a period of 20 years. The only remedy against this would be for the owner of the supporting building to seek a declaration during the 20 years that the supported building has no right to support. It should be noted that where two detached buildings adjoin on separate plots an easement cannot be acquired requiring a person who removes his abutting wall to weatherproof the exposed flank wall of the remaining building (but if the wall is a party wall, other rules apply; paragraph 2.05).

Rights of light

3.08 To a considerable extent the law relating to rights of light has been rendered of secondary importance by daylighting regulations under planning legislation (Chapter 11), but a knowledge of the law is still required. There is no right to light generally, but only in respect of some definite opening, such as a window or skylight. The owner of the dominant tenement has a right only to such amount of light as is necessary for 'ordinary purposes'. Many years' user of an exceptional amount of light does not prevent an adjoining owner from building so as to reduce light; this was held in a case where an architect claimed that he had enjoyed and needed more light for his office than for ordinary office purposes (*Ambler* v *Gordon* [1905] 1 KB 417).

The decision whether or not enough light is left for ordinary purposes must, therefore, depend on observation, and on all the scientific methods now available for measuring light. The so-called 45° rule from the centre of a window can do no more than help the judge make up his mind, although a reduction of more than 50% of previous light will often be actionable. It should also be noted that if light could be obtained from an existing but blocked skylight, then this must be counted as an available alternative source.

3.09 Under the Prescription Act 1832, as amended by the Rights of Light Act 1959, it was provided that an absolute right of light could be obtained only after 20 years uninterrupted user. Because of the possibility of prescriptive rights being acquired over bomb-damaged sites, the 1959 Act provided a temporary extension of the period to 27 years for actions alleging infringement beginning before that date. The 1959 Act also provided for registration as a local land charge (paragraph 1.08) of a theoretical wall of stated dimensions in such a position as would prevent an adjoining owner from claiming a prescriptive right of light because the owner of the servient tenement did not erect a permanent structure to the registered dimensions. This useful provision avoids the cumbersome procedure by which screens and hoardings had to be erected by the person seeking to prevent a right of light being acquired over his land; in any case such hoardings would now be subject to planning control (Chapter 13).

4 Restrictive covenants

4.01 A restrictive covenant is a covenant which restricts an owner of the servient tenement in some way in his use and enjoyment of his land. The covenant must be made for the benefit of the dominant land belonging to the covenantee. Typical examples are covenants not to build above a given height or in a given place, or covenants restricting the user of the land to given purposes. Although to some extent superseded by planning controls, restrictive covenants still have a valuable role to play, particularly in preserving the character of housing estates. The essentials of a restrictive covenant are:

1. That it is in substance negative.
2. That it is made between the covenantor and the covenantee for the benefit of the covenantee's land.
3. That the parties intend the burden of the covenant to run with the covenantor's land so as to bind not only the covenantor but also his successors in title.

4.02 A restrictive convenant is an equitable interest and therefore requires registration as a land charge in unregistered land unless the covenant is contained in a lease when registration is not required. In registered land a restrictive covenant is protected by registering a notice or caution against the servient land on the Register. If a restrictive covenant complies with the requirements listed in paragraph 4.01 and is properly protected, it will bind the covenantor's successors in title. The usual remedy for infringement of a restrictive covenant is an injunction to restrain further breaches, but the court may give damages either in addition to or in lieu of an injunction.

The rules on the passing of the benefit of restrictive covenants are complex and need not be considered here.

4.03 Architects should request that their clients obtain confirmation that there are no restrictive covenants applying to a site that could affect the proposed design of a building or indeed whether a building could be constructed at all. An architect must proceed with caution. Although the point has never been tested in court, an architect who continued to act for a client in designing a building that was known by both of them to contravene a restrictive covenant, might be liable jointly with his client for the tort of conspiracy, i.e. of agreeing to do an unlawful act.

Discharge of restrictive covenants

4.04 Many restrictive covenants imposed in former years are no longer of real benefit to the owners of adjoining lands and may indeed be anti-social or in conflict with reasonable redevelopment proposals. Power is given to the Lands Tribunal by Section 84 of the Law of Property Act 1925, as amended by Section 28 of the Law of Property Act 1969, for the discharge or modification of any covenant if the Tribunal is satisfied that, *inter alia*, changes in the neighbourhood make the covenant obsolete or that the restriction does not now secure practical advantages of substantial value to the person entitled to its benefit or is contrary to public policy (i.e. planning policy). Compensation may be awarded in lieu of the covenant.

5 Landlord and tenant covenants

5.01 The vast majority of leases with which architects are concerned on behalf of their clients, particularly of trade and business premises, are the subject of formal agreements defining precisely the respective rights and obligations of the parties. Whether the architect's client is a tenant who wishes to rebuild, alter, or repair premises, or a landlord who requires evidence to recover damages from a tenant who has failed to observe a covenant for repair, regard must be had first to the express terms of the lease, and the client's solicitor should be asked to advise on the meaning and extent of the terms. The following general remarks, except where otherwise stated, introduce the law only in so far as the lease has not stated to the contrary.

Doctrine of waste

5.02 'Waste' consists of an act or omission which causes or is likely to cause a lasting alteration to the nature of the land and premises to the prejudice of the landlord. A tenant of land for more than one year is, apart from statute and any terms of the lease, liable for voluntary waste (any positive act such as pulling down or altering the premises) and permissive waste (allowing the premises to fall into disrepair). In practice, a lease will always contain repairing covenants. Normally the landlord is responsible for external repairs and the tenant for internal repairs. In any event, in respect of a lease of a dwelling house for less than seven years, the landlord is obliged to keep the exterior in repair and to keep in repair and working order all installations relating to heating and the supply of services: Housing Act 1985, Section 11. There is a third type of waste: ameliorating waste – some change which will improve the value of the reversion. The courts are very unlikely to restrain the commission of this form of waste.

Fixtures

5.03 Prima facie anything that is attached to the land becomes part of the land and therefore the property of the landowner. If, therefore, a tenant attaches something to the land that has been leased to him, it will, presumptively, become the property of the landlord. However, two questions arise: Is the addition in truth a fixture, or does it remain a chattel? Even if it is a fixture, is it one which a tenant may remove?

1. Fixture or chattel? In deciding whether something attached to the land is a fixture or chattel, two matters are considered:
   (a) How is the thing attached to the land? Is it attached so that it can be removed readily without damaging the fabric? If so, it may still be regarded as a chattel, and therefore the property of the tenant.
   (b) Why is the thing attached? This is now the more important text (*Berkeley* v *Poulett* (1976) 241 EG 911). If the thing is attached to the land simply because it cannot otherwise be enjoyed as a chattel (e.g. a tapestry fixed to a wall), then it remains a chattel. If the thing is attached in order to improve the land permanently, then it is a fixture.
2. Tenant's fixtures. Even if the thing is a fixture, a tenant who has attached it may be able to remove it. In the case of non-agricultural holdings, the tenant may remove trade, domestic and ornamental fixtures before the expiry of the tenancy. He must make good any damage to the premises occasioned by the removal of fixtures. If the tenancy is of agricultural land, the tenant can remove *all* fixtures which he has attached within two months of the lease expiring. The landlord has the option to purchase them if he wishes.

Alterations and improvements

5.04 In the absence of any term in the lease regulating the matter, the tenant should obtain the landlord's consent to any alterations. This is because any alteration to the premises will constitute waste (voluntary or ameliorating). It is common for a lease to contain an express condition that no alterations shall be made without the landlord's consent. It is provided by the Landlord and Tenant Act 1927, Section 19 that such consent shall not be unreasonably withheld where the alteration constitutes an improvement. Whether a proposed alteration is an improvement is a question of fact to be considered from the tenant's point of view. It should be noted that it is the tenant's responsibility to prove that the landlord's consent is being unreasonably withheld, that the landlord may object on aesthetic, artistic, and even sentimental grounds, and that although the Act forbids the taking of any payment as a condition of giving consent, the landlord may reasonably require the tenant to pay the landlord's legal and other expenses (including architects' and surveyors' fees) plus a reasonable amount for any diminution in the value not only of the leased premises but also of any adjoining premises of the landlord.

Repairing covenants

Surveys

5.05 Architects are frequently asked to prepare a schedule of dilapidations at the beginning of a tenancy, during the course of, or at the end of the lease. The importance of initial schedules is that in the absence of any covenant to do works as a condition of the grant of the lease, any repairing covenant must be construed with reference to the original condition of the premises. Different phrases may be used, but generally the tenant's obligation is to 'repair, keep in repair and deliver the premises in repair at the end of the term'. Repair may include the replacement or renewal of parts but not renewal of the whole or substantially the whole of the premises.

5.06 A term to 'keep and deliver up premises in good and tenantable repair' is used almost exclusively in leases of houses and flats, and in such cases (unless the amount of the rent brings the premises within the restrictions of the Housing Acts with the statutory implications that the premises were and will be kept fit for human habitation) the covenant could include an obligation to put the premises into repair as well as to keep them in repair. That repair must be such 'as having regard to the age, character and locality of the premises would make it reasonably fit for occupation by another reasonably minded tenant of the same class' (*Proudfoot* v *Hart* (1890) 25 QBD 42, 55). The standard of repair is neither increased by an improvement, nor decreased by a deterioration in the class of tenants (*Lord Calthorpe* v *McOscar* [1924] 1 KB 716).

5.07 It is the tenant's responsibility to prove that a bad state of repair is within the exception of 'fair wear and tear'. In general terms the phrase means that the tenant is not responsible for damage resulting from exposure to the natural elements or reasonable use. Although not liable for direct damage the tenant could be liable for consequential damages – e.g. he might not be liable for repair of tiles slipping from a roof after a storm, but he would be liable for damage to the interior of the premises from flooding resulting from his failure to take steps to prevent rain entering.

Enforcement of repairing covenants

5.08 Under the Leasehold Property (Repairs) Act 1938, as extended by the Landlord and Tenant Act 1954, a landlord cannot forfeit the lease or even begin an action for damages in respect of a tenant's failure to observe a repairing covenant unless he has first served on the tenant a notice under section 146 of the Law of Property Act 1925 clearly specifying the breach. If the tenant serves a counter-notice within 28 days the landlord cannot take any action without the consent of the court. Architects are frequently asked to produce a schedule of defects to accompany such a notice (see also paragraph 5.11).

Consents

5.09 It is emphasized that what has been stated is always subject to the express wording of the lease and also to the many statutory provisions for the protection of tenants of certain types of premises, particularly houses. Architects should remember that a client's tenancy may come at the end of a long line of underleases, and the consents of superior landlords may be required for any work which the client has requested.

Mortgages

5.10 It is not proposed to discuss this subject in detail, but architects should remember that alteration to premises will alter the value of the mortgagee's security. For this reason most mortgages contain covenants requiring the mortgagee's consent to works. As with leases, there may be several mortgagees having different priorities of charge on the premises, and the architect should ask the client whether the property is mortgaged, and if it is request him to obtain any necessary consents.

Architect's responsibilities for surveys

Dilapidations

5.11 If asked to prepare a schedule of dilapidations, an archiect should first find out from his client's solicitor the terms of the lease, so that he is clear as to which portions of the building come within the repairing covenant. These are the only portions he need examine. As tenant's fixtures are removable by the tenant, only dilapidations to landlord's fixtures need usually be catalogued, but because of the difficulties of assessing ownership of fixtures, it is often wise to examine dilapidations on anything that is at all doubtful.

5.12 Estimates of cost of making good dilapidations are often required. Unless an architect has much experience of this kind of work, it is advisable to involve a quantity surveyor. When lessor and lessee cannot agree about the extent of damages or the extent

of responsibility for making them good, their dispute may have to be resolved in the courts. In such cases the schedule of dilapidations becomes evidence, and it is therefore important that it is very clearly drawn. When making a survey for a schedule the possibility that matters might come to court should be borne in mind.

Where the parties agree to appoint an architect or surveyor to prepare a schedule of dilapidations, then, by analogy with the cases on valuations, if no reasons for the schedule are given and it was made honestly and in good faith, it cannot be set aside, even though it turns out to be mistaken: *Campbell* v *Edwards* [1976] 1 WLR 403. If reasons are given for the schedule and they are fundamentally erroneous, it may be set aside: *Burgess* v *Purchase & Sons (Farms) Ltd* [1983] Ch 216.

Surveys of property to be purchased

5.13 Architects are often asked to inspect property for clients who intend to purchase it or take a lease. An examination of the property is required, bearing in mind the proposed use and taking into account all defects and dilapidations. Useful guides to technical points to be noted in such a survey are given in *Architectural Practice and Procedure* and in *Guide to Domestic Building Surveys*.

5.14 It is important to note that if defects are not observed, the architect may be held to be negligent. For example, where a surveyor failed to report that the timbers of a house were badly affected by death-watch beetle and worm, he was held liable in negligence to the purchaser of that property (*Phillips* v *Ward* [1956] 1 WLR 471). The measure of damages in such a case is the difference between the market value of the property with the defect and the purchase price. It is *not* the difference between the market value with the defect and the value of the property as it would have been if it had been as described (*Perry* v *Sidney Phillips & Son* [1982] 1 WLR 1297).

Hidden defects

5.15 It is often wise, particularly when investigating old property, to open up and inspect hidden portions of the building. If this is not done, the limitations of the investigation should be clearly pointed out to the client, and he should be asked to take a decision as to whether the expense of opening up is worthwhile. He must of course be informed of the probability or otherwise of e.g. rot. If rot is discovered and it was not mentioned in the survey and the architect did not recommend opening up to check, he is almost certainly negligent.

6 Business tenancies – architects' offices

6.01 This review of business tenancies can be in outline only, and it is written from the point of view of architects as tenants of office premises. Two preliminary matters which recent cases involving architect tenants have shown to be of importance concern landlords' rights of forfeiture and rights of assignment.

1. An architect should be careful if a lease includes an absolute right of forfeiture in the event of bankruptcy, as he will find that he cannot raise finance from either a building society or a bank on the security of such a lease.
2. Care should be taken to check the wording of covenants empowering assignment or subletting, not only in the immediate lease offered (where the landlord may have only a right of reasonable objection) but also in any superior lease (where the superior landlord may have reserved an absolute right of refusal without reasonable cause). Consent may be obtained from the immediate landlord but refused by the superior landlord, thus preventing a subsequent assignment of the lease.

Protection of business tenants

6.02 Part II of the Landlord and Tenant Act 1954, as amended by Part I of the Law of Property Act 1969, provides a substantial measure of protection to occupiers of business premises by providing in effect that the tenant may continue in occupancy indefinitely, unless the landlord satisfies the court that a new tenancy ought not to be granted for certain defined statutory reasons (paragraph 6.03). If the tenant receives notice of determination (not less than six nor more than twelve months' notice) expiring not earlier than the existing tenancy would otherwise have ended, he may within two months of receipt serve a counter-notice on the landlord that he is unwilling to leave and then apply to the court for a new tenancy.

6.03 There are seven reasons which might prevent the grant of a new tenancy, the first three of which, if proved, prevent the grant absolutely, the latter four being left to the discretion of the court.

1. If, on termination of the existing tenancy, the landlord intends to demolish or reconstruct the premises and could not reasonably do so without possession of the whole. (Since the 1969 Act, this does not prevent a new tenancy of the whole or part of the premises if the landlord will be able to do the work without seriously 'interfering' with the tenant's business.)
2. If the landlord proves that he intends to occupy the premises for his own business or as a residence. (Since 1969 the landlord may successfully resist if he intends the premises to be occupied by a company in which he has a controlling interest.)
3. If the landlord proves the premises are part of a larger holding for which he could obtain a substantially larger rent than for the individual parts.
4. If the tenant fails to keep the premises in repair.
5. If there are persistent delays in paying rent.
6. If there are breaches of covenant.
7. If the landlord is willing to provide suitable alternative accommodation on reasonable terms.

Compensation

6.04 If the court cannot grant a new tenancy for any of the first three reasons above, the tenant will be entitled to compensation at the rateable value or twice the rateable value where the tenant and his predecessors in the same business have occupied for 14 years or more.

New tenancy

6.05 The length of a new tenancy (but not exceeding 14 years), the rent, and other terms are fixed by the court.

6

Scots land law

ANGUS STEWART QC

1 Introduction

1.01 The term 'property' is used in Scots law to denote both a right and the subject of a right. The right can be described as the right of using and disposing of a thing as one's own. This may be subject to many different statutory, contractual, or other restrictions. Property as the subject of the right is classified either as heritable or movable. Heritable property is property which by its nature is immovable, for example, land or buildings, while movable property consists of things such as furniture or motor cars, which by their nature can be moved.

Heritable and movable property

1.02 Movable property may become heritable through attachment to heritable property. Building materials are movable until they are incorporated in the building, when they become part of the heritage. Articles such as light fittings, a central heating system, or machinery, which are installed in a building, become part of the heritable property if they are sufficiently attached to or connected with the building. The question whether or not movable property has become heritable in this way, i.e. has become a 'fixture', depends on the whole circumstances and has given rise to a large body of case law. The important point in deciding this is generally the degree of attachment to the heritage (whether, for example, the thing in question can be removed without damage to itself or the heritage). Things may also be heritable because they are essential accessories of the heritage as, for example, the keys of a house, or unattached articles essential for the operation of fixed machinery. Articles such as pictures or fitted carpets are not regarded as fixtures, since they are only lightly attached. Fitted cupboards, and gas or electric fires which are built in, would be.

1.03 In certain circumstances heritable property may become movable. Examples are minerals removed from the land, or standing timber which is felled.

1.04 Whether property is heritable or movable may be of considerable importance in, among others, questions of valuation for rating and in interpretation of contracts for the sale of heritage, where it is necessary to know what is included in the sale. Houses, for example, are often sold 'complete with fixtures and fittings'. Felled timber or harvested crops would not in the absence of express provision in the contract be included in a sale of land.

Corporeal and incorporeal

1.05 Heritable and movable property are both further classified as corporeal or incorporeal property, the former being tangible, the latter consisting of intangible rights. Examples of incorporeal property are servitude rights (paragraph 3.08), such as rights of way-leave for pipes, or certain security rights in heritage, which

are heritable, and patent or copyright rights (Chapter 24), which are movable.

2 Corporeal heritable property and feudal law

2.01 For centuries a valid title to heritage in Scotland has been obtained only by having the disposition, contract, or other deed publicly recorded. Traditionally, deeds have been recorded in the Register of Sasines. If a deed recorded in the Register appears good and has been followed by possession for ten years, the title cannot be challenged. Under the Land Registration (Scotland) Act 1979, the traditional system is being replaced, in one area after another, by a new system of registration of titles in the Land Register for Scotland. In general, an entry in the title sheet made up by the Keeper will represent an unchallengeable entitlement to the registered interest, be it a right of ownership, of security or wayleave, and so on. Entries in the title sheet will be conclusive of the location and extent of the property and of all interests affecting it. The technical content of deeds will be reduced and conveyancing simplified. Registered titles will be backed by a State guarantee. In exceptional circumstances the Keeper may decline to guarantee a title. Possession for ten years after registration will make such a title unchallengeable.

2.02 The terminology and technicalities of Scots land law still owe something to the feudal system of land holding. Under feudal law, all rights to land derive from the Crown, the paramount feudal 'superior'. Historically, grants of land were made by the Crown to its 'vassals' in return for military or other services. A Crown vassal might in turn make land grants for services and in turn stand in the position of superior to his vassals.

Feuing

2.03 The Crown is still in theory the paramount superior of all land, although the practical importance of this is probably limited to the fact that certain types of property, such as the foreshore, are assumed to be vested in the Crown. Most privately owned land and buildings are held on a feu. However, the distinctive feudal element of the system of holding has been modified and now greatly attenuated by a number of statutes.

2.04 Today the vassal who holds property on feu may have to pay a feu-duty. Frequently this is purely nominal. Provided he pays his feu-duty his successors (whether they succeed on his death or through a purchase of his interest) hold the land in perpetuity. The vassal may sell his interest in the land, or part of it, or feu the whole or parts to other persons, himself retaining an interest as mid-superior. If he sells or feus parts he may still be liable to his

superior for the whole feu-duty. But he may make an arrangement with him to allocate the feu-duty so that each part of the land is liable for a proportion only. If he does not do so, each part and each proprietor is liable for the whole. Under the Conveyancing and Feudal Reform (Scotland) Act 1970, he can now compel the superior to come to such an arrangement.

2.05 The Land Tenure Reform (Scotland) Act 1974, although it has not abolished feu-duties outright, has done much to pave the way for their eventual disappearance by (1) banning the creation of new feu-duties, (2) making it compulsory to redeem existing feu-duties when properties are sold (the purchaser makes a lump sum payment which is fixed according to a statutory formula), and (3) allowing the vassal to insist on redemption, in return for a lump sum payment, at other times. The Act also introduces elaborate provisions to prevent superiors from frustrating the purpose of the reform by exacting other kinds of periodic payment, for example by creating long leases for dwelling houses. It may happen that several houses, for example in one tenement, together make up a single feu burdened by a single feu-duty which has not been formally allocated among the individual flats. In such a case the provisions for redemption do not apply. But as has already been mentioned, the 1970 Act allows any single proprietor to insist on allocation; and once the feu-duty has been allocated, the provisions of the 1974 Act will apply.

Restrictions on ownership by vassals

2.06 Although in many respects the vassal is in the position of absolute owner of the land, his right of ownership may be subject to many conditions and restrictions contained in his title. The disposition of the property may, for example, regulate the number and type of buildings the vassal may erect, and the use to which the property may be put. It may require the vassal to keep any buildings in good repair, insure them with an approved company, and rebuild them within a certain time in the event of their destruction. It may also require the vassal to contribute to the cost of building or maintaining roads serving the feu. These are examples of conditions which, if properly framed in a feudal title, can be enforced by the superior against all vassals in perpetuity. When ground is feued for building it is practice to impose a deadline for the completion of the building with a condition that if the deadline is not met ownership will revert to the grantor. Before starting to design, architects should suggest to their clients that the feudal title of the property be examined to check for conditions. The client's solicitor will do this.

Pre-emption

2.07 The superior may also insert a clause of pre-emption, stipulating that if the vassal wishes to sell he must first offer the property to the superior, either at a fixed price or, more commonly, at a price which he has been offered and for which he would sell if the superior does not exercise his right. Such a right is now exercisable on the occasion of the first sale only and must be exercised within 21 days of the vassal's offer to the superior.

2.08 Not any and every condition is enforceable by the superior, however. The superior must have an interest to enforce the condition, which in fact is fairly readily assumed, and the condition must be precise in its terms so that the vassal will be able to ascertain, through reading the condition, what is required of him. There is a presumption that the vassal is free to do as he wishes with his property, and when a condition is being interpreted he will always receive the benefit of the doubt if there is any ambiguity.

Jus quaesitum tertio

2.09 Some feuing conditions are enforceable by persons other than the superior; this right is called *jus quaesitium tertio* (Chapter 4, paragraph 4.04). If, for example, a superior feus out lots of land on which buildings are to be erected according to a uniform plan, one feuar may in certain circumstances object to another feuar breaching the feuing conditions. The breach must affect him directly in some way, for instance, by damaging his amenity. If it is stated in the title that certain things may be done only with the permission of the superior, however, other vassals may not object to these things if the superior's permission is obtained. Otherwise the fact that a superior acquiesces in a breach of the conditions is of no consequence in a question between vassals.

Altering and discharging conditions

2.10 A superior may alter or discharge feuing conditions, though, if other vassals have a right to object to a breach, their consent must be obtained. In return for waiving conditions, the superior may demand a lump payment or, indeed, any other consideration he thinks he can obtain but not, since the 1974 Act, any increase in feu-duty or other periodic payment or the imposition of such a payment. The situation where desirable development could be obstructed by superiors led to statutory reform in the shape of the Conveyancing and Feudal Reform (Scotland) Act 1970. Under sections 1 and 2 of the Act the Lands Tribunal has power to vary or discharge any 'land obligations' (including feuing conditions and rights such as servitudes) which for a variety of reasons have become unreasonable, or unduly burdensome compared with any benefit they might bring, or the existence of which impedes some reasonable use of the land. This includes powers formerly held by a sheriff (Chapter 4) under the Housing (Scotland) Act 1966 to allow the division of a single dwelling house into two or more dwellings in breach of the feuing conditions, and the sheriff's power has thus ended. The Lands Tribunal has power to order payment of compensation and to add or substitute different provisions. It is of course still open to the parties to come to a private arrangement, and there may be situations in which such an arrangement is more convenient than an application to the Tribunal.

Leases

2.11 A proprietor may lease his property to another, the basis of the contract being that the tenant has the right to occupy and make use of the property in return for payment of rent. There are numerous statutory provisions regulating leases of various kinds, mainly by restricting rents or providing some degree of security of tenure for the tenant. It is not proposed to deal with this subject in the present chapter in any detail.

Business tenancies

2.12 It should be noted, however, that the statutory provisions relating to security of tenure in business tenancies which apply in England (Chapter 5) do not extend to Scotland. Thus the architect in Scotland who rents his office premises relies wholly on his contract with his landlord for security of tenure, there being no corresponding Scottish legislation.

Surveys

2.13 The responsibilities of Scottish architects with regard to surveys are the same as for English architects (Chapter 22, paragraph 3.03).

Non-feudal tenure

2.14 A distinctive system of non-feudal ownership survives here and there in the Northern Isles. It is known as udal tenure. Udal owners hold their land outright of no superior and the ultimate superiority of the Crown is not acknowledged. Udal titles include foreshore. The validity of a udal title depends on possession rather than recording. In other parts of Scotland there are isolated instances of non-feudal tenures and tenures whose origins pre-date the feudal system. Parish churches and lands are said to be held of no superior. Compulsory purchase or other statutory acquisition of feudal lands is said to eliminate all mid-superiorities but not the ultimate superiority of the Crown. Council house sales tend to be on the feudal model so that the Council may keep an interest in the use and development of the property.

3 Other restrictions of corporeal heritable property

3.01 Apart from any restrictions in his title, numerous other restrictions, both statutory and otherwise, may affect the proprietor of heritable property.

Statutory restrictions

3.02 It is not proposed to enter into the statutory restrictions in detail, but obvious examples of these are the Town and Country Planning Acts and the numerous statutes and regulations governing compulsory purchase (Chapter 13). In addition various bodies have power to enter land or premises compulsorily (Chapter 17). A number of uses are not permitted except under licence (sale of alcohol, gaming, sex shops, etc.). The Public Health (Scotland) Acts prohibit the carrying on of a large number of activities, defined as statutory nuisances, on various kinds of property. A proprietor is also subject to building regulations administered by the appropriate local authority in respect of any building operations he may wish to carry out (Chapter 15). A statutory right to continue in occupation of the family home is given to the spouse of the owner or tenant by the Matrimonial Homes (Family Protection) Scotland Act 1981. The right can be enforced against third parties who should protect their interest by getting the protected spouse's consent to any transaction in accordance with the statutory formalities. Unless 'de-crofted', croft land and buildings continue subject to the statutory crofting regime even after purchase by the crofting tenant.

3.03 In addition the occupier of premises is obliged under the Occupiers' Liability (Scotland) Act 1960 to take reasonable care to see that persons entering the premises (which include land and other types of property) do not suffer injury owing to the state of the premises. His failure to do so may result in his being liable.

Common structures

3.04 In his use of his property the proprietor may also have to take into account the interests of his neighbours in a variety of ways. Where there is a common gable or dividing wall between two properties, either proprietor may object to the other carrying out operations which may be injurious to it, since it is common property. Where the property is a flatted or tenement building in which each house is owned separately, each proprietor has a common interest in the property outwith his own, so far as necessary for his support and shelter. Thus although the external walls of each property belong to individual proprietors, they may not interfere with them in such a way as to endanger the other properties. Similarly each proprietor is sole owner of his floors and ceilings, to the mid-point of the joists, but must not interfere with them in such a way as to weaken his neighbour's floor or ceiling. The roof of a tenement property belongs to the owner of the top storey, but all proprietors in the building have a common interest in seeing that it is properly maintained, and they may compel the owner to keep it in repair and to refrain from damaging it. Common stairs and passages are the common property of all to whose premises they form an access, and all are obliged to maintain them. If alterations to common property or the roof are contemplated it is often (though not always) necessary to obtain the consent of all proprietors. Clients should be advised to consult their solicitors who can check the feudal titles and, if necessary, attempt to obtain consents.

3.05 These rules apply to all tenement property in Scotland, unless, as frequently happens, there is express provision to the contrary in the titles (see paragraphs 2.06 ff), in which case the provisions in the titles prevail over the common law rules. A check on the feudal titles by the client's solicitor should reveal feuing conditions which may affect design.

3.06 It often happens that there are difficulties in getting all proprietors in a tenement building to agree to mutual repairs. There may be difficulty in deciding, without legal advice, whether a particular repair is a mutual responsibility or in agreeing how the cost of the repair should be allocated. Local authorities have statutory powers to carry out repairs and charge the cost to all proprietors in proportion to the rateable value of their properties. The local authority should be applied to in the case of deadlock among the proprietors. Under the Civic Government (Scotland) Act 1982 councils have powers to light common stairs and passages and to require common areas to be kept clean and properly decorated. Fire authorities have power to deal with fire hazards in common areas.

Natural rights

3.07 A proprietor may also have to take account of servitude rights and natural rights of his neighbours or others. Natural rights arise independently of any separate contract or title, through ownership of the land. They include right of support of land. Thus a proprietor may not quarry up to the boundary of his land if this would lead to subsidence of his neighbour's land. He is not entitled to interfere with a stream flowing through his land in such a way as to change its natural flow as it comes to his neighbour's land, since all the riparian proprietors have a common interest in the stream and may object if they are deprived of its natural flow. He may not carry on operations on his property which constitute a 'nuisance', i.e. which interfere with his neighbour's right to the comfortable enjoyment of his property. What is or is not a nuisance at common law depends on the nature of the neighbourhood, but it may consist of excessive noise or foul smells. If a nuisance has existed without challenge for a period of 20 years or more, however, it cannot be objected to.

Servitudes

3.08 A servitude, in contrast to a natural right, is founded on agreement, whether express or implied. A servitude may be positive or negative; a positive servitude entitles the person who has right to the servitude to do certain things, such as obtaining access to his property over his neighbour's; a negative servitude entitles one proprietor to insist that another refrain from certain acts, for example, erecting buildings over a certain height. Property may be subject to many different kinds of servitude, including servitudes of support, stillicide (which entitles the proprietor of property to let rainwater from his own house fall on his neighbour's ground), and light, affecting mainly urban property, and servitudes of way or access, pasturage, and drawing or conducting water, affecting land.

Express or implied servitudes

3.09 Servitudes may be constituted either by express agreement, which may be followed by recording in the Register of Sasines (nowadays Registration) so that the servitude appears in the title, or by implied agreement. For example, where A sells part of his land to B and the only means of access is over A's land, there is an implied agreement that B has a servitude right of access over A's land. Positive servitudes may also be constituted by uninterrupted use for a period of 20 years, and may lapse if not exercised for that period. Negative servitudes lapse only if a breach is allowed to continue for 20 years without interruption.

Defeating acquisition of implied servitudes

3.10 Servitudes roughly correspond to easements in England. Methods of preventing easements being obtained by prescription (i.e. long use) are discussed in Chapter 7, but these are not applicable in Scotland to servitudes. However, many of the matters which are subjects of servitudes, including support, stillicide, and light, are within the provisions of the Scottish Building Regulations (Chapter 15), which are much more comprehensive and detailed than the English ones. In most cases, the regulations prevent new buildings being designed so that their proprietors acquire onerous servitudes by implication over their neighbours' properties.

Rights of way

3.11 Land may be subject to a public right of way, which is a right for members of the public to pass by a definite route over land from one public place to another. Such a right is almost invariably constituted by use for a period of 20 years, and lapses if not used for that period.

3.12 The Prescription and Limitation (Scotland) Act 1973 now gives in one statute the various periods of occupation or use required to set up rights over land, from ownership to rights of way, and conversely the periods of non-use which will defeat claims, for example, of servitude.

4 Sale of land and buildings

4.01 The law does not recognize verbal agreements for the sale of land or buildings. Agreements for the sale of heritage must be in writing, signed and witnessed. Agreements once completed in normal Scottish form are binding and cannot be withdrawn from unilaterally. But such agreements do not of themselves effect a transfer of the property. Property is transferred when the title is delivered and recorded. Purchasers should normally not alter or spend money on property until they have a title. Since the title supersedes the sale agreement, purchasers' legal advisers should ensure that all sale conditions which are meant to have continuing effect are either incorporated in the title or otherwise kept in force.

4.02 The contract of sale is concluded and is binding on the purchaser and the seller when a written offer to purchase has been accepted in writing. It is too late thereafter for the purchaser to complain about the structural state of the property or that it is less extensive than he believed or is subject to feudal conditions that prevent his using it in the way he intended.

4.03 Normally missives of sale are concluded by solicitors acting for the parties. Prospective purchasers would be well advised not to sign agreements prepared by house builders or developers without taking legal advice.

5 Incorporeal heritable property

5.01 This type of property consists, broadly speaking, of rights over heritage. Servitudes are one example, and rights to leases and feu-duties are others. Security rights over land are another, as, for example, the right of a building society over property on the security of which it has granted a mortgage (Chapter 5).

6 Corporeal movable property

6.01 Ownership of movable property does not depend, as does that of heritage, on possession of a documentary title. The posses-sor of an article is presumed to be the owner in the absence of proof to the contrary. A person is the legal possessor of an article even if he has placed it in the hands of some other person who is his agent or servant, or whom he places in the position of custodier of the property for some reason. Thus a person taking a car to a garage for repair puts the garage in the position of custodier and does not in the eyes of the law lose possession of his car. Accordingly he continues to be the presumed owner. Similarly if an article is on hire, the legal possessor is the person who hires it out and not the person to whom it is hired. Conversely property in movables does not pass by mere agreement. There must be some element of delivery to and possession by the transferee. This aspect of Scots law has important practical implications, e.g. in relation to the effectiveness of clauses in building contracts purporting to transfer ownership of plant and materials.

7 Incorporeal movable property

7.01 This type of property consists of rights which are not, generally speaking, directly connected with heritage. Shares in a limited company and a partner's interest in his firm (Chapter 20) are both movable, even though the company or firm may own heritage. Other examples are rights to debts or rights under contracts. Trade names and trade-marks are further legal examples, as are rights to designs and copyright (Chapter 24).

Part Two

The law of building contracts

7

Introduction to building contracts

ANTHONY SPEAIGHT QC

1 The nature of building contracts

1.01 The general principles of the English law of contract were discussed in Chapter 2. A building contract is a particular type of contract governed by those general principles. Contracts for building work can vary greatly. Many such contracts are made every week by word of mouth between homeowners and self-employed sole builders: in such cases the only express terms will be a brief description of the work to be done and a price. Other building contracts are so complicated that the documents embodying the contract contain more words than the entire works of Shakespeare. However, most contracts for building work have certain characteristics in common. The contract will usually be one for the undertaking of labour and the supply of materials. The person who is engaging and paying the builder is normally referred to as 'the employer': in most, though not quite every, case this is the person who owns the site or the building at which the construction works are to be carried out. The builder is traditionally referred to as 'the contractor'. In many such contracts there is a certifying officer who plays a role in fixing the amounts of instalment payments and other matters of importance to the project, such as the date of completion, by the issue of certificates. The person who performs the certification function is very frequently an architect; and is sometimes referred to as 'the architect' even when he is not.

1.02 Assuming that the parties who are proposing to enter into a building contract have decided that they will record their agreement in writing, there is no reason why they should not sit down and draft a written agreement for themselves in their own words. But in practice that rarely happens. Because building contracts have so many standard features, and because the complexity of the building process is such that a comprehensive contract is likely to be a lengthy document, standard forms are generally used. Typically such a form will be the subject of a few minor alterations, and certain additions, negotiated between the parties. If parties decide that they will use a standard form, they have complete freedom what form to choose. There is nothing to prevent an enterprising individual publishing his own form, and selling as many copies as he can to anybody whom he can convince of the merits of his draft. Indeed, in 1982 the Association of Consultant Architects (ACA) did just that: disliking the 1980 Joint Contracts Tribunal Form which had just been published, the ACA published their own standard form (see Chapter 9). More recently, Sir Michael Latham's report 'Constructing the Team' published by HMSO in 1994 proposed a new family of interlocking building contracts developed from the New Engineering Contract (see Chapter 9). However, for most practical purposes the use of a standard form means the use of a form published by the body now known as the Joint Contracts Tribunal (JCT).

2 History of the Joint Contracts Tribunal

2.01 By the end of the nineteenth century a standard form of building contract was in fairly common use. For many years it was known as 'the RIBA form of contract'. Indeed, that title achieved such currency that it continued to be used in some quarters long after the correct name of the form had become 'the JCT form'. The JCT was established in 1931. It consisted at that time of the RIBA and the NFBTE, which is now known as the Building Employers Confederation, with the object of publishing and where necessary amending a standard form of building contract. The JCT published important new editions of the form in 1939 and in 1963.

2.02 Over the years the JCT expanded to include in addition to its original constituent bodies the RICS, the RIBA, the Building Engineers Confederation, the Association of County Councils, the Association of Metropolitan Authorities, the Association of District Councils, the Confederation of Associations of Specialist Engineering Contractors, the Federation of Associations of Specialists and Subcontractors, the Association of Consulting Engineers, the British Property Federation and the Scottish Building Contract Committee. The CBI has observer status. The JCT is therefore now broad-based and comprehensive.

2.03 In 1964 an official report entitled 'The Placing and Management of Contracts for Building of Civil Engineering Works' was published (the Banwell Report). This report recommended inter alia that the conditions on which sub-contractors tender and enter into contracts should be standardized. Accordingly, in 1966 the JCT obtained authority from its constituent members to assume responsibility for the production of standard forms of sub-contract; at the same time (again on a recommendation contained in the Banwell Report) the FASS and CASEC were invited to become members of the JCT.

2.04 In 1980 the JCT published a new standard form; at the same time it published its first set of sub-contract documents. The standard form was much longer than the 1963 form, and many practitioners found it daunting and unmanageable. At first there was some doubt how widely it would be used, and for a number of years the 1963 form continued to be adopted on projects quite frequently. However, with time the 1980 form has become established. In relation to sub-contracts the JCT published not only a standard from of sub-contract, which interlocked with the standard form of main contract, but also a set of supplementary documents for the submission of tenders, making nominations and the like. The main contract has been the subject of a number of amendments.

The commentary in Chapter 8 discusses the form as amended up to and including Amendment 13 issued in 1994.

3 The JCT family of forms

3.01 The number of versions and forms published by the JCT has been growing over the last 15 years. Currently it publishes the following forms and associated documents:

1. The Standard Form of Building Contract in the following variants:
   (a) local authorities edition with quantities;
   (b) local authorities edition with approximate quantities;
   (c) local authorities edition without quantities;
   (d) private edition with quantities;
   (e) private edition with approximate quantities;
   (f) private edition without quantities.
2. Fluctuation Clauses (Clauses 38, 39 and 40 as referred to in Clause 37):
   (a) for use with all versions of the local authorities edition;
   (b) for use with all versions of the private edition.
3. Contractor's Designed Portion Supplement:
   (a) with quantities;
   (b) without quantities.
4. Sectional Completion Supplement:
   (a) with quantities and with approximate quantities;
   (b) without quantities.
5. Formula Rules for use with all versions of the Standard Form of Building Contract.
6. Standard Form with Contractor's Design (CD81).
7. Fixed Fee Form of Prime Cost Contract (1987).
8. Standard Form of Prime Contract (1992).
9. Intermediate Form of Building Contract (IFC84).
10. Agreement for Minor Works (MW80).
11. Management Contract (MC87).
12. JCT Measured Form Contract.
13. Sub-contract documents:
    (a) NSC/T Part 1: Invitation to Tender;
    (b) NSC/T Part 2: Tender;
    (c) NSC/T Part 3: Particular conditions;
    (d) NSC/W: Standard Form of Employer/Nominated Sub-contractor Agreement;
    (e) NSC/N: Standard Form of Nomination for Sub-contractor;
    (f) NSC/A: Standard Form of Articles of Nominated Sub-Contract Agreement between a Contractor and a Nominated Sub-contractor;
    (g) NSC/C: Standard Conditions of Nominated Sub-Contract (incorporated by reference into NSC/A).
14. Formula Rules for use with Standard Form of Sub-Contract.

3.02 A prospective employer looking for a way through the maze of forms which now exist might find it useful to take the following approach, in order to decide which form will be best suited to his requirements in any particular situation.

First decision: who will design the works?

3.03 First, decide who is going to design the proposed building. The broad options are between the traditional approach of engaging an architect to design a building and then employing a building contractor to construct in accordance with the designs; and handing the entire package of the project over to a contractor who is engaged both to design and to build on the basis of a relatively brief statement of the employer's requirements. In the latter case, the appropriate form is the Standard Form of Building Contract With Contractor's Design which was published in 1981.

3.04 A variant on the design-and-build option sometimes arises when within a project being carried out with an architect's design it is desired that the contractor should himself design one portion. In that case the employer should be advised to use the standard form coupled with the Contractor's Designed Portion Supplement. In 1981 such a supplement was published for use with the 'with

quantities' form; in 1993 a separate supplement was published for use with the 'without quantities' form.

Second decision: will the works be designed before the start of the contract?

3.05 If the employer decides that the works are to be designed by an architect or some other professional consultant on his behalf, rather than the building contractor, the next question is whether the employer is content to wait for the works to be designed before he engages a building contractor to start work. In the traditional scheme of a building project the works were designed as the first stage, and thereafter the employer sought tenders for executing the designs. That arrangement continues to offer a prospective employer many advantages, notably cost control. But in recent years different contractual arrangements have often been used by developers for whom speed of start and completion of a project have for sound commercial reasons been more important than the optimum control of the building costs component of expenditure: particularly at times of high interest rates, developers may judge speed of completion to be the paramount commercial consideration.

3.06 The pure option of a contract to suit the employer who wants to embark on a project in advance of a design is the JCT Standard Form of Prime Cost Contract, the present version of which was published in 1992. Under this form of contract the building contractor is entitled to be paid whatever turns out to be the cost to him of doing the work ('the prime cost') plus a fixed fee. In practice this form is often thought of as appropriate when work is very urgently required, such as after fire damage, or when the scope of the work cannot be ascertained until the work has been commenced.

3.07 An alternative option for an employer who is able to have some limited design work carried out is a management contract, under which a building contractor undertakes to organize other contractors, known as 'works contractors' to carry out a building project. During the 1980s large contractors who were undertaking work in this way provided their own forms of contract, and the arrangement's popularity grew. In 1987 the JCT published a Standard Form of Management Contract. The 'management contractor' is paid a fixed fee plus the prime cost of his own on-site management staff and of the works contractors. This arrangement has appealed to a number of developers in recent years. It enables a quick start to be made on a project, as the design need not be particularly detailed when the management contractor is engaged. It also tends to promote a speedy completion. The management contractor may be able to effect very good supervision and management of all the works on site, and the contract may contain incentives to him to secure a speedy completion.

Third decision: how firm a price is required?

3.08 If the works are to be designed by an architect and to be designed before the making of the building contract, the next consideration is how firm a price the employer wants. If he wants certainty, then he should put out to tender a set of drawings and bills of quantities which specify the works in terms of quality and quantity. That process should lead to the making of a contract in the Standard Form With Quantities, which may be regarded as the basic form of 'lump sum', i.e. fixed price, contract.

3.09 Another kind of fixed price is obtained from the Standard Form Without Quantities, but it is a type of fixed price under which paradoxically the total paid is not ascertained until after completion of the works. The price to be paid is then worked out by remeasurement, the prices in the contract being simply rates.

3.10 An employer who for the sake of a slightly earlier start is willing to embark on a project with only an indication of the likely price may, instead of either of the above versions of the contract, use a bill of approximate quantities. The difference from a normal bill of quantities is that it is prepared from less complete design information, and so can be drafted at a slightly earlier stage. The price ultimately to be paid will again be based on remeasurement.

Fourth decision: how large is the project?

3.11 All the standard forms so far mentioned are far too complicated for small projects. In 1980 the JCT published an Agreement for Minor Works (labelled 'MW 80'). The advice of the JCT is that this form be used on contracts up to the value of £70 000 (at 1992 prices). Perhaps the easiest way to state a lawyer's assessment of when this form is suitable is to identify when it is not suitable. It is not appropriate,

– when a project will go on so long that fluctuations are required;
– when the employer wishes to nominate sub-contractors;
– when the works have not yet been sufficiently designed to enable a fixed price to have been tendered, or when pricing against a detailed bill of quantities is required.

3.12 In 1984 the JCT published a form for medium-sized contracts, which required a contract more detailed than MW 80 but did not require the full complexities of the standard forms. This was called the Intermediate Form of Building Contract (IFC 84). The JCT's advice in its Practice Note 20 is that this form would be suitable when the value is not more than £280 000 (at 1992 prices) and the contract period is not more than 12 months. The JCT consider that IFC 84 may also be suitable for larger or longer contracts provided that the works are,

'1. Of simple content involving the normally recognised basic trades and skills of the industry; and
2. Without any building service installations of a complex nature, or other specialist work of a similar nature; and
3. Adequately specified, or specified and billed, as appropriate prior to the invitation of tenders.'

3.13 Where an employer has a regular flow of minor works, such as regular maintenance jobs, there is now an alternative to entering a separate contract for each such job. The JCT in 1989 published a form intended to be suitable for an employer who wished to engage a contractor under a single contract to undertake all the small jobs which might arise in relation to a particular property over a specific period. This is called the 1989 Measured Term Contract.

3.14 An employer who wants to make a distinct contract for a small maintenance item may, as an alternative to MW 80, use the recently published 1990 Jobbing Agreement. This is suitable only for employers who are large organizations, such as local authorities, or who have experience in ordering small jobbing work and dealing with contractors' accounts. The terms of this contract provide for a single payment following checking by the employer of the contractor's account. The JCT recommends its use for work worth up to £10 000 (at 1990 prices) and of duration not exceeding one month.

4 The JCT Standard Form of Contract, 1980 edition

4.01 The 1980 edition of the Standard Form, often referred to as 'JCT 1980', is the direct successor of the 1963 Form, but with some major changes of the form and content. In form, one major change has been the adoption of a system of subordinate decimal numbering in the interest of clarity (though one must now be careful for example, not to confuse Clause 35.18.1.2 with Clause 35.1.8.12 or even Clause 3.5.18.1!).

4.02 The conditions of contract themselves are now divided into five parts: Part 1, General matters; Part 2, Nominated sub-contractors

and nominated suppliers; Part 3, Fluctuations; Part 4, Arbitration and Part 5, Performance specified work.

4.03 The main changes in substance from the 1963 edition are:

1. The greatly expanded provisions relating to nominated sub-contractors and suppliers contained in Part 2.
2. The expansion of the definition of variations.
3. New provisions relating to extensions of time.
4. New provisions relating to loss and expense.
5. New provisions relating to performance specified work.

These and other provisions of the Standard Form are discussed in more detail in the commentary which follows.

4.04 The various forms relating to nominated sub-contractors are intended for use with the Standard Form of Main Contract; very broadly the Standard Form of Sub-contract is the successor of the 'green form' of sub-contract previously issued by the NFBTE, now the BEC. This form, together with its associated documentation, is considered more fully in the commentary which follows.

4.05 There are virtually no differences of substance between the private and local authority variants of the Standard Form Main Contract; such divergences as there are are designed to bring the local authorities' variants into line with local authority law and practice. In the 'with quantities' versions, a bill of quantities forms part of the contract documentation, and the rates contained in the bills of quantities are used for pricing variations and omissions to the contract. In principle the contract is a 'fixed price' contract, i.e. one in which the contractor takes the risk that the work may prove more costly or extensive than he had foreseen. It should, however, be noted that the effect of the relevant contractual provisions (discussed in the commentary) is that the employer guarantees that the bills have been accurately prepared, and therefore the contractor is entitled to extra payment if the bills of quantities do not fully or accurately describe the work included in the contract. The 'without quantities' variants incorporate, instead of bills of quantities, a specification describing the work, and a schedule of rates which is used for the valuation of variations. Again, the contract is a fixed price one. The 'with approximate quantities' variant is a remeasurement contract rather than a fixed price one. In this variant a bill of quantities is prepared, showing the approximate amount of work which is estimated to be required. When the work is completed it is remeasured, and the contract sum recalculated by reference to the amount of work actually done in accordance with the bill rates. These variants are suitable for situations where it is impossible or impracticable to estimate with accuracy the amount of work required in advance.

4.06 Because the Standard Form takes effect by agreement and not by statute, it can be amended in any way the parties choose, but care should be taken when attempting any amendment lest unintended ambiguities and inconsistencies are introduced. Further, any amendment in order to be effective must be in or referred to in the document itself and not merely in the contract bills (or specification where applicable). In the case of *Gleesons v London Borough of Hillingdon* (1970) 215 EG 165, the conditions were not amended, and in the appendix completion was stated to be 24 months after possession. The contract bills provided for completion in stages from 12 to 24 months. It was held that having regard to what is now Clause 2 the bills must be ignored so that liquidated damages were not recoverable until the completion date specified in the appendix had passed. The special Sectional Completion Supplement is available for dealing with this specific situation. (See also *Bramall and Ogden Ltd v Sheffield City Council* (1983) 29 BLR 73.)

4.07 Chapter 8 gives a full commentary on the 1980 main contract form as currently amended. Chapter 9 discusses the sub-contract documentation published by the JCT and other standard forms.

8

The JCT Standard Form of Building Contract, 1980 edition

STEPHEN BICKFORD-SMITH
LANA WOOD*

The text of the Standard Form reproduced in this chapter is from the Private With Quantities edition. The commentary, where appropriate, takes account of variations in the other versions.

1 Articles of Agreement

1.01 The recitals begin by naming the parties to the contract, the employer and the contractor, and go on to record certain matters, including the nature of the intended works. Articles 1 and 2 define the basic obligations of the parties: the contractor agrees to carry out and complete the works in compliance with the contract document and the employer agrees to pay the contractor the contract sum at the times and in the manner specified in the conditions.

1.02 Article 3A identifies the architect, and only applies where the person concerned is entitled to use the name 'architect' under and in accordance with the Architects Registration Acts 1931–1969. Article 3B is for use where the person charged with the duties normally performed by the architect under the contract is not entitled to call himself 'architect' within these Acts and such person is referred to as the contract administrator. For convenience in this chapter the term 'architect' will be used throughout. Article 4 identifies the quantity surveyor.

1.03 The Court of Appeal held in *Croudace* v *London Borough of Lambeth* (1986) 33 BLR 20 that if the architect ceases to act, the employer comes under a duty to appoint another, and if he fails to do so he will be in breach of contract. Amendment 4: 1987 introduced a timescale for the replacement of architects, contract administrators and quantity surveyors. The employer is now required to nominate a replacement within a reasonable time and in any case not later than 21 days after cessation. Unless the nominee is an official of the local authority the contractor has a right to object to the nominee within 7 days. If he chooses to do so the dispute will be referred to an arbitrator under Article 5. There is no right of objection where the nominee is an official of the local authority. The private edition does not have Article 3B or footnote [e], so there will always be an opportunity for the contractor to object to any nominee.

1.04 Article 5 constitutes an Arbitration Agreement within the terms of Section 32 of the Arbitration Act 1950. Any dispute which arises during the progress of the works or after the completion or abandonment of the works is automatically referred to arbitration in accordance with Clause 41, subject to the exceptions

---

Articles of Agreement

made the _____ day of _____ 19 _____

BETWEEN _____

_____

of (or whose registered office is situated at) _____

_____

_____

(hereinafter called 'the Employer') of the one part

AND _____

_____

of (or whose registered office is situated at) _____

_____

(hereinafter called 'the Contractor') [a] of the other part.

Whereas

First   the Employer is desirous of [b] _____

_____

_____

at _____

_____

and has caused Drawings and Bills of Quantities showing and describing the work to be done to be prepared by or under the direction of

_____

Second   the Contractor has supplied the Employer with a fully priced copy of the said Bills of Quantities (which copy is hereinafter referred to as 'the Contract Bills');

Third   the said Drawings numbered _____

_____

(hereinafter referred to as 'the Contract Drawings') and the Contract Bills have been signed by or on behalf of the parties hereto;

Fourth   the status of the Employer, for the purposes of the statutory tax deduction scheme under the Finance (No. 2) Act, 1975, as at the Base Date is stated in the Appendix;

---

* In early editions this chapter was written by Donald Keating QC. In the preparation of the commentary for later editions considerable use has been made by permission of Mr Keating's text from the second edition.

Fifth the extent of the application of the Construction (Design and Management) Regulations 1994 (the 'CDM Regulations') to the work referred to in the First recital is stated in the Appendix;

Now it is hereby agreed as follows

Article 1
For the consideration hereinafter mentioned the Contractor will upon and subject to the Contract Documents carry out and complete the Works shown upon, described by or referred to in those Documents.

Article 2
The Employer will pay to the Contractor the sum of _____

_____

_____ (£ _____ . _____)
(hereinafter referred to as 'the Contract Sum') or such other sum as shall become payable hereunder at the times and in the manner specified in the Conditions.

Article 3
The term 'the Architect' in the Conditions shall mean the said

_____

of _____

_____

or, in the event of his death or ceasing to be the Architect for the purpose of this Contract, such other person as the Employer shall nominate within a reasonable time but in any case no later than 21 days after such death or cessation for that purpose, not being a person to whom the Contractor no later than 7 days after such nomination shall object for reasons considered to be sufficient by an Arbitrator appointed in accordance with article 5. Provided always that no person subsequently appointed to be the Architect under this Contract shall be entitled to disregard or overrule any certificate or opinion or decision or approval or instruction given or expressed by the Architect for the time being.

Article 4
The term 'the Quantity Surveyor' in the Conditions shall mean

_____

of _____

_____

or, in the event of his death or ceasing to be the Quantity Surveyor for the purpose of this Contract, such other person as the Employer shall nominate within a reasonable time but in any case no later than 21 days after such death or cessation for that purpose, not being a person to whom the Contractor no later than 7 days after such nomination shall object for reasons considered to be sufficient by an Arbitrator appointed in accordance with article 5.

Article 5
If any dispute or difference as to the construction of this Contract or any matter or thing of whatsoever nature arising thereunder or in connection therewith shall arise between the Employer or the Architect on his behalf and the Contractor either during the progress or after the completion or abandonment of the Works or after the determination of the employment of the Contractor, except under clause 31 (*statutory tax deduction scheme*) to the extent provided in clause 31·9 or under clause 3 of the VAT Agreement, it shall be and is hereby referred to arbitration in accordance with clause 41.

Article 6·1
The term 'the Planning Supervisor' in the Conditions shall mean the Architect

or _____

of _____

_____

or in the event of the death of the Planning Supervisor or his ceasing to be the Planning Supervisor such other person as the Employer shall appoint as the Planning Supervisor pursuant to regulation 6(5) of the CDM Regulations.

Article 6·2
The term 'the Principal Contractor' in the Conditions shall mean the Contractor, or, in the event of his ceasing to be the Principal Contractor, such other contractor as the Employer shall appoint as the Principal Contractor pursuant to regulation 6(5) of the CDM Regulations.

[A1] AS WITNESS THE HANDS OF THE PARTIES HERETO

[A1] Signed by or on behalf of the Employer _____

in the presence of:

[A1] Signed by or on behalf of the Contractor _____

in the presence of: _____

— —

[A2] EXECUTED AS A DEED BY THE EMPLOYER
hereinbefore mentioned namely

[A3] by affixing hereto its common seal

[A4] in the presence of: _____

* OR —

[A5] acting by a director and its secretary*/two directors* whose signatures are here subscribed:
namely _____

[Signature] _____ DIRECTOR

and _____

[Signature] _____ SECRETARY */DIRECTOR*

[A2] AND AS A DEED BY THE CONTRACTOR
hereinbefore mentioned namely _____

[A3] by affixing hereto its common seal

[A4] in the presence of:

* OR —

[A5] acting by a director and its secretary*/two directors* whose signatures are here subscribed:
namely _____

[Signature] _____ DIRECTOR

and _____

[Signature] _____ SECRETARY*/DIRECTOR*

discussed below. If either party commences proceedings in a court, the other party can apply to have the action stayed, on the ground that the proper forum for resolution of such disputes is by arbitration.

1.05 Disputes under Clause 31 relating to the statutory tax deduction scheme (except to the extent provided in Clause 31.9), and under Clause 3 of the VAT agreement are excluded from the arbitration provisions. The object of these exclusions is clear: statute provides alternative methods of resolving disputes relating to these matters, which would bind the parties irrespective of the arbitrator's decision.

1.06 The articles conclude with a space for the appropriate attestation clause. If the contract is to be executed by an individual as a deed following the Law of Property (Miscellaneous Provisions) Act 1989 there is no longer any requirement that it be executed under seal (although the use of a seal will not invalidate it). The instrument must make it clear on its face that it is intended to be a deed and must be signed by the person in the presence of a witness who attests the signature, (or if it is signed at the person's direction in his presence it must be attested by two witnesses). Further, the instrument must be delivered as a deed by the person or by a person authorized to do so on his behalf. If the contract is to be executed by a company, the Companies Act 1989

provides that a document executed by a company which makes it clear on its face that it is intended to be a deed has effect, upon delivery, as a deed, and it is presumed to be delivered upon execution, unless a contrary intention is proved. A document may be executed by a company by affixing its seal but, irrespective of whether or not the company has a seal, a document signed by a director and the secretary of the company or by two directors and expressed to be executed by the company has the same effect as if executed under the common seal of the company.

Part 1 Conditions: General

2 Clause 1: Interpretation, definitions, etc.

2.01 This clause calls for very little comment. Its purpose is to provide a helpful list of definitions of the main terms used in the contract. Note that a 'person' may be an individual, firm (partnership) or body corporate. It is therefore possible for the architect, under Clause 8.6, to issue an instruction for the exclusion from the works of an entire firm of sub-contractors, for example.

3 Clause 2: Contractor's obligations

3.01 In carrying and completing the contract works, the contractor is both entitled to the benefit of the conditions and subject to the obligations which they impose upon him.

The position of the architect

3.02 The architect is the employer's agent with authority to exercise those powers conferred on him by the contract. As such, he is both entitled and obliged to protect the employer's interests. Formerly the courts took the view that because of the grave disadvantages which would be suffered by the contractor if the architect failed to certify properly or otherwise exercise in a proper manner duties given to him by the contract, the architect was to some extent in a independent 'quasi-judicial' position, and immune from actions for negligence by either party when performing functions requiring the exercise of his independent professional judgement and the application of his mind fairly and impartially between the parties. However in *Sutcliffe* v *Thackrah* [1974] AC 727, it was held that an architect was liable to his employer for negligently over-certifying on interim certificates, and the House of Lords said that the architect enjoyed no such 'quasi-judicial' immunity.

Part 1: General

1 Interpretation, definitions etc.

1·1 Unless otherwise specifically stated a reference in the Articles of Agreement, the Conditions or the Appendix to any clause means that clause of the Conditions.

1·2 The Articles of Agreement, the Conditions and the Appendix are to be read as a whole and the effect or operation of any article or clause in the Conditions or item in or entry in the Appendix must therefore unless otherwise specifically stated be read subject to any relevant qualification or modification in any other article or any of the clauses in the Conditions or item in or entry in the Appendix.

1·3 Unless the context otherwise requires or the Articles or the Conditions or an item in or entry in the Appendix specifically otherwise provides, the following words and phrases in the Articles of Agreement, the Conditions and the Appendix shall have the meanings given below or as ascribed in the article, clause or Appendix item to which reference is made:

Word or phrase	Meaning
3·3A Quotation:	a Quotation by a Nominated Sub-Contractor pursuant to **clause 3·3A** of Conditions NSC/C (*Conditions of Nominated Sub-Contract*).
13A Quotation:	see **clause 13A·1·1**.
All Risks Insurance:	see **clause 22·2**.
Analysis:	see **clause 42·13**.
Appendix:	the Appendix to the Conditions as completed by the parties.
Approximate Quantity:	a quantity in the Contract Bills identified therein as an approximate quantity.*
Arbitrator:	the person appointed under **clause 41** to be the Arbitrator.
Architect:	the person entitled to the use of the name 'Architect' and named in **article 3** or any successor duly appointed under **article 3** or otherwise agreed as the person to be the Architect.
Articles or Articles of Agreement:	the Articles of Agreement to which the Conditions are annexed, and references to any recital are to the recitals set out before the Articles.
Base Date:	the date stated in the Appendix.
CDM Regulations:	the Construction (Design and Management) Regulations 1994 or any remaking thereof or any amendment to a regulation therein.
Certificate of Completion of Making Good Defects:	see **clause 17·4**.
Completion Date:	the Date for Completion as fixed and stated in the Appendix or any date fixed either under **clause 25** or in a confirmed acceptance of a 13A Quotation.
Conditions:	the clauses 1 to 37, either clause 38 or 39 or 40, clauses 41 and 42 and the Supplemental Provisions ('the VAT Agreement') annexed to the Articles of Agreement.
Contract Bills:	the Bills of Quantities referred to in the **First recital** which have been priced by the Contractor and signed by or on behalf of the parties to this Contract.
Contract Documents:	the Contract Drawings, the Contract Bills, the Articles of Agreement, the Conditions and the Appendix.
Contract Drawings:	the Drawings referred to in the **First recital** which have been signed by or on behalf of the parties to this Contract.
Contract Sum:	the sum named in **article 2** but subject to **clause 15·2**.
Contractor:	the person named as Contractor in the Articles of Agreement.
Contractor's Statement:	see **clause 42**.
Date for Completion:	the date fixed and stated in the Appendix.
Date of Possession:	the date stated in the Appendix under the reference to **clause 23·1**.
Defects Liability Period:	the period named in the Appendix under the reference to **clause 17·2**.
Domestic Sub-Contractor:	see **clause 19·2**.
Employer:	the person named as Employer in the Articles of Agreement.
Excepted Risks:	ionising radiations or contamination by radioactivity from any nuclear fuel or from any nuclear waste from the combustion of nuclear fuel, radioactive toxic explosive or other hazardous properties of any explosive nuclear assembly or nuclear component thereof, pressure waves caused by aircraft or other aerial devices travelling at sonic or supersonic speeds.

Final Certificate:	the certificate to which **clause 30·8** refers.
Health and Safety Plan:	where it is stated in the Appendix that all the CDM Regulations apply, the plan provided to the Principal Contractor and developed by him to comply with regulation 15(4) of the CDM Regulations and, for the purpose of regulation 10 of the CDM Regulations, received by the Employer before any construction work under the Contract has started; and any further development of that plan by the Principal Contractor during the progress of the Works.
Interim Certificate:	any one of the certificates to which **clauses 30·1** and **30·7** and the entry in the **Appendix** under the reference to **clause 30·1·3** refer.
Joint Names Policy:	a policy of insurance which includes the Contractor and the Employer as the insured.
Nominated Sub-Contract:	an Agreement NSC/A (*Articles of Nominated Sub-Contract Agreement*), the Conditions NSC/C (*Conditions of Nominated Sub-Contract*) incorporated therein and the documents annexed thereto.
Nominated Sub-Contractor:	see **clause 35·1**.
Nominated Supplier:	see **clause 36·1·1**.
Numbered Documents:	the Numbered Documents annexed to Agreement NSC/A (*Articles of Nominated Sub-Contract Agreement*).
Performance Specified Work:	see **clause 42·1**.
Period of Interim Certificates:	the period named in the **Appendix** under the reference to **clause 30·1·3**.
person:	an individual, firm (partnership) or body corporate.
Planning Supervisor:	the Architect or the other person named in Article 6·1 or any successor duly appointed by the Employer as the Planning Supervisor pursuant to regulation 6(5) of the CDM Regulations.
Practical Completion:	see **clause 17·1**.
Principal Contractor:	the Contractor or any other contractor duly appointed by the Employer as the Principal Contractor pursuant to regulation 6(5) of the CDM Regulations.
provisional sum:	includes a sum provided for work whether or not identified as being for defined or undefined work* and a provisional sum for Performance Specified Work: see **clause 42·7**.
Quantity Surveyor:	the person named in **article 4** or any successor duly appointed under **article 4** or otherwise agreed as the person to be the Quantity Surveyor.
Relevant Event:	any one of the events set out in **clause 25·4**.
Retention:	see **clause 30·2**.
Retention Percentage:	see **clause 30·4·1·1** and any entry in the Appendix under the reference to **clause 30·4·1·1**.
Site Materials:	all unfixed materials and goods delivered to, placed on or adjacent to the Works and intended for incorporation therein.
Specified Perils:	fire, lightning, explosion, storm, tempest, flood, bursting or overflowing of water tanks, apparatus or pipes, earthquake, aircraft and other aerial devices or articles dropped therefrom, riot and civil commotion, but excluding Excepted Risks.
Statutory Requirements:	see **clause 6·1·1**.
Valuation:	see **clause 13·4·1·1**.
Variation:	see **clause 13·1**.
VAT Agreement:	see **clause 15·1**.
Works:	the works briefly described in the **First recital** and shown upon, described by or referred to in the Contract Documents and including any changes made to these works in accordance with this Contract.

1·4 Notwithstanding any obligation of the Architect to the Employer and whether or not the Employer appoints a clerk of works, the Contractor shall remain wholly responsible for carrying out and completing the Works in all respects in accordance with clause 2·1, whether or not the Architect or the clerk of works, if appointed, at any time goes on to the Works or to any workshop or other place where work is being prepared to inspect the same or otherwise, or the Architect includes the value of any work, materials or goods in a certificate for payment, save as provided in clause 30·9·1·1 with regard to the conclusiveness of the Final Certificate.

1·5 If the Employer pursuant to Article 6·1 or to Article 6·2 by a further appointment replaces the Planning Supervisor referred to in, or appointed pursuant to, Article 6·1 or replaces the Contractor or any other contractor appointed as the Principal Contractor, the Employer shall immediately upon such further appointment notify the Contractor in writing of the name and address of the new appointee.

3.03 The architect must at all times seek to perform as exactly as possible his duties under the contract. Thus, for example, it is wrong to permit a contractor to carry out work to a standard lower than that required by the contract because the architect discovers that the contractor has tendered low. It is also wrong to insist on a standard of work higher than the contract standard because the employer demands it. Architects are reminded that quite apart from what the courts have explained as their role under the Building Contract, Rule 1.4 of the RIBA Code of Professional Conduct requires all members and students of the RIBA to act impartially in all matters of dispute between the building owner and the contractor and to interpret the conditions of the Building Contract with entire fairness as between the parties.

2		Contractor's obligations

2·1 The Contractor shall upon and subject to the Conditions carry out and complete the Works in compliance with the Contract Documents, using materials and workmanship of the quality and standards therein specified, provided that where and to the extent that approval of the quality of materials or of the standards of workmanship is a matter for the opinion of the Architect such quality and standards shall be to the reasonable satisfaction of the Architect.

2·2 ·1 Nothing contained in the Contract Bills shall override or modify the application or interpretation of that which is contained in the Articles of Agreement, the Conditions or the Appendix.

2·2 ·2 Subject always to clause 2·2·1:

·2 ·1 the Contract Bills (or any addendum bill issued as part of the information referred to in clause 13A·1·1 for the purpose of obtaining a 13A Quotation), unless otherwise specifically stated therein in respect of any specified item or items, are to have been prepared in accordance with the Standard Method of Measurement of Building Works, 7th Edition, published by the Royal Institution of Chartered Surveyors and the Building Employers Confederation;

·2 ·2 if in the Contract Bills (or in any addendum bill issued as part of the information referred to in clause 13A·1·1 for the purpose of obtaining a 13A Quotation which Quotation has been accepted by the Employer) there is any departure from the method of preparation referred to in clause 2·2·2·1 or any error in description or in quantity or omission of items (including any error in or omission of information in any item which is the subject of a provisional sum for defined work*) then such departure or error or omission shall not vitiate this Contract but the departure or error or omission shall be corrected; where the description of a provisional sum for defined work* does not provide the information required by General Rule 10·3 in the Standard Method of Measurement the correction shall be made by correcting the description so that it does provide such information; any such correction under this clause 2·2·2·2 shall be treated as if it were a Variation required by an instruction of the Architect under clause 13·2.

2·3 If the Contractor shall find any discrepancy in or divergence between any two or more of the following documents, including a divergence between parts of any one of them or between documents of the same description, namely:

2·3 ·1 the Contract Drawings,

2·3 ·2 the Contract Bills,

2·3 ·3 any instruction issued by the Architect under the Conditions (save insofar as any such instruction requires a Variation in accordance with the provisions of clause 13·2),

2·3 ·4 any drawings or documents issued by the Architect under clause 5·3·1·1, 5·4 or 7, and

2·3 ·5 the Numbered Documents,

he shall immediately give to the Architect a written notice specifying the discrepancy or divergence, and the Architect shall issue instructions in regard thereto.

2·4 ·1 If the Contractor shall find any discrepancy or divergence between his Statement in respect of Performance Specified Work and any instruction of the Architect issued after receipt by the Architect of the Contractor's Statement, he shall immediately give to the Architect a written notice specifying the discrepancy or divergence, and the Architect shall issue instructions in regard thereto.

2·4 ·2 If the Contractor or the Architect shall find any discrepancy in the Contractor's Statement, the Contractor shall correct the Statement to remove the discrepancy and inform the Architect in writing of the correction made. Such correction shall be at no cost to the Employer.

3.04 This duty to act fairly is often extremely difficult for a client to appreciate, but is essential to the correct functioning of the contract. The foregoing does not mean that the architect may not consult with the employer on matters within the sphere of his independent duty, but obliges the architect when he comes to make his decision to make up his own mind, doing the best to decide what the parties must have intended according to the contract document and circumstances prevailing at the time of entering into the contract. He should then certify or give his decision accordingly whether or not he thinks it will please the employer.

It is in this way that the architect must act in an independent manner.

3.05 Clause 2.1 provides that where and to the extent that approval of the quality of materials or of the standards of workmanship is a matter for the opinion of the architect, such policy and standards shall be to the reasonable satisfaction of the architect. Under Clause 30.8 the effect of the final certificate is conclusive evidence that the quality of materials or standard of workmanship are to the reasonable satisfaction of the architect, where they are required to be so. It was held in *Crown Estates* v *John Mowlem & Co Limited* [1994] 10 Const LJ 311 (CA) that the scheme of the contract is that the architect must be satisfied as to the quality of all materials and standards of workmanship and must form the opinion that they conform to those required by the contractual terms. This duty extends to:

1. Goods, materials or workmanship for which criteria is stipulated in the contract documents, for example 'to British Standard Specifications';
2. Goods, materials or workmanship for which criteria is not stipulated in the contract documents, there being an implied term that goods and materials are of reasonable quality and fit for their purpose;
3. Goods, materials or workmanship in relation to which standards and quality are expressed to be to the architect's reasonable satisfaction.

The architect's standard of satisfaction in each of these instances must be reasonable and not subjective or arbitrary – it is this with which Clause 2.1.4 is concerned.

3.06 It is not the architect's function to direct the contractor in the way he shall carry out the works, save where the conditions expressly give him this power (see Clause 13).

Liability for design

3.07 It is thought that provided the contractor carries out the work strictly in accordance with the contract documents, he is not responsible if the works prove to be unsuitable for the purpose which the employer or architect had in mind. In relation to performance specified work, Clause 42.17.1.2 specifically provides that nothing in the contract is to operate as a guarantee of fitness for purpose of performance specified work. Further, Clause 6.1.5 provides that as long as the contractor complies with Clause 6.1.2 (which requires him to report any divergences he finds between the statutory requirements and the works as proposed), he will not be liable to the employer if the works do not comply with the statutory requirements. The contractor is required under Clause 2.3 to bring to the architect's attention any dicrepancies between the various documents. It is probably also the contractor's implied duty to bring any obvious errors in the architect's design of which the contractor had actual knowledge to the architect's attention.

3.08 Clause 2.2.1 provides that nothing in the bills shall override or modify the interpretation of the articles, conditions or appendix. Thus if a provision in the bills conflicts with anything in these latter documents, the latter prevails as a matter of interpretation (see *Gleesons* v *Hillingdon* [1970] 215 EG 165, *English Industrial Estates* v *George Wimpey* [1973] 1 Lloyd's Reports 118 and *Henry Boot Construction Limited* v *Central Lancashire New Town Development Corporation* [1980] 15 BLR 1).

3.09 Under Clause 2.2.2.1 (unless otherwise expressly stated in respect of any specified item or items), the contract bills are deemed to have been prepared in accordance with the principles of the *Standard Method of Measurement*, seventh edition (SMM). If they have not been so prepared, this constitutes an error which must be corrected. The correction is to be treated as though it were a variation required by the architect by virtue of Clause 2.2.2.2. SMM expressly requires bills fully and accurately to describe the work. Thus, for example, if there is no provision in the contract bills for excavation in rock, but in carrying out the work it becomes clear that such excavation is necessary, then it seems that the bills must be read as if they had included an item for excavation in rock and the contract will become entitled to extra payment (see *Bryant & Son Limited* v *Birmingham Hospital Saturday Fund* [1938] All ER 503).

4 Clause 3: Contract sum – additions or deductions – adjustment – interim certificates

4.01 This clause makes it clear that where adjustments are made in the contract sum, as soon as the adjustment has been quantified, whether in whole or in part, it is to be taken into account in computing the next interim certificate, not left until the final certificate.

---

3   Contract Sum – additions or deductions – adjustment – Interim Certificates

Where in the Conditions it is provided that an amount is to be added to or deducted from the Contract Sum or dealt with by adjustment of the Contract Sum then as soon as such amount is ascertained in whole or in part such amount shall be taken into account in the computation of the next Interim Certificate following such whole or partial ascertainment.

---

5 Clause 4: Architect's/contract administrator's instructions

5.01 The contractor must comply with the architect's instructions. Failure to do so gives rise to the right under Clause 4.1.2 to have work carried out by others, and in some circumstances can result in the employer having the right to determine the contractor's employment (see Clause 27.1.3).

Power to issue instructions

5.02 The architect can only issue instructions where express power is given. The most important instances are:

1. Clause 2.3 (discrepancies in documents).
2. Clause 2.4 (divergence between performance specified work and architect's instructions).
3. Clause 6.1.3 (divergence between statutory requirements and documents).
4. Clause 6.1.6 (divergence between statutory requirements and contractor's statement).
5. Clause 7 (levels) – but only with employer's consent.
6. Clause 8.4 (removal of work, materials and goods).
7. Clause 8.4.4 (inspections and tests).
8. Clause 8.5 (failure to comply with Clause 8.1.3).
9. Clause 8.6 (exclusions of persons from the works).
10. Clause 13.2 (variations) – subject to right of reasonable objection in Clause 4.1.1.
11. Clause 13.3 (instructions on provisional sums).
12. Clause 17.2 (defects, shrinkages or other faults) – but only with employer's consent.
13. Clause 17.3 (rectification of defects).
14. Clause 23.2 (postponement of work).
15. Clause 34.2 (antiquities).
16. Clause 35.6 (nomination of sub-contractor).
17. Clause 35.24.6.1 (notice specifying default of nominated sub-contractor).
18. Clause 36.2 (nominating a supplier).
19. Clause 42.11 (variations to performance specified work).

5.03 Under Clause 4.2 the contractor may request the architect to specify in writing the provision of the conditions which empower the issue of an instruction. If the architect specifies a provision and the contractor then obeys the instruction, the instruction is deemed to be empowered by the provision in the contract specified

---

4   Architect's instructions

4·1 ·1 The Contractor shall forthwith comply with all instructions issued to him by the Architect in regard to any matter in respect of which the Architect is expressly empowered by the Conditions to issue instructions; save that:

·1 ·1 where such instruction is one requiring a Variation within the meaning of clause 13·1·2 the Contractor need not comply to the extent that he makes reasonable objection in writing to the Architect to such compliance;

·1 ·2 where pursuant to clause 13·2·3 clause 13A applies to an instruction, the Variation to which that instruction refers shall not be carried out until

– the Architect has issued to the Contractor a confirmed acceptance of the 13A Quotation

or

– an instruction in respect of the Variation has been issued under clause 13A·4·1.

4·1 ·2 If within 7 days after receipt of a written notice from the Architect requiring compliance with an instruction the Contractor does not comply therewith, then the Employer may employ and pay other persons to execute any work whatsoever which may be necessary to give effect to such instruction; and all costs incurred in connection with such employment may be deducted by him from any monies due or to become due to the Contractor under this Contract or may be recoverable from the Contractor by the Employer as a debt.

4·2 Upon receipt of what purports to be an instruction issued to him by the Architect the Contractor may request the Architect to specify in writing the provision of the Conditions which empower the issue of the said instruction. The Architect shall forthwith comply with any such request, and if the Contractor shall thereafter comply with the said instruction (neither party before such compliance having given to the other a written request to concur in the appointment of an Arbitrator under clause 41 in order that it may be decided whether the provision specified by the Architect empowers the issue of the said instruction), then the issue of the same shall be deemed for all the purposes of this Contract to have been empowered by the provision of the Conditions specified by the Architect in answer to the Contractor's request.

4·3 ·1 All instructions issued by the Architect shall be issued in writing.

4·3 ·2 If the Architect purports to issue an instruction otherwise than in writing it shall be of no immediate effect, but shall be confirmed in writing by the Contractor to the Architect within 7 days, and if not dissented from in writing by the Architect to the Contractor within 7 days from receipt of the Contractor's confirmation shall take effect as from the expiration of the latter said 7 days. Provided always:

·2 ·1 that if the Architect within 7 days of giving such an instruction otherwise than in writing shall himself confirm the same in writing, then the Contractor shall not be obliged to confirm as aforesaid, and the said instruction shall take effect as from the date of the Architect's confirmation; and

·2 ·2 that if neither the Contractor nor the Architect shall confirm such an instruction in the manner and at the time aforesaid but the Contractor shall nevertheless comply with the same, then the Architect may confirm the same in writing at any time prior to the issue of the Final Certificate, and the said instruction shall thereupon be deemed to have taken effect on the date on which it was issued otherwise than in writing by the Architect.

---

in the architect's answer. If the contractor is not satisfied with the architect's answer, the matter may be referred to arbitration during the progress of the works in accordance with Article 5.

Form of instructions

5.04 Under Clause 4.3.1, instructions are to be in writing, but note the elaborate provisions in Clause 4.3.2 for confirmation in writing if the architect purports to issue an oral instruction.

Site meeting minutes

5.05 Sometimes the architect and the contractor expressly agree that site meeting minutes are to operate as the confirmation of oral instructions contemplated by Clause 4.3. If there is no express agreement as to the status of the minute, in each case it must be decided whether in fact it was intended that the minutes should act as written confirmation of the instructions. Significant factors to take into account would be the authorship of the minutes and whether they are accepted by all parties as a true record of the meeting.

6 Clause 5: Contract documents – other documents – issue of certificates

6.01 This clause is concerned with matters of contract administration, namely the custody and issue of the contract and other

5	**Contract Documents – other documents – issue of certificates**
5·1	The Contract Drawings and the Contract Bills shall remain in the custody of the Architect or the Quantity Surveyor so as to be available at all reasonable times for the inspection of the Employer and of the Contractor.
5·2	Immediately after the execution of this Contract the Architect without charge to the Contractor shall provide him (unless he shall have been previously so provided) with:
5·2 ·1	one copy certified on behalf of the Employer of the Contract Documents;
5·2 ·2	two further copies of the Contract Drawings; and
5·2 ·3	two copies of the unpriced Bills of Quantities.
5·3 ·1	So soon as is possible after the execution of this Contract:
·1 ·1	the Architect without charge to the Contractor shall provide him (unless he shall have been previously so provided) with 2 copies of any descriptive schedules or other like documents necessary for use in carrying out the Works; and
·1 ·2	the Contractor without charge to the Employer shall provide the Architect (unless he shall have been previously so provided) with 2 copies of his master programme for the execution of the Works and within 14 days of any decision by the Architect under clause 25·3·1 or of the date of issue of a confirmed acceptance of a 13A Quotation with 2 copies of any amendments and revisions to take account of that decision or of that confirmed acceptance. [h]
5·3 ·2	Nothing contained in the descriptive schedules or other like documents referred to in clause 5·3·1·1 (nor in the master programme for the execution of the Works or any amendment to that programme or revision therein referred to in clause 5·3·1·2) shall impose any obligation beyond those imposed by the Contract Documents. [i]
5·4	As and when from time to time may be necessary the Architect without charge to the Contractor shall provide him with 2 copies of such further drawings or details as are reasonably necessary either to explain and amplify the Contract Drawings or to enable the Contractor to carry out and complete the Works in accordance with the Conditions.
5·5	The Contractor shall keep one copy of the Contract Drawings, one copy of the unpriced Bills of Quantities, one copy of the descriptive schedules or other like documents referred to in clause 5·3·1·1, one copy of the master programme referred to in clause 5·3·1·2 (unless clause 5·3·1·2 has been deleted) and one copy of the drawings and details referred to in clause 5·4 upon the site so as to be available to the Architect or his representative at all reasonable times.
5·6	Upon final payment under clause 30·8 the Contractor shall if so requested by the Architect forthwith return to him all drawings, details, descriptive schedules and other documents of a like nature which bear the name of the Architect.
5·7	None of the documents mentioned in clause 5 shall be used by the Contractor for any purpose other than this Contract, and neither the Employer, the Architect nor the Quantity Surveyor shall divulge or use except for the purposes of this Contract any of the rates or prices in the Contract Bills.
5·8	Except where otherwise specifically so provided any certificate to be issued by the Architect under the Conditions shall be issued to the Employer, and immediately upon the issue of any such certificate the Architect shall send a duplicate copy thereof to the Contractor.
5·9	Before the date of Practical Completion the Contractor shall without further charge to the Employer supply to the Employer such drawings and information showing or describing any Performance Specified Work as built, and concerning the maintenance and operation of any Performance Specified Work including any installations forming a part thereof, as may be specified in the Contract Bills or in an instruction on the expenditure of the provisional sum for the Performance Specified Work.

6	**Statutory obligations, notices, fees and charges**
6·1 ·1	Subject to clause 6·1·5 the Contractor shall comply with, and give all notices required by, any Act of Parliament, any instrument, rule or order made under any Act of Parliament, or any regulation or byelaw of any local authority or of any statutory undertaker which has any jurisdiction with regard to the Works or with whose systems the same are or will be connected (all requirements to be so complied with being referred to in the Conditions as 'the Statutory Requirements').
6·1 ·2	If the Contractor shall find any divergence between the Statutory Requirements and all or any of the documents referred to in clause 2·3 or between the Statutory Requirements and any instruction of the Architect requiring a Variation issued in accordance with clause 13·2, he shall immediately give to the Architect a written notice specifying the divergence.
6·1 ·3	If the Contractor gives notice under clause 6·1·2 or if the Architect shall otherwise discover or receive notice of a divergence between the Statutory Requirements and all or any of the documents referred to in clause 2·3 or between the Statutory Requirements and any instruction requiring a Variation issued in accordance with clause 13·2, the Architect shall within 7 days of the discovery or receipt of a notice issue instructions in relation to the divergence. If and insofar as the instructions require the Works to be varied, they shall be treated as if they were Architect's instructions requiring a Variation issued in accordance with clause 13·2.
6·1 ·4 ·1	If in any emergency compliance with clause 6·1·1 requires the Contractor to supply materials or execute work before receiving instructions under clause 6·1·3 the Contractor shall supply such limited materials and execute such limited work as are reasonably necessary to secure immediate compliance with the Statutory Requirements.
·4 ·2	The Contractor shall forthwith inform the Architect of the emergency and of the steps that he is taking under clause 6·1·4·1.
·4 ·3	Work executed and materials supplied by the Contractor under clause 6·1·4·1 shall be treated as if they had been executed and supplied pursuant to an Architect's instruction requiring a Variation issued in accordance with clause 13·2 provided that the emergency arose because of a divergence between the Statutory Requirements and all or any of the documents referred to in clause 2·3 or between the Statutory Requirements and any instruction requiring a Variation issued in accordance with clause 13·2, and the Contractor has complied with clause 6·1·4·2.
6·1 ·5	Provided that the Contractor complies with clause 6·1·2, the Contractor shall not be liable to the Employer under this Contract if the Works do not comply with the Statutory Requirements where and to the extent that such non-compliance of the Works results from the Contractor having carried out work in accordance with the documents referred to in clause 2·3 or with any instruction requiring a Variation issued by the Architect in accordance with clause 13·2.
6·1 ·6	If the Contractor or the Architect shall find any divergence between the Statutory Requirements and any Contractor's Statement he shall immediately give the other a written notice specifying the divergence. The Contractor shall inform the Architect in writing of his proposed amendment for removing the divergence; and the Architect shall issue instructions in regard thereto. The Contractor's compliance with such instructions shall be subject to clause 42·15 and at no cost to the Employer save as provided in clause 6·1·7.
6·1 ·7	If after the Base Date there is a change in the Statutory Requirements which necessitates some alteration or modification to any Performance Specified Work such alteration or modification shall be treated as if it were an instruction of the Architect under clause 13·2 requiring a Variation.
6·2	The Contractor shall pay and indemnify the Employer against liability in respect of any fees or charges (including any rates or taxes) legally demandable under any Act of Parliament, any instrument, rule or order made under any Act of Parliament, or any regulation or byelaw of any local authority or of any statutory undertaker in respect of the Works. The amount of any such fees or charges (including any rates or taxes other than value added tax) shall be added to the Contract Sum unless they:
6·2 ·1	arise in respect of work executed or materials or goods supplied by a local authority or statutory undertaker as a Nominated Sub-Contractor or as a Nominated Supplier; or
6·2 ·2	are priced in the Contract Bills; or
6·2 ·3	are stated by way of a provisional sum in the Contract Bills.
6·3	The provisions of clauses 19 and 35 shall not apply to the execution of part of the Works by a local authority or a statutory undertaker executing such work solely in pursuance of its statutory obligations and such bodies shall not be sub-contractors within the terms of this Contract.
6A	**Provisions for use where the Appendix states that all the CDM Regulations apply**
6A·1	The Employer shall ensure:
	that the Planning Supervisor carries out all the duties of a planning supervisor under the CDM Regulations; and
	where the Contractor is not the Principal Contractor, that the Principal Contractor carries out all the duties of a principal contractor under the CDM Regulations.
6A·2	Where the Contractor is and while he remains the Principal Contractor, the Contractor shall comply with all the duties of a principal contractor set out in the CDM Regulations; and in particular shall ensure that the Health and Safety Plan has the features required by regulation 15(4) of the CDM Regulations. Any amendment by the Contractor to the Health and Safety Plan shall be notified to the Employer, who shall where relevant thereupon notify the Planning Supervisor and the Architect.

documents. Clause 5.3.1.2 in particular should be noted: this requires the contractor to supply the architect with two copies of his master programme for the execution of the works and to update it to take account of extensions of time granted under Clause 25. This master programme does not, however, impose any obligation beyond those imposed by the contract documents (Clause 5.3.2). Clause 5.9 provides that the contractor is also required to supply as-built drawings for performance specified work before the date of practical completion.

6.02 All certificates which the conditions require to be issued by the architect are to be issued to the employer with a copy to the contractor.

7 Clause 6: Statutory obligations, notices, fees and charges

7.01 This clause imposes heavy obligations. The contractor has to comply with and give all relevant statutory notices and also comply with relevant statutory requirements, including the Building Regulations 1991. Within inner London the construction of buildings is regulated by the Building (Inner London) Regulations 1985 and 1987.

6A·3 Clause 6A·3 applies from the time the Employer pursuant to Article 6A·2 appoints a successor to the Contractor as the Principal Contractor. The Contractor shall comply at no cost to the Employer with all the reasonable requirements of the Principal Contractor to the extent that such requirements are necessary for compliance with the CDM Regulations; and, notwithstanding clause 25, no extension of time shall be given in respect of such compliance.

6A·4 Within the time reasonably required in writing by the Planning Supervisor to the Contractor, the Contractor shall provide, and shall ensure that any subcontractor, through the Contractor, provides, such information to the Planning Supervisor or, if the Contractor is not the Principal Contractor, to the Principal Contractor as the Planning Supervisor reasonably requires for the preparation, pursuant to regulations 14(d), 14(e) and 14(f) of the CDM Regulations, of the health and safety file required by the CDM Regulations.

7 **Levels and setting out of the Works**

The Architect shall determine any levels which may be requried for the execution of the Works, and shall provide the Contractor by way of accurately dimensioned drawings with such information as shall enable the Contractor to set out the Works at ground level. The Contractor shall be responsible for and shall, at no cost to the Employer, amend any errors arising from his own inaccurate setting out. With the consent of the Employer the Architect may instruct that such errors shall not be amended and an appropriate deduction for such errors not required to be amended shall be made from the Contract Sum.

7.02 Under Section 71 of the Health and Safety etc. at Work Act 1974, 'subject to the provisions of this section, breach of duty imposed by building regulations shall so far as it causes damage be actionable except insofar as the regulations provide otherwise'. Where the architect's design does not comply with the regulations, the contractor may be entitled to an indemnity against any claim for breach of this clause, thus effectively relieving him of liability: *EDAC v William Moss* (1984) Const LJ 1. A contractor does not owe a duty at common law to take reasonable care to comply with the Building Regulations, however breach of these duties, in addition to giving rise to the possibility of criminal proceedings, makes the contractor liable in damages to the employer. The architect may also be liable to the employer and in some circumstances to the contractor (see *Townsend (Builders) Limited v Cinema News Etc Limited* [1959] 1 WLR 119).

7.03 By Clause 6.1.2 the contractor is required to give written notice to the architect of any divergence between the statutory requirements and the documents referred to in Clause 2.3 or any instruction requiring a variation issued in accordance with Clause 13.2. The architect is required to issue instructions in relation to the divergence, and this instruction will be treated as an instruction requiring a variation under Clause 13.2.

7.04 By Clause 6.1.6 the contractor and the architect are required to give written notice to the other of any divergence they may find between the statutory requirements and the contractor's statement in respect of performance specified work. The contractor is required to inform the architect in writing of his proposed amendment and the architect then must issue instructions in relation to the divergence. In this case the compliance with the instructions will be at no cost to the employer unless the divergence has resulted from a change in the statutory requirements after the base date.

7.05 Work carried out by local authorities or statutory undertakers in pursuance of their statutory obligations is excluded by Clause 6.3 from the provisions of Clauses 19 and 35 which relate to domestic and nominated sub-contractors respectively. It is important to note that this applies only where the work is being carried out by the local authority or statutory undertaker 'solely in pursuance of its statutory obligations' and would not apply where, for example, an electricity board were carrying out works as subcontractors in the normal way (see *Henry Boot Construction Limited v Central Lancashire New Town Development Corporation* (1980) 15 BLR 1).

8 Clause 7: Levels and setting out of the works

8.01 Unless the architect with the employer's consent instructs that any errors arising from inaccurate setting out by the contractor are not to be amended, the contractor must amend them at his own cost. If the architect does instruct that the errors need not be amended, an appropriate deduction in respect of the errors is to be made from the contract sum.

9 Clause 8: Work, materials and goods

9.01 This clause defines the kinds and standards of materials and workmanship which are required by the contract and gives the architect certain important powers. The contractor cannot be required to provide that which may have become unobtainable since the date of tender. However, he is not permitted to substitute an alternative without the architect's consent in writing, such consent not to be unreasonably withheld or delayed.

Express obligations

9.02 It is an express term of the contract that all work must be carried out in a proper and workmanlike manner (Clause 8.1.3). If there is any failure to comply with this obligation the architect has a power under Clause 8.5 to issue any instructions which are necessary as a result, including an instruction requiring a variation. No addition to the contract sum shall be made in respect of compliance with such an instruction and no extension of time will be given.

Implied obligations

9.03 In so far as the contract bills do not describe standards of materials or goods, the contractor must supply them in accordance with the standards implied by law, that is materials or goods which are reasonably fit for the purpose for which they will be used and are of good quality. However these implied obligations may be excluded if the circumstances show that the parties did not intend them to apply. Thus:

1. There is no obligation as to fitness for a particular purpose if that purpose was not made known to the contractor at the time of making the contract.
2. There is no obligation as to fitness for purpose of materials where there was no reliance upon the skill and judgement of the contractor in the choice of those materials, Thus, for example, if an architect, without reliance on a contractor, specified for use on a roof 'Somerset 13' tiles, then the contractor is not liable if Somerset 13 tiles of good quality are not fit for use on that roof. The contractor is, however, liable if the tiles fail because, for example, they laminate owing to some latent defect of quality even though the defect could not have been detected by the exercise of proper care and skill on his part (see *Young and Marten v McManus Childs Limited* [1968] 2 All ER; *Norta Wallpapers v John Sisk* [1978] 1 IR 114 (an Irish case); and *Comyn Ching & Co (London) Limited v Oriental Tube Co Limited* (1979) 17 BLR 47).
3. There is no obligation as to latent defects of quality of materials where the circumstances show that the parties do not intend the contractor to accept such obligations. Thus it seems (though the point is not clear) that in the example just cited the contractor would not have been liable for the latent defects in the tiles if the employer (or the architect on his behalf) had required the contractor to purchase them from a supplier who, to the knowledge of the parties, would only supply them upon terms which substantially limited the contractor's remedies against the supplier in respect of such defects (see *Young and Marten* (above) and *Gloucestershire County Council v Richardson* [1969] 2 All ER 1181).
4. In the case of a nominated supplier whose sale contract restricts, limits or excludes liability to the contractor, where the architect specifically has approved such restriction, limitation

8		Work, materials and goods

8·1   ·1   All materials and goods shall, so far as procurable, be of the kinds and standards described in the Contract Bills, and also, in regard to any Performance Specified Work, in the Contractor's Statement, provided that materials and goods shall be to the reasonable satisfaction of the Architect where and to the extent that this is required in accordance with clause 2·1.

8·1   ·2   All workmanship shall be of the standards described in the Contract Bills, and also, in regard to any Performance Specified Work, in the Contractor's Statement, or, to the extent that no such standards are described in the Contract Bills, or, in regard to any Performance Specified Work, in the Contractor's Statement, shall be of a standard appropriate to the Works, provided that workmanship shall be to the reasonable satisfaction of the Architect where and to the extent that this is required in accordance with clause 2·1.

8·1   ·3   All work shall be carried out in a proper and workmanlike manner and in accordance with the Health and Safety Plan.

8·1   ·4   The Contractor shall not substitute any materials or goods described in any Contractor's Statement for Performance Specified Work without the Architect's consent in writing which consent shall not be unreasonably withheld or delayed. No such consent shall relieve the Contractor of any other obligation under this Contract.

8·2   ·1   The Contractor shall upon the request of the Architect provide him with vouchers to prove that the materials and goods comply with clause 8·1.

8·2   ·2   In respect of any materials, goods or workmanship, as comprised in executed work, which are to be to the reasonable satisfaction of the Architect in accordance with clause 2·1, the Architect shall express any dissatisfaction within a reasonable time from the execution of the unsatisfactory work.

8·3   The Architect may issue instructions requiring the Contractor to open up for inspection any work covered up or to arrange for or carry out any test of any materials or goods (whether or not already incorporated in the Works) or of any executed work, and the cost of such opening up or testing (together with the cost of making good in consequence thereof) shall be added to the Contract Sum unless provided for in the Contract Bills or unless the inspection or test shows that the materials, goods or work are not in accordance with this Contract.

8·4   If any work, materials or goods are not in accordance with this Contract the Architect, without prejudice to the generality of his powers, may:

8·4   ·1   issue instructions in regard to the removal from the site of all or any of such work, materials or goods; and/or

8·4   ·2   after consultation with the Contractor (who shall immediately consult with any relevant Nominated Sub-Contractor) and with the agreement of the Employer, allow all or any of such work, materials or goods to remain and confirm this in writing to the Contractor (which shall not be construed as a Variation) and where so allowed and confirmed an appropriate deduction shall be made in the adjustment of the Contract Sum; and/or

8·4   ·3   after consultation with the Contractor (who shall immediately consult with any relevant Nominated Sub-Contractor) issue such instructions requiring a Variation as are reasonably necessary as a consequence of such an instruction under clause 8·4·1 or such confirmation under clause 8·4·2 and to the extent that such instructions are so necessary and notwithstanding clauses 13·4, 25 and 26 no addition to the Contract Sum shall be made and no extension of time shall be given; and/or

8·4   ·4   having had due regard to the Code of Practice appended to these Conditions *(following clause 42)*, issue such instructions under clause 8·3 to open up for inspection or to test as are reasonable in all the circumstances to establish to the reasonable satisfaction of the Architect the likelihood or extent, as appropriate to the circumstances, of any further similar non-compliance. To the extent that such instructions are so reasonable, whatever the results of the opening up for inspection or test, and notwithstanding clauses 8·3 and 26 no addition to the Contract Sum shall be made. Clause 25·4·5·2 shall apply unless as stated therein the inspection or test showed that the work, materials or goods were not in accordance with this Contract.

8·5   Where there is any failure to comply with clause 8·1·3 in regard to the carrying out of the work in a proper and workmanlike manner the Architect, without prejudice to the generality of his powers, may, after consultation with the Contractor (who shall immediately consult with any relevant Nominated Sub-Contractor), issue such instructions whether requiring a Variation or otherwise as are reasonably necessary as a consequence thereof. To the extent that such instructions are so necessary and notwithstanding clauses 13·4 and 25 and 26 no addition to the Contract Sum shall be made and no extension of time shall be given in respect of compliance by the Contractor with such instruction.

8·6   The Architect may (but not unreasonably or vexatiously) issue instructions requiring the exclusion from the site of any person employed thereon.

	Code of Practice: referred to in clause 8·4·4

1   This is the Code of Practice referred to in clause 8·4·4. The purpose of the Code is to help in the fair and reasonable operation of the requirements of clause 8·4·4.

2   The Architect and the Contractor should endeavour to agree the amount and method of opening up or testing but in any case in issuing his instructions pursuant to clause 8·4·4 the Architect is required to consider the following criteria:

·1   the need in the event of non-compliance to demonstrate at no cost to the Employer either that it is unique and not likely to occur in similar elements of the Works or alternatively the extent of any similar non-compliance in the Works already constructed or still to be constructed;

·2   the need to discover whether any non-compliance in a primary structural element is a failure of workmanship and/or materials such that rigorous testing of similar elements must take place; or where the non-compliance is in a less significant element whether it is such as is to be statistically expected and can be simply repaired; or whether the non-compliance indicates an inherent weakness such as can only be found by selective testing the extent of which must depend upon the importance of any detail concerned;

·3   the significance of the non-compliance having regard to the nature of the work in which it has occurred;

·4   the consequence of any similar non-compliance on the safety of the building, its effect on users, adjoining property, the public, and compliance with any Statutory Requirements;

·5   the level and standard of supervision and control of the Works by the Contractor;

·6   the relevant records of the Contractor and where relevant of any sub-contractor resulting from the supervision and control referred to in paragraph 2·5 above or otherwise;

·7   any Codes of Practice or similar advice issued by a responsible body which are applicable to the non-complying work, materials or goods;

·8   any failure by the Contractor to carry out, or to secure the carrying out of, any tests specified in the Contract Documents or in an instruction of the Architect;

·9   the reason for the non-compliance when this has been established;

·10   any technical advice that the Contractor has obtained in respect of the non-complying work, materials or goods;

·11   current recognised testing procedures;

·12   the practicability of progressive testing in establishing whether any similar non-compliance is reasonably likely;

·13   if alternative testing methods are available, the time required for and the consequential costs of such alternative testing methods;

·14   any proposals of the Contractor;

·15   any other relevant matters.

---

not accept liability, one way of protecting the employer is to obtain a warranty direct from the supplier or sub-contractor concerned. The JCT issue a Standard Form of Employer/Nominated Sub-contractor Agreement (NSC/W) and a Standard Form of Tender by Nominated Supplier (TNS/1) which contain such 'direct warranties'.

Effect of price on standards

9.05   The question of whether the price for a piece of work is low or high should be ignored when considering the required standard, unless the parties have expressly or by implication agreed that prices should be considered. However it seems that the architect can accept a lower standard than usual where the parties have agreed at the time of the contract the price is low and that the contractor is to 'build down to a price'. A suitable term should be included in the contract documents to make the intentions of the parties clear.

Effect of proposed use of works on standards

9.06   Where the use is known to the contractor at the time of contract it can, probably, be taken into account in considering the requisite standard where the bills are silent. But it is better to have express agreements for possible matters of dispute, for example, as to tolerances and how far they are cumulative.

Clause 8.3: Testing

9.07   The architect is not bound to order tests under this clause before saying that he is not reasonably satisfied with any work. If

---

or exclusion, the employer's rights against the contractor are restricted, limited or excluded to the same extent – see Clause 36.5.1.

5.   By virtue of Clause 42.17.1.2, nothing in the contract is to operate as a guarantee of fitness for purpose of performance specified work.

Position of employer

9.04   If there is no breach of an express or implied term, the employer normally has no remedy against the contractor, sub-contractor or supplier under the terms of the contract. This is a situation which should be avoided if possible. If the contractor will he does order a test, and the work, materials or goods are found to be satisfactory, the contractor has a right to an extension of time (Clause 25.4.5.2), payment of loss and expense (Clause 26.2.2), and the cost of the tests. It is thought that where tests of part of a class of work, e.g. piling, show that the whole must be rejected, the contractor is not entitled to payment for tests in respect of those parts, e.g. individual piles, which pass the test or to the other rights set out above.

Clause 8.4: Removal

9.08 The architect must order removal from site of defective work. It is not sufficient merely to order correction (see *Holland Hernani & Cubitts (Northern) Limited* v *Welsh Health Technical Services Organisation* (1981) 18 BLR 80). There is no provision for re-execution, because upon the removal of the unsatisfactory work, materials or goods, the contractor's duty to complete remains and no further instruction is necessary. See Clauses 4.1.2, 27.2.3 and 30.2.1.1 for the architect's remedies for non-compliance. Defects which appear after practical completion are dealt with under Clause 17.

9.09 In 1988 a Code of Practice was introduced to help in the fair and reasonable operation of the provisions in Clause 8.4.4 for opening up. The architect is required to have due regard for this code, but its terms are not as such a mandatory part of the contract.

10 Clause 9: Royalties and patent rights

10.01 The contractor is by this clause obliged to indemnify the employer in respect of any infringement of patent rights. However, if the use of a patented article by the contractor was in compliance with an instruction of the architect, then the contractor has no such liability, and, indeed, is entitled to be repaid by the employer any liability which he has incurred. In practice, the erection of new buildings rarely involves an infringement of patent rights, which essentially protect the intellectual property in new inventions.

---

9 Royalties and patent rights

9·1 All royalties or other sums payable in respect of the supply and use in carrying out the Works as described by or referred to in the Contract Bills of any patented articles, processes or inventions shall be deemed to have been included in the Contract Sum, and the Contractor shall indemnify the Employer from and against all claims, proceedings, damage, costs and expense which may be brought or made against the Employer or to which he may be put by reason of the Contractor infringing or being held to have infringed any patent rights in relation to any such articles, processes or inventions.

9·2 Provided that where in compliance with Architect's instructions the Contractor shall supply and use in carrying out the Works any patented articles, processes or inventions, the Contractor shall not be liable in respect of any infringement or alleged infringement of any patent rights in relation to any such articles, processes or inventions and all royalties damages or other monies which the Contractor may be liable to pay to the persons entitled to such patent rights shall be added to the Contract Sum.

---

11 Clause 10: Person-in-charge

11.01 The person-in-charge is the contractor's agent to receive instructions. To avoid confusion he should be named.

---

10 Person-in-charge

The Contractor shall constantly keep upon the site a competent person-in-charge and any instructions given to him by the Architect or directions given to him by the clerk of works in accordance with clause 12 shall be deemed to have been issued to the Contractor.

---

12 Clause 11: Access for architect/contract administrator to the works

12.01 In the absence of express provision doubts might arise as to the architect's right of access to the site, since the contractor is entitled as against the employer to free and uninterrupted possession of the site during the progress of the works. Therefore Clause 11 reserves to the architect and his representative a right of access

to the works and a similar right of access in relation to workshops and other places in the possession of the contractor where work is being prepared for final incorporation in the works. This right is subject to such reasonable restrictions of the contractor and nominated or domestic sub-contractor as are necessary to protect any proprietary right in the work for the contract. The provisions relating to domestic and nominated sub-contractors do not, of course, directly affect the obligations of the sub-contractors, but the contractor would be liable in damages to the employer if he could establish damage flowing from failure by the contractor to ensure that the appropriate terms were included in the sub-contracts.

---

11 Access for Architect to the Works

The Architect and his representatives shall at all reasonable times have access to the Works and to the workshops or other places of the Contractor where work is being prepared for this Contract, and when work is to be so prepared in workshops or other places of a Domestic Sub-Contractor or a Nominated Sub-Contractor the Contractor shall by a term in the sub-contract so far as possible secure a similar right of access to those workshops or places for the Architect and his representatives and shall do all things reasonably necessary to make such right effective. Access in accordance with clause 11 may be subject to such reasonable restrictions of the Contractor or any Domestic Sub-Contractor or any Nominated Sub-Contractor as are necessary to protect any proprietary right of the Contractor or of any Domestic or Nominated Sub-Contractor in the work referred to in clause 11.

---

13 Clause 12: Clerk of works

13.01 The clerk of works is to act 'solely as inspector'. He is not the architect's agent to give instructions, and it will be a source of confusion and dispute if he purports to do so. If the clerk of works gives 'directions' they are to be of no effect unless converted into architect's instructions by the architect within two working days. Such directions can lead to uncertainty on the part of the contractor. It is suggested that the clerk of works be discouraged from giving directions in ordinary circumstances. However, if directions are to be given, the problems will be minimized if they are in writing and the architect immediately confirms, amends or rejects them.

13.02 In *Kensington and Chelsea and Westminster Area Health Authority* v *Wettern Composites* (1984) 31 BR 57 it was held that the employer is vicariously liable for the negligence of the clerk of works. Responsibility for his acts was not borne by the architect, even though he was acting under the direction and control of the architect.

---

12 Clerk of works

The Employer shall be entitled to appoint a clerk of works whose duty shall be to act solely as inspector on behalf of the Employer under the directions of the Architect and the Contractor shall afford every reasonable facility for the performance of that duty. If any direction is given to the Contractor by the clerk of works the same shall be of no effect unless given in regard to a matter in respect of which the Architect is expressly empowered by the Conditions to issue instructions and unless confirmed in writing by the Architect within 2 working days of such direction being given. If any such direction is so given and confirmed then as from the date of issue of that confirmation it shall be deemed to be an Architect's instruction.

Work done before confirmation of directions

13.03 The architect can, if the work done before confirmation of directions constitutes a variation, subsequently sanction it in writing under Clause 13.2. This may be particularly appropriate where the contractor has carried out extra work in an emergency upon the direction of the clerk of works.

Resident architect

13.04 A person so entitled is sometimes appointed to the site of a large contract. His position should be sharply distinguished from that of the clerk of works and should be defined in a communication to the contractor stating clearly how far, if at all, he is not to have all the powers to issue architect's instructions given by the terms of the contract.

14 Clause 13: Variations and provisional sums

14.01 This clause is essentially concerned with three matters:

1. Defining what constitutes a variation.
2. Defining the method in which variations are to be ordered.
3. Laying down the rules for valuing variations.

---

13   **Variations and provisional sums**

13·1   The term 'Variation' as used in the Conditions means:

13·1   ·1   the alteration or modification of the design, quality or quantity of the Works including

   ·1   ·1   the addition, omission or substitution of any work,

   ·1   ·2   the alteration of the kind or standard of any of the materials or goods to be used in the Works,

   ·1   ·3   the removal from the site of any work executed or materials or goods brought thereon by the Contractor for the purposes of the Works other than work materials or goods which are not in accordance with this Contract;

13·1   ·2   the imposition by the Employer of any obligations or restrictions in regard to the matters set out in clauses 13·1·2·1 to 13·1·2·4 or the addition to or alteration or omission of any such obligations or restrictions so imposed or imposed by the Employer in the Contract Bills in regard to:

   ·2   ·1   access to the site or use of any specific parts of the site;

   ·2   ·2   limitations of working space;

   ·2   ·3   limitations of working hours;

   ·2   ·4   the execution or completion of the work in any specific order;

   but excludes

13·1   ·3   nomination of a sub-contractor to supply and fix materials or goods or to execute work of which the measured quantities have been set out and priced by the Contractor in the Contract Bills for supply and fixing or execution by the Contractor.

13·2   ·1   The Architect may issue instructions requiring a Variation.

13·2   ·2   Any instruction under clause 13·2·1 shall be subject to the Contractor's right of reasonable objection set out in clause 4·1·1.

13·2   ·3   The valuation of a Variation instructed under clause 13·2·1 shall be in accordance with clause 13·4·1 unless the instruction states that the treatment and valuation of the Variation are to be in accordance with clause 13A or unless the Variation is one to which clause 13A·8 applies. Where the instruction so states, clause 13A shall apply unless the Contractor within 7 days (or such other period as may be agreed) of receipt of the instruction states in writing that he disagrees with the application of clause 13A to such instruction. If the Contractor so disagrees, clause 13A shall not apply to such instruction and the Variation shall not be carried out unless and until the Architect instructs that the Variation is to be carried out and is to be valued pursuant to clause 13·4·1.[i·1]

13·2   ·4   The Architect may sanction in writing any Variation made by the Contractor otherwise than pursuant to an instruction of the Architect.

13·2   ·5   No Variation required by the Architect or subsequently sanctioned by him shall vitiate this Contract.

13·3   The Architect shall issue instructions in regard to:

13·3   ·1   the expenditure of provisional sums included in the Contract Bills; [j] and

13·3   ·2   the expenditure of provisional sums included in a Nominated Sub-Contract.

13·4   ·1   ·1   Subject to clause 13·4·1·2

   all Variations required by the Architect or subsequently sanctioned by him in writing and all work executed by the Contractor in accordance with instructions by the Architect as to the expenditure of provisional sums which are included in the Contract Bills shall be valued by the Quantity Surveyor and

   all work executed by the Contractor for which an Approximate Quantity is included in the Contract Bills shall be measured and valued by the Quantity Surveyor

   and such valuation (in the Conditions called 'the Valuation') shall, unless otherwise agreed by the Employer and the Contractor or unless the Architect has issued to the Contractor a confirmed acceptance of a 13A Quotation for such Variation or it is a Variation to which clause 13A·8 applies, be made in accordance with the provisions of clauses 13·5·1 to 13·5·5 and, in respect of Performance Specified Work, with the provisions of clauses 13·5·6 and 13·5·7.

   ·1   ·2   The valuation of Variations to the sub-contract works executed by a Nominated Sub-Contractor in accordance with instructions of the Architect and of all instructions issued under clause 13·3·2 and all work executed by a Nominated Sub-Contractor for which an Approximate Quantity is included in any bills of quantities included in the Numbered Documents shall (unless otherwise agreed by the Contractor and the Nominated Sub-Contractor concerned with the approval of the Employer) be made in accordance with the relevant provisions of Conditions NSC/C (*Conditions of Nominated Sub-Contract*).

13·4   ·2   Where under the instruction of the Architect as to the expenditure of a provisional sum a prime cost sum arises and the Contractor under clause 35·2 tenders for the work covered by that prime cost sum and that tender is accepted by or on behalf of the Employer, that work shall be valued in accordance with the accepted tender of the Contractor and shall not be included in the Valuation of the instruction of the Architect in regard to the expenditure of the provisional sum.

13·5   ·1   To the extent that the Valuation relates to the execution of additional or substituted work which can properly be valued by measurement or to the execution of work for which an Approximate Quantity is included in the Contract Bills such work shall be measured and shall be valued in accordance with the following rules:

   ·1   ·1   where the additional or substituted work is of similar character to, is executed under similar conditions as, and does not significantly change the quantity of, work set out in the Contract Bills the rates and prices for the work so set out shall determine the Valuation;

   ·1   ·2   where the additional or substituted work is of similar character to work set out in the Contract Bills but is not executed under similar conditions thereto and/or significantly changes the quantity thereof, the rates and prices for the work so set out shall be the basis for determining the valuation and the valuation shall include a fair allowance for such difference in conditions and/or quantity;

   ·1   ·3   where the additional or substituted work is not of similar character to work set out in the Contract Bills the work shall be valued at fair rates and prices;

   ·1   ·4   where the Approximate Quantity is a reasonably accurate forecast of the quantity of work required the rate or price for the Approximate Quantity shall determine the Valuation;

   ·1   ·5   where the Approximate Quantity is not a reasonably accurate forecast of the quantity of work required the rate or price for that Approximate Quantity shall be the basis for determining the Valuation and the Valuation shall include a fair allowance for such difference in quantity.

   Provided that clause 13·5·1·4 and clause 13·5·1·5 shall only apply to the extent that the work has not been altered or modified other than in quantity.

13·5   ·2   To the extent that the Valuation relates to the omission of work set out in the Contract Bills the rates and prices for such work therein set out shall determine the valuation of the work omitted.

13·5   ·3   In any valuation of work under clauses 13·5·1 and 13·5·2:

   ·3   ·1   measurement shall be in accordance with the same principles as those governing the preparation of the Contract Bills as referred to in clause 2·2·2·1;

   ·3   ·2   allowance shall be made for any percentage or lump sum adjustments in the Contract Bills; and

   ·3   ·3   allowance, where appropriate, shall be made for any addition to or reduction of preliminary items of the type referred to in the Standard Method of Measurement, 7th Edition, Section A (Preliminaries/General Conditions); provided that no such allowance shall be made in respect of compliance with an Architect's instruction for the expenditure of a provisional sum for defined work.*

13·5   ·4   To the extent that the Valuation relates to the execution of additional or substituted work which cannot properly be valued by measurement the Valuation shall comprise:

   ·4   ·1   the prime cost of such work (calculated in accordance with the 'Definition of Prime Cost of Daywork carried out under a Building Contract' issued by the Royal Institution of Chartered Surveyors and the Building Employers Confederation which was current at the Base Date) together with percentage additions to each section of the prime cost at the rates set out by the Contractor in the Contract Bills; or

   ·4   ·2   where the work is within the province of any specialist trade and the said Institution and the appropriate [k] body representing the employers in that trade have agreed and issued a definition of prime cost of daywork, the prime cost of such work calculated in accordance with that definition which was current at the Base Date together with percentage additions on the prime cost at the rates set out by the Contractor in the Contract Bills.

   Provided that in any case vouchers specifying the time daily spent upon the work, the workmen's names, the plant and the materials employed shall be delivered for verification to the Architect or his authorised representative not later than the end of the week following that in which the work has been executed.

13·5   ·5   If

   compliance with any instruction requiring a Variation or

   compliance with any instruction as to the expenditure of a provisional sum for undefined work* or

   compliance with any instruction as to the expenditure of a provisional sum for defined work* to the extent that the instruction for that work differs from the description given for such work in the Contract Bills or

   the execution of work for which an Approximate Quantity is included in the Contract Bills to such extent as the quantity is more or less than the quantity ascribed to that work in the Contract Bills

   substantially changes the conditions under which any other work is executed, then such other work shall be treated as if it had been the subject of an instruction of the Architect requiring a Variation under clause 13·2 which shall be valued in accordance with the provisions of clause 13.

13·5 ·6 ·1 The Valuation of Performance Specified Work shall include allowance for the addition or omission of any relevant work involved in the preparation and production of drawings, schedules or other documents;

·6 ·2 the Valuation of additional or substituted work related to Performance Specified Work shall be consistent with the rates and prices of work of a similar character set out in the Contract Bills or the Analysis making due allowance for any changes in the conditions under which the work is carried out and/or any significant change in the quantity of the work set out in the Contract Bills or in the Contractor's Statement. Where there is no work of a similar character set out in the Contract Bills or the Contractor's Statement a fair valuation shall be made;

·6 ·3 the Valuation of the omission of work relating to Performance Specified Work shall be in accordance with the rates and prices for such work set out in the Contract Bills or the Analysis;

·6 ·4 any valuation of work under clauses 13·5·6·2 and 13·5·6·3 shall include allowance for any necessary addition to or reduction of preliminary items of the type referred to in the Standard Method of Measurement, 7th Edition, Section A (Preliminaries/General Conditions);

·6 ·5 where an appropriate basis of a fair valuation of additional or substituted work relating to Performance Specified Work is daywork the Valuation shall be in accordance with clauses 13·5·4·1 or 13·5·4·2 and the proviso to clause 13·5·4 shall apply;

·6 ·6 if

compliance with any instruction under clause 42·11 requiring a Variation to Performance Specified Work or

compliance with any instruction as to the expenditure of a provisional sum for Performance Specified Work to the extent that the instruction for that Work differs from the information provided in the Contract Bills pursuant to clause 42·7·2 and/or 42·7·3 for such Performance Specified Work

substantially changes the conditions under which any other work is executed (including any other Performance Specified Work) then such other work (including any other Performance Specified Work) shall be treated as if it had been the subject of an instruction of the Architect requiring a Variation under clause 13·2 or, if relevant, under clause 42·11 which shall be valued in accordance with the provisions of clause 13·5.

13·5 ·7 To the extent that the Valuation does not relate to the execution of additional or substituted work or the omission of work or to the extent that the valuation of any work or liabilities directly associated with a Variation cannot reasonably be effected in the Valuation by the application of clauses 13·5·1 to ·6 a fair valuation thereof shall be made.

Provided that no allowance shall be made under clause 13·5 for any effect upon the regular progress of the Works or for any other direct loss and/or expense for which the Contractor would be reimbursed by payment under any other provision in the Conditions.

13·6 Where it is necessary to measure work for the purpose of the Valuation the Quantity Surveyor shall give to the Contractor an opportunity of being present at the time of such measurement and of taking such notes and measurements as the Contractor may require.

13·7 Effect shall be given to a Valuation under clause 13·5, to an agreement by the Employer and the Contractor to which clause 13·4·1·1 refers, to a 13A Quotation for which the Architect has issued to the Contractor a confirmed acceptance and to a valuation pursuant to clause 13A·8 by addition to or deduction from the Contract Sum.

Definition of variation

14.02 Clause 13.1 defines variation in wide terms. Not only does it include alterations in the work itself (Clause 13.1.1), but also, by Clause 13.1.2, alterations in obligations or restrictions imposed in the contract bills by the employer in relation to such matters as site access, working space, working hours and work sequence. It would appear that the architect has no power to vary such obligations or restrictions if they are not set out in the contract bills. Clause 13.1.3 excludes from the definition of variation nomination of a sub-contractor to supply and fix materials or goods or to execute work for which the measured quantities have been set out and priced by the contractor in the contract bills for supply and fixing or execution by the contractor. Thus the employer is not entitled to vary the work by ordering the omission of work and nominating a sub-contractor to carry it out.

14.03 Disputes frequently arise between employer and contractor as to whether work constitutes a variation and such disputes are frequently referred to arbitration. The architect's decision as to what constitutes and does not constitute a variation is subject to review by the arbitrator appointed under Clause 41, although the reference will not be opened until after practical completion, unless the employer and the contractor agree otherwise.

14.04 The same instruction may amount both to another order and to a postponement of work within Clause 23.2 (see *M Harrison & Co v Leeds City Council* (1980) 14 BLR 118).

Deemed variations

14.05 This term is frequently used to denote an occurrence which entitles (or is alleged to entitle) the contractor to extra payments even though the requirements of Clause 13 have not been complied with. There are two principal occurrences which often give rise to a deemed variation:

1. The bills of quantities are inaccurate and fail to record correctly the quantity of work actually required. In these circumstances, the contractor is entitled to extra payment under Clause 2.2.2.2, since the Standard Method of Measurement (SMM) referred to in Clause 2.2.2.1 requires bills of quantities to describe the work fully and accurately.
2. Mis-statements or inaccuracies in the bills of quantities may constitute an actionable misrepresentation for which the contractor is entitled to damages under the Misrepresentation Act 1967.

Limits on the architect's powers

14.06 Despite the apparent breadth of the architect's powers to order variations, it is generally thought he cannot order variations of such extent or nature as to alter the nature of the works as originally contemplated. The architect's powers are limited to those given by the conditions, which he has no power to vary or waive. Thus he cannot without the contractor's agreement require work that is the subject matter of a prime cost sum (Clause 35) to be carried out by the contractor, and (see Clause 13.1.5) cannot omit work in order to have it carried out by another contractor or nominated sub-contractor (see *Commissioner for Main Roads v Reed & Stuart Property* (1974) 48 ALJR 461). He cannot, it is thought, order variations after practical completion. He is, however, entitled to vary work which is to be carried out by nominated sub-contractors.

Prime costs, provisional sums and approximate quantities

14.07 Where work can be described but the quantity of work required cannot be accurately determined, an estimate of the quantity is to be given. This is identified as an approximate quantity. A provisional sum represents a sum which is included to meet unforeseen contingencies (which may not arise). Prime cost sums are pre-estimates of expenditure which it is known will be incurred when the contract is entered into. More detailed definitions of these terms are set out in SMM, General Rules 10.1 to 10.6.

Procedure

14.08 Clause 13.2 lays down the procedure for requiring a variation. All variations require the issue of an architect's instruction. Varied work may be sanctioned subsequently by the architect, as well as in advance of its being undertaken. In principle in the absence of an architect's instruction, the contractor is not entitled to extra payment for any increased costs due to variations (although the architect's decision not to give a certificate sanctioning the variation is subject to review by an arbitrator). Merely permitting the contractor to alter the proposed method of construction at the contractor's request does not ordinarily amount to a variation, although the particular circumstances must always be considered (see *Simplex Concrete Piles v Borough of St Pancras* (1958) 14 BLR 80.

Valuation rules

14.09 Clause 13.5 lays down the rules for valuing variations and work for which an approximate quantity has been included. Clause 13.5.1 deals with the situation where the additional or substituted work is capable of measurement. The task of measurement is to be carried out by the quantity surveyor, who is to value the work in accordance with the rules laid down in Clauses 13.5.1–5, whichever is appropriate.

14.10 Under Clause 13.5.2 where work is omitted from the contract bills, the amount of the omission is to be determined by the rates and prices for such work in the contract bills. By Clause 13.5.3 measurement of variations is to be carried out in accordance with SMM, allowance is to be given for any percentage of lump sum adjustment, and preliminary items are also subject to adjustment. Preliminary items defined by SMM consist broadly of overhead items which the contractor will incur, such as plant, site establishment, etc. Where work is incapable of valuation by measurement, Clause 13.5.4 requires it to be valued at day work rates.

14.11 Clause 13.5.5 deals with what might be termed indirect variations, where a variation which directly affects one aspect of the work also has indirect effects on another aspect. For example, the Architect may require work to be carried out in a different sequence from that envisaged, resulting in certain finishing trades being obliged to work in parts of the building which are not fully watertight. In such circumstances the contractor would be entitled to be paid as if the altered work were itself the subject of a variation by virtue of Clause 13.5.5.

14.12 Clause 13.5.7 provides a 'fall back' method of valuing a variation where none of the other methods can be applied to produce a fair result. The proviso to Clause 13.5.7 excludes additional payment for items for which the contractor would be able to claim as loss and/or expense under any other provision of the contract. Thus the policy of the 1980 JCT Form is to divorce completely claims for variations from claims for loss and expense (under the 1963 JCT Form they were to some extent confused – see Clauses 11(6) and 24(1) of that form). This divorce is in line with the recommendations of the Banwell Report.

Sub-contract work

14.13 Under Clause 13.4.1 variations to nominated sub-contract works are to be valued in accordance with the provisions of the nominated sub-contract (see NSC/C). Where the contractor tenders for provisional work which has become the subject of a prime cost sum and that tender is accepted, any variation is to be valued in accordance with the contractor's tender for that work.

Disputes about valuations

14.14 The rule of valuation contained in Clause 13.5.1.3 (work not of similar character to work set out in the contract bills) is in practice probably the most difficult to apply. It is necessary to decide firstly whether it applies and then, if it does, how to apply it. It seems that one must look at the position at the time of acceptance of the tender and consider the character of the work then priced and the conditions under which the parties must have contemplated it would be carried out. If the character of the various works or the conditions under which they were carried out differ, then this rule applies. The following, it is thought, may be examples of its application: material change in quantities; winter working instead of summer working; wet instead of dry; high instead of low; confined working space instead of ample working space. If it does apply, it is necessary to look at its effect, which must vary according to circumstances. In some cases a 'fair valuation' may result in no or very little change from bill rates. Indeed, the wording of this sub-clause is so wide that the payment of less than bill rates might be justified. Note, however, that a claim under Clause 13.5.1.3 must be sharply differentiated from a claim for loss and expense (see above).

Daywork

14.15 Subject to any special agreement, the quantity surveyor must carry out the valuation in accordance with the rules laid down in this clause, but the architect is not bound to follow the quantity surveyor's valuation. The responsibility for valuation rests ultimately with the architect, who may in a particular case take the view that the quantity surveyor has failed to apply the rules laid down correctly in principle. He may, for example, consider that

varied work should have been valued at bill rates, whereas the quantity surveyor has valued it at 'fair' rates. In these circumstances the architect is entitled and bound to overrule the quantity surveyor (*R B Burden Limited* v *Swansea Corporation* (1957) 3 All ER 243). The quantity surveyor has no authority to vary the terms of the contract (see *John Laing Construction Limited* v *County and District Properties Limited* (1982) 23 BLR 1).

Errors in the bills

14.16 The contractor may have made errors in pricing his tender on the basis of the bills of quantities, either by totalling figures incorrectly or by inserting a rate for a particular item which is manifestly excessive or too low. The parties are precluded from disputing the total contract sum by the wording of Clause 14. Where a particular item is priced manifestly too low, contractors sometimes argue that if work the subject of the uneconomic rate becomes the subject of variation it should be valued at an economic rate and not at the bill rate. It is submitted that in the absence of any claim for rectification being sustainable an architect would be in breach of his duty to his employer were he to agree to this course without the employer's express agreement.

15 Clause 13A: Variation instruction – contractor's quotation in compliance with the instruction

15.01 Clause 13A was introduced by Amendment 13 issued in January 1994. It provides a new method of valuing a variation. The new method is an alternative to the traditional method of valuing in accordance with the valuation rules in Clause 13.5. It is for the architect in the first instance to decide whether he wishes Clause 13A to be used. If he wishes the Clause 13A method to apply, he must specify this in his instruction. If he does so, the clause 13A method will apply, unless within seven days the contractor states in writing that he disagrees with the application of Clause 13A to the instruction. If the contractor does that, then the valuation rules in Clause 13.5 will apply.

15.02 At the heart of the Clause 13A method of valuing is what is called a '13A Quotation'. This is a quotation to be provided by the contractor. If the system is to work properly the architect's variation instruction must give the contractor sufficient information to provide a quotation; and Clause 13A.1.1 specifically directs this. The JCT suggests that the information be in a similar format to that provided at tender stage, such as drawings, an addendum bill of quantities or a specification. If the contractor considers that the information provided is insufficient, then he has the right within 7 days to request further information. The Contractor is allowed 21 days from receipt of the instruction to provide the information. But if there has been a request by him for further information, the 21 day period runs from the receipt of the further information.

13A   **Variation instruction – Contractor's quotation in compliance with the instruction**

13A   Clause 13A shall only apply to an instruction where pursuant to clause 13·2·3 the Contractor has not disagreed with the application of clause 13A to such instruction.

13A·1 ·1   The instruction to which clause 13A is to apply shall have provided sufficient information [i·2] to enable the Contractor to provide a quotation, which shall comprise the matters set out in clause 13A·2 (a '13A Quotation'), in compliance with the instruction; and in respect of any part of the Variation which relates to the work of any Nominated Sub-Contractor sufficient information to enable the Contractor to obtain a 3·3A Quotation from the Nominated Sub-Contractor in accordance with clause 3·3A·1·2 of the Conditions NSC/C (*Conditions of Nominated Sub-Contract*). If the Contractor reasonably considers that the information provided is not sufficient, then, not later than 7 days from the receipt of the instruction, he shall request the Architect to supply sufficient further information.

13A·1 ·2   The Contractor shall submit to the Quantity Surveyor his 13A Quotation in compliance with the instruction and shall include therein 3·3A Quotations in respect of any parts of the Variation which relate to the work of Nominated Sub-Contractors not later than 21 days from

the date of receipt of the instruction

or if applicable, the date of receipt by the Contractor of the sufficient further information to which clause 13A·1·1 refers

whichever date is the later and the 13A Quotation shall remain open for acceptance by the Employer for 7 days from its receipt by the Quantity Surveyor.

13A·1 ·3 The Variation for which the Contractor has submitted his 13A Quotation shall not be carried out by the Contractor or as relevant by any Nominated Sub-Contractor until receipt by the Contractor of the confirmed acceptance issued by the Architect pursuant to clause 13A·3·2.

13A·2 The 13A Quotation shall separately comprise:

13A·2 ·1 the value of the adjustment to the Contract Sum (other than any amount to which clause 13A·2·3 refers) including therein the effect of the instruction on any other work including that of Nominated Sub-Contractors supported by all necessary calculations by reference, where relevant, to the rates and prices in the Contract Bills and including, where appropriate, allowances for any adjustment of preliminary items;

13A·2 ·2 any adjustment to the time required for completion of the Works (including where relevant stating an earlier Completion Date than the Date for Completion given in the Appendix) to the extent that such adjustment is not included in any revision of the Completion Date that has been made by the Architect under clause 25·3 or in his confirmed acceptance of any other 13A Quotation;

13A·2 ·3 the amount to be paid in lieu of any ascertainment under clause 26·1 of direct loss and/or expense not included in any other accepted 13A Quotation or in any previous ascertainment under clause 26;

13A·2 ·4 a fair and reasonable amount in respect of the cost of preparing the 13A Quotation;

and, where specifically required by the instruction, shall provide indicative information in statements on

13A·2 ·5 the additional resources (if any) required to carry out the Variation; and

13A·2 ·6 the method of carrying out the Variation.

Each part of the 13A Quotation shall contain reasonably sufficient supporting information to enable that part to be evaluated by or on behalf of the Employer.

13A·3 ·1 If the Employer wishes to accept a 13A Quotation the Employer shall so notify the Contractor in writing not later than the last day of the period for acceptance stated in clause 13A·1·2.

13A·3 ·2 If the Employer accepts a 13A Quotation the Architect shall, immediately upon that acceptance, confirm such acceptance by stating in writing to the Contractor (in clause 13A and elsewhere in the Conditions called a 'confirmed acceptance'):

·2 ·1 that the Contractor is to carry out the Variation;

·2 ·2 the adjustment of the Contract Sum, including therein any amounts to which clause 13A·2·3 and clause 13A·2·4 refer, to be made for complying with the instruction requiring the Variation;

·2 ·3 any adjustment to the time required by the Contractor for completion of the Works and the revised Completion Date arising therefrom (which, where relevant, may be a date earlier than the Date for Completion given in the Appendix) and, where relevant, any revised period or periods for the completion of the Nominated Sub-Contract work of each Nominated Sub-Contractor; and

·2 ·4 that the Contractor, pursuant to clause 3·3A·3 of the Conditions NSC/C *(Conditions of Nominated Sub-Contract),* shall accept any 3·3A Quotation included in the 13A Quotation for which the confirmed acceptance has been issued.

13A·4 If the Employer does not accept the 13A Quotation by the expiry of the period for acceptance stated in clause 13A·1·2, the Architect shall, on the expiry of that period

either

13A·4 ·1 instruct that the Variation is to be carried out and is to be valued pursuant to clause 13·4·1;

or

13A·4 ·2 instruct that the Variation is not to be carried out.

13A·5 If a 13A Quotation is not accepted a fair and reasonable amount shall be added to the Contract Sum in respect of the cost of preparation of the 13A Quotation provided that the 13A Quotation has been prepared on a fair and reasonable basis. The non-acceptance by the Employer of a 13A Quotation shall not of itself be evidence that the Quotation was not prepared on a fair and reasonable basis.

13A·6 If the Architect has not, under clause 13A·3·2, issued a confirmed acceptance of a 13A Quotation neither the Employer nor the Contractor may use that 13A Quotation for any purpose whatsoever.

13A·7 The Employer and the Contractor may agree to increase or reduce the number of days stated in clause 13A·1·1 and/or in clause 13A·1·2 and any such agreement shall be confirmed in writing by the Employer to the Contractor. Where relevant the Contractor shall notify each Nominated Sub-Contractor of any agreed increase or reduction pursuant to this clause 13A·7.

13A·8 If the Architect issues an instruction requiring a Variation to work for which a 13A Quotation has been given and in respect of which the Architect has issued a confirmed acceptance to the Contractor such Variation shall not be valued under clause 13·5; but the Quantity Surveyor shall make a valuation of such Variation on a fair and reasonable basis having regard to the content of such 13A Quotation and shall include in that valuation the direct loss and/or expense, if any, incurred by the Contractor because the regular progress of the Works or any part thereof has been materially affected by compliance with the instruction requiring the Variation.

15.03 The 13A Quotation must provide not merely a price for the variation. It must give the value of the entire adjustment to the contract sum including the effect on any other work. In addition it must give all the other matters listed in Clause 13A.2, including any adjustment to the time required for completion of the works, any sum by way of 'direct loss and expense' (see Clause 26) and a fee for preparing the 13A Quotation.

15.04 On receipt of the 13A Quotation the employer must choose to accept it or not to accept it. If the employer decides to accept it, he should notify the contractor directly. The Architect should then confirm the acceptance by giving the contractor in writing the information specified in Clause 13A.3.2. It might be thought that the effect of such acceptance would be that the contractor's price became binding: that, after all, is the normal meaning in law of accepting a quotation. But that is not quite so. The price to be paid for the varied work is a valuation to be made in due course by the quantity surveyor on a fair and reasonable basis: however, the quantity surveyor is directed to make that assessment having regard to the content of the 13A Quotation and disregarding the normal valuation rules in Clause 13.5.

15.05 The alternative course for the employer is not to accept the 13A Quotation. That may happen for two different reasons. One is simply that the employer considers the contractor's price excessive. In that case the architect should instruct that the variation is to be carried out in any event and to be valued in accordance with the normal valuation rules. The other reason is that, having seen the cost or delay implications, the Employer decides that he does not want to have the varied work after all. In that case the architect should instruct the contractor that the varied work is not to be carried out. Whatever the reason for the non-acceptance of a 13A Quotation, the contractor is entitled to be paid a fair and reasonable fee for preparing it.

15.06 If the variation affects work by a nominated sub-contractor, then the contractor may seek a similar quotation from the sub-contractor. A similar amendment has been made to the Conditions of Sub-Contract (NSC/C). The sub-contractor's quotation is called a 3.3A Quotation, which, of course, is a reference to the new clause number in NSC/C. The contractor will use the contents of the 3.3A Quotation when preparing his 13A Quotation.

15.07 Architects should not seek to employ the 13A Quotation procedure in the following situations, to which it is inappropriate:

• to a variation instruction which requires virtually immediate compliance;

• to a variation which amounts to a minor amendment or correction to information in the contract documents;

• when using the With Approximate Quantities version of JCT 80, under which variations are not separately valued.

16 Clause 14: Contract sum

16.01 Unless there is a case for rectification the parties are bound by any errors incorporated into the contract sum. Rectification is available either where the document fails to record the mutual intentions of the parties or where it fails to record accurately the intention of one party only, where the other with knowledge of the other party's error has nevertheless stood by and allowed the other to sign the agreement (see *Bates* v *Wyndhams* [1981] 1 All ER 1077).

---

14 Contract Sum

14·1 The quality and quantity of the work included in the Contract Sum shall be deemed to be that which is set out in the Contract Bills.

14·2 The Contract Sum shall not be adjusted or altered in any way whatsoever otherwise than in accordance with the express provisions of the Conditions, and subject to clause 2·2·2·2 any error whether of arithmetic or not in the computation of the Contract Sum shall be deemed to have been accepted by the parties hereto.

17 Clause 15: Value added tax – supplemental provisions

17.01 When value added tax was introduced the Joint Contracts Tribunal decided that the contract sum, that is the sum in Article 2, should be exclusive of VAT. A separate document was issued by the JCT originally entitled 'Supplemental VAT Agreement'. The general intention was that the contractor should be entitled to recover from the employer, as an additional sum, such VAT as he might have to pay to H M Customs and Excise on his supply of goods and services to the employer. The agreement also provided machinery for dealing with difficulties which might arise. Today the equivalent document is entitled 'Supplemental Provisions (the VAT Agreement)'. It is normally to be found at the back of JCT contracts. The view is taken that Clause 15.1 sufficiently incorporates it, and that there is no need for parties separately to execute it.

---

15 Value added tax – supplemental provisions

15·1 In clause 15 and in the supplemental provisions pursuant hereto (hereinafter called the 'VAT Agreement') 'tax' means the value added tax introduced by the Finance Act 1972 which is under the care and management of the Commissioners of Customs and Excise (hereinafter and in the VAT Agreement called 'the Commissioners').

15·2 Any reference in the Conditions to 'Contract Sum' shall be regarded as such Sum exclusive of any tax and recovery by the Contractor from the Employer of tax properly chargeable by the Commissioners on the Contractor under or by virtue of the Finance Act 1972 or any amendment or re-enactment thereof on the supply of goods and services under this Contract shall be under the provisions of clause 15 and of the VAT Agreement. Clause 1A of the VAT Agreement shall only apply where so stated in the Appendix. [k·1]

15·3 To the extent that after the Base Date the supply of goods and services to the Employer becomes exempt from the tax there shall be paid to the Contractor an amount equal to the loss of credit (input tax) on the supply to the Contractor of goods and services which contribute exclusively to the Works.

17.02 In the early days of VAT a considerable amount of building work was outside the scope of VAT. The scheme then was the contractor would analyse each supply into that element which attracted VAT and that which was zero-rated. Progressively, more and more building work has come within the scope of VAT. Therefore, in 1989 a simpler alternative was introduced, contained in Clause 1A of the supplemental provisions. That provides a scheme for use when the contractor is aware at the outset that *all* supplies will be standard rated, or, in occasional cases, zero-rated. The Appendix now contains an entry for the parties to indicate whether or not the simpler Clause 1A scheme is to apply.

17.03 Tax is a complicated subject, and one wholly outside the scope of this book. For that reason the supplemental provisions are not printed here. On any point of the remotest difficulty architects should take advice from an accountant, or a solicitor or barrister specializing in tax matters.

18 Clause 16: Materials and goods unfixed or off-site

18.01 This clause should be read in conjunction with Clause 30.2. The position as to materials and goods intended for the works is as follows:

1. As soon as materials or goods are brought onto or adjacent to the works, they must not be removed without the architect's consent (Clause 16.1).
2. As soon as materials or goods are paid for, property passes to the employer (Clause 16.1).
3. As soon as materials or goods are incorporated into the works, property passes to the owner of the land by operation of law whether the goods are paid for or not.

---

16 Materials and goods unfixed or off-site

16·1 Unfixed materials and goods delivered to, placed on or adjacent to the Works and intended therefor shall not be removed except for use upon the Works unless the Architect has consented in writing to such removal which consent shall not be unreasonably withheld. Where the value of any such materials or goods has in accordance with clause 30·2 been included in any Interim Certificate under which the amount properly due to the Contractor has been paid by the Employer, such materials and goods shall become the property of the Employer, but, subject to clause 22B or 22C (if applicable), the Contractor shall remain responsible for loss or damage to the same.

16·2 Where the value of any materials or goods intended for the Works and stored off-site has in accordance with clause 30·3 been included in any Interim Certificate under which the amount properly due to the Contractor has been paid by the Employer, such materials and goods shall become the property of the Employer and thereafter the Contractor shall not, except for use upon the Works, remove or cause or permit the same to be moved or removed from the premises where they are, but the Contractor shall nevertheless be responsible for any loss thereof or damage thereto and for the cost of storage, handling and insurance of the same until such time as they are delivered to and placed on or adjacent to the Works whereupon the provisions of clause 16·1 (except the words 'Where the value' to the words' the property of the Employer, but,') shall apply thereto.

18.02 The architect has a discretion as to whether to certify for the value of goods and materials 'off-site' under Clause 30.3. If off-site materials are certified for, the property passes to the employer (Clause 16.2). The employer does not in any circumstances have an interest in or right to retain the contractor's plant and equipment.

19 Clause 17: Practical completion and defects liability

19.01 This clause provides for a certificate of practical completion when, in the opinion of the architect, practical completion is achieved, if the contractor has complied with Clause 5.9 if applicable. This is to be followed by the delivery of a schedule of defects which is usually delivered at the end of the defects liability period (specified in the Appendix) but in any event not later than 14 days after its expiration. Instructions may be issued from time to time to make good particular defects appearing during the defects liability period, after which a certificate of completion of making defects is issued. The contractor is not required to make good damage caused by frost occurring after practical completion, unless the architect certifies otherwise.

---

17 Practical Completion and defects liability

17·1 When in the opinion of the Architect Practical Completion of the Works is achieved and the Contractor has complied sufficiently with clause 6A·4, and, if relevant, the Contractor has complied with clause 5·9 *(Supply of as-built drawings etc. – Performance Specified Work)*, he shall forthwith issue a certificate to that effect and Practical Completion of the Works shall be deemed for all the purposes of this Contract to have taken place on the day named in such certificate.

17·2 Any defects, shrinkages or other faults which shall appear within the Defects Liability Period and which are due to materials or workmanship not in accordance with this Contract or to frost occurring before Practical Completion of the Works, shall be specified by the Architect in a schedule of defects which he shall deliver to the Contractor as an instruction of the Architect not later than 14 days after the expiration of the said Defects Liability Period, and within a reasonable time after receipt of such schedule the defects, shrinkages and other faults therein specified shall be made good by the Contractor at no cost to the Employer unless the Architect with the consent of the Employer shall otherwise instruct; and if the Architect does so otherwise instruct then an appropriate deduction in respect of any such defects, shrinkages or other faults not made good shall be made from the Contract Sum.

17·3 Notwithstanding clause 17·2 the Architect may whenever he considers it necessary so to do issue instructions requiring any defect, shrinkage or other fault which shall appear within the Defects Liability Period and which is due to materials or workmanship not in accordance with this Contract or to frost occurring before Practical Completion of the Works, to be made good, and the Contractor shall within a reasonable time after receipt of such instructions comply with the same at no cost to the Employer unless the Architect with the consent of the Employer shall otherwise instruct; and if the Architect does so otherwise instruct then an appropriate deduction in respect of any such defects, shrinkages or other faults not made good shall be made from the Contract Sum. Provided that no such instructions shall be issued after delivery of a schedule of defects or after 14 days from the expiration of the Defects Liability Period.

17·4 When in the opinion of the Architect any defects, shrinkages or other faults which he may have required to be made good under clauses 17·2 and 17·3 shall have been made good he shall issue a certificate to that effect, and completion of making good defects shall be deemed for all the purposes of this Contract to have taken place on the day named in such certificate (the 'Certificate of Completion of Making Good Defects').

17·5 In no case shall the Contractor be required to make good at his own cost any damage by frost which may appear after Practical Completion, unless the Architect shall certify that such damage is due to injury which took place before Practical Completion.

Meaning of practical completion

19.02 The term 'practical completion' is not defined in the contract, but it has been said (by Lord Dilhorne in *Westminster City Council* v *Jarvis Limited* [1970] 1 All ER 943 at 948) that it does not mean the stage when the work 'was almost but not entirely finished', but 'the completion of all the construction work that has to be done'. Such completion is subject to defects which may thereafter appear and require action under Clause 17. In the same case in the Court of Appeal, Salmon LJ said: 'I take these words to mean completion for all practical purposes, i.e. for the purpose of allowing [the employer] to take possession of the works and use them as intended. If "completion" in Clause 21 [Clause 23 of the 1980 JCT Form] means completion down to the last detail, however trivial and unimportant, then Clause 22 [Clause 24 of the 1980 Form] would be a penalty clause and as such unenforceable'. Neither explanation is binding as to the meaning of the words for the purposes of considering whether the contractor has reached the stage of practical completion. However, it is suggested that the architect can issue his certificate despite minor defects if:

1. He is reasonably satisfied the works accord with the contract.
2. There is adequate retention.
3. The employer will not suffer loss due to disturbance or otherwise.
4. He obtains a written acknowledgment of the existence of the defect and an undertaking to put it right from the contractor. If the defects are other than trivial, the views of the employer should first be obtained.

Form of certificate

19.03 This is not prescribed by the contract, but it should be clear and definite. The RIBA issue suitable forms.

Effect of certificate of practical completion

19.04 The practical completion certificate has the following important effects:

1. It fixes the commencement of the defects liability period (as defined in the Appendix)
2. It fixes the period of final measurement laid down by Clause 30.
3. It gives rise to the rights to the release of the first half of the retention percentage (Clause 30.4.1)
4. It marks the time for the release of the obligation to insure under Clause 22A.1 where this applies.
5. It marks the end of liability for liquidated damages under Clause 24.
6. It marks the end of liability for frost damage (Clause 17.2).

The employer's remedies for defective work are not limited to those contained in the clause (i.e. requiring the contractor to make good defects and non-release of retention). He may additionally sue for damages for breach of contract (*HW Nevill (Sunblest) Limited* v *Wm Press & Son Limited* (1981) 20 BLR 78).

Meaning of defects

19.05 For the contractor's obligation as to standards of workmanship, materials, and goods, see Clauses 2 and 8, and the notes thereto. Defects are, generally, work, materials and goods which are not in conformity with the contract documents.

The contractor is not obliged to remedy work left defective by a Nominated Sub-contractor (see *Fairclough* v *Rhuddlan Borough Council* (1985) 30 BLR 26).

19.06 It is, in general, no excuse for a contractor to say that the architect or the Clerk of Works ought to have observed bad work during site inspections. See Clause 30 for the effect of the final certificate.

Frost damage

19.07 The contractor is not responsible for frost damage after practical completion unless the architect certifies that the damage is due to injury which took place before practical completion.

Instructions under 17.3 making good defects

19.08 This clause enables the architect to issue instructions before the delivery of the schedule of defects when he 'considers it necessary so to do'. One of the matters to be taken into account in considering whether it is necessary to issue such instructions is whether it is reasonable to leave the defect unremedied until after the issue of the schedule.

Architect's remedies

19.09 A notice under Clause 4.1.2 can be given for breach of an instruction to make good defects. If the notice is not complied with, others can be employed to do the necessary work and the cost deducted from the retention percentage. Further, until defects have been made good, the architect need not and should not issue his certificate of completion of making good defects. The second half of the retention percentage will not be released, and issue of the final certificate with the protection it usually affords to the contractor (see Clause 30) may be delayed. It is not clear whether the power of determination under Clause 27 can be exercised after practical completion; however, the remedies set out above ought to be sufficient to make it unnecessary to attempt to rely on Clause 27.

Irremediable breach

19.10 The architect may include a defect in an instruction or in the schedule, but then find on representation by the contractor that it cannot be remedied except at a cost which is unreasonable in comparison with the loss to the employer and the nature of the defect. In such circumstances the Architect has, it is thought, a discretion to issue his certificate under Clause 17.4 and to make a reduction of the amount certified for payment in respect of the works not properly carried out, being the amount by which the works are reduced in value by reason of the unremedied defect. Where the approval of the quality of any material or the standards of any workmanship is a matter for his opinion, however, the architect would be wise to consider carefully the implications of issuing a final certificate (see Clauses 2.1 and 30.9).

Defects appearing after the expiry of the defects liability period

19.11 If defects appear after the issue of the certificate under Clause 17.4, the architect can no longer issue instructions under Clause 17, but the appearance of the defect is the disclosure of a breach of contract by the contractor. The employer is entitled to damages, and the architect should adjust any further certificate to reflect the effect on the value of the works. In accordance with common law rules as to mitigation of damages, the contractor, if it is reasonable to do so, should be given the opportunity of rectifying the defects. An unqualified final certificate should not be issued if the defects are unremedied (see Clause 30.9).

Practical completion of part

19.12 Clause 18 makes provision for 'partial' practical completion where the employer takes possession of part of the work before completion of the work as a whole. Therefore, the procedure laid down under Clause 17 may be applied a number of times during the course of the contract.

20 Clause 18: Partial possession by employer

20.01 This clause provides for the situation where, before the works are completed, the employer, with the consent of the contractor, takes possession of part or parts of the works. It provides provisions as to practical completion, defects, insurance, and retention percentage for application to each part analogous to those which apply to the whole, and for proportionate reduction of any liquidated damages payable. The appropriate Appendix entry must be completed so as to allow the proper operation of Clause 18.1.4, otherwise liquidated damages will not be enforceable. In *Bramall & Ogden Limited* v *Sheffield City Council* (1983) 29 BLR 73 (a case on JCT 63), the Appendix was completed so as to allow a sum in damages for each uncompleted dwelling. This was held to be inconsistent with Clause 16(e) (equivalent to JCT 80 Clause 18.1.4). If possession is given in sections, the architect must apply Clause 18 and has no power without the consent of the parties to issue a certificate of practical completion for an average date of completion.

---

18   Partial possession by Employer

18·1   If at any time or times before the date of issue by the Architect of the certificate of Practical Completion the Employer wishes to take possession of any part or parts of the Works and the consent of the Contractor (which consent shall not be unreasonably withheld) has been obtained, then, notwithstanding anything expressed or implied elsewhere in this Contract, the Employer may take possession thereof. The Architect shall thereupon issue to the Contractor on behalf of the Employer a written statement identifying the part or parts of the Works taken into possession and giving the date when the Employer took possession (in clauses 18,20·3, 22·3·1 and 22C·1 referred to as 'the relevant part' and 'the relevant date' respectively).

18·1   ·1   For the purposes of clauses 17·2, 17·3, 17·5 and 30·4·1·2 Practical Completion of the relevant part shall be deemed to have occurred and the Defects Liability Period in respect of the relevant part shall be deemed to have commenced on the relevant date.

18·1   ·2   When in the opinion of the Architect any defects, shrinkages or other faults in the relevant part which he may have required to be made good under clause 17·2 or clause 17·3 shall have been made good he shall issue a certificate to that effect.

18·1   ·3   As from the relevant date the obligation of the Contractor under clause 22A or of the Employer under clause 22B·1 or clause 22C·2 whichever is applicable to insure shall terminate in respect of the relevant part but not further or otherwise; and where clause 22C applies the obligation of the Employer to insure under clause 22C·1 shall from the relevant date include the relevant part.

18·1   ·4   In lieu of any sum to be paid or allowed by the Contractor under clause 24 in respect of any period during which the Works may remain incomplete occurring after the relevant date there shall be paid or allowed such sum as bears the same ratio to the sum which would be paid or allowed apart from the provisions of clause 18 as the Contract Sum less the amount contained therein in respect of the relevant part bears to the Contract Sum.

Duty to complete in sections

20.02 This clause does not impose a duty to complete in sections. Equally, if the contractor is delayed and therefore subject to liquidated damages, he is not entitled to any contra-credit for having completed some of the work before the contractual completion date. If sectional completion is required, the JCT Sectional Completion Supplement should be employed.

Use, but not possession

20.03 Neither the Standard Form nor the Sectional Completion Supplement makes provision for the situation where the employer, without taking possession of a part, requires use of it (for example, for storage purposes). If such an arrangement is desired, specific amendments to the form of contract must be made (see *English Industrial Estates* v *George Wimpey* [1973] 1 Lloyd's Reports 118).

21 Clause 19: Assignment and sub-contracts

21.01 At law, a party may assign the benefit of a contract on giving notice of the assignment to the other party, but may not assign the burden without the other party's consent. This clause prohibits either party making any assignment without the written consent of the other. The rationale behind this is to ensure that the original contracting parties are not brought into direct contractual relations with third parties with whom they may not wish to contract. The House of Lords held in *Linden Garden Trust Limited* v

Lenesta Sludge Disposals Limited [1993] 3 All ER 417 that any purported assignment would be invalid under this clause, and therefore not effective to transfer any rights of action under the contract.

---

19   Assignment and sub-contracts

19·1   ·1   Neither the Employer nor the Contractor shall, without the written consent of the other, assign this Contract.

19·1   ·2   Where clause 19·1·2 is stated in the Appendix to apply then, in the event of transfer by the Employer of his freehold or leasehold interest in, or of a grant by the Employer of a leasehold interest in, the whole of the premises comprising the Works, the Employer may at any time after Practical Completion of the Works assign to any such transferee or lessee the right to bring proceedings in the name of the Employer (whether by arbitration or litigation) to enforce any of the terms of this Contract made for the benefit of the Employer hereunder. The assignee shall be estopped from disputing any enforceable agreements reached between the Employer and the Contractor and which arise out of and relate to this Contract (whether or not they are or appear to be a derogation from the right assigned) and made prior to the date of any assignment.

19·2   ·1   A person to whom the Contractor sub-lets any portion of the Works other than a Nominated Sub-Contractor is in this Contract referred to as a 'Domestic Sub-Contractor'.

19·2   ·2   The Contractor shall not without the written consent of the Architect (which consent shall not be unreasonably withheld) sub-let any portion of the Works. The Contractor shall remain wholly responsible for carrying out and completing the Works in all respects in accordance with clause 2·1 notwithstanding the sub-letting of any portion of the Works.

19·3   ·1   Where the Contract Bills provide that certain work measured or otherwise described in those Bills and priced by the Contractor must be carried out by persons named in a list in or annexed to the Contract Bills and selected therefrom by and at the sole discretion of the Contractor the provisions of clause 19·3 shall apply in respect of that list.

19·3   ·2   ·1   The list referred to in clause 19·3·1 must comprise not less than three persons. Either the Employer (or the Architect on his behalf) or the Contractor shall be entitled with the consent of the other, which consent shall not be unreasonably withheld, to add [I] additional persons to the list at any time prior to the execution of a binding sub-contract agreement.

·2   ·2   If at any time prior to the execution of a binding sub-contract agreement and for whatever reason less than three persons named in the list are able and willing to carry out the relevant work then

either the Employer and the Contractor shall by agreement (which agreement shall not be unreasonably withheld) add [I] the names of other persons so that the list comprises not less than three such persons

or the work shall be carried out by the Contractor who may sub-let to a Domestic Sub-Contractor in accordance with clause 19·2.

19·3   ·3   A person selected by the Contractor under clause 19·3 from the aforesaid list shall be a Domestic Sub-Contractor.

19·4   It shall be a condition in any sub-letting to which clause 19·2 or 19·3 refers that:

19·4   ·1   the employment of the Domestic Sub-Contractor under the sub-contract shall determine immediately upon the determination (for any reason) of the Contractor's employment under this Contract; and

19·4   ·2   the sub-contract shall provide that:

·2   ·1   Subject to clause 16·1 of these Conditions (in clauses 19·4·2·2 to ·4 called 'the Main Contract Conditions'), unfixed materials and goods delivered to, placed on or adjacent to the Works by the sub-contractor and intended therefore shall not be removed except for use on the Works unless the Contractor has consented in writing to such removal, which consent shall not be unreasonably withheld.

·2   ·2   Where, in accordance with clause 30·2 of the Main Contract Conditions, the value of any such materials or goods shall have been included in any Interim Certificate under which the amount properly due to the Contractor shall have been discharged by the Employer in favour of the Contractor, such materials or goods shall be and become the property of the Employer and the sub-contractor shall not deny that such materials or goods are and have become the property of the Employer.

·2   ·3   Provided that if the Main Contractor shall pay the sub-contractor for any such materials or goods before the value therefor has, in accordance with clause 30·2 of the Main Contract Conditions, been included in any Interim Certificate under which the amount properly due to the Contractor has been discharged by the Employer in favour of the Contractor, such materials or goods shall upon such payment by the Main Contractor be and become the property of the Main Contractor.

·2   ·4   The operation of clauses 19·4·2·1 to ·3 hereof shall be without prejudice to any property in any materials or goods passing to the Contractor as provided in clause 30·3·5 of the Main Contract Conditions (off-site materials or goods).

19·5   ·1   The provisions of this Contract relating to Nominated Sub-Contractors are set out in Part 2 of the Conditions. Save as otherwise expressed in the Conditions the Contractor shall remain wholly responsible for carrying out and completing the Works in all respects in accordance with clause 2·1, notwithstanding the nomination of a sub-contractor to supply and fix materials or goods or to execute work.

19·5   ·2   Subject to clause 35·2 the Contractor is not himself required, unless otherwise agreed, to supply and fix materials or goods or to execute work which is to be carried out by a Nominated Sub-Contractor.

21.02 In addition, Clauses 19.2, 19.3 and 19.4 make specific provision for 'domestic sub-contractors', i.e. sub-contractors to whom the contractor delegates part of the work but who are not nominated pursuant to Clause 35 (see paragraph 39). Clause 19.2.2 imposes a general prohibition on subletting any portion of the works without the consent of the architect, whose consent shall not be unreasonably withheld. Any person other than a nominated sub-contractor to whom a portion of the work is sublet is called a domestic sub-contractor (19.2.1).

Lists of domestic sub-contractors

21.03 Clause 19.3 makes further provision for domestic sub-contractors. It applies whenever the bills provide in respect of any work that the work is to be carried out by a person selected from a list contained in or annexed to the contract bills at the sole discretion of the contractor. This recognizes a practice which has been adopted by some employers. Clause 19.3.2.1 provides that this list must comprise not less than three persons and is subject to amendment by either the employer or the contractor with the consent of the other so as to add further names to the list at any time prior to the execution of a binding sub-contract. If at any time prior to the sub-contract being entered into less than three persons on the list are prepared to carry out the work in question by virtue of Clause 19.3.2.2 either further names are to be added to the list or the work is to be carried out by the contractor who may, if he wishes, sublet to a domestic sub-contractor under Clause 19.2 (subject to the architect's approval).

21.04 This procedure is only available where the work is measured or described in the bills and priced by the contractor, therefore it can never apply where the work in question is the subject of a provisional or prime cost sum or where for some other reason the work is not included in the bills.

21.05 Clause 19.4.1 provides, perhaps unnecessarily, that any domestic sub-contract is subject to a condition that the domestic sub-contractor's employment shall determine if the contractor's employment under the main contract is determined. Since domestic sub-contractors will not, of course, be parties to this contract, any rights they may have in fact against the main contractor on such determination would not be affected by this clause.

20.06 Clause 19.4.2 makes provision for the passing of property. These provisions are without prejudice to the provisions of Clause 30.3.5 as to the passing of property in materials which are included in an interim certificate when stored off site.

21.07 Clause 19.5.2 makes it clear that apart from the provisions of Clause 35.2 the contractor is not himself required to carry out work for which provision is made for execution by a nominated sub-contractor. This confirms the position as laid down in *North West Metropolitan Hospital Board* v *T A Bickerton & Son Limited* [1970] 1 WLR 607, where it was held that where a nominated sub-contractor failed to perform, it was the duty of the employer to renominate a further nominated sub-contractor. However, Clause 19.5.1 (inserted by amendment 9: 1990) provides that the contractor remains wholly responsible for the carrying out and completing of the works to the standards required by Clause 2.1, notwithstanding the nomination of a sub-contractor who will actually supply and fix materials or goods or to execute work.

22 Clause 20: Injury to persons and property and indemnity to employer

Contractor's liability under Clauses 20.1 and 20.2 in respect of personal injury and injury or damage to property

22.01 These clauses require the contractor to indemnify the employer, subject to two provisos, against expenses, etc. arising from the death or injury to any person or damage to property occa-

sioned by the carrying out of the works. However, the contractor is not liable and the indemnity cannot be invoked, except to the extent that the employer can show that the injury or damage was due to negligence, breach of statutory duty, omission or default on the part of the contractor or those for whom he is responsible. The contractor is not liable for any injury or damage caused by the negligence, breach of statutory duty, omission or default of those persons employed engaged or authorized by the employer.

20	Injury to persons and property and indemnity to Employer
20·1	The Contractor shall be liable for, and shall indemnify the Employer against, any expense, liability, loss, claim or proceedings whatsoever arising under any statute or at common law in respect of personal injury to or the death of any person whomsoever arising out of or in the course of or caused by the carrying out of the Works, except to the extent that the same is due to any act or neglect of the Employer or of any person for whom the Employer is responsible including the persons employed or otherwise engaged by the Employer to whom clause 29 refers.
20·2	The Contractor shall, subject to clause 20·3 and, where applicable, clause 22C·1, be liable for, and shall indemnify the Employer against, any expense, liability, loss, claim or proceedings in respect of any injury or damage whatsoever to any property real or personal in so far as such injury or damage arises out of or in the course of or by reason of the carrying out of the Works, and to the extent that the same is due to any negligence, breach of statutory duty, omission or default of the Contractor, his servants or agents or of any person employed or engaged upon or in connection with the Works or any part thereof, his servants or agents or of any other person who may properly be on the site upon or in connection with the Works or any part thereof, his servants or agents, other than the Employer or any person employed, engaged or authorised by him or by any local authority or statutory undertaker executing work solely in pursuance of its statutory rights or obligations.
20·3 ·1	Subject to clause 20·3·2 the reference in clause 20·2 to 'property real or personal' does not include the Works, work executed and/or Site Materials up to and including the date of issue of the certificate of Practical Completion or up to and including the date of determination of the employment of the Contractor (whether or not the validity of that determination is disputed) under clause 27 or clause 28 or clause 28A or, where clause 22C applies, under clause 27 or clause 28 or clause 28A or clause 22C·4·3, whichever is the earlier.
20·3 ·2	If clause 18 has been operated then, in respect of the relevant part and as from the relevant date, such relevant part shall not be regarded as 'the Works' or 'work executed' for the purpose of clause 20·3·1.

22.02 'Property, real or personal' does not include the works, work executed or site materials before the issue of the Certificate of Practical Completion or the determination of the employment of the contractor (Clause 20.3), nor does it include existing structures on the site. If Clauses 22B or 22C apply, the contractor is liable under this clause for: claims by third parties whose property is damaged; claims by the employer in respect of his own property; and, it seems, damage to the works. However, this clause is not wide enough to cover the situation where the work is defectively executed as a result of the contractor's negligence (see *City of Manchester* v *Fram Gerrard* 6 BLR 70). Further, in *Ossery Road (Skelmersdale) Limited* v *Balfour Beatty Building Limited* [1993] CILL 882, it was held that where work is to an existing structure and damage to it is caused by the negligence of the contractor, and such damage was not caused by a specified peril, the contractor will be exempted from all liability to the employer for loss or damage suffered and from his obligations to indemnify the employer against third party claims.

22.03 In addition to his liability under Clause 20.2, the contractor must as an incident of his duty to complete make good any damage to the works such as that due to vandalism or theft occurring before practical completion and not caused by the employer's negligence or default or within the risks accepted by the employer where Clause 22B or 22C is used. The contractor's plant, equipment, and unfixed goods and materials are at his risk. Goods and materials when certified for remain at his risk.

22.04 Where by virtue of Clause 20.3 the contractor is not responsible for damage, the employer may be unable to recover damages from a sub-contractor who caused the damage in question (see *Norwich City Council* v *Harvey* (1987) 39 BLR 75).

Employer and contractor liable to third party

22.03 In *A M F International* v *Magnet Bowling* [1968] 1 WLR 1028, both employer and contractor were held liable to a third party for damage to the third party's property; it was held the employer could not recover under the indemnity in what is now Clause 20.2 because the indemnity did not apply where, as was the case, the third party's loss arose partly as a result of the employer's negligence. The employer succeeded in recovering from the contractor the sum he had to pay the third party because the damage arose from the contractor's failure to comply with items in the bills requiring the diversion of storm water and the protection of the works.

23 Clause 21: Insurance against injury to person or property

23.01 Clause 21 imposes certain duties to insure on the contractor. Clause 21.1 requires the contractor to take out and maintain employers' liability insurance in respect of death or injury to the employees of the contractor or any sub-contractor. Clause 21.2 relates to damage to third party property caused by the actual execution of the works, subject to certain exceptions, which include damage caused by the contractor's own negligence.

24 Clauses 22 to 22D: Insurance of the works

24.01 Clause 22 provides for all-risks insurance of the works. There are three alternatives, any one of which may be stated in the Appendix to apply. Two (22A and B) are to be used for new works, (the contractor accepting the risk of the Clause 22 perils if 22A is used and the employer if 22B is used) and the third (22C) relates to works to existing buildings. In practice insurance brokers and companies provide standard form policies with wording corresponding to the alternatives provided for in Clause 22. Clause 22D allows the employer, should he so wish, to have effected on his behalf an insurance covering the loss or damage he will suffer as a result of late possession of the works in the event of an extension of time under Clause 25.3.

21			Insurance against injury to persons or property
21·1	·1	·1	Without prejudice to his obligation to indemnify the Employer under clause 20 the Contractor shall take out and maintain insurance which shall comply with clause 21·1·1·2 in respect of claims arising out of his liability referred to in clauses 20·1 and 20·2.
	·1	·2	The insurance in respect of claims for personal injury to or the death of any person under a contract of service or apprenticeship with the Contractor, and arising out of and in the course of such person's employment, shall comply with the Employer's Liability (Compulsory Insurance) Act 1969 and any statutory orders made thereunder or any amendment or re-enactment thereof. For all other claims to which clause 21·1·1·1 applies the insurance cover:
			– shall indemnify the Employer in like manner to the Contractor but only to the extent that the Contractor may be liable to indemnify the Employer under the terms of this Contract; and
			– shall be not less than the sum stated in the Appendix [I·1] for any one occurrence or series of occurrences arising out of one event.
21·1	·2		As and when he is reasonably required to do so by the Employer the Contractor shall send to the Architect for inspection by the Employer documentary evidence that the insurances required by clause 21·1·1·1 have been taken out and are being maintained, but at any time the Employer may (but not unreasonably or vexatiously) require to have sent to the Architect for inspection by the Employer the relevant policy or policies and the premium receipts therefor.
21·1	·3		If the Contractor defaults in taking out or in maintaining insurance as provided in clause 21·1·1·1 the Employer may himself insure against any liability or expense which he may incur arising out of such default and a sum or sums equivalent to the amount paid or payable by him in respect of premiums therefor may be deducted by him from any monies due or to become due to the Contractor under this Contract or such amount may be recoverable by the Employer from the Contractor as a debt.
21·2	·1		Where it is stated in the Appendix that the insurance to which clause 21·2·1 refers may be required by the Employer the Contractor shall, if so instructed by the Architect, take out and maintain a Joint Names Policy for such amount of indemnity as is stated in the Appendix in respect of any expense, liability, loss, claim or proceedings which the Employer may incur or sustain by reason of injury or damage to any property other than the Works and Site Materials caused by collapse, subsidence, heave, vibration, weakening or removal of support or lowering of ground water arising out of or in the course of or by reason of the carrying out of the Works excepting injury or damage:
	·1	·1	for which the Contractor is liable under clause 20·2;
	·1	·2	attributable to errors or omissions in the designing of the Works;
	·1	·3	which can reasonably be foreseen to be inevitable having regard to the nature of the work to be executed or the manner of its execution;
	·1	·4	which it is the responsibility of the Employer to insure under clause 22C·1 (if applicable);
	·1	·5	arising from war risks or the Excepted Risks.
21·2	·2		Any such insurance as is referred to in clause 21·2·1 shall be placed with insurers to be approved by the Employer, and the Contractor shall send to the Architect for deposit with the Employer the policy or policies and the premium receipts therefor.
21·2	·3		The amounts expended by the Contractor to take out and maintain the insurance referred to in clause 21·2·1 shall be added to the Contract Sum.
21·2	·4		If the Contractor defaults in taking out or in maintaining the Joint Names Policy as provided in clause 21·2·1 the Employer may himself insure against any risk in respect of which the default shall have occurred.
21·3			Notwithstanding the provisions of clauses 20·1, 20·2 and 21·1·1, the Contractor shall not be liable either to indemnify the Employer or to insure against any personal injury to or the death of any person or any damage, loss or injury caused to the Works or Site Materials, work executed, the site, or any property, by the effect of an Excepted Risk.

22			Insurance of the Works [m]
22·1			Clause 22A or clause 22B or clause 22C shall apply whichever clause is stated to apply in the Appendix.
22·2			In clauses 22A, 22B, 22C and, so far as relevant, in other clauses of the Conditions the following phrase shall have the meaning given below:
	All Risks Insurance: [n]		insurance which provides cover against any physical loss or damage to work executed and Site Materials but excluding the cost necessary to repair, replace or rectify
		1	property which is defective due to
		·1	wear and tear,
		·2	obsolescence,
		·3	deterioration, rust or mildew;
	All Risks Insurance: [m·1]	2	any work executed or any Site Materials lost or damaged as a result of its own defect in design, plan, specification, material or workmanship or any other work executed which is lost or damaged in consequence thereof where such work relied for its support or stability on such work which was defective;
		3	loss or damage caused by or arising from
		·1	any consequence of war, invasion, act of foreign enemy, hostilities (whether war be declared or not), civil war, rebellion, revolution, insurrection, military or usurped power, confiscation, commandeering, nationalisation or requisition or loss or destruction of or damage to any property by or under the order of any government de jure or de facto or public, municipal or local authority;
		·2	disappearance or shortage if such disappearance or shortage is only revealed when an inventory is made or is not traceable to an identifiable event;
		·3	an Excepted Risk (as defined in clause 1·3);
			and if the Contract is carried out in Northern Ireland
		·4	civil commotion;
		·5	any unlawful, wanton or malicious act committed maliciously by a person or persons acting on behalf of or in connection with an unlawful association; 'unlawful association' shall mean any organisation which is engaged in terrorism and includes an organisation which at any relevant time is a proscribed organisation within the meaning of the Northern Ireland (Emergency Provisions) Act 1973; 'terrorism' means the use of violence for political ends and includes any use of violence for the purpose of putting the public or any section of the public in fear.
22·3	·1		The Contractor where clause 22A applies, and the Employer where either clause 22B or clause 22C applies, shall ensure that the Joint Names Policy referred to in clause 22A·1 or clause 22A·3 or the Joint Names Policies referred to in clause 22B·1 or in clauses 22C·1 and 22C·2 shall
		either	provide for recognition of each sub-contractor nominated by the Architect as an insured under the relevant Joint Names Policy
		or	include a waiver by the relevant insurers of any right of subrogation which they may have against any such Nominated Sub-Contractor

in respect of loss or damage by the Specified Perils to the Works and Site Materials where clause 22A or clause 22B or clause 22C·2 applies and, where clause 22C·1 applies, in respect of loss or damage by the Specified Perils to the existing structures (which shall include from the relevant date any relevant part to which clause 18·1·3 refers) together with the contents thereof owned by the Employer or for which he is responsible; and that this recognition or waiver shall continue up to and including the date of issue of the certificate of practical completion of the sub-contract works (as referred to in clause 2·11 of Conditions NSC/C *(Conditions of Nominated Sub-Contract)* or the date of determination of the employment of the Contractor (whether or not the validity of that determination is contested) under clause 27 or clause 28 or clause 28A or, where clause 22C applies, under clause 27 or clause 28 or clause 28A or clause 22C·4·3, whichever is the earlier. The provisions of clause 22·3·1 shall apply also in respect of any Joint Names Policy taken out by the Employer under clause 22A·2 or by the Contractor under clause 22B·2 or under clause 22C·3 in respect of a default by the Employer under clause 22C·2.

22·3 ·2 Except in respect of the Joint Names Policy referred to in clause 22C·1 (or the Joint Names Policy referred to in clause 22C·3 in respect of a default by the Employer under clause 22C·1) the provisions of clause 22·3·1 in regard to recognition or waiver shall apply to Domestic Sub-Contractors. Such recognition or waiver for Domestic Sub-Contractors shall continue up to and including the date of issue of any certificate or other document which states that the domestic sub-contract works are practically complete or the date of determination of the employment of the Contractor as referred to in clause 22·3·1, whichever is the earlier.

22A Erection of new buildings – All Risks Insurance of the Works by the Contractor [m]

22A·1 The Contractor shall take out and maintain a Joint Names Policy for All Risks Insurance for cover no less than that defined in clause 22·2 [n] [o·1] for the full reinstatement value of the Works (plus the percentage, if any, to cover professional fees stated in the Appendix) and shall (subject to clause 18·1·3) maintain such Joint Names Policy up to and including the date of issue of the certificate of Practical Completion or up to and including the date of determination of the employment of the Contractor under clause 27 or clause 28 or clause 28A (whether or not the validity of that determination is contested), whichever is the earlier.

22A·2 The Joint Names Policy referred to in clause 22A·1 shall be taken out with insurers approved by the Employer and the Contractor shall send to the Architect for deposit with the Employer that Policy and the premium receipt therefor and also any relevant endorsement or endorsements thereof as may be required to comply with the obligation to maintain that Policy set out in clause 22A·1 and the premium receipts therefor. If the Contractor defaults in taking out or in maintaining the Joint Names Policy as required by clauses 22A·1 and 22A·2 the Employer may himself take out and maintain a Joint Names Policy against any risk in respect of which the default shall have occurred and a sum or sums equivalent to the amount paid or payable by him in respect of premiums therefor may be deducted by him from any monies due or to become due to the Contractor under this Contract or such amount may be recoverable by the Employer from the Contractor as a debt.

22A·3 ·1 If the Contractor independently of his obligations under this Contract maintains a policy of insurance which provides *(inter alia)* All Risks Insurance for cover no less than that defined in clause 22·2 for the full reinstatement value of the Works (plus the percentage, if any, to cover professional fees stated in the Appendix) then the maintenance by the Contractor of such policy shall, if the policy is a Joint Names Policy in respect of the aforesaid Works, be a discharge of the Contractor's obligation to take out and maintain a Joint Names Policy under clause 22A·1. If and so long as the Contractor is able to send to the Architect for inspection by the Employer as and when he is reasonably required to do so by the Employer documentary evidence that such a policy is being maintained then the Contractor shall be discharged from his obligation under clause 22A·2 to deposit the policy and the premium receipt with the Employer but on any occasion the Employer may (but not unreasonably or vexatiously) require to have sent to the Architect for inspection by the Employer the policy to which clause 22A·3·1 refers and the premium receipts therefor. The annual renewal date, as supplied by the Contractor, of the insurance referred to in clause 22A·3·1 is stated in the Appendix.

22A·3 ·2 The provisions of clause 22A·2 shall apply in regard to any default in taking out or in maintaining insurance under clause 22A·3·1.

22A·4 ·1 If any loss or damage affecting work executed or any part thereof or any Site Materials is occasioned by any one or more of the risks covered by the Joint Names Policy referred to in clause 22A·1 or clause 22A·2 or clause 22A·3 then, upon discovering the said loss or damage, the Contractor shall forthwith give notice in writing both to the Architect and to the Employer of the extent, nature and location thereof.

22A·4 ·2 The occurrence of such loss or damage shall be disregarded in computing any amounts payable to the Contractor under or by virtue of this Contract.

22A·4 ·3 After any inspection required by the insurers in respect of a claim under the Joint Names Policy referred to in clause 22A·1 or clause 22A·2 or clause 22A·3 has been completed the Contractor with due diligence shall restore such work damaged, replace or repair any such Site Materials which have been lost or damaged, remove and dispose of any debris and proceed with the carrying out and completion of the Works.

22A·4 ·4 The Contractor, for himself and for all Nominated and Domestic Sub-Contractors who are, pursuant to clause 22·3, recognised as an insured under the Joint Names Policy referred to in clause 22A·1 or clause 22A·2 or clause 22A·3, shall authorise the insurers to pay all monies from such insurance in respect of the loss or damage referred to in clause 22A·4·1 to the Employer. The Employer shall pay all such monies (less only the percentage, if any, to cover professional fees stated in the Appendix) to the Contractor by instalments under certificates of the Architect issued at the Period of Interim Certificates.

22A·4 ·5 The Contractor shall not be entitled to any payment in respect of the restoration, replacement or repair of such loss or damage and (when required) the removal and disposal of debris other than the monies received under the aforesaid insurance.

22B Erection of new buildings – All Risks Insurance of the Works by the Employer [m]

22B·1 The Employer shall take out and maintain a Joint Names Policy for All Risks Insurance for cover no less than that defined in clause 22·2 [n] [o·1] for the full reinstatement value of the Works (plus the percentage, if any, to cover professional fees stated in the Appendix) and shall (subject to clause 18·1·3) maintain such Joint Names Policy up to and including the date of issue of the certificate of Practical Completion or up to and including the date of determination of the employment of the Contractor under clause 27 or clause 28 or clause 28A (whether or not the validity of that determination is contested) whichever is the earlier.

22B·2 The Employer shall, as and when reasonably required to do so by the Contractor, produce documentary evidence and receipts showing that the Joint Names Policy required under clause 22B·1 has been taken out and is being maintained. If the Employer defaults in taking out or in maintaining the Joint Names Policy required under clause 22B·1 then the Contractor may himself take out and maintain a Joint Names Policy against any risk in respect of which a default shall have occurred and a sum or sums equivalent to the amount paid or payable by him in respect of the premiums therefor shall be added to the Contract Sum.

22B·3 ·1 If any loss or damage affecting work executed or any part thereof or any Site Materials is occasioned by any one or more of the risks covered by the Joint Names Policy referred to in clause 22B·1 or clause 22B·2 then, upon discovering the said loss or damage, the Contractor shall forthwith give notice in writing both to the Architect and to the Employer of the extent, nature and location thereof.

22B·3 ·2 The occurrence of such loss or damage shall be disregarded in computing any amounts payable to the Contractor under or by virtue of this Contract.

22B·3 ·3 After any inspection required by the insurers in respect of a claim under the Joint Names Policy referred to in clause 22B·1 or clause 22B·2 has been completed the Contractor with due diligence shall restore such work damaged, replace or repair any such Site Materials which have been lost or damaged, remove and dispose of any debris and proceed with the carrying out and completion of the Works.

22B·3 ·4 The Contractor, for himself and for all Nominated and Domestic Sub-Contractors who are, pursuant to clause 22·3, recognised as an insured under the Joint Names Policy referred to in clause 22B·1 or clause 22B·2, shall authorise the insurers to pay all monies from such insurance in respect of the loss or damage referred to in clause 22B·3·1 to the Employer.

22B·3 ·5 The restoration, replacement or repair of such loss or damage and (when required) the removal and disposal of debris shall be treated as if they were a Variation required by an instruction of the Architect under clause 13·2.

22C Insurance of existing structures – insurance of Works in or extensions to existing structures [m]

22C·1 The Employer shall take out and maintain a Joint Names Policy in respect of the existing structures (which shall include from the relevant date any relevant part to which clause 18·1·3 refers) together with the contents thereof owned by him or for which he is responsible, for the full cost of reinstatement, repair or replacement of loss or damage due to one or more of the Specified Perils [o·2] up to and including the date of issue of the certificate of Practical Completion or up to and including the date of determination of the employment of the Contractor under clause 22C·4·3 or clause 27 or clause 28 or clause 28A (whether or not the validity of that determination is contested) whichever is the earlier. The Contractor, for himself and for all Nominated Sub-Contractors who are, pursuant to clause 22·3·1, recognised as an insured under the Joint Names Policy referred to in clause 22C·1 or clause 22C·3 shall authorise the insurers to pay all monies from such insurance in respect of loss or damage to the Employer. [o·2A]

22C·2 The Employer shall take out and maintain a Joint Names Policy for All Risks Insurance for cover no less than that defined in clause 22·2 [n] [o·2] for the full reinstatement value of the Works (plus the percentage, if any, to cover professional fees stated in the Appendix) and shall (subject to clause 18·1·3) maintain such Joint Names Policy up to and including the date of issue of the certificate of Practical Completion or up to and including the date of determination of the employment of the Contractor under clause 22C·4·3 or clause 27 or clause 28 or clause 28A (whether or not the validity of that determination is contested) whichever is the earlier.

22C·3 The Employer shall, as and when reasonably required to do so by the Contractor, produce documentary evidence and receipts showing that the Joint Names Policy required under clause 22C·1 or clause 22C·2 has been taken out and is being maintained. If the Employer defaults in taking out or in maintaining the Joint Names Policy required under clause 22C·1 the Contractor may himself take out and maintain a Joint Names Policy against any risk in respect of which the default shall have occurred and for that purpose shall have such right of entry and inspection as may be required to make a survey and inventory of the existing structures and the relevant contents. If the Employer defaults in taking out or in maintaining the Joint Names Policy required under clause 22C·2 the Contractor may take out and maintain a Joint Names Policy against any risk in respect of which the default shall have occurred. A sum or sums equivalent to the premiums paid or payable by the Contractor pursuant to clause 22C·3 shall be added to the Contract Sum.

22C·4 If any loss or damage affecting work executed or any part thereof or any Site Materials is occasioned by any one or more of the risks covered by the Joint Names Policy referred to in clause 22C·2 or clause 22C·3 then, upon discovering the said loss or damage, the Contractor shall forthwith give notice in writing both to the Architect and to the Employer of the extent, nature and location thereof and

22C·4 ·1 the occurrence of such loss or damage shall be disregarded in computing any amounts payable to the Contractor under or by virtue of this Contract;

22C·4 ·2 the Contractor, for himself and for all Nominated and Domestic Sub-Contractors who are, pursuant to clause 22·3, recognised as an insured under the Joint Names Policy referred to in clause 22C·2 or clause 22C·3, shall authorise the insurers to pay all monies from such insurance in respect of the loss or damage referred to in clause 22C·4 to the Employer;

22C·4	·3	·1	if it is just and equitable so to do the employment of the Contractor under this Contract may within 28 days of the occurrence of such loss or damage be determined at the option of either party by notice by registered post or recorded delivery from either party to the other. Within 7 days of receiving a notice (but not thereafter) either party may give to the other a written request to concur in the appointment of an Arbitrator under clause 41 in order that it may be determined whether such determination will be just and equitable;
	·3	·2	upon the giving or receiving by the Employer of such a notice of determination or, where a reference to arbitration is made as aforesaid, upon the Arbitrator upholding the notice of determination, the provisions of clauses 28A·4 and 28A·5 (except clause 28A·5·5) shall apply.
22C·4	·4		If no notice of determination is served under clause 22C·4·3·1, or, where a reference to arbitration is made as aforesaid, if the Arbitrator decides against the notice of determination, then
	·4	·1	after any inspection required by the insurers in respect of a claim under the Joint Names Policy referred to in clause 22C·2 or clause 22C·3 has been completed, the Contractor with due diligence shall restore such work damaged, replace or repair any such Site Materials which have been lost or damaged, remove and dispose of any debris and proceed with the carrying out and completion of the Works; and
	·4	·2	the restoration, replacement or repair of such loss or damage and (when required) the removal and disposal of debris shall be treated as if they were a Variation required by an instruction of the Architect under clause 13·2.

22D   **Insurance for Employer's loss of liquidated damages – clause 25·4·3**

22D·1   Where it is stated in the Appendix that the insurance to which clause 22D refers may be required by the Employer then forthwith after the Contract has been entered into the Architect shall either inform the Contractor that no such insurance is required or instruct the Contractor to obtain a quotation for such insurance. This quotation shall be for an insurance on an agreed value basis [o·3] to be taken out and maintained by the Contractor until the date of Practical Completion and which will provide for payment to the Employer of a sum calculated by reference to clause 22D·3 in the event of loss or damage to the Works, work executed, Site Materials, temporary buildings, plant and equipment for use in connection with or on or adjacent to the Works by any one or more of the Specified Perils and which loss or damage results in the Architect giving an extension of time under clause 25·3 in respect of the Relevant Event in clause 25·4·3. The Architect shall obtain from the Employer any information which the Contractor reasonably requires to obtain such quotation. The Contractor shall send to the Architect as soon as practicable the quotation which he has obtained and the Architect shall thereafter instruct the Contractor whether or not the Employer wishes the Contractor to accept that quotation and such instruction shall not be unreasonably withheld or delayed. If the Contractor is instructed to accept the quotation the Contractor shall forthwith take out and maintain the relevant policy and send it to the Architect for deposit with the Employer, together with the premium receipt therefor and also any relevant endorsement or endorsements thereof and the premium receipts therefor.

22D·2   The sum insured by the relevant policy shall be a sum calculated at the rate stated in the Appendix as liquidated and ascertained damages for the period of time stated in the Appendix.

22D·3   Payment in respect of this insurance shall be calculated at the rate referred to in clause 22D·2 (or any revised rate produced by the application of clause 18·1·4) for the period of any extension of time finally given by the Architect as referred to in clause 22D·1 or for the period of time stated in the Appendix, whichever is the less.

22D·4   The amounts expended by the Contractor to take out and maintain the insurance referred to in clause 22D·1 shall be added to the Contract Sum. If the Contractor defaults in taking out or in maintaining the insurance referred to in clause 22D·1 the Employer may himself insure against any risk in respect of which the default shall have occurred.

24.02 In April 1994 the JCT published amendments labelled 'TC/94' concerned with terrorism cover. These amendments are not being incorporated in reprints of the form, and are described as 'not intended to be permanent'. The background to these amendments is as follows. In 1992 reinsurers informed leading British insurers that in future they would not be prepared to reinsure in respect of fire and explosion damage caused by terrorism. The Government then established a company called Pool Reinsurance Company Limited (or 'Pool Re') to act as a Government-backed reinsurer of last resort. Members of the public who wish to purchase terrorism damage insurance pay additional premiums at standard rates, which are passed on by the insurers to Pool Re. JCT contracts require insurance in respect of fire and explosion (see, e.g. Clause 22C.1), and so this new form of insurance is relevant to parties to JCT contracts. This scheme provides wholly satisfactory insurance for the public against terrorism damage, so long as it remains in force. So long as it is in force, no amendment is necessary to the JCT contract. The concern of the JCT is simply that the Government might withdraw support from Pool Re, as it is entitled to do under the terms of its agreement with Pool Re on 120 days' notice. Many people may consider that the contingency of the Government withdrawing terrorism reinsurance of last resort is so remote that it may reasonably be ignored. But the amendments

in TC/94 may be used by parties who share the worry of the JCT that the Government might do that: they are not published in this book, but are readily available from RIBA Publications.

25   Clause 23: Date of possession, completion and postponement

25.01 This clause should be read in conjunction with Clause 24 (damages for non-completion) and Clause 25 (extension of time).

25.02 If 'possession of the site' cannot be given on the date for possession, the employer is in serious breach of contract and the contractor is entitled to claim damages. In addition the employer would be unable to deduct liquidated damages for non-completion on the due date. There is no contractual provision enabling the architect to award an extension of time in such circumstances (the provision enabling the architect to postpone the 'work' gives him no power to postpone possession of the site). The best that can be done is to reach an agreement between the contractor and the employer to alter the dates for possession and completion.

23		**Date of Possession, completion and postponement**
23·1	·1	On the Date of Possession possession of the site shall be given to the Contractor who shall thereupon begin the Works, regularly and diligently proceed with the same and shall complete the same on or before the Completion Date.
23·1	·2	Where clause 23·1·2 is stated in the Appendix to apply the Employer may defer the giving of possession for a period not exceeding six weeks or such lesser period stated in the Appendix calculated from the Date of Possession.
23·2		The Architect may issue instructions in regard to the postponement of any work to be executed under the provisions of this Contract.
23·3	·1	For the purposes of the Works insurances the Contractor shall retain possession of the site and the Works up to and including the date of issue of the certificate of Practical Completion, and, subject to clause 18, the Employer shall not be entitled to take possession of any part or parts of the Works until that date.
23·3	·2	Notwithstanding the provisions of clause 23·3·1 the Employer may, with the consent in writing of the Contractor, use or occupy the site or the Works or part thereof whether for the purposes of storage of his goods or otherwise before the date of issue of the certificate of Practical Completion by the Architect. Before the Contractor shall give his consent to such use or occupation the Contractor or the Employer shall notify the insurers under clause 22A or clause 22B or clause 22C·2 to ·4 whichever may be applicable and obtain confirmation that such use or occupation will not prejudice the insurance. Subject to such confirmation the consent of the Contractor shall not be unreasonably withheld.
23·3	·3	Where clause 22A·2 or clause 22A·3 applies and the insurers in giving the confirmation referred to in clause 23·3·2 have made it a condition of such confirmation that an additional premium is required the Contractor shall notify the Employer of the amount of the additional premium. If the Employer continues to require use or occupation under clause 23·3·2 the additional premium required shall be added to the Contract Sum and the Contractor shall provide the Employer, if so requested, with the additional premium receipt therefor.

Postponement

25.03 However, if Clause 23.2 is stated in the Appendix to apply, the employer may defer giving possession for a limited period, as specified or up to six weeks.

25.04 Note the contractor's right to extension of time (Clause 25.4.5.1) and to claim loss and expense (Clause 26.2.5), and if the whole of the works are suspended beyond the period of delay stated in the Appendix, to determination (Clause 28.1.3.5). For circumstances when a variation order may also amount to a postponement of work, see *M Harrison & Co* v *Leeds City Council* (1980) 14 BLR 118.

26   Clause 24: Damages for non-completion

26.01 This clause gives the employer the right, if the architect certifies under this clause that the contractor has failed to achieve practical completion by the completion date, to deduct or claim liquidated and ascertained damages at the rate stated in the Appendix. The certificate is, it seems, required in order to ensure that the architect has properly considered any notices of delay under Clause 25 and has granted all extensions of time to which the contractor is entitled. Under Clause 25 provision is made for re-assessment of the need for extension of time throughout the contract period, and therefore Clause 24.2.2 makes provision for the situation where, after liquidated damages have been deducted, a later completion date is fixed under Clause 25.3.3 than that on the basis of which liquidated damages were deducted. In these circumstances, the employer would be obliged to pay or repay to the contractor amounts in respect of the period up to such later completion date. Clause 24.3.3 does not state whether the employer must pay interest on any damages repaid and it is unclear at present what the correct interpretation of the clause is.

26.02 The issue of a certificate under Clause 24.1 is a condition precedent to the employer's right to deduct liquidated damages (see *Ramac Construction* v *Lesser* [1975] 2 Lloyd's Reports 430). It was further held in *J F Finnigan Limited* v *Community Housing Association Limited* (1993) 8 Const LJ 311 that the provision in Clause 24.2.1 that 'the Employer may require in writing' a sum to be paid or allowed as liquidated damages operated as a condition precedent to the employer's entitlement to deduct liquidated damages. A form of certificate of non-completion is available from RIBA Publications Ltd.

---

24   Damages for non-completion

24·1   If the Contractor fails to complete the Works by the Completion Date then the Architect shall issue a certificate to that effect. In the event of a new Completion Date being fixed after the issue of such a certificate such fixing shall cancel that certificate and the Architect shall issue such further certificate under clause 24·1 as may be necessary.

24·2   ·1   Subject to the issue of any certificate under clause 24·1 the Contractor shall, as the Employer may require in writing not later than the date of the Final Certificate, pay or allow to the Employer liquidated and ascertained damages at the rate stated in the Appendix (or at such lesser rate as may be specified in writing by the Employer) for the period between the Completion Date and the date of Practical Completion and the Employer may deduct the same from any monies due or to become due to the Contractor under this Contract (including any balance stated as due to the Contractor in the Final Certificate) or the Employer may recover the same from the Contractor as a debt.

24·2   ·2   If, under clause 25·3·3, the Architect fixes a later Completion Date or a later Completion Date is stated in a confirmed acceptance of a 13A Quotation the Employer shall pay or repay to the Contractor any amounts recovered allowed or paid under clause 24·2·1 for the period up to such later Completion Date.

24·2   ·3   Notwithstanding the issue of any further certificate of the Architect under clause 24·1 any requirement of the Employer which has been previously stated in writing in accordance with clause 24·2·1 shall remain effective unless withdrawn by the Employer.

Advantage of liquidated damages

26.03 If there is no provision for liquidated damages, ascertainment of the damage suffered by reason of non-completion can involve the parties in long and costly proceedings. Where the parties have made and agreed upon a genuine pre-estimate of damages, such proceedings are avoided. The rate agreed, termed here 'liquidated and ascertained damages', will be given effect to by the courts without enquiring into the actual loss suffered.

Liquidated damages and penalties distinguished

26.04 In circumstances where the liquidated damages are construed as a penalty, the contractor can have the agreed rate of liquidated damages set aside and make the employer prove and be limited to his actual loss. It is therefore extremely important that liquidated damages should be stated in the Appendix in such a way as they cannot be construed as being a penalty. This is particularly likely to happen, as it did in *Bramall & Ogden Limited* v *Sheffield City Council* (1983) 29 BLR 73 where the sectional completion is required, but the Sectional Completion Supplement is not used.

Delay partly employer's fault

26.05 At common law an employer who is partly responsible for delay could not rely on a liquidated damages clause. However, under Clause 25 extensions of time may be granted in respect of

relevant events which include delay caused by the employer's fault, and, provided such extensions are properly granted, the right to liquidated damages is preserved. However, failure to grant proper extensions of time in respect of such relevant events as arise through the employer's fault will disentitle him from claiming liquidated damages. In *Percy Bilton Limited* v *Greater London Council* [1982] 2 All ER 623 (HL), it was held that delay caused by the bankruptcy of a nominated sub-contractor (for which no provision for extension is made by Clause 25) did not arise through any fault of the employer, so as to disentitle him from claiming liquidated damages. Failure to give possession of the site on the due date or within the period allowed under Clause 23.1.2, if applicable, could result in the right to liquidated damages being lost, as this is not a ground for extension under Clause 25, but is a fault of the employer (see *Rapid Building Group Ltd* v *Ealing Family Housing Association Ltd* (1984) 29 BLR 5).

Procedure

26.06 The employer has a discretion as to whether to deduct liquidated damages. In practice, although this is not required by the contract, it is convenient for the architect to set out his calculation of the employer's right to liquidated damages and send a copy to each party when giving his certificate. Under the 1963 JCT Form it has been held that no certificate under Clause 22 of that form (the equivalent clause to Clause 24) could be issued after the issue of the final certificate (*Fairweather* v *Asden Securities* (1979) 12 BLR 40). It is thought the position is the same under the 1980 Form.

27 Clause 25: Extension of time

27.01 Clause 25 makes provisions for extensions of time through delay caused by 'relevant events' as defined in Clause 25.4. When it becomes reasonably apparent that the progress of the works is being or is likely to be delayed, the contractor is obliged to give written notice forthwith to the architect of the material circumstances identifying:

1. The cause or causes of the delay.
2. Any event which in his opinion is a relevant event.

27.02 Clause 25.2.2 requires the contractor to give particulars of the expected effects of the cause of delay and an estimate of the extent of delay in completion of the works beyond the completion date which will result from that particular delay, whether or not that delay will be concurrent with a delay resulting from any other relevant event. This information should be included in the notice where possible, alternatively it should be given in writing as soon as possible after the issue of the notice.

---

25   Extension of time [p]

25·1   In clause 25 any reference to delay, notice or extension of time includes further delay, further notice or further extension of time.

25·2   ·1   ·1   If and whenever it becomes reasonably apparent that the progress of the Works is being or is likely to be delayed the Contractor shall forthwith give written notice to the Architect of the material circumstances including the cause of delay and identify in such notice any event which in his opinion is a Relevant Event.

·1   ·2   Where the material circumstances of which written notice has been given under clause 25·2·1·1 include reference to a Nominated Sub-Contractor, the Contractor shall forthwith send a copy of such written notice to the Nominated Sub-Contractor concerned.

25·2   ·2   In respect of each and every Relevant Event identified in the notice given in accordance with clause 25·2·1·1 the Contractor shall, if practicable in such notice, or otherwise in writing as soon as possible after such notice:

·2   ·1   give particulars of the expected effects thereof; and

·2   ·2   estimate the extent, if any, of the expected delay in the completion of the Works beyond the Completion Date resulting therefrom whether or not concurrently with delay resulting from any other Relevant Event and shall give such particulars and estimate to any Nominated Sub-Contractor to whom a copy of any written notice has been given under clause 25·2·1·2.

25·2 ·3   The Contractor shall give such further written notices to the Architect, and send a copy to any Nominated Sub-Contractor to whom a copy of any written notice has been given under clause 25·2·1·2, as may be reasonably necessary or as the Architect may reasonably require for keeping up-to-date the particulars and estimate referred to in clauses 25·2·2·1 and 25·2·2·2 including any material change in such particulars or estimate.

25·3 ·1   If, in the opinion of the Architect, upon receipt of any notice, particulars and estimate under clauses 25·2·1·1 and 25·2·2,

·1 ·1   any of the events which are stated by the Contractor to be the cause of the delay is a Relevant Event and

·1 ·2   the completion of the Works is likely to be delayed thereby beyond the Completion Date

the Architect shall in writing to the Contractor give an extension of time by fixing such later date as the Completion Date as he then estimates to be fair and reasonable. The Architect shall, in fixing such new Completion Date, state:

·1 ·3   which of the Relevant Events he has taken into account and

·1 ·4   the extent, if any, to which he has had regard to any instruction under clause 13·2 requiring as a Variation the omission of any work issued since the fixing of the previous Completion Date,

and shall, if reasonably practicable having regard to the sufficiency of the aforesaid notice, particulars and estimates, fix such new Completion Date not later than 12 weeks from receipt of the notice and of reasonably sufficient particulars and estimate, or, where the period between receipt thereof and the Completion Date is less than 12 weeks, not later than the Completion Date.

If, in the opinion of the Architect, upon receipt of any such notice, particulars and estimate, it is not fair and reasonable to fix a later date as a new Completion Date, the Architect shall if reasonably practicable having regard to the sufficiency of the aforesaid notice, particulars and estimate so notify the Contractor in writing not later than 12 weeks from receipt of the notice, particulars and estimate, or, where the period between receipt thereof and the Completion Date is less than 12 weeks, not later than the Completion Date.

25·3 ·2   After the first exercise by the Architect of his duty under clause 25·3·1 or after any revision to the Completion Date stated by the Architect in a confirmed acceptance of a 13A Quotation in respect of a Variation the Architect may in writing fix a Completion Date earlier than that previously fixed under clause 25 or than that stated by the Architect in a confirmed acceptance of a 13A Quotation if in his opinion the fixing of such earlier Completion Date is fair and reasonable having regard to the omission of any work or obligation instructed or sanctioned by the Architect under clause 13 after the last occasion on which the Architect fixed a new Completion Date.

Provided that no decision under clause 25·3·2 shall alter the length of any adjustment to the time required by the Contractor for the completion of the Works in respect of a Variation for which a 13A Quotation has been given and which has been stated in a confirmed acceptance of a 13A Quotation.

25·3 ·3   After the Completion Date, if this occurs before the date of Practical Completion, the Architect may, and not later than the expiry of 12 weeks after the date of Practical Completion shall, in writing to the Contractor either

·3 ·1   fix a Completion Date later than that previously fixed if in his opinion the fixing of such later Completion Date is fair and reasonable having regard to any of the Relevant Events, whether upon reviewing a previous decision or otherwise and whether or not the Relevant Event has been specifically notified by the Contractor under clause 25·2·1·1; or

·3 ·2   fix a Completion Date earlier than that previously fixed under clause 25 or stated in a confirmed acceptance of a 13A Quotation if in his opinion the fixing of such earlier Completion Date is fair and reasonable having regard to the omission of any work or obligation instructed or sanctioned by the Architect under clause 13 after the last occasion on which the Architect fixed a new Completion Date; or

·3 ·3   confirm to the Contractor the Completion Date previously fixed or stated in a confirmed acceptance of a 13A Quotation.

Provided that no decision under clause 25·3·3·1 or clause 25·3·3·2 shall alter the length of any adjustment to the time required by the Contractor for the completion of the Works in respect of a Variation for which a 13A Quotation has been given and which has been stated in a confirmed acceptance of a 13A Quotation.

25·3 ·4   Provided always that:

·4 ·1   the Contractor shall use constantly his best endeavours to prevent delay in the progress of the Works, howsoever caused, and to prevent the completion of the Works being delayed or further delayed beyond the Completion Date;

·4 ·2   the Contractor shall do all that may reasonably be required to the satisfaction of the Architect to proceed with the Works.

25·3 ·5   The Architect shall notify in writing to every Nominated Sub-Contractor each decision of the Architect under clause 25·3 fixing a Completion Date and each revised Completion Date stated in the confirmed acceptance of a 13A Quotation together with, where relevant, any revised period or periods for the completion of the work of each Nominated Sub-Contractor stated in such confirmed acceptance.

25·3 ·6   No decision of the Architect under clause 25·3·2 or clause 25·3·3·2 shall fix a Completion Date earlier than the Date for Completion stated in the Appendix.

25·4   The following are the Relevant Events referred to in clause 25:

25·4 ·1   force majeure;

25·4 ·2   exceptionally adverse weather conditions;

25·4 ·3   loss or damage occasioned by any one or more of the Specified Perils;

25·4 ·4   civil commotion, local combination of workmen, strike or lock-out affecting any of the trades employed upon the Works or any of the trades engaged in the preparation, manufacture or transportation of any of the goods or materials required for the Works;

25·4 ·5   compliance with the Architect's instructions

·5 ·1   under clauses 2·3, 2·4·1, 13·2 (except for a confirmed acceptance of a 13A Quotation), 13·3 (except compliance with an Architect's instruction for the expenditure of a provisional sum for defined work or of a provisional sum for Performance Specified Work), 13A·4·1, 23·2, 34, 35 or 36; or

·5 ·2   in regard to the opening up for inspection of any work covered up or the testing of any of the work, materials or goods in accordance with clause 8·3 (including making good in consequence of such opening up or testing) unless the inspection or test showed that the work, materials or goods were not in accordance with this Contract;

25·4 ·6   the Contractor not having received in due time necessary instructions (including those for or in regard to the expenditure of provisional sums), drawings, details or levels from the Architect for which he specifically applied in writing provided that such application was made on a date which having regard to the Completion Date was neither unreasonably distant from nor unreasonably close to the date on which it was necessary for him to receive the same;

25·4 ·7   delay on the part of Nominated Sub-Contractors or Nominated Suppliers which the Contractor has taken all practicable steps to avoid or reduce;

25·4 ·8 ·1   the execution of work not forming part of this Contract by the Employer himself or by persons employed or otherwise engaged by the Employer as referred to in clause 29 or the failure to execute such work;

·8 ·2   the supply by the Employer of materials and goods which the Employer has agreed to provide for the Works or the failure so to supply;

25·4 ·9   the exercise after the Base Date by the United Kingdom Government of any statutory power which directly affects the execution of the Works by restricting the availability or use of labour which is essential to the proper carrying out of the Works or preventing the Contractor from, or delaying the Contractor in, securing such goods or materials or such fuel or energy as are essential to the proper carrying out of the Works;

25·4 ·10 ·1   the Contractor's inability for reasons beyond his control and which he could not reasonably have foreseen at the Base Date to secure such labour as is essential to the proper carrying out of the Works; or

·10 ·2   the Contractor's inability for reasons beyond his control and which he could not reasonably have foreseen at the Base Date to secure such goods or materials as are essential to the proper carrying out of the Works;

25·4 ·11   the carrying out by a local authority or statutory undertaker of work in pursuance of its statutory obligations in relation to the Works, or the failure to carry out such work;

25·4 ·12   failure of the Employer to give in due time ingress to or egress from the site of the Works or any part thereof through or over any land, buildings, way or passage adjoining or connected with the site and in the possession and control of the Employer, in accordance with the Contract Bills and/or the Contract Drawings, after receipt by the Architect of such notice, if any, as the Contractor is required to give, or failure of the Employer to give such ingress or egress as otherwise agreed between the Architect and the Contractor;

25·4 ·13   where clause 23·1·2 is stated in the Appendix to apply, the deferment by the Employer of giving possession of the site under clause 23·1·2;

25·4 ·14   by reason of the execution of work for which an Approximate Quantity is included in the Contract Bills which is not a reasonably accurate forecast of the quantity of work required;

25·4 ·15   delay which the Contractor has taken all practicable steps to avoid or reduce consequent upon a change in the Statutory Requirements after the Base Date which necessitates some alteration or modification to any Performance Specified Work;

25·4 ·16   the use or threat of terrorism and/or the activity of the relevant authorities in dealing with such use or threat;

25·4 ·17   compliance or non-compliance by the Employer with clause 6A·1.

27.03 It is clear that the contractor is required to give full particulars and all details of the delay, even if the delay is the contractor's own fault. Obviously, more than one notice under Clause 25 may be served during the currency of the contract.

27.04 It was held in *Balfour Beatty Building Limited* v *Chestermount Properties Limited* (1993) 9 Const LJ that where the works are delayed as a result of the contractor's fault, so that the original completion date has passed, the architect still has power on the happening of a relevant event to refix the completion date. The appropriate way to do this is to take the original completion date and add the number of days which the architect regards as fair and reasonable in all the circumstances, even if the effect of this is that the new completion date has already passed before the happening of the relevant event. It would be wrong in principle to refix the completion date by starting at the date of the relevant event and adding days to that date.

Position of sub-contractors

27.05 Where any notice by the contractor makes reference to a nominated sub-contractor, the contractor must serve a copy of the notice and the details given under Clause 25.2.2 on the nominated sub-contractor. The purpose of this provision is to protect the position of a nominated sub-contractor on whom the main contractor is seeking to cast blame for the delay.

Architect's action

27.06 On receipt of the contractor's notice, particulars, and estimate, the architect must firstly decide whether the contractor is entitled to an extension of time in principle (i.e. whether the delay is caused by a relevant event as defined by Clause 25.4) and secondly, whether the occurrence of the relevant event will, in fact, cause delay beyond the completion date. Having decided these two points, the architect grants an extension of time if he thinks that it is fair and reasonable to do so, by fixing a new completion date which is notified to the contractor in writing. His notice must state which of the relevant events he has taken into account and the extent, if any, to which he has had regard to any instruction issued since the fixing of the previous completion date under Clause 13.2 requiring as a variation the omission of any work (Clause 25.3.1.4). He is not bound, however, to allocate the extension period between the relevant events, e.g. by awarding so many weeks for adverse weather or for some variations, etc. He must either issue a new completion date or notify the contractor of his decision not to do so no later than 12 weeks from receipt of the contractor's notice, reasonably sufficient particulars and estimate or (where there are fewer than 12 weeks to completion) not later than the completion date.

27.07 Under Clause 25.3.2, if the architect has already exercised his power to grant an extension he may fix a completion date which is earlier than the previously extended completion date if he thinks it fair and reasonable, having regard to variations requiring the omission of work which have been issued after the last occasion on which an extension of time was granted. This is, however, subject to the proviso that (under Clause 25.3.6) no completion date can be fixed earlier than the date for completion stated in the Appendix. Thus the architect is entitled to reduce a previously granted extension of time if work is subsequently ordered to be omitted, thereby reducing the amount of the contractor's commitments and justifying an earlier completion date. RIBA Publications Ltd publish a form of 'Notification of Revision to Completion Date'.

Duties of architect after practical completion

27.08 When practical completion has occurred, provision is made for the architect finally to review the position as regards extensions of time. He may fix a later completion date than that previously fixed and in so doing take into account all relevant events whether or not specifically notified by the contractor. It is also open to him to fix an earlier completion date, having regard to omissions which have occurred since the last occasion when an extension of time was granted. Alternatively, he may simply confirm the previously fixed completion date.

The relevant events

Clause 25.4.1

27.09 The meaning of the term 'force majeure' is difficult to state exactly, but very broadly the words extend to special circumstances quite outside the control of the contractor proceeding from a cause which is inevitable and unforeseeable. Such happenings will not by their very nature have been dealt with elsewhere in the contract. Interference by government and the effect of epidemics are examples of events which are probably within this clause. Financial difficulties experienced by the contractor are equally clearly not within this definition.

Clause 25.4.2

27.10 Exceptionally adverse weather conditions require quite unusual severity: it will frequently be necessary to establish this with the aid of weather charts covering a considerable period. Note that the definition includes exceptional extremes of heat and dryness, as well as the more normal British weather; such extremes of heat and dryness can, of course, have a serious effect on progress.

Clause 25.4.3

27.11 These contingencies are very wide, and in some instances may be due to an act of negligence on the part of the contractor, at any rate in their underlying causes.

Clause 25.4.6

27.12 Although this clause provides for non-receipt of necessary drawings, details or levels following an application 'neither unreasonably distant from nor unreasonably close to the date on which it was necessary for him to receive the same', it is suggested that if the receipt was in fact late, the architect should not refuse to consider whether to make an extension merely because the contractor has failed to make a specific application at the time required, but should take into account the effect, if any, of such failure when considering the amount of any extension. It was held in *Percy Bilton Limited* v *Greater London Council* that delay by the Employer in nominating a replacement for a nominated sub-contractor fell within the predecessor of this sub-clause. It should be noted that a default by the employer of the kind described in this sub-clause gives rise to a right in the contractor to determine his employment under Clause 28.3.2.

Clause 25.4.7

27.13 Where this sub-clause applies, neither the nominated sub-contractor, the nominated supplier nor the contractor has to pay liquidated damages. The extension must be granted whatever the cause of the delay, including the making good by a nominated sub-contractor of his own bad work before completion of the sub-contract work (see *Westminster City Council* v *Jarvis Limited* [1970] 1 All ER 943). But where defects are discovered in the sub-contract works after the nominated sub-contractor has purported to complete the works and the works have been accepted by the architect and the contractor, there is no right to an extension even where the work has been accepted with some suspicions (see *Westminster County Council* above). The employer's interests in respect of loss caused by delay on the part of nominated sub-contractors and nominated suppliers can be protected by obtaining warranties of timely completion from them. These forms of direct warranty (TNS/1 in the case of nominated suppliers, NSC/W in the case of nominated sub-contractors) are discussed later in this chapter.

Clause 25.4.8

27.14 In *Henry Boot Construction Limited* v *Central Lancashire New Town Development Corporation* (1980) 15 BLR 1, it was held that work carried out by statutory undertakers under contracts with the employer fell within this sub-clause rather than Clause 25.4.11, even though the work was referred to in the bills of quantities as work in respect of which direct payment would be made by the employer and the amounts deducted from the final account.

Clause 25.4.10

27.15 Although the wording of this sub-clause is, on the face of it, wide, it is thought that it is not of as great assistance to contractors as it may first appear: the requirement is the contractor's 'inability for reasons beyond his control' to procure the necessary labour or materials. A contractor could not bring himself within this sub-clause merely because performance had become more difficult (because, for example, labour rates had risen and it was therefore necessary for the contractor to pay uneconomically high prices for labour or materials having regard to his tender).

Clause 25.4.11

27.16 This sub-clause covers delay caused by local authorities and statutory undertakers in performing their statutory obligations. Where the contractor has no choice but to employ these local authorities or statutory undertakers, it is thought unjust that he should be penalized for their delay. This sub-clause does not apply where such a body is carrying out work extending beyond its statutory obligations as sub-contractors (see *Henry Boot Construction Limited* v *Central Lancashire New Town Development Corporation* (1980) 15 BLR 1, discussed above).

Clause 25.4.12

27.17 This clause applies if the employer is in possession and control of the land in question, which must adjoin the site, and fails to give access in accordance with the contract bills and/or the contract drawings after any required notice given by the contractor. Alternatively, it would apply if the employer failed to give access as otherwise agreed between the architect, presumably acting with the consent of the employer, and the contractor. This latter situation may cover agreed wayleaves, etc.

Danger in amending Clause 25

27.18 If Clause 25 is amended, Clause 39.5.8.1 provides in effect that fluctuations are not to be 'frozen' as at the completion date, but that the contractor is entitled to claim fluctuations even though the completion date has passed. Therefore, if Clause 25 is to be amended, Clause 39.5.8.1 should also be changed.

28 Clause 26: Loss and expense caused by matters materially affecting regular progress of the works

Nature of Clause 26

28.01 Clause 26 entitles the contractor to claim direct loss and/or expense arising as a result of the regular progress of the works or part of them being materially affected by any of the list of matters contained in Clause 26.2. Under Clause 26.6 the provisions of Clause 26 are without prejudice to any other rights and remedies which the contractor may possess, and therefore the provisions of Clause 26 do not preclude any claim by the contractor for damages for breach of contract, negligence, misrepresentation, etc. The word 'direct' excludes claims for consequential loss (see *Cawoods* v *Croudace* [1978] 2 Lloyd's Reports 55). It is thought that in general the computation of the amount of direct loss and/or expense is to follow the lines for computation for ordinary damages for breach of contract, although, of course, a claim under Clause 26 is not a claim for breach of contract as such. See *Wright Limited* v *PH & T (Holdings) Limited* (1980) 13 BLR 26. In *Minter* v *Welsh Health Technical Services Organisation* 13 BLR 1, it was held that under the 1963 JCT Form Clause 24(1) that the contractor could claim as part of his direct loss and/or expense the amount of finance charges he incurred in respect of the amount of such loss and expense.

---

26   Loss and expense caused by matters materially affecting regular progress of the Works

26·1   If the Contractor makes written application to the Architect stating that he has incurred or is likely to incur direct loss and/or expense in the execution of this Contract for which he would not be reimbursed by a payment under any other provision in this Contract due to deferment of giving possession of the site under clause 23·1·2 where clause 23·1·2 is stated in the Appendix to be applicable or because the regular progress of the Works or of any part thereof has been or is likely to be materially affected by any one or more of the matters referred to in clause 26·2; and if and as soon as the Architect is of the opinion that the direct loss and/or expense has been incurred or is likely to be incurred due to any such deferment of giving possession or that the regular progress of the Works or of any part thereof has been or is likely to be so materially affected as set out in the application of the Contractor then the Architect from time to time thereafter shall ascertain, or shall instruct the Quantity Surveyor to ascertain, the amount of such loss and/or expense which has been or is being incurred by the Contractor; provided always that:

26·1   ·1   the Contractor's application shall be made as soon as it has become, or should reasonably have become, apparent to him that the regular progress of the Works or of any part thereof has been or was likely to be affected as aforesaid; and

26·1   ·2   the Contractor shall in support of his application submit to the Architect upon request such information as should reasonably enable the Architect to form an opinion as aforesaid; and

26·1   ·3   the Contractor shall submit to the Architect or to the Quantity Surveyor upon request such details of such loss and/or expense as are reasonably necessary for such ascertainment as aforesaid.

26·2   The following are the matters referred to in clause 26·1:

26·2   ·1   the Contractor not having received in due time necessary instructions (including those for or in regard to the expenditure of provisional sums), drawings, details or levels from the Architect for which he specifically applied in writing provided that such application was made on a date which having regard to the Completion Date was neither unreasonably distant from nor unreasonably close to the date on which it was necessary for him to receive the same;

26·2   ·2   the opening up for inspection of any work covered up or the testing of any of the work, materials or goods in accordance with clause 8·3 (including making good in consequence of such opening up or testing), unless the inspection or test showed that the work, materials or goods were not in accordance with this Contract;

26·2   ·3   any discrepancy in or divergence between the Contract Drawings and/or the Contract Bills and/or the Numbered Documents;

26·2   ·4   ·1   the execution of work not forming part of this Contract by the Employer himself or by persons employed or otherwise engaged by the Employer as referred to in clause 29 or the failure to execute such work;

·4   ·2   the supply by the Employer of materials and goods which the Employer has agreed to provide for the Works or the failure so to supply;

26·2   ·5   Architect's instructions under clause 23·2 issued in regard to the postponement of any work to be executed under the provisions of this Contract;

26·2   ·6   failure of the Employer to give in due time ingress to or egress from the site of the Works or any part thereof through or over any land, buildings, way or passage adjoining or connected with the site and in the possession and control of the Employer, in accordance with the Contract Bills and/or the Contract Drawings, after receipt by the Architect of such notice, if any, as the Contractor is required to give, or failure of the Employer to give such ingress or egress as otherwise agreed between the Architect and the Contractor;

26·2   ·7   Architect's instructions issued

under clause 13·2 or clause 13A·4·1 requiring a Variation (except for a Variation for which the Architect has given a confirmed acceptance of a 13A Quotation or for a Variation thereto) or

under clause 13·3 in regard to the expenditure of provisional sums (other than instructions to which clause 13·4·2 refers or an instruction for the expenditure of a provisional sum for defined work or of a provisional sum for Performance Specified Work);

26·2   ·8   the execution of work for which an Approximate Quantity is included in the Contract Bills which is not a reasonably accurate forecast of the quantity of work required;

26·2   ·9   compliance or non-compliance by the Employer with clause 6A·1.

26·3   If and to the extent that it is necessary for ascertainment under clause 26·1 of loss and/or expense the Architect shall state in writing to the Contractor what extension of time, if any, has been made under clause 25 in respect of the Relevant Event or Events referred to in clause 25·4·5·1 (so far as that clause refers to clauses 2·3, 13·2, 13·3 and 23·2) and in clauses 25·4·5·2, 25·4·6, 25·4·8 and 25·4·12.

26·4   ·1   The Contractor upon receipt of a written application properly made by a Nominated Sub-Contractor under clause 4·38·1 of Sub-Contract Conditions NSC/C *(Conditions of Nominated Sub-Contract)* shall pass to the Architect a copy of that written application. If and as soon as the Architect is of the opinion that the loss and/or expense to which the said clause 4·38·1 refers has been incurred or is likely to be incurred due to any deferment of the giving of possession where clause 23·1·2 is stated in the Appendix to apply or that the regular progress of the sub-contract works or of any part thereof has been or is likely to be materially affected as referred to in clause 4·38·1 of Sub-Contract Conditions NSC/C *(Conditions of Nominated Sub-Contract)* and as set out in the application of the Nominated Sub-Contractor then the Architect shall himself ascertain or shall instruct the Quantity Surveyor to ascertain, the amount of loss and/or expense to which the said clause 4·38·1 refers.

26·4	**·2**	If and to the extent that it is necessary for the ascertainment of such loss and/or expense the Architect shall state in writing to the Contractor with a copy to the Nominated Sub-Contractor concerned what was the length of the revision of the period or periods for completion of the sub-contract works or of any part thereof to which he gave consent in respect of the Relevant Event or Events set out in clause 2·6·5·1 (so far as that clause refers to clauses 2·3, 13·2, 13·3 and 23·2 of the Main Contract Conditions) 2·6·5·2, 2·6·6, 2·6·8, 2·6·12 and 2·6·15 of Conditions NSC/C *(Conditions of Nominated Sub-Contract).*
26·5		Any amount from time to time ascertained under clause 26 shall be added to the Contract Sum.
26·6		The provisions of clause 26 are without prejudice to any other rights and remedies which the Contractor may possess.

Notice

28.02 Clause 26.1 requires the contractor to make a written application to the architect stating that he has incurred or is likely to incur such loss and expense. Once a notice has been given, the loss and expense must be ascertained from time to time by the architect or quantity surveyor. Only one such notice need be given (reversing the position under the previous JCT Form) (see *Minter v Welsh Health Technical Services Organisation*). Under Clause 26.1 the application must be made as soon as it has become or should reasonably have become apparent to the contractor that regular progress is being affected. The contractor must submit information in support of his application, and must on request supply a breakdown of the loss and/or expense (see Clause 26.1.3). It is thought that the requirement of a notice is a condition precedent to the contractor's rights under this clause.

28.03 All that is required under Clause 26 is that direct loss and/or expense arises because 'regular progress of the works' is 'materially affected' or because giving possession of the site has been deferred under Clause 23.1.2. There is no requirement that progress be delayed, or that the whole of the works be affected. It could apply, for example, where the contractor is obliged to bring extra operatives on site, or where there is a loss of productivity of certain trade.

28.04 It should be noted that any possible overlap between the operation of Clause 26 and Clause 13 is precluded by the proviso contained in Sub-clause 13.5.6.

Claims generally

28.05 The term 'claim' has no exact meaning, but for present purposes it may be considered any claim for payment by the contractor in respect of the original contract work arising other than under Clause 30. Any such claims fall under one of the following categories:

1. A right to payment arising under a clause of the contract.
2. A claim for damages ordinarily for breach of contract.
3. A claim under neither 1 nor 2.

If a claim comes within 1, the architect follows whatever procedure the contract prescribes according to the clause relied on by the contractor. The architect need not consult the employer, although he may do so if he thinks it desirable. If the claim falls within 2, the architect should consult the employer and should not include in a certificate any sum in respect of such a claim without the employer's agreement, as the contract gives him no power to certify in respect of the claim for damages. If the claim falls within 3, the contractor has no right to payment. The architect cannot certify save on the employer's direction, and any payment made will be ex gratia.

Provisions relating to nominated sub-contractors

28.06 Clause 26.4 contains provisions to deal with the situation where a nominated sub-contractor claims loss and expense under Clause 4.38.1 of Sub-contract Conditions NSC/C. The contractor is under an obligation to pass such application on to the architect, who then reaches a decision on it and instructs the quantity surveyor to ascertain the amount of loss and expense incurred (or he

may carry out this exercise himself). To the extent that it is necessary for the ascertainment of such loss and expense, the architect must state in writing to the contractor (with a copy to the sub-contractor) the revised period for completion of the sub-contract works to which he gave consent in respect of each event set out in Clauses 2.6.5.1 (so far as that clause refers to Clauses 2.3, 13.2, 13.3 and 23.2 of the main contract conditions), 2.6.5.2, 2.6.6, 2.6.8, 2.6.12 and 2.6.15 of Conditions NSC/C. This applies to such matters as discrepancies in sub-contract documents, variations, expenditure of provisional sums, postponement, exceptionally adverse weather conditions, delayed instructions, delay caused by the employer carrying out work not forming part of the main contract, and delay in giving access, etc. to the sub-contractor.

28.07 The provisions of Clause 26 are without prejudice to any other rights and remedies which the contractor may possess. The contractor may pursue a claim for damages, even if a claim under Clause 26 fails (see *Fairclough* v *Vale of Belvoir Superstore* [1991] 56 BLR 74), or may even make a claim under Clause 26 in order to obtain prompt reimbursement and later claim damages for breach of contract taking into account the amount awarded under Clause 26 (*London Borough of Merton* v *Leach* (1985) 32 BLR 51).

29 Clause 27: Determination by the employer

29.01 This clause makes provision for the following matters:

1. Discretionary determination by the employer in event of certain defaults by the contractor.
2. Automatic determination of the contractor's employment in the event of bankruptcy or liquidation (subject to an option to reinstate if the employer and contractor so agree).
3. The rights and duties of the parties following determination of the contractor's employment.

Determination on notice

29.02 The employer is entitled to determine the contractor's employment in the circumstances specified in Clause 27.2, subject to the giving of the notices to be issued by the architect required by the clause. Since Amendment 11: 1992, all notices under Clauses 27.2.1–4 must, by virtue of Clause 27.1 be in writing and be given by actual delivery, by registered post or by recorded delivery.

29.03 It was held in *West Faulkner Associates* v *London Borough of Newham* (1993) 8 Const LJ 232, a case on JCT 63 Clause 25(1)(b), which is in identical terms to Clause 27.2.1.2 that 'regularly and diligently' meant that a contractor must go about his way in such a way as to achieve his contractual obligations. This clause requires a contractor to plan work, to lead and manage his workforce, to provide sufficient and proper materials and to employ competent tradesmen so that the works are fully carried out to an acceptable standard and that all time, sequence and other provisions of the contract are fulfilled. The architect will be in breach of contract if he fails to serve a notice under the clause if an ordinarily competent architect would have done so in the same circumstances.

29.04 At common law a party is entitled to treat a contract as repudiated and therefore at an end if the other party so conducts himself as to show no intention to go on with the contract (see *Universal Cargo Carriers* v *Citati* [1957] 2 QB 401). The purpose of Clause 27 is to confer on the employer additional and alternative rights by which he may determine the contractor's employment, without having to prove that the contractor has repudiated the contract. However, having regard to the provision of Clause 27.2.4 (which requires that notice should not be given unreasonably or vexatiously), there is sometimes uncertainty as to whether the circumstances which exist justify determination of the contractor's employment. See *J M Hill & Sons Limited* v *London Borough of Camden* (1980) 18 BLR 31, CA; see also *John Jarvis*

27   Determination by Employer

27·1   Any notice or further notice to which clauses 27·2·1, 27·2·2, 27·2·3 and 27·3·4 refer shall be in writing and given by actual delivery, or by registered post or by recorded delivery. If sent by registered post or recorded delivery the notice or further notice shall, subject to proof to the contrary, be deemed to have been received 48 hours after the date of posting (excluding Saturday and Sunday and public holidays).

27·2   ·1   If, before the date of Practical Completion, the Contractor shall make a default in any one or more of the following respects:

·1   ·1   without reasonable cause he wholly or substantially suspends the carrying out of the Works; or

·1   ·2   he fails to proceed regularly and diligently with the Works; or

·1   ·3   he refuses or neglects to comply with a written notice or instruction from the Architect requiring him to remove any work, materials or goods not in accordance with this Contract and by such refusal or neglect the Works are materially affected; or

·1   ·4   he fails to comply with the provisions of clause 19·1·1 or clause 19·2·2; or

·1   ·5   he fails pursuant to the Conditions to comply with the requirements of the CDM Regulations,

the Architect may give to the Contractor a notice specifying the default or defaults (the 'specified default or defaults').

27·2   ·2   If the Contractor continues a specified default for 14 days from receipt of the notice under clause 27·2·1 then the Employer may on, or within 10 days from, the expiry of that 14 days by a further notice to the Contractor determine the employment of the Contractor under this Contract. Such determination shall take effect on the date of receipt of such further notice.

27·2   ·3   If

the Contractor ends the specified default or defaults, or

the Employer does not give the further notice referred to in clause 27·2·2

and the Contractor repeats a specified default (whether previously repeated or not) then, upon or within a reasonable time after such repetition, the Employer may by notice to the Contractor determine the employment of the Contractor under this Contract. Such determination shall take effect on the date of receipt of such notice.

27·2   ·4   A notice of determination under clause 27·2·2 or clause 27·2·3 shall not be given unreasonably or vexatiously.

27·3   ·1   If the Contractor

makes a composition or arrangement with his creditors, or becomes bankrupt, or

being a company,

makes a proposal for a voluntary arrangement for a composition of debts or scheme of arrangement to be approved in accordance with the Companies Act 1985 or the Insolvency Act 1986 as the case may be or any amendment or re-enactment thereof, or

has a provisional liquidator appointed, or

has a winding-up order made, or

passes a resolution for voluntary winding-up (except for the purposes of amalgamation or reconstruction), or

under the Insolvency Act 1986 or any amendment or re-enactment thereof has an administrator or an administrative receiver appointed

then:

27·3   ·2   the Contractor shall immediately inform the Employer in writing if he has made a composition or arrangement with his creditors, or being a company, has made a proposal for a voluntary arrangement for a composition of debts or scheme of arrangement to be approved in accordance with the Companies Act 1985 or the Insolvency Act 1986 as the case may be or any amendment or re-enactment thereof;

27·3   ·3   where a provisional liquidator or trustee in bankruptcy is appointed or a winding-up order is made or the Contractor passes a resolution for voluntary winding-up (except for the purposes of amalgamation or reconstruction) the employment of the Contractor under this Contract shall be forthwith automatically determined but the said employment may be reinstated if the Employer and the Contractor [p·1] shall so agree;

27·3   ·4   where clause 27·3·3 does not apply the Employer may at any time, unless an agreement to which clause 27·5·2·1 refers has been made, by notice to the Contractor determine the employment of the Contractor under this Contract and such determination shall take effect on the date of receipt of such notice.

27·4   The Employer shall be entitled to determine the employment of the Contractor under this or any other contract, if the Contractor shall have offered or given or agreed to give to any person any gift or consideration of any kind as an inducement or reward for doing or forbearing to do or for having done or forborne to do any action in relation to the obtaining or execution of this or any other contract with the Employer, or for showing or forbearing to show favour or disfavour to any person in relation to this or any other contract with the Employer, or if the like acts shall have been done by any person employed by the Contractor or acting on his behalf (whether with or without the knowledge of the Contractor), or if in relation to this or any other contract with the Employer the Contractor or any person employed by him or acting on his behalf shall have committed an offence under the Prevention of Corruption Acts 1889 to 1916.

27·5   Clauses 27·5·1 to 27·5·4 are only applicable where clause 27·3·4 applies.

27·5   ·1   From the date when, under clause 27·3·4, the Employer could first give notice to determine the employment of the Contractor, the Employer, subject to clause 27·5·3, shall not be bound by any provisions of this Contract to make any further payment thereunder and the Contractor shall not be bound to continue to carry out and complete the Works in compliance with clause 2·1.

27·5   ·2   Clause 27·5·1 shall apply until

either

·2   ·1   the Employer makes an agreement (a '27·5·2·1 agreement') with the Contractor on the continuation or novation or conditional novation of this Contract, in which case this Contract shall be subject to the terms set out in the 27·5·2·1 agreement

or

·2   ·2   the Employer determines the employment of the Contractor under this Contract in accordance with clause 27·3·4, in which case the provisions of clause 27·6 or clause 27·7 shall apply.

27·5   ·3   Notwithstanding clause 27·5·1, in the period before either a 27·5·2·1 agreement is made or the Employer under clause 27·3·4 determines the employment of the Contractor, the Employer and the Contractor may make an interim arrangement for work to be carried out. Subject to clause 27·5·4 any right of set-off which the Employer may have shall not be exercisable in respect of any payment due from the Employer to the Contractor under such interim arrangement.

27·5   ·4   From the date when, under clause 27·3·4, the Employer may first determine the employment of the Contractor (but subject to any agreement made pursuant to clause 27·5·2·1 or arrangement made pursuant to clause 27·5·3) the Employer may take reasonable measures to ensure that Site Materials, the site and the Works are adequately protected and that Site Materials are retained in, on the site of or adjacent to the Works as the case may be. The Contractor shall allow and shall in no way hinder or delay the taking of the aforesaid measures. The Employer may deduct the reasonable cost of taking such measures from any monies due or to become due to the Contractor under this Contract (including any amount due under an agreement to which clause 27·5·2·1, or under an interim arrangement to which clause 27·5·3, refers) or may recover the same from the Contractor as a debt.

27·6   In the event of the determination of the employment of the Contractor under clause 27·2·2, 27·2·3, 27·3·3, 27·3·4 or 27·4 and so long as that employment has not been reinstated then:

27·6   ·1   the Employer may employ and pay other persons to carry out and complete the Works and to make good defects of the kind referred to in clause 17 and he or they may enter upon the site and the Works and use all temporary buildings, plant, tools, equipment and Site Materials, and may purchase all materials and goods necessary for the carrying out and completion of the Works and for the making good of defects as aforesaid; provided that where the aforesaid temporary buildings, plant, tools. equipment and Site Materials are not owned by the Contractor the consent of the owner thereof to such use is obtained by the Employer;

27·6   ·2   ·1   except where an insolvency event listed in clause 27·3·1 (other than the Contractor being a company making a proposal for a voluntary arrangement for a composition of debts or scheme of arrangement to be approved in accordance with the Companies Act 1985 or the insolvency Act 1986 as the case may be or any amendment or re-enactment) has occurred the Contractor shall, if so required by the Employer or by the Architect on behalf of the Employer within 14 days of the date of determination, assign to the Employer without payment the benefit of any agreement for the supply of materials or goods and/or for the execution of any work for the purposes of this Contract to the extent that the same is assignable;

·2   ·2   except where the Contractor has a trustee in bankruptcy appointed or being a company has a provisional liquidator appointed or has a petition alleging insolvency filed against it and which is subsisting or passes a resolution for voluntary winding-up (other than for the purposes of amalgamation or reconstruction) which takes effect as a creditors voluntary liquidation the Employer may pay any supplier or sub-contractor for any materials or goods delivered or works executed for the purposes of this Contract before or after the date of determination in so far as the price thereof has not already been discharged by the Contractor. Payments made under clause 27·6·2·2 may be deducted from any sum due or to become due to the Contractor or may be recoverable from the Contractor by the Employer as a debt;

27·6   ·3   the Contractor shall, when required in writing by the Architect so to do (but not before), remove from the Works any temporary buildings, plant, tools, equipment, goods and materials belonging to him and the Contractor shall have removed by their owner any temporary buildings, plant, tools, equipment, goods and materials not owned by him. If within a reasonable time after such requirement has been made the Contractor has not complied therewith in respect of temporary buildings, plant, tools, equipment, goods and materials belonging to him, then the Employer may (but without being responsible for any loss or damage) remove and sell any such property of the Contractor, holding the proceeds less all costs incurred to the credit of the Contractor.

27·6   ·4   ·1   Subject to clauses 27·5·3 and 27·6·4·2 the provisions of this Contract which require any further payment or any release or further release of Retention to the Contractor shall not apply; provided that clause 27·6·4·1 shall not be construed so as to prevent the enforcement by the Contractor of any rights under this Contract in respect of amounts properly due to be discharged by the Employer to the Contractor which the Employer has unreasonably not discharged and which, where clause 27·3·4 applies, have accrued 28 days or more before the date when under clause 27·3·4 the Employer could first give notice to determine the employment of the Contractor or, where clause 27·3·4 does not apply, which have accrued 28 days or more before the date of determination of the employment of the Contractor.

·4 **·2** Upon the completion of the Works and the making good of defects as referred to in clause 27·6·1 (but subject, where relevant, to the exercise of the right under clause 17·2 and/or clause 17·3 of the Architect, with the consent of the Employer, not to require defects of the kind referred to in clause 17 to be made good) then within a reasonable time thereafter an account in respect of the matters referred to in clause 27·6·5 shall be set out either in a statement prepared by the Employer or in a certificate issued by the Architect.

27·6 **·5** **·1** The amount of expenses properly incurred by the Employer including those incurred pursuant to clause 27·6·1 and of any direct loss and/or damage caused to the Employer as a result of the determination;

·5 **·2** the amount of any payment made or otherwise discharged in favour of the Contractor;

·5 **·3** the total amount which would have been payable for the Works in accordance with this Contract.

27·6 **·6** If the sum of the amounts stated under clauses 27·6·5·1 and 27·6·5·2 exceeds or is less than the amount stated under clause 27·6·5·3 the difference shall be a debt payable by the Contractor to the Employer or by the Employer to the Contractor as the case may be.

27·7 **·1** If the Employer decides after the determination of the employment of the Contractor not to have the Works carried out and completed, he shall so notify the Contractor in writing within 6 months from the date of such determination. Within a reasonable time from the date of such written notification the Employer shall send to the Contractor a statement of account setting out:

·1 **·1** the total value of work properly executed at the date of determination of the employment of the Contractor, such value to be ascertained in accordance with the Conditions as if the employment of the Contractor had not been determined, together with any amounts due to the Contractor under the Conditions not included in such total value;

·1 **·2** the amount of any expenses properly incurred by the Employer and of any direct loss and/or damage caused to the Employer as a result of the determination.

After taking into account amounts previously paid to or otherwise discharged in favour of the Contractor under this Contract, if the amount stated under clause 27·7·1·2 exceeds or is less than the amount stated under clause 27·7·1·1 the difference shall be a debt payable by the Contractor to the Employer or by the Employer to the Contractor as the case may be.

27·7 **·2** If after the expiry of the 6 month period referred to in clause 27·7·1 the Employer has not begun to operate the provisions of clause 27·6·1 and has not given a written notification pursuant to clause 27·7·1 the Contractor may require by notice in writing to the Employer that he states whether clauses 27·6·1 to 27·6·6 are to apply and, if not to apply, require that a statement of account pursuant to clause 27·7·1 be prepared by the Employer for submission to the Contractor.

27·8 The provisions of clauses 27·2 to 27·7 are without prejudice to any other rights and remedies which the Employer may possess.

Limited v *Rochdale Housing Association Limited* (1986) 36 BLR 48, CA, on the corresponding provisions in Clause 28.

29.05 Under Clause 27.4 the employer is entitled to determine the contractor's employment on discovery of any corrupt practices by the contractor, and in this case the requirements of Clause 27.1 do not have to be complied with.

Bankruptcy

29.05 If the contractor makes a composition or arrangement with his creditors or, if a company, has made a proposal for a voluntary arrangement for a composition of debts or scheme of arrangement for approval under the Insolvency Act 1986 or the Companies Act 1985, he must immediately inform the employer in writing. The employer then has a right under Clause 27.3.4 to determine the employment of the contractor by notice. If he chooses not to do so, then all rights and duties under the contract are effectively suspended pending the making of an agreement under Clause 27.5.2.1 or the determination of the employment by notice.

29.06 The employment of the contractor determines automatically if a provisional liquidator or trustee in bankruptcy is appointed or a winding up order is made, or the contractor passes a resolution for voluntary winding up (except for the purposes of amalgamation or reconstruction), subject to the option of reinstatement.

Rights of parties after determination

29.07 Clause 27.6 governs the rights of the parties after determination. Briefly, the position is that:

1. The employer is entitled to get the work completed by others and to take an assignment of contracts for supply of materials and sub-contracts (except where the determination occurs by reason of the contractor's bankruptcy).
2. The employer is entitled to make direct payment to suppliers or sub-contractors, again except where determination occurs by reason of the contractor's bankruptcy.
3. The contractor is obliged within a reasonable time of notice being given by the architect to remove all temporary buildings, plant, tools, equipment, goods and materials belonging to him and to have removed all such items which do not belong to him by their owner.

29.08 Typically, the employer will obtain a new contractor to carry out and complete the work. Under Clause 27.6.4.1, the employer is not bound to make any further payments to the contractor whose employment has been determined until completion of the work. On completion an account will be taken by the architect: if the employer has in fact got the work completed for less than he would have had to pay the contractor, the contractor is in principle entitled to be paid the difference, but if (as is far more likely) the work has cost more than the contractor would have charged, the contractor is obliged to pay the difference to the employer. In addition the architect must certify the amount of direct loss and/or damage caused to the employer by the determination, and this will be taken into account. It was held in *Emson Eastern Limited (in receivership)* v *E M E Developments Limited* (55) BLR 114 that 'completion of the works' means the date of practical completion rather than the date of issue of the final certificate. However, this decision has been criticized as unsatisfactory, because it fails to take account of the contractor's continuing obligation during the defects liability period to make good any defects which occur, although the employer would be able to rely on his common law claims for the cost of completion and defences by way of abatement, set-off or counterclaim.

30 Clause 28: Determination by contractor

30.01 This clause, which should be compared with Clause 27, entitles the contractor to determine his own employment in certain events. Clause 28.2.1.1 provides for determination for non-payment of amounts due on a certificate; Clause 28.2.1.2 deals with obstruction of certificates; Clause 28.2.1.3 deals with failure to comply with Clause 19.1.1 (prohibition against assigning without consent). Clause 28.2.2 deals with suspension of the work.

Non-payment of certificates

30.02 The contract does not deal in express terms with the position where the employer does not pay the amount of a certificate by reason of a bona fide counterclaim for defective work, for example, or by reason of some matter arising under some express provision of the contract. It is thought that a purported determination under this sub-clause would not be valid or would ordinarily be held to be unreasonable or vexatious if based solely upon a deduction which the employer was entitled to make, or considered himself entitled to make in good faith.

Obstruction of certificates

30.03 Interference with or obstruction of issue of certificates by the employer includes preventing the architect from performing his duties, directing the architect as to the amount for which he is to give his certificate or as to the decision he should arrive at on matters which are within the sphere of the architect's independent duty.

Suspension of work

30.04 Clause 28.2.2 relates to suspension of the works for a continuous period of the length stated in the Appendix. Care must be taken to ensure that the periods in the Appendix are reasonably

28   Determination by Contractor

28·1   Any notice or further notice to which clauses 28·2·1, 28·2·2, 28·2·3, 28·2·4 and 28·3 refer shall be in writing and given by actual delivery or by registered post or by recorded delivery. If sent by registered post or recorded delivery the notice or further notice shall, subject to proof to the contrary, be deemed to have been received 48 hours after the date of posting (excluding Saturday and Sunday and public holidays).

28·2   ·1   If the Employer shall make default in any one or more of the following respects:

·1   ·1   he does not discharge in accordance with this Contract the amount properly due to the Contractor in respect of any certificate and/or any VAT due on that amount pursuant to the VAT Agreement; or

·1   ·2   he interferes with or obstructs the issue of any certificate due under this Contract; or

·1   ·3   he fails to comply with the provisions of clause 19·1·1; or

·1   ·4   he fails pursuant to the Conditions to comply with the requirements of the CDM Regulations,

the Contractor may give to the Employer a notice specifying the default or defaults (the 'specified default or defaults').

28·2   ·2   If, before the date of Practical Completion, the carrying out of the whole or substantially the whole of the uncompleted Works is suspended for the continuous period of the length stated in the Appendix by reason of one or more of the following events:

·2   ·1   the Contractor not having received in due time necessary instructions, drawings, details or levels from the Architect for which he specifically applied in writing provided that such application was made on a date which having regard to the Completion Date was neither unreasonably distant nor unreasonably close to the date on which it was necessary for him to receive the same; or

·2   ·2   Architect's instructions issued under clause 2·3, 13·2 or 23·2 unless caused by reason of some negligence or default of the Contractor, his servants or agents or of any person employed or engaged upon or in connection with the Works or any part thereof, his servants or agents other than a Nominated Sub-Contractor, the Employer or any person employed or engaged by the Employer; or

·2   ·3   delay in the execution of work not forming part of this Contract by the Employer himself or by persons employed or otherwise engaged by the Employer as referred to in clause 29 or the failure to execute such work or delay in the supply by the Employer of materials and goods which the Employer has agreed to supply for the Works or the failure so to supply; or

·2   ·4   failure of the Employer to give in due time ingress to or egress from the site of the Works or any part thereof through or over any land, buildings, way or passage adjoining or connected with the site and in the possession and control of the Employer, in accordance with the relevant Contract Documents, after receipt by the Architect of such notice, if any, as the Contractor is required to give, or failure of the Employer to give such ingress or egress as otherwise agreed between the Architect and the Contractor,

the Contractor may give to the Employer a notice specifying the event or events ('the specified suspension event or events').

28·2   ·3   If

– the Employer continues a specified default, or

– a specified suspension event is continued

for 14 days from receipt of the notice under clause 28·2·1 or clause 28·2·2 then the Contractor may on, or within 10 days from, the expiry of that 14 days by a further notice to the Employer determine the employment of the Contractor under this Contract. Such determination shall take effect on the date of receipt of such further notice.

28·2   ·4   If

– the Employer ends the specified default or defaults, or

– the specified suspension event or events cease, or

– the Contractor does not give the further notice referred to in clause 28·2·3

and

– the Employer repeats (whether previously repeated or not) a specified default, or

– a specified suspension event is repeated for whatever period (whether previously repeated or not), whereby the regular progress of the Works is or is likely to be materially affected

then, upon or within a reasonable time after such repetition, the Contractor may by notice to the Employer determine the employment of the Contractor under this Contract. Such determination shall take effect on the date of receipt of such notice.

28·2   ·5   A notice of determination under clause 28·2·3 or clause 28·2·4 shall not be given unreasonably or vexatiously.

28·3   ·1   If the Employer [p·2]

makes a composition or arrangement with his creditors, or becomes bankrupt,

or being a company,

makes a proposal for a voluntary arrangement for a composition of debts or scheme of arrangement to be approved in accordance with the Companies Act 1985 or the Insolvency Act 1986 as the case may be or any amendment or re-enactment thereof, or

has a provisional liquidator appointed, or

has a winding-up order made, or

passes a resolution for voluntary winding-up (except for the purposes of amalgamation or reconstruction), or

under the Insolvency Act 1986 or any amendment or re-enactment thereof has an administrator or an administrative receiver appointed

then:

28·3   ·2   the Employer shall immediately inform the Contractor in writing if he has made a composition or arrangement with his creditors, or, being a company, has made a proposal for a voluntary arrangement for a composition of debts or scheme of arrangement to be approved in accordance with the Companies Act 1985 or the Insolvency Act 1986 or any amendment or re-enactment thereof as the case may be;

28·3   ·3   the Contractor may by notice to the Employer determine the employment of the Contractor under this Contract. Such determination shall take effect on the date of receipt of such notice. Provided that after the occurrence of any of the events set out in clause 28·3·1 and before the taking effect of any notice of determination of his employment issued by the Contractor pursuant to clause 28·3·3 the obligation of the Contractor to carry out and complete the Works in compliance with clause 2·1 shall be suspended.

28·4   In the event of the determination of the employment of the Contractor under clauses 28·2·3, 28·2·4 or 28·3·3 and so long as that employment has not been reinstated the provisions of clauses 28·4·1, 28·4·2 and 28·4·3 shall apply; such application shall be without prejudice to the accrued rights or remedies of either party or to any liability of the classes mentioned in clause 20 which may accrue either before the Contractor or any sub-contractors, their servants or agents or others employed on or engaged upon or in connection with the Works or any part thereof other than the Employer or any person employed or engaged by the Employer shall have removed his or their temporary buildings, plant, tools, equipment, goods or materials (including Site Materials) or by reason of his or their so removing the same. Subject to clauses 28·4·2 and 28·4·3 the provisions of this Contract which require any payment or release or further release of Retention to the Contractor shall not apply.

28·4   ·1   The Contractor shall with all reasonable dispatch and in such manner and with such precautions as will prevent injury, death or damage of the classes in respect of which before the date of determination he was liable to indemnify the Employer under clause 20 remove from the site all his temporary buildings, plant, tools, equipment, goods and materials (including Site Materials) and shall ensure that his sub-contractors do the same, but subject always to the provisions of clause 28·4·3·5.

28·4   ·2   Within 28 days of the determination of the employment of the Contractor the Employer shall pay to the Contractor the Retention deducted by the Employer prior to the determination of the employment of the Contractor but subject to any right of the Employer of deduction therefrom which has accrued before the date of determination of the Contractor's employment.

28·4   ·3   The Contractor shall with reasonable dispatch prepare an account setting out the sum of the amounts referred to in clauses 28·4·3·1 to 28·4·3·5 which shall include as relevant amounts in respect of all Nominated Sub-Contractors:

·3   ·1   the total value of work properly executed at the date of determination of the employment of the Contractor, such value to be ascertained in accordance with the Conditions as if the employment of the Contractor had not been determined, together with any amounts due to the Contractor under the Conditions not included in such total value; and

·3   ·2   any sum ascertained in respect of direct loss and/or expense under clauses 26 and 34·3 (whether ascertained before or after the date of determination); and

·3   ·3   the reasonable cost of removal pursuant to clause 28·4·1; and

·3   ·4   any direct loss and/or damage caused to the Contractor by the determination; and

·3   ·5   the cost of materials or goods (including Site Materials) properly ordered for the Works for which the Contractor shall have paid or for which the Contractor is legally bound to pay, and on such payment in full by the Employer such materials or goods shall become the property of the Employer.

After taking into account amounts previously paid to or otherwise discharged in favour of the Contractor under this Contract the Employer shall pay to the Contractor the amount properly due in respect of this account within 28 days of its submission by the Contractor to the Employer but without any deduction of Retention.

28·5   The provisions of clauses 28·2 to 28·4 are without prejudice to any other rights and remedies which the Contractor may possess.

sufficient. Clause 28.2.2 has been amended following the decision in *John Jarvis Ltd* v *Rochdale Housing Association Limited* (1986) 36 BLR 48, CA, in which it was held that the words 'unless caused by some negligence or default of the contractor' did not include nominated sub-contractors. This is now expressly spelt out by the sub-clause. Therefore the main contractor is entitled to determine his employment if the work is suspended by reason of the default of a nominated Sub-contractor.

30.05 In the same case it was held that notice under clause the previous Clause 28.1.3 (now 28.2.3) was not given 'unreasonably or vexatiously' unless a reasonable contractor in the same circumstances would have thought it unreasonable or vexatious to give the notice.

Bankruptcy of employer

30.06 Clause 28.3 provides that the employer must inform the contractor immediately in writing if any of the following events happen:

Being an individual:
1. He makes a composition or arrangement with his creditors.
2. He becomes bankrupt.

Being a company:
1. It makes a proposal for a voluntary arrangement for a composition of debts or a scheme of arrangement for approval under the Insolvency Act 1986 or the Companies Act 1985.
2. It has a provisional liquidator appointed.
3. It has a winding up order made.
4. It passes a resolution for voluntary winding up (except for the purposes of amalgamation or reconstruction).
5. It has an administrator or administrative receiver appointed under the Insolvency Act 1986.

Unlike the provisions under Clause 27 in relation to the insolvency of the contractor, in none of these circumstances is the contract automatically brought to an end, but instead the contractor has a right to determine his employment by notice in the event of the insolvency of the employer.

Rights of parties after determination

Clause 28.4 governs the rights of the parties after determination. In summary:

1. The contractor is to remove his temporary buildings, plant, etc. from the site with all reasonable dispatch and give facilities for his sub-contractors to do the same.
2. Within 28 days of the determination the employer must pay to the contractor the retention held at the date of the determination, less any amounts which have accrued due to the employer.
3. The contractor is to prepare an account of sums due to him for the items set out in Sub-clause 28.4.3.
4. The employer shall pay the amount properly due in respect of the items in Sub-clause 28.4.3 within 28 days of the submission of the account.

31 Clause 28A: Determination by employer or contractor

31.01 Either party may determine the employment of the contractor where the works have been suspended for the relevant continuous period stated in the Appendix by reason of one of the events specified in 28A.1.1. Again, care should be taken to ensure that the periods provided in the Appendix are reasonably sufficient.

Rights of parties after determination

31.02 The rights and duties of the parties after determination may be summarized as follows:

28A	Determination by Employer or Contractor
28A·1 ·1	If, before the date of Practical Completion, the carrying out of the whole or substantially the whole of the uncompleted Works is suspended for the relevant continuous period of the length stated in the Appendix by reason of one or more of the following events:
·1 ·1	force majeure; or
·1 ·2	loss or damage to the Works occasioned by any one or more of the Specified Perils; or

·1 ·3	civil commotion; or
·1 ·4	Architect's instructions issued under clause 2·3, 13·2 or 23·2 which have been issued as a result of the negligence or default of any local authority or statutory undertaker executing work solely in pursuance of its statutory obligations; or
·1 ·5	hostilities involving the United Kingdom (whether war be declared or not); or
·1 ·6	terrorist activity

then the Employer or the Contractor may upon the expiry of the aforesaid relevant period of suspension give notice in writing to the other by actual delivery or by registered post or recorded delivery that unless the suspension is terminated within 7 days after the date of receipt of that notice the employment of the Contractor under this Contract will determine 7 days after the date of receipt of the aforesaid notice; and the employment of the Contractor shall so determine 7 days after receipt of such notice. If sent by registered post or recorded delivery the notice shall, subject to proof to the contrary, be deemed to have been received 48 hours after the date of posting (excluding Saturday and Sunday and public holidays).

28A·1 ·2 The Contractor shall not be entitled to give notice under clause 28A·1·1 in respect of the matter referred to in clause 28A·1·1·2 where the loss or damage to the Works occasioned by any one or more of the Specified Perils was caused by some negligence or default of the Contractor, his servants or agents or of any person employed or engaged upon or in connection with the Works or any part thereof, his servants or agents other than the Employer or any person employed or engaged by the Employer or by any local authority or statutory undertaker executing work solely in pursuance of its statutory obligations.

28A·1 ·3 A notice of determination under clause 28A·1·1 shall not be given unreasonably or vexatiously.

28A·2 Upon determination of the employment of the Contractor under clause 28A·1·1 the provisions of this Contract which require any further payment or any release or further release of Retention to the Contractor shall not apply; and the provisions of clauses 28A·3 to 28A·6 shall apply.

28A·3 The Contractor shall with all reasonable dispatch and in such manner and with such precautions as will prevent injury, death or damage of the classes in respect of which before the date of determination of his employment he was liable to indemnify the Employer under clause 20, remove from the site all his temporary buildings, plant, tools, equipment, goods and materials (including Site Materials) and shall ensure that his sub-contractors do the same, but subject always to the provisions of clause 28A·5·4.

28A·4 The Employer shall pay to the Contractor one half of the Retention deducted by the Employer prior to the determination of the employment of the Contractor within 28 days of the date of determination of the Contractor's employment and the other half as part of the account to which clause 28A·5 refers but subject to any right of deduction therefrom which has accrued before the date of such determination.

28A·5 The Contractor shall, not later than 2 months after the date of the determination of the Contractor's employment, provide the Employer with all documents (including those relating to Nominated Sub-Contractors and Nominated Suppliers) necessary for the preparation of the account to which this clause refers. Subject to due discharge by the Contractor of this obligation the Employer shall with reasonable dispatch prepare an account setting out the sum of the amounts referred to in clauses 28A·5·1 to 28A·5·4 and, if clause 28A·6 applies, clause 28A·5·5, which shall include as relevant amounts in respect of all Nominated Sub-Contractors:

28A·5 ·1 the total value of work properly executed at the date of determination of the employment of the Contractor, such value to be ascertained in accordance with the Conditions as if the employment of the Contractor had not been determined, together with any amounts due to the Contractor under the Conditions not included in such total value; and

28A·5 ·2 any sum ascertained in respect of direct loss and/or expense under clauses 26 and 34·3 (whether ascertained before or after the date of determination); and

28A·5 ·3 the reasonable cost of removal under clause 28A·3; and

28A·5 ·4 the cost of materials or goods (including Site Materials) properly ordered for the Works for which the Contractor shall have paid or for which the Contractor is legally bound to pay, and on such payment in full by the Employer such materials or goods shall become the property of the Employer; and

28A·5 ·5 any direct loss and/or damage caused to the Contractor by the determination.

After taking into account amounts previously paid to or otherwise discharged in favour of the Contractor under this Contract the Employer shall pay to the Contractor the amount properly due in respect of this account within 28 days of its submission by the Employer to the Contractor but without deduction of any Retention.

28A·6 Where determination of the employment of the Contractor has occurred in respect of the matter referred to in clause 28A·1·1·2 and the loss or damage to the Works occasioned by any one or more of the Specified Perils was caused by some negligence or default of the Employer or of any person for whom the Employer is responsible, then upon such determination of the employment of the Contractor the account prepared under clause 28A·5 shall include the amount, if any, to which clause 28A·5·5 refers.

28A·7 The Employer shall inform the Contractor in writing which part or parts of the amounts paid or payable under clause 28A·5 is or are fairly and reasonably attributable to any Nominated Sub-Contractor and shall so inform each Nominated Sub-Contractor in writing.

1. The contractor is to remove his temporary buildings, plant, etc. from the site with all reasonable dispatch.
2. Within 28 days of the determination of the employment the employer is to pay one half of the retention monies held at the date of determination to the contractor, less any monies which have accrued to the employer.
3. The contractor is to provide the employer within two months after the determination with all documents necessary for the preparation of an account by the employer.
4. The employer shall pay the contractor within 28 days the amounts properly due in respect of the items listed in Clause 28A.5.

32 Clause 29: Works by employer or person employed or engaged by the employer

32.01 This clause governs the position where the employer wishes to carry out certain work himself (or via persons employed by him) while the contractor is engaged on the works. Where this work is described in the bills the contractor is obliged to permit the employer to carry the work out, but where it is not, the contractor is required to give his consent, which must not be unreasonably withheld. Clause 29.3 makes it clear that there is no relationship between the Contractor and persons so employed. (For the meaning of 'work not forming part of this contract' see *Henry Boot Construction Limited* v *Central Lancashire New Town Development Corporation* (1980) 15 BLR 1).

---

29   Works by Employer or persons employed or engaged by Employer

29·1 Where the Contract Bills, in regard to any work not forming part of this Contract and which is to be carried out by the Employer himself or by persons employed or otherwise engaged by him, provide such information as is necessary to enable the Contractor to carry out and complete the Works in accordance with the Conditions, the Contractor shall permit the execution of such work.

29·2 Where the Contract Bills do not provide the information referred to in clause 29·1 and the Employer requires the execution of work not forming part of this Contract by the Employer himself or by persons employed or otherwise engaged by the Employer, then the Employer may, with the consent of the Contractor (which consent shall not be unreasonably withheld) arrange for the execution of such work.

29·3 Every person employed or otherwise engaged by the Employer as referred to in clauses 29·1 and 29·2 shall for the purpose of clause 20 be deemed to be a person for whom the Employer is responsible and not to be a sub-contractor.

---

33 Clause 30: Certificates and payments

33.01 This clause provides for:

1. Interim certificates (Clause 30.1).
2. Rules for ascertainment of amounts due in interim certificates (Clause 30.2).
3. Rules for valuing off-site materials or goods (Clause 30.3).
4. Rules for ascertainment of retention (Clause 30.4).
5. Rules on treatment of retention (Clause 30.5).
6. Final adjustment of contract sum (Clause 30.6).
7. Final adjustment of nominated sub-contract sums (Clause 30.7).
8. Issue of an effect of final certificate (Clauses 30.8 and 30.9).

Interim certificates

33.02 The architect is under a duty to issue certificates showing the amount due from time to time; if he certifies an excessive amount, he may be liable to the employer in damages (see *Sutcliffe* v *Thackrah* [1974] AC 727). Certificates are payable within 14 days of issue, but under Clause 30.1.1.2, the employer is entitled to make a deduction from interim certificates, including retention money included in such certificates, subject to a restriction in relation to retention payable to a nominated sub-contractor. The employer is obliged to give reasons for such deduction (see Clause 30.1.1.3).

Amounts due in interim certificates

33.03 The amount to be included in interim certificates is defined by Clauses 30.2.1 and 30.2.2, which deal with matters which are

---

30   Certificates and payments

30·1 ·1 ·1 The Architect shall from time to time as provided in clause 30 issue Interim Certificates stating the amount due to the Contractor from the Employer and the Contractor shall be entitled to payment therefor within 14 days from the date of issue of each Interim Certificate. [q]

·1 ·2 Notwithstanding the fiduciary interest of the Employer in the Retention as stated in clause 30·5·1 the Employer is entitled to exercise any right under this Contract of deduction from monies due or to become due to the Contractor against any amount so due under an Interim Certificate whether or not any Retention is included in that Interim Certificate by the operation of clause 30·4. Such deduction is subject to the restriction set out in clause 35·13·5·3·2.

·1 ·3 Where the Employer exercises any right under this Contract of deduction from monies due or to become due to the Contractor he shall inform the Contractor in writing of the reason for that deduction.

30·1 ·2 Interim valuations shall be made by the Quantity Survey or whenever the Architect considers them to be necessary for the purpose of ascertaining the amount to be stated as due in an Interim Certificate. [r]

30·1 ·3 Interim Certificates shall be issued at the Period of Interim Certificates specified in the Appendix up to and including the end of the period during which the Certificate of Practical Completion is issued. Thereafter Interim Certificates shall be issued as and when further amounts are ascertained as payable to the Contractor from the Employer and after the expiration of the Defects Liability Period named in the Appendix or upon the issue of the Certificate of Completion of Making Good Defects (whichever is the later) provided always that the Architect shall not be required to issue an Interim Certificate within one calendar month of having issued a previous Interim Certificate.

30·2 The amount stated as due in an Interim Certificate, subject to any agreement between the parties as to stage payments, shall be the gross valuation as referred to in clause 30·2 less

any amount which may be deducted and retained by the Employer as provided in clause 30·4 (in the Conditions called 'the Retention') and

the total amount stated as due in Interim Certificates previously issued under the Conditions.

The gross valuation shall be the total of the amounts referred to in clauses 30·2·1 and 30·2·2 less the total of the amounts referred to in clause 30·2·3 and applied up to and including a date not more than 7 days before the date of the Interim Certificate.

30·2 ·1 There shall be included the following which are subject to Retention:

·1 ·1 the total value of the work properly executed by the Contractor including any work so executed to which clause 13·5 refers but excluding any restoration, replacement or repair of loss or damage and removal and disposal of debris which in clauses 22B·3·5 and 22C·4·4·2 are treated as if they were a Variation, together with, where applicable, any adjustment of that value under clause 40;

·1 ·2 the total value of the materials and goods delivered to or adjacent to the Works for incorporation therein by the Contractor but not so incorporated, provided that the value of such materials and goods shall only be included as and from such times as they are reasonably, properly and not prematurely so delivered and are adequately protected against weather and other casualties;

·1 ·3 the total value of any materials or goods other than those to which clause 30·2·1 refers where the Architect in the exercise of his discretion under clause 30·3 has decided that such total value shall be included in the amount stated as due in an Interim Certificate;

·1 ·4 the amounts referred to in clause 4·17·1 of Conditions NSC/C *(Conditions of Nominated Sub-Contract)* in respect of each Nominated Sub-Contractor;

·1 ·5 the profit of the Contractor upon the total of the amounts referred to in clauses 30·2·1·4 and 30·2·5 less the total of the amount referred to in clause 30·2·3·2 at the rates included in the Contract Bills, or, in the case where the nomination arises from an instruction as to the expenditure of a provisional sum, at rates related thereto, or, if none, at reasonable rates.

30·2 ·2 There shall be included the following which are not subject to Retention:

·2 ·1 any amounts to be included in Interim Certificates in accordance with clause 3 as a result of payments made or costs incurred by the Contractor under clauses 6·2, 8·3, 9·2, 21·2·3, 22B·2 and 22C·3;

·2 ·2 any amounts ascertained under clause 26·1 or 34·3 or in respect of any restoration, replacement or repair of loss or damage and removal and disposal of debris which in clauses 22B·3·5 and 22C·4·4·2 are treated as if they were a Variation;

·2 ·3 any amount to which clause 35·17 refers;

·2 ·4 any amount payable to the Contractor under clause 38 or 39, if applicable;

·2 ·5 the amounts referred to in clause 4·17·2 of Conditions NSC/C *(Conditions of Nominated Sub-Contract)* in respect of each Nominated Sub-Contractor.

30·2 ·3 There shall be deducted the following which are not subject to Retention:

·3 ·1 any amount deductible under clause 7 or 8·4·2 or 17·2 or 17·3 or any amount allowable by the Contractor to the Employer under clause 38 or 39, if applicable;

·3 ·2 any amount referred to in clause 4·17·3 of Conditions NSC/C *(Conditions of Nominated Sub-Contract)* in respect of each Nominated Sub-Contractor.

30·3 The amount stated as due in an Interim Certificate may in the discretion of the Architect include the value of any materials or goods before delivery thereof to or adjacent to the Works (in clause 30·3 referred to as 'the materials') provided that:

30·3 ·1 the materials are intended for incorporation in the Works;

30·3 ·2 nothing remains to be done to the materials to complete the same up to the point of their incorporation in the Works;

30·3 ·3 the materials have been and are set apart at the premises where they have been manufactured or assembled or are stored, and have been clearly and visibly marked, individually or in sets, either by letters or figures or by reference to a pre-determined code, so as to identify:

   ·3 ·1 the Employer, where they are stored on the premises of the Contractor, and in any other case the person to whose order they are held; and

   ·3 ·2 their destination as the Works;

30·3 ·4 where the materials were ordered from a supplier by the Contractor or by any sub-contractor, the contract for their supply is in writing and expressly provides that the property therein shall pass unconditionally to the Contractor or the sub-contractor (as the case may be) not later than the happening of the events set out in clauses 30·3·2 and 30·3·3;

30·3 ·5 where the materials were ordered from a supplier by any sub-contractor, the relevant sub-contract between the Contractor and the sub-contractor is in writing and expressly provides that on the property in the materials passing to the sub-contractor the same shall immediately thereon pass to the Contractor;

30·3 ·6 where the materials were manufactured or assembled by any sub-contractor, the sub-contract is in writing and expressly provides that the property in the materials shall pass unconditionally to the Contractor not later than the happening of the events set out in clauses 30·3·2 and 30·3·3;

30·3 ·7 the materials are in accordance with this Contract;

30·3 ·8 the Contractor provides the Architect with reasonable proof that the property in the materials is in him and that the appropriate conditions set out in clauses 30·3·1 to ·7 have been complied with;

30·3 ·9 the Contractor provides the Architect with reasonable proof that the materials are insured against loss or damage for their full value under a policy of insurance protecting the interests of the Employer and the Contractor in respect of the Specified Perils, during the period commencing with the transfer of property in the materials to the Contractor until they are delivered to, or adjacent to, the Works.

30·4 ·1 The Retention which the Employer may deduct and retain as referred to in clause 30·2 shall be such percentage of the total amount included under clause 30·2·1 in any Interim Certificate as arises from the operation of the following rules:

   ·1 ·1 the percentage (in the Conditions and Appendix called 'the Retention Percentage') deductible under clause 30·4·1·2 shall be 5 per cent (unless a lower rate shall have been agreed between the parties and specified in the Appendix as the Retention Percentage); and the percentage deductible under clause 30·4·1·3 shall be one half of the Retention Percentage; [s]

   ·1 ·2 [t] the Retention Percentage may be deducted from so much of the said total amount as relates to:

     work which has not reached Practical Completion (as referred to in clauses 17·1, 18·1·1 or 35·16); and

     amounts in respect of the value of materials and goods included under clauses 30·2·1·2, 30·2·1·3 and 30·2·1·4 (so far as that clause relates to materials and goods as referred to in clause 4·17·1 of Conditions NSC/C *(Conditions of Nominated Sub-Contract)*;

   ·1 ·3 [t] half the Retention Percentage may be deducted from so much of the said total amount as relates to work which has reached Practical Completion (as referred to in clauses 17·1, 18·1·1 or 35·16) but in respect of which a Certificate of Completion of Making Good Defects under clause 17·4 or a certificate under clause 18·1·2 or an Interim Certificate under clause 35·17 has not been issued.

30·4 ·2 The Retention deducted from the value of work executed by the Contractor or any Nominated Sub-Contractor, and from the Value of materials and goods intended for incorporation in the Works but not so incorporated, and specified in the statements issued under clause 30·5·2·1, is hereinafter referred to as the 'Contractor's retention' and the 'Nominated Sub-Contract retention' respectively.

30·5 The Retention shall be subject to the following rules:

30·5 ·1 the Employer's interest in the Retention is fiduciary as trustee for the Contractor and for any Nominated Sub-Contractor (but without obligation to invest);

30·5 ·2 ·1 at the date of each Interim Certificate the Architect shall prepare, or instruct the Quantity Surveyor to prepare, a statement specifying the Contractor's retention and the Nominated Sub-Contract retention for each Nominated Sub-Contractor deducted in arriving at the amount stated as due in such Interim Certificate;

   ·2 ·2 such statement shall be issued by the Architect to the Employer, to the Contractor and to each Nominated Sub-Contractor whose work is referred to in the statement.

30·5 ·3 The Employer shall, to the extent that the Employer exercises his right under clause 30·4, if the Contractor or any Nominated Sub-Contractor so requests, at the date of payment under each Interim Certificate place the Retention in a separate banking account (so designated as to identify the amount as the Retention held by the Employer on trust as provided in clause 30·5·1) and certify to the Architect with a copy to the Contractor that

such amount has been so placed. The Employer shall be entitled to the full beneficial interest in any interest accruing in the separate banking account and shall be under no duty to account for any such interest to the Contractor or any sub-contractor.

30·5 ·4 Where the Employer exercises the right to deduct referred to in clause 30·1·1·2 against any Retention he shall inform the Contractor of the amount of that deduction from either the Contractor's retention or the Nominated Sub-Contract retention of any Nominated Sub-Contractor by reference to the latest statement issued under clause 30·5·2·1.

30·6 ·1 ·1 Not later than 6 months after Practical Completion of the Works the Contractor shall provide the Architect, or, if so instructed by the Architect, the Quantity Surveyor, with all documents necessary for the purposes of the adjustment of the Contract Sum including all documents relating to the accounts of Nominated Sub-Contractors and Nominated Suppliers.

   ·1 ·2 Not later than 3 months after receipt by the Architect or by the Quantity Surveyor of the documents referred to in clause 30·6·1·1

     ·2 ·1 the Architect, or, if the Architect has so instructed, the Quantity Surveyor, shall ascertain (unless previously ascertained) any loss and/or expense under clauses 26·1, 26·4·1 and 34·3, and

     ·2 ·2 the Quantity Surveyor shall prepare a statement of all adjustments to be made to the Contract Sum as referred to in clause 30·6·2 other than any to which clause 30·6·1·2·1 applies

     and the Architect shall forthwith send a copy of any ascertainment to which clause 30·6·1·2·1 refers and of the statement prepared in compliance with clause 30·6·1·2·2 to the Contractor and the relevant extract therefrom to each Nominated Sub-Contractor.

30·6 ·2 The Contract Sum shall be adjusted by:

   – the amount of any Valuations agreed by the Employer and the Contractor to which clause 13·4·1·1 refers, and

   – the amounts stated in any 13A Quotations for which the Architect has issued to the Contractor a confirmed acceptance pursuant to clause 13A·3·2 and for the amount of any Variations thereto as valued pursuant to clause 13A·8

and as follows:

There shall be deducted:

   ·2 ·1 all prime cost sums, all amounts in respect of sub-contractors named as referred to in clause 35·1, the certified value of any work by a Nominated Sub-Contractor, whose employment has been determined in accordance with clause 35·24, which was not in accordance with the relevant Sub-Contract but which has been paid or otherwise discharged by the Employer, and any Contractor's profit thereon included in the Contract Bills;

   ·2 ·2 all provisional sums and the value of all work for which an Approximate Quantity is included in the Contract Bills;

   ·2 ·3 the amount of the valuation under clause 13·5·2 of items omitted in accordance with a Variation required by the Architect under clause 13·2, or subsequently sanctioned by him in writing, together with the amount included in the Contract Bills for any other work as referred to in clause 13·5·5 which is to be valued under clause 13·5;

   ·2 ·4 any amount deducted or deductible under clause 7 or 8·4·2 or 17·2 or 17·3 or any amount allowed or allowable to the Employer under clause 38, 39 or 40, whichever is applicable;

   ·2 ·5 any other amount which is required by this Contract to be deducted from the Contract Sum;

There shall be added:

   ·2 ·6 the amounts of the nominated sub-contract sums or tender sums for all Nominated Sub-Contractors as finally adjusted or ascertained under all relevant provisions of Conditions NSC/C *(Conditions of Nominated Sub-Contract)*;

   ·2 ·7 the tender sum (or such other sum as is appropriate in accordance with the terms of the tender as accepted by or on behalf of the Employer) for any work for which a tender made under clause 35·2 has been accepted;

   ·2 ·8 any amounts properly chargeable to the Employer in accordance with the nomination instruction of the Architect in respect of materials or goods supplied by Nominated Suppliers; such amounts shall include the discount for cash of 5 per cent referred to in clause 36 but shall exclude any value added tax which is treated, or is capable of being treated, as input tax (as referred to in the Finance Act 1972) by the Contractor;

   ·2 ·9 the profit of the Contractor upon the amounts referred to in clauses 30·6·2·6, 30·6·2·7 and 30·6·2·8 at the rates included in the Contract Bills or in the cases where the nomination arises from an instruction as to the expenditure of a provisional sum at rates related thereto or if none at reasonable rates;

   ·2 ·10 any amounts paid or payable by the Employer to the Contractor as a result of payments made or costs incurred by the Contractor under clauses 6·2, 8·3, 9·2 and 21·2·3;

   ·2 ·11 the amount of the Valuation under clause 13·5 of any Variation, including the valuation of other work as referred to in clause 13·5·5, other than the amount of the valuation of any omission under clause 13·5·2;

   ·2 ·12 the amount of the Valuation of work executed by, or the amount of any disbursements by, the Contractor in accordance with instructions of the Architect as to the expenditure of provisional sums included in the Contract Bills and of all work for which an Approximate Quantity is included in the Contract Bills;

·2 ·13 any amount ascertained under clause 26·1 or 34·3;

·2 ·14 any amount paid by the Contractor under clause 22B or clause 22C which the Contractor is entitled to have added to the Contract Sum;

·2 ·15 any amount paid or payable to the Contractor under clause 38, 39 or 40, whichever is applicable;

·2 ·16 any other amount which is required by this Contract to be added to the Contract Sum.

30·7 So soon as is practicable but not less than 28 days before the date of issue of the Final Certificate referred to in clause 30·8 and notwithstanding that a period of one month may not have elapsed since the issue of the previous Interim Certificate, the Architect shall issue an Interim Certificate the gross valuation for which shall include the amounts of the sub-contract sums for all Nominated Sub-Contracts as finally adjusted or ascertained under all relevant provisions of Conditions NSC/C *(Conditions of Nominated Sub-Contract).*

30·8 The Architect shall issue the Final Certificate (and inform each Nominated Sub-Contractor of the date of its issue) not later than 2 months after whichever of the following occurs last:

the end of the Defects Liability Period;

the date of issue of the Certificate of Completion of Making Good Defects under clause 17·4;

the date on which the Architect sent a copy to the Contractor of any ascertainment to which clause 30·6·1·2·1 refers and of the statement prepared in compliance with clause 30·6·1·2·2.

The Final Certificate shall state:

30·8 ·1 the sum of the amounts already stated as due in Interim Certificates, and

30·8 ·2 the Contract Sum adjusted as necessary in accordance with clause 30·6·2

and the difference (if any) between the two sums shall (without prejudice to the rights of the Contractor in respect of any Interim Certificates which have not been paid by the Employer) be expressed in the said Certificate as a balance due to the Contractor from the Employer or to the Employer from the Contractor as the case may be, and, subject to any deductions authorised by the Conditions, the said balance shall as from the 28th day after the date of the said Certificate be a debt payable as the case may be by the Employer to the Contractor or by the Contractor to the Employer.

30·9 ·1 Except as provided in clauses 30·9·2 and 30·9·3 (and save in respect of fraud), the Final Certificate shall have effect in any proceedings arising out of or in connection with this Contract (whether by arbitration under article 5 or otherwise) as

·1 ·1 conclusive evidence that where and to the extent that the quality of materials or the standard of workmanship is to be to the reasonable satisfaction of the Architect the same is to such satisfaction, and

·1 ·2 conclusive evidence that any necessary effect has been given to all the terms of this Contract which require that an amount is to be added to or deducted from the Contract Sum or an adjustment is to be made of the Contract Sum save where there has been any accidental inclusion or exclusion of any work, materials, goods or figure in any computation or any arithmetical error in any computation, in which event the Final Certificate shall have effect as conclusive evidence as to all other computations, and

·1 ·3 conclusive evidence that all and only such extensions of time, if any, as are due under clause 25 have been given, and

·1 ·4 conclusive evidence that the reimbursement of direct loss and/or expense, if any, to the Contractor pursuant to clause 26·1 is in final settlement of all and any claims which the Contractor has or may have arising out of the occurrence of any of the matters referred to in clause 26·2 whether such claim be for breach of contract, duty of care, statutory duty or otherwise.

30·9 ·2 If any arbitration or other proceedings have been commenced by either party before the Final Certificate has been issued the Final Certificate shall have effect as conclusive evidence as provided in clause 30·9·1 after either

·2 ·1 such proceedings have been concluded, whereupon the Final Certificate shall be subject to the terms of any award or judgment in or settlement of such proceedings, or

·2 ·2 a period of 12 months during which neither party has taken any further step in such proceedings, whereupon the Final Certificate shall be subject to any terms agreed in partial settlement,

whichever shall be the earlier.

30·9 ·3 If any arbitration or other proceedings have been commenced by either party within 28 days after the Final Certificate has been issued, the Final Certificate shall have effect as conclusive evidence as provided in clause 30·9·1 save only in respect of all matters to which those proceedings relate.

30·10 Save as aforesaid no certificate of the Architect shall of itself be conclusive evidence that

30·10 ·1 any works, materials or goods

or

30·10 ·2 any Performance Specified Work

to which it relates are in accordance with this Contract.

and are not subject to retention respectively. The principal item in Clause 30.2.1 is the total value of work properly executed by the contractor (Clause 30.2.1.1). This means that the amounts certified should take into account adjustments for variation, price fluctuations, and defects. RIBA Publications Ltd publish forms of interim certificate and direction, and a statement of retention.

33.04 Clause 30.2.2 deals with matters which are not subject to retention. Broadly, retention is to be deducted where the contractor has some responsibility for the matters in question so that the employer's interests have to be protected by making the deduction. There will be no retention in instances where the employer's interests do not require such protection: thus, for example, amounts of direct loss and/or expense payable to the contractor and included in interim certificates are not subject to retention (see Clause 30.2.2.2).

33.05 Clause 30.1.2 requires that valuations must be carried out by the quantity surveyor, although the architect should ensure that the quantity surveyor adopts the correct principles when making such valuations.

Valuation of off-site materials

33.06 Clause 30.3 confers on the architect a discretion to certify for payment in respect of goods and materials not on the site. If goods and materials are not on the site, the employer has less protection in the event of the contractor's insolvency and certain other circumstances than if they are on the site. It is suggested that instead of the code allowed by Clause 30.3.3, it is better to use plain language such as 'SOLD the property of [the employer] for use at [the works]'.

33.07 Architects must be extremely careful in deciding whether to exercise their power to certify for off-site materials or goods: in general, it is suggested that this power should not be exercised in respect of what might be termed 'ordinary' goods or materials, such as bricks, timber, concrete, etc. It may, however, prove of assistance where some particularly large or costly purpose-made component is required for the work, and the contractor would otherwise be obliged to incur the expense of purchasing it a considerable time before it can be incorporated in the works and certified for payment, e.g. a large purpose-made central heating boiler. It is unlikely that such a component could readily be adapted for use elsewhere, and thus the risk in certifying for payment in respect of such an item is relatively small. The subject is covered in JCT Practice Note 5.

Set-off

33.08 There are conflicting views regarding the employer's right to set-off against monies due to the contractor on interim certificates, the amount of any counter-claim he has in respect of such matters as defects in the work. It is widely held that *Gilbert-Ash (Northern) Ltd* v *Modern Engineering (Bristol) Limited* [1974] AC 689 supports the right to set-off, but in that case there was an express provision allowing such deduction. The later *Mottram Consultants Ltd* v *Bernard Sunley & Sons Limited* [1975] 2 Lloyd's Reports 197 suggests that set-off can only be allowed if an express term is included. However, the employer cannot withhold payment on the ground of a counterclaim having been made against the contractor by a nominated sub-contractor (see *George E Taylor* v *Percy Trentham* (1980) 16 BLR 15).

Retention

33.09 The purpose of retention is to provide the employer with security for the contractor's due performance of his obligations in relation to the quality of the work. The percentage of retention is 5% on work which has not reached practical completion (Clause 30.4.1.1), and 2.5% on work which has reached practical completion. When the certificate of making good defects is issued, it has the effect of releasing the retention in respect of the works or that part of them to which that certificate relates. See also JCT Practice Note 18.

Rules on treatment of retention

33.10 Under Clause 30.5.1, the employer holds the retention monies on trust for the contractor and any nominated sub-contractor. In *Wates Construction Limited* v *Franthom Property Limited* (1991) 53 BLR 23, CA, it was held that Clause 30.5.1 had the effect of requiring the employer to place the retention monies in a separate bank account if so required. The intention is that the retention money should, in effect, be set aside as a separate fund to be used only for the purpose of providing the Employer with security against the making good of defects, and the purpose of making the employer a trustee is to protect the retention money against his liquidation. If no actual separate fund is set up, in the event of the employer's liquidation there will be no effective trust, and therefore the contractor will have to prove for his retention monies along with the general creditors (see *MacJordan Construction Limited* v *Brookmount Erostin Limited* [1992] BCLC 350, CA) so it is important to ensure that the exercise of setting up a separate fund is carried out. If the employer fails to do this the court will grant a mandatory injunction enforcing the obligation before liquidation, but the Court of Appeal considered that it would be likely to do so after liquidation, as to do so might constitute a preference under the Insolvency Act 1986. If the case involved a solvent employer but an insolvent contractor, and the employer had failed in his contractual obligation to set the retention monies aside, the court would treat the fund as having been set aside to prevent the employer relying on his breach of contract. However, the court will not grant an injunction compelling the employer to set aside the retention money in a separate fund where the employer has a claim against the contractor for a greater amount (see *Henry Boot Building Ltd* v *The Croydon Hotel and Leisure Co Ltd* (1985) 36 BLR 41).

33.11 In *Re Arthur Sanders Limited* (1981) 17 BLR 125, it was held that where the contractor has gone into liquidation, its liquidator was entitled to recover from the employer a sum representing the amount of retention due to a nominated sub-contractor notwithstanding that the liquidator conceded that the employer was entitled to withhold that part of the retention which related to the value of the contractor's own work. The reason given in that case by the employer for withholding the retention was that the contractor owed the employer money in respect of damages sustained by the employer as a result of the contractor's default on another contract. It is, however, doubtful that the employer is entitled to withhold retention money due to a contractor on the grounds that the employer has a claim against the contractor in relation to some other contract, since the employer's right to retention monies is restricted to claims arising out of the failure by the contractor to execute correctly the work covered by the contract in question (see *National Westminster Bank* v *Halesowen Pressworks and Assemblies Limited* [1972] AC 785).

Final adjustment of contract sum

33.12 Clause 30.6 provides a detailed guide as to how the final account is to be prepared. Subject to the architect's decision on matters of principle, this will be prepared by the quantity surveyor. In the private edition Clause 30.6.2.14 deals with reimbursement of the contractor if he has to insure the works following the employer's default.

Final adjustment of sub-contract sum

33.13 Clause 30.7 relates to the final adjustment or ascertainment of nominated sub-contract sums. This must be carried out not less than 28 days before the date of issue of the final certificate.

Final certificate

33.14 The responsibility for issuing this certificate is a heavy one, and the architect should not issue it unless he is satisfied that the contract has been fully complied with. It must be issued within two months of the latest of the following events:

1. The end of the defects liability period.
2. The issue of the Certificate of Completion of making good defects under Clause 17.4.
3. Receipt by the architect or the quantity surveyor of the documents referred to in Sub-clauses 30.6.1.2.1 and 30.6.1.2.2.

The form of the final certificate is governed by Clauses 30.8.1 and 30.8.2. Note that the final certificate may show a balance in favour of the employer if monies have been overpaid in earlier certificates. It is not necessary to hold back payment from earlier certificates merely to keep something in reserve for the purposes of the final certificate, although it is often considered prudent. RIBA Publications Ltd publish a form of Final Certificate.

Effect of final certificate

33.15 The final certificate is not merely the last certificate; it is, if properly issued in accordance with the contract, a document of considerable legal importance. Subject to certain qualifications, it is conclusive evidence of the following matters:

1. Where the quality of materials or the standards of workmanship are to be to the reasonable satisfaction of the architect, they are to his reasonable satisfaction (Clause 30.9.1.1).
2. All the terms of the contract which require an adjustment to be made of the contract sum have been complied with (Clause 30.9.1.2).
3. All and only such extensions of time as are due under Clause 25 have been given (Clause 30.9.1.3).
4. The reimbursement of direct loss and/or expense, if any, to the contractor pursuant to Clause 26.1 is in final settlement of all claims arising out of the matters referred to in Clause 26.2 (Clause 30.9.1.4).

33.16 In summary the qualifications are:

1. Where proceedings have been commenced by either party before the issue of the final certificate, the conclusiveness of the certificate becomes limited as set out in Clause 30.9.2.
2. Where proceedings have been commenced by either party within 14 days of its issue, the final certificate is then conclusive save only in respect of all matters to which the proceedings relate (see Clause 30.9.3).
3. Fraud (Clause 30.9.1).
4. Mathematical error (Clause 30.9.1.2).

33.17 The question of the width of construction to be given to Clause 30.9.1.1 was considered in *Crown Estates* v *John Mowlem & Co Limited* (1994) 10 Const LJ 311 (CA). It was held that the clause should be given a wide interpretation and that the conclusive evidence provision applied to the quality of all materials and the standard of all workmanship, in relation to which, under various provisions of the contract, the architect was required to form an opinion as to whether or not they complied with the contract requirements.

33.18 It was further held in *Crown Estates* that Clause 30.9 does not impose a time limit of 28 days within which arbitration proceedings should be brought, as had previously been thought, but that proceedings could be brought at any time. The effect of Clause 30.9.1 is to provide an evidential bar, from which Clauses 30.9.2 and 30.9.3 afford limited relief.

33.19 The *Crown Estates* decision was a considerable surprise. The Court's interpretation of Clause 30 was contrary both to the general understanding of construction lawyers, and to the intentions of the JCT. In December 1994 the RIBA circulated a note in which it advised users to make the following alterations to the Standard Form:

• delete Clause 30.9.1.1;
• at the beginning of Clause 30.10 delete the words 'Save as aforesaid';

- at the end of Clause 1.4 delete the words 'save as provided in Clause 30.9.1.1 with regard to the conclusiveness of the Final Certificate'.

34 Clause 31: Finance (No. 2) Act 1975 – statutory tax deduction

34.01 The provisions of Clause 31 are of relevance to accountants rather than to architects, and do not justify commentary in this book.

34.02 Clause 32, which concerned outbreak of hostilities, and Clause 33, which concerned war damage, were deleted in 1992 by Amendment 11. There is now no Clause 32 or 33 in this contract.

35 Clause 34: Antiquities

35.01 The words 'direct loss and expense' bear the same meaning as in Clause 26, as to which see the discussion in the notes to that clause.

Part 2 Conditions: Nominated sub-contractors and nominated suppliers

36 Clause 35: Nominated sub-contractors
General introduction

36.01 This clause, which is for use when the architect has reserved to himself the final selection of sub-contractors to supply and fix goods or execute work, is one of the most elaborate in the whole contract, being very considerably longer than the equivalent clause, Clause 27, in the 1963 JCT Form. This reflects the growing importance of nominated sub-contractors in the building industry: frequently work carried out by nominated sub-contractors forms a high proportion of the value of the contract as a whole, and they play an especially large role in such areas as foundation construction and mechanical and electrical services.

36.02 The clause is primarily concerned with the following areas:

1. Ways of nomination.
2. Procedure for nomination.
3. Payment of nominated sub-contractor.
4. Extensions of time.
5. Failure to complete nominated sub-contract works and the consequences thereof.
6. Practical completion of nominated sub-contract works.
7. Final payment to nominated sub-contractor.
8. Renomination.
9. Determination of employment of nominated sub-contractor.

Ways of nomination

36.03 There are now eight ways in which a sub-contractor can be nominated:

1. By the use of a prime cost sum in the contract bills.
2. By naming a sub-contractor in the contract bills.
3. By the use of a prime cost sum in any instruction issued under Clause 13.3.1 in relation to the expenditure of a provisional sum (except a provisional sum relating to performance specified work) included in the contract bills.
4. By naming a sub-contractor in a similar instruction.
5. By the use of a prime cost sum in any instruction issued under Clause 13.2 requiring a variation to be effected (provided that the work is both additional to that in the contract drawings and bills and is of a similar kind to that which the contract bills stated would be supplied and fixed or executed by a nominated sub-contractor).

---

31   Finance (No.2) Act 1975 – statutory tax deduction scheme

31·1   In this Condition 'the Act' means the Finance (No·2) Act 1975; 'the Regulations' means the Income Tax (Sub-Contractors in the Construction Industry) Regulations 1975 S.I. No. 1960; ' "contractor" ' means a person who is a contractor for the purposes of the Act and the Regulations; 'evidence' means such evidence as is required by the Regulations to be produced to a 'contractor' for the verification of a 'sub-contractor's' tax certificate; 'statutory deduction' means the deduction referred to in S.69(4) of the Act or such other deduction as may be in force at the relevant time; ' "sub-contractor" ' means a person who is a sub-contractor for the purposes of the Act and the Regulations; 'tax certificate' is a certificate issuable under S.70 of the Act.

31·2   ·1   Clauses 31·3 to ·9 shall not apply if, in the Appendix, the Employer is stated not to be a 'contractor'.

31·2   ·2   If in the Appendix the words 'is a "contractor" ' are deleted, nevertheless if, at any time up to the issue and payment of the Final Certificate, the Employer becomes such a 'contractor', the Employer shall so inform the Contractor and the provisions of clause 31 shall immediately thereupon become operative.

31·3   ·1   Not later than 21 days before the first payment under this Contract is due to the Contractor or after clause 31·2·2 has become operative the Contractor shall:

either

  ·1   ·1   provide the Employer with the evidence that the Contractor is entitled to be paid without the statutory deduction;

  or

  ·1   ·2   inform the Employer in writing, and send a duplicate copy to the Architect, that he is not entitled to be paid without the statutory deduction.

31·3   ·2   If the Employer is not satisfied with the validity of the evidence submitted in accordance with clause 31·3·1·1, he shall within 14 days of the Contractor submitting such evidence notify the Contractor in writing that he intends to make the statutory deduction from payments due under this Contract to the Contractor who is a 'sub-contractor' and give his reasons for that decision. The Employer shall at the same time comply with clause 31·6·1.

31·4   ·1   Where clause 31·3·1·2 applies, the Contractor shall immediately inform the Employer if he obtains a tax certificate and thereupon clause 31·3·1·1 shall apply.

31·4   ·2   If the period for which the tax certificate has been issued to the Contractor expires before the final payment is made to the Contractor under this Contract the Contractor shall not later than 28 days before the date of expiry:

either

  ·2   ·1   provide the Employer with evidence that the Contractor from the said date of expiry is entitled to be paid for a further period without the statutory deduction in which case the provisions of clause 31·3·2 shall apply if the Employer is not satisfied with the evidence;

  or

  ·2   ·2   inform the Employer in writing that he will not be entitled to be paid without the statutory deduction after the said date of expiry.

31·4   ·3   The Contractor shall immediately inform the Employer in writing if his current tax certificate is cancelled and give the date of such cancellation.

31·5   The Employer shall, as a 'contractor' in accordance with the Regulations, send promptly to the Inland Revenue any voucher which, in compliance with the Contractor's obligations as a 'sub-contractor' under the Regulations, the Contractor gives to the Employer.

31·6   ·1   If at any time the Employer is of the opinion (whether because of the information given under clause 31·3·1·2 or of the expiry or cancellation of the Contractor's tax certificate or otherwise) that he will be required by the Act to make a statutory deduction from any payment due to be made the Employer shall immediately so notify the Contractor in writing and require the Contractor to state not later than 7 days before each future payment becomes due (or within 10 days of such notification if that is later) the amount to be included in such payment which represents the direct cost to the Contractor and any other person of materials used or to be used in carrying out the Works.

31·6   ·2   Where the Contractor complies with clause 31·6·1 he shall indemnify the Employer against loss or expense caused to the Employer by any incorrect statement of the amount of direct cost referred to in clause 31·6·1.

31·6   ·3   Where the Contractor does not comply with clause 31·6·1 the Employer shall be entitled to make a fair estimate of the amount of direct cost referred to in clause 31·6·1.

31·7   Where any error or omission has occurred in calculating or making the statutory deduction the Employer shall correct that error or omission by repayment to, or by deduction from payments to, the Contractor as the case may be subject only to any statutory obligation on the Employer not to make such correction.

31·8   If compliance with clause 31 involves the Employer or the Contractor in not complying with any other of the Conditions, then the provisions of clause 31 shall prevail.

31·9   The provisions of article 5 shall apply to any dispute or difference between the Employer or the Architect on his behalf and the Contractor as to the operation of clause 31 except where the Act or the Regulations or any other Act of Parliament or statutory instrument, rule or order made under an Act of Parliament provide for some other method of resolving such dispute or difference.

34   Antiquities

34·1 All fossils, antiquities and other objects of interest or value which may be found on the site or in excavating the same during the progress of the Works shall become the property of the Employer and upon discovery of such an object the Contractor shall forthwith:

34·1 ·1 use his best endeavours not to disturb the object and shall cease work if and insofar as the continuance of work would endanger the object or prevent or impede its excavation or its removal;

34·1 ·2 take all steps which may be necessary to preserve the object in the exact position and condition in which it was found; and

34·1 ·3 inform the Architect or the clerk of works of the discovery and precise location of the object.

34·2 The Architect shall issue instructions in regard to what is to be done concerning an object reported by the Contractor under clause 34·1, and (without prejudice to the generality of his power) such instructions may require the Contractor to permit the examination, excavation or removal of the object by a third party. Any such third party shall for the purposes of clause 20 be deemed to be a person for whom the Employer is responsible and not to be a sub-contractor.

34·3 ·1 If in the opinion of the Architect compliance with the provisions of clause 34·1 or with an instruction issued under clause 34·2 has involved the Contractor in direct loss and/or expense for which he would not be reimbursed by a payment made under any other provision of this Contract then the Architect shall himself ascertain or shall instruct the Quantity Surveyor to ascertain the amount of such loss and/or expense.

34·3 ·2 If and to the extent that it is necessary for the ascertainment of such loss and/or expense the Architect shall state in writing to the Contractor what extension of time, if any, has been made under clause 25 in respect of the Relevant Event referred to in clause 25·4·5·1 so far as that clause refers to clause 34.

34·3 ·3 Any amount from time to time so ascertained shall be added to the Contract Sum.

Part 2: Nominated Sub-Contractors and Nominated Suppliers

Nominated Sub-Contractors

35   GENERAL

35·1 Where

35·1 ·1 in the Contract Bills; or

35·1 ·2 in any instruction of the Architect under clause 13·3 on the expenditure of a provisional sum included in the Contract Bills; or

35·1 ·3 in any instruction of the Architect under clause 13·2 requiring a Variation to the extent, but not further or otherwise,

·3 ·1 that it consists of work additional to that shown upon the Contract Drawings and described by or referred to in the Contract Bills and

·3 ·2 that any supply and fixing of materials or goods or any execution of work by a Nominated Sub-Contractor in connection with such additional work is of a similar kind to any supply and fixing of materials or the execution of work for which the Contract Bills provided that the Architect would nominate a sub-contractor; or

35·1 ·4 by agreement (which agreement shall not be unreasonably withheld) between the Contractor and the Architect on behalf of the Employer

the Architect has, whether by the use of a prime cost sum or by naming a sub-contractor, reserved to himself the final selection and approval of the sub-contractor to the Contractor who shall supply and fix any materials or goods or execute work, the sub-contractor so named or to be selected and approved shall be nominated in accordance with the provisions of clause 35 and a sub-contractor so nominated shall be a Nominated Sub-Contractor for all the purposes of this Contract. The provisions of clause 35·1 shall apply notwithstanding the requirement in rule A51 of the Standard Method of Measurement, 7th Edition, for a PC sum to be included in the Bills of Quantities in respect of Nominated Sub-Contractors; where however such sum is included in the Contract Bills the provisions of the aforesaid rule A51 shall apply in respect thereof.

35·2 ·1 Where the Contractor in the ordinary course of his business directly carries out works included in the Contract Bills and to which clause 35 applies, and where items of such works are set out in the Appendix and the Architect is prepared to receive tenders from the Contractor for such items, then the Contractor shall be permitted to tender for the same or any of them but without prejudice to the Employer's right to reject the lowest or any tender. If the Contractor's tender is accepted, he shall not sub-let the work to a Domestic Sub-Contractor without the consent of the Architect. Provided that where an item for which the Architect intends to nominate a sub-contractor is included in Architect's instructions issued under clause 13·3 it shall be deemed for the purposes of clause 35·2·1 to have been included in the Contract Bills and the item of work to which it relates shall likewise be deemed to have been set out in the Appendix.

35·2 ·2 It shall be a condition of any tender accepted under clause 35·2 that clause 13 shall apply in respect of the items of work included in the tender as if for the reference therein to the Contract Drawings and the Contract Bills there were references to the equivalent documents included in or referred to in the tender submitted under clause 35·2.

35·2 ·3 None of the provisions of clause 35 other than clause 35·2 shall apply to works for which a tender of the Contractor is accepted under clause 35·2.

PROCEDURE FOR NOMINATION OF A SUB-CONTRACTOR

35·3 The nomination of a sub-contractor to which clause 35·1 applies shall be effected in accordance with clauses 35·4 to 35·9 inclusive.

35·4 The following documents relating to Nominated Sub-Contractors are issued by the Joint Contracts Tribunal for the Standard Form of Building Contract and are referred to in the Conditions and in those documents either by the use of the name or of the identification term:

Name of document	Identification term
The Standard Form of Nominated Sub-Contract Tender 1991 Edition which comprises:	NSC/T
Part 1: The Architect's Invitation to Tender to a Sub-Contractor	– Part 1
Part 2: Tender by a Sub-Contractor	– Part 2
Part 3: Particular Conditions (to be agreed by a Contractor and a Sub-Contractor nominated under clause 35·6)	– Part 3
The Standard Form of Articles of Nominated Sub-Contract Agreement between a Contractor and a Nominated Sub-Contractor, 1991 Edition	Agreement NSC/A
The Standard Conditions of Nominated Sub-Contract, 1991 Edition, incorporated by reference into Agreement NSC/A	Conditions NSC/C
The Standard Form of Employer/ Nominated Sub-Contractor Agreement, 1991 Edition	Agreement NSC/W
The Standard Form of Nomination Instruction for a Sub-Contractor	Nomination NSC/N

35·5 ·1 No person against whom the Contractor makes a reasonable objection shall be a Nominated Sub-Contractor. The Contractor shall make such reasonable objection in writing at the earliest practicable moment but in any case not later than 7 working days from receipt of the instruction of the Architect under clause 35·6 nominating the sub-contractor.

35·5 ·2 Where such reasonable objection is made the Architect may either issue further instructions to remove the objection so that the Contractor can then comply with clause 35·7 in respect of such nomination instruction or cancel such nomination instruction and issue an instruction either under clause 13·2 omitting the work which was the subject of that nomination instruction or under clause 35·6 nominating another sub-contractor therefor. A copy of any instruction issued under clause 35·5·2 shall be sent by the Architect to the sub-contractor.

35·6 The Architect shall issue an instruction to the Contractor on Nomination NSC/N nominating the sub-contractor which shall be accompanied by:

35·6 ·1 NSC/T Part 1 *(Invitation to Tender)* completed by the Architect and NSC/T Part 2 *(Tender by a Sub-Contractor)* completed and signed by the sub-contractor and signed by or on behalf of the Employer as 'approved' together with a copy of the numbered tender documents listed in and enclosed with NSC/T Part 1 together with any additional documents and/or amendments thereto as have been approved by the Architect;

35·6 ·2 a copy of the completed Agreement NSC/W *(Employer/Nominated Sub-Contractor Agreement)* entered into between the Employer and the sub-contractor; and

35·6 ·3 confirmation of any alterations to the information given in NSC/T Part 1 *(Invitation to Tender)*

item 7: obligations or restrictions imposed by the Employer
item 8: order of Works: Employer's requirements
Item 9: type and location of access

35·6 ·4 the Principal Contractor's Health and Safety Plan.

A copy of the instruction shall be sent by the Architect to the sub-contractor together with a copy of the completed Appendix for the Main Contract.

35·7 The Contractor shall forthwith upon receipt of such instruction:

35·7 ·1 complete in agreement with the sub-contractor NSC/T Part 3 *(Particular Conditions)* and have that completed NSC/T Part 3 signed by or on behalf of the Contractor and by or on behalf of the sub-contractor; and

35·7 ·2 execute Agreement NSC/A *(Articles of Nominated Sub-Contract Agreement)* with the sub-contractor

and thereupon shall send a copy of the completed Agreement NSC/A and of the agreed and signed NSC/T Part 3 (but **not** the other Annexures to Agreement NSC/A) to the Architect.

35·8 If the Contractor, having used his best endeavours, has not, within 10 working days from receipt of such instruction, complied with clause 35·7, the Contractor shall thereupon by a notice in writing inform the Architect

either

35·8 ·1 of the date by which he expects to have complied with clause 35·7

or

35·8 ·2 that the non-compliance is due to other matters identified in the Contractor's notice. [u·1]

35·9 Within a reasonable time after receipt of a notice under clause 35·8 the Architect shall:

35·9 ·1 where **clause 35·8·1 applies**, after consultation with the Contractor and so far as he considers it reasonable, fix a later date by which the Contractor shall have complied with clause 35·7;

35·9 ·2   where **clause 35·8·2 applies**, inform the Contractor in writing

either that he does not consider that the matters identified in the notice justify non-compliance by the Contractor with such nomination instruction in which case the Contractor shall comply with clause 35·7 in respect of such nomination instruction

or   that he does consider that the matters identified in the notice justify non-compliance by the Contractor with such nomination instruction in which case the Architect shall either issue further instructions so that the Contractor can then comply with clause 35·7 in respect of such nomination instruction or cancel such nomination instruction and issue an instruction either under clause 13·2 omitting the work which was the subject of the nomination instruction or under clause 35·6 nominating another sub-contractor therefor. A copy of any instruction issued under clause 35·9·2 shall be sent by the Architect to the sub-contractor.

35·10   [Number not used]

35·11   [Number not used]

35·12   [Number not used]

PAYMENT OF NOMINATED SUB-CONTRACTOR

35·13 ·1   The Architect shall on the issue of each Interim Certificate:

·1 ·1   direct the Contractor as to the amount of each interim or final payment to Nominated Sub-Contractors which is included in the amount stated as due in Interim Certificates and the amount of such interim or final payment shall be computed by the Architect in accordance with the relevant provisions of Conditions NSC/C *(Conditions of Nominated Sub-Contract)*; and

·1 ·2   forthwith inform each Nominated Sub-Contractor of the amount of any interim or final payment directed in accordance with clause 35·13·1·1.

35·13 ·2   Each payment directed under clause 35·13·1·1 shall be duly discharged by the Contractor in accordance with Conditions NSC/C *(Conditions of Nominated Sub-Contract)*.

35·13 ·3   Before the issue of each Interim Certificate (other than the first Interim Certificate) and of the Final Certificate the Contractor shall provide the Architect with reasonable proof of discharge by the Contractor pursuant to clause 35·13·2.

35·13 ·4   If the Contractor is unable to provide the reasonable proof referred to in clause 35·13·3 because of some failure or omission of the Nominated Sub-Contractor to provide any document or other evidence to the Contractor which the Contractor may reasonably require and the Architect is reasonably satisfied that this is the sole reason why reasonable proof is not furnished by the Contractor, the provisions of clause 35·13·5 shall not apply and the provisions of clause 35·13·3 shall be regarded as having been satisfied.

35·13 ·5 ·1   If the Contractor fails to provide reasonable proof under clause 35·13·3, the Architect shall issue a certificate to that effect stating the amount in respect of which the Contractor has failed to provide such proof, and the Architect shall issue a copy of the certificate to the Nominated Sub-Contractor concerned.

·5 ·2   Provided that the Architect has issued the certificate under clause 35·13·5·1, and subject to clause 35·13·5·3, the amount of any future payment otherwise due to the Contractor under this Contract (after deducting any amounts due to the Employer from the Contractor under this Contract) shall be reduced by any amounts due to Nominated Sub-Contractors which the Contractor has failed to discharge (together with the amount of any value added tax which would have been due to the Nominated Sub-Contractor) and the Employer shall himself pay the same to the Nominated Sub-Contractor concerned. Provided that the Employer shall in no circumstances be obliged to pay amounts to Nominated Sub-Contractors in excess of amounts available for reduction as aforesaid.

·5 ·3   The operation of clause 35·13·5·2 shall be subject to the following:

·3 ·1   where the Contractor would otherwise be entitled to payment of an amount stated as due in an Interim Certificate under clause 30, the reduction and payment to the Nominated Sub-Contractor referred to in clause 35·13·5·2 shall be made at the same time as the Employer pays the Contractor any balance due under clause 30 or, if there is no such balance, not later than the expiry of the period of 14 days within which the Contractor would otherwise be entitled to payment;

·3 ·2   where the sum due to the Contractor is the Retention or any part thereof, the reduction and payment to the Nominated Sub-Contractor referred to in clause 35·13·5·2 shall not exceed any part of the Contractor's retention (as defined in clause 30·4·2) which would otherwise be due for payment to the Contractor;

·3 ·3   where the Employer has to pay 2 or more Nominated Sub-Contractors but the amount due or to become due to the Contractor is insufficient to enable the Employer to pay the Nominated Sub-Contractors in full, the Employer shall apply the amount available pro rata to the amounts from time to time remaining undischarged by the Contractor or adopt such other method of apportionment as may appear to the Employer to be fair and reasonable having regard to all the relevant circumstances;

·3 ·4   clause 35·13·5·2 shall cease to have effect absolutely if at the date when the reduction and payment to the Nominated Sub-Contractor referred to in clause 35·13·5·2 would otherwise be made there is in existence

either a Petition which has been presented to the Court for the winding up of the Contractor

or a resolution properly passed for the winding up of the Contractor other than for the purposes of amalgamation or reconstruction

whichever shall have first occurred. [v]

35·13 ·6   Where, in accordance with clause 2·2 of Agreement NSC/W *(Employer/ Nominated Sub-Contractor Agreement)*, the Employer, before the date of the issue of an instruction nominating a sub-contractor, has paid to him an amount in respect of design work and/or materials or goods and/or fabrication which is/are included in the subject of the sub-contract sum or tender sum:

·6 ·1   the Employer shall send to the Contractor the written statement of the Nominated Sub-Contractor of the amount to be credited to the Contractor, and

·6 ·2   the Employer may make deductions up to the amount of such credit from the amounts stated as due to the Contractor in any of the Interim Certificates which include amounts of interim or final payment to the Nominated Sub-Contractor; provided that the amount so deducted from that stated as due in any one Interim Certificate shall not exceed the amount of payment to the Nominated Sub-Contractor included therein as directed by the Architect.

EXTENSION OF PERIOD OR PERIODS FOR COMPLETION OF NOMINATED SUB-CONTRACT WORKS

35·14 ·1   The Contractor shall not grant to any Nominated Sub-Contractor any extension of the period or periods within which the sub-contract works (or where the sub-contract works are to be completed in parts any part thereof) are to be completed except in accordance with the relevant provisions of Conditions NSC/C *(Conditions of Nominated Sub-Contract)* which require the written consent of the Architect to any such grant.

35·14 ·2   The Architect shall operate the relevant provisions of Conditions NSC/C *(Conditions of Nominated Sub-Contract)* upon receiving any notice, particulars and estimate and a request from the Contractor and any Nominated Sub-Contractor for his written consent to an extension of the period or periods for the completion of the sub-contract works or any part thereof as referred to in clause 2·3 of Conditions NSC/C *(Conditions of Nominated Sub-Contract)*.

FAILURE TO COMPLETE NOMINATED SUB-CONTRACT WORKS

35·15 ·1   If any Nominated Sub-Contractor fails to complete the sub-contract works (or where the sub-contract works are to be completed in parts any part thereof) within the period specified in the Nominated Sub-Contract or within any extended time granted by the Contractor with the written consent of the Architect, and the Contractor so notifies the Architect with a copy to the Nominated Sub-Contractor,

then, provided that the Architect is satisfied that clause 35·14 has been properly applied, the Architect shall so certify in writing to the Contractor. Immediately upon the issue of such a certificate the Architect shall send a duplicate thereof to the Nominated Sub-Contractor.

35·15 ·2   The certificate of the Architect under clause 35·15·1 shall be issued not later than 2 months from the date of notification to the Architect that the Nominated Sub-Contractor has failed to complete the sub-contract works or any part thereof.

PRACTICAL COMPLETION OF NOMINATED SUB-CONTRACT WORKS

35·16   When in the opinion of the Architect practical completion of the works executed by a Nominated Sub-Contractor is achieved and the Sub-Contractor has complied sufficiently with clause 5E·5 of Conditions NSC/C *(Conditions of Nominated Sub-Contract)* he shall forthwith issue a certificate to that effect and practical completion of such works shall be deemed to have taken place on the day named in such certificate, a duplicate copy of which shall be sent by the Architect to the Nominated Sub-Contractor; where clause 18 applies practical completion of works executed by a Nominated Sub-Contractor in a relevant part shall be deemed to have occurred on the relevant date to which clause 18·1 refers and the Architect shall send to the Nominated Sub-Contractor a copy of the written statement which he has issued pursuant to clause 18·1.

EARLY FINAL PAYMENT OF NOMINATED SUB-CONTRACTORS

35·17   Provided clause 5 of Agreement NSC/W *(Employer/Nominated Sub-Contractor Agreement)* remains in force unamended, then at any time after the day named in the certificate issued under clause 35·16 the Architect may, and on the expiry of 12 months from the aforesaid day shall, issue an Interim Certificate the gross valuation for which shall include the amount of the relevant sub-contract sum or ascertained final sub-contract sum as finally adjusted or ascertained under the relevant provisions of Conditions NSC/C *(Conditions of Nominated Sub-Contract)*; provided always that the Nominated Sub-Contractor:

35·17 ·1   has in the opinion of the Architect and the Contractor remedied any defects, shrinkages or other faults which have appeared and which the Nominated Sub-Contractor is bound to remedy under the Nominated Sub-Contract; and

35·17 ·2   has sent through the Contractor to the Architect or the Quantity Surveyor all documents necessary for the final adjustment of the sub-contract sum or the computation of the ascertained final sub-contract sum referred to in clause 35·17.

35·18   Upon due discharge by the Contractor to the Nominated Sub-Contractor ('the original sub-contractor') of the amount certified under clause 35·17 then:

35·18 ·1 ·1   if the original sub-contractor fails to rectify any defect, shrinkage or other fault in the sub-contract works which he is bound to remedy under the Nominated Sub-Contract and which appears before the issue of the Final Certificate under clause 30·8 the Architect shall issue an instruction nominating a person ('the substituted sub-contractor') to carry out such rectification work and all the provisions relating to

Nominated Sub-Contractors in clause 35 shall apply to such further nomination;

·1 ·2 the Employer shall take such steps as may be reasonable to recover, under the Agreement NSC/W *(Employer/Nominated Sub-Contractor Agreement)*, from the original sub-contractor a sum equal to the sub-contract price of the substituted sub-contractor. The Contractor shall pay or allow to the Employer any difference between the amount so recovered by the Employer and the sub-contract price of the substituted sub-contractor provided that, before the further nomination has been made, the Contractor has agreed (which agreement shall not be unreasonably withheld) to the sub-contract price to be charged by the substituted sub-contractor.

35·18 ·2 Nothing in clause 35·18 shall override or modify the provisions of clause 35·21.

35·19 Notwithstanding any final payment to a Nominated Sub-Contractor under the provisions of clause 35:

35·19 ·1 until the date of Practical Completion of the Works or the date when the Employer takes possession of the Works, whichever first occurs, the Contractor shall be responsible for loss or damage to the sub-contract works for which a payment to which clause 35·17 refers has been made to the same extent but not further or otherwise than he is responsible for that part of the Works for which a payment as aforesaid has not been made;

35·19 ·2 the provisions of clause 22A or 22B or 22C whichever is applicable shall remain in full force and effect.

POSITION OF EMPLOYER IN RELATION TO NOMINATED SUB-CONTRACTOR

35·20 Neither the existence nor the exercise of the powers in clause 35 nor anything else contained in the Conditions shall render the Employer in any way liable to any Nominated Sub-Contractor except by way and in the terms of the Agreement NSC/W *(Employer/Nominated Sub-Contractor Agreement)*.

CLAUSE 2·1 OF AGREEMENT NSC/W – POSITION OF CONTRACTOR

35·21 Whether or not a Nominated Sub-Contractor is responsible to the Employer in the terms set out in clause 2·1 of Agreement NSC/W *(Employer/Nominated Sub-Contractor Agreement)* the Contractor shall not be responsible to the Employer in respect of any nominated sub-contract works for anything to which such terms relate. Nothing in clause 35·21 shall be construed so as to affect the obligations of the Contractor under this Contract in regard to the supply of workmanship, materials and goods.

RESTRICTIONS IN CONTRACTS OF SALE ETC. – LIMITATION OF LIABILITY OF NOMINATED SUB-CONTRACTORS

35·22 Where any liability of the Nominated Sub-Contractor to the Contractor is limited under the provisions of clause 1·7 of Conditions NSC/C *(Conditions of Nominated Sub-Contract)* the liability of the Contractor to the Employer shall be limited to the same extent.

35·23 [Number not used]

CIRCUMSTANCES WHERE RE-NOMINATION NECESSARY

35·24 If in respect of any Nominated Sub-Contract:

35·24 ·1 the Contractor informs the Architect that in the opinion of the Contractor the Nominated Sub-Contractor has made default in respect of any one or more of the matters referred to in clauses 7·1·1·1 to 7·1·1·4 of Conditions NSC/C *(Conditions of Nominated Sub-Contract)*; and the Contractor has passed to the Architect any observations of the Nominated Sub-Contractor in regard to the matters on which the Contractor considers the Nominated Sub-Contractor is in default; and the Architect is reasonably of the opinion that the Nominated Sub-Contractor has made default; or

35·24 ·2 the Contractor informs the Architect that one of the insolvency events referred to in clause 7·2·1 of Conditions NSC/C *(Insolvency of Nominated Sub-Contractor)* has occurred and **either** that under clause 7·2·3 of the aforesaid Conditions the employment of the Nominated Sub-Contractor has been automatically determined **or** that under clause 7·2·4 of those Conditions the Contractor has an option, with the written consent of the Architect, to determine the employment of the Nominated Sub-Contractor; or

35·24 ·3 the Nominated Sub-Contractor determines his employment under clause 7·7 of Conditions NSC/C *(Conditions of Nominated Sub-Contract)*; or

35·24 ·4 the Contractor has been required by the Employer to determine the employment of the Nominated Sub-Contractor under clause 7·3 of Conditions NSC/C *(Conditions of Nominated Sub-Contract)* and has so determined that employment; or

35·24 ·5 work properly executed or materials or goods properly fixed or supplied by the Nominated Sub-Contractor have to be taken down and/or re-executed or re-fixed or re-supplied ('work to be re-executed') as a result of compliance by the Contractor or by any other Nominated Sub-Contractor with any instruction or other exercise of a power of the Architect under clauses 7 or 8·4 or 17·2 or 17·3 and the Nominated Sub-Contractor cannot be required under the Nominated Sub-Contract and does not agree to carry out the work to be re-executed;

then:

35·24 ·6 Where **clause 35·24·1 applies:**

·6 ·1 the Architect shall issue an instruction to the Contractor to give to the Nominated Sub-Contractor the notice specifying the default or defaults to which clause 7·1·1 of Conditions NSC/C *(Conditions of Nominated Sub-Contract)* refers; and may in that instruction state that the Contractor must obtain a further instruction of the Architect before determining the employment of the Nominated Sub-Contractor under clause

7·1·2 or 7·1·3 of Conditions NSC/C *(Conditions of Nominated Sub-Contract)*; and

·6 ·2 the Contractor shall inform the Architect whether, following the giving of that notice for which the Architect has issued an instruction under clause 35·24·6·1, the employment of the Nominated Sub-Contractor has been determined by the Contractor under clause 7·1·2 or 7·1·3 of Conditions NSC/C *(Conditions of Nominated Sub-Contract)*; or where the further instruction referred to in clause 35·24·6·1 has been given by the Architect the Contractor shall confirm that the employment of the Nominated Sub-Contractor has been determined; then

·6 ·3 if the Contractor informs or confirms to the Architect that the employment of the Nominated Sub-Contractor has been so determined the Architect shall make such further nomination of a sub-contractor in accordance with clause 35 as may be necessary to supply and fix the materials or goods or to execute the work and to make good or re-supply or re-execute as necessary any work executed by or any materials or goods supplied by the Nominated Sub-Contractor whose employment has been determined which were not in accordance with the relevant Nominated Sub-Contract.

35·24 ·7 ·1 Where **clause 35·24·2 applies** and the Contractor has an option under clause 7·2·4 of Conditions NSC/C *(Insolvency of Nominated Sub-Contractor)* to determine the employment of the Nominated Sub-Contractor, clause 35·24·7·2 shall apply in respect of the written consent of the Architect to any determination of the employment of the Nominated Sub-Contractor.

·7 ·2 Where

– the administrator or the administrative receiver of the Nominated Sub-Contractor, or

– the Nominated Sub-Contractor after making a composition or arrangement with his creditors or, being a company, after making a voluntary arrangement for a composition of debts or a scheme of arrangement approved in accordance with the Companies Act 1985 or the Insolvency Act 1986 or any amendment or re-enactment thereof as the case may be

is, to the reasonable satisfaction of the Contractor and the Architect, prepared and able to continue to carry out the relevant Nominated Sub-Contract and to meet the liabilities thereunder, the Architect may withhold his consent. Where continuation on such terms does not apply the Architect shall give his consent to a determination by the Contractor of the employment of the Nominated Sub-Contractor unless the Employer and the Contractor otherwise agree.

·7 ·3 Where the written consent of the Architect to the determination of the employment of the Nominated Sub-Contractor has been given and the Contractor has determined that employment or where, under clause 7·2·3 of the Conditions NSC/C *(Conditions of Nominated Sub-Contract)*, the employment of the Nominated Sub-Contractor has been automatically determined the following shall apply. The Architect shall make such further nomination of a sub-contractor in accordance with clause 35 as may be necessary to supply and fix the materials or goods or to execute the work and to make good or re-supply or re-execute as necessary any work executed by or any materials or goods supplied by the Nominated Sub-Contractor whose employment has been determined which were not in accordance with the relevant Nominated Sub-Contract.

·7 ·4 Where **clause 35·24·4 applies** the Architect shall make such further nomination of a sub-contractor in accordance with clause 35 as may be necessary to supply and fix the materials or goods or to execute the work and to make good or re-supply or re-execute as necessary any work executed by or any materials or goods supplied by the Nominated Sub-Contractor whose employment has been determined which were not in accordance with the relevant Nominated Sub-Contract.

35·24 ·8 ·1 Where **clause 35·24·3 applies** the Architect shall make such further nomination of a sub-contractor in accordance with clause 35 as may be necessary to supply and fix the materials or goods or to execute the work and to make good or re-supply or re-execute as necessary any work executed by or any materials or goods supplied by the Nominated Sub-Contractor who has determined his employment which were not in accordance with the relevant Nominated Sub-Contract.

·8 ·2 Where **clause 35·24·5 applies** the Architect shall make such further nomination of a sub-contractor in accordance with clause 35 as may be necessary to carry out the work to be re-executed referred to in clause 35·24·5.

35·24 ·9 The amount properly payable to the Nominated Sub-Contractor under the Nominated Sub-Contract resulting from such further nomination under clause 35·24·6·3 or 35·24·7·3 or 35·24·7·4 shall be included in the amount stated as due in Interim Certificates and added to the Contract Sum. Where clauses 35·24·3 and 35·24·8·1 apply any extra amount, payable by the Employer in respect of the sub-contractor nominated under the further nomination over the price of the Nominated Sub-Contractor who has validly determined his employment under his Nominated Sub-Contract, and where clauses 35·24·5 and 35·24·8·2 apply the amount payable by the Employer, resulting from such further nomination may at the time or any time after such amount is certified in respect of the sub-contractor nominated under the further nomination be deducted by the Employer from monies due or to become due to the Contractor under this Contract or may be recoverable from the Contractor by the Employer as a debt.

35·24 ·10 The Architect shall make the further nomination of a sub-contractor as referred to in clauses 35·24·6·3, 35·24·7, 35·24·8·1 and 35·24·8·2 within a reasonable time, having regard to all the circumstances, after the obligation to make such further nomination has arisen.

DETERMINATION OR DETERMINATION OF EMPLOYMENT OF NOMINATED SUB-CONTRACTOR – ARCHITECT'S INSTRUCTIONS

35·25 The Contractor shall not determine any Nominated Sub-Contract by virtue of any right to which he may be or may become entitled without an instruction from the Architect so to do.

35·26 **·1**   Where the employment of the Nominated Sub-Contractor is determined under clauses 7·1 to 7·5 of Conditions NSC/C *(Conditions of Nominated Sub-Contract)* the Architect shall provide the Contractor with the information and with the direction in an Interim Certificate to enable the Contractor to comply with clause 7·5·2 of Conditions NSC/C: namely the amount of expenses properly incurred by the Employer and the amount of direct loss and/or damage caused to the Employer by the determination of the employment of the Nominated Sub-Contractor; and shall, pursuant to clause 35·13·1, issue an Interim Certificate which certifies the value of any work executed or goods and materials supplied by the Nominated Sub-Contractor to the extent that such value has not been included in previous Interim Certificates.

35·26 **·2**   Where the employment of the Nominated Sub-Contractor is determined under clause 7·7 of Conditions NSC/C *(Conditions of Nominated Sub-Contract)* and clause 7·8 of those Conditions applies, the Architect shall, pursuant to clause 35·13·1, issue an Interim Certificate which certifies the value of any work executed or goods and materials supplied by the Nominated Sub-Contractor to the extent that such value has not been included in previous Interim Certificates.

6. By naming a sub-contractor in a similar instruction.
7. By the use of a prime cost sum by agreement with the contractor.
8. By naming a sub-contractor by agreement with the contractor.

36.04 Under Clause 35.2 the architect has a discretion to allow the contractor to tender for work which it is proposed should be carried out by a nominated Sub-contractor if 'in the ordinary course of his business' he 'directly carries out works' of the type in question.

Procedure

36.05 Since Amendment 10: 1991 there has only been one procedure for nomination of a sub-contractor, which is as follows:

36.06 The architect sends to all sub-contractors whom he wishes to invite to tender a completed form NSC/T Part 1 (Invitation to Tender), the numbered tender documents, a copy of the Appendix to the main contract as completed and a Form NSC/W (Employer/ Nominated Sub-contractor Agreement).

36.07 The sub-contractor submits a tender on Form NSC/T Part 2 and returns the executed NSC/W.

36.08 The architect decides which of the tenderers he proposes to nominate and the employer executes the relevant NSC/W and signs as approved the relevant NSC/T Part 2. The architect then issues an instruction to the contractor on NSC/N, the nomination instruction, enclosing with it copies of NSC/T Parts 1 and 2, the numbered tender documents and NSC/W. The architect must also send a copy of NSC/N to the successful tenderer.

Contractor's right of objection

36.09 The contractor then has a right of 'reasonable objection' to any proposed Nominated Sub-contractor under Clause 35.5.1. The Contractor should not be allowed to use this right so as to endeavour to place himself in a better position for tendering for the work himself under Clause 35.2.

Completion of Agreement

36.10 If the contractor does not object, the Contractor must complete in agreement with the Nominated Sub-contractor NSC/T Part 3, and must execute NSC/A with the sub-contractor within 10 working days of receipt of NSC/N and send a copy of each to the Architect.

Payment of nominated sub-contractor

36.11 Under Clause 35.13.3, the contractor is obliged to provide the architect with reasonable proof that sums previously certified to the nominated sub-contractor have been paid to him before the issue of the next interim certificate; failure to provide such proof entitles the employer to make direct payment to the sub-contractor of an amount which the contractor has failed to pass on to the

nominated sub-contractor. Before the employer does this, however, the architect is obliged to issue a certificate under Clause 35.13.5.1 stating the amount in respect of which the contractor has failed to provide proof of payment to the nominated sub-contractor. This amount is then deducted from money which would otherwise be due to the contractor and paid direct to the nominated sub-contractor (Clause 35.13.5.2). The detailed machinery for operating Clause 35.13.5.2 is set out in Clause 35.13.5.3.

Architects should ensure that:

1. Nominated sub-contractors are informed of the amount shown as due to them in interim certificates issued to the contractor.
2. Proof is required from the contractor that nominated sub-contractors have been paid sums previously shown as due to them in interim certificates before issuing a new certificate.
3. If necessary, Clause 35.13.5.2 is operated and direct payment made to the nominated sub-contractors concerned.

36.12 Under Clause 35.13.4, the contractor is relieved from the obligation to furnish reasonable proof of payment if this is due to some failure or omission of the nominated sub-contractor.

36.13 Under Clause 35.13.5.3.4, the right to make direct payments ceases on the bankruptcy or liquidation of the contractor.

Extensions of time

36.14 Extensions of time for the sub-contract works can only be granted with the consent of the architect under the relevant terms of NSC/C. Clause 35.14.1 makes it clear that the contractor cannot give an extension of time to the sub-contractor on his own without the architect's consent. Under Clause 35.14.2, the architect is obliged to operate the relevant provisions of NSC/C upon receipt of any notice, particulars, estimate and request for extension of time from the contractor or sub-contractor.

Failure to complete nominated sub-contract works

36.15 If the nominated sub-contractor fails to complete the sub-contract works within the sub-contract period or any extended time granted by the contractor with the architect's consent and the architect is satisfied that Clause 35.14 has been properly applied, then the architect must certify this to the contractor (see Clause 35.15.1). This certificate is important since under NSC/C, the contractor will be entitled to damages equivalent to any loss or damage suffered by him as a result of the sub-contractor's failure to complete. It is a condition precedent to the right under NSC/ C that a certificate is issued under this clause of the main contract (see *Brightside Kilpatrick Engineering* v *Mitchell Construction (1973) Limited* [1975] 2 Lloyd's Reports 493).

Practical completion of nominated sub-contract works

36.16 Each nominated sub-contract is the subject of a separate certificate of practical completion under Clause 35.16. The issue of this certificate brings into operation the machinery for:

Final payment of nominated sub-contractors

36.17 Where a certificate of practical completion of nominated sub-contract works has been issued, the architect may (and must within 12 months) issue an interim certificate including the amount of the relevant sub-contract sum or ascertained final sub-contract sum as finally adjusted under the relevant provisions of the nominated sub-contract, provided that the sub-contractor has made good defects and provided all documents necessary for the final adjustment of the sub-contract sum to take place (see Clause 35.17).

36.18 This procedure is conditional on Clause 5 of Agreement NSC/W (Employer/ Nominated Sub-contractor Agreement) remaining in force unamended. This clause imposes on the nominated sub-contractor an obligation to indemnify the employer against any failure by the nominated sub-contractor to remedy defects which occur between the final payment to the nominated sub-contractor and the issue of the final certificate relating to the work as a whole, and thus protects the employer's rights in the event of the nominated sub-contractor failing to remedy such defects.

36.19 By Clause 35.18 if the nominated sub-contractor fails to remedy such defects, the architect must issue an instruction nominating a substituted sub-contractor to make them good. This substituted sub-contractor is to be regarded as a nominated sub-contractor.

36.20 The primary liability for defective work, including defective work carried out by nominated sub-contractors, rests with the contractor, but the effect of these provisions is that the employer agrees with the contractor first to seek to pursue his remedies against the nominated sub-contractor under NSC/W in respect of the failure to make good the defects. Thereafter, the employer is entitled to look to the contractor for reimbursement, provided the contractor has agreed (which agreement is not to be unreasonably withheld) to the sub-contract prices charged by the substituted sub-contractor.

36.21 Under Clause 35.19, notwithstanding any final payment to a nominated sub-contractor, the contractor remains responsible for loss or damage to the sub-contract works until practical completion to the same extent as he was responsible before the payment was made. JCT Practice Note 12 deals with direct payment and final payment to nominated sub-contractors.

Renomination

36.22 Under Clause 27 of the 1963 JCT Form it was held that where a nominated sub-contractor failed to complete his work the employer was under a duty to nominate a new nominated sub-contractor (see *North West Metropolitan Hospital Board* v *T A Bickerton & Son Limited* [1970] 1 WLR 607). Another case under JCT 63 (*Fairclough Building Limited* v *Rhuddlan Borough Council* (1985) 30 BLR 26, CA), established that the duty extended to a duty to nominate a new nominated sub-contractor to carry out any necessary remedial work to the sub-contract works. The contractor is entitled to an extension of time if the renomination does not match the original programme. This remains the position under the 1980 JCT Form.

The duty to renominate may arise in five circumstances:

1. Where the architect is reasonably of the opinion that the sub-contractor has made default, following the contractor informing him that in the contractor's opinion the nominated sub-contractor has made default in respect of any one or more of the matters referred to in Clauses 7.1.1.1–4 of NSC/C and passing on to the architect any observations of the sub-contractor in regard to the matters in question.
2. Where one of the insolvency events in Clause 7.2.1 of NSC/C has happened to the nominated sub-contractor (Clause 35.24.2).
3. Where the nominated sub-contractor has determined his employment under Clause 7.7 of NSC/C.
4. Where the contractor has been required by the employer to determine the employment of the sub-contractor under Clause 7.3 of NSC/C and has done so.
5. Where work, etc. properly executed has to be re-executed as a result of compliance with an instruction by the architect under Clause 7, 8.4, 17.2 or 17.3 and the nominated sub-contractor cannot be required to carry out the work under the sub-contract and does not agree to do so.

36.23 Where 1 above applies, prior to determination, provision is made by Clause 35.24.6 for the following procedure to be adopted: the architect first instructs the contractor to give a notice to the sub-contractor specifying the default. The architect may instruct the contractor to include in that notice a statement that the contractor requires a further instruction of the architect before determining the sub-contractor's employment. Then the contractor informs the architect whether he has determined the sub-contractor's employ-

ment; where the further instruction from the architect is required and has been given, the contractor is to confirm that the employment of the sub-contractor has been determined. Thereafter, the architect is obliged to nominate a new sub-contractor. Where the sub-contractor's employment has been determined for failure to remove defective work or to remedy defects, the contractor is to be given the opportunity to agree a price to be charged by the substituted sub-contractor.

36.24 The contractor is not entitled to determine a nominated sub-contractor's employment under Clause 35.24.1 for default without an architect's instruction, and the procedure for determining a nominated sub-contractor's employment is as laid down in Clause 35.24. Architects must be careful to ensure that where it is sought to determine the sub-contractor's employment under Clause 35.24.1, they fully investigate the circumstances before issuing an instruction to determine the sub-contractor's employment. In particular, they must ensure that they receive all representations which the sub-contractor wishes to make as to his alleged default. Where the sub-contractor's employment is determined, the architect must make clear to the contractor which amounts included in the amount stated as due in an interim certificate are due in respect of the value of work executed or materials or goods supplied by the nominated sub-contractor.

36.25 Clause 7.5.2 of NSC/C entitles the architect to certify in respect of the amount of expenses properly incurred by the employer and the amount of direct loss and/or damage caused to the employer by the determination of the sub-contract. When the sub-contractor's employment is determined, the employer is entitled to deduct from sums otherwise payable to the sub-contractor the amount of any damage suffered by him. The contractor is obliged by this provision to give effect to this deduction.

36.26 Where 2 above applies, the architect is obliged to nominate a new sub-contractor only if he consents to the determination of the employment of the insolvent nominated sub-contractor. Clause 35.24.7 provides for circumstances in which the architect's consent may be withheld and the option to determine the contract consequently not exercised. This clearly may be advantageous in some circumstances.

36.27 Where 3 above applies, the architect is to nominate a new sub-contractor, but the extra cost of employing the new sub-contractor is to be deducted from money otherwise payable to the contractor.

37 Clause 36: Nominated suppliers

37.01 There are four ways in which a supplier may be nominated, as set out in Clauses 36.1.1.1–4. The first three (Clauses 36.1.1.1–3) all have as their hallmark the inclusion of a prime cost or provisional sum in the bills. The fourth, contained in Clause 36.1.1.4, deals with the situation where a variation occurs and the architect specifies materials or goods for which there is a sole supplier, in which case those goods are to be made the subject of a prime cost sum, and the sole supplier is deemed to have been nominated as a nominated supplier by the architect. Clause 36.1.2 makes it clear that apart from this situation, no nominated supplier situation arises unless goods are the subject of a prime cost sum, even though there is a 'sole supplier' as defined by Clause 36.1.1.3.

Clause 36.1.1.3: Sole supplier

37.02 The meaning of these words is unclear: if there is only one supplier of the goods in the whole country, clearly that would constitute a sole supplier, but where there is more than one, it would presumably be a question of fact and degree as to whether the contractor could obtain the material in question from only one of those suppliers. The number of suppliers and their physical proximity to the work would be factors in deciding whether there is a sole supplier.

37.03 Clause 36.3 lays down rules for ascertaining the amount to be set against prime cost sums in respect of nominated suppliers' materials. In addition, under Clause 36.3.2, the contractor is entitled to recover expenses properly incurred and which he would not have incurred had he not obtained the materials or goods from the nominated supplier. This would include, for example, extra travelling costs in the case where a supplier is nominated whose distance from the works was more than an alternative source of supply of the same or similar materials.

Terms of nominated supplier's contracts

37.04 Under Clause 36.4, the architect is not (save by agreement with the contractor) to nominate a supplier whose terms of sale do not conform to certain criteria. These cover such matters as standard of materials, replacement of defective materials, delivery times, discount, passing of property on delivery, and submission to the arbitration provisions in Article 5 of the contract.

Contractor's liability for goods supplied by nominated supplier

37.05 Nomination itself ordinarily shows that there has been no reliance on the contractor's skill and judgement so that the contractor is not liable if the goods of the nominated supplier of good quality are unfit for their intended purpose. Clause 36.5.1 expressly exempts the contractor from liability to the employer in respect of defects in goods supplied by a nominated supplier to the extent that the contract between the contractor and the nominated supplier contains similar exemptions, provided that the exemptions have been specifically approved by the architect. Even without such a provision it is unlikely that the contractor would be held responsible to the employer if the goods supplied by the nominated supplier failed to answer to their purpose (see *Young and Marten* v *McManus Childs*, [1968] 2 All ER 1181). The employer's interests vis-à-vis the nominated supplier are to be protected by the direct warranty Tender TNS/1. It is therefore of the utmost importance that the architect should ensure that this form of direct warranty is entered into in all cases where nominated suppliers are involved.

Part 3 Conditions: Fluctuations

38 Clauses 37 to 40

38.01 Clause 37.1 identifies three different bases, namely those set out in Clauses 38, 39, and 40, by reference to which fluctuations are to be calculated. Clause 37.2 provides that Clause 38 shall apply where neither Clause 39 nor 40 is identified in the Appendix.

Nominated Suppliers

36·1 ·1 In the Conditions 'Nominated Supplier' means a supplier to the Contractor who is nominated by the Architect in one of the following ways to supply materials or goods which are to be fixed by the Contractor:

·1 ·1 where a prime cost sum is included in the Contract Bills in respect of those materials or goods and the supplier is either named in the Contract Bills or subsequently named by the Architect in an instruction issued under clause 36·2;

·1 ·2 where a provisional sum is included in the Contract Bills and in any instruction by the Architect in regard to the expenditure of such sum the supply of materials or goods is made the subject of a prime cost sum and the supplier is named by the Architect in that instruction or in an instruction issued under clause 36·2;

·1 ·3 where a provisional sum is included in the Contract Bills and in any instruction by the Architect in regard to the expenditure of such a sum materials or goods are specified for which there is a sole source of supply in that there is only one supplier from whom the Contractor can obtain them, in which case the supply of materials or goods shall be made the subject of a prime cost sum in the instructions issued by the Architect in regard to the expenditure of the provisional sum and the sole supplier shall be deemed to have been nominated by the Architect;

·1 ·4 where the Architect requires under clause 13·2, or subsequently sanctions, a Variation and specifies materials or goods for which there is

---

a sole supplier as referred to in clause 36·1·1·3, in which case the supply of the materials or goods shall be made the subject of a prime cost sum in the instruction or written sanction issued by the Architect under clause 13·2 and the sole supplier shall be deemed to have been nominated by the Architect.

36·1 ·2 In the Conditions the expression 'Nominated Supplier' shall not apply to a supplier of materials or goods which are specified in the Contract Bills to be fixed by the Contractor unless such materials or goods are the subject of a prime cost sum in the Contract Bills, notwithstanding that the supplier has been named in the Contract Bills or that there is a sole supplier of such materials or goods as defined in clause 36·1·1·3.

36·2 The Architect shall issue instructions for the purpose of nominating a supplier for any materials or goods in respect of which a prime cost sum is included in the Contract Bills or arises under clause 36·1.

36·3 ·1 For the purposes of clause 30·6·2·8 the amounts 'properly chargeable to the Employer in accordance with the nomination instruction of the Architect' shall include the total amount paid or payable in respect of the materials or goods less any discount other than the discount referred to in clause 36·4·4, properly so chargeable to the Employer and shall include where applicable:

·1 ·1 any tax (other than any value added tax which is treated, or is capable of being treated, as input tax (as referred to in the Finance Act 1972) by the Contractor) or duty not otherwise recoverable under this Contract by whomsoever payable under or by virtue of any Act of Parliament on the import, purchase, sale, appropriation, processing, alteration, adapting for sale or use of the materials or goods to be supplied; and

·1 ·2 the net cost of appropriate packing, carriage and delivery after allowing for any credit for return of any packing to the supplier; and

·1 ·3 the amount of any price adjustment properly paid or payable to, or allowed or allowable by, the supplier less any discount other than a cash discount for payment in full within 30 days of the end of the month during which delivery is made.

36·3 ·2 Where in the opinion of the Architect the Contractor properly incurs expense, which would not be reimbursed under clause 36·3·1 or otherwise under this Contract, in obtaining the materials or goods from the Nominated Supplier such expense shall be added to the Contract Sum.

36·4 Save where the Architect and the Contractor shall otherwise agree, the Architect shall only nominate as a supplier a person who will enter into a contract of sale with the Contractor which provides, inter alia:

36·4 ·1 that the materials or goods to be supplied shall be of the quality and standard specified provided that where and to the extent that approval of the quality of materials or of the standards of workmanship is a matter for the opinion of the Architect such quality and standards shall be to the reasonable satisfaction of the Architect;

36·4 ·2 that the Nominated Supplier shall make good by replacement or otherwise any defects in the materials or goods supplied which appear up to and including the last day of the Defects Liability Period under this Contract and shall bear any expenses reasonably incurred by the Contractor as a direct consequence of such defects provided that:

·2 ·1 where the materials or goods have been used or fixed such defects are not such that reasonable examination by the Contractor ought to have revealed them before using or fixing;

·2 ·2 such defects are due solely to defective workmanship or material in the materials or goods supplied and shall not have been caused by improper storage by the Contractor or by misuse or by any act or neglect of either the Contractor, the Architect or the Employer or by any person or persons for whom they may be responsible or by any other person for whom the Nominated Supplier is not responsible;

36·4 ·3 that delivery of the materials or goods supplied shall be commenced, carried out and completed in accordance with a delivery programme to be agreed between the Contractor and the Nominated Supplier including, to the extent agreed, the following grounds on which that programme may be varied:

force majeure; or

civil commotion, local combination of workmen, strike or lock-out; or

any instruction of the Architect under clause 13·2 *(Variations)* or clause 13·3 *(provisional sums)*; or

failure of the Architect to supply to the Nominated Supplier within due time any necessary information for which he has specifically applied in writing on a date which was neither unreasonably distant from nor unreasonably close to the date on which it was necessary for him to receive the same; or

exceptionally adverse weather conditions

or, if no such programme is agreed, delivery shall be commenced, carried out and completed in accordance with the reasonable directions of the Contractor;

36·4 ·4 that the Nominated Supplier shall allow the Contractor a discount for cash of 5 per cent on all payments if the Contractor makes payment in full within 30 days of the end of the month during which delivery is made;

36·4 ·5 that the Nominated Supplier shall not be obliged to make any delivery of materials or goods (except any which may have been paid for in full less only a discount for cash) after the determination (for any reason) of the Contractor's employment under this Contract;

36·4 ·6 that full discharge by the Contractor in respect of payments for materials or goods supplied by the Nominated Supplier shall be effected within 30 days of the end of the month during which delivery is made less only a discount for cash of 5 per cent if so paid;

36·4 ·7 that the ownership of materials or goods shall pass to the Contractor upon delivery by the Nominated Supplier to or to the order of the Contractor, whether or not payment has been made in full;

36·4 ·8 ·1 that in any dispute or difference between the Contractor and the Nominated Supplier which is referred to arbitration the Contractor and the Nominated Supplier agree and consent pursuant to Sections 1(3)(a) and 2(1)(b) of the Arbitration Act 1979 that either the Contractor or the Nominated Supplier

– may appeal to the High Court on any question of law arising out of an award made in the arbitration and

– may apply to the High Court to determine any question of law arising in the course of the arbitration;

and that the Contractor and the Nominated Supplier agree that the High Court should have jurisdiction to determine any such questions of law;

·8 ·2 that if any dispute or difference between the Contractor and the Nominated Supplier raises issues which are substantially the same as or are connected with issues raised in a related dispute between the Employer and the Contractor under this Contract then, where clauses 41·2·1 and 41·2·2 apply, such dispute or difference shall be referred to the Arbitrator to be appointed pursuant to clause 41; that the Arbitrator shall have power to make such directions and all necessary awards in the same way as if the procedure of the High Court as to joining one or more defendants or joining co-defendants or third parties was available to the parties; that the agreement and consent referred to in clause 36·4·8·1 on appeals or applications to the High Court on any question of law shall apply to any question of law arising out of the awards of such arbitrator in respect of all related disputes referred to him or arising in the course of the reference of all the related disputes referred to him; and that in any case, subject to the agreement referred to in clause 36·4·8·1, the award of such Arbitrator shall be final and binding on the parties;

36·4 ·9 that no provision in the contract of sale shall override, modify or affect in any way whatsoever the provisions in the contract of sale which are included therein to give effect to clauses 36·4·1 to 36·4·9 inclusive.

36·5 ·1 Subject to clauses 36·5·2 and 36·5·3, where the said contract of sale between the Contractor and the Nominated Supplier in any way restricts, limits or excludes the liability of the Nominated Supplier to the Contractor in respect of materials or goods supplied or to be supplied, and the Architect has specifically approved in writing the said restrictions, limitations or exclusions, the liability of the Contractor to the Employer in respect of the said materials or goods shall be restricted, limited or excluded to the same extent.

36·5 ·2 The Contractor shall not be obliged to enter into a contract with the Nominated Supplier until the Architect has specifically approved in writing the said restrictions, limitations or exclusions.

36·5 ·3 Nothing in clause 36·5 shall be construed as enabling the Architect to nominate a supplier otherwise than in accordance with the provisions stated in clause 36·4.

Part 3: Fluctuations

37 ·1 Fluctuations shall be dealt with in accordance with whichever of the following alternatives[w]
clauses 38; or
clause 39; or
clause 40[y]
is identified in the Appendix. The provisions so identified shall be [x] deemed to be incorporated with the Conditions as executed by the parties hereto.

37 ·2 Clauses 38 shall apply where neither clause 39 nor clause 40 is identified in the Appendix.

37 ·3 Neither clause 38 nor clause 39 nor clause 40 shall apply in respect of the work for which the Architect has issued to the Contractor a confirmed acceptance of a 13A Quotation or in respect of a Variation to such work.

38.02 Clause 38 allows fluctuations in prices arising from changes in the matters specified in Clause 38.1.1, namely rates of contribution, levy, or tax payable by the contractor. These cover such matters as national insurance contributions. VAT is dealt with specifically by the VAT agreement and is not within Clause 38. Apart from changes in tax rates, no other price changes are taken into account where the parties contract on the basis that fluctuations are to be governed by Clause 38.

38.03 Clause 39 and Clause 40 both provide for what are known as 'full' fluctuations entitling the contractor to recover extra costs of labour and materials as from a date specified in the contract. The system under Clause 39 is as follows:

38.04 In respect of labour costs, extra costs as a result of awards by the National Joint Council for the Building Industry are recoverable – this also applies to reimbursement of travelling charges (see Clause 39.1.5).

Clause 38 – For use with the Private Edition With Quantities

38 Contribution, levy and tax fluctuations

38·1 The Contract Sum shall be deemed to have been calculated in the manner set out below and shall be subject to adjustment in the events specified hereunder:

38·1 ·1 The prices contained in the Contract Bills are based upon the types and rates of contribution, levy and tax payable by a person in his capacity as an employer and which at the Base Date are payable by the Contractor. A type and rate so payable are in clause 38·1·1 referred to as a 'tender type' and a 'tender rate'.

38·1 ·2 If any of the tender rates other than a rate of levy payable by virtue of the Industrial Training Act 1964 is increased or decreased or if a tender type ceases to be payable or if a new type of contribution, levy or tax which is payable by a person in his capacity as an employer becomes payable after the Base Date, then in any such case the net amount of the difference between what the Contractor actually pays or will pay in respect of

·2 ·1 workpeople engaged upon or in connection with the Works either on or adjacent to the site, and

·2 ·2 workpeople directly employed by the Contractor who are engaged upon the production of materials or goods for use in or in connection with the Works and who operate neither on nor adjacent to the site and to the extent that they are so engaged

or because of his employment of such workpeople and what he would have paid had the alteration, cessation or new type of contribution, levy or tax not become effective, shall, as the case may be, be paid to or allowed by the Contractor.

38·1 ·3 There shall be added, to the net amount paid to or allowed by the Contractor under clause 38·1·2, in respect of each person employed by the Contractor who is engaged upon or in connection with the Works either on or adjacent to the site and who is not within the definition of 'workpeople' in clause 38·6·3 the same amount as is payable or allowable in respect of a craftsman under clause 38·1·2 or such proportion of that amount as reflects the time (measured in whole working days) that each such person is so employed.

38·1 ·4 For the purposes of clause 38·1·3:

no period less than 2 whole working days in any week shall be taken into account and periods less than a whole working day shall not be aggregated to amount to a whole working day;

the phrase 'the same amount as is payable or allowable in respect of a craftsman' shall refer to the amount in respect of a craftsman employed by the Contractor or by any Domestic Sub-Contractor under a sub-contract to which clause 38·3 refers) under the rules or decisions or agreements of the National Joint Council for the Building Industry or other wage-fixing body and, where the aforesaid rules or decisions or agreements provide for more than one rate of wage emolument or other expense for a craftsman, shall refer to the amount in respect of a craftsman employed as aforesaid to whom the highest rate is applicable; and

the phrase 'employed by the Contractor' shall mean an employment to which the Income Tax (Employment) Regulations 1973 (the PAYE Regulations) under S·204 of the Income and Corporation Taxes Act 1970, apply.

38·1 ·5 The prices contained in the Contract Bills are based upon the types and rates of refund of the contributions, levies and taxes payable by a person in his capacity as an employer and upon the types and rates of premium receivable by a person in his capacity as an employer being in each case types and rates which at the Base Date are receivable by the Contractor. Such a type and such a rate are in clause 38·1·6 referred to as a 'tender type' and a 'tender rate'.

38·1 ·6 If any of the tender rates is increased or decreased or if a tender type ceases to be payable or if a new type of refund of any contribution, levy or tax payable by a person in his capacity as an employer becomes receivable or if a new type of premium receivable by a person in his capacity as an employer becomes receivable after the Base Date, then in any such case the net amount of the difference between what the Contractor actually receives or will receive in respect of workpeople as referred to in clauses 38·1·2·1 and 38·1·2·2 or because of his employment of such workpeople and what he would have received had the alteration, cessation or new type of refund or premium not become effective, shall, as the case may be, be paid to or allowed by the Contractor.

38·1 ·7 The references in clauses 38·1·5 and 38·1·6 to premiums shall be construed as meaning all payments howsoever they are described which are made under or by virtue of an Act of Parliament to a person in his capacity as an employer and which affect the cost to an employer of having persons in his employment.

38·1 ·8 Where employer's contributions are payable by the Contractor in respect of workpeople as referred to in clauses 38·1·2·1 and 38·1·2·2 whose employment is contracted-out employment within the meaning of the Social Security Pensions Act 1975 the Contractor shall for the purpose of recovery or allowance under clause 38·1 be deemed to pay employer's contributions as if that employment were not contracted-out employment.

38·1 ·9 The reference in clause 38·1 to contributions, levies and taxes shall be construed as meaning all impositions payable by a person in his capacity as an employer howsoever they are described and whoever the recipient which are imposed under or by virtue of an Act of Parliament and which affect the cost to an employer of having persons in his employment.

38·2 The Contract Sum shall be deemed to have been calculated in the manner set out below and shall be subject to adjustment in the events specified hereunder:

38·2 ·1 The prices contained in the Contract Bills are based upon the types and rates of duty if any and tax if any (other than any value added tax which is treated, or is capable of being treated, as input tax (as referred to in the Finance Act 1972) by the Contractor) by whomsoever payable which at the Base Date are payable on the import, purchase, sale, appropriation, processing or use of the materials, goods, electricity and, where so specifically stated in the Contract Bills, fuels specified in a list submitted by the Contractor and attached to the Contract Bills under or by virtue of any Act of Parliament. A type and a rate so payable are in clause 38·2·2 referred to as a 'tender type' and a 'tender rate'.

38·2   **·2**   If in relation to any materials or goods specified as aforesaid, or any electricity or fuels specified as aforesaid and consumed on site for the execution of the Works including temporary site installations for those Works, a tender rate is increased or decreased or a tender type ceases to be payable or a new type of duty or tax (other than any value added tax which is treated, or is capable of being treated, as input tax as referred to in the Finance Act 1972) by the Contractor) becomes payable on the import, purchase, sale, appropriation, processing or use of those materials, goods, electricity or fuels after the Base Date; then in any such case the net amount of the difference between what the Contractor actually pays in respect of those materials, goods, electricity or fuels and what he would have paid in respect of them had the alteration, cessation or imposition not occurred, shall, as the case may be, be paid to or allowed by the Contractor. In clause 38·2·2 the expression 'a new type of duty or tax' includes an additional duty or tax and a duty or tax imposed in regard to specified materials, goods, electricity or fuels in respect of which no duty or tax whatever was previously payable (other than any value added tax which is treated, or is capable of being treated, as input tax (as referred to in the Finance Act 1972) by the Contractor).

38·3   **Fluctuations – work sub-let – Domestic Sub-Contractors**

38·3   **·1**   If the Contractor is obliged by clause 19·3, or shall decide subject to clause 19·2, to sublet any portion of the Works to a Domestic Sub-Contractor he shall incorporate in the sub-contract provisions to the like effect as the provisions of

clause 38 (excluding clause 38·3) including the percentage stated in the Appendix pursuant to clause 38·7

which are applicable for the purposes of this Contract.

38·3   **·2**   If the price payable under such a sub-contract as referred to in clause 38·3·1 is increased above or decreased below the price in such sub-contract by reason of the operation of the said incorporated provisions, then the net amount of such increase or decrease shall, as the case may be, be paid to or allowed by the Contractor under this Contract.

38·4 to ·6   **Provisions relating to clause 38**

38·4   **·1**   The Contractor shall give a written notice to the Architect of the occurrence of any of the events referred to in such of the following provisions as are applicable for the purposes of this Contract:

·1   ·1   clause 38·1·2;

·1   ·2   clause 38·1·6;

·1   ·3   clause 38·2·2;

·1   ·4   clause 38·3·2.

38·4   **·2**   Any notice required to be given under clause 38·4·1 shall be given within a reasonable time after the occurrence of the event to which the notice relates, and the giving of a written notice in that time shall be a condition precedent to any payment being made to the Contractor in respect of the event in question.

38·4   **·3**   The Quantity Surveyor and the Contractor may agree what shall be deemed for all the purposes of this Contract to be the net amount payable to or allowable by the Contractor in respect of the occurrence of any event such as is referred to in any of the provisions listed in clause 38·4·1.

38·4   **·4**   Any amount which from time to time becomes payable to or allowable by the Contractor by virtue of clauses 38·1 and ·2 or clause 38·3 shall, as the case may be, be added to or deducted from:

·4   ·1   the Contract Sum; and

·4   ·2   any amounts payable to the Contractor and which are calculated in accordance with either clauses 28·2·2·1 or 28·2·2·2.

The addition or deduction to which clause 38·4·4 refers shall be subject to the provisions of clauses 38·4·5 to ·4·7.

38·4   **·5**   As soon as is reasonably practicable the Contractor shall provide such evidence and computations as the Architect or the Quantity Surveyor may reasonably require to enable the amount payable to or allowable by the Contractor by virtue of clauses 38·1 and ·2 or clause 38·3 to be ascertained; and in the case of amounts payable to or allowable by the Contractor under clause 38·1·3 (or clause 38·3 for amounts payable to or allowable by the Domestic Sub-Contractor under provisions in the sub-contract to the like effect as clauses 38·1·3 and 38·1·4) – employees other than workpeople – such evidence shall include a certificate signed by or on behalf of the Contractor each week certifying the validity of the evidence reasonably required to ascertain such amounts.

38·4   **·6**   No addition to or deduction from the Contract Sum made by virtue of clause 38·4·4 shall alter in any way the amount of profit of the Contractor included in that Sum.

38·4   **·7**   Subject to the provisions of clause 38·4·8 no amount shall be added or deducted in the computation of the amount stated as due in an Interim Certificate or in the Final Certificate in respect of amounts otherwise payable to or allowable by the Contractor by virtue of clauses 38·1 and ·2 or clause 38·3 if the event (as referred to in the provisions listed in clause 38·4·1) in respect of which the payment or allowance would be made occurs after the Completion Date.

38·4   **·8**   Clause 38·4·7 shall not be applied unless:

·8   ·1   the printed text of clause 25 is unamended and forms part of the Conditions; and

·8   ·2   the Architect has, in respect of every written notification by the Contractor under clause 25, fixed or confirmed in writing such Completion Date as he considers to be in accordance with clause 25.

38·5   Clauses 38·1 to ·3 shall not apply in respect of:

38·5   **·1**   work for which the Contractor is allowed daywork rates under clause 13·5·4;

38·5   **·2**   work executed or materials or goods supplied by any Nominated Sub-Contractor or Nominated Supplier (fluctuations in relation to Nominated Sub-Contractors and Nominated Suppliers shall be dealt with under any provision in relation thereto which may be included in the appropriate sub-contract or contract of sale);

38·5   **·3**   work executed by the Contractor for which a tender made under clause 35·2 has been accepted (fluctuations in relation to such work shall be dealt with under any provision in the accepted tender of the Contractor);

38·5   **·4**   changes in the rate of value added tax charged on the supply of goods or services by the Contractor to the Employer under this Contract.

38·6   In clause 38:

38·6   **·1**   the expression the 'Base Date' means the Date stated in the Appendix;

38·6   **·2**   the expressions 'materials' and 'goods' include timber used in formwork but do not include other consumable stores, plant and machinery (save that electricity and, where specifically so stated in the Contract Bills, fuels are dealt with in clause 38·2);

38·6   **·3**   the expression 'workpeople' means persons whose rates of wages and other emoluments (including holiday credits) are governed by the rules or decisions or agreements of the National Joint Council for the Building Industry or some other wage-fixing body for trades associated with the building industry;

38·6   **·4**   the expression 'wage-fixing body' shall mean a body which lays down recognised terms and conditions of workers. For the purposes of clause 38 'recognised terms and conditions' means terms and conditions of workers in comparable employment in the trade or industry, or section of trade and industry, in which the employer in question is engaged, which have been settled by an agreement or award, to which the parties are employers' associations and independent trade unions which represent (generally, or in the district in question, as the case may be) a substantial proportion of the employers and of the workers in the trade, industry or section being workers of the description to which the agreement or award relates.

38·7   **Percentage addition to fluctuation payments or allowances**

38·7   **·1**   There shall be added to the amount paid to or allowed by the Contractor under:

·1   ·1   clause 38·1·2,

·1   ·2   clause 38·1·3,

·1   ·3   clause 38·1·6,

·1   ·4   clause 38·2·2

the percentage stated in the Appendix.

Clause 39 – For use with the Private Edition With Quantities

39   **Labour and materials cost and tax fluctuations**

39·1   The Contract Sum shall be deemed to have been calculated in the manner set out below and shall be subject to adjustment in the events specified hereunder:

39·1   **·1**   The prices (including the cost of employer's liability insurance and of third party insurance) contained in the Contract Bills are based upon the rates of wages and the other emoluments and expenses (including holiday credits) which will be payable by the Contractor to or in respect of

·1   ·1   workpeople engaged upon or in connection with the Works either on or adjacent to the site, and

·1   ·2   workpeople directly employed by the Contractor who are engaged upon the production of materials or goods for use in or in connection with the Works and who operate neither on nor adjacent to the site and to the extent that they are so engaged

in accordance with:

·1   ·3   the rules or decisions of the National Joint Council for the Building Industry or other wage-fixing body which will be applicable to the Works and which have been promulgated at the Base Date; and

·1   ·4   any incentive scheme and/or productivity agreement under the provisions of Rule 1·16 or any successor to this Rule (Productivity Incentive Schemes and/or Productivity Agreements) of the Rules of the National Joint Council for the Building Industry (including the General Principles covering Incentive Schemes and/or Productivity Agreements published by the aforesaid Council to which Rule 1·16 or any successor to this Rule refers) or provisions on incentive schemes and/or productivity agreements contained in the rules or decisions of some other wage-fixing body; and

·1   ·5   the terms of the Building and Civil Engineering Annual and Public Holidays Agreements (or the terms of agreements to similar effect in respect of workpeople whose rates of wages and other emoluments and expenses (including holiday credits) are in accordance with the rules or decisions of a wage-fixing body other than the National Joint Council for the Building Industry) which will be applicable to the Works and which have been promulgated at the Base Date;

and upon the rates or amounts of any contribution, levy or tax which will be payable by the Contractor in his capacity as an employer in respect of, or calculated by reference to, the rates of wages and other emoluments and expenses (including holiday credits) referred to herein.

39·1 ·2 If any of the said rates of wages or other emoluments and expenses (including holiday credits) are increased or decreased by reason of any alteration in the said rules, decisions or agreements promulgated after the Base Date, then the net amount of the increase or decrease in wages or other emoluments and expenses (including holiday credits) together with the net amount of any consequential increase or decrease in the cost of employer's liability insurance, of third party insurance, and of any contribution, levy or tax payable by a person in his capacity as an employer shall, as the case may be, be paid to or allowed by the Contractor.

39·1 ·3 There shall be added, to the net amount paid to or allowed by the Contractor under clause 39·1·2, in respect of each person employed by the Contractor who is engaged upon or in connection with the Works either on or adjacent to the site and who is not within the definition of 'workpeople' in clause 39·7·3 the same amount as is payable or allowable in respect of a craftsman under clause 39·1·2 or such proportion of that amount as reflects the time (measured in whole working days) that each such person is so employed.

39·1 ·4 For the purposes of clauses 39·1·3 and 39·2·3:

no period less than 2 whole days in any week shall be taken into account and periods less than a whole working day shall not be aggregated to amount to a whole working day;

the phrase 'the same amount as is payable or allowable in respect of a craftsman' shall refer to the amount in respect of a craftsman employed by the Contractor (or by any Domestic Sub-Contractor under a sub-contract to which clause 39·4 refers) under the rules or decisions or agreements of the National Joint Council for the Building Industry or other wage-fixing body and, where the aforesaid rules or decisions or agreements provide for more than one rate of wage, emolument or other expenses for a craftsman, shall refer to the amount in respect of a craftsman employed as aforesaid to whom the highest rate is applicable; and

the phrase 'employed by the Contractor' shall mean an employment to which the Income Tax (Employment) Regulations 1973 (the PAYE Regulations) under S·204 of the Income and Corporation Taxes Act 1970, apply.

39·1 ·5 The prices contained in the Contract Bills are based upon:

the transport charges referred to in a basic transport charges list submitted by the Contractor and attached to the Contract Bills and incurred by the Contractor in respect of workpeople engaged in either of the capacities referred to in clauses 39·1·1·1 and 39·1·1·2; or

the reimbursement of fares which will be reimbursable by the Contractor to workpeople engaged in either of the capacities referred to in clauses 39·1·1·1 and 39·1·1·2 in accordance with the rules or decisions of the National Joint Council for the Building Industry which will be applicable to the Works and which have been promulgated at the Base Date or, in the case of workpeople so engaged whose rates of wages and other emoluments and expenses are governed by the rules or decisions of some wage-fixing body other than the National Joint Council for the Building Industry, in accordance with the rules or decisions of such other body which will be applicable and which have been promulgated as aforesaid.

39·1 ·6 If:

·6 ·1 the amount of transport charges referred to in the basic transport charges list is increased or decreased after the Base Date; or

·6 ·2 the reimbursement of fares is increased or decreased by reason of any alteration in the said rules or decisions promulgated after the Base Date or by any actual increase or decrease in fares which takes effect after the Base Date,

then the net amount of that increase or decrease shall, as the case may be, be paid to or allowed by the Contractor.

39·2 The Contract Sum shall be deemed to have been calculated in the manner set out below and shall be subject to adjustment in the events specified hereunder:

39·2 ·1 The prices contained in the Contract Bills are based upon the types and rates of contribution, levy and tax payable by a person in his capacity as an employer and which at the Base Date are payable by the Contractor. A type and a rate so payable are in clause 39·2·2 referred to as a 'tender type' and a 'tender rate'.

39·2 ·2 If any of the tender rates other than a rate of levy payable by virtue of the Industrial Training Act 1964 is increased or decreased or if a tender type ceases to be payable or if a new type of contribution, levy or tax which is payable by a person in his capacity as an employer becomes payable after the Base Date, then in any such case the net amount of the difference between what the Contractor actually pays or will pay in respect of workpeople as referred to in clauses 39·1·1·1 and 39·1·1·2 or because of his employment of such workpeople and what he would have paid had the alteration, cessation or new type of contribution, levy or tax not become effective, shall, as the case may be, be paid to or allowed by the Contractor.

39·2 ·3 There shall be added, to the net amount paid to or allowed by the Contractor under clause 39·2·2, in respect of each person employed by the Contractor who is engaged upon or in connection with the Works either on or adjacent to the site and who is not within the definition of 'workpeople' in clause 39·7·3, the same amount as is payable or allowable in respect of a craftsman under clause 39·2·2 or such proportion of that amount as reflects the time (measured in whole working days) that each such person is so employed. The provisions of clause 39·1·4 shall apply to clause 39·2·3.

39·2 ·4 The prices contained in the Contract Bills are based upon the types and rates of refund of the contributions, levies and taxes payable by a person in his capacity as an employer and upon the types and rates of premium receivable by a person in his capacity as an employer being in each case types and rates which at the Base Date are receivable by the Contractor. Such a type and such a rate are in clause 39·2·5 referred to as a 'tender type' and a 'tender rate'.

39·2 ·5 If any of the tender rates is increased or decreased or if a tender type ceases to be payable or if a new type of refund of any contribution, levy or tax payable by a person in his capacity as an employer becomes receivable or if a new type of premium receivable by a person in his capacity as an employer becomes receivable after the Base Date, then in any such case the net amount of the difference between what the Contractor actually receives or will receive in respect of workpeople as referred to in clauses 39·1·1·1 and 39·1·1·2 or because of his employment of such workpeople, and what he would have received had the alteration, cessation or new type of refund or premium not become effective, shall, as the case may be, be paid to or allowed by the Contractor.

39·2 ·6 The reference in clauses 39·2·4 and 39·2·5 to premiums shall be construed as meaning all payments howsoever they are described which are made under or by virtue of an Act of Parliament to a person in his capacity as an employer and which affect the cost to an employer of having persons in his employment.

39·2 ·7 Where employer's contributions are payable by the Contractor in respect of workpeople as referred to in clauses 39·1·1·1 and 39·1·1·2 whose employment is contracted-out employment within the meaning of the Social Security Pensions Act 1975, the Contractor shall, subject to the proviso hereto, for the purpose of recovery or allowance under clause 39·2 be deemed to pay employer's contributions as if that employment were not contracted-out employment; provided that clause 39·2·7 shall not apply where the occupational pension scheme, by reference to membership of which the employment of workpeople is contracted-out employment, is established by the rules of the National Joint Council for the Building Industry or of some other wage-fixing body so that contributions to such occupational pension scheme are within the payment and allowance provisions of clause 39·1.

39·2 ·8 The reference in clauses 39·2·1 to 39·2·5 and 39·2·7 to contributions, levies and taxes shall be construed as meaning all impositions payable by a person in his capacity as an employer howsoever they are described and whoever the recipient which are imposed under or by virtue of an Act of Parliament and which affect the cost to an employer of having persons in his employment.

39·3 The Contract Sum shall be deemed to have been calculated in the manner set out below and shall be subject to adjustment in the events specified hereunder:

39·3 ·1 The prices contained in the Contract Bills are based upon the market prices of the materials, goods, electricity and, where specifically so stated in the Contract Bills, fuels, specified in a list submitted by the Contractor and attached to the Contract Bills, which were current at the Base Date. Such prices are hereinafter referred to as 'basic prices' and the prices set out by the Contractor on the said list shall be deemed to be the basic prices of the specified materials, goods, electricity and fuels.

39·3 ·2 If after the Base Date the market price of any of the materials or goods specified as aforesaid increases or decreases, or the market price of any electricity or fuels specified as aforesaid and consumed on site for the execution of the Works (including temporary site installations for those Works) increases or decreases, then the net amount of the difference between the basic price thereof and the market price payable by the Contractor and current when the materials, goods, electricity or fuels are bought shall, as the case may be, be paid to or allowed by the Contractor.

39·3 ·3 The references in clauses 39·3·1 and 39·3·2 to 'market prices' shall be construed as including any duty or tax (other than value added tax which is treated, or is capable of being treated as input tax (as referred to in the Finance Act 1972) by the Contractor) by whomsoever payable which is payable under or by virtue of any Act of Parliament on the import, purchase, sale, appropriation, processing or use of the materials, goods, electricity or fuels specified as aforesaid.

39·4 **Fluctuations – work sub-let – Domestic Sub-Contractors**

39·4 ·1 If the Contractor is obliged by clause 19·3, or shall decide subject to clause 19·2, to sub-let any portion of the Works to a Domestic Sub-Contractor he shall incorporate in the sub-contract provisions to the like effect as the provisions of

clause 39 (excluding clause 39·4) including the percentage stated in the Appendix pursuant to clause 39·8

which are applicable for the purposes of this Contract.

39·4 ·2 If the price payable under such a sub-contract as referred to in clause 39·4·1 is increased above or decreased below the price in such sub-contract by reason of the operation of the said incorporated provisions, then the net amount of such increase or decrease shall, as the case may be, be paid to or allowed by the Contractor under this Contract.

39·5 to ·7 **Provisions relating to clause 39**

39·5 ·1 The Contractor shall give a written notice to the Architect of the occurrence of any of the events referred to in such of the following provisions as are applicable for the purposes of this Contract:

·1 ·1 clause 39·1·2;

·1 ·2 clause 39·1·6;

·1 ·3 clause 39·2·2;

·1 ·4 clause 39·2·5;

·1 ·5 clause 39·3·2;

·1 ·6 clause 39·4·2.

39·5 ·2 Any notice required to be given by clause 39·5·1 shall be given within a reasonable time after the occurrence of the event to which the notice relates and the giving of written notice in that time shall be a condition precedent to any payment being made to the Contractor in respect of the event in question.

39·5 **·3** The Quantity Surveyor and the Contractor may agree what shall be deemed for all the purposes of this Contract to be the net amount payable to or allowable by the Contractor in respect of the occurrence of any event such as is referred to in any of the provisions listed in clause 39·5·1.

39·5 **·4** Any amount which from time to time becomes payable to or allowable by the Contractor by virtue of clause 39·1 to ·3 or clause 39·4 shall, as the case may be, be added to or deducted from:

 ·4 **·1** the Contract Sum; and

 ·4 **·2** any amounts payable to the Contractor and which are calculated in accordance with either clauses 28·2·2·1 or 28·2·2·2.

The addition or deduction to which clause 39·5·4 refers shall be subject to the provisions of clauses 39·5·5 to ·5·7.

39·5 **·5** As soon as is reasonably practicable the Contractor shall provide such evidence and computations as the Architect or the Quantity Surveyor may reasonably require to enable the amount payable to or allowable by the Contractor by virtue of clauses 39·1 to ·3 or clause 39·4 to be ascertained; and in the case of amounts payable to or allowable by the Contractor under clause 39·1·3 (or clause 39·4 for amounts payable to or allowable by the Domestic Sub-Contractor under provisions in the sub-contract to the like effect as clauses 39·1·3 and 39·1·4) – employees other than workpeople – such evidence shall include a certificate signed by or on behalf of the Contractor each week certifying the validity of the evidence reasonably required to ascertain such amounts.

39·5 **·6** No addition to or deduction from the Contract Sum made by virtue of clause 39·5·4 shall alter in any way the amount of profit of the Contractor included in that Sum.

39·5 **·7** Subject to the provisions of clause 39·5·8 no amount shall be added or deducted in the computation of the amount stated as due in an Interim Certificate or in the Final Certificate in respect of amounts otherwise payable to or allowable by the Contractor by virtue of clauses 39·1 to ·3 or clause 39·4 if the event (as referred to in the provisions listed in clause 39·5·1) in respect of which the payment or allowance would be made occurs after the Completion Date.

39·5 **·8** Clause 39·5·7 shall not be applied unless:

 ·8 **·1** the printed text of clause 25 is unamended and forms part of the Conditions; and

 ·8 **·2** the Architect has, in respect of every written notification by the Contractor under clause 25, fixed or confirmed in writing such Completion Date as he considers to be in accordance with clause 25.

39·6 Clauses 39·1 to ·4 shall not apply in respect of:

39·6 **·1** work for which the Contractor is allowed daywork rates under clause 13·5·4;

39·6 **·2** work executed or materials or goods supplied by any Nominated Sub-Contractor or Nominated Supplier (fluctuations in relation to Nominated Sub-Contractors and Nominated Suppliers shall be dealt with under any provision in relation thereto which may be included in the appropriate sub-contract or contract of sale);

39·6 **·3** work executed by the Contractor for which a tender made under clause 35·2 has been accepted (fluctuations in relation to such works shall be dealt with under any provision in the accepted tender of the Contractor);

39·6 **·4** changes in the rate of value added tax charged on the supply of goods or services by the Contractor to the Employer under this Contract.

39·7 In clause 39:

39·7 **·1** the expression the 'Base Date' means the Date stated in the Appendix;

39·7 **·2** the expressions 'materials' and 'goods' include timber used in formwork but do not include other consumable stores, plant and machinery (save that electricity and, where specifically so stated in the Contract Bills, fuels are dealt with in clause 39·3);

39·7 **·3** the expression 'workpeople' means persons whose rates of wages and other emoluments (including holiday credits) are governed by the rules or decisions or agreements of the National Joint Council for the Building Industry or some other wage-fixing body for trades associated with the building industry;

39·7 **·4** the expression 'wage-fixing body' shall mean a body which lays down recognised terms and conditions of workers. For the purposes of clause 39 'recognised terms and conditions' means terms and conditions of workers in comparable employment in the trade or industry, or section of trade and industry, in which the employer in question is engaged, which have been settled by an agreement or award, to which the parties are employers' associations and independent trade unions which represent (generally, or in the district in question, as the case may be) a substantial proportion of the employers and of the workers in the trade, industry or section being workers of the description to which the agreement or award relates.

39·8 **Percentage addition to fluctuation payments or allowances**

39·8 **·1** There shall be added to the amount paid to or allowed by the Contractor under:

 ·1 **·1** clause 39·1·2,

 ·1 **·2** clause 39·1·3,

 ·1 **·3** clause 39·1·6,

 ·1 **·4** clause 39·2·2,

 ·1 **·5** clause 39·2·5,

 ·1 **·6** clause 39·3·2

the percentage stated in the Appendix.

Clause 40 – For use with the Private Edition With Quantities

40 **Use of price adjustment formulae**

40·1 **·1** **·1** The Contract Sum shall be adjusted in accordance with the provisions of clause 40 and the Formula Rules current at the Base Date issued for use with clause 40 by the Joint Contracts Tribunal for the Standard Form of Building Contract (hereinafter called 'the Formula Rules').

 ·1 **·2** Any adjustment under clause 40 shall be to sums exclusive of value added tax and nothing in clause 40 shall affect in any way the operation of clause 15 and the VAT Agreement.

40·1 **·2** The Definitions in rule 3 of the Formula Rules shall apply to clause 40.

40·1 **·3** The adjustment referred to in clause 40 shall be effected in all certificates for payment issued under the provisions of the Conditions.

40·1 **·4** If any correction of amounts of adjustment under clause 40 included in previous certificates is required following any operation of rule 5 of the Formula Rules such correction shall be given effect in the next certificate for payment to be issued.

40·2 Interim valuations shall be made before the issue of each Interim Certificate and accordingly the words 'whenever the Architect considers them to be necessary' shall be deemed to have been deleted in clause 30·1·2.

40·3 For any article to which rule 4 (ii) of the Formula Rules applies the Contractor shall insert in a list attached to the Contract Bills the market price of the article in sterling (that is the price delivered to the site) current at the Base Date. If after that Date the market price of the article inserted in the aforesaid list increases or decreases then the net amount of the difference between the cost of purchasing at the market price inserted in the aforesaid list and the market price payable by the Contractor and current when the article is bought shall, as the case may be, be paid to or allowed by the Contractor. The reference to 'market price' in clause 40·3 shall be construed as including any duty or tax (other than any value added tax which is treated, or is capable of being treated, as input tax (as defined in the Finance Act 1972) by the Contractor) by whomsoever payable under or by virtue of any Act of Parliament on the import, purchase, sale, appropriation or use of the article specified as aforesaid.

40·4 [Number not used.]

40·5 The Quantity Surveyor and the Contractor may agree any alteration to the methods and procedures for ascertaining the amount of formula adjustment to be made under clause 40 and the amounts ascertained after the operation of such agreement shall be deemed for all the purposes of this Contract to be the amount of formula adjustment payable to or allowable by the Contractor in respect of the provisions of clause 40. Provided always:

40·5 **·1** that no alteration to the methods and procedures shall be agreed as aforesaid unless it is reasonably expected that the amount of formula adjustment so ascertained will be the same or approximately the same as that ascertained in accordance with Part I or Part II of Section 2 of the Formula Rules whichever Part is stated to be applicable in the Contract Bills; and

40·5 **·2** that any agreement under clause 40·5 shall not have any effect on the determination of any adjustment payable by the Contractor to any sub-contractor to whom clause 40·4 refers.

40·6 **·1** If at any time prior to the issue of the Final Certificate under clause 30·8 formula adjustment is not possible because of delay in, or cessation of, the publication of the Monthly Bulletins, adjustment of the Contract Sum shall be made in each Interim Certificate during such period of delay on a fair and reasonable basis.

40·6 **·2** If publication of the Monthly Bulletins is recommenced at any time prior to the issue of the Final Certificate under clause 30·8 the provisions of clause 40 and the Formula Rules shall apply for each Valuation Period as if no delay or cessation as aforesaid had occurred and the adjustment under clause 40 and the Formula Rules shall be substituted for any adjustment under clause 40·6·1.

40·6 **·3** During any period of delay or cessation as aforesaid the Contractor and Employer shall operate such parts of clause 40 and the Formula Rules as will enable the amount of formula adjustment due to be readily calculated upon recommencement of publication of the Monthly Bulletins.

40·7 **·1** **·1** If the Contractor fails to complete the Works by the Completion Date, formula adjustment of the Contract Sum under clause 40 shall be effected in all Interim Certificates issued after the aforesaid Completion Date by reference to the Index Numbers applicable to the Valuation Period in which the aforesaid Completion Date falls.

 ·1 **·2** If for any reason the adjustment included in the amount certified in any Interim Certificate which is or has been issued after the aforesaid Completion Date is not in accordance with clause 40·7·1·1, such adjustment shall be corrected to comply with that clause.

40·7 **·2** Clause 40·7·1 shall not be applied unless:

 ·2 **·1** the printed text of clause 25 is unamended and forms part of the Conditions; and

 ·2 **·2** the Architect has, in respect of every written notification by the Contractor under clause 25, fixed or confirmed in writing such Completion Date as he considers to be in accordance with clause 25.

38.05 Tax increases are recoverable under Clause 38. JCT Practice Note 17 gives guidance on the choice of fluctuations provisions. NJCC Procedure Note 7 contains information about Clauses 38.7 and 39.8.

38.06 Material increases are recoverable based on the increases over a price list to be submitted by the contractor and attached to the contract bills current at the date of tender. This forms a list of basic prices, and if an increase above the basic prices occurs, the contractor is entitled to reimbursement.

38.07 Under Clause 40, adjustment of prices takes place in accordance with the formula rules issued by the JCT, using those current at the date of tender. Monthly bulletins are issued by the JCT giving details of price changes, and the contract sum falls to be adjusted in accordance with these.

Fluctuations where contractor is guilty of delay

38.08 In principle, the contractor is not entitled to price increases under the fluctuations clauses where these price increases arise during a period after the contractual completion date: this provides an added incentive to the contractor to meet the completion date. This is subject, however, to no amendments having been made to Clause 25, and to the architect having, in respect of every written notification by the contractor under Clause 25, fixed or confirmed in writing a completion date in accordance with that clause (see Clause 38.4.8, Clause 39.5.8, and Clause 40.7.2). It is therefore incumbent on the architect to ensure that Clause 25 is properly administered, and that no amendments have been made to Clause 25, or alternatively that the appropriate parts of the fluctuations clauses are amended so as to delete the provision removing the 'freeze' on fluctuations if Clause 25 is amended.

38.09 In *J Murphy & Sons* v *Southwark London Borough Council* (1982) 22 BLR 41, CA, it was held that under the predecessor of what is now Clause 39 the contractor was not entitled to recover increases in rates of wages, etc., payable to work people who were self-employed, since their wages were not 'governed by' the rules or decisions or agreements of the National Joint Council for the Building Industry within what is now Clause 39.7.3. However, this anomaly has been rectified in the 1980 JCT Form by the wording of Clause 39.1.3.

Part 4 Conditions: Arbitration

39 Clause 41: Settlement of disputes – arbitration

39.01 Clause 41 provides the procedural rules governing a dispute referred to arbitration under Article 5. Clause 41.1 sets out the types of dispute which are intended to come within the operation of Article 5 and Clause 41 and provides that where the employer or the contractor requires such a dispute to be referred to arbitration he is to give written notice to the other. The parties must then agree on an arbitrator, or if they fail to do so within 14 days, the person named in the Appendix as appointer shall appoint an arbitrator.

Part 4: Settlement of disputes – Arbitration

41·1 When the Employer or the Contractor requires a dispute or difference as referred to in article 5 including:

 any matter or thing left by this Contract to the discretion of the Architect, or

 the withholding by the Architect of any certificate to which the Contractor may claim to be entitled, or

 the adjustment of the Contract Sum under clause 30·6·2, or

 the rights and liabilities of the parties under clauses 27 or 28, or

 unreasonable withholding of consent or agreement by the Employer or the Architect on his behalf or by the Contractor

to be referred to arbitration then either the Employer or the Contractor shall give written notice to the other to such effect and such dispute or difference shall be referred to the arbitration and final decision of a person to be agreed between the parties as the Arbitrator, or, upon failure so to agree within 14 days after the date of the aforesaid written notice, of a person to be appointed as the Arbitrator on the request of either the Employer or the Contractor by the person named in the Appendix.

41·2 ·1 Provided that if the dispute or difference to be referred to arbitration under this Contract raises issues which are substantially the same as or connected with issues raised in a related dispute between:

 the Employer and Nominated Sub-Contractor under Agreement NSC/W *(Employer/Nominated Sub-Contractor Agreement)*, or

 the Contractor and any Nominated Sub-Contractor under a Nominated Sub-Contract, or

 the Contractor and/or the Employer and any Nominated Supplier whose contract of sale with the Contractor provides for the matters referred to in clause 36·4·8·2,

and if the related dispute has already been referred for determination to an Arbitrator, the Employer and the Contractor hereby agree

 that the dispute or difference under this Contract shall be referred to the Arbitrator appointed to determine the related dispute;

 that the JCT Arbitration Rules applicable to the related dispute shall apply to the dispute under this Contract;

 that such Arbitrator shall have power to make such directions and all necessary awards in the same way as if the procedure of the High Court as to joining one or more defendants or joining co-defendants or third parties was available to the parties and to him; and

 that the agreement and consent referred to in clause 41·6 on appeals or applications to the High Court on any question of law shall apply to any question of law arising out of the awards of such Arbitrator in respect of all related disputes referred to him or arising in the course of the reference of all the related disputes referred to him;

41·2 ·2 save that the Employer or the Contractor may require the dispute or difference under this Contract to be referred to a different Arbitrator (to be appointed under this Contract) if either of them reasonably considers that the Arbitrator appointed to determine the related dispute is not appropriately qualified to determine the dispute or difference under this Contract.

41·2 ·3 Clauses 41·2·1 and 41·2·2 shall apply unless in the Appendix the words 'clauses 41·2·1 and 41·2·2 apply' have been deleted.

41·3 Such reference, except

 ·1 on article 3 or article 4; or

 ·2 on the questions

  whether or not the issue of an instruction is empowered by the Conditions; or
  whether or not a certificate has been improperly withheld; or
  whether a certificate is not in accordance with the Conditions; or
  whether a determination under clause 22C·4·3·1 will be just and equitable; or

 ·3 on any dispute or difference under clause 4·1 in regard to a reasonable objection by the Contractor, under clause 8·4, under clause 8·5, under clause 18·1 or under clause 23·3·2 in regard to withholding of consent by the Contractor, or under clause 25,

shall not be opened until after Practical Completion or alleged Practical Completion of the Works or termination or alleged termination of the Contractor's employment under this Contract or abandonment of the Works, unless with the written consent of the Employer or the Architect on his behalf and the Contractor.

41·4 Subject to the provisions of clauses 4·2, 30·9, 38·4·3, 39·5·3 and 40·5 the Arbitrator shall, without prejudice to the generality of his powers, have power to rectify this Contract so that it accurately reflects the true agreement made by the Employer and the Contractor, to direct such measurements and/or valuations as may in his opinion be desirable in order to determine the rights of the parties and to ascertain and award any sum which ought to have been the subject of or included in any certificate and to open up, review and revise any certificate, opinion, decision (except, where clause 8·4 is relevant, a decision of the Architect to issue instructions pursuant to clause 8·4·1), requirement or notice and to determine all matters in dispute which shall be submitted to him in the same manner as if no such certificate, opinion, decision, requirement or notice had been given.

41·5 Subject to clause 41·6 the award of such Arbitrator shall be final and binding on the parties.

41·6 The parties hereby agree and consent pursuant to Sections 1(3)(a) and 2(1)(b) of the Arbitration Act, 1979, that either party

 ·1 may appeal to the High Court on any question of law arising out of an award made in an arbitration under this Arbitration Agreement; and

 ·2 may apply to the High Court to determine any question of law arising in the course of the reference;

and the parties agree that the High Court should have jurisdiction to determine any such question of law.

41·7 Whatever the nationality, residence or domicile of the Employer, the Contractor, any sub-contractor or supplier or the Arbitrator, and wherever the Works or any part thereof are situated, the law of England shall be the proper law of this Contract and in particular (but not so as to derogate from the generality of the foregoing) the provisions of the Arbitration Acts 1950 (notwithstanding anything in S.34 thereof) to 1979 shall apply to any arbitration under this Contract wherever the same, or any part of it, shall be conducted. [y·2]

41·8 If before making his final award the Arbitrator dies or otherwise ceases to act as the Arbitrator, the Employer and the Contractor shall forthwith appoint a further Arbitrator, or, upon failure so to appoint within 14 days of any such death or cessation, then either the Employer or the Contractor may request the person named in the Appendix to appoint such further Arbitrator. Provided that no such further Arbitrator shall be entitled to disregard any direction of the previous Arbitrator or to vary or revise any award of the previous Arbitrator except to the extent that the previous Arbitrator had power so to do under the JCT Arbitration Rules and/or with the agreement of the parties and/or by the operation of law.

41·9 The arbitration shall be conducted in accordance with the JCT Arbitration Rules current at the Base Date. [y·3] Provided that if any amendments to the Rules so current have been issued by the Joint Contracts Tribunal after the Base Date the Employer and the Contractor may, by a joint notice in writing to the Arbitrator, state that they wish the arbitration to be conducted in accordance with the JCT Arbitration Rules as so amended.

'Third party' proceedings

39.02 Clause 41.2 provides a form of 'third party' procedure, similar to that possible in normal litigation. If a dispute or difference arises between the employer and the contractor and:

1. There has already been referred to arbitration a dispute between
   (a) the employer and a nominated sub-contractor; or
   (b) the contractor and any nominated sub-contractor; or
   (c) the contractor and/or the employer and any nominated supplier; and
2. The dispute which arises between the employer and the contractor raises issues which are substantially the same as or connected with issues raised in the existing arbitration,

then the matter is to be referred to the arbitrator dealing with the existing dispute, unless the saving in Clause 41.2.2 applies (arbitrator not appropriately qualified). The arbitrator is given powers equivalent to those of High Court procedures in relation to joining defendants or co-defendants and the issue of third-party proceedings.

Matters which may be opened during the currency of the works

39.03 Clause 41.3 governs the matters which may, having been referred to arbitration, be opened during the currency of the works. Other matters may not be opened unless both the employer or the architect on his behalf and the contractor give their consent in writing. Matters on which references may be open are:

1. References on Articles 3 or 4.
2. References on the questions:
   (a) whether or not the issue of an instruction is empowered by the conditions;
   (b) whether or not a certificate has been improperly withheld;
   (c) whether a certificate is not in accordance with the conditions;
   (d) whether a determination under Clause 22C.4.3.1 will be just and equitable.
3. Any dispute or difference under Clause 4.1 in regard to a reasonable objection by the contractor.
4. Any dispute under Clause 8.4 or 8.5.
5. Any dispute under Clause 18.1.
6. Any dispute under Clause 23.3.2 in regard to withholding of consent by the contractor.
7. Any dispute under Clause 25.

Powers of the arbitrator

39.04 The arbitrator may:

1. Rectify the contract.
2. Order measurements and valuations to help him determine the rights of the parties.
3. Ascertain and award any sums which should have been the subject of or included in any certificate.
4. Open up, review and revise any certificate, opinion, decision (except a decision of the architect to issue instructions pursuant to Clause 8.4.1, if applicable), requirement or notice.
5. Determine all matters in dispute as if no such certificate, opinion, decision, requirement or notice had been given.

39.05 The award of the arbitrator is final and binding on the parties (although it should be noted that, unlike a court judgment, it will only be binding on the parties to it), subject to rights of appeal on questions of law and applications for determination of questions of law under Sections 1(3)(a) and 2(1)(b) of the Arbitration Act 1979.

Part 5 Conditions: Performance specified work
40 Clause 42

40.01 This clause was introduced by Amendment 12: 1993. Practice Note 25 explains what is meant by performance specified work. Performance specified work must be identified as such in the Appendix, and will normally comprise materials and components or assemblies of a kind or standard to satisfy design requirements given in the tender documents for the contract, for example trussed rafters or precast concrete floor units. The provisions for performance specified work should not be used for items which will materially affect the appearance of the building or which may result in changes in the design of other work (except at the point of interface with the performance specified work), or which will affect the use of the finished building, so that it would be essential to examine and accept the contractor's proposals for the work before acceptance of the tender. Performance specified work may not be provided by a nominated sub-contractor or by a nominated supplier.

Part 5: Performance Specified Work [ee]

42·1 The term 'Performance Specified Work' means work:

42·1 ·1 identified in the Appendix, and

42·1 ·2 which is to be provided by the Contractor, and

42·1 ·3 for which certain requirements have been predetermined and are shown on the Contract Drawings, and

42·1 ·4 in respect of which the performance which the Employer requires from such work and which the Contractor, by this Contract and subject to the Conditions, is required to achieve has been stated in the Contract Bills and these Bills have included

either information relating thereto sufficient to have enabled the Contractor to price such Performance Specified Work

or a provisional sum in respect of the Performance Specified Work together with the information relating thereto as referred to in clause 42·7.

42·2 Before carrying out any Performance Specified Work, the Contractor shall provide the Architect with a document or set of documents, referred to in these Conditions as the 'Contractor's Statement'. Before so providing the Contractor shall have referred the draft of such Statement to the Planning Supervisor and shall have made such amendments, if any, as may have been necessary to take account of the comments of the Planning Supervisor. Subject to the Conditions the Contractor shall carry out the Performance Specified Work in accordance with that Statement.

42·3 The Contractor's Statement shall be sufficient in form and detail adequately to explain the Contractor's proposals for the execution of the Performance Specified Work. It shall include any information which is required to be included therein by the Contract Bills or, where there is a provisional sum for the Performance Specified Work, by the instruction of the Architect on the expenditure of that sum; and may include information in drawn or scheduled form and a statement of calculations.

42·4 The Contractor's Statement shall be provided to the Architect:

– by any date for its provision given in the Contract Bills or

– by any reasonable date for its provision given in the instruction by the Architect on the expenditure of a provisional sum for Performance Specified Work.

If no such date is given it shall be provided at a reasonable time before the Contractor intends to carry out the Performance Specified Work.

42·5 Within 14 days after receipt of the Contractor's Statement the Architect may, if he is of the opinion that such Statement is deficient in form and/or detail adequately to explain the Contractor's proposals for the execution of the Performance Specified Work, by notice in writing require the Contractor to amend such Statement so that it is in the opinion of the Architect not deficient. A copy of the Statement as so amended shall be provided to the Architect. Whether or not an amendment is required by the Architect, the Contractor is responsible in accordance with the Conditions for any deficiency in such Statement and for the Performance Specified Work to which such Statement refers.

42·6 If the Architect shall find anything in the Contractor's Statement which appears to the Architect to be a deficiency which would adversely affect the performance required by the Employer from the relevant Performance Specified Work, he shall immediately give notice to the Contractor specifying the deficiency. Whether or not a notice is given by the Architect, the Contractor is responsible in accordance with the Conditions for the Performance Specified Work.

42·7 A provisional sum for Performance Specified Work means a sum provided in the Contract Bills for Performance Specified Work where the following information has been provided in the Contract Bills:

42·7 ·1 the performance which the Employer requires from such work;

42·7 ·2 the location of such Performance Specified Work in the building;

42·7 ·3 information relating thereto sufficient to have enabled the Contractor to have made due allowance in programming for the execution of such Performance Specified Work and for pricing all preliminary items relevant to such Performance Specified Work.

42·8 No instruction of the Architect pursuant to clause 13·3·1 on the expenditure of provisional sums included in the Contract Bills shall require Performance Specified Work except an instruction on the expenditure of a provisional sum included in the Contract Bills for Performance Specified Work.

42·9 The inclusion of Performance Specified Work in the Contract Bills shall not be regarded as a departure from the method of preparation of these Bills referred to in clause 2·2·2·1.

42·10 If in the Contract Bills there is any error or omission in the information which, pursuant to clause 42·7·2 and/or 42·7·3, is to be included in the Contract Bills in respect of a provisional sum for Performance Specified Work such error or omission shall be corrected so that it does provide such information; and any such correction shall be treated as if it were a Variation required by an instruction of the Architect under clause 13·2.

42·11 Subject to clause 42·12 the Architect may issue instructions under clause 13·2 requiring a Variation to Performance Specified Work.

42·12 No instruction of the Architect under clause 13·2 may require as a Variation the provision by the Contractor of Performance Specified Work additional to that which has been identified in the Appendix unless the Employer and the Contractor otherwise agree.

42·13 Where the Contract Bills do not provide an analysis of the portion of the Contract Sum which relates to any Performance Specified Work the Contractor shall provide such an analysis ('the Analysis') within 14 days of being required to do so by the Architect.

42·14 The Architect shall, within a reasonable time before the Contractor intends to carry out the Performance Specified Work, give any instructions necessary for the integration of such Performance Specified Work with the design of the Works. The Contractor shall, subject to clause 42·15, comply with any such instruction.

42·15 If the Contractor is of the opinion that compliance with any instruction of the Architect injuriously affects the efficacy of the Performance Specified Work, he shall within 7 days of receipt of the relevant instruction specify by notice in writing to the Architect such injurious affection. Except where the Architect amends the instruction to remove such injurious affection, the instruction shall not have effect without the written consent of the Contractor which consent shall not be unreasonably withheld or delayed.

42·16 Except for any extension of time in respect of the Relevant Event stated in clause 25·4·15 an extension of time shall not be given under clause 25·3 and clauses 26·1 and 28·2·2 shall not have effect where and to the extent that the cause of the progress of the Works having been delayed, affected or suspended is that the Architect has not received the Contractor's Statement by the time referred to in clause 42·4 or any amendment to the Contractor's Statement pursuant to clause 42·5.

42·17 ·1 The Contractor shall exercise reasonable skill and care in the provision of Performance Specified Work provided that:

 ·1 ·1 clause 42·17 shall not be construed so as to affect the obligations of the Contractor under this Contract in regard to the supply of workmanship, materials and goods; and

 ·1 ·2 nothing in this Contract shall operate as a guarantee of fitness for purpose of the Performance Specified Work.

42·17 ·2 The Contractor's obligation under clause 42·17·1 shall in no way be modified by any service in respect of any Performance Specified Work which he has obtained from others and, in particular, the Contractor shall be responsible for any such service as if such services had been undertaken by the Contractor himself.

42·18 Performance Specified Work pursuant to clause 42 shall not be provided by a Nominated Sub-Contractor under a Nominated Sub-Contract or by a Nominated Supplier under a contract of sale to which clause 36 refers.

40.04 The architect must issue instructions necessary for the integration of the performance specified works within the works under Clause 43.14 within a reasonable time before the contractor intends to carry out the work.

40.05 The contractor's price for the work will only be adjustable in the event of variation of the work by the architect under Clause 13.5.6, a correction under Clause 2.2.2.2, a change in statutory requirements or the application to the work of the fluctuations provisions or Clause 26.

41 Appendix

41.01 Architects should ensure that the Appendix is completed. It is not unknown for this to be overlooked. Care should be taken to follow the format and instructions. In *Temloc* v *Errill Properties* (1987) 39 BLR 30 an entry of the word 'nil' was made in respect of the liquidated and ascertained damages. Did this mean that there were to be no damages for delay payable at all, no matter how late completion? Or did it mean that damages for delay were not to be at a pre-agreed rate, but were left to be assessed, if they arose, on normal common law principles, namely to compensate for any actual loss which could be proved? The Court of Appeal held that it meant there were to be no damages for delay at all. Obviously, parties should try to avoid creating uncertainties of that character.

40.02 The architect will prepare or direct the preparation of drawings or written or other documents showing or describing the requirements for the components or assemblies comprised in the performance specified work, and these documents, which should include enough information for the tenderer to include or allow for the price or rates for the item if required to do so, will be included in the tender documents for the main contract. The contractor may then tender for the performance specified work.

Contractor's statement

40.03 The contractor will be required to provide the architect with a statement at the time stated in the contract bills, including information in drawn, diagrammatic or scheduled form and with calculations as required, more particularly showing or describing the performance specified work as the contractor intends to carry it out (Clause 42.2). The architect may require this statement to be amended by written notice if it is in his opinion deficient in form or detail, or if it contains a deficiency which would adversely affect the performance required by the employer from that work.

Appendix		
	Clause etc.	
Statutory tax deduction scheme – Finance (No.2) Act 1975	Fourth recital and 31	Employer at Base Date *is a 'contractor'/ is not a 'contractor' for the purposes of the Act and the Regulations
CDM Regulations	Fifth recital	*all the CDM Regulations apply/ regulations 7 and 13 only of the CDM Regulations apply
Base Date	1·3	
Date for Completion	1·3	

VAT Agreement	15·2	Clause 1A of the VAT Agreement *applies/does not apply [k·1]
Defects Liability Period (if none other stated is 6 months from the day named in the Certificate of Practical Completion of the Works)	17·2	_____
Assignment by Employer of benefits after Practical Completion	19·1·2	Clause 19·1·2 *applies/does not apply
Insurance cover for any one occurrence or series of occurrences arising out of one event	21·1·1	£ _____
Insurance – liability of Employer	21·2·1	Insurance *may be required/ is not required Amount of indemnity for any one occurrence or series of occurrences arising out of one event £ _____ [y·1]
Insurance of the Works – alternative clauses	22·1	*Clause 22A/Clause 22B/ Clause 22C applies (See Footnote [m] to clause 22)
Percentage to cover professional fees	*22A 22B·1 22C·2	_____
Annual renewal date of insurance as supplied by Contractor	22A·3·1	_____
Insurance for Employer's loss of liquidated damages – clause 25·4·3	22D	Insurance *may be required/ is not required
	22D·2	Period of time _____
Date of Possession	23·1·1	_____
Deferment of the Date of Possession	23·1·2 25·4·13 26·1	Clause 23·1·2 *applies/does not apply Period of deferment if it is to be less than 6 weeks is _____

Liquidated and ascertained damages	24·2	at the rate of £ _____ per _____
Period of suspension (if none stated is 1 month)	28·2·2	
Period of delay (if none stated is, in respect of clauses 28A·1·1·1 to 28A·1·1·3, 3 months, and, in respect of clauses 28A·1·1·4 to 28A·1·1·6, 1 month)	28A·1·1·1 to 28A·1·1·3 28A·1·1·4 to 28A·1·1·6	_____ _____
Period of Interim Certificates (if none stated is 1 month)	30·1·3	_____
Retention Percentage (if less than 5 per cent) [aa]	30·4·1·1	_____
Work reserved for Nominated Sub-Contractors for which the Contractor desires to tender	35·2	_____
	Clause etc.	
Fluctuations: (if alternative required is not shown clause 38 shall apply)	37	clause 38 [cc] clause 39 clause 40
Percentage addition	38·7 or 39·8	_____
Formula Rules	40·1·1·1	
	rule 3	Base Month _____ 19 _____
	rules 10 and 30(i)	Part I/Part II [dd] of Section 2 of the Formula Rules is to apply
Settlement of disputes – Arbitration – appointor (if no appointor is selected the appointor shall be the President or a Vice-President, Royal Institute of British Architects)	41·1	President or a Vice-President: *Royal Institute of British Architects *Royal Institution of Chartered Surveyors *Chartered Institute of Arbitrators
Settlement of disputes – Arbitration	41·2	Clauses 41·2·1 and 41·2·2 apply (See clause 41·2·3)
Performance Specified Work	42·1·1	Identify below or on a separate sheet each item of Performance Specified Work to be provided by the Contractor and insert the relevant reference in the Contract Bills [ee]

9

Other standard forms of building contract

ANTHONY SPEAIGHT QC

1 Introduction

1.01 This chapter discusses standard forms of building contract other than the JCT Standard Form of Contract (reproduced with a commentary in Chapter 8). Most other forms in regular use are published by the Joint Contracts Tribunal (JCT), which has now produced an extensive family of forms, each intended to meet a slightly different situation. In addition, a number of forms have been published by other bodies, such as the Association of Consultant Architects (ACA) and the Institution of Civil Engineers (ICE). It is becoming increasingly difficult for any ordinary practitioner to keep up with all the standard forms of contract which are now available. Almost every year some new form is published, quite apart from the regular updating which occurs to the existing forms. The question of which JCT form is best suited to a particular situation has been discussed in Chapter 7.

1.02 It would be an impossible task in any book, and certainly in one of the scale of this work, to provide a commentary on every standard form. So what can sensibly be attempted? Nominated sub-contracting under JCT 80 has a special importance. It is now so closely connected with JCT 80 that an understanding of the main contract without a serious assessment of nominated sub-contracting would be thoroughly incomplete. Furthermore, an understanding of the most important scheme for employer-controlled sub-contracting provides a useful grounding when confronted with sub-contracts issued for use under other forms of contract. In addition to a reasonably comprehensive look at such sub-contracting, a brief discussion of some of the more important of the other forms must be a worthwhile task, with an attempt to identify their various advantages and disadvantages. Therefore, the purpose of this chapter is:

1. To describe in some detail the procedures for nominated sub-contracting under the JCT Standard Form of Contract (JCT 80), and the provisions of the Nominated Sub-Contract Conditions.
2. To indicate briefly the salient features of some of the other more important contracts.

2 JCT documents for entering into nominated sub-contracts

2.01 For many years the standard form of sub-contract was a document published by the NFBTE and FASS known as 'the green form': it was intended for use when the Main Contract was in the JCT 1963 standard form. In 1980 the JCT for the first time published its own documents for nominated sub-contracts. This comprised documents labelled NSC/1, NSC/2 and 2a, NSC/3 and NSC/4. They provided two alternative procedures known as 'the basic method' and 'the alternative method'. Many users found these documents exceedingly complicated. In 1991 the JCT reviewed

the nominated sub-contracts documents with a view to their simplification. As a result JCT published a new set of documents: the two previous procedures were replaced by a single method known as 'the 1991 method'. See the discussion under Clause 35 of the main contract at paragraph 36.05 in Chapter 8.

2.02 For the purpose of this family of JCT documents a nominated sub-contractor has a definition, which is contained in Clause 35.1 of the main contract. Where the architect has by the use of a prime cost sum or by naming a sub-contractor reserved to himself the final selection and approval of a sub-contractor, that sub-contractor is a 'nominated sub-contractor'.

2.03 A book entitled *Revised Procedure for Nomination of a Sub-Contractor* has been published by RIBA Publications for the JCT. This book provides the texts of the NSC documents, which otherwise are available only in the form of multi-copy pads.

The Invitation to Tender NSC/T Part 1

2.04 The normal first step in the 1991 procedure is for the architect to complete the Invitation to Tender form, which is labelled NSC/T, and to send it to the prospective sub-contractors, from whom he would be pleased to receive a tender. The architect has to fill in a certain number of details on the form before issuing it. The principal matters are:

- description and location of the main contract works;
- the identity of the main contractor and design team;
- form of main contract, any changes from the printed form;
- earliest and latest starting dates;
- certain proposed details of the sub-contract, including attendance items, fluctuations.

The form requests the tendering of a VAT-exclusive price.

2.05 It is intended that the architect should issue drawings, specification, bill of quantities and/or a schedule of rates with this form in order to describe the sub-contract works in sufficient detail to permit a tender to be prepared. It is also intended that the architect should send out a copy of the Appendix to the Main Contract as it has been, or is intended to be, completed. It is likely to be in the interests of the employer for the sub-contractor to enter into a direct warranty agreement. If that is planned, the architect should at the same time send out a copy of the Employer/Nominated Sub-Contractor Agreement, known as NSC/W (see below).

2.06 Nervous architects will be reassured by the declaration in the fourth recital to the Employer/Nominated Sub-Contractor Agreement, which it is envisaged will be executed in the course of this procedure, that nothing in NSC/T Part 1 is intended to render the architect liable to the sub-contractor. In truth, it is hard to see how such liability could arise, although on extreme facts an employer has been held to owe a duty to a person invited to tender to give proper consideration to the tender.

Tender by a Sub-Contractor NSC/T Part 2

2.07 This document is provided for the sub-contractor to complete with details of his tender. The form provides for the submission of the following:

- a VAT-exclusive sum
- a schedule of rates
- daywork percentages, or alternatively a schedule of daywork prices;
- fluctuations basis;
- requirements for general attendance by the main contractor if outside the scope of general attendance;
- earliest and latest starting times;
- periods required for submission for approval of all necessary sub-contractor drawings;
- period required for the execution of the sub-contract works off-site and on-site; any special conditions or arrangements required.

2.08 If the sub-contractor does not know the identity of the main contractor when he submits the tender, he is allowed seven days after he discovers the identity of the main contractor in which he may withdraw his tender.

2.09 When the architect and the employer have considered the tenders received from prospective sub-contractors, and have reached a decision on which one to appoint, the architect should arrange for the employer to sign the tender of the sub-contractor in question as having been approved. The form provides a space for such approval at the very end. Alternatively, the architect may be authorized to sign on behalf of the employer.

2.10 Rather than immediately make the formal nomination, the architect has the alternative option of ordering design work or the fabrication of components from the proposed sub-contractor, provided both sub-contractor and employer have completed the Employer/Sub-Contractor Agreement NSC/W. That possibility arises because Clause 2.2.1–2 of NSC/W permits direct employment of the sub-contractor by the employer prior to the issue of the Nomination Instruction.

Nomination Instruction NSC/N

2.11 When the decision has been made as to which sub-contractor is to be appointed, the architect should prepare this nomination form. It is perfectly possible for all the NSC procedure steps up to this point to have been carried out prior to the engagement of a main contractor. But the Nomination Instruction cannot, of its nature, be issued until there is a main contractor to receive the instruction. The form is to be sent to the main contractor together with the completed NSC/T Parts 1 and 2 and NSC/W in respect of that sub-contractor, together with sub-contract tender drawings, specification and bill of quantities. He should also send this form directly to the sub-contractor together with a completed copy of the Appendix to the main contract and the Employer/Sub-Contractor Agreement as executed by the employer.

2.12 The purpose of NSC/N is to constitute the notice of nomination stipulated by Clause 35.6 of the JCT 80 main contract. The text to be filled in on NSC/N by the architect amounts to no more than simple details which have already been given on NSC/T Part 1. The main contractor is then required by his own contractual obligations in Clause 35.7 of the JCT 80 main contract, and reminded by the text of NSC/N, to take the following steps:

1. To complete in agreement with the sub-contractor the document known as NSC/T Part 3, and have the completed document executed by both main contractor and sub-contractor; and
2. To execute the Standard Form of Articles of Nominated Sub-Contract Agreement between a contractor and a nominated sub-contractor, known as NSC/A.

The architect should ensure that the main contractor sends him a copy of the completed NSC/T Part 3 and NSC/A.

2.13 The main contractor is allowed the opportunity to register an objection to the identity of the proposed nominated sub-contractor named on the Nomination Instruction. But it must be a 'reasonable objection', it must be made in writing, it must be made at the earliest practicable moment, and in any event it must be within seven working days of receipt of the Nomination Instruction (Clause 35.5 of Main Contract JCT 80).

Particular Conditions to be Agreed between a Contractor and a Sub-Contractor NSC/T Part 3

2.14 The procedure places the obligation on the main contractor and the sub-contractor to attempt to agree between themselves on certain matters of some importance which the NSC documents call the 'Particular Conditions'. These matters are the following:

1. Programme details. Once specified, the dates on this document will assume contractual effect. For clause 2.1 of NSC/C states that the sub-contractor shall carry out and complete the works in accordance with these programme details. The components of the programme details are:
    Earliest and latest starting date on site. This is the third occasion that such dates will have been given under the procedure. But on the previous two occasions, that is by the architect on NSC/T Part 1 and by the sub-contractor on NSC/T Part 2, they were indicative only: they had no contractual effect. On this third occasion the dates will have contractual effect.
    Periods required for submission of all necessary sub-contractor drawings, etc., for off-site works, and for on-site works. It is envisaged that a notice will be given to the sub-contractor to commence on-site works, and that the length of this notice period will also be a 'Particular Condition'.
    Other details and arrangements. If the main contractor and sub-contractor can agree a programme for the sub-contract works, it may be attached.
2. Amount of insurance cover for any one occurrence.
3. Appointment of persons to assist in the resolution of disputes. The NSC procedure now envisages that the contractor and sub-contractor will at the outset appoint:
    An adjudicator. The Building Employers Confederation maintains a list of suitable adjudicators. This individual's role is to make a decision on how disputed sums of money are to be dealt with pending the decision of an arbitrator. There are basically three possibilities: the main contractor retains the money; or the money is paid to the sub-contractor; or the money is paid to an independent trustee-stakeholder.
    A trustee-stakeholder. This should normally be a deposit-taking bank. This person's role is to hold funds in accordance with the directions of the adjudicator pending the decision of an arbitrator.
4. VAT regime. There are a number of variants.
5. Any other matters, including special conditions or agreements on employment of labour, limitation of working hours, safety or site security.
6. Changes to information given in NSC/T Part 1. The employer or architect may have changed their minds since the Invitation to Tender about the obligations, the order of the works, or the type and location of access. Any such alteration should have been specified on an enclosure with the Nomination Instruction NSC/N.
7. Appointer of arbitrator. If nobody is named, the default appointer will be the President of the RICS. This contrasts with the position under the main contract JCT 80 where the default appointer is the President of the RIBA.

2.15 If the main contractor has not been able to agree the Particular Conditions within 10 days of receipt of the Nomination Instruction, he should report in writing to the architect (Clause 35.8 of the Main Contract JCT 80). Unless the contractor's notice is merely by way of an application for extension of time, the architect will then have to decide how to break the impasse (Clause 35.9). His options are in effect to decree that the point does not matter; or to decree that it does matter, and to issue a further instruction, or, in a more extreme case, to order omission of the item of work or to nominate another sub-contractor. If he is minded to issue an instruction, he should bear in mind that he has no power to order a proposed sub-contractor to do things until that person has signed a contract with either the employer or the main contractor.

Articles of Nominated Sub-Contract Agreement NSC/A

2.16 This is the formal sub-contract itself. Its function largely is to identify the other sub-contract documents. It will state, if correctly completed, whether the sectional completion supplement or self-vouching applies. It will state that the standard Conditions NSC/C are to apply unamended; or, if amended, what the amendments are. The numbered tender documents will be annexures, as will NSC/T Part 3. It is also prescribed that NSC/T Parts 1 and 2 will be annexures, but that does not mean that in all cases the proposals in them will have been adopted or will be terms of the contract.

3 The Nominated Sub-Contract Conditions NSC/C

3.01 The JCT first published a form of Nominated Sub-Contract in 1980 called NSC/4. There was a variant for use when the nominated sub-contractor had not been nominated by NSC/1, which was labelled NSC/4a. Between 1983 and 1990 there were nine amendments to NSC/4 and NSC/4a. In 1991 the JCT published a revised edition of Nominated Sub-Contract Conditions labelled NSC/C. Whereas NSC/4 had some 38 clauses and was found to be a form of massive complexity, NSC/C, although still lengthy, has the material rearranged into 8 sections. Many users will find the new format easier. However, there is an unnecessary confusion through the use of both the term 'Section' and the term 'clause' in respect of the divisions. Each part of the form is called a 'Section', within which the text is broken down by decimal markings into 1.1, 1.2, etc. Those divisions are called Clause 1.1, Clause 1.2, etc.

Section 1: Intentions of the Parties

3.02 This section begins with definitions. Most are straightforward. An exception, and worthy of mention are 'Sub-Contract Sum' and 'Tender Sum', which are the two alternative ways of expressing the price in tender documents and the Articles. The reader is simply referred to Clauses 4.2 and 4.3, which in turn refer him to Articles 3.1 and 3.2 in NSC/A, which baldly use the terms without explanation. The difference, in fact, is as follows. A 'Sub-Contract Sum' is a lump sum price where the price tendered and agreed will be the sum paid, subject to changes by variations. A 'Tender Sum', on the other hand, is the expression used where the contract is on a remeasurement basis: the contractor will be paid according to the work actually done, as ascertained by remeasurement.

3.03 This section attempts two things which any good contract ought to achieve – namely, to identify the sub-contract documents, and to express an order of priority between them, that is to say which is to prevail in the case of inconsistency. By Clause 1.5 the sub-contract documents are listed as NSC/C, NSC/A and the documents annexed to NSC/A. The last-mentioned category includes NSC/T Parts 1 and 2, which contain proposals which may well be different from the terms on which the parties ultimately settled. Therefore, it is important that the instructions given in the JCT scheme be followed in respect of deleting and altering the text of NSC/T Part 2 before annexing to NSC/A. The main contract is given top place in the priority, but since this will presumably be

JCT 80, there ought not to be any conflict between it and the sub-contract documents. No priority is expressed between drawings and specifications.

3.04 Clause 1.9 contains the fundamental obligation of the sub-contractor.

Execution of the Sub-Contract Works – Sub-Contractor's obligations

1.9   1   The Sub-Contractor shall carry out and complete the Sub-Contract Works in compliance with the Sub-Contract Documents and in conformity with all reasonable directions and requirements of the Contractor (so far as they may apply) regulating for the time being the due carrying out of the Works.

    2   All materials and goods shall, so far as procurable, be of the kinds and standards described in the Sub-Contract Documents provided that where and to the extent that approval of the quality and standards of materials and goods is a matter for the opinion of the Architect such quality and standards shall be to the reasonable satisfaction of the Architect.

    3   All workmanship shall be of the standards described in the Sub-Contract Documents, or, to the extent that no such standards are described in the Sub-Contract Documents, shall be of a standard appropriate to the Sub-Contract Works provided that where and to the extent that approval of workmanship is a matter for the opinion of the Architect such workmanship shall be to the reasonable satisfaction of the Architect.

    4   All work shall be carried out in a proper and workmanlike manner.

3.05 Clause 1.13 is one of a number of provisions aimed at overcoming problems which the sub-contractor may face by reason of not having a direct contractual nexus with the employer (save on the limited matters that the direct Employer/Nominated Sub-Contractor Agreement NSC/W covers). In *Gordon Durham* v *Haden Young* (1990) 52 BLR 61 H H Judge Thayne Forbes held that one of the rights under the main contract to which a similarly worded clause in the 'green form' could apply was the power of an arbitrator to open up, review and revise certificates.

Benefits under Main Contract

1.13   The Contractor will so far as he lawfully can at the request of the Sub-Contractor obtain for him any rights or benefits of the provisions of the Main Contract so far as the same are applicable to the Sub-Contract Works and not inconsistent with the express terms of the Sub-Contract but not further or otherwise. Any action taken by the Contractor in compliance with any aforesaid request shall be at the cost of the Sub-Contractor and may include the provision by the Sub-Contractor of such indemnity and security as the Contractor may reasonably require.

Section 2: Commencement and completion

3.06 By Clause 2.1 the sub-contractor's fundamental obligation is to carry out and complete the sub-contract works 'in accordance with the agreed programme details in NSC/T Part 3 item 1'. Often there will be a programme document; and, if there is, it ought to have been referred to in item 1 of NSC/T Part 3 amongst the Particular Conditions. But such a programme is not obligatory. If there is no such programme document, the 'programme details' must mean the statement in NSC/T Part 3 of the period required for on-site works. If there is a programme document, then Clause 2.1 would seem to require the sub-contractor not merely to finish on time, but also to proceed towards completion at the speed and in the manner indicated on the programme. On the other hand, if there is no programme document, the bare obligation in NSC/T Part 3 is to finish within a stated number of weeks: in that case, it seems the sub-contractor may be entitled to carry out his work, if he so chooses, in an almighty last minute scramble. Clause 2.1 specifically refers to the notice to start which is mentioned in the standard form of NSC/T Part 3 (see above).

3.07 The remainder of this section is concerned with extensions of time. The procedure seems cumbersome, but it has not been easy to think of a simpler one which would meet all the conflicting interests of different parties when works have become delayed. The steps are as follows:

1. The sub-contractor gives written notice to the main contractor of material circumstances including the cause of delay. He must as soon as possible give full particulars of the expected effects and estimate the extent of delay (Clause 2.2).
2. The main contractor must inform the architect of such notice and send on the particulars and estimate; and he may submit his own representations (Clause 2.2).

3. The architect forms an opinion whether delay has been caused by a 'relevant event'. If he decides that it has, he gives written consent to the contractor to give an extension of time, mentioning the amount of extension he considers fair and reasonable (Clause 2.3).
4. The main contractor is then required to grant an extension of time (Clause 2.3).

The main contractor is prohibited by the terms of the main contract JCT 80 from granting an extension of time to a sub-contractor other than with the written consent of the architect (see Chapter 8 paragraph 36.14). However, in practice it is more likely that the main contractor will try to prevent the sub-contractor obtaining an extension of time, rather than that he will be over-enthusiastic about allowing an extension. For often, when a delay has occurred, the main contractor and sub-contractor will be blaming each other as responsible for it.

3.08 What can the sub-contractor do if he is dissatisfied with the architect's decision on his application for an extension of time? If a main contractor feels aggrieved by an architect's decision he may commence an arbitration against the employer, in which the arbitrator will have power to open up, review and revise the certificate, opinion or decision in question. But the sub-contractor has no direct contractual relationship with the employer (save in respect of the limited matters covered by the direct NSC/W agreement), and, therefore, there could be some difficulty in the sub-contractor commencing an arbitration directly against the employer. The JCT family of forms' solution to this situation is to permit the sub-contractor to 'borrow' the main contractor's name, and, in his name, to arbitrate against the employer. There are other situations in which it has been found satisfactory for the law to permit one person to step into the shoes of another for the purposes of litigation: an obvious example is when an insurance company, which has paid out to an insured, seeks to recover its outlay from a third party responsible for the loss using the insured's name. But the arrangement for a sub-contractor to use a main contractor's name against an employer seems far less happy. Sir John Donaldson said in *Northern Regional Health Authority* v *Derek Crouch Construction* [1984] 1 QB 644 that every conceivable complication would arise if a main contractor disagreed with the case which a sub-contractor wished to submit in its name. Be that as it may, name-borrowing is the regime which exists. If a sub-contractor wishes to challenge the architect's decision on an extension of time, he uses the main contractor's name to do so. It has been held that there is an implied term of this sub-contract that, if the sub-contractor exercises his right to commence a name-borrowing arbitration, the main contractor 'will render to the sub-contractor such assistance and co-operation as may be necessary in order to enable the sub-contractor properly to conduct the arbitration' (*Lorne Stewart* v *William Sindall* (1986) 35 BLR 109).

3.09 If the sub-contractor fails to complete on time, he becomes liable to pay to the main contractor 'a sum equivalent to any loss and/or damage suffered or incurred by the Contractor and caused by the failure of the Sub-Contractor as aforesaid' (Clause 2.9). The main contractor's right to such payment is subject to the architect having certified the sub-contractor's failure to complete in accordance with Clause 2.8–9. This certificate is indispensable: in legal parlance it is a 'condition precedent' to the right (see *Brightside Kirkpatrick* v *Mitchell Construction* [1975] 2 Lloyd's Reports 493). A bald statement by the architect that the sub-contractor is in delay is probably insufficient. The certificate should state that the sub-contract works ought to have been completed within the period for completion stated in the programme details in NSC/T Part 3 item 1 or any revised or extended period.

3.10 Practical completion of the works of a nominated sub-contractor is certified by the architect (Clause 2.11, Clause 35.16 of JCT 80).

3.11 A Supplement is provided listing modifications to the text of NSC/C if there is to be sectional completion.

2·6   The following are the Relevant Events referred to in clause 2·3·1:

·1   force majeure;

·2   exceptionally adverse weather conditions;

·3   loss or damage occasioned by any one or more of the Specified Perils;

·4   civil commotion, local combination of workmen, strike or lock-out affecting any of the trades employed upon the Works or any of the trades engaged in the preparation, manufacture or transportation of any of the goods or materials required for the Works;

·5   compliance by the Contractor and/or the Sub-Contractor with the Architect's instructions:

   ·1   under clauses 2·3, 13·2, 13·3 (except, where bills of quantities are included in the Numbered Documents, compliance with an Architect's instruction for the expenditure of a provisional sum for defined work*), 23·2, 34, 35 or 36 of the Main Contract Conditions, or

   ·2   in regard to the opening up for inspection of any work covered up or the testing of any of the work, materials or goods in accordance with clause 8·3 of the Main Contract Conditions (including making good in consequence of such opening up or testing) unless the inspection or test showed that the work, materials or goods were not in accordance with the Main Contract or the Sub-Contract as the case may be;

·6   the Contractor, or the Sub-Contractor through the Contractor, not having received in due time necessary instructions (including those for or in regard to the expenditure of provisional sums), drawings, details or levels from the Architect for which the Contractor, or the Sub-Contractor through the Contractor, specifically applied in writing provided that such application was made on a date which having regard to the Completion Date or the period or periods for the completion of the Sub-Contract Works was neither unreasonably distant from nor unreasonably close to the date on which it was necessary for the Contractor or the Sub-Contractor to receive the same;

·7   delay on the part of nominated sub-contractors (other than the Sub-Contractor) or of nominated suppliers in respect of the Works which the Contractor has taken all practicable steps to avoid or reduce;

·8   ·1   the execution of work not forming part of the Main Contract by the Employer himself or by persons employed or otherwise engaged by the Employer as referred to in clause 29 of the Main Contract Conditions or the failure to execute such work;

   ·2   the supply by the Employer of materials and goods which the Employer has agreed to provide for the Works or the failure so to supply;

·9   the exercise after the Base Date by the United Kingdom Government of any statutory power which directly affects the execution of the Works by restricting the availability or use of labour which is essential to the proper carrying out of the Works, or preventing the Contractor or the Sub-Contractor from, or delaying the Contractor or the Sub-Contractor in, securing such goods or materials or such fuel or energy as are essential to the proper carrying out of the Works;

·10   ·1   the Contractor's or the Sub-Contractor's inability for reasons beyond his control and which he could not reasonably have foreseen at the Base Date for the purposes of the Main Contract or the Sub-Contract as the case may be to secure such labour as is essential to the proper carrying out of the Works; or

   ·2   the Contractor's or the Sub-Contractor's inability for reasons beyond his control and which he could not reasonably have foreseen at the Base Date for the purposes of the Main Contract or the Sub-Contract as the case may be to secure such goods or materials as are essential to the proper carrying out of the Works;

·11   the carrying out by a local authority or statutory undertaker of work in pursuance of its statutory obligations in relation to the Works, or the failure to carry out such work;

·12   failure of the Employer to give in due time ingress to or egress from the site of the Works or any part thereof through or over any land, buildings, way or passage adjoining or connected with the site and in the possession and control of the Employer, in accordance with the Contract Bills and/or the Contract Drawings, after receipt by the Architect of such notice, if any, as the Contractor is required to give, or failure of the Employer to give such ingress or egress as otherwise agreed between the Architect and the Contractor;

·13   the valid exercise by the Sub-Contractor of the right in clause 4·21 to suspend the further execution of the Sub-Contract Works;

·14   Where it is stated in the completed Appendix of the Main Contract Conditions (attached to NSC/T Part 1 or, if different, in the completed Appendix of the Main Contract Conditions enclosed with the copy of Nomination NSC/N sent to the Sub-Contractor by the Architect) that clause 23·1·2 of the Main Contract Conditions applies to the Main Contract, any deferment by the Employer in giving possession of the site of the Works to the Contractor.

·15   where bills of quantities are included in the Numbered Documents, by reason of the execution of work for which an Approximate Quantity is included in those bills which is not a reasonably accurate forecast of the quantity of work required.

·16   the use or threat of terrorism and/or the activity of the relevant authorities in dealing with such use or threat;

·17   compliance or non-compliance by the Employer with clause 6A.1 of the Main Contract Conditions; (*Employer's obligation – Planning Supervisor – Principal Contractor where not the Contractor*)

Section 3: Control of the works

3.12 The architect acting under JCT 80 can give 'instructions' to the main contractor. If the architect wishes to give an instruction related to sub-contract work, he must do so via the main contractor. When the main contractor receives an instruction from the architect which relates to the work of a nominated sub-contractor, he is entitled – indeed, he is required – to pass the instruction on to the nominated sub-contractor (Clause 3.3.1), who is required to comply with it (Clause 3.3.2). Thereby, the architect has as much control over the work of the nominated sub-contractor as he has over the work of the main contractor, notwithstanding that the sub-contractor is not (save for the limited matters covered by NSC/W) in direct contractual relations with the employer, whose agent the architect is.

3.13 The main contractor is entitled to give a further type of order to a nominated sub-contractor called a 'reasonable direction' (Clause 3.3.1). It is believed that this provision is intended to cover such matters as the general organization of the site.

3.14 If the architect issues an instruction in respect of 'non-complying work' under clause 8.4 or 8.5 of the Main Contract JCT 80, and the work in question was work of a sub-contractor, then the sub-contractor must comply with the architect's instruction (Clauses 3.4 to 3.9).

3.15 The sub-contractor is given the right to request, via the main contractor, that the architect specify in writing the provision under which any instruction has been issued. He is also given the right to commence a name-borrowing arbitration in the name of the main contractor to have the question determined 'whether the provision specified by the architect empowers the issue of the said instruction' (Clause 3.12). It would seem that an arbitrator is thereby given jurisdiction not merely to decide whether the architect has specified 'the right clause' in answer to the challenge, but also whether on the facts of the case the giving of the instruction was justified.

3.16 The sub-contractor requires the written consent of both architect and main contractor to sub-let any portion of the work, but such consent shall not be unreasonably withheld (Clause 3.14).

Section 4: Payment

3.17 As already mentioned there are two different ways in which the contract price can be expressed:

1. 'Sub-Contract Sum'. This is a fixed lump sum price. The final payment will vary from it only to the extent that the contract works were varied or that there were provisional sums.
2. 'Tender Sum'. This is the method of payment where the price ultimately to be paid will be determined by remeasurement at the conclusion of the works. In this case the price actually payable is called the 'Ascertained Final Sub-Contract Sum'.

A choice between these two options is made by the architect at the outset when he completes NSC/T Part 1. There is lengthy text in NSC/C explaining how both options are to be carried out. Depending on which of these two options had been chosen, one or other of these chunks of text will be deemed to be deleted: happily there is no need for the parties actually to strike a line through any parts of the text.

3.18 In the case of a lump sum contract, a valuation function is carried out by the quantity surveyor who was named in NSC/T Part 1 as the quantity surveyor named in the main contract. He values variations, expenditure of provisional sums, and work for which an approximate quantity was indicated in bills of quantities which were a numbered document annexed to NSC/A.

3.19 In the case of a remeasurement contract, it is again the same quantity surveyor who is responsible for determining the ascertained final Sub-Contract Sum. If the sub-contractor has attached a schedule of rates to NSC/T Part 2, this will be used in determining the valuation (Clause 4.12). The fact that it is a remeasurement sub-contract does not affect the sub-contractor's obligation to complete the work (*Ibmac* v *Marshall* [1968] EGD 218, 611).

3.20 The main contract JCT 80 requires the architect to include in interim certificates the amounts due to a nominated sub-contractor without application (Clause 30.2 of JCT 80). Within the curious period of two weeks and three days the main contractor must inform the sub-contractor of sums included in an interim certificate in respect of the nominated sub-contractor (Clause 4.16.1.1). The main contractor is under no obligation to the sub-contractor

to pay sums other than those certified in an interim certificate (Clause 4.16.2.1). There is a right for the sub-contractor to suspend work if he is not paid (Clause 4.21).

3.21 The main contractor's payment obligation to the sub-contractor is 'to discharge' the amount certified (Clause 4.16.2.1). In most cases that will be done by actually making payment. But can a good discharge be effected by the main contractor 'setting-off' a sum due from the sub-contractor to him, that is deducting a cross-claim? If the cross-claim is as certain as the debt certified then there would be obvious injustice in denying the right to set-off. At the other end of the spectrum, it is equally clearly unjust to allow a specious complaint to stand as an excuse for not paying a certified sum. But in the face of the complexity of most building projects how is a court to know whether an alleged cross-claim is specious without embarking on a full investigation of the merits? And the time involved in doing that will provide to the person putting up a specious cross-claim the very delay in payment which is his aim. In the early 1970s the courts' policy was that such delay in payment of a certified sum was to be avoided by giving summary judgment on any certified sum, irrespective of any alleged cross-claim (*Dawnays* v *Minter* [1971] 1 WLR 1205). In 1974 the House of Lords reversed that policy in favour refusing summary judgment where a party wished to advance a cross-claim (*Modern Engineering (Bristol)* v *Gilbert-Ash* [1974] AC 689), but it is uncertain how far that decision depends on express wording in a contract. The JCT has sought to achieve a middle position. NSC/C permits a main contractor to set off in just three situations:

1. A sum agreed by the sub-contractor to be due (Clause 4.26).
2. A sum awarded in arbitration of litigation (Clause 4.26).
3. Loss and expense suffered by the main contractor provided that:
   (a) The architect has certified that the sub-contractor has failed to complete (Clause 35.15 of JCT 80);
   (b) The main contractor has quantified his claim with precision;
   (c) The main contractor has given notice in writing as prescribed by Clause 4.27.2.

3.22 A significant hole was knocked in the balanced arrangements which the JCT thought it had thus achieved by the Court of Appeal decision in *Acsim (Southern)* v *Danish Contracting* (1989) 47 BLR 55: it was there held that a person who being sued for the price of work could defend himself by showing that the work was worth less than the price claimed, and that a contract provision limiting the scope of set-off did not limit the scope of that defence, which is sometimes called 'abatement'. In practice many consider there to be only the most slender distinction between saying that by reason of defects work is worth less than the certified value, and saying that there is a cross-claim for damages for the cost of rectifying the defects.

3.33 If the employer has exercised a right under the Main Contract to deduct monies due to a main contractor, and the reason for the deduction was a default of a sub-contractor, then the amount of such deduction may also be deducted by the main contractor from monies paid on by him to the sub-contractor (Clause 4.16.1.2). The provisions for giving notices of set-offs under Clause 4.27.2 do not apply to a deduction of this character (*Mellowes PPG* v *Snelling Construction* (1989) 49 BLR 109). It has been commented that the combined effect of this right and the right of abatement is to weaken the protection for sub-contractors which the notice scheme might have been thought to give.

3.34 NSC/C provides for a person called an 'adjudicator' to fulfil a role aimed at securing short-term rough and ready fairness when there is a dispute between a sub-contractor and a main contractor about a loss and expense claim which is being relied on for a set-off. He can direct that pending an arbitration decision disputed funds shall be treated in any combination of three different ways:

1. retained by the main contractor;
2. paid over to the sub-contractor;

3. lodged with a trustee-stakeholder to await the outcome of arbitration.

An adjudicator is not an arbitrator, and his decision cannot be enforced as an arbitrator's award (*A Cameron v John Mowlem & Co* (1990) 52 BLR 24).

3.35 The right to recover direct loss and expense between contractor and sub-contractor is mutual. If either the main contractor or the sub-contractor is responsible for materially affecting the progress of the works, the other, by following prescribed procedures, can make financial recovery (Clauses 4.38–4.41).

3.36 There is a provision for the Final Certificate issued in respect of the main contract under Clause 30.8 of JCT 80 to have effect as conclusive evidence of the quality of the sub-contract works in a similar way to its conclusive evidential effect in relation to the main contractor's works (Clause 4.25). In the light of the Court of Appeal's surprising decision in *Crown Estates* v *Mowlem* that the Final Certificate, in effect, creates a bar on any claim in respect of defective work, even if undiscovered and undiscoverable, (see Chapter 8 paragraphs 33.17–19) architects should advise employers that NSC/C should be amended. An appropriate amendment to NSC/C would be simply to delete Clause 4.25.1.1.

3.37 Specific provision is made by NSC/C in regard to the passing of property. The general law is that if a builder incorporates a building material into a property, ownership of that material passes to the owner of the property, whether he has been paid for his work or not. But there have been cases where there was a conflict between that principle and another fundamental principle of the law: that nobody can give something which does not belong to him. A related difficulty was illustrated by *Dawber Williamson* v *Humberside County Council* (1979) 14 BLR 70: a roofing sub-contractor delivered materials to the site; prior to their fixing, their value was certified and paid by the employer to the main contractor; but the main contractor went into liquidation without paying for the materials. So the question arose: who owned the materials? The court accepted the sub-contractor's argument that he still owned them. Happy result as that was for the sub-contractor who would otherwise have lost any realistic prospect of payment, it meant that the employer had to pay out for them a second time. The JCT decided that their policy towards the problem of which innocent party should lose out when a main contractor becomes insolvent was that it should be the sub-contractor rather than the employer: that is to say, that as soon as the employer has paid the main contractor for a material, even if not yet fixed, and even if the material belongs to a sub-contractor, 'property' in it, i.e. ownership, should pass to him. The implementation of that policy required provisions in both the main contract (Clause 16.1 of JCT 80, and see Section 18 of Chapter 8)) and in NSC/C (Clause 4.15.4).

3.38 There is a further name-borrowing provision whereby a sub-contractor can use the main contractor's name in an arbitration against the employer if he feels aggrieved by any decision as to the amount certified by the architect (Clause 4.20).

Sections 4A, 4B, 4C: Fluctuations

3.39 There are three different regimes offered for dealing with fluctuations. NSC/T Parts 1 and 2 should specify which is to apply. They are known as:

1. Contribution, levy and tax fluctuations (Clause 4A).
2. Labour and materials cost and tax fluctuations (Clause 4B).
3. Formula adjustment (Clause 4C).

Section 5: Statutory obligations

3.40 NSC/C makes provision for:

1. Value added tax – standard arrangements (Clause 5A).
2. Value added tax – special arrangements (Clause 5B).

3. Income and Corporation Taxes Act 1988 – tax deduction scheme (Clauses 5C and 5D).

This book does not deal with tax law, which is a highly specialist subject.

Section 6: Injury, damage and insurance

3.41 The sub-contractor undertakes to indemnify the main contractor against personal injury or death caused by the carrying out of the sub-contract works unless such occurred as result of the fault of the main contractor or employer: in other words the sub-contractor is liable unless he can prove that it was the fault of one of the other parties to the contracts (Clause 6.2). The sub-contractor undertakes to indemnify the main contractor in respect of damage to property provided that this is due to the negligence, omission or default of the sub-contractor: in other words, the sub-contractor is liable only if somebody else can prove that it was the sub-contractor's fault (Clause 6.3).

3.42 The sub-contractor undertakes to insure in respect of his liability for personal injury, death and damage to property (Clause 6.5). Depending on which of the insurance options in the main contract has been selected, that is Clauses 22A, 22B and 22C (see Chapter 8 paragraph 24), there is an appropriate passage of text in NSC/C.

Section 7: Determination

3.43 There is a scheme for a sub-contractor to be sacked from a project where his work is unsatisfactory. The grounds for such dismissal are:

1. wholly suspending work;
2. failing to proceed in accordance with the programme details in NSC/T Part 3;
3. neglecting after notice in writing from the main contractor to remove defective work or materials;
4. assigning the sub-contract or sub-letting part without consent.

For such a dismissal to be carried out, both architect and main contractor must be involved. The main contractor must inform the architect that the sub-contractor is in default in one of these respects. If the matter is to go any further, the architect must then instruct the main contractor to proceed; if the architect does so, the main contractor serves a formal notice on the sub-contractor. When the matter is referred to him, the architect must decide whether the main contractor should be allowed to determine the sub-contractor's contract without more ado upon default after the formal notice, or whether the main contractor must obtain the architect's sanction before proceeding to that step. If the power to determine is exercised by the main contractor for no good reason, the main contractor is likely to be liable to the sub-contractor in damages. But this may not be so if the main contractor genuinely, but wrongly, believes he is entitled to determine (*Woodar* v *Wimpey* [1980] 1 AER 571).

3.44 Insolvency and corruption are also grounds on which a sub-contractor's employment can be ended.

3.45 The sub-contractor has his own right to end his employment. Grounds for doing so are that the main contractor has wholly suspended work, or unreasonably failed to proceed.

3.46 If the main contractor's employment under the main contract is ended, then the sub-contract automatically ends.

Section 9: Settlement of disputes – arbitration

3.47 There is an arbitration clause similar to that in the main contract JCT 80. There is a provision to enable two arbitrations to be dealt with by the same arbitrator if connected disputes are the subject of arbitration. This can arise if there is a connected dispute being submitted to arbitration between the employer and the main contractor; or between the main contractor and another nominated sub-contractor; or between the sub-contractor and the employer under NSC/W.

4 JCT Intermediate Form of Building Contract (IFC 84)

4.01 This form was published in 1984. Between 1986 and 1994 there were seven amendments. The genesis of the form owes something to the disenchantment of the construction industry with JCT 80 on its publication. Many people found JCT 80 so daunting and complicated that they went on using JCT 1963. For such persons IFC 84 was offered as a form of contract which in terms of length and complexity resembled JCT 1963, but in essentials had the benefit of up-to-date drafting. In most significant respects the characteristics of the contract created by IFC 84 correspond to JCT 80. The principal difference from JCT 80 is in respect of the nomination of sub-contractors: in this respect IFC 84 does not correspond with JCT 1963.

4.02 Sub-contracting under IFC 84 is thus its one distinctive characteristic. A new animal has been created, 'the named sub-contractor'. The lengthy discussion on earlier pages of this chapter will have shown just how complicated nominating sub-contracting under JCT 80 has become, and, therefore, one can applaud the initiative to provide a simpler alternative. However, there are those who consider that unnecessary confusion has been created by the introduction of yet another species of sub-contractor, whose distinction from the recognized categories of nominated and domestic sub-contractors is imperfectly drawn. A new family of sub-contract documents has been spawned, namely:

NAM/T: Tender and Agreement for named sub-contractor;
NAM/SC: Sub-Contract Conditions for named sub-contractor;
NAM/FR: Formula Rules for named sub-contractors;
ESA/1: Employer/Specialist Agreement to provide a direct warranty where a portion of the design is provided by a named sub-contractor.

IFC also has its own Fluctuations Supplement and Sectional Completion Supplement.

4.03 Other differences from JCT 80 are:

1. Certification procedures are simpler; 95% of the value of work executed and materials on site is included in interim certificates, 97.5% at practical completion.
2. There is no provision for nominated suppliers.
3. There is no provision for performance specified work.
4. There is no restraint on opening an arbitration whilst the works are in progress.

Advantages

4.04 It is less complex than JCT 80 but still covers most of the same ground. It is a well drafted form in the sense that it should ensure smooth administration, and that it has been well thought out.

Disadvantages

4.05 Although not quite so complex as JCT 80, it is still a very complicated contract. By reason of its central importance in the JCT family, most people working in construction will have some familiarity with JCT 80, and they may find the differences between JCT 80 and IFC 84 simply a distraction. The 'named sub-contractor' arrangements are a potential source of complication.

5 JCT Agreement for Minor Building Works 1980 (MW 80)

5.01 The first form intended for minor works was published in 1968: it was said to be designed for works up to a value of £8 000,

because above that figure bills of quantities were thought to be necessary. The present form (MW 80) was published in 1980, and has proved very popular. There have been eight amendments between 1985 and 1994.

5.02 It is a fixed price lump sum contract. The works must be sufficiently clearly defined to permit accurate tendering, but it is not envisaged that there will be bills of quantities. The contract is to be administered by an architect who will issue certificates, but the scale of contract administration is much less than under JCT 80. For example, there is no provision for the architect to certify that works have not been completed by the completion date. The general theme of the contract is simplicity.

5.03 MW 80 is different from IFC 84, generally in the direction of greater simplification, in the following respects:

1. Extension of time. There is no list of circumstances justifying an extension. Instead the contractor is entitled to an extension if the delay is for 'reasons beyond the control of the Contractor'. An amendment of 1991 provides: 'Reasons within the control of the Contractor include default of the Contractor or of others employed or engaged by or under him for or in connection with the Works and of any supplier of goods or materials for the Works'.
2. No provision for 'named sub-contractors'. There is no scope for the employer to direct the use of a particular sub-contractor.
3. Retention fees are not treated as trust moneys.
4. Valuation is given a much more rough and ready treatment: 'on a fair and reasonable basis using where relevant prices in the priced specification/schedules/schedule of rates'.
5. Loss and expense. There is a limited provision for the contractor to be reimbursed if the regular progress of the works is affected, but broadly speaking the only ground for such is variations and the method of assessment is much more rough and ready.
6. No provision for partial possession or sectional completion.
7. No provisions for opening up and testing.
8. Ownership of unfixed materials. There is no provision requiring the contractor to include a clause in sub-contracts that ownership of unfixed materials will pass to the employer as soon as paid for.
9. No fluctuations save that changes in contributions, levies and taxes will be allowed.

Advantages

5.04 Simplicity and ease of administration.

Disadvantages

5.05 Many matters are left sketchily defined.

6 JCT Conditions of Contract for Building Works of a Jobbing Character (JA/C 90)

6.01 In simple terms this may be said to be a contract for even smaller jobs than MW 80. It is intended to be used by organizations such as local authorities, who regularly employ building contractors to carry out small works, for example, maintenance jobs on a stock of houses. Unlike MW 80, there is no architect or other professional contract administrator. The JCT suggest its use for jobs up to £10 000 in value (at 1990 prices) with a duration of up to one month.

6.02 JA/C 90 can be used with either the employer's own works order or with a JCT four-page document entitled Standard Form of Tender and Agreement for Building Works of a Jobbing Character (JA/T 90). With an economy not found in most other JCT documentation this document is designed to serve three separate purposes at three successive stages: as an invitation to tender, a returned tender and an executed agreement.

6.03 Amongst differences from MW 80 are the following:

1. Extension of time. In the absence of a certifier, the employer decides in the first instance whether an extension of time is justified; that decision is subject to arbitration.
2. There are no interim payments. The contractor is to submit one invoice after completion of the works.
3. Valuation. If the parties cannot agree, the employer values in the first instance, subject to arbitration.
4. There is no certificate of practical completion.
5. There is no retention.
6. There are no grounds for termination, other than corruption.

7 JCT Standard Form of Measured Term Contract 1989

7.01 This form is intended for use by the same kind of employers as JA/C 90, that is large organizations who are accustomed to employing building contractors on small jobs. Typical would be the owner of a housing stock, on which there are regular maintenance jobs. This form is for use if such an employer wishes to enter an umbrella contract with a building contractor to cover a series of such small jobs, rather than enter a separate JA/C 90 contract for each individual job. Measured term contracts have for some years been in use by housing authorities and other commercial organizations with regular maintenance programmes.

7.02 This contract is quite unlike any other in that it does not involve an obligation by the contractor to carry out any item of work at all. Rather it creates a framework for subsequent orders. Unlike JA/C 90, this contract does involve a contract administrator: he, rather than the employer, places the order which initiates each job, and he values the work in accordance with an agreed schedule of rates. The contractor is obliged to carry out any order which is given. But he does not have exclusive claim to all jobs within the 'contract area', that is the district, estate or whatever, which is identified in the recitals as the geographical territory of the contract.

7.03 The Appendix to this form of contract is unusually important. It identifies a list of properties which may be the location of works ordered under the contract. It states the period over which work may be ordered under the contract, normally at least one year. It gives an indication, though not a guarantee of the value of work which will be ordered. It mentions the type of work which may be ordered under the contract.

8 JCT Standard Form of Building Contract with Contractor's Design 1981 (CD 81)

8.01 There emerged in the 1970s the concept of a contract under which a package deal of both design and build would be provided. The notion was supported by a NEDO report 'Construction for Industrial Recovery'. Originally it was envisaged that it would be used by local authorities for public housing projects. In fact, it has been more used for commercial light industrial building and by developers for offices and shops. In 1981 the JCT published its design and build form (now labelled 'CD 81'); there have been seven amendments between 1986 and 1994.

8.02 The basic problem of a fixed price package deal contract for a new building is that, unless the building is to some extent defined in the contract, the employer has no certainty what he will be provided with for his money. On the other hand, if the building is described in detail in the contract, then one has not moved far from the traditional procurement method of design before contract. CD 81 tackles this problem by the concept of a statement of 'Employer's Requirements'. This statement can, at the employer's choice, be anything from a three-line performance specification to a completely developed scheme design, with outline specifications and drawings. It must be stated clearly whether employer or contractor is responsible for obtaining approvals.

8.03 It would have been perfectly feasible to leave the contractor to implement the 'Employer's Requirements' as he saw fit. But CD 81 carries the pre-contractual definition of the project a stage further by a second concept, the 'Contractor's Proposals'. These are drafted by the prospective contractor in response to the employer's requirements and supplied together with a tender figure. The employer must examine these proposals: indeed, a recital in the articles declares that the employer has done so. Obviously the proposals should respond to, and be compatible with, the employer's requirements. But what if there is some divergence? The contract provides that the proposals prevail. Therefore, in his own interests the employer must consider the proposals very carefully before entering into a CD 81 contract.

8.04 The contract is a lump sum contract, payable in stages or periodically. It is not envisaged that there will be a bill of quantities or schedule of rates. There is no architect, contract administrator or other certifier.

8.05 The contractor assumes a liability, wholly alien to a contractor's obligation under a traditional contract, for the design. He warrants that the design work has been done with reasonable skill and care (Clause 2.5). Therefore, his liability is similar to that of an architect. This clause may not be the limit of his responsibility in law for design work. For example, in the case of housing work, he will have assumed responsibility under the Defective Premises Act 1972, which probably involves an absolute obligation that work has been done so as to make the dwelling reasonably fit for human habitation.

Advantages

8.06 The employer can look to one person as responsible for all aspects of the project. If defects later come to light, he does not have to work out whether it has been caused by bad design or bad workmanship before he knows against whom to complain.

Disadvantages

8.07 The employer does not know quite what the building presented at the end of the project will be like, unless he has spelled out his employer's requirements in a very detailed manner. If he has done that, much of the point of a design-and-build contract may be thought to be lost. Similarly, the employer has little control over what happens during the course of the project. He does not have somebody looking after his interests when design decisions are taken, and endeavouring to satisfy his requirements, in the same way as he would if his own architect was running the contract.

9 JCT 80 – Contractor's Designed Portion Supplement 1981 (CDPS 81)

9.01 This supplement is intended to be used where the contractor is required to design one element in a contract, the remainder of which will be a traditional contract. An example would be the erection of a building with a standard steel structural frame, where the main contractor was a specialist in such frames.

9.02 CDPS 81 is a nine-page document to be used in conjunction with the JCT Standard Form. It modifies JCT 80 to make the contractor responsible for the design of the identified portion. The integration of this design into the works as a whole is the responsibility of the architect. There are 'Employer's Requirements' and 'Contractor's Proposals' in relation to this portion, reminiscent of the statements which form the foundation of CD 81.

10 JCT Standard Form of Management Contract (MC 87)

10.01 At much the same time as 'design-and-build' was emerging, there was also another new procurement method starting to appear, known as 'management contracting'. Under this arrangement a large firm of building contractors would assume responsibility to an employer for the erection of a building but, rather than carrying out construction work themselves, would sub-contract the entire works to others, known as 'works contractors', reserving to themselves a role as managers and for the provision of basic site services. This form of arrangement was attractive to developers for whom speed of commencement and completion was of paramount importance. The arrangement was also potentially attractive to an employer who was undertaking a particularly complex project on which strong management will be advantageous. During the 1970s and 1980s the large companies, which in the main were the bodies carrying out management contracting, developed their own forms of contract.

10.02 There was no standard form, nor one negotiated between representatives of different interests, until the publication by the JCT in 1987 of its Standard Form of Management Contract. The only amendments so far published concern the peripheral matters of arbitration rules and VAT. There is a family of documents for use in connection with the works contractors' contracts:

WKS/1 Section 1: Invitation to Tender;
WKS/1 Section 2: Tender by Works Contractor;
WKS/1 Section 3: Agreement;
WKS/2 Conditions of Contract;
WKS/3 Employer/Works Contractor Agreement.

It will be seen that they follow the scheme of the JCT 80 nominated sub-contractor documents.

10.03 This is a 'cost plus' type of contract. The management contractor is entitled to be reimbursed whatever he has to pay to the works contractors. In addition he is entitled to be reimbursed his own costs for providing site services and to be paid a fee. The contract envisages the appointment of an architect and other design professionals by the employer: the management contractor will work in liaison with them. Since the paramount concern of employers using this form of contract tends to be speed, the management contractor is often appointed at much the same time as the architect. The contract envisages that the management contractor will perform services in the pre-construction, as well as the construction, period.

10.04 The dominant obligation of the management contractor tends to be get the project completed by the contractual completion date. There is provision for extension of time and liquidated damages. There is also provision for the recovery of loss and expense upon the regular progress of the works being disrupted, but, since it is the works contractors who are doing the construction work, it is they, rather than the management contractor, who will in the first instance make such applications. Consistent with the general theme of reimbursement to the management contractor of his outlay, he will be entitled to recover from the employer payments of this character which he has had to make to works contractors.

10.05 The management contractor also has an obligation under the contract to achieve as cheap an outcome as possible. He undertakes to ensure that the project is carried through in an economical and expeditious manner. A 'Contract Cost Plan' is annexed to the contract.

10.06 Most unusually for a standard form contract, but again consistent with the priority attached to speed, a jurisdiction is conferred on the architect to require an acceleration of the works.

Advantages

10.07 It is an attractive choice for a property developer for whom interest charges are a major commercial consideration, since this is the method of procurement which tends to allow the speediest start to the works and has been found by many developers to offer the best prospect of a speedy completion. This arrangement provides stronger management of the works than any other: since the management contractor has no responsibility for any construction he has nothing to distract him from using his experience of running construction projects to drive the project to an efficient and speedy completion. The arrangement is attractive to management contractors because they assume virtually no financial risk.

Disadvantages

10.08 The employer does not have any certainty as to the cost of the project. The employer cannot look to one person for the assumption of design as well as construction responsibility.

11 GC/Works/1 (third edition)

11.01 The Government works or GC family of forms of contract are publications by the Government. There has been a little consultation, but no negotiation, in their drafting. In 1973 the Government issued GC/Works/1 which was a lump sum with quantities contract. In 1989 a third edition of this form was issued. The form is intended for use both on building and engineering work. The form is intended for projects worth £150 000 or more. There is another government form for minor works, namely GC/Works/2. Related documents have been published for sub-contracts on building projects being carried out under GC/Works/1:

GW/Sa: Government Works Sub-Contract Articles of Agreement and Appendix;
GW/Sc: Government Works Sub-Contract Conditions;
GW/S/FR: Price Adjustment Formula provisions.

12 ACA Form of Building Agreement

12.01 In 1982 the Association of Consultant Architects (ACA) published its own form of contract. Many members of ACA were deeply dissatisfied with JCT 80 by reason of its complexity. At the same time they recognized that continuing to use JCT 1963 would with the passage of time become increasingly unwise. In 1984 ACA published a second edition. In 1990 they published a revision of the second edition.

12.02 There is also an ACA Form of Sub-Contract. Again the current issue is the 1990 revision of the second edition.

12.03 The contract is basically a lump sum 'with quantities' type of contract. But the contractor does not take the risk of errors in the bills of quantities: if there is an error the architect shall determine a fair adjustment. There is an option to cater for a portion of contractor design. A simple fluctuations clause is available.

12.04 The ACA form is the only standard form which recognizes that many people in the construction industry do not regard arbitration as the most desirable form of dispute resolution. Those who have had experience of both often say that litigation before an official referee provides a cheaper, quicker and higher quality decision. Hence the ACA form requires the parties to choose between three options of dispute resolution: litigation, straight arbitration, or adjudication with arbitration to follow.

Advantages

12.05 The ACA form has many of the good points of the New Engineering Contract (NEC) without the bad points. It has the merits of brevity, simplicity and clarity, but not to such a striking degree as to be likely to create problems. It avoids the generalized, vague statements of the NEC, which pose a high risk of creating unnecessary litigation over contract meaning. It is a contract of similar length, and degree of detail, to IFC 84, but its drafting is regarded by many as easier to understand. There is far less detail to be entered by the parties than required by the NEC's Contract Data. Despite 13 years of use, there is no known occasion on which the meaning of any part of the contract has had to be litigated – but that may merely reflect the relatively limited use which has been made of this form.

Disadvantages

12.06 The ACA contract is not the product of negotiation, and some commentators regard that as a criticism. It is said that the ACA form is more favourable to the employer than the JCT form. For example, there is no restriction on assignment by the employer after completion of the works.

13 The New Engineering Contract

13.01 In 1993 the Institution of Civil Engineers published a contract which had 'New' in its title and was new in its nature. Unlike the JCT contracts which have all evolved from the old RIBA forms, it acknowledged no ancestry among previous forms. The New Engineering Contract (NEC) consciously turned its back on all previous forms. Its authors believed that the existing forms promoted a confrontational culture in the construction industry. Despite its genesis in a working party of the Institution of Civil Engineers, the NEC can be used on building contracts as well as on engineering contracts. Strong encouragement to use it in building projects was given by the report of Sir Michael Latham, 'Constructing the Team' (1994). Amongst construction lawyers there are currently two schools of thought about NEC: there are some great enthusiasts, and a large number of mild sceptics.

13.02 For architects who have become familiar with any of the JCT contracts, the NEC involves a massive leap into uncharted territory. Apart from the fact that the parties are still called 'the Employer' and 'the Contractor', almost every other expression is different. Instead of an 'architect' or 'engineer', there are two different actors called respectively, 'the Supervisor' and 'the Project Manager'. Some of the new expressions are just new labels for recognized concepts, whilst others connote novel concepts.

13.03 The drafting of the clauses is also novel. Instead of indicating a contractual undertaking by an expression connoting obligation such as, 'X shall perform Y', NEC says 'X performs Y'. This may generate confusion, since any contract contains text which does not connote obligations, such as statements of what parties may do, but are not obliged to do. The numbering of clauses is to be applauded for avoiding the multiple decimal points of recent JCT contracts, although strangely the first clause is number 10.

13.04 There is no agreement as such. That is to say, there is no form to fulfil the role of 'Articles of Agreement' in a JCT contract, where the parties enter their signatures or affix their seals to bring the contract into being. Those who use the NEC will have to exercise care to record in some way if and when they are committing themselves to a contract, and which options they are selecting.

13.05 There is a nine-page section entitled 'Contract Data', which is reminiscent of the Appendix to a JCT contract. Part is completed by the employer, part by the contractor. The details to be inserted are quite complicated. For example, in relation to 'Compensation events' (read: 'relevant event' in JCT-speak), there must be an entry for 'days with rainfall greater than 5 mm (nr) . . .' and 'days with snow lying at . . . hours GMT (nr) . . .'.

13.06 An 'Adjudicator' is appointed from the start of the contract. Whenever the contractor dislikes a decision of the supervisor or project manager, he may refer the issue to the adjudicator. Either party may refer a decision of the adjudicator, if it dislikes it, to arbitration. However, the drafting of the arbitration clause is skimpy, and the mode of appointment of arbitrator, and other provisions concerning arbitration, left for the parties to specify.

13.07 The NEC can be regarded as comprising three elements:

1. Nine 'core clauses'. These will be used in every contract.
2. Six 'main options'. One, but only one, of these must be chosen.
3. Thirteen 'secondary options'. These may be regarded as optional add-ons. It is not necessary to use any of them. Save that a few cannot be used with some of the main options, the parties can pick as many or as few of these as they want.

13.08 The six main options, of which one must be chosen, are:

Option A   Priced contract with activity schedule
Option B   Priced contract with bill of quantities
Option C   Target contract with activity schedule
Option D   Target contract with bill of quantities
Option E   Cost reimbursable contract
Option F   Management contract

Broadly speaking, this allows a lump sum contract, a remeasurement contract, a cost plus contract or a management contract. Through the use of secondary options the parties can add sectional completion and fluctuations. The NEC takes a contractor's designed portion in its stride by simply stating 'The Contractor designs the parts of the works which the Works Information states he is to design' (Clause 21.1).

Advantages

13.09 The two great virtues of the NEC are, firstly, its simplicity and clarity of expression, and, secondly, its policy of promoting a co-operative, as opposed to a confrontational, approach.

Disadvantages

13.10 The meaning of some clauses is vague by reason of the brief, generalized, or novel way in which they are expressed: some lawyers predict that there will have to be litigation to resolve uncertainties of meaning. Those who embark on a contract under NEC have to learn a new contractual language.

10

Contractor and sub-contractor collateral warranties

E ANN MINOGUE

1 Architects and collateral warranties

1.01 Architects are likely to encounter collateral warranties in two circumstances. Firstly, and most importantly, they themselves may be asked to provide collateral warranties to third parties (such as potential purchasers), and secondly they may be expected to advise their clients – the employer under the building contract – on collateral warranties to be given by contractors and sub-contractors either to the employer or to third parties. Although in most cases employers will take direct legal advice on the provision of collateral warranties to third parties, architects should still be aware of the nature of contractor/sub-contractor collateral warranties in case advice is required. In addition, architects should satisfy themselves that the appropriate collateral warranties are obtained from contractors or sub-contractors in favour of the employer. Architect's collateral warranties are dealt with elsewhere in this book, and this chapter, although looking at collateral warranties generally, will concentrate in particular on contractor/sub-contractor collateral warranties.

2 What is a collateral warranty?

2.01 A collateral warranty is a form of contract which runs alongside, and is usually supplemental to, another contract. Usually a collateral warranty creates a contractual relationship between two parties where none would otherwise exist. This takes the form of a contract between one of the parties to the underlying contract and a third party who has an interest in the performance of that contract. In this text, the person giving the collateral warranty will be called the 'warrantor' and the person to whom it is given the 'beneficiary'.

3 Why have collateral warranties become so important?

3.01 The legal doctrine of privity of contract means that liability for the improper performance of obligations under a contract is limited to the parties to that contract. For example, under the JCT 80 Standard Form of Building Contract, if no collateral warranty is obtained and a sub-contractor is in breach of his sub-contract, the employer will not be able to sue him for breach of contract as the employer is not a party to the sub-contract. The employer would have to make his claim against the main contractor with whom he would have a contractual link. A particular problem arises where the sub-contractor's default does not place the main contractor in breach of the main contract: the clearest example is where a nominated sub-contractor provides late or incorrect design information. Even where this problem does not arise, if the contractor is insolvent, the employer will find himself unable to

recover any of his losses. The risk of insolvency has always existed but the need to establish a contractual link with sub-contractors has grown due to recently decided cases.

3.02 It was a desire to circumvent the legal problems that stem from the law of privity of contract that led to the development of the tort of negligence as set out in the famous case of *Donoghue v Stevenson* (1932) AC 562. That case established the 'neighbour principle' which obliges a party to take care to avoid acts which it can reasonably foresee are likely to injure its 'neighbour'. 'Neighbour' was defined as those so closely affected by a party's act that that party ought to have had them in contemplation when carrying out the act in question. 'Injury' initially meant physical harm but the courts came to extend it to financial loss. A 'duty of care' in negligence is owed only to neighbours. There is no need for the two parties to be contractually linked.

3.03 For many years the tort of negligence applied to cases of defective buildings, the leading case being *Anns v Merton London Borough Council* (1978) AC 728. Builders, architects and others involved in the construction process were held to owe fairly wide duties of care to all those who might reasonably be expected to be affected by their negligent actions. This duty of care served to protect tenants and purchasers of developments and other third parties. Therefore, parties who needed to be protected from negligent and defective building design or work were advised that they had adequate legal protection under the tort of negligence without needing any direct contractual link with the builders and designers.

3.04 The cases of *D & F Estates Limited and Others v The Church Commissioners of England and Others* (1988) 49 BLR 1 and *Murphy v Brentwood District Council* (1990) 50 BLR 1 dramatically altered the established legal position relating to defective buildings and negligence so that a builder would not be liable in tort to successive owners of a building (i.e. those with no contractual link to him) for any defects in the building itself. It was held that the cost of rectifying defects was economic loss and that this type of loss was not ordinarily compensatable in the tort of negligence. The builder would only be liable to successive owners if any defect caused personal injury or damage to 'other property' (i.e. something other than the building). (By way of aside, professional designers who give negligent advice can still be held liable for pure economic loss, even to persons with whom they have no contract: *Hedley Byrne & Co v Heller & Partners* (1964) AC 465).

3.05 The decisions in *D & F Estates* and *Murphy* left third parties legally exposed. As a result, collateral warranties became increasingly important as the only means of protection for third parties who were prevented by the doctrine of privity of contract and *D & F Estates* and *Murphy* from recovering losses suffered due to defective building work. It has now become common practice for employers, purchasers, tenants, funders and others to require contractors, sub-contractors, and professional consultants engaged in building and design work with whom they do not have a contractual link to provide collateral warranties to enable them to recover directly for any defects arising.

3.06 Although a recent decision of the House of Lords (*St Martin's Property Corporation Ltd* v *Sir Robert McAlpine Ltd* (1994) AC 85) may enable contractual claims to be pursued on behalf of subsequent purchasers of a defective building, even though the purchaser has no contractual link with the contractor, the extent of the comfort afforded by that decision is so imprecise that clients should still ask for collateral warranties from contractors and sub-contractors on behalf of purchasers, tenants and funders.

4 Who needs the benefit of collateral warranties?

Employers

4.01 As noted in Section 1 above, employers require collateral warranties in two different circumstances, either:

* To supplement and reinforce their direct contractual rights from those ultimately responsible for design and construction work. So, for example, the employer may seek collateral warranties from key sub-contractors and suppliers in respect of materials and workmanship supplied or carried out by them even though he also has contractual rights against the main contractor. The main advantage to the employer of obtaining collateral warranties in such circumstances is that if such workmanship or materials were to prove defective, proceedings could be brought directly against the party responsible in addition to the contractor. This will be particularly useful if the main contractor has gone into liquidation.
* Where, but for the collateral warranty, the employer may have no enforceable contractual right against anyone for the design and construction work. This is most commonly the case where 'nominated' or specialist sub-contractors carry out design work in connection with the development, but the main contractor has no responsibility for such design (as is the case if JCT 80 is used without Contractor's Designed Portion Supplement). If a collateral warranty was not obtained here from the sub-contractor concerned, the employer would have no remedy at all. Equally, an employer would also require collateral warranties if he uses management contracting to procure his development. Otherwise, he may find himself without any remedy since the management contractor's liability for works contractors' shortcomings is limited by the terms of the management contract.

As noted above, in the first case, it is really for the employer to decide whether he feels he needs this supplemental protection. In the second case, though, there is a much greater obligation on the architect to ensure that the correct collateral warranties are in place since, if they are not, the employer may well be left without any contractual remedy at all in respect of parts of the design of the development where the architect has agreed that such design will be carried out by the sub-contractor. In these circumstances, there must be a good argument that the architect has failed in his duties to the employer if he does not advise him that collateral warranties should be obtained.

Purchasers

4.02 Purchasers cannot generally sue vendors for defects in the development in the absence of express contractual undertakings from the vendor. A purchaser from an original employer would have no direct contractual link with those involved in the construction process unless the benefits of the construction contracts and the various consultancy agreements were assigned to him. In many cases, this may not be possible without the prior consent of the contractor or consultants. Purchasers from original developers

were specifically mentioned in *D & F Estates* and *Murphy* as having no rights in negligence against contractors for any defects arising in any building purchased. In lieu of an assignment of the various contracts, and sometimes in addition to the same, purchasers will often require collateral warranties to ensure that they are fully protected. Collateral warranties can provide better protection than assignment when it comes to claiming for costs incurred by the beneficiary as an assignee is normally limited to claiming what could have been claimed by the original employer, although the terms of such collateral warranties will usually try to limit the beneficiary's recovery to costs which could have been recovered by the original employer. This can be significantly less than the losses actually suffered by an incoming purchaser whose business may be disrupted by the need to repair defects.

Tenants

4.03 A prospective tenant of a new development may require collateral warranties if the lease is to be granted on a full repairing basis, so that the landlord accepts no liability for defects in the building and the tenant becomes liable to carry out repairs at his own cost. Such leases also often contain clauses requiring the tenant to indemnify the landlord for any losses or costs that the landlord may incur as a result of building defects. With full repairing leases it is desirable that the tenant obtains collateral warranties from those involved in the construction process in order that he can recover, via a direct contractual link, repair costs from those responsible. Even where the landlord does accept some liability for defects in the building, tenants will usually also want a collateral warranty from the design and construction team in order to protect themselves against insolvency of the landlord, an event not unknown in recent years.

Funders

4.04 Where a bank or institution provides finance for a development and takes a legal charge over the property to be developed, the funder will be concerned that on completion it is free of defects and is of a sufficient quality and value to provide adequate security for the loan. Without a collateral warranty, a funder will have no direct contractual relationship with any of those involved in the design and construction of the development. A funder will usually want any collateral warranty to contain 'step-in' rights so that, should the employer/borrower default under the funding agreement, or act in such a way that would enable the contractor to terminate the building contract, the funder could step-in and take over the completion of the development.

Other third parties

4.05 Collateral warranties may be required in a number of other circumstances. For instance, where development work is dependent on the consent of a neighbouring landholder, that neighbouring landholder may require a collateral warranty from those involved in the construction process to ensure that, should any damage occur to his property or should his business be disrupted as a result of the works, he would be able to recover from those responsible any costs incurred in repairing the damage and any loss of profit. Collateral warranties may also be required where a developer lets a development to a tenant who carries out fitting-out works. In such circumstances the developer may require a collateral warranty from the tenant's designer and fit-out contractor to ensure such works are performed correctly.

5 Who should provide collateral warranties?

5.01 Exactly which contractor or sub-contractor provides warranties depends upon the form of contractual procurement used.

JCT 80 (and traditional forms of contracting)

5.02 Under traditional forms of contract the main contractor is fully responsible for his own and his sub-contractors' or suppliers' standard of workmanship and for the quality of all materials used but not for any sub-contractor's or supplier's design. The main contractor can, moreover, claim loss and expense for delay or errors in the design of nominated sub-contractors. JCT warranty forms NSC/W (for nominated sub-contractors) and TNS/W (for nominated suppliers) were specifically drafted to give the employer redress in such circumstances.

NSC/W and TNS/W provide a direct contractual link between a nominated sub-contractor or supplier and the employer. As both forms of warranty are broadly similar, this section will concentrate on NSC/W. Under Clause 2.1 of NSC/W the nominated sub-contractor warrants that he has exercised reasonable skill and care in the design of the sub-contract works, in the selection of the goods and materials to be used in the sub-contract works and in the satisfaction of any performance specification set out in the sub-contract. It is important to note that the warranty provided only extends to reasonable skill and care, rather than a warranty of suitability for required purpose, independent of fault, which would, if the design formed part of a contract for the supply of goods and services and if the employer was relying on the skill and knowledge of the sub-contractor, be implied by the Supply of Goods and Services Act 1982. Accordingly, an employer seeking to rely on NSC/W would have to prove that the sub-contractor was negligent in designing the sub-contract works, selecting materials, etc., rather than merely having to show that the design or the goods and materials selected were unsuitable. In addition, the wording of Clause 2.1 ensures that NSC/W provides no protection in respect of latent defects in workmanship which ought to be covered by the Main Contract. This can of course present difficulties if the main contractor goes into liquidation or if there is confusion as to whether the main cause of, say, a latent defect is design errors or poor workmanship.

Under Clauses 25.4.7 and 26.4 of JCT 1980, the main contractor will be able to claim an extension of time and loss and expense from the employer due to delay caused by the nominated sub-contractor. To provide the employer with some redress, Clauses 3.2 and 3.3 of NSC/W make the nominated sub-contractors liable to the employer for any delay in issuing sub-contract design information to the architect; any delay which may result in the determination of the sub-contract under Clause 35.24 of the JCT 80 main contract; and any delay that may allow the main contractor to claim an extension of time under the main contract.

Clause 11 of NSC/W provides that all disputes are to be referred to arbitration. A major disadvantage of arbitration is that, as the Arbitration Act 1950 makes no provision for proceedings between more than two parties, arbitration is not well suited to dealing with multi-party proceedings of the type common in complicated construction disputes where it is often unclear as to who is responsible for any particular defect. To overcome these problems the JCT have attempted to draft Clause 11 of NSC/W to allow for multi-party arbitrations. However, the relevant provisions are highly complicated and it is very unclear as to whether or not they would work in practice. If multi-party proceedings are envisaged it would be easier to try and ensure such disputes are heard in the courts.

If the specialist design element of the project is significant, it may be prudent for the employer to appoint a separate design consultant, or to use the Contractor's Design Portion Supplement produced by the JCT.

Third parties may require warranties from the main contractor as well as the various design sub-contractors as noted in Section 4 above. A purchaser may also seek an assignment of the building contract from the employer in addition to, or in substitution for, a collateral warranty. Such an assignment requires the contractor's consent at the time of assignment or the Building Contract may be amended so that the contractor is obliged to consent to the assignment in advance of it.

JCT 81 (and other design-and-build contracts)

5.03 Under design-and-build contracts, the contractor usually has the main responsibility for both the design and construction of the works. It is common for contractors, however, to sub-let the

design of the works to independent firms of consultants. Employers and third parties may seek a warranty from the design consultants in case, at a future date, defects arise in the works due to the design which cause losses that can not be recovered due to the contractor's liquidation, due to the inadequacy of the contractor's insurance cover, or due to a contractual cap on the contractor's liability.

JCT 1987 (and other forms of management contract)

5.04 In the JCT Management Contract, and in most other similar forms, the management contractor is liable for all the work carried out by the works contractors, including any design work. It provides, however, that the employer will (in certain circumstances) have to pay the management contractor to remedy any default of the works contractors. This rule applies where the management contractor is unable to recover from a defaulting works contractor. This can obviously present problems to the employer should the management contractor be unable to recover or if the management contractor becomes insolvent. To deal with this problem a form of direct warranty agreement known as WC/3 (the JCT Standard Form of Employer/Works Contractor Agreement) has been prepared for use with JCT 1987. This form is in many ways similar to NSC/W and TNS/W and imposes on the works contractors a duty to use all reasonable skill and care in the design of any part of the works he designs and in the selection of any materials or goods he may select. Form WC/3 also obliges the works contractor to provide any design information to the management contractor on time. It does not, however, extend to matters other than design so that the employer would have no direct claim against a works contractor in respect of simple delay in the carrying out of the work on site. It would be prudent to amend Form WC/3 to protect the employer against any breach by the works contractor of his obligations.

Construction management

5.05 In construction management contracts the employer engages a construction manager and also directly engages the contractors, usually known as trade contractors, who are actually to undertake the on-site works. As the construction manager will not ordinarily be liable for breaches of the trade contracts, the employer bears the risk of trade contractor insolvency and has no main contractor to sue for such breaches. It will therefore be usual for any third party with an interest in a development to seek collateral warranties from all the principal trade contractors as well as the construction manager.

6 Standard forms of collateral warranty

6.01 Initially collateral warranties tended to be tailor-made, usually to suit the requirements of particular employers. As they reallocate risk amongst the parties, they are often the subject of extensive negotiation. Non-standard warranties can vary greatly in scope and complexity with some drafted to be more favourable to beneficiaries and some to warrantors. They can also be known by a variety of names such as 'Duty of Care Agreement', or simply 'Warranty Agreement' and can be drafted as deeds or simple contract letter form agreements. As tailor-made warranties can be very diverse and negotiating them can lead to extensive argument before a development is begun, a number of standard forms have been drafted and are being increasingly used. The main standard form contractor and sub-contractor warranties are set out below.

Contractor's warranties

6.02 The JCT have produced warranties to be given by contractors to funders and purchasers/tenants. These warranties, MCWa/F and MCWa/P&T can be used with the Standard Form of Building Contract JCT 80, the Design and Build Contract JCT 81 and the Intermediate Form of Building Contract IFC 84. The warranties were first published in 1993 and are still in their first edition.

They are intended to be compatible with the standard form of Consultants Warranties CoWa/P/T and CoWa/F issued by the BPF.

Sub-contractor's warranties

6.03 NSC/W and TNS/W for use with JCT 80 have already been mentioned and are currently in their first edition. The JCT Standard Form of 'Employer/Works Contractor Agreement' WC/3 for use with JCT 87 is in its first edition but has been the subject of one amendment.

7 Key clauses of the JCT Standard Form of Main Contractor Warranty

7.01 It is not proposed to comment in detail on the NSC/W and TNS/W forms of sub-contractor warranty which are discussed generally in Section 5.02. This section will be confined to commenting on the Standard Forms of Main Contractor Warranty, MCWa/P&T and MCWa/F, although comparative reference will also be made to consultants' warranties.

The warranty itself

7.02 Most forms of warranty start by imposing a contractual obligation on the warrantor in favour of the beneficiary. Such a warranty in a contractor collateral warranty usually refers to the terms of the main contract. Clause 1 of MCWa/P&T states: 'The Contractor warrants that it has carried out the Works in accordance with the Building Contract.' This wording reflects the fact that such warranties are intended to be given *after* practical completion. The contractor's liability under the warranty to the third party will be the same as its obligations under the main contract to the employer. The contractor's obligations under JCT 80, JCT 81 and IFC 84 are similar in that the contractor has an absolute duty to complete the contract works in accordance with the contract and specification. This position contrasts with a consultant's obligations under consultancy appointments and warranties that are usually limited to a need to exercise reasonable skill and care in the performance of his duties.

Economic and consequential loss

7.03 Under the law of negligence, losses which are deemed to be purely economic are generally not recoverable. Under contract law, however, such economic loss can be recoverable. Therefore, if an employer suffers a loss of profit, a loss of rent revenue, or a diminution in value in his property due to a negligent act of the contractor which amounts to a breach of contract, he can claim such loss from the contractor in contract, although not in negligence. Contractors have resisted the imposition of such all-embracing liability in collateral warranties. As a result of this, Clause 1(a) of MCWa/P&T restricts any damages recoverable to the cost of repairing any defects or damage caused. The wording is:

'... the Contractor shall be liable for the reasonable costs of repair and renewal and/or reinstatement of any part or parts of the Works ... The Contractor shall not be liable for other losses incurred by the Purchaser/the Tenant;'

Where an architect is asked to advise the employer on the acceptability of a contractor warranty, it is important to make it clear to the employer that such a limitation seriously restricts a purchaser or tenant's ability to recover any losses which he may suffer.

Joint liability and contribution clauses

7.04 A further limitation on the beneficiary's right to claim damages from a contractor applies in the case where the contractor is not in fact (as opposed to in law) the only person responsible for the defect. MCWa/P&T contains a 'net contribution' clause which limits the liability of the warrantor to the proportion of the costs

incurred by the beneficiary which it would be fair for him to pay having regard to his own and the other parties' share of the blame. The relevant clause is Clause 1(b) which states:

(b) the Contractor's liability for costs under this Agreement shall be limited to that proportion of such costs which it would be just and equitable to require the Contractor to pay having regard to the extent of the Contractor's responsibility for the same on the basis that [insert names of consultants] shall be deemed to have provided contractual undertakings in the terms of the Warranty CoWa/P&T to the Purchaser/the Tenant in respect of the performance of their services in connection with the works and shall be deemed to have paid to the Purchaser/the Tenant such proportion which it would be just and equitable for them to pay having regard to the extent of their responsibility;'

This clause operates by deeming the consultants to have assumed a legal liability to the beneficiary, even if in fact the beneficiary has not obtained collateral warranties from those other parties. The purpose of the deeming clause is to entitle the court to calculate what percentage of the blame should be apportioned to those other parties. This is a calculation which the court is used to making under the Civil Liability (Contribution) Act 1978 where, for instance, two drivers negligently contribute to causing the same crash. Clause 1(b) is simply intended to cap the damages for which the contractor is liable, and it is a significant limitation on the value to a beneficiary of the MCWa warranties.

Deleterious material clauses

7.05 Most forms of collateral warranty (with the notable exceptions of NSC/W, TNS/W and the JCT 87 Works Contractor/ Employer Agreement), contain a deleterious materials list and provisions. Clause 2 of the MCWa warranties contains deleterious materials provisions whereby the contractor warrants absolutely that none of the deleterious materials named has been used in the works. The situation is different with consultants' collateral warranties as consultants only warrant in their appointments that they have exercised reasonable skill and care in the performance of their services and they therefore cannot offer an absolute warranty as to the use of deleterious materials. They therefore tend to warrant only that they have not specified such materials for use in the development. The deleterious materials provisions in contractor and consultant warranties are intended to complement each other.

Step-in rights

7.06 Where a warranty is to be provided to a funder or funding institution it is common for the warranty to contain 'step-in rights'. Clauses 4 to 6 of MCWa/F enable the funder to step into the employer's shoes should the employer behave in such a way as would enable the contractor to terminate the contract. This is most likely to occur if the employer encounters financial difficulties and is unable to pay the contractor. Step-in provisions such as these permit the fund actually to take on the duties, rights and responsibilities of the employer.

Insurance clauses

7.07 Contractors' warranties will not usually contain insurance clauses unless the contractor is to be responsible for some elements of the design of the works. Where such design obligations exist, insurance provisions backed by professional indemnity insurance are very common and the contractor will often have to rely on the contractor's professional indemnity insurance to pay any award. The relevant clause of the MCWa warranties is Clause 6 in MCWa/ P&T and Clause 8 in MCWa/F. These clauses are intended to be linked to the JCT 1981 form of contract.

It is important to ensure that the insurance will be available up to the limit stated in the clause for *any one claim* rather than up to that limit for *all* claims. The insurance clauses contain provisions requiring the contractor to maintain the insurance for a certain period. This time limit should be at least as long as the contractor's liability under the warranty, if the warranty contains an expiry date. The clauses state that insurance shall be maintained 'so long as it is available at commercially reasonable rates'. This allows contractors to cease maintaining insurance if insurance premiums rise to an exorbitant level. However, the warranty also requires the contractor to notify the beneficiary if such insurance is no longer available.

Limitation

7.08 Most standard forms of warranty allow for the execution of a warranty as either a simple contract or as a deed under seal or under hand. Where a warranty is signed as a simple contract consideration is required (see for example the consideration recital immediately before Clause 1 of the MCWa warranties), and the limitation period for the warranty will run for six years from the date of any breach of the warranty. Where a warranty is executed as a deed, no consideration is required and the limitation period will run for 12 years from any breach. For this reason, beneficiaries tend to favour the execution of warranties as deeds, although the method of execution of the warranty should reflect that of the underlying contract to ensure that the warrantor's liability under the warranty lasts for a similar period as his liability under the contract. It is common to see clauses in warranties which limit the liability of the warrantor to a specific period of time, often calculated as a certain number of years following practical completion. For example, Clause 9 in MCWa/P&T states that:

'No action or proceedings for any breach of this Agreement shall be commenced against the Contractor after the expiry of [ ] years from the date of Practical Completion of the Works . . .'

The advantage to a contractor of such a clause is that it provides a fixed period under which the contractor will be liable and the contractor knows exactly when his liability under the warranty will end. The inclusion of such a clause can significantly reduce the potential liability of the contractor to the beneficiary.

Assignment

7.09 When developments are sold, or some other change of ownership takes place, it is common for the potential purchaser to request that any existing warranties are assigned to him. Under common law the benefits of a contract can be assigned unless there is an express prohibition against assignment in the contract. Sometimes, the warrantor may require that assignments be permissible only with his consent, which shall not be unreasonably withheld. Alternatively the warrantor may only allow the assignment of the warranty a limited number of times, for example twice, or to purchasers or tenants of a specified part of the development. The standard form contemplates assignment without consent, but only on a limited number of occasions. The client should be advised that such limiting provisions may affect the marketability of a development as potential future purchasers may be put off if they are unable to obtain the comfort of the relevant collateral warranties.

11

Arbitration

M. S. MATHEOU

1 The relevance of arbitration law to architects' practice

1.01 As a result of a number of factors, the UK construction industry has, for many years, been a fertile source of disputes. If a construction industry dispute cannot be settled by an 'amicable' agreement, then, most commonly, it is dealt with by the process of 'arbitration'. This means that architects are almost bound to come across 'arbitration' at some point during their professional careers. In particular:

(a) it is likely that the terms of engagement of an architect will contain an arbitration clause;
(b) construction contracts (both Main Contracts and Sub-contracts) almost invariably provide that disputes should be resolved by arbitration;
(c) an architect may have to give factual evidence at an arbitration arising out of a project in which he or she has been involved;
(d) an architect may be called upon to give 'expert evidence' at an arbitration arising out of a project in which he or she has not been involved;
(e) an architect may be appointed to be an arbitrator.

1.02 The purpose of this chapter is to provide architects with an overview of what is involved in the process of arbitration and the legal framework in which arbitrators operate. Particular consideration is given to the various ways in which an architect may become involved in an arbitration as outlined above. This chapter is specifically *not* intended to be a manual on how to conduct an arbitration, nor is it a comprehensive reference work on the topic. There are many substantial books which fulfil these roles and interested readers should refer to the bibliography at the end of this chapter for more information.

1.03 The chapter concludes with a section on 'alternative dispute resolution' (ADR). It was once the case that the 'arbitration' process was said to be the only alternative to resolving disputes by litigation in court. In fact, that has never been the case because it was always possible for the parties to resolve their disputes by agreement. However, achieving an agreement is often difficult and this has led to the growth of a number of techniques designed to help the parties to attain this position. Those techniques have become known by the collective name of alternative dispute resolution or ADR. The more formal recognition of ADR has only started to occur in the past decade or so although ADR is a process which has already been reflected in some construction industry standard forms, and the use of ADR in the construction industry is likely to increase rather than decrease in the future.

1.04 At the time of writing the Department of Trade and Industry has issued a draft Arbitration Bill as a discussion document. The draft bill is to some extent simply a consolidation measure but it also contains some changes of substance. It clearly requires considerable further thought and its ultimate fate is, as yet, unknown. It is thought to be unlikely that legislative time will be found for the bill before the autumn of 1995.

2 What is 'arbitration'?

2.1 There is no statutory or generally accepted definition of 'arbitration'. For these purposes, the essence of 'arbitration' is that it is a process of resolving a dispute by obtaining a binding decision from one or more other persons which is used when the parties to the dispute have agreed to use that process. To explain this by an example, if a creditor claims that a debtor owes him money, unless the parties have agreed to resolve their disputes in a different way, the creditor can start a court action to recover the debt and the debtor cannot prevent this from happening. However, the creditor could not unilaterally refer the dispute to arbitration. Parties resolve their disputes by arbitration because that is what they have agreed to do.

2.2 An 'arbitration agreement' is one which provides that a dispute between the parties (which may be a dispute which already exists, or may be a dispute which might arise in the future) shall be referred to and decided by arbitration. The parties may create an arbitration agreement either by including a clause to refer future disputes to arbitration in a substantive contract, or by agreeing to refer a dispute to arbitration after the dispute has arisen.

2.3 The person or persons who make the decision in an arbitration are called 'the arbitration tribunal'. Subject to a limited exception referred to below, the job of the arbitration tribunal is to hear and weigh up the evidence and arguments submitted by each party to the dispute, to make certain findings of facts and law and, as a result of that, to make an 'arbitration award' which is binding on the parties.

The importance of deciding whether a process is or is not 'arbitration'

2.4 The most important reason for distinguishing 'arbitration' from other decision making or dispute resolution processes is that if the process is arbitration, and in particular, if it is governed by the Arbitration Acts (see paragraphs 2.16 and 2.17 below) the parties will be afforded a number of legal rights and remedies in respect of the process, and, the parties may seek to use the powers of the courts to enforce those rights or obtain the remedies. If the process is not 'arbitration' the parties will only be entitled to whatever rights they have under the terms of the contract between them and their remedies will be limited to those available for breaches of contract: i.e. claims for damages or, in limited circumstances, for an injunction (see Chapter 2).

How to decide whether a process is or is not 'arbitration'

2.5 In most circumstances it will be quite clear whether or not a dispute resolution process constitutes 'arbitration'. In almost all of the cases an architect is likely to come across, it will be clear beyond doubt that the dispute resolution process under consideration is an arbitration and that will mean that, even if the features set out below (such as the requirement that an arbitrator shall be impartial and fair) are not expressly covered by the arbitration agreement, they are likely to be implied into that agreement.

2.6 In cases where there is any doubt as to whether the parties intend the dispute resolution process to be 'arbitration' the courts will look to see whether (expressly or impliedly) the following features exist.

(a) There must be a valid agreement to arbitrate. An arbitration agreement itself must either form part of a valid, binding contract between the parties or it must amount to such a contract. In other words, the parties must have the relevant capacity to make a contract, the terms of the contract must be sufficiently clear for it to be enforceable and there must be consideration, etc. All these issues are dealt with in respect of contracts generally elsewhere in this book. Arbitration agreements are considered in more detail below (see Section 3).

(b) It must be intended that the decision made by the process will be a binding determination of the parties' legal rights. This is to be contrasted with, for example, an agreement to engage in mediation (a form of ADR) where it is of the essence of the process that any view about the dispute expressed by the mediator will *not* be binding on the parties. A process of 'adjudication' is now found in a number of construction contracts. However it is clear from these clauses that, although it may be intended that the adjudicator's decision should have some limited binding effect, the clause in the contract usually provides that the decision is to be binding only until the dispute is heard by an arbitrator. This makes it clear that the adjudication process is not intended to be arbitration (see *A Cameron* v *John Mowlem & Co* (1990) 52 BLR 42).

(c) The arbitration tribunal is under a duty to act impartially. Not only must the arbitrator act impartially in making procedural decisions, he must also refrain from expressing any verbal partiality towards the parties. In some cases the arbitration agreement provides that each party shall nominate an arbitrator and there may then be provision for an umpire or a third arbitrator to be appointed. However (with the exception of certain arbitrations in the shipping and commodities industries) it is specifically not the function of the appointed arbitrators to act in any way as an advocate of the party who has appointed them.

(d) It must be intended that the arbitration tribunal will carry out its functions in a judicial manner in accordance with the rules of natural justice. This feature distinguishes the arbitration process from various other dispute resolution processes which are to be found in commercial contracts. It should be noted that there are procedures which are properly called arbitrations which have been applied in the shipping and commodities industries but which do not possess the full extent of this feature. However, with respect to the construction industry for practical purposes it is safe to say that an arbitration tribunal must only decide disputes in accordance with the evidence presented by the parties and it must not hear evidence or arguments from one party in the absence of the other, at least without giving the other party an opportunity to comment on what has been said.

Arbitration tribunals must also obey the rules of evidence which apply in court (unless the parties agree to waive this requirement). This is one feature that makes it clear that an architect who carries out valuation and certification functions under a building contract, or decides upon an application for an extension of time, is not acting as an arbitrator (architects are often said to be acting in an arbitral or 'quasi arbitral' capacity in this context but such statements are quite wrong). The architect in this context has a duty to act *fairly* but he does not have a duty to act *judicially*. The requirement to act

judicially also distinguishes arbitration from provisions commonly found in contracts whereby an independent third party can be appointed to decide matters 'as an expert'. Such a provision is often found in rent review clauses in leases. An expert can resolve a dispute by making his own enquiries or by using the knowledge which he already has about the subject matter of the dispute. Apart from the exceptional cases of some shipping and commodities arbitration referred to above, an arbitrator must not do this.

(e) The arbitration tribunal must be appointed by the parties, or by a method to which they have consented. This emphasises the consensual nature of the whole process.

(f) The parties to the arbitration process must be the same as the parties whose rights are being determined, and who will be bound by the arbitration award. In most construction industry arbitrations there will be little doubt that this requirement has been met.

The advantages and disadvantages of arbitration compared with resolving disputes in Court

2.7 As stated above, for this purpose, arbitrations arise from the consent of the parties. This means that at some point, either when they are making a contract incorporating an arbitration clause, or later on after a dispute has arisen, the parties have a choice. They must decide whether they should choose arbitration as the process by which to resolve their disputes or whether to make no such choice, in which case disputes which cannot be resolved amicably must be dealt with by litigation in the courts.

2.8 Arbitration is said to have a number of advantages over court proceedings:

(a) Technical expertise of the arbitrator: The parties may feel that they would prefer technical disputes to be decided by an arbitrator with the relevant technical expertise. This is, of course, a point of particular relevance in the construction industry where disputes about the construction process may often involve technical, architectural, engineering or quantity surveying/valuation issues. It should be noted that, notwithstanding any technical expertise the arbitrator may have, he should only decide the dispute in accordance with the evidence presented to him by the parties.

(b) Privacy: Arbitration proceedings are private and confidential as between the parties. Proceedings in court are (in general) open to the public. The fact that a writ has been issued by one party against another is a matter of public record. It is often important to parties that their 'dirty washing' should not be aired in the public forum of the courts and it is for this reason that arbitration clauses are often found in partnership agreements (including architectural partnerships) where it is felt that public knowledge of a dispute between partners could be very damaging for the partnership business.

(c) Flexibility: The parties can have a great deal of control over the procedure, for example, by choosing their own arbitrator, fixing the venue for the hearing and setting the timetable for the dispute to be dealt with.

(d) The ability to exclude appeals: Parties are sometimes keen that, whatever the decision on a particular dispute may be, it should be final and binding in the sense that it is not subject to an appeal. It is not possible to agree to exclude rights of appeal from a decision of the courts but such agreements are possible with respect to arbitrations (see below).

(e) It is often said that arbitration proceedings offer the advantage of speed.

(f) It is often said that arbitration proceedings can be more economical than equivalent proceedings in court.

2.9 In general it is true that arbitration proceedings can often offer many of these advantages. However, arbitration is a process which is used in connection with a very wide range of disputes, even within the construction industry. Some disputes may be of a very limited scope and in those circumstances resolving the dispute by arbitration is likely to offer many of the advantages listed above. However, construction industry disputes are often extremely complex.

2.10 In the case of complex disputes (for example disputes about entitlements to extensions of time, liquidated damages and defects in buildings) the arbitration process bears a very close resemblance to equivalent proceedings in court. The issues will be defined by pleadings, there will be discovery of documents, expert evidence will be served in the form of reports and there will be a substantial hearing, usually involving lawyers representing each party and the consideration of both oral and written evidence (see Section 4 below). In this type of case, arbitration is rarely faster than litigation and it is often more rather than less expensive. The main reason for the greater expense is that parties to an arbitration must pay (often quite substantial) fees to the arbitrator and they must hire the room or rooms in which the arbitration will take place. In contrast, the fees for issuing proceedings in court and obtaining a hearing date are almost nominal, so much so that it is fair to say that for all practical purposes the State provides judges and their court rooms for no charge.

2.11 So far as construction industry disputes are concerned, the point, often made, that the judge may have less technical knowledge than an arbitrator carries less weight than it might do in other cases. The Official Referees' Court (which is a part of the Queen's Bench Division of the High Court) has now developed into what is, in practice, a specialist construction industry court. Although the judges who sit as Official Referees are not necessarily qualified as construction industry professionals, their experience in dealing with a large range of construction industry disputes means that they are well aware of the terms of most of the standard forms used by the industry and they can quickly grasp the technical issues which arise in construction industry cases.

2.12 There are some drawbacks to be set against the advantages which can be obtained from the process of arbitration. Some of these are set out below.

2.13 A particular disadvantage of arbitration proceedings is the lack of effective means to deal with disputes involving more than two parties. This is particularly important in the construction industry where similar issues may arise between the employer and the contractor and also between the contractor and one or more sub-contractors. There may also be cases where (for example) the employer wishes to recover damages in respect of a defect but the contractor maintains the defect was caused by bad design whilst the architect claims the defect was due to a failure of workmanship. Unless special provision is made in *all* of the arbitration agreements these disputes cannot be heard together. Even where such special provision is made, the drafting must be extremely carefully carried out (see also paragraph 3.19 below). Unless there are effective procedures written into the arbitration agreements, even if the same arbitrator is appointed to deal with the various disputes between the different parties, he does not have power to order the various arbitrations to be heard at the same time unless all the parties consent (*Oxford Shipping Co Ltd* v *Nippon Yusen Kaisha, The Eastern Saga* [1984] 2 Lloyd's Reports 373).

2.14 It is often the case that debtors in times of economic depression will try and raise a number of weak defences or counterclaims simply as a means of delaying the evil day when they will have to pay their creditors. The courts provide procedures for dealing with those defences which are obviously weak, in addition to providing a range of sanctions which can be used to prevent one of the parties from 'dragging its feet' during the litigation process. The equivalent procedures and sanctions in the context of arbitrations are much less effective. An arbitrator who is bold enough to adopt a summary procedure to dispose of a weak defence or to deal with a recalcitrant respondent may risk his reputation being damaged by an application to the court on the basis that his award should be set aside for misconduct.

2.15 Notwithstanding some of the drawbacks of arbitration as compared with litigation in the courts, there is no doubt that arbitration can be used to great advantage, and in cases where the parties make sensible use of procedures which may be available (such as the possibility of adopting a 'short form' procedure under Rules 5 or 7 of the JCT Arbitration Rules) the process can offer an efficient and economical way of resolving a dispute. What is certain is that, whatever advantages or disadvantages there may be in practice, arbitration clauses will continue to be incorporated into construction industry standard forms, so the process of arbitration will continue to be important to the industry.

Arbitrations and the Arbitration Acts of 1950, 1975 and 1979 (together referred to as 'the Arbitration Acts')

2.16 Although not all arbitrations are governed by the Arbitration Acts, the vast majority of arbitrations fall within their ambit. The Arbitration Acts apply to arbitrations which are conducted pursuant to written arbitration agreements. It is not necessary that the arbitration agreement should be signed. It is also not necessary that the agreement itself to arbitrate is contained within the underlying contract. For example, it would be sufficient if by an agreement in writing an employer and a main contractor agreed to carry out building works 'pursuant to the Articles and Conditions of the JCT standard form of building contract 1980 edition including all amendments up to amendment 12'. Such an agreement would amount to a written arbitration agreement even if not actually written on the standard form because of the express reference to the articles of the JCT form (Article 5 being the arbitration clause).

2.17 The Arbitration Acts provide a 'legal infrastructure' which allows the courts in England and Wales to support the arbitration process. If an arbitration agreement is not subject to the Arbitration Acts then this legal infrastructure is not available and a number of practical difficulties might arise. For example, if one of the parties to an oral arbitration agreement started proceedings in court in breach of that agreement, it might not be possible for the arbitration agreement to be enforced by obtaining an order staying (i.e. suspending) the court action (see below, paragraphs 5.2–5.12). However, even in these circumstances, the courts have some residual inherent jurisdiction and a remedy might be available.

In the remainder of this chapter the term 'arbitration agreement' means an agreement in writing which is subject to the Arbitration Acts. The individual Arbitration Acts are referred to as 'the 1950 Act', 'the 1975 Act' and 'the 1979 Act'.

3 The arbitration agreement

3.1 As stated above, the arbitration process is, in essence, a consensual way of resolving disputes so the very foundation of the process is the arbitration agreement itself. Arbitration agreements can fulfil four functions:

(a) They establish the jurisdiction of the arbitration tribunal. The existence of the agreement is the foundation of the arbitration tribunal's powers and defines the category of disputes which the parties have agreed will be resolved by arbitration.

(b) They establish the composition of the arbitration tribunal. That is to say the contents of the arbitration agreement dictate the number of arbitrators, whether they are to have any particular qualifications and how they are to be appointed.

(c) They may prescribe the procedure which the arbitrators are to follow. This may be done by setting out the procedure extensively or by reference to some other document containing the procedure.

(d) They may make other provisions in relation to the rules of law which the arbitration tribunal will apply.

Each of these matters is considered below.

The jurisdiction of the arbitration tribunal

3.2 There are two aspects to the issue of an arbitration tribunal's jurisdiction. There must, as a matter of fact, be an arbitration agreement for the arbitration tribunal to have any jurisdiction to determine anything at all and, if there is an arbitration agreement, the particular dispute must fall within the scope of disputes covered by that agreement or the matters which have been referred to the arbitrator for his decision. If an arbitration tribunal which does not actually have jurisdiction to resolve a particular dispute nevertheless proceeds to hear the dispute and makes an award then, unless the parties have, by their conduct, relinquished the right to argue that the arbitrator had no jurisdiction, the arbitration process, and the award which results from it will be a nullity.

3.3 Perhaps the classic example of this situation in the construction industry is where a project has been started (perhaps on the basis of a 'letter of intent') at a time when negotiations about the terms of the main contract are incomplete. In these circumstances, the employer might argue that a contract (including an arbitration clause) did come into existence and, on that basis, the employer might seek to start an arbitration. If the contractor took the view that there was no contract then he could simply refuse to take part in the arbitration and object to the enforcement of the arbitration award when that award was finally made. However, this is a risky course for the party denying the arbitration tribunal jurisdiction to take, and a more sensible course is for that party to seek to persuade the arbitration tribunal that it has no jurisdiction and if the arbitration tribunal does not agree with him then to apply to the court for a declaration to that effect.

3.4 The position where the contract incorporating the arbitration agreement never came into existence in the first place is, therefore, reasonably clear and logical: if there was never any contract then there was never any arbitration agreement therefore the arbitration tribunal has no jurisdiction. However, the position is less logical where there once was a contract but the contract *no longer* exists. This situation can come about in a number of circumstances: a contract may be voidable (as opposed to being void from the outset) if, for example, one of the parties was induced to enter into the contract as a result of a misrepresentation. In other circumstances a perfectly valid contract can be brought to an end as a result, for example, of the 'innocent' party accepting the repudiatory breach of the contract by the other party, or as a result of some subsequent event causing the contract to be legally 'frustrated'. Logic might dictate that if the contract has come to an end in any of these ways then the arbitration agreement (being part of the contract) must also have come to an end. However, the courts have taken the much more pragmatic (if logically unsatisfying) view that arbitration clauses in contracts fall into a special category which survive when the remainder of the contract has come to an end. Even in the case of contracts which, as a matter of law, are void from the outset, in some cases the arbitration agreements have been held to have a separate existence.

3.5 As stated above, the second aspect of the subject of jurisdiction is whether the dispute in question falls into the category of disputes which is covered by the arbitration agreement. In most construction contracts which adopt one of the standard forms there will not be a great deal of doubt about this issue. The arbitration agreement in Article 5 of the JCT Standard Form of Building Contract 1980 applies to any dispute or difference as to the construction of the contract or '. . . any matter or thing of whatsoever nature arising [under the contract] or in connection [therewith] including any matter or thing left by [the Contract] to the discretion of the Architect . . .'. It is hard to imagine any dispute between the employer and the contractor relating to the particular contract which might fall outside the scope of this arbitration clause.

3.6 The arbitration clause in Condition 1.8.1 of the RIBA Standard Form of Agreement for the Appointment of an Architect (SFA/92) provides that '. . . any difference or dispute arising out of the Appointment shall be referred . . .' to arbitration. The expression 'arising out of' has been held to have a very wide meaning but it might possibly exclude some claims against the architect such as claims for damages in tort caused by the architect's negligence.

3.7 As stated above, most arbitrations which architects will come across are likely to arise out of arbitration clauses in standard form contracts. These clauses are, of necessity, agreements to refer future disputes to arbitration (as opposed to agreements to refer a particular dispute to arbitration which must be made after the dispute has arisen). The significance of this is that, in the case of most agreements to refer future disputes to arbitration, the arbitration tribunal's jurisdiction will be defined not only by the arbitration agreement itself, but by another document (referred to in this chapter as an 'arbitration notice') which must be served by one of the parties on the other in order to refer to arbitration a particular dispute which falls within the scope of the arbitration agreement. For the arbitration tribunal to have jurisdiction over a dispute, therefore, the dispute must be both within the scope of the arbitration agreement *and* within the scope of the arbitration notice.

3.8 The practical significance of this point arises in connection with amendments to claims and counterclaims. To take an example, where an employer under a building contract has disputed claims for liquidated damages for late completion it might serve an arbitration notice on the contractor referring to arbitration the dispute concerning the employer's right to the liquidated damages. The contractor may wish to make counterclaims. It is open to the contractor in these circumstances to run any defence available to him. However, the employer's arbitration notice does not cover the contractor's claim for payment of the retention monies so, strictly speaking, the employer would be able to object that the arbitrator appointed pursuant to his notice would have no jurisdiction to hear the contractor's counterclaim.

3.9 In practice, issues such as this can be dealt with by agreeing (either formally, or simply by not arguing the point) that the jurisdiction of the arbitration tribunal should be enlarged to cover the additional disputes. However, this point about jurisdiction becomes very important when arbitration proceedings have been started within the time permitted by the Limitation Act 1980 but one or other of the parties wishes to introduce the new claims or counterclaims after that period has expired. If the arbitration tribunal has no jurisdiction in respect of the new claims or counterclaims because they were not covered by the arbitration notice, then any claim started by a fresh arbitration notice would be defeated by the Limitation Act defence.

The composition of the arbitration tribunal

3.10 As stated above, the second function of the arbitration agreement is to deal with the number of arbitrators, whether they are to have any particular qualifications and how they are to be appointed. It is possible for the arbitration agreement to be silent on all of these matters. If that is the case, and there is nothing else in the agreement which is impliedly contrary to the following matters, then:

(a) Section 6 of the 1950 Act provides that the reference to arbitration shall be deemed to be a reference to a sole arbitrator;

(b) if the parties have not specified how the arbitrators are to be appointed then, in default of agreement between the parties, Section 10 of the 1950 Act provides that the court may appoint the arbitration tribunal by appointing a sole arbitrator, or one of three arbitrators, or an umpire;

(c) it is not necessary for an arbitrator to have any particular qualification.

The number of arbitrators

3.11 It is possible for an arbitration agreement to specify that the arbitration tribunal should be composed of any number of arbitrators. However, it is very rare for there to be more than three arbitrators. This is sensible for the practical reasons of cost and avoiding the difficulties of co-ordinating a large number of arbitrators to attend preliminary meetings and the hearing itself.

3.12 Where an arbitration agreement specifies that three arbitrators should be appointed, then the most common method of appointing the tribunal is that each party appoints one arbitrator, and those two appoint the third by agreement, and in default of agreement the third arbitrator is appointed by some independent third party, or by the court. When three arbitrators are appointed, unless a contrary intention is expressed, the award of the majority of them will be binding.

3.13 It is also possible to specify that the tribunal should be made up of only two arbitrators, one appointed by each party. The two arbitrators then hear the dispute. If they agree on an award then their award is binding. If they do not agree then the dispute is referred to a third person called an 'umpire'. The umpire then hears the dispute (in the case of some arbitrations he may do this by reviewing the papers referred to the two arbitrators, and not by a full rehearing of the arbitration) and makes his decision. In order to ascertain whether the umpire is under an obligation to agree with one of the arbitrators or whether he may make an independent decision it is necessary to look at the arbitration agreement itself. Should this not specify the position, Section 8(1) of the 1950 Arbitration Act makes it clear that where two arbitrators are at deadlock, they must appoint an umpire who will effectively take up the reference as if he were a sole arbitrator, and the powers of the original two arbitrators will fall away.

3.14 Although in some cases an arbitrator may have been appointed by only one of the parties, it is not that arbitrator's function to act as a 'champion' of the party who appointed him. He must hear the evidence, listen to the argument, and then make his decision in the proper way. There is a limited exception to this rule in the case of some shipping and commodities arbitrations where, if two arbitrators fail to agree, they then become 'advocates' of their appointing parties to argue the case before the umpire. However, this sort of procedure is unlikely to be of any relevance in the sort of cases which architects are likely to come across.

3.15 Although some construction industry disputes (particularly international disputes) are dealt with by an arbitration tribunal of three arbitrators, it is most common to provide that disputes shall be resolved by a sole arbitrator. This is the provision which is found in SFA/2 and also in the various JCT forms of contract. In Clause 1.8.1 of SFA/2 it is provided that if there is no agreement on the identity of the sole arbitrator within 14 days of the notice served by one party on the other then either party may request the President of the Chartered Institute of Arbitrators to make the appointment. JCT 80 now provides that if there is no agreement on the identity of the sole arbitrator within 14 days of notice served by one party on the other then either party may request a person named in the Appendix to the contract to make the appointment. The Appendix leaves a space for the parties to identify the appointing person but provides that if there is nothing entered at this point in the Appendix then the person shall be the President or Vice-President of the RIBA.

The qualification of arbitrators

3.16 As stated above, it is not necessary for an arbitrator to have any particular qualification unless the agreement so provides. Nevertheless, it would be extremely unwise for parties agreeing or appointing an arbitrator, or for a third party making an appointment in default of agreement, to appoint someone with no experience of the arbitration process. Similarly, it would be unwise for such a person to accept an appointment. Where the appointing body is one which maintains a list of arbitrators (such as the Chartered Institute of Arbitrators, or the RIBA or the RICS) it is likely that the appointed arbitrator will, in fact, have such experience and, in the case of the Chartered Institute, the person nominated will almost certainly be an associate or fellow of the Chartered Institute, which can only be the case if he has satisfied the Chartered

Institute that he has a certain amount of knowledge and experience of the arbitration process.

3.17 In this context the term 'qualification' may cover not only academic or other qualifications to act as an arbitrator, but also any other particular quality that the arbitration agreement specifies that the arbitrator should have. For example, SFA/2 provides that if the difference or dispute is one which arises out of the conditions relating to copyright then the arbitrator shall, unless otherwise agreed, be an architect. In default of such agreement, the appointment of someone who was not an architect to deal with a dispute of this type would be void, even if it were made by the person named in the clause as the appointing body.

3.18 Another example is often found in international contracts where provision is made for the appointment of three arbitrators and it is specified that the one arbitrator may be nominated by each of the parties but that the third arbitrator (however he is appointed) shall not have the same nationality as either of the parties, or shall be of some specified independent nationality.

Multi-party disputes

3.19 A further point which can be viewed as an aspect of the appointment and/or qualification of an arbitrator is the machinery found in some contracts to attempt to deal with multi-party disputes. As stated above, one aspect of construction industry disputes is that there are often more than two parties involved in a particular dispute. One way of dealing with a limited category of multi-party disputes is found in the JCT 80 forms of contract and the associated contract forms relating to nominated sub-contractors (NSC2, NSC2a, NSC4 and NSC4a). Clause 41.2 of the JCT 80 form provides an option to allow the employer and the contractor to agree that a dispute between them related to a dispute which either of them have with a nominated sub-contractor or supplier may be referred to an arbitrator appointed to deal with that other dispute. The clause is not particularly powerful or ideal. First, either the employer or the contractor may require that the 'main contract dispute' should not be referred to the other arbitrator if they reasonably consider that the other arbitrator is not appropriately qualified. Second, the clause is expressly optional, and a provision in the Appendix expressly allows the parties to agree when making the contract that the clause shall not apply. Third, the clause does not operate in the reverse situation, to allow the employer or the contractor to refer a dispute which one of them has with a nominated sub-contractor to an arbitrator appointed under the main contract. An example of a set of contracts which is even less satisfactory is the ICE sixth edition Civil Engineering Conditions and the FCEC 'blue form' of sub-contract where the sub-contract envisages multi-party arbitration but no provision at all is made in the main contract.

3.20 Where no provision is made for multi-party disputes (or where provision is made but it does not cover the circumstances which have arisen) then the party who is 'common' to both disputes may consider that he may be prejudiced by the risk of inconsistent decisions between the various arbitration tribunals. This issue is dealt with in the context of seeking a stay of court proceedings pursuant to Clause 4 of the 1950 Act (see paragraph 5.2 below).

Prescribing the arbitration procedure

3.21 This is the third possible function of the arbitration agreement referred to above. If no procedure is referred to in the arbitration agreement, then the arbitration tribunal is said to be 'master of its own procedure'. In other words, subject to rules about fairness, giving the parties the opportunity to present their cases, and complying with the law of evidence, the arbitration tribunal can follow whatever procedure it considers to be just and convenient to deal with the dispute. The arbitration clause in SFA/2 is an example of an arbitration agreement which is silent as to the procedure which the arbitrator must follow.

3.22 Theoretically, leaving the procedure to be worked out by an experienced arbitrator should introduce the flexibility for the arbitrator to 'tailor' the procedure to deal with the particular dispute before him. However, this does not always happen. First, the absence of guidance has, in the past, lead to arbitrators adopting procedures which were perhaps surprising to one or other of the parties. Conversely, some arbitrators, concerned perhaps that they should not suffer the embarrassment of an application to court on the basis that some novel procedure which they had adopted amounted to misconduct, were inflexible and adopted an excessively rigid view of the procedure, adding to the expense and delay attached to the proceedings. Accordingly, it is becoming more common for procedures to be laid down in the arbitration agreement. For example, the various JCT forms of contract now provide that disputes shall be dealt with in accordance with the JCT Arbitration Rules 1988 and the various forms of contract published by the ICE provide for the dispute to be dealt with in accordance with the ICE Arbitration Procedure 1983. These procedures present a range of options for the parties and for the arbitrator, giving the parties the advantage of some certainty, and the arbitrators the comfort that if they adopt an option envisaged by the prescribed rules then it is unlikely that they could be said to have misconducted themselves. Arbitration procedure is dealt with in a little more detail in Section 4.

Other provisions which may be found in arbitration agreements

3.23 The range of other provisions which may be found in arbitration agreements is potentially very large, although at least in construction industry arbitrations, there are not many other provisions which are commonly found.

3.24 One point which may be covered in arbitration agreements is the rules of law which must be applied. In most arbitration agreements nothing is said on this topic so the arbitrators must follow all of the rules of English law. There is, in some quarters, a misconception that, as well as procedural flexibility and informality, arbitrators are somehow permitted to be legally flexible to come to a 'fair' result notwithstanding the rules of law governing the dispute. This is not the case. Arbitrators must apply the law. There have been some arbitration agreements which purport to permit the arbitration tribunal to decide the dispute 'ex aqueo et bono' (meaning according to equity and good conscience). These are not recognized as arbitration agreements by English law.

3.25 A more common provision is that the arbitration tribunal need not apply the strict rules of evidence. The rules of evidence are an extremely technical branch of the law which have been developed for the most part in the context of trials before juries. The effect of some of the rules has been reduced to some extent in the various Civil Evidence Acts (in particular the Act of 1968). Nevertheless, even the Civil Evidence Act rules are complex to understand and to apply so parties commonly agree that the arbitration tribunal shall hear and consider any evidence laid before it by the parties and it will be for the tribunal to consider what weight, if any, it attaches to any particular item of evidence.

3.26 Although not expressed as derogations from the requirement that arbitrators must obey the law of evidence, it is possible that the various 'short forms' of arbitration procedure envisaged by the JCT Arbitration Rules and the ICE Arbitration Procedure impliedly mean that an arbitrator following those procedures need not follow the strict rules of evidence: for example, a 'documents only' arbitration would probably be impossible in many cases if the arbitration tribunal had to ignore documents which were, technically, 'hearsay evidence'.

4 Arbitration procedure

4.1 As stated above, if nothing is specified in the arbitration agreement, then the arbitration tribunal is master of its own procedure and is free, within the bounds of fairness and complying with the rules of natural justice, to adopt any expeditious procedure to resolve the dispute. Nevertheless, most arbitrations in the construction industry follow a pattern modelled on the procedure for High Court litigation found in the Rules of the Supreme Court. The objectives of the procedures can be summarized as follows:

(a) First, to define the issues in the arbitration with sufficient precision so that each side can prepare the evidence and argument which it will rely upon to prove its case and disprove the other party's case and (which is, in effect, the correlative of this point) so that neither side can be said to be taken by surprise by evidence or argument presented by its opponent.
(b) Second, to make provision for the preparation of evidence and the way in which evidence must be presented.
(c) Third, to make provision for the way in which the hearing itself will be conducted (if, indeed, a hearing is held).

In practice, provision for most of these issues will be dealt with by the arbitration tribunal making an 'order for directions' after a preliminary meeting with the parties which is held at an early stage of the arbitration. In substantial cases, these directions, and the need for further directions, are reviewed at a 'pre-trial review' or a 'hearing for directions' which is held by the arbitration much nearer to the trial date.

Definition of the issues

4.2 In the simplest of cases, arbitrators sometimes order that each side should serve upon the other a 'statement of case'. Such a document often sets out the nature of each side's case in summary form and identifies, in a mixture of argument and references to evidence, how the party will prove its case.

4.3 Unfortunately, construction industry cases are rarely this simple. It is more common to find that the arbitrator orders that documents should be served sequentially by the parties setting out the case of each in the form of 'pleadings' such as would be found in the High Court. The claimant serves its 'Points of Claim'. The respondent serves 'Points of Defence' and the same document may also include 'Points of Counterclaim'. The claimant then responds with 'Points of Reply' or 'Points of Reply and Defence to Counterclaim'.

4.4 In each case, these pleadings should set out, as concisely as possible, the material facts on which the party serving the document relies in support of its case. Notwithstanding the general rule that the pleadings should be concise, it is frequently the case that the pleadings in construction industry cases run to several volumes with numbers of appendices and/or schedules. One reason for the length of pleadings is the need to deal with *every* material fact. In cases involving multiple defects in a building, each and every defect must be precisely specified, and the particular term of the contract which is said to have been broken must be identified, together with the loss which the claimant states that he has suffered as a result of the defect. In cases involving delay and/or loss and expense it is now clear, following *Wharf Properties v Eric Cumine Associates* (No 2) (1991) 52 Build. L. R. 1 (PC) that a claimant must do his best to ascertain precisely the cause of delay which he says leads to the loss and expense which he claims, and his pleadings, and the evidence called in support of the pleaded case must establish 'cause and effect' to the best of the ability of the claimant.

4.5 The result of this need to be specific is that it is common to prepare a document called a 'Scott Schedule' (after the judge who invented the concept). A Scott Schedule is a table which becomes part of the pleadings in which the claimant enters each circumstance which he claims have caused him to suffer loss, and the loss which he claims to have suffered in the first two columns of the table. Subsequent columns are completed by the respondent, and there is usually a column at the end allowing the arbitration tribunal to enter its conclusion on each issue.

Preparation of evidence
Discovery

4.6 The first aspect to be dealt with under this heading is 'discovery of documents'. This is a step almost invariably found in high court proceedings and in arbitration proceedings of any complexity. Each party must make a list of all documents in its possession, custody or power relevant to the matters at issue (as defined by the pleadings on statements of case). The list must include 'internal' documents (such as internal memoranda commenting on claims made by the other party, or minutes of meetings of the board of directors).

4.7 Once the list of documents has been prepared by each party, the lists are then exchanged (occasionally provision is made for the lists also to be delivered to the arbitrator). The parties to the arbitration are then entitled to inspect and take copies of any of the documents listed by their opponent.

4.8 The test for 'relevance' of documents is very wide indeed. The documents which are relevant and must be disclosed are not limited to documents which would be admissible in evidence nor to those which would prove or disprove any matter in question. Any document must be disclosed which, it is reasonable to suppose, contains information which may enable the party to whom discovery is given either to advance his own case or to damage that of his adversary, or if it is a document which may fairly lead him to a train of enquiry which may have either of these two consequences. Clearly, this process can be a very powerful tool to enable a party to obtain internal documentation from his opponent which might seriously damage his opponent's case. However, the scope of the process means that compiling the list is very time consuming and expensive.

4.9 Only documents which are 'privileged from production' need not be disclosed. For most practical circumstances which architects are likely to come across, the only relevant categories of privilege are legal professional privilege and communications between the parties on a 'without prejudice' basis.

4.10 Documents covered by legal professional privilege are communications between clients and their qualified lawyers which come into existence for the purpose of providing the client with legal advice. Documents produced by the lawyers, or at their request in order to collect or prepare evidence for the arbitration are also privileged. It should be noted, however, that legal professional privilege *only* applies to communications between clients and their qualified lawyers and to documents prepared by or at the request of qualified lawyers. There are a great number of construction industry arbitrations where lawyers are not involved but other consultants are engaged. Communications with such consultants and documents prepared by them will not be covered by legal professional privilege (see *New Victoria Hospital v Ryan* (Court of Appeal) 4th December 1992).

4.11 Without prejudice communications are communications between the parties or their advisers, whether or not marked 'without prejudice', which comprise negotiations to settle the dispute or part of the dispute and which are intended to be made on a 'without prejudice basis' (in other words on the basis that they should not be referred to in the arbitration).

4.12 It is frequently the case that once a party has inspected the list of documents provided by his opponent he concludes that there are likely to be other documents or categories of documents which are relevant (according to the test referred to above) and which have not been disclosed. If the parties cannot reach agreement about any further disclosure which might be required then the party seeking discovery will make an application to the arbitrator to ask for an order that the further discovery should be made available.

Evidence of fact and expert evidence

4.13 The process of preparing and collecting evidence for the hearing is one which continues throughout the arbitration process.

Of course, it is impossible for the parties to draft their pleadings or their statements of case unless they have an idea about what they will seek to prove and how they will seek to prove it. However, it is at the stage in the proceedings following discovery that the final preparation of the evidence is completed. For the purposes of this discussion, the categories of evidence to be considered are evidence of fact and expert evidence.

4.14 The distinction between these two categories of evidence arises from the general rule that a witness's opinion about a matter in issue in an arbitration is generally inadmissible. It is the job of the arbitrator to form opinions about those matters and to decide the arbitration based on the facts which are laid before him. So, for example, in a dispute about the workmanlike construction of a concrete structure, a witness's statement that when the shuttering was removed from the concrete all the reinforcement could be seen on the surface with no concrete cover would be admissible evidence but, if the witness went on to say that in his opinion there had been a clear breach of contract, that statement would not be admissible because it represented a conclusion which the arbitrator was asked to make. However, it has always been recognized that there are certain issues of a technical nature on which a judge or an arbitrator will be unable to reach a conclusion without hearing the opinion of appropriately qualified experts. It is the opinion evidence given by such experts in respect of these specialist technical matters that is described as expert evidence. All other evidence is evidence of fact.

4.15 Because expert evidence is an exception to the rule that evidence of opinion is inadmissible, expert evidence is only admissible in an arbitration with leave of the arbitrator. (See Sections 2, 3 and 5 of the Civil Evidence Act 1972 which apply the relevant rules of court to arbitration proceedings.)

4.16 Accordingly, a party who wants to call expert evidence must apply to the arbitrator for leave and the arbitrator must order as a condition of giving such leave that the expert evidence should be disclosed to the other party in the form of a report to be served at some specified time before the hearing. Such orders are almost invariably made in construction industry arbitrations. It is now also the almost invariable practice to require the experts to meet 'without prejudice' for the purpose of identifying those parts of their evidence which they agree and those parts which are in issue. If used properly this procedure can be helpful in limiting the issues which have to be examined in detail at the arbitration hearing itself.

4.17 Until relatively recently there were no pre-hearing steps which were to be taken with regard to the evidence of witnesses of fact. These witnesses simply appeared at the arbitration and gave their evidence orally. However, it is now almost the invariable practice that the arbitrator orders that statements of the evidence in chief to be given by witnesses should be exchanged between the parties and served on the arbitrator at some specified time before the hearing of the arbitration. This is part of a trend away from the old practices where parties at an arbitration often sought to 'ambush' each other with surprise witnesses and towards procedures governed by openness. The practice also assists early settlement of cases because once the parties have seen each other's witness statements they will have a much clearer understanding of both the strengths and weaknesses of their own case and of their opponent's case.

Submissions of law

4.18 It is also now very frequently the case that the arbitrator directs that the parties should deliver to him and to each other a written summary of the submissions which they will make both on the facts, the expert evidence and the law. Again this is part of a trend towards greater openness in the arbitration procedure and towards shortening the duration of the hearing itself.

The arbitration hearing

4.19 Following on from the practice of exchanging submissions, statements of witnesses of fact and other documents before the hearing itself, a description of the procedure at the arbitration hearing is now rather different from what would have been the case less than ten years ago. At that time the procedure in almost all construction industry arbitrations was that the claimant's representative would open the arbitration by explaining the whole of the case to the arbitrator and taking the arbitrator through all of the relevant documents and correspondence. The claimant would then call his witnesses of fact and expert witnesses. Each witness would give their evidence in chief orally. The witness would then be cross-examined by the respondent's representative and might then be re-examined by the claimant's representative. Today this 'traditional' approach is very rare. The arbitrator will have received all the papers before the hearing and he will have read the parties' written submissions so the claimant can proceed to call his witnesses without a lengthy opening. It is almost always the case that the witness statements which have already been served are ordered to stand as the evidence in chief of the witness so when each witness is called he is almost immediately cross-examined by the representative of the opponent of the party calling the witness.

4.20 The sequence in which witnesses are called by the parties is very much a matter for them. Most commonly the claimant calls all of his witnesses of fact and expert witnesses and then the respondent calls all of his witnesses. However, sometimes it is the case that the claimant will call all of his witnesses dealing with a particular topic (whether a factual topic or an issue of expert evidence) and the respondent will then call his witnesses dealing with that particular topic. The most appropriate procedure varies from case to case.

4.21 After the arbitrator has heard the evidence, the representatives of the parties will make their closing submissions. Again, it is common for these submissions to be put in writing and in more complex cases the arbitrator may order a short adjournment to give the parties the chance to prepare their submissions in the light of all the evidence which has been given and ask for those submissions to be delivered to him in writing. The arbitrator may then ask for a further short hearing to deal with any questions which he has on the written submissions.

The award

4.22 The minimum formal requirements for an arbitration award, subject to any express provisions in the arbitration agreement or rules governing the arbitration, are that arbitration awards:

- are normally in writing, dated and signed by all members of the arbitration tribunal (the date is important as it will fix time from which interest on the award is calculated);
- identify the parties by name;
- state the arbitration tribunal's *decision* (as opposed to the reasons for the decision; see below) on all matters which have been referred to it.

4.23 In addition to these bare formal requirements, the award should have a number of substantive characteristics. These all refer to the nature of the decision or decisions recorded in the award. The first point to note is that the award need not contain reasons if there is a valid exclusion agreement, or the dispute is solely concerned with fact, or neither party gave notice before the award was made that reasons would be required. However, it is common practice, even in these cases for the arbitration tribunal's reasons to be set out in a document which is expressed not to be part of the award.

4.24 In cases where reasons are required, it should be borne in mind that the objective of giving reasons as part of the award is to allow the court to consider any appeal. Accordingly, the arbitrator must state all his findings of fact (although he need not recite all the evidence which leads to the findings) and briefly state his reasoning on the issues of law.

4.25 All awards, whether including reasons or not, should be certain (in the sense of being sufficiently clear and unambiguous),

and final (unless clearly intended to be an interim award). If the reference to arbitration calls for an award in money terms, then the award should be in an appropriate form to allow it to be enforced as if it were a judgment of the High Court i.e. it should specify precisely the sum of money found to be due, and which of the parties is to make the payment.

Arbitration procedures found in construction industry cases

4.26 There are two sets of rules commonly applied in construction industry cases as a result of their being referred to in building and civil engineering standard forms. These are the JCT Arbitration Rules 1988 (the JCT Rules) and ICE Arbitration Procedure (England & Wales) (1983) (the ICE Procedure). Both the JCT Rules and the ICE Procedure cover in express terms many of the powers impliedly given to arbitrators and/or the courts by the Arbitration Acts and by the general law. Some particularly notable features of each set of rules which do not necessarily fall into the category of express statements of powers which an arbitrator would have in any event are referred to below.

4.27 The JCT Arbitration Rules 1988 offer three options as to how the arbitration will be conducted. Provision is made for:

- a procedure without a hearing;
- a full procedure with a hearing;
- a short procedure with a hearing.

4.28 If there is no joint decision by the parties as to which procedure shall apply then the arbitrator shall direct that the procedure without a hearing shall be followed unless, having regard to information supplied or representations made by the parties, he directs that the arbitration shall follow the full procedure with a hearing. This is an interesting point of policy because, without the sanction of a reference in rules accepted by the parties, it would be misconduct for an arbitrator to refuse to have a hearing.

4.29 The procedure without a hearing depends on the service of statements of case and supporting documents by the parties on the arbitrator and on each other. Subject, to the right of the arbitrator to ask for clarification, he then proceeds directly to make his award.

4.30 In general the ICE Procedure allows the arbitrator the flexibility to handle the case in what he considers to be an appropriate way. The arbitrator may order the parties to define their cases by delivering pleadings, or statements of case or whatever other means the arbitrator considers to be appropriate. Express provision is made for discovery of particular documents at an early stage in the proceedings.

4.31 A particularly interesting feature of the ICE Procedure is that there are two optional procedures which may be adopted when the parties so agree (the arbitrator may invite the parties to agree to these procedures but he cannot order them to do so):

- there is provision for a 'short procedure': according to this procedure each side delivers to each other and to the arbitrator a file containing a statement as to orders sought, reasons relied upon by the parties and copies of any documents relied upon. The arbitrator then fixes a date for the hearing for oral submissions, for putting questions to witnesses or for the parties' representatives. However, the short procedure can be 'disapplied' on the insistance of any party, merely by serving notice, without the need to give reasons;
- there is a 'special procedure for experts': according to this procedure, parties submit a file containing a statement of factual findings sought, a report or statement from an expert and any other document relied upon by the parties. There is then a hearing for experts to express their views and be examined by the arbitrator. The rules provide that no costs of legal representation are allowed if their procedure is followed but the validity of this stipulation must be doubtful in the light of Section 18(3) of the 1950 Act.

5 The relationship between arbitration and the courts

The role of the courts in arbitration proceedings

5.1 As stated above, the Arbitration Acts provide a 'legal infrastructure' for arbitrations which are subject to those acts. The Arbitration Acts operate by giving the court powers to enforce this legal infrastructure. These powers can be loosely divided into four categories:

- powers to enforce the arbitration agreement;
- powers to assist in the running of the arbitration process;
- powers to supervise the arbitration process; and
- powers to decide points of law.

Notwithstanding these powers, it remains the policy of the courts that if the parties have agreed that their disputes should be resolved by arbitration then that agreement should be upheld. It can be seen from the description of the categories of the court's powers that it is only in the last of these categories that the courts are involved in deciding part of the dispute itself. For the rest of the categories, the objective of the court's powers is to ensure that the arbitration process runs smoothly. Even if the court intervenes in the arbitration process it is the arbitration tribunal, not the court, which resolves the dispute. As will appear below, even in the case of the power of the courts to deal with points of law, those powers will now be exercised only on a very limited basis, and the powers can, by agreement be excluded altogether.

Each of the four categories of the court's powers is dealt with separately below.

Powers to enforce the arbitration agreement – 'staying' of court proceedings in favour of arbitration

5.2 If a party to an arbitration agreement starts proceedings in court in respect of a matter covered by the arbitration agreement then the Arbitration Acts give the courts the power to hold that party to his agreement to arbitrate by ordering a 'stay' (which means a suspension) of the court proceedings. The effect of the stay will be that if the party who started the court action still wishes to pursue his claim, he will only be able to do so by arbitration.

5.3 The Acts distinguish between 'domestic' arbitration agreements and other arbitration agreements. An arbitration agreement is not a domestic arbitration agreement if either it provides for

arbitration outside the UK, or if one of the parties to the arbitration agreement is a national of or habitually resident in a state outside the UK or is a corporation incorporated outside the UK or whose central management and control is outside the UK. Domestic arbitration agreements are covered by Section 4 of the 1950 Act and other arbitration agreements are covered by Section 1 of the 1975 Act.

5.4 There are certain conditions which must exist before the court's powers under either Act can be invoked. These are:

(a) the proceedings in which a stay is sought must be legal proceedings in any court;

(b) the proceedings must be in respect of a matter covered by the arbitration agreement;

(c) the proceedings must be brought by a party to the arbitration agreement, or by a person claiming under or through such a party such as an assignee;

(d) the person making the application for the stay must be a party to the court proceedings, in other words he must be the person against whom the court proceedings are brought;

(e) the person making the application for the stay must be a party to the arbitration agreement or a person claiming through or under such a party;

(f) the application must be made after acknowledging service of the court proceedings but before delivering any pleadings or taking any other steps in the proceedings.

5.5 In the case of arbitration agreements which are not domestic arbitration agreements, if the conditions listed above are fulfilled, unless the court is satisfied that the arbitration agreement is null and void, inoperative, or incapable of being performed or that there is not in fact any dispute between the parties, the court *must* stay the court proceedings.

5.6 For domestic arbitration agreements, if the conditions are fulfilled, and the court is satisfied that the applicant was and remains ready to do all things necessary for the proper conduct of an arbitration, and there is no sufficient reason why the matter should not be referred in accordance with the arbitration agreement, then the court *may* stay the court proceedings. In other words, in the case of domestic arbitration agreements, the court has a discretion as to whether a stay should be ordered.

5.7 The issue of whether there is some sufficient reason why the dispute should not be referred to arbitration and the court's discretion as to whether or not a stay to arbitration should be ordered are, in practice, the same issue. There is now a very pronounced bias in favour of enforcing the arbitration agreement so, if the other conditions are satisfied, a plaintiff will have to show strong reasons why the action should not be referred to arbitration before the court would exercise its discretion to refuse a stay. Two examples of reasons commonly relied upon by plaintiffs are cases where the plaintiff seeks summary judgment under Order 14 of the Rules of the Supreme Court and 'multi-party' situations.

5.8 In cases where a plaintiff seeks summary judgment, the court has, until very recently, accepted the argument in the case of both domestic and non-domestic arbitrations that if it is right for summary judgment to be given on the basis that there is no arguable defence to the claim, then the claim is 'indisputable' and the matter should not be referred to arbitration because there is no dispute to be referred. This argument applied to both domestic and non-domestic arbitration agreements. In such cases, the questions of whether there should be summary judgment or whether there should be a stay to arbitration have been regarded as opposite sides of the same coin. Some doubt has been thrown on this approach by the case of *Hayter* v *Nelson* [1990] 2 Lloyd's LR 265 at first instance. The judge supported the view that there was a dispute which should be referred to arbitration unless the plaintiff's claim was admitted. Notwithstanding that, the Court of Appeal in the case of *The John C Helmsing* [1990] 2 Lloyd's LR 290 did not feel able to give approval to this line of argument.

5.9 Where a plaintiff claims against a number of defendants in respect of matters arising out of the same set of facts, it may be that the plaintiff has an arbitration agreement with one of the parties but not with the others. For example, in the case of defects in a building, it may be unclear whether the defects have arisen because of bad design by the architect, or bad workmanship by the building contractor, or both.

5.10 A plaintiff may bring an action against both of these parties in court. However, if he only has an arbitration agreement with one of them, the grant of a stay by the court would involve the plaintiff in extra expense in calling the same evidence about the defects in the court proceedings and in the arbitration and would expose him to the risk that the court and the arbitrator would reach inconsistent decisions concerning the cause of the defects. In such cases, the court will often refuse a stay to arbitration (see *Taunton-Collins* v *Cromie* [1964] 2 All ER 332) but this is not always the case. The case *Wharf Properties Ltd* v *Eric Cummine and Associates and Ors* [1984] HKLR 211 concerned a building dispute with 17 defendants. The main contractor, who was one of the defendants, applied for a stay to arbitration which was resisted by the plaintiff, who was the developer, on the ground that the developer would be involved in a multiplicity of proceedings. The judge attached weight to the consideration that the plaintiffs had themselves created the risk of a multiplicity of proceedings by failing to agree the same mechanism for resolving disputes with all of the defendants so he proceeded to grant the stay requested by the main contractor.

5.11 A particular point relevant to whether or not there should be a stay of court proceedings in favour of arbitration in many construction industry cases arises out of the process of certification and decision making written into many of the industry's contracts. It is usual for arbitration clauses to contain a power for the arbitrator to open up, review and revise such certificates and decisions. In this context, although the arbitrator is deciding disputes, he is not deciding whether or not there was a breach of contract: he is substituting his own decision for that of the original certifier or decision-maker. This is not a function which can be carried out by the courts unless that power is conferred on the court by agreement between the parties (*Northern Regional health Authority* v *Derek Crouch Construction* [1984] 2 All ER 175 and Section 43A of the Supreme Court Act 1981).

5.12 Other examples of cases where the court may exercise its discretion to refuse a stay of court proceedings in favour of arbitration include cases where there are allegations of impropriety or fraud against the defendant.

The court's powers to assist the arbitration process

Appointment of arbitrators

5.13 In various cases where the parties do not agree upon the appointment of an arbitrator and there is no machinery in the arbitration agreement for some other body to make an appointment in default of agreement between the parties, any party may apply to the High Court for the appointment of an arbitrator, umpire, or third arbitrator. This right also extends to cases where an appointed arbitrator refuses to act, is incapable of acting, or dies; where an arbitration agreement provides for the appointment of an arbitrator by some third party and he refuses to make the appointment or does not make it within a reasonable time; and where two arbitrators are required or are at liberty to appoint an umpire or third party and do not appoint him (1950 Act, Section 10).

Extension of time limits for commencing arbitration proceedings

5.14 Where the terms of an arbitration agreement provide that any claim shall be barred unless the proceedings are commenced within a time fixed by the agreement, the court may, if it is of the opinion that undue hardship would otherwise be caused, extend

the time for commencing the arbitration for such period as it thinks proper. This provision does not, however, allow the court to extend the time for commencing an arbitration beyond the time limited by the Limitation Act 1980 (1950 Act, Section 27).

Requiring witnesses to attend arbitrations and/or provide documents

5.15 The arbitrator has wide powers to make orders requiring the parties to attend an arbitration, but he has no power to make an order affecting any person who was not a party to the arbitration agreement. Section 12(4) of the Arbitration Act 1950 provides that the court has power to issue a 'writ of subpoena *ad testificandum*' or a 'writ of subpoena *duces tecum*'. These documents are court orders requiring people who are not parties to the arbitration to appear at the hearing to give oral evidence, or bring documentary evidence respectively.

Provision of other procedural assistance

5.16 Section 12(6) of the Arbitration Act 1950 provides that the High Court shall have the same powers for making certain orders in respect of an arbitration as it has for the purpose of a matter in court. These orders are for:

(a) security for costs;
(b) the giving of evidence by affidavit;
(c) the examination on oath of any witness before an officer of the High Court or any other person and the issue of a commission or request for the examination of a witness out of the jurisdiction;
(d) the preservation, interim custody, or sale of any goods which are the subject matter of the reference;
(e) securing the amount in dispute in the reference;
(f) detention, preservation, or inspection of any property or thing which is the subject matter of the reference, or as to which any question may arise therein (with ancillary orders authorizing persons to enter upon land, etc.); and
(g) interim injunctions or the appointment of a receiver.

5.17 In many cases, these powers overlap with the powers of the arbitrator and in such cases an application should be made to the arbitrator in the first instance. For example, it would be a very rare occurrence for the court to order that evidence should be given in affidavit where an arbitrator had refused to make such an order. For other orders the application can only be made to the court, for example, an application for an interim injunction. In such cases, the court will consider whether or not to make the order requested using the same principles which apply to an equivalent application made during the course of court proceedings.

Extension of arbitrator's powers where parties are in default

5.18 If any party fails within the time specified in an arbitrator's order (or within a reasonable time if no time is specified) to comply with the arbitrator's order, then on the application of the arbitrator or any party, the court can make an order extending the powers of the arbitrator (Section 5 of the 1979 Act). If an order is made, then the arbitrator may continue with the reference in the same manner as a judge of the High Court might continue with proceedings where a party fails to comply with an order of that court, or with a requirement of the Rules of the Supreme Court. The effect of this is that if there is a major failure by the claimant to comply with procedural directions, the arbitrator may order summary dismissal of the claim. If there is a major failure by the respondent, the arbitrator may make an immediate award for the amount claimed, or an interim award on liability, followed by assessment of damages.

Taxation of costs

5.19 Any costs directed by an award to be paid are, unless the award otherwise dictates, taxable in the High Court in the same way that costs of an action are subject to taxation. The court may also tax the fees of an arbitrator (1950 Act, Sections 18 and 19).

Enforcement of arbitration awards

5.20 Arbitration awards may, with leave of the court, be enforced in the same manner as a judgment of the High Court (1950 Act, Section 26). Obtaining leave is almost always a pure formality unless the respondent can say that there was some severe defect in the arbitration process, such as problems with the arbitration tribunal's jurisdiction.

The court's powers to supervise the arbitration process

Determination of the validity of an arbitration agreement

5.21 As stated above, even if an arbitration agreement purports to give an arbitrator power to determine the validity of the arbitration agreement or the scope of the arbitrator's jurisdiction, it remains the case that if there is no valid arbitration agreement or if the matter is, in fact, outside an arbitrator's jurisdiction (although the arbitrator himself may have made a determination to the contrary), any purported award made by the arbitrator will be a nullity. The only final way in which to determine the validity of an arbitration agreement is by an application to court seeking a declaration concerning the existence of the arbitration agreement and/or the arbitrator's jurisdiction.

Revocation of the arbitrator's authority

5.22 Section 1 of the 1950 Act provides that the authority of an arbitrator or umpire is irrevocable except by leave of the court. Granting leave to revoke the authority of an arbitrator is an extreme remedy which is rarely used, given the other specific powers of the court in respect of arbitrations and the reluctance of courts to interfere in a pending arbitration. Where the authority of an arbitrator is revoked under Section 1 of the 1950 Act, Section 10 provides that the court may either appoint a sole arbitrator in place of the person or persons removed, or order that the arbitration agreement shall cease to have effect with respect to the dispute referred.

Removal of an arbitrator for misconduct

5.23 This power is given to the court by Section 23 of the 1950 Act. The meaning of misconduct is considered in the next paragraph. The remedy may be sought during the course of the arbitration, but the courts will be reluctant to grant this remedy except in extreme cases. There are two reasons for this. First, the effect of the order is to require a new arbitrator to be appointed which may mean that a significant amount of costs have been incurred and wasted. Second, even if there has been misconduct, it will not be apparent until the award is made whether the misconduct has caused a party to suffer some prejudice; so, given the drastic effect of removing the arbitrator, the court may refuse to make the order.

Remitting or setting aside an arbitration award

5.24 The court has a statutory jurisdiction under Section 22 of the 1950 Act to remit all or any of the matters referred to arbitration, to the reconsideration of the arbitrator. The court has a statutory jurisdiction under Section 23 of the 1950 Act to set aside an award where an arbitrator has misconducted himself or the proceedings, or where the award has been improperly procured. These two remedies are often treated as different versions of the same remedy, setting aside being considered a more drastic remedy than remission. However, the effect of setting aside an award is probably that a new arbitration tribunal must be constituted to hear the case afresh. The effect of remission is that the arbitrator is given the power to rewrite the relevant part of his award.

5.25 The grounds on which this jurisdiction can be exercised emphatically do not include errors of law or fact. The only remedy in those cases is an appeal in the circumstances where appeals are permitted (see below, paragraphs 5.29–5.32). The circumstances do include misconduct, cases where the arbitrator acts outside his jurisdiction, cases of obvious defects in the award (such as failure to give a decision on all the issues submitted to arbitration), and cases where a mistake is admitted by the arbitrator. 'Misconduct' in these circumstances need not mean personal misconduct by the arbitrator but can simply mean conducting the proceedings otherwise than in the manner required by the law. For example, a failure by the arbitration tribunal to act impartially or judicially will amount to misconduct.

Removal of an arbitrator for delay

5.26 Section 13(3) of the 1950 Act provides that the court may, on the application of a party, remove an arbitrator who fails to use all reasonable dispatch in entering on and proceeding with the reference and making an award.

Lack of impartiality, or fraud

5.27 Section 24(1) of the 1950 Act provides that a party may apply for leave to revoke the authority of an arbitrator, or for an injunction to restrain any other party or the arbitrator from proceeding with the arbitration on the ground that the arbitrator is or may not be impartial. Section 24(2) of the 1950 Act provides that, where a dispute arises involving a question of whether any party has been guilty of fraud, the court may order that the arbitration agreement shall cease to have effect and may give leave to revoke the authority of an arbitrator or umpire appointed under the agreement.

The court's powers to decide points of law

5.28 Circumstances where a party may appeal from a valid arbitration award or obtain a court's decision on a point of law arising in an arbitration are very limited. Provision is made for appeals in Section 1 of the 1979 Act and for determination of preliminary points of law in Section 2 of the 1979 Act. Appeals and preliminary points of law may only be brought to court with the consent of all of the other parties to the reference or with leave of the court, and then only if there is not a valid exclusion agreement excluding the right of appeal or to refer points to the court.

5.29 The court will not grant leave to appeal or leave to apply for the determination of a preliminary point unless it considers that the determination of the question of law could substantially affect the rights of one or more of the parties to the arbitration agreement. Following the decisions of the House of Lords in the cases of *The Nema* [1981] 3 WLR 292 and *The Antaios* [1985] AC 191 it is clear that the philosophy adopted by the courts is that, in agreeing to have their disputes decided by an arbitrator, the parties must accept the risk that the arbitrator may make an incorrect decision both as to the law and as to the facts of the case.

5.30 Leave to appeal will only be granted in respect of a question of law concerning the construction of a 'one-off' clause in a contract (that is to say, a clause which is not part of a standard form for a particular industry) if it is apparent to the judge that the meaning given to the clause by the arbitrator is obviously wrong. Even then, if the judge considers that it is possible that argument could persuade him that the arbitrator might be right, he should not grant leave. In cases concerning the meaning of standard terms in contracts, the judge should take an approach which is less strict, but leave should not be given even in those cases, unless the judge considers that a strong prima facie case has been made out that the arbitrator was wrong in his construction of the contract. When the events to which the standard clause were applied in the particular arbitration were themselves 'one-off' events, the stricter criteria would, nevertheless, be applied.

5.31 Accordingly, cases where an appeal to the court under Section 1 of the 1979 Act may be permitted and cases where the court will agree to decide a preliminary question of law under Section 2 of the 1970 Act are very rare indeed. If an appeal is permitted, the court may confirm, vary, set aside, or remit the award for the reconsideration of the arbitrator, together with the court's opinion on the question of law which was the subject of the appeal.

5.32 In addition to these difficulties, Section 3(1) of the 1979 Act provides that if the parties have entered into an agreement which excludes the right of appeal or a determination of a preliminary question of law, then the court will not grant leave to appeal, nor will it consider an application for the determination of a preliminary question. Subject to certain exceptions not relevant to construction industry disputes, such an exclusion agreement is only effective if it is entered into after the commencement of the arbitration in which the award is made or the question of law arises.

6 The architect as arbitrator

When to accept an appointment

6.1 As can be seen from the relatively brief description of the law of arbitration set out in this chapter, the acceptance of the position of arbitrator is not something to be undertaken lightly. An architect who undertakes arbitrations should have a good working knowledge of the law and practice of arbitrations in addition to the law and practice of the construction industry. Furthermore, acting as an arbitrator can be time-consuming. Time must be made available out of an architect's practice so that he can deal with any preliminary applications which may be necessary as well as the time required for hearing the arbitration and subsequently for writing the arbitration award.

6.2 There are now a number of organizations which run courses to train would-be arbitrators and attendance at such courses is most advisable before embarking on a career as an arbitrator.

Fees

6.3 When an arbitrator undertakes his appointment he is impliedly entitled to a reasonable level of remuneration to be paid by the parties. If nothing is agreed between the arbitrator and the parties when he accepts his appointment then the arbitrator usually assesses what he considers to be a reasonable sum for his services and makes that sum, and the identity of the person who is liable to pay that sum, part of his award. The actual recovery of his fees is usually dealt with by notifying the parties that the arbitration award is available to be collected on payment of his fees. This is usually a sufficient incentive for the claimant to pay the arbitrator's fees (whether or not he is made liable for them by the award) so that he may obtain the award and (if he has been successful) proceed to enforce it.

6.4 The position is less clear where the parties settle their dispute before the completion of the arbitration process. It should be borne in mind that this is what happens in the vast majority of construction industry arbitrations. In these circumstances the law probably is that the arbitrator is entitled to reasonable remuneration from the parties in respect of the work which he has carried out but that he is not entitled to payment (either as 'remuneration' or as 'damages' for lost opportunity) in respect of the money which he would have made had the arbitration run to its completion.

6.5 If there is a dispute between the arbitrators and the parties with regard to the level of his remuneration then there are various ways for that to be determined by the court, depending on the circumstances of the case.

6.6 With all these matters, it is by far the best procedure for the arbitrator and the parties to agree the precise terms of his remuneration at the outset rather than to leave matters to what is to be implied by the law. It is common for arbitrators and parties to agree that there should be hourly remuneration rates for preparatory reading and interlocutory hearings and daily rates of remuneration for the hearing of the arbitration itself. It is also now common for 'cancellation charges' to be stipulated by arbitrators to protect them from loss of revenue in the event that the arbitration is settled before the award is made. Arbitrators often also stipulate that they require some security on account of likely fees. It is also common for arbitrators to stipulate that they should receive interim payments on a month-by-month basis. This can be particularly relevant in some substantial disputes where the pre-hearing procedure may take many months, and the hearing itself may last a number of weeks.

The arbitrator's personal liability for his mistakes

6.7 Until recently it had been thought that a person acting as an arbitrator was immune from being sued by one of the parties on the basis that the arbitrator had made a mistake which had caused the party to suffer loss. The rationale for this immunity was that the effect of allowing actions against arbitrators in this way would be to allow the unsuccessful party in the arbitration to re-argue his case in front of the courts with the objective of recovering his losses from the arbitrator (or his insurers) rather than the other party to the arbitration. As a matter of public policy this was not thought to be desirable: rather it was thought that the parties who had selected arbitration as their dispute resolution process should be held to their decision and to have undertaken the risk that the arbitration tribunal might 'get it wrong'. Such rights of redress as were available to the parties would be limited to their rights of appeal or their rights to have the arbitration award remitted or set aside.

6.8 Recent judicial statements have thrown some doubt on the scope of the immunity of the arbitrator but it is probably still the case that unless an arbitrator has acted in bad faith he will not be liable to the parties in respect of the subject matter of the arbitration. However, slightly different considerations apply to the level of the arbitrator's fees and to the arbitrator's liability for the costs incurred by the parties in fighting the arbitration.

6.9 The position is unclear as to what happens with regard to the fees payable by the parties if an arbitrator makes procedural errors. Mere procedural errors are probably not sufficient to justify any reduction in the fees of the arbitrator but if he makes a series of continual glaring errors so that either his authority to act is revoked with leave of the court or his award is ultimately set aside (as opposed to merely being remitted) then it may be that the arbitrator could be held to be liable to return any fees which had been paid to him and possibly to be liable to the parties for the legal costs for which they have incurred in running the arbitration. Bearing in mind such costs can amount to thousands of pounds (or in very large cases hundreds of thousands of pounds) this is potentially a significant risk.

6.10 Perhaps the best advice for an architect contemplating and accepting an appointment as an arbitrator (in addition to the advice in paragraph 6.1 above) is to ensure that he is covered by appropriate professional indemnity insurance.

Can an architect acting as an arbitrator seek legal advice?

6.11 Although it is not particularly common for architect–arbitrators to seek legal advice with regard to the questions of law they have to decide, it is clear that they are entitled to do so provided that certain safeguards are observed. The safeguards arise in respect of:

- the way in which the legal advice is sought;
- the way in which the legal advice is used;
- the recovery by the arbitrator of the fees payable to the legal adviser.

6.12 The issue in this context is that it must be the arbitrator, and not the legal adviser, who makes decisions, even on points of law. Furthermore, the rules of natural justice require that the parties have the opportunity to deal with all of the arguments and other matters considered by the arbitrator. Accordingly, if an arbitrator wishes to take legal advice during the course of an arbitration then he should consult the parties both with regard to the definition of the question or questions to be put to the legal adviser and the nature of the advice which the arbitrator receives. Ideally the arbitrator should invite comments from the parties both with regard to the definition of the questions and with regard to the legal adviser's answers to the questions. It should be made clear that it is the arbitrator who takes the decision so he must not (and must be seen not to) merely adopt the views put forward by the legal adviser without considering the matter himself.

6.13 As stated above, the arbitrator is entitled to recover reasonable remuneration from the parties together with any out of pocket expenses which he incurs. The extent to which is reasonable for him to obtain independent legal advice will vary from case to case, but, on the assumption that legal advice was reasonably obtained then the arbitrator should be able to recover these expenses from the parties.

6.14 As with all matters relating to remuneration and fees, if an arbitrator anticipates at the outset that he is likely to require legal advice then the best thing for him to do is to obtain agreement from the parties both with regard to the principle that he may take legal advice and the manner in which the advice should be sought together with the way in which the fees for the legal adviser would be dealt with.

7 The architect as expert witness

7.1 The need for expert evidence is referred to above in paragraphs 4.13–4.18. The importance of expert evidence in the preparation and presentation of most construction industry arbitrations cannot be understated.

7.2 Whereas an architect should not undertake the role of arbitrator without special training and previous experience of the arbitration process, quite different considerations apply to the role of expert witness. The function of an expert witness is to state his professional opinion on the relevant issues in the arbitration. The opinion should be stated clearly, first in writing in the report prepared for submission prior to the hearing itself and then orally at the hearing.

7.3 Expert evidence is not given in a vacuum. The evidence can only be based on facts and the facts and/or assumptions relied upon by an expert must be clearly set out.

7.4 A set of guidelines for expert witnesses in litigation and arbitrations were set out in the case of *National Justice Compania Naviera SA* v *The Prudential Assurance Company Limited (the Ikarian Reefer)* [1993] 2 Lloyd's Reports 68 (QBD) as follows:

- Expert evidence to be presented to the court should be and should be seen to be independently produced by the expert witness, albeit that the expert is giving evidence on behalf of one of the parties and he should co-operate with the party's legal team in identifying the issues which he is to address and on the overall structure for his report.
- The expert witness should present an objective unbiased opinion to the court regarding matters which fall within his expertise.
- An expert witness should never assume the role of advocate.
- Any facts or assumptions upon which the expert witness's opinion is founded must be stated together with any material facts which could detract from his concluded opinion.
- Any photographs, survey reports, plans and any other document upon which the expert witness has relied in his evidence must be provided to the other parties in the arbitration at the same time as expert reports are exchanged.

- If the expert witness does not have sufficient data available to him to form a properly researched conclusion, this fact must be revealed to the court together with an indication that the opinion is no more than provisional.
- If any of the subject matter of the dispute falls outside the area of the expert witness's expertise, he is under a duty to inform the arbitration tribunal in his report. Likewise, he should make it clear if, when under cross-examination, he is asked questions which are not within the area of his expertise.
- Where the expert witness is unable to swear on oath that his report contains the truth, the whole truth, and nothing but the truth, this qualification must be stated in the report.
- If an expert witness changes his mind with respect to a material issue of his evidence after reports have been exchanged, this change of view should immediately be communicated through the parties' representatives to the other side, and where appropriate to the arbitration tribunal.

8 Alternative dispute resolution
Introduction

8.1 The vast majority of civil disputes which are dealt with by means of litigation or arbitration are settled before a full hearing because the parties reach agreement. In many cases the best overall result for a party may involve accepting an outcome which obtains rather less than would be the case if he were entirely successful at a full hearing of the dispute in court or in an arbitration. The negotiated outcome may well be acceptable having regard to matters such as the risk of failure at the hearing, the delay in achieving a resolution of the dispute, and legal costs.

8.2 These factors led to recognition, originally in the United States, that litigation and arbitration had become unwieldy, inefficient, and expensive and were, therefore, inappropriate methods for resolving many commercial disputes. In addition to the factors set out above, the damage which the litigation or arbitration process often does to commercial relationships and the heavy time commitment required from the management of companies to deal with litigation were also influential considerations.

8.3 This recognition led to a search for a means of bringing forward the time when a settlement could be agreed between the parties and a means to promote the achievement of such a settlement. The result was the development of the techniques now collectively known as 'alternative dispute resolution' (ADR). Those techniques do not emphasize how to get the best trial results but how to achieve the best possible settlement. The difference in emphasis is important because in litigation and arbitration, the procedures are directed towards enforcing rights, and compromise and settlements happen, in a sense, as a by-product of all the factors referred to above. The point about ADR techniques, however, is that they are directed at compromise and settlement and not at the enforcement of rights.

Common factors in ADR techniques

8.4 The objective of all the ADR techniques is to bring the parties together with a view to the parties agreeing settlement of the dispute between themselves, rather than submitting the dispute to a third party, such as a judge or an arbitrator, who makes a decision which is binding on them. There are, in essence, two forms of ADR:

(a) mediation/conciliation;
(b) the 'mini-trial' or 'executive conference'.

8.5 The common factors in both these techniques are as follows:

(a) **The process is voluntary:** there is no obligation to take part in an ADR process. However, it is now becoming common to include ADR clauses in contracts, in particular in the construction industry, and where such clauses are expressed to be mandatory the courts may be persuaded to stay court proceedings to allow the ADR exercise to be completed.

(b) **There is no binding result without the consent of the parties:** this is of the essence of the process – parties do not give up their legal rights or become bound by any obligations unless they agree to the result of the process.

(c) **The process is commercial:** the parties are free to negotiate any settlement they require and they may include in the settlement provisions which would not be available in a court order. For example, in a dispute between a supplier of raw materials and a contractor, the parties may agree to settle the dispute on terms that the contractor will purchase materials from the supplier in the future at some advantageous or discounted rate.

(d) **The participants from each party have the power to conclude a binding agreement to end the dispute:** this feature is also crucial to the success of the process. The involvement of executives from each party with sufficient seniority and authority to conclude an agreement in itself increases the likelihood that an agreement will be reached.

Mediation/conciliation

8.6 The terms 'mediation' and 'conciliation' are often used interchangeably to describe a process where the parties meet in the presence of a neutral person (the 'mediator' or 'conciliator') to discuss the dispute and to attempt to reach a settlement. For the sake of convenience, in the remainder of this section the terms 'mediation' and 'mediator' will be used, but these terms should be taken to include references to 'conciliation' and 'conciliator'.

8.7 It should be mentioned that the process outlined in the ICE Conciliation Procedure 1988 does not fit into the definition set out above. According to the ICT Conciliation Procedure, the mediator receives from the parties a relatively quick explanation of the dispute, and reviews 'evidence' and arguments put forward by the parties. The mediator then produces a report setting out his view of the dispute which he submits to the parties. The ICE Conditions of Contract then provide that, unless one of the parties dissents from the view in the report within a specified period the decision in the report becomes binding on the parties.

8.8 A common procedure for a mediation is for the parties to meet together with the mediator. At that meeting the parties may be given the opportunity to make an opening statement in each other's presence. The mediator then meets separately and privately with each of the parties. Such private meetings are often described as 'caucuses'. This caucus procedure allows each party to state in confidence to the mediator what his real position is so that the mediator can assess the true distance between the parties. This also allows the mediator to act as a devil's advocate to test privately the strengths and weaknesses of the parties' cases and to help to define what, for each party, is the real issue in the dispute. The starting position is often that one side wants more than their claim is worth, while the other side is offering less than anyone would settle for and the real skill of the mediator is to bring the parties away from these entrenched positions. The mediator should not, generally, disclose what he is told without the consent of the party who gave him the information.

8.9 The mediator may, in his separate meetings with each party, be able to suggest ways in which the dispute should be settled. Some mediation rules provide that the mediator is to conclude the mediation process by producing a report which will become binding upon the parties unless they indicate that they do not accept the mediator's solution to the dispute. This moves the process away from the objective of getting the parties themselves to agree to the settlement, but it can also have the result of promoting a settlement.

8.10 Mediation rules often provide that each of the parties should send the documents which they will refer to at the mediation to the mediator and the other party some time before the mediation itself. This is so that the mediator will have the opportunity to familiarize himself with the dispute in advance of the meeting.

8.11 The adoption of some sort of mediation rules is desirable as a guide to the parties on procedure. However, the parties should not become hidebound by the guidelines; they must give the mediator sufficient flexibility to do his job properly.

'Mini-trials' or 'executive conferences'

8.12 The 'mini-trial' is a procedure which is not a trial at all – there is no judge, and there will be no 'findings'. It is for those reasons that the name 'executive conference' is increasingly being used to describe this process and will be used in the rest of this chapter. In the executive conference procedure, each party is represented, generally by a lawyer. The representatives make a truncated presentation of the parties' best case to the 'executive panel'. The panel consists of executives from the parties who have the power to settle the dispute, and often includes a neutral chairman. The neutral chairman is either selected by the parties, or they may provide for him to be selected by some independent body such as CEDR, the Centre for Dispute Resolution (a non-profit making organization set up by interested parties to promote ADR in the UK) or the Chartered Institute of Arbitrators.

8.13 The essential feature of the executive conference is that it has an abbreviated procedure throughout. The parties will be limited as to the time they will be allowed for presenting their case. This is intended to force them to concentrate on the real issues and on the strongest features of their respective cases.

8.14 The objective is that after the presentation of each party's case, the executives from the parties may negotiate to agree upon a settlement. They may also ask the neutral chairman to assist them by giving his opinion about the case as a whole or about certain issues in the case.

When to consider the use of ADR techniques

8.15 There are a number of situations in which parties might consider using ADR techniques either before litigation or arbitration has started, or during the course of such proceedings. These circumstances include:

(a) when making the first move towards negotiations might be perceived as a sign of weakness by the other party, particularly when previous negotiations have broken down;

(b) when the parties' true position is probably much closer than they actually admit;

(c) where there is a personality clash between individuals so that the introduction of a neutral person acting as a buffer between the parties might assist the progress of negotiations;

(d) where it is suspected that the client on the other side is not being given an accurate assessment of the case by his advisers or does not, for some other reason, properly understand the realities of the case (a procedure such as the executive conference enables a party to address his arguments directly to the opposing party without the intervention of that party's advisers);

(e) in multi-party situations; where there are a number of parties to a dispute, it can often be difficult to start settlement negotiations involving all of the parties and then maintain the negotiations until a settlement is achieved. Involving all the parties in a mediation or an executive tribunal process has the advantage of bringing all the decision makers into the same room at the same time.

8.16 However, there are cases where it would often not be appropriate to use ADR techniques. These cases include:

(a) **where the dispute between the parties only concerns points of law:** in such cases it will be reasonably cheap and expeditious to obtain a decision of the court or an arbitrator and there may be no real scope for negotiation;

(b) **where one of the parties considers that his case is very strong indeed:** a plaintiff who considers that he should be able to obtain summary judgment in court or a defendant who considers that if the case were taken to court the plaintiff's claim ought to be struck out, might well take the view that he should make the relevant application rather than negotiate in the context of ADR;

(c) **where a party has already offered what is, in reality, as much as he can or should offer:** the reality of a situation which involves negotiation, such as ADR, is that there will be pressure on each party during the course of the negotiations to move away from their starting positions. If this simply will not happen, then engaging in ADR will be pointless and will only cause delay. Furthermore, it is also the case that where negotiations have failed, the last positions of the parties in the failed negotiations almost inevitably become the starting positions for the next round. Accordingly, where one party has gone as far as he can go, and will not give way any further, it is probably best to avoid the delay while the ADR process operates and simply get on with litigation or arbitration.

12

Building contracts and arbitration in Scotland

PETER ANDERSON

1 Introduction

1.01 The Standard Form of Building Contract published by the Joint Contracts Tribunal (JCT) has for the last 27 years, as amended by the Scottish supplement, been the accepted set of contract conditions for building contracts in Scotland.

1.02 The Scottish supplement to the JCT Standard Form is published by the Scottish Building Contracts Committee (SBCC) set up in 1964. The current membership of the SBCC is made up of representatives of the Royal Incorporation of Architects in Scotland; the Scottish Building Employers Federation; the Institution of Chartered Surveyors in Scotland; the Confederation of Association of Specialist Engineering Contractors; the Convention of the Scottish Open Authorities; the Federation of Association of Specialist and Sub-contractors; the Association of Consulting Engineers; the Scottish Office Environment Department; the Department of the Environment; the Confederation of British Industry and the Association of Scottish Chambers of Commerce.

After the 1963 first edition of the Standard Form for which a Scottish supplement was published, there have been almost annual revisions to match with the revisions issued by JCT until the publication of the 1980 Standard Form. Since 1980, however, despite efforts to restrict the issue of amendments to January or July each year, there has been a continual tide of changes often generated by changes in the law and the effect of judicial decisions as well as developments in practice. The 1980 edition contained a number of important amendments as compared with the 1963 version, the most important of which related to the procedure for nomination of a sub-contractor and the publication of a Standard Form of Sub-contract for a Nominated Sub-contractor more fully described in Chapters 8 and 9.

In September, 1993 SBCC produced a guide to the Scottish Building Contracts Committee/JCT documents applicable for use in Scotland and that updated loose leaf volume is highly recommended.

1.03 The 1980 edition of the Standard Form is still the current version and is in widespread use. In Scotland it should be taken together with the Scottish supplement and the series of documents for nominated sub-contractors. Despite the availability of the Standard Form, it is still relatively common to find contracts are established by exchange of letters or that although reference is made to the Standard Form, no executed version of the document is ever prepared. Although the Standard Form is not without its difficulties, it is suggested that it should always be used and completed because it is drafted to include all matters likely to arise and has been the subject of extensive interpretation in the courts, both in England and Scotland as well as commentary from authors. The Standard Form has the further advantage that it is subject to frequent detailed review by SBCC and JCT and therefore does respond surprisingly quickly to difficulties encountered in practice. Further, where projects involve large contract sums with heavy obligations both on employers and contractors, there is merit in

expressing rights and duties within a single document which has recognized interpretations and consequences.

1.04 It is also important to sign the SBCC formal contracted documents to apply the law of Scotland to the contract. That is of particular importance where the work is being done in Scotland and the parties are effectively resident in Scotland. To use the JCT Standard Form means that the parties subject themselves to the law of England in relation to the arbitration or for that matter in a subsequent litigation which itself might nevertheless have to have raised in the Scots courts. It is not enough to make reference to Scots law as the proper law of the contract in the contract bills.

1.05 The Scottish supplement to the 1980 edition of the Standard Form (JCT 80) is known generically as 'the Scottish Building Contract' and it consists of:

1. The formal building contract between the employer and the contractor.
2. Appendix No. I containing the Scottish supplement.
3. Appendix No. II containing an Abstract of Conditions similar to the appendix in JCT 80.

When first issued there was only one version which could be adapted for use in either Local Authority or Private Contracts With or Without Quantities, but with the proliferation of different types of contract issued by the JCT over the last ten years or so, there are now no less than six editions of the Scottish Building Contract as follows:

1. With Quantities – either Local Authority or Private.
2. Without Quantities – either Local Authority or Private.
3. With Approximate Quantities – either Local Authority or Private.
4. Sectional Completion – either Local Authority or Private.
5. With Contractor's Design where an Architect/Contract Administrator has not been appointed.
6. Contractor's Designed Portion.

Up to the time of writing, the latest revision of the first four of the above is January 1992 and numbers 5 and 6 were revised as at January 1993. To aid visual identification each edition is printed in paper of a different colour.

2 The Building Contract

2.01 The contents of the Building Contract are virtually the same in all six editions and it is important to note the new treatment of the arbitration clause. As in earlier editions it is still found in Clause 4 but only to the extent that the employer and the contractor agree to refer disputes to arbitration in accordance with Clause 41 of Appendix I which contains the detailed arrangements for arbitration. Originally the arbitration clause was the last Clause 35 of JCT 80, then after some five or six years it was transferred to the Articles of Agreement (in England) and the Building Contract (in Scotland) and now it appears in both the Contract and Appendix No. I.

2.02 Clause 6 is the same as in earlier editions, namely 'Both parties consent to registration hereof for preservation and execution'. This gives the parties to the contract a useful additional course of action outside any course open to them in terms of the Contract Conditions, and furthermore it is open only to parties contracting under Scots law.

2.03 After an initial complaint has been investigated by a committee of RIAS made up of senior practitioners, they formulate a report for the Secretary and Counsel. If in their view, a *prima facie* case of dishonourable conduct has been made out, Counsel are advised of this and they in turn then instruct the RIAS Legal Adviser to act as prosecutor and to formulate a charge which is considered by a panel of members of Counsel. That panel convenes a Hearing after written Defences to the charges that have been lodged. Evidence is heard as necessary. The Respondent has

[Facsimile of SBCC Scottish Building Contract Without Quantities (January 1992 Revision) form — "Building Contract" between Employer and Contractor.]

> **6** This Contract shall be regarded as a Scottish Contract and shall be construed and the rights of parties and all matters arising hereunder shall be determined in all respects according to the Law of Scotland.
>
> **7** Both parties consent to registration hereof for preservation and execution:
>
> ¹Refer to SBCC 'Note to Users: Attestation' for guidance
>
> IN WITNESS WHEREOF¹
>
> *In addition, both parties sign on pages 12 and 14.*

the opportunity to be legally represented and after hearing all of the facts and representations the panel reaches its view. It has no power to award costs but does publicize its decisions.

2.04 The Building Contract registered as above is then ready for use, but three requirements must be fulfilled:

1. The parties concerned must be clearly identifiable. In the case of the Building Contract there is no doubt on this score, since the parties concerned are the employer and the contractor.
2. The sum of money payable must be clearly identifiable. Again in the case of a Building Contract where there is a sum of money due to a contractor, the sum concerned would be the amount brought out, for example, in an architect's certificate.
3. The date from which the sum is owed must be capable of being fixed. The date would be 14 days from the issue of an architect's certificate.

2.05 This little-known facility is rarely, if ever, employed by the parties to a Building Contract, but it is perhaps surprising that contractors do not see fit to make use of it when an employer delays in paying a certificate.

2.06 The final clause in the Building Contract is known as 'the testing clause' and attention is drawn to the note at the bottom of p. 3 in the following terms:

> 'This document is set out for execution by individuals or firms. Where Limited Companies or Local Authorities are involved amendment will be necessary and the appropriate officials should be consulted or legal advice taken.'

This note is added because a limited company executes formal documents in accordance with the provisions of its Memorandum and Articles of Association, which may vary from one company to another, and a local authority in accordance with its standing orders, which may likewise be different.

2.07 Finally, it is worth mentioning that the process of executing a document 'under Seal' which extends the length of time under which parties are bound by it, is not applicable to Scotland.

2.08 The habit of the JCT to issue frequent amendments to JCT 80 (often forced upon them by government legislation or court decisions) undoubtedly causes much confusion and at times irritation, especially when, as is invariably the case, the amendments appear in a separate amendment sheet and may not be incorporated into the printed document for some considerable time.

2.09 The SBCC January 1992 document with Scottish supplement does make a valiant attempt to incorporate all of the relevant amendments to JCT (1980) prior to the date of that revisal. SBCC amendment sheet number 2, October 1993, incorporates Amendment 11 JCT (July 1992) into the Scottish Building Contract. The amendment sheet should be signed by the employer and the contractor and attached to the Scottish Building Contract. JCT 12 (July 1993) is also incorporated. Amendments 11 and 12 are given effect by amending Clause 3.2 and other appropriate clauses of the Standard Form.

3 The Scottish supplement – Appendix I

Part 1: General

Clause 1: Interpretation, definitions, etc.

3.01 The 1980 edition of the Standard Form contains an interpretation and definition clause (see Chapter 8). This has been adopted in the Scottish supplement subject to the amendments shown and with the addition of a small number of further definitions, all of which are self-explanatory. It might perhaps be convenient at this stage to mention that the series of documents produced by the SBCC for the process of nomination of a sub-contractor have retained the titles and numbering of the English documents with the addition of the word 'Scot' after the appropriate number.

Clause 5: Contract documents – other documents

3.02 This amendment makes clear whether the contractor is to be required to comply with the new requirement for a master programme or progress schedule which has been introduced into the 1980 edition of the Standard Form.

> **5 Contract Documents – other documents**
> 5.3.1.2 shall apply³
> Clause 5.3.1.2 shall not apply and in clause 5.3.2 the words '(nor in the master programme for the execution of the Works or any amendment to that programme or revision therein referred to in clause 5.3.1.2)' shall be deleted.³

Clause 14: Contract sum

3.03 The words added to Clause 14.2 ensure that an employer is not debarred from deducting liquidate damages following on the decision in the *Robert Paterson* v *Household Supplies* case (paragraph 3.16).

> **14 Contract Sum**
> 14.2 line 2 There shall be added after the word 'Conditions' the words 'including without prejudice thereto clause 30.11.'

Clause 16: Materials and goods unfixed or off-site

3.04 Two amendments have been made to Clause 16 of the Standard Form: an addition to the end of 16.1, and a provision deleting 16.2 (paragraph 3.14).

> **16 Materials and goods unfixed or off-site**
> 16.1 There shall be added at the end 'and for any materials and/or goods purchased prior to their delivery to the site under the separate Contract referred to in clause 30.3 hereof.'
> 16.2 shall be deleted.
> N.B. – See clause 30 – Certificates and Payments below.

Clause 19: Assignations and sub-contracts

3.05 This amendment introduced in the January 1988 Revision deletes Clause 19.1.2 of JCT 80 added by JCT Amendment 4 – the terminology of which was not applicable to Scotland. The new clause introduces into Scotland a similar provision by which an employer who disposes of his interest in the works after practical completion may assign his rights to initiate proceedings to that person. Clauses 19.4.2.1, .2, .3 and .4 are also deleted.

> **19 Assignation and Sub-Contracts**
> 19.1.2 shall be deleted and the following substituted:
> Where clause 19.1.2 is stated in Appendix II to apply, then in the event of the Employer alienating by the sale or lease or otherwise disposing of his interest in the Works, the Employer may at any time after the issue of the Certificate of Practical Completion assign to the person acquiring his interest in the Works, his right, title and interest to bring proceedings in the name of the Employer (whether in arbitration or court proceedings) to enforce any of the rights of the Employer arising under or by reason of breach of this Contract.
> 19.4.2.1, .2, .3 and .4 shall be deleted.

Clause 27: Determination by employer

3.06 The amendment made to this clause is similar to previous editions, but it should be noted in the amended Clause 27.2.2 reference is now made to the Insolvency Act 1986 and the appointment of an administrator or an administrative receiver as defined in that Act. It is important to note that Clause 27 of JCT is substantially re-written in the SBCC version of all of the standard form contracts. There is an amendment sheet dated May 1994 which incorporates the SBCC amendment sheets of May and October 1993.

> **27 Determination by Employer**
> 27.2 shall be deleted and the following substituted:
> 27.2.1 In the event of a provisional liquidator being appointed to control the affairs of the Contractor, the Employer may determine the employment of the Contractor under this Contract by giving him seven days written notice sent by registered post or recorded delivery of such determination.
> 27.2.2 In the event of the Contractor becoming bankrupt or making a composition or arrangement with his creditors or having a proposal in respect of his Company for a voluntary arrangement for a composition of debts or scheme of arrangement approved in accordance with the Insolvency Act 1986 or having an application made under the Insolvency Act 1986 in respect of his Company to the Court for the appointment of an administrator or having his estate sequestrated or becoming apparently insolvent or entering into a trust deed for his creditors or having a winding up order made or (except for the purposes of reconstruction) a resolution for voluntary winding up passed or a receiver or manager of his business or undertaking duly appointed or having an administrative receiver, as defined in the Insolvency Act 1986, appointed, or possession being taken by or on behalf of the holder of any debenture secured by a floating charge, the employment of the Contractor under this Contract shall be forthwith automatically determined.
> 27.2.3 In the event of the employment of the Contractor being determined under clauses 27.2.1 or 27.2.2 hereof the said employment may be reinstated and continued if the Employer and the Contractor, his trustee in bankruptcy, provisional liquidator, liquidator, receiver, manager or administrative receiver as the case may be shall so agree.
> 27.4.3 The words 'and sell any such property of the Contractor' shall be deleted and the words 'and sell any such property so far as belonging to the Contractor' substituted.

3.07 An amendment has also been made to Clause 27.4.3 to meet the requirements of Scots law: there has been added the words 'so far as belonging to the Contractor'. This makes it clear that the employer is entitled only in the event of the bankruptcy of the main contractor to sell property (i.e. temporary plant buildings, tools, equipment, goods, and materials) which actually belong to the contractor.

Clause 28: Determination by contractor

3.08 This amendment which applies only to Private Editions again reflects the terms of the Insolvency Act 1986.

> **28 Determination by Contractor**
> Clause 28.1.4 (Private Editions only) The whole clause shall be deleted and the following substituted:
> 28.1.4 the Employer becomes bankrupt or makes a composition or arrangement with his creditors or has a proposal in respect of his Company for a voluntary arrangement for a composition of debts or scheme of arrangement approved in accordance with the Insolvency Act 1986 or has an application made under the Insolvency Act 1986 in respect of his Company to the Court for the appointment of an administrator or has his estate sequestrated or becomes apparently insolvent or enters into a trust deed for his creditors or has a winding up order made or (except for the purposes of reconstruction) a resolution for voluntary winding up is passed or a receiver or manager of his business or undertaking is duly appointed or has an administrative receiver, as defined in the Insolvency Act 1986, appointed, or possession is taken by or on behalf of the holder of any debenture secured by a floating charge.

Clause 30: Certificates and payments

3.09 A number of important amendments have been made to Clause 30 of the Standard Form where these deal with the architect's discretionary power to certify payment for off-site goods and materials because of the differences between Scots law and English law. It should be noted that the Scottish supplement provides for the total deletion of Clause 30.2.1.3 as contained in the 1980 edition of the Standard Form.

> **30 Certificates and Payments**
> 30.2.1.3 shall be deleted.
> 30.3 shall be deleted and the following substituted:
> If the Architect'/the Contract Administrator is of the opinion that it is expedient to do so the Employer may enter into a separate contract for the purchase from the Contractor or any Sub-Contractor of any materials and/or goods prior to their delivery to the site, which the Contractor is under obligation to supply in terms of this Contract, and upon such contract being entered into the purchase of the said materials and/or goods shall be excluded altogether from this Contract and the Contract Sum shall be adjusted accordingly. Provided that when the Employer enters into a separate contract with any Sub-Contractor
> 30.3.1 he shall do so only with the consent of the Contractor, which consent shall not be unreasonably withheld, and
> 30.3.2 payment by the Employer to the Sub-Contractor for any of the said materials and/or goods shall in no way affect any cash discount or other emolument to which the Contractor may be entitled and which shall be paid by the Employer to the Contractor.
> The following clause shall be added:
> 30.11 Nothing in clauses 30.6.2 or 30.9.1.2 shall prevent the Employer deducting or adding liquidate and ascertained damages in accordance with clause 24 hereof from any sum due by him to the Contractor or by the Contractor to the Employer as the case may be under the Final Certificate.

3.10 Under English law it is understood that provided the stringent provisions of Clause 30.2.1.3 are followed, the right of property in off-site materials and goods is satisfactorily transferred from the main contractor to the employer. This is not the position under Scots law because, except in a contract of sale or purchase (which a building contract is not), the right of property in an article does not necessarily pass from A to B simply because A has paid B for it. Clauses seeking to retain the title to Goods (Romalpa clauses) are of doubtful validity in Scotland.

3.11 Recognizing the need to have a similar provision in the Scottish supplement, the problem has been solved in Scotland by taking the specific off-site materials and goods out of the Building Contract and transferring them into a contract of sale. Two special documents are available in Scotland to effect this: a contract of sale between an employer and a main contractor, and a contract of sale among an employer, a main contractor, and a sub-contractor. These two contracts are the means by which the transaction dealing with off-site goods and materials is taken out of the Building Contract, with the result that the contract sum in the Building Contract is reduced by the amount paid for them, and the architect issues a variation order to this effect.

3.12 There are a number of important points to note in connection with both contracts of sale:

1. The conditions listed in the instructions attached to the contract must be carefully complied with, particularly those regarding the contract between the main contractor and the sub-contractor or supplier. These instructions are in fact identical to those contained in Clause 30.2.1.3 of the Standard Form.
2. The architect must, as has been said before, reduce the contract sum by means of a variation order, the reduction being equivalent to the total cost of the materials and goods being purchased. The purchase price is paid for in two instalments – 95%, normally, at the time of the purchase and 5%, normally, at the end of the defects liability period – and it is essential that a receipt for the price is obtained from the contractor or sub-contractor, as the case may be.
3. The materials and goods concerned must be fully described in the contract.
4. A separate contract is required for each purchase separated by a period of time, although several items can be included in each contract.

3.13 The risk an employer runs in paying a contractor or sub-contractor for materials and goods before they have been delivered to the site arises in the event of the bankruptcy of either the contractor or the sub-contractor. If, for example, a main contractor went bankrupt, unless the right of property had been legally transferred to the employer, the liquidator could successfully resist any attempt by the employer to claim these goods as his own, even though the employer had paid for them.

3.14 Clause 30.3 of the Scottish supplement gives the architect the power to recommend the employer to enter into a separate contract with either a contractor or a sub-contractor for the purchase of certain materials and goods prior to their delivery to the site, although there is no obligation on the employer to do so if he does not wish it. In this connection should be noted the amendment made to Clause 16.1 which deals with the main contractor's continuing responsibility for the insurance of off-site materials and goods after their purchase.

3.15 When the employer wishes to enter into a contract of purchase with a sub-contractor, it should be carefully noted that by Clause 30.3.1 of the Scottish supplement he may do so only with the consent of the main contractor, which shall not be unreasonably withheld, and that by Clause 30.3.2 payment by the employer to the sub-contractor for any of the materials and goods does not affect any cash discount or other emolument to which the main contractor is entitled.

3.16 The second amendment made to Clause 30 – the addition of a new Clause 30.11, which confirms the employer's right to deduct or add liquidate damages from any sums due by him to the contractor or by the contractor to the employer under a final certificate – has been added because of the decision in the Scottish case of *Robert Paterson* v *Household Supplies*, which seemed to suggest that unless specific reference was made to the damages in the final certificate, the employer's right to deduct them was lost.

Part 2: Nominated sub-contractors and nominated suppliers

3.17 The 1980 edition of the Standard Form is in three parts – Part 1 dealing with the main contract, Part 2 containing all the provisions appropriate to the nomination of a sub-contractor or supplier, and Part 3 fluctuations. The same procedure has been adopted in the 1980 Scottish supplement, although a Part 4 has been added.

3.18 The amendments required for Scottish contracts to either Clause 35 or Clause 36 are relatively few, and dealing first with Clause 35 (nominated sub-contractors) they are as follows:

Clause 35: Nominated sub-contractors

3.19 Clause 35.3 has been deleted, and a reference to the corresponding Scottish documents substituted.

PART 2 – NOMINATED SUB-CONTRACTORS AND NOMINATED SUPPLIERS

35 Nominated Sub-Contractors – Procedure for nomination of a Sub-Contractor

35.4 shall be deleted and the following substituted:

The following documents relating to Nominated Sub-Contractors are issued by the Scottish Building Contract Committee and are referred to in the Conditions and in the documents themselves as

The Standard Form of Nominated Sub-Contract Tender for use in Scotland which comprises:	Tender NSC/T/Scot
Part 1: The Architect's/the Contract Administrator's Invitation to Tender to a Sub-Contractor	– Part 1
Part 2: Tender by a Sub-Contractor	– Part 2
Part 3: Particular Conditions to be agreed by a Contractor and a Sub-Contractor nominated under clause 35.6	– Part 3
The Scottish Building Sub-Contract between a Contractor and a Nominated Sub-Contractor	Sub-Contract NSC/A/Scot
The Standard Conditions of Nominated Sub-Contract incorporated by reference into Sub-Contract NSC/A/Scot	Conditions NSC/C
The Standard Form of Employer/Nominated Sub-Contractor Agreement for use in Scotland	Agreement NSC/W/Scot
The Standard Form of Nomination Instruction for a Sub-Contractor for use in Scotland	Nomination NSC/N/Scot

and throughout Part 2 of the Conditions, NSC/T/Scot, NSC/A/Scot, NSC/W/Scot and NSC/N/Scot shall be substituted for NSC/T, NSC/A, NSC/W and NSC/N respectively: NSC/A/Scot shall be read in conjunction with NSC/C.

35.13.5.3.4 shall be deleted and the following substituted:

Clause 35.13.5.2 shall not apply if at the date when the reduction and payment to the Nominated Sub-Contractor referred to in clause 35.13.5.2 would otherwise be made the Contractor has become bankrupt or made a composition or arrangement with his creditors or had his estate sequestrated or become apparently insolvent or entered into a trust deed for his creditors or had a winding up order made or a resolution for winding up passed (except for the purposes of reconstruction).

35.24.2 shall be deleted and the following substituted:

the Nominated Sub-Contractor becomes bankrupt or makes a composition or arrangement with his creditors or has a proposal in respect of his Company for a voluntary arrangement for a composition of debts or scheme of arrangement approved in accordance with the Insolvency Act 1986 or has an application made under the Insolvency Act 1986 in respect of his Company to the Court for the appointment of an administrator or has his estate sequestrated or becomes apparently insolvent or enters into a trust deed for his creditors or has a winding up order made or (except for the purposes of reconstruction) has a resolution for voluntary winding up passed or a receiver or manager of his business or undertaking duly appointed or has an administrative receiver or an administrator as defined in the Insolvency Act 1986 appointed, or possession is taken by or on behalf of any holder of any debenture secured by a floating charge; or

The following clause shall be added:

35.27 Determination of employment of Contractor

The Nominated Sub-Contractor shall recognise an Assignation by the Contractor in favour of the Employer in terms of clause 27.4.2.1.

3.20 Clause 35.13.5.4.4 has been deleted and the alternative clause is similar to early editions although the reference in the fourth line to the contractor being 'apparently insolvent' should be noted. This is to comply with the new bankruptcy laws.

3.21 The amendments to Clauses 35.13.6 and 35.17 are necessary owing to different clause numbers in NSC/2/Scot and NSC/2a/Scot.

3.22 Clause 35.24.2 has been deleted, and the substituted clause in the Scottish supplement uses Scottish legal phraseology.

3.23 Finally, Clause 35.27 has been added requiring a nominated sub-contractor to recognize an assignation by the contractor in favour of the employer in terms of Clause 27.4.2.1. This additional clause is required to clarify the situation and to conform with the requirements of Scots law.

Clause 36: Nominated suppliers

3.24 The two amendments made to this section are as follows:

1. Clause 36.4.8 has been deleted, and the clause now provides that if the dispute between the contractor and the nominated supplier is substantially the same as a dispute under the Building Contract, then it should be referred to the arbiter appointed by Clause 4 of the Building Contract.
2. The second amendment is the addition of Clause 36.6, which like Clause 35.27 requires the nominated supplier to recognize an assignation by the contractor in favour of the employer.

36 Nominated Suppliers

36.4.8.1 and 36.4.8.2 shall be deleted and the following substituted:

36.4.8.1 that in any dispute or difference between the Contractor and the Nominated Supplier which is referred to arbitration the Contractor and the Nominated Supplier agree and consent that either the Contractor or the Nominated Supplier may require the Arbiter to state a case under Section 3 of the Administration of Justice (Scotland) Act 1972 on any question of law arising out of a proposed award made in the arbitration, and that the Contractor and the Nominated Supplier agree that the Court of Session should have jurisdiction to determine any questions of law;

***The Architect/the Contract Administrator should state whether in Appendix II the words 'Clauses 41.2.1 and 41.2.2' have been deleted; if so then clause 36.4.8.2 will not apply to the Nominated Supplier**

36.4.8.2 that if any dispute or difference between the Employer and/or the Contractor and the Nominated Supplier raises predominantly issues which are substantially the same as or are connected with issues raised in a related dispute between the Employer and the Contractor under this Contract then, where *clauses 41.2.1 and 41.2.2 apply, such dispute or difference shall be referred to the Arbiter already appointed pursuant to clause 41; and the Employer and/or the Contractor and the Nominated Supplier agree that such Arbiter shall have the same powers and discretions as are enjoyed by the Court of Session in respect of the joining of one or more defenders or joining co-defenders or third parties and he and the parties shall be entitled to apply the same procedures with appropriate modifications as are available under rules of court for such purposes and he may make all directions and awards including part, interim and final awards as he considers appropriate for these purposes;

– that the agreement and consent referred to in clause 36.4.8.1 on a stated case under Section 3 of the Administration of Justice (Scotland) Act 1972 to the Court of Session on any question of law shall apply to any question of law arising out of the proposed awards of such Arbiter in respect of all related disputes referred to him or arising in the course of the reference of all related disputes referred to him;

– and that in any case, subject to the agreement referred to in clause 36.4.8.1, the award of such Arbiter shall be final and binding on the parties.

When the Employer and/or the Contractor or the Nominated Supplier require such dispute or difference to be referred to arbitration, then either the Employer and/or the Contractor or the Nominated Supplier shall give written notice to the other to such effect and such dispute or difference shall be referred to the arbitration and final decision of the already appointed Arbiter. Arbitration proceedings shall be deemed to have been instituted on the date when such notice is given. The written notice shall also be given to the already appointed Arbiter and his appointment as Arbiter between the Employer and/or the Contractor and the Nominated Supplier shall take effect when the Arbiter gives the parties notice in writing that he accepts the appointment. If he does not give such notice of acceptance within 28 days after receipt of notice from the Employer and/or the Contractor or the Nominated Supplier, he shall be deemed to have declined the appointment. Any such appointment shall extend to and include the power to determine whether the issues predominantly raised between the Employer and/or the Contractor and the Nominated Supplier are substantially the same as or are connected with issues in the related dispute on which he has already been appointed Arbiter or if having regard to the limited scope of the convergence between the related dispute and the dispute or difference under this Agreement, it is more appropriate that this dispute or difference be referred to a different Arbiter. Save that either the Employer or the Contractor or the Nominated Supplier may require the dispute or difference arising under the Supply Contract to be referred to a different Arbiter (to be appointed under the Supply Contract) if any of them reasonably considers that the Arbiter appointed to determine the related dispute is not appropriately qualified to determine the dispute or difference under the Supply Contract and it is more appropriate that this dispute or difference is referred to a different Arbiter.

Any dispute or difference as to the applicability of clause 36.4.8.2 shall be referred to the determination of the Arbiter appointed to deal with the related dispute. If the Arbiter already appointed declines to deal with the related dispute or determines that the dispute is sufficiently different and shall be referred to another Arbiter, then, failing agreement between the parties upon another Arbiter within 14 days of said declinature or determination, the matter shall be referred to an Arbiter appointed by the Chairman or Vice-Chairman of the Scottish Building Contract Committee.

36.4.8.3 Unless otherwise agreed, the Arbiter may if he thinks fit award simple interest at such rate as he thinks fit (a) on any sum which is subject to the reference but which is paid before the award for such period commencing not earlier than the date on which the right to payment in respect of any part of the said sum (whether then quantified or not) first arose and ending not later than the date of payment as he thinks fit and (b) on any sum which he awards for such period commencing not earlier than the date on which the right to payment first arose in respect of any part of the said sum (whether then quantified or not) and ending not later than the date of his award as he thinks fit; and he may fix different periods for different parts of said sum all as he thinks fit.

36.4.8.3.1 The foregoing power to award interest shall be equally applicable to sums awarded by way of interim and part awards as to sums awarded as final awards, and shall apply irrespective of the basis in law upon which the said sums are awarded.

36.4.8.3.2 The foregoing power to award interest shall be exerciseable notwithstanding that the principal sum requires to be quantified or that the debtor has claims by way of retention or set off.

36.4.8.3.3 The foregoing powers to award interest conferred on the Arbiter are without prejudice to any other power of an Arbiter to award interest.

36.4.8.3.4 A sum directed to be paid by an award shall, unless the award otherwise directs, carry interest as from the date of the award at the same rate as the Court of Session judicial rate applying at the date of the commencement of the arbitration.

36.4.8.4 Any party to subsisting arbitration proceedings may apply to the Chairman or Vice-Chairman of the Scottish Building Contract Committee for the office of Arbiter to be declared vacant and the Chairman or Vice-Chairman, as appropriate, may declare the office of Arbiter vacant should any of the following circumstances occur:–

36.4.8.4.1 The Arbiter refuses to act or delays unreasonably to act;

36.4.8.4.2 The Arbiter resigns or withdraws from acting;

36.4.8.4.3 The Arbiter becomes incapacitated by reason of mental or physical infirmity from discharging the duties of Arbiter;

36.4.8.4.4 The Arbiter is disqualified for whatever reason from performing the duties of his office;

36.4.8.4.5 The Arbiter dies.

36.4.8.5 The Chairman or Vice-Chairman of the Scottish Building Contract Committee acting under the provisions of clause 36.4.8 is hereby empowered and shall be entitled to apply the Facilitating Regulations of the Scottish Building Contract Committee's Arbitration Service.

36.4.8.6 Any Arbiter appointed for the purposes of clause 36.4.8 shall have the same powers as an Arbiter appointed and acting under the provisions of clause 41 hereof and, without prejudice to the foregoing generality, clauses 41.2.3, 41.3, 41.5 and 41.6.

The following clause shall be added:

36.6 Determination of Employment of Contractor

The Nominated Supplier shall recognise an Assignation by the Contractor in favour of the Employer in terms of clause 27.4.2.1.

Part 3: Fluctuations

3.25 It is not necessary to make any amendments to this part in the Scottish supplement, but attention is drawn to the appropriate entry in Appendix II, page 8, by which the applicable fluctuation clause is identified.

Part 4: Settlement of disputes – arbitration

3.26 Part 4 of early editions of the Scottish Building Contract was only introduced for those who chose to create the contract between the employer and the contractor by an exchange of letters (see paragraph 1.03) so that they could incorporate it into their contract by reference, but in the January 1988 Revision, Part 4 contains the full arbitration Clause 41, replacing the corresponding English clause of JCT 80.

PART 4 – SETTLEMENT OF DISPUTES – ARBITRATION

41 shall be deleted and the following substituted therefor:

41 In the event of any dispute or difference between the Employer and the Contractor arising during the progress of the Works or after completion or abandonment thereof in regard to any matter or thing whatsoever arising out of this Contract or in connection therewith including:

any matter or thing left by this Contract to the discretion of the Architect/the Contract Administrator, or

the withholding by the Architect/the Contract Administrator of any certificate to which the Contractor may claim to be entitled, or

– the adjustment of the Contract Sum under clause 30.6.2, or

– the rights and liabilities of the parties under clauses 27, 28, 32 or 33, or

unreasonable withholding of consent or agreement by the Employer or the Architect/the Contract Administrator on his behalf or by the Contractor (but excluding any such dispute or difference arising under clause 31 to the extent provided in clause 31.9 and under clause 3 of the VAT Agreement), then the said dispute or difference shall be and is hereby referred to the arbitration of such person as the parties may agree to appoint as Arbiter or failing agreement within 14 days after either party has given to the other written notice to concur in the appointment of an Arbiter as may be appointed by the person named in Appendix II whom failing by the Chairman or Vice-Chairman of the Scottish Building Contract Committee. Arbitration proceedings shall be deemed to have been instituted on the date on which the said written notice has been given.

41.1 No arbitration shall commence without the written consent of the parties until after determination or alleged determination of the Contractor's employment or until after Practical Completion or alleged Practical Completion or abandonment of the Works unless it relates to

41.1.1 the nominations of an Architect/the Contract Administrator or Quantity Surveyor to a vacant appointment

41.1.2 whether or not the issue of an instruction is empowered by these Conditions

41.1.3 whether or not a certificate has been improperly withheld or is not in accordance with these Conditions

41.1.4 Clause 4.1 in regard to a reasonable objection by the Contractor, clauses 8.4, 8.5, 18.1 or 23.3.2 (so far as these relate to the Contractor's withholding of consent) and clauses 25, 32 and 33

41.1.5 whether a determination under clause 22C.4.3.1 will be just and equitable.

41.2.1 Provided that if the dispute or difference to be referred to arbitration under this Contract raises predominantly issues which are substantially the same as or are connected with issues raised in a related dispute between

the Employer and any Nominated Sub-Contractor under Agreement NSC/W/Scot as applicable, or

the Contractor and any Nominated Sub-Contractor under Sub-Contract NSC/A/Scot, or

the Contractor and/or the Employer and any Nominated Supplier whose contract of sale with the Contractor provides for the matters referred to in clause 36.4.8.2,

and if the related dispute has already been referred for determination to an Arbiter who has already been appointed, the Employer and the Contractor hereby agree

that the dispute or difference under this Contract shall be referred to the Arbiter appointed to determine the related dispute,

that such Arbiter shall have the same powers and discretions as are enjoyed by the Court of Session in respect of the joining of one or more defenders or joining co-defenders or third parties and he and the parties shall be entitled to apply the same procedures with appropriate modifications as are available under rules of court for such purposes and he may make all directions and awards including part, interim and final awards as he considers appropriate for these purposes,

and that the provisions of Section 3 of the Administration of Justice (Scotland) Act 1972 shall apply to any question of law arising out of the awards of such Arbiter in respect of all related disputes referred to him or arising in the course of the reference of all related disputes referred to him.

When the Employer or the Contractor requires such dispute or difference to be referred to arbitration, then either the Employer or the Contractor shall give written notice to the other to such effect and such dispute or difference shall be referred to the arbitration and final decision of the already appointed Arbiter. Arbitration proceedings shall be deemed to have been instituted on the date when such notice is given. The written notice shall also be given to the already appointed Arbiter and his appointment as Arbiter between the Employer and the Contractor shall take effect when the Arbiter gives the parties notice in writing that he accepts the appointment. If he does not give such notice of acceptance within 28 days after receipt of notice from the Employer or the Contractor, he shall be deemed to have declined the appointment. Any such appointment shall extend to and include the power to determine whether the issues predominantly raised between the Employer and the Contractor are substantially the same as or are connected with issues in the related dispute on which he has already been appointed Arbiter or if having regard to the limited scope of the convergence between the related dispute and the dispute or difference under this Agreement, it is more appropriate that this dispute or difference be referred to a different Arbiter. Any dispute or difference as to the applicability of clause 41.2.2 shall be referred to the determination of the Arbiter appointed to deal with the related dispute.

41.2.2 Save that the Employer or the Contractor may require the dispute or difference under this Contract to be referred to a different Arbiter (to be appointed under this Contract) if either of them reasonably considers that the Arbiter appointed to determine the related dispute is not appropriately qualified to determine the dispute or difference under this Contract. The reference to an already appointed Arbiter shall include a reference of any question whether the issues raised predominantly are substantially the same or connected with those raised in the related dispute.

41.2.3 Clauses 41.2.1 and 41.2.2 shall apply unless in Appendix II the words 'Clauses 41.2.1 and 41.2.2 apply' have been deleted.

41.2.4 If the Arbiter already appointed referred to in clause 41.2.1 declines to deal with the related dispute or determines that the dispute is sufficiently different and should be referred to another Arbiter, then, failing agreement between the parties upon another Arbiter within 14 days of said declinature or determination, the matter shall be referred to an Arbiter appointed by the Chairman or Vice-Chairman of the Scottish Building Contract Committee.

41.3 Subject to the provisions of clauses 4.2, 30.9, 38.4.3, 39.5.3 and 40.5 the Arbiter shall have power to

41.3.1 direct such measurements and/or valuations as may in his opinion be desirable in order to determine the rights of the parties

41.3.2 ascertain and award any sum which ought to have been referred to or included in any certificate

41.3.3 open up, review and revise any certificate, opinion, decision, requirement or notice (except where clause 8.4 is relevant, a decision of the Architect/the Contract Administrator to issue instructions pursuant to clause 8.4.1)

41.3.4 determine all matters in dispute which shall be submitted to him in the same manner as if no such certificate, opinion, decision, requirement or notice had been given

41.3.5 award compensation or damages and expenses to or against any of the parties to the arbitration.

41.4 The Law of Scotland shall apply to all arbitrations in terms of this clause and the award of the Arbiter shall be final and binding on the parties subject to the provisions of Section 3 of the Administration of Justice (Scotland) Act 1972.

41.5 The Arbiter shall be entitled to appoint a Clerk to assist him in accordance with normal arbitration practice, to issue interim, part or final awards as well as proposed findings, to remuneration and reimbursement of his outlays, and to find the parties jointly and severally liable therefor, and to decern; and to dispense with a Deed of Submission.

41.6 Unless otherwise agreed, the Arbiter may if he thinks fit award simple interest at such rate as he thinks fit (a) on any sum which is subject to the reference but which is paid before the award for such period commencing not earlier than the date on which the right to payment in respect of any part of the said sum (whether then quantified or not) first arose and ending not later than the date of payment as he thinks fit and (b) on any sum which he awards for such period commencing not earlier than the date on which the right to payment first arose in respect of any part of the said sum (whether then quantified or not) and ending not later than the date of his award as he thinks fit; and he may fix different periods for different parts of said sum all as he thinks fit.

41.6.1 The foregoing power to award interest shall be equally applicable to sums awarded by way of interim and part awards as to sums awarded as final awards, and shall apply irrespective of the basis in law upon which the said sums are awarded.

41.6.2 The foregoing power to award interest shall be exerciseable notwithstanding that the principal sum requires to be quantified or that the debtor has claims by way of retention or set off.

41.6.3 The foregoing powers to award interest conferred on the Arbiter are without prejudice to any other power of an Arbiter to award interest.

41.6.4 A sum directed to be paid by an award shall, unless the award otherwise directs, carry interest as from the date of the award at the same rate as the Court of Session judicial rate applying at the date of the commencement of the arbitration.

41.7 Any party to subsisting arbitration proceedings may apply to the Chairman or Vice-Chairman of the Scottish Building Contract Committee for the office of Arbiter to be declared vacant and the Chairman or Vice-Chairman, as appropriate, may declare the office of Arbiter vacant should any of the following circumstances occur:–

41.7.1 The Arbiter refuses to act or delays unreasonably to act;

41.7.2 The Arbiter resigns or withdraws from acting;

41.7.3 The Arbiter becomes incapacitated by reason of mental or physical infirmity from discharging the duties of Arbiter;

41.7.4 The Arbiter is disqualified for whatever reason from performing the duties of his office;

41.7.5 The Arbiter dies.

41.8 The Chairman or Vice-Chairman of the Scottish Building Contract Committee acting under the provisions of clause 41 is hereby empowered and shall be entitled to apply the Facilitating Regulations of the Scottish Building Contract Committee's Arbitration Service.

3.27 There are some important changes in the current arbitration clause as compared with earlier versions:

1. In place of the traditional arrangement that the arbiter, failing agreement by the parties, should be appointed by the Sheriff of the Sheriffdom in which the works are being carried out, the arbiter is now in these circumstances appointed by one of either the Sheriff, the Dean of the Faculty of Advocates or the Chairman or Vice-Chairman of the SBCC as may be indicated in the Abstract of Conditions comprising Appendix no. II. Failing such indication the appointee is the Chairman or Vice-Chairman of the SBCC. In July 1988 the JCT issued Arbitration Rules which are obligatory for parties conducting arbitrations under JCT 80. These Rules were not adopted by the SBCC but instead the SBCC has created an arbitration appointment service in conjunction with which it has published a series of forms aimed at facilitating the appointment of an arbiter. These forms are as follows:

   1. ARB.1 – Notice to Consent in the Appointment of an Arbiter.
   2. ARB.2 – Application to the Chairman, SBCC for the Appointment of an Arbiter.
   3. ARB.3 – Form of Notice of Unilateral Application for the Appointment of an Arbiter.
   4. ARB.4 – Form of Notice of Appointment.
   5. ARB.5 – Form of Objection to Nomination.
   6. ARB.6 – Notice of Decision following Objection to nominated Arbiter.
   7. ARB.7 – Form of Application to declare Office of Arbiter vacant.
   8. ARB.8 – Form of Intimation of Notice of Application to declare the Office of Arbiter vacant.

9. ARB.9 – Notice of Decision following Application to Declare the Office of Arbiter vacant.
10. ARB.10 – Notice of Hearing.

2. New grounds for the appointment of an arbiter have been added in Clauses 41.1.4 and 41.1.5.
3. A new Clause 41.5 has been added giving the arbiter power, for example to appoint a clerk, to find the parties jointly and severally liable and to dispense with a Deed of Submission. In practice any properly drawn Deed of Submission will contain all the powers given to the arbiter under this clause and as the majority of arbitrations entered into in terms of the Scottish Building Contract will be initiated by a Deed of Submission, this clause may well be seldom invoked.

Part 5: Proper law

This is a new Part added in the January 1988 Revision and repeats Clause 5 of the Building Contract for the convenience of those who do not choose to use it.

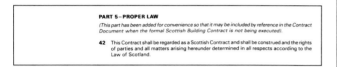

> **PART 5 – PROPER LAW**
> *(This part has been added for convenience so that it may be included by reference in the Contract Document when the formal Scottish Building Contract is not being executed).*
>
> 42 This Contract shall be regarded as a Scottish Contract and shall be construed and the rights of parties and all matters arising hereunder determined in all respects according to the Law of Scotland.

4 The Scottish supplement – Appendix II

4.01 This appendix is similar to the appendix annexed to JCT 80 with the exception of the final entry dealing with the method of appointment of an arbiter to which reference has already been made (see paragraph 3.27) and which obviously is unique to Scotland.

5 Different editions of the Standard Form

5.01 The above comments apply equally to the With Quantities Edition and the Without Quantities Edition except for the reference in the Building Contract for the latter to the method by which the contract sum has been calculated, i.e. by pricing the Specification/Schedule of Works or by a Contract Sum Analysis.

5.02 The same pattern is followed in the other four editions but note that in the case of the With Contractor's Design edition the name of the Employer's agent for the purposes of the contract requires to be inserted in Clause 3 of the Building Contract since in this type of contract an architect is not engaged by the employer.

6 The alternative method of nomination

6.01 Reference was made earlier in this chapter to an alternative method of nomination available to employers and architects under JCT 80. The documents used in Scotland for the alternative are distinguished from those for use with the Basic Method by the addition of an 'a' after the identifying number and they are all printed on yellow paper to aid identification. When originally published they did not include a Tender document but in March 1989 an optional Form of Tender was published by the JCT and the SBCC and is recommended as ensuring that the same information is given to each Tenderer.

Tender NSC/1a/Scot

6.02 This differs substantially in format from Tender NSC/1/Scot and is divided into two sections:

1. Section 1: The Invitation to Tender on pages 1–10. This comprises a description of the works for which a tender is required and gives full details of the main contract.
2. Section 2: The Tender by the Sub-contractor on pages 11–17. This contains the sub-contractor's tender and gives details which he requires to agree with the main contractor.

APPENDIX II

ABSTRACT OF CONDITIONS

	Clause	
Statutory tax deduction scheme – Finance (No. 2) Act 1975	31	Employer at Base Date is a 'contractor'³/is not a 'contractor' for the purposes of the Act and the Regulations
Base Date	1.3	
¹Clause 1A can only apply where the Contractor is satisfied at the date the Contract is entered into that his output tax on all supplies to the Employer under the Contract will be at either a positive or a zero rate of tax. VAT Agreement	15.2	Clause 1A of the VAT Agreement applies¹ – does not apply¹
Defects Liability Period (If none other stated is 12 months from the day named in the Certificate of Practical Completion of the Works)	17.2	
Assignation by Employer of benefits after Practical Completion	19.1.2	Clause 19.1.2 applies³/does not apply
Insurance cover for any one occurrence or series of occurrences arising out of one event	21.1.1	£
²If the indemnity is to be for an aggregate amount and not for any one occurrence or series of occurrences the entry should make this clear Insurance – Liability of Employer	21.2.1	Insurance may be²/is not required Amount of indemnity for any one occurrence or series of occurrences arising out of one event² £
Insurance of the Works – Alternative clauses	22.1	Clause 22A³/22B³/22C applies
³No percentage should be inserted if those concerned are all Employees of a Local Authority, but the sum assured should cover the cost of professional services Percentage to cover Professional fees	22A³/22B³/22C.2	%³
Annual renewal date of insurance as supplied by the Contractor	22A.3.1	
Insurance for Employer's loss of liquidated and ascertained damages – Clause 25.4.3	22D	Insurance may be³/is not required
	22D.2	Period of time
Date of Possession	23.1.1	
Date for Completion	1.3	
Deferment of Date of Possession	23.1.2 25.4.13	Clause 23.1.2 applies³/does not apply
	26.1	Period of deferment if it is to be less than 6 weeks is
Liquidate and Ascertained Damages	24.2	at the rate of £ per
⁴It is suggested the periods should be 28.1.3 one month; 28A.1.1 and 28A.1.3 one month; 28A.1.2 three months Period of delay	28.1.3	⁴
It is essential that periods be inserted since otherwise no period of delay would be prescribed Period of delay	28A.1.1 28A.1.3	⁴
Period of delay	28A.1.2	⁴
Period of Interim Certificates (if none stated is one month)	30.1.3	
Retention Percentage (if less than five per cent)	30.4.1.1	
Work reserved for Nominated Sub-Contractors for which the Contractor desires to tender	35.2	
Fluctuations (if alternative required is not shown clause 38 shall apply)	37	Clause 38³/Clause 39³/Clause 40
Percentage addition	38.7 or 39.8	%
Formula Rules Rule 3	40.1.1.1 Base Month	19
⁵Not to exceed 10% Rule 3		⁵Non-Adjustable Element % (Local Authorities Edition only)
Rule 10 and 30(i)		Part I³/Part II of Section 2 of the Formula Rules is to apply.
Settlement of disputes – Arbitration – if no appointor is selected the appointor shall be the Chairman or Vice-Chairman, The Scottish Building Contract Committee	41	The Chairman or Vice-Chairman of the Scottish Building Contract Committee³/The Dean of the Faculty of Advocates³/The Sheriff of the Sheriffdom in which the Works are situated.
Settlement of disputes – Arbitration	41.2	Clauses 41.2.1 and 41.2.2 apply (See Clause 41.2.3)

There seems to be no particular reason why the two forms of tender should be so different in style and with comparatively little amendment Tender NSC/1a/Scot could readily be used with the Basic Method of Nomination when the Basic Method is being followed.

Agreement NSC/2A/Scot

6.03 This document is similar in many respects to Agreement NSC/2/Scot, the comments on which should be read in conjunction with this document, particularly those concerning Clause 2 of the latter, which is Clause 1 of Agreement NSC/2a/Scot. However, Agreement NSC/2A/Scot contains two fewer clauses than Agreement NSC/2/Scot, both of which refer to the formal tender which is not used when the alternative procedure is being employed – but see above: when Tender NGC/1a/Scot is used Clause 12 of NSC/2/Scot should be added.

Nomination NSC/3a/Scot

6.04 This document, which, as has already been noted, has no counterpart in England, corresponds to Nomination NSC/3/Scot and requires no comment.

Sub-contract NSC/4a/Scot

6.05 Apart from the opening narrative of the Building Sub-contract which now makes a reference to Tender NSC/1a/Scot this document is identical to NSC/4/Scot and also makes provision in italics for sectional completion. When Tender NSC/1a/Scot *has* been completed it is not necessary to complete the complicated provisions of the lengthy Appendix No. II (because this information is already included in the Tender) but three items of Appendix No. III require completion giving (a) the amount of insurance cover required; (b) the period when the sub-contract works can be carried out; and (c) any other special conditions.

7 Scottish Minor Works Contract

7.01 This form is not a supplement to a JCT form but a separate form of contract altogether, intended for use when the works are of a simple straightforward content and of a duration which does not require full labour and material fluctuations. Unlike its English equivalent it does contain provisions for the use of bills of quantities and the employment of sub-contractors. Clause 4.01 states that if the contract documents provide that certain works are to be carried out by a sub-contractor taken from a list of not less than three, the selection is to be at the sole discretion of the contractor. This is similar to the provisions of Clause 19.3 of JCT 80.

The SBCC has also published the Scottish Minor Works Sub-contract for use by sub-contractors selected as above.

8 Sub-contracts for Domestic Sub-contractors

8.01 There are two editions of this form of sub-contract:

1. DOM/1/Scot where a sub-contractor is selected under the provisions of 19.2 and 19.3 of JCT 80.

2. DOM/2/Scot where the main contract is under the Scottish Building Contract With Contractor's Design and the sub-contractor is appointed under Clause 18.2 of that contract.

Both forms comprise the traditional format of a formal building sub-contract followed by an appendix containing the amendments required to DOM/1 and DOM/2 respectively.

9 Scottish Management Contract

9.01 Mention should also be made of the above form of contract issued to meet the growing demand in Scotland for management contracts where the main contractor accepts responsibility for wide management duties set out in Clauses 1.4 to 1.8 of the contract and enters into a series of works contracts with individual contractors who actually carry out the construction of the works.

It is not possible within the confines of this article to do more than draw the reader's attention to the existence of this form of contract when its use is intended in Scotland.

10 Scottish Measured Term Contract

At the time of going to press the SBCC has just issued this form of contract intended for use by an employer (e.g. a local authority) who needs regular maintenance and minor works including improvements to be carried out in respect of their properties within a defined area and who wants also to engage one contractor to carry out such work for a specified period on receipt of individual orders for those works.

Part Three

Statute law affecting architects

13

Planning law

SIR DESMOND HEAP

Note

Throughout this chapter the following abbreviations are used:
TP = The Town and Country Planning Act 1990;
The 1990 Act = The Town and Country Planning Act 1990, except in Section 5 of this chapter where it means the Planning (Listed Buildings and Conservation Areas) Act 1990.

1 Introduction

1.01 Town and country planning control over the development of all land (including buildings) in England and Wales* is an administrative process deriving from the Town and Country Planning Act 1947. It has operated since 1 July 1948 and was brought about (to mention no other matter) for the simple reason that in England and Wales there is a limited amount of land for an increasing number of people who wish to live and work upon it and who, increasingly, call for more space both for working and for leisure. Thus the pressure on a limited acreage of land is great and is getting greater.

1.02 Today the principal Act on the subject is the Town and Country Planning Act 1990. It contains 337 sections and 17 schedules and came into operation on 24 August 1990.

Associated with the principal Act are three further Acts related to planning, namely, the Planning (Listed Buildings and Conservation Areas) Act 1990, the Planning (Hazardous Substances) Act 1990 and the Planning (Consequential Provisions) Act 1990. These four Acts are defined (TP s. 336(1)) as 'the Planning Acts'.

1.03 No sooner were 'the Planning Acts' on the Statute Book than the Government had further thoughts about the control of land development. This led to the Planning and Compensation Act 1991 which has rewritten (with important alterations) many of the provisions of the Town and Country Planning Acts of 1990. But the Town and Country Planning Act 1990 itself still remains the principal Act on the subject. It is emphasized that any references in this chapter to sections in, or to the contents of, the 1990 Acts are references to those sections and to those contents *as amended by the 1991 Act*. Accordingly the reader is warned that if he is buying Queen's Printers' copies of Town and Country Planning Acts from Her Majesty's Stationery Office, High Holborn, London WC1V 6BH, or copies of subordinate rules, regulations and codes (statutory instruments) made under such Acts, he must remember that what he is buying is *not* an updated, current version of how the document he is buying *must* be read today.

1.04 Planning control over land development is rooted in central government policy. Accordingly, attention is drawn to the various

---

* There is a similar, but separate, statutory Code for Scotland. The Secretary of State for Wales acts for Wales as the Secretary of State for the Environment does for England.

Planning Policy Guidance Notes (PPG) first issued in 1988. These are issued by the Department of the Environment from time to time. The following notes have been issued so far:

1992/PPG1	General Policy and Principles (superseding *General Policy and Principles, 1988*)
1988/PPG2	Green Belts
1992/PPG3	Housing (superseding *Land for Housing, 1988*)
1992/PPG3	(Wales) Land for Housing in Wales
1992/PPG4	Industrial and Commercial Development and Small Firms (*revised*)
1992/PPG5	Simplified Planning Zones (*revised*)
1993/PPG6	Town Centres and Retail Developments (superseding *Major Retail Development*, 1988)
1992/PPG7	The Countryside and the Rural Economy (superseding *Rural Enterprise and Development, 1988*)
1992/PPG8	Telecommunications (*revised*)
1994/PPG9	Nature Conservation
1989/PPG9	Regional Guidance for the South East (*revised*)
1988/PPG10	Strategic Guidance for the West Midlands
1988/PPG11	Strategic Guidance for Merseyside
1992/PPG12	Development Plans and Regional Planning Guidance (superseding *Local Plans, 1988*)
1992/PPG12	(Wales) Development Plans in Wales
1994/PPG13	Transport
1990/PPG14	Development on Unstable Land
1994/PPG15	Planning and the Historic Environment
1990/PPG16	Archaeology and Planning
1991/PPG17	Sport and Recreation
1992/PPG18	Enforcing Planning Control
1992/PPG19	Outdoor Advertisement Control
1992/PPG20	Coastal Planning
1992/PPG21	Tourism
1993/PPG22	Renewable Energy
1994/PPG23	Planning and Pollution Control
1994/PPG24	Planning and Noise

Attention is also drawn to the following two Development Control Policy Notes:

1969/8	Caravan sites
1985/16	Access for the disabled

Planning control process

1.05 The planning control process is a bifurcated process involving, on the one hand, the making of development plans (that is to say, blueprints for the future) that seek to show what the state of affairs will be when all foreseeable development (or non-development) in the area covered by the plan has been achieved. On the other prong of the bifurcated process there is the day-to-day control over the carrying out of development through the medium of a grant or a refusal of planning permission for development. All this is a highly simplified, not to say over-simplified, statement of the entire complicated and sophisticated process of town planning control as it functions today.

1.06 In the ultimate analysis, all this control is done by the minister for town and country planning by whatever name he may be known. At the moment he is known as the Secretary of State for the Environment, but this does not alter the fact that, under the Secretary of State for the Environment Order 1970 (S.I. 1970 No. 1681), one minister of the Crown is, by law, rendered responsible ultimately for the way in which all town planning control is carried out in England and Wales. For his actions he is answerable to the Sovereign Parliament. Thus the control is exercised, in the ultimate analysis, in accordance with the town and country planning policies of the central government for the time being functioning at Westminster.

1.07 In this chapter no attention is given to the first prong of the aforementioned bifurcated process, namely, the making, approving, and bringing into operation of development plans comprising 'structure plans', 'local plans' and 'unitary development plans'. It is assumed for the purpose of this chapter that all the requisite development plans are in operation. Accordingly, attention in succeeding paragraphs is given to the day-to-day process of development control through the medium of grants or refusals of planning permission for development.

1.08 Moreover, it should be made clear at the start that this chapter is written primarily for the guidance of architects; it is deliberately slanted in the direction of architects. An effort has been made to pick out from the surging cauldron of town planning controls some of the more important controls and particularly those that would affect an architect seeking to organize development on behalf of a client. Thus the chapter does not purport to deal with control over advertisements, caravans, mineral workings or hazardous substances.

1.09 Accordingly, there will be found in succeeding paragraphs a brief statement on local planning authorities (paragraph 2.09) and what they can do when faced with an application for planning permission for development (paragraph 4.06). Development itself is treated in some detail (paragraph 3.01) though, maybe, not in all the detail into which the expression breaks up once it is investigated. The method of making planning applications is dealt with, as are the consequences of a refusal or a grant of permission subject to conditions (paragraph 4.04). Special reference is made to buildings of special architectural or historic interest (paragraph 5.01) because these are matters which, although standing outside the main stream of town planning control, are nevertheless highly important matters to a developer and to any architect advising him.

There is a brief reference (paragraph 6.01) to the three new concepts in the planning field of urban development areas and corporations, of enterprise zones, and of simplified planning zones.

There is reference to the enforcement of planning control over the development of land (paragraph 7.01) or, in other words, there is a statement on what happens, or does not happen, if a person does indeed carry out development without getting the appropriate planning permission in advance. Finally, a few personal thoughts of the writer appear in paragraph 8.01.

1.10 The length of this chapter has been limited. This means that it has not been possible in every instance to put in all the qualifications, exceptions, reservations, and so forth which, in a more categorical statement, would necessarily be appended to the general statements set out in the paragraphs which follow.

Accordingly, it is emphasized that this chapter is in the nature of a guide – a guide for architects. It is hoped that it will be helpful to them, but in the limited space available it cannot be an exhaustive statement on everything on which the chapter touches. Further information can be obtained from the author's *An Outline of Planning Law* (10th edn, Sweet & Maxwell, London).

2 Local planning authorities; or who is to deal with planning applications?

2.01 The first thing an architect seeking to carry out development must do is to inspect the site of the proposed development. It is most important nowadays to discover:

1. whether it is a cleared site; or
2. whether it contains a building and, if it does, whether that building is a building of special architectural or historic interest (see paragraph 5.01).

2.02 Second, the architect must consider carefully the definition of 'development' in the 1990 Act (Section 55) and in the Town and Country Planning (Use Classes) Order 1987*. Many building operations and changes of use do not constitute development by virtue of the definitions and provisions of this section and the 1987 Order. If they do not, then nothing in the town planning Acts applies to them. 'Development' is defined in paragraph 3.01. Copies of the Town and Country Planning (Use Classes) Order 1987 (S.I. 1987 No. 764) and its two amending orders of 1992 (S.I. 1992 Nos 610 and 657) are available from HMSO, High Holborn, London WC1V 6BH.

2.03 Third, the architect must examine closely the type of development which is sought to be carried out. Is it development which can be dealt with in the normal run of planning control, or will it be subject to some additional control over and above the normal run? It certainly will be if it happens to be development of land occupied by a building of special architectural or historic interest (paragraph 5.01) which has been listed by the Secretary of State.

2.04 Fourth, the architect must satisfy himself whether the site for the development does, or does not:

1. Comprise 'Article 1(4) land' (as defined in article 1(4) of the T & CP (General Permitted Development) Order 1995 (S.I. 1995 No. 418).
2. Comprise 'Article 1(5) land' (as defined in article 1(5) of the Town and Country Planning (General Permitted Development) Order 1995), which land includes land within:
   (a) a national park declared under the National Parks and Access to the Countryside Act 1949;
   (b) an area of outstanding natural beauty (AONB) declared under the same Act of 1949;
   (c) an area designated as a conservation area under Section 69 of the Planning (Listed Buildings in Conservation Areas) Act 1990;
   (d) an area specified for the purposes of the Wildlife and Countryside Act 1981, Section 41(3); and
   (e) the Broads as defined in the Norfolk and Suffolk Broads Act 1988.
3. Comprise 'Article 1(6) land' (as defined in article 1(6) of the aforesaid Order 1995) which land includes:
   (a) land in a National Park
   (b) in the Norfolk and Suffolk Broads (as defined above); and
   (c) in land outside a national park but within an area (specified in Article 1(6)) as set out in Schedule 1, Part 3, of the aforesaid 1995 Order.

If the development site is on 'Article 1(4)' land or on 'Article 1(5) land' or on 'Article 1(6) land' then the amount of 'permitted development' (see paragraph 2.05) allowed on the site is constricted by the said 1995 Order. Copies of the Town and Country Planning (General Permitted Development) Order 1995 are obtainable from HMSO (see paragraph 2.02).

2.05 Fifth, the architect must investigate generally the Town and Country Planning (General Permitted Development) Order 1995. It will be necessary to do this sort of investigation in order to ascertain whether the development is 'permitted development' under the Order because, if it is, it gets automatic planning permission and there is no need to make any application to a local planning

---

* This Use Classes Order of 1987 is currently under review.

authority (see paragraph 4.02). But it is to be remembered that the important widening of the field of 'permitted development' brought about in 1981 does *not* apply to 'Article 1(4) land' nor to 'Article 1(5) land' nor to 'Article 1(6) land' each as above described. Any such land falls within what are nowadays called 'sensitive areas' and the relaxation of development control brought about by the General Development (Amendment) Order 1981 was denied to them – and is still denied to them by the Town and Country Planning (General Permitted Development) Order 1995.

2.06 Sixth, the architect must ascertain whether the development site is in an Urban Development Area (see paragraph 6.01); in an Enterprise Zone (see paragraph 6.09); or in a Simplified Planning Zone (see paragraph 6.12). If the site is in any one of these areas or zones, then the normal constraints of development control (e.g. the need to obtain, from a local planning authority, planning permission for development (see paragraph 2.10)) are relaxed (see paragraphs 6.01, 6.09 and 6.12).

2.07 All these are preliminary matters about which the architect should become fully informed at the outset. In this article it will be assumed, for the moment, that the architect is dealing with a cleared site (or, at least, a site *not* containing anything in the nature of a special building), and that the development he wishes to carry out is development that can be dealt with under the general run of town planning control and does *not* attract any additional, i.e. special, control. (The *special* control over development which is going to occupy the site of an existing building of architectural or historic interest is dealt with later.) For the moment it is assumed that the development which the architect is considering is straightforward building development not subject to any special form of control, but only to *general* town planning control under the Town and Country Planning Act 1990.

Which authority?

2.08 This being the case, the next thing which the architect must consider is the local government authority to whom the applica-

tion for planning permission is to be made. It must be made to the local planning authority.

2.09 The local government system in England and Wales was completely reorganized as from 1 April 1974 under the provision of the Local Government Act 1972. It was further reorganized as from the 1 April 1986 by the Local Government Act 1985 which abolished the Greater London Council and the 6 metropolitan county councils (but not the metropolitan counties themselves) of Greater Manchester, Merseyside, South Yorkshire, Tyne and Wear, West Midlands, and West Yorkshire respectively.

2.10 After all the foregoing reorganizations the system (outside Greater London) provided for local government to be discharged at three separate tiers, namely:

1. By 47 non-metropolitan county councils popularly called 'shire' county councils;
2. By 369 district councils (36 metropolitan district councils if they happen to be in a metropolitan county and 333 'shire' district councils if they happen to be in a 'shire' county) some of which have borough status; and
3. By parish councils.
4. In Greater London local government was (and still is) carried out by each of the 32 London borough councils plus the Corporation of the City of London.

2.11 In July 1992 the entire organization of local government in England was referred by the central government for comprehensive review by the Local Government Commission for England whose Progress Report, dated March 1995, is available from HMSO. This contains a number of recommendations for amending the structure of local government in certain areas. The Commission issued a further Report in September 1995. As and when the Government takes action on any of the Commission's recommendations (it is not obliged to take any action at all) such action would lead to the establishing of *unitary* local government authorities. A *unitary* authority would prepare a *unitary* development plan (a mixture of both structure and local plan) and be responsible for all other planning matters. All this must be borne in mind when the reader is studying paragraphs 2.12 to 2.28 of this chapter.

2.12 The county councils and the district councils and the unitary councils (when established) are all local planning authorities and thus current nomenclature speaks of the 'county planning authority', the 'district planning authority' and the 'unitary planning authority'. A purchaser or a developer of land must, *at the very start*, ascertain which is the local planning authority for the purpose of whatever he wishes to do.

2.13 All applications for planning permission will go to the district planning authority or the unitary planning authority except (in the area of a shire district council) when the application relates to a 'County matter' (see TP Schedule 1, paragraph 1) in which event the application is to be made to the shire county council (see paragraph 2.14). When an application is made to the district council, it is to be remembered that there are seven specified categories of development in which the interests of the county council receive special protection and in which consultation *by* the district council *with* the county council *must* take place. These refer to:

1. Development, the carrying out of which would 'materially conflict with or prejudice the implementation'
   (a) of any policy or general proposal in a structure plan (whether approved or merely proposed);
   (b) of any proposal to include in a structure plan any matter publicized by the county council;
   (c) of any 'fundamental provision' in an approved development plan;
   (d) of any proposal in a local plan prepared by the county council (whether or not it has yet been adopted);
   (e) of any publicized proposal by the county council for inclusion in a local plan being prepared by them;
   (f) of any publicized proposal by the county council for alterations to a local plan;

2. Any development which by reason of its scale, nature, or location would be of 'major importance' for the implementation of an approved structure plan;
3. Any development likely to affect, or be affected by, mineral workings 'other than coal';
4. Any development of land the county council wishes to develop themselves;
5. Any development which would prejudice development proposed by the county council;
6. Any development of land in England which is land the county council propose shall be used for waste disposal;
7. Any development which would prejudice a proposed use of land for waste disposal.

In each of the foregoing cases (the details of which are to be found in paragraph 7 of Schedule 1 to the Town and Country Planning Act 1990), where special protection is given to the interests of the county council, the district council *must* consult with the county council and take into account any representations made by the county council before they (the district council) determine the planning application. How long must these complicated consultations continue? That period has been fixed by the Town and Country Planning (General Development Procedure) Order 1995, article 11, as 14 days after notification to the county council.

2.14 The instances of 'county matters' when, in a *shire* county, the application for planning permission goes in the first place *not* to the district planning authority but to the county planning authority, are (TP Schedule 1, paragraph 1):

1. applications relating to mineral mining, working, and development (including the construction of cement works) (TP Schedule 1, paragraph 1(1) (a)–(h) inclusive);
2. applications relating to development straddling the boundary of a national park (TP Schedule 1, paragraph 1(1) (i)); and
3. applications in England relating to waste disposal matters (TP Schedule 1, paragraph 1(1) (j)) and Town and Country Planning (Prescription of County Matters) Regulations 1980 (S.I. 1980 No. 2010) which does not apply to Greater London.

2.15 Parish councils are not local planning authorities but, even so, have the right (if they have claimed it) to be consulted by the district council about planning applications for development falling within the area of the parish council (TP Schedule 1, paragraph 8).

2.16 In Greater London the 32 London boroughs (each for its own borough) with the Common Council (for the City of London) are all local planning authorities (1990 Act, s. 1(2)).

2.17 Although the application for planning permission will formally be made to a local planning authority it will often be the case that a good deal of 'negotiation' relating to the application will take place between the applicant's architect and officers of the local planning authority. The power of a planning officer, acting within the scope of his duties as such to bind the planning authority in whose service he functions, is well illustrated in the important case of *Lever (Finance) Ltd* v *Westminster (City) London Borough Council* [1970] 3 All ER 496.

2.18 In this case certain developers, who proposed developing a piece of land by building 14 houses on it, applied for planning permission to the local planning authority, attaching to the application a detailed plan of the development showing one of the houses, house G, as sited 40ft away from all existing houses. Permission for the development in accordance with the detailed plan was given by the planning authority on 24 March 1969. A month later the developers' architect made some variations to the detailed plan submitted to the authority. The variations included altering the site of house G so that it was sited only 23ft away from existing houses. A further site plan showing this variation was sent to the planning authority.

2.19 The authority's planning officer had lost the file containing the original plan approved by the planning authority. Because of this he had made a mistake and told the architect over the telephone that the variation was not material and that no further planning consent was required. The telephone conversation took place in May 1969, and the developers acted on this representation and went ahead with the development, including the erection of house G, which was started in September 1969.

2.20 The residents of the existing houses made representations to the planning authority about the variation of the site of house G. The planning authority suggested to the developers that they should apply for planning permission for the variation. On 17 March 1970 the developers did so apply, the application being supported by the authority's planning officer, but the planning authority refused the application. It also refused a further application, made in April 1970, to sanction a variation in the structure of house G, and resolved that an enforcement notice should be issued to take down the house. By this time house G had been erected but not glazed.

2.21 The developers brought an action against the planning authority, claiming a declaration that they were entitled to complete the house on the site where it was, and an injunction restraining the authority from serving an enforcement notice.

2.22 It was the practice of many planning authorities, after detailed planning permission had been given, to allow their planning officers to decide whether any proposed minor modifications to the detailed plan were material or not, and where the planning officer said that a variation was not material, for the developer to proceed with the work as varied without applying for any further permission.

2.23 On the foregoing facts the Court of Appeal held that there was a valid planning permission for the erection of house G on the site as varied and that an enforcement notice should not be served. The court came to that conclusion because (per Lord Denning, Master of the Rolls, and Lord Justice Megaw) a planning permission covered work specified in the detailed plans and any immaterial variation therein; and, having regard to the practice of planning authorities allowing their officers to decide on the materiality of minor alterations to an approved plan (a practice which should be affirmed), the planning officer's decision that the variation of the site of house G was not a material variation was a representation *within the officer's ostensible authority*; and, having been acted on by the developers, it was binding on the planning authority.

2.24 As already stated, this case is an important one. It warrants the closest reading and consideration because it illustrates how easily, in these days, a planning officer can bind the local planning authority in whose service he functions. It should be added that throughout the case mention is made of Section 64 of the Town and Country Planning Act 1968, which later became Section 4 of the Town and Country Planning Act 1971. That Section 4 (relating to the delegation of functions of officers of local authorities) was repealed by the Local Government Act 1972, but this does not detract from the general principles enunciated in the *Lever* case. (See Section 101 of the Local Government Act 1972.)

2.25 It is becoming more and more the custom for developers to engage, through their architects, in repeated interchanges with the planning staff of local planning authorities as to how, in detail, a piece of development shall be carried out. Do these interchanges bind the local planning authority? That is the question. There is no entirely clear answer. The position today, as a result of the case discussed above, is that such interchanges are *more prone* to bind the local authority than ever before. Even so, the ancient doctrine of *caveat emptor* may still be quoted as a warning to the developer and his architect. The purpose of negotiations with the planning staff of local planning authorities should be made clear; are negotiations intended to be binding or not? The architect (if he is the one doing the talking) owes to his client the duty of getting this important point made quite clear.

2.26 Fees are payable since 1 April 1981 to local planning authorities in respect of applications for planning permission, applications for approval of matters reserved in an outline planning permission, or applications for consent to display advertisements. The amount of the fees is set out in Schedule 1, Part II and Schedule 2 to the Town and Country Planning (Fees for Applications and Deemed Applications) Regulations 1989 (S.I. 1989 No. 193) as amended several times. Each of the amendments has led to a progressive increase in the fees the latest rates operating as from 3 January 1995 (S.I. 1993 No. 3170 reg. 5(b)).

2.27 A reduced planning fee is payable, in certain circumstances, where more than one application for planning permission is made for the same development or for approval of the same reserved matters provided all the applications are made by the same applicant within a period of 28 days.

2.28 Certain applications are exempt from liability to a fee. These are

1. certain applications on behalf of a disabled person;
2. applications to renew a temporary permission;
3. certain revised applications; and
4. applications relating to 'permitted development' prevented by a direction under Article 4 of the (General Permitted Development) Order 1995.

There are no exemptions in respect of applications to display advertisements.

3 The meaning of development

3.01 The question as to whether that which the architect seeks to carry out is or is not development is a considerable one. The meaning of 'development' is amply defined in the Town and Country Planning Act 1990, Section 55, and it is a question of taking the relevant provisions of this Act, working carefully through them, and then applying the appropriate parts of these provisions to the matter in hand to ascertain if that which it is sought to do is, *in law* as well as in fact, development.

3.02 Putting the matter quite briefly, development consists of:

1. the carrying out of *operations* (that is to say, building, mining, engineering or other operations), or
2. the making of any *material change in the use* of land (including buildings on land).

It will be seen that the big cleavage in the definition is between the carrying out of *operations*, on the one hand, and the making of a *material change of use*, on the other.

What is an operation?

3.03 If the definitions of what constitutes development is important, it may be said that the definition of what does *not* constitute development is equally important. Section 55 of the 1990 Act contains quite a list of operations and uses which do *not* amount to development. If that which the architect seeks to do falls within this particular list, then he need worry no more about the 1990 Act or any part of it.

What is a change of use?

3.04 This list of exceptions in Section 55 of the 1990 Act must be read with the Town and Country Planning (Use Classes) Order 1987, which contains 16 classes of use. If that which the architect seeks to do is, in fact, a material change of use, then if the existing use is any one of those specified in the 1987 Order, and if the change of use will still leave the use within the same use-class, the proposed change of use will *not*, in law, constitute development. In short, a use may switch around without planning permission,

provided its total manoeuvring does not take it out of its use-class as set out in the 1987 Order.

3.05 However, since the case of *City of London Corporation* v *Secretary of State for the Environment and Watling Street Properties Ltd* (1971) 23 P. and C.R. 169, it is clear that, on granting planning permission, a local planning authority may impose such conditions as would prevent any future change of use, notwithstanding that any such change would *not* constitute development of land by virtue of the provisions of the Use Classes Order 1987 and Section 55 (2) (f) of the 1990 Act. This decision, in respect of which no appeal was made, would seem to be a memorable decision when it is remembered that the whole object of the Town and Country Planning Act 1990 is to exercise control over things which do constitute *development* and not over things which do not.

3.06 For the purpose of removing all doubt, Section 55 (3) of the 1990 Act specifically states that merely using a single dwelling house as two or more separate dwelling houses *does* involve making a material change of use and it is 'development' needing planning permission before it can take place. Thus the architect may carry out, at ground level or above, *internal* building operations (not affecting the exterior elevations) on a single house in order to adapt it for use as two houses. Such building operations will *not* need planning permission. However, when it comes to inaugurating the *use* of the former single house as two houses, this change of use *will* call for planning permission which may or may not be granted.

3.07 If the architect has any doubts as to whether that which he seeks to do is or is not 'development', he can apply (1990 Act, Section 192) to the local planning authority for a certificate of lawfulness relating to any *proposed* use or development of land. Such a certificate relating to any *existing* use or development can be made under Section 191 of the 1990 Act. In either case there is a right of appeal to the Secretary of State for the Environment (hereinafter referred to as 'the Secretary of State') against the decision of the authority (TP Section 195). Alternatively, an application may be made to the High Court to determine the point. The jurisdiction of the court is not ousted by Section 78 of the 1990 Act, as is shown by the case of *Pyx Granite Co Ltd* v *Ministry of Housing and Local Government* [1958] 1 QB 554, CA.

4 Control of development in general

4.01 Once the architect is satisfied that that which he seeks to do is indeed *development*, but is not an Enterprise Zone (see paragraphs 6.09 to 6.11 of this chapter) *nor* a Simplified Planning Zone (see paragraphs 6.12 to 6.15 of this chapter), he must next ascertain whether it falls within the privileged category of 'permitted development'. For this he will have to investigate the Town and Country Planning (General Permitted Development) Order 1995.

Permitted development

4.02 The 1995 Order, carries no less than 84 separate classes of development which are categorized as *permitted* development, that is to say, they comprise development for which a grant of planning permission is automatically given by virtue of the General Permitted Development Order 1995 itself (TP Sections 58, 59, 60). If development falls within any one of these 84 classes of permitted development there is no need to make any application to any local planning authority for planning permission for the development. If the development is *not* permitted development, then a formal application must be made (TP Sections 58, 62).

4.03 It is to be stressed that the General Permitted Development Order of 1995 is a most important document. The 84 classes of permitted development are spread across 33 Parts – Part 1 to Part 33 respectively – as set out in Schedule 2 to the Order as follows:

Permitted Development Order 1995

Part	Class	Permitted development
1	A	Development within the curtilage of a dwellinghouse. The enlargement, improvement or other alteration of a dwellinghouse
1	B	The enlargement of a dwellinghouse consisting of an addition or alteration to its roof
1	C	Any other addition to the roof of a dwellinghouse
1	D	The erection or construction of a porch outside any external door of a dwellinghouse
1	E	The provision within the curtilage of a dwellinghouse, of any building or enclosure, swimming or other pool required for a purpose incidental to the enjoyment of the dwellinghouse, or the maintenance, improvement or other alteration of such a building or enclosure
1	F	The provision within the curtilage of a dwellinghouse of a hard surface for any purpose incidental to the enjoyment of the dwellinghouse
1	G	The erection or provision within the curtilage of a dwellinghouse of a container for the storage of oil for domestic heating
1	H	The installation, alteration or replacement of a satellite antenna on a dwellinghouse or within the curtilage of a dwellinghouse
2	A to C	Minor operations
3	A to G	Changes of use
4	A to B	Temporary buildings and uses
5	A to B	Caravan sites
6	A to C	Agricultural buildings and operations
7	A	Forestry buildings and operations
8	A to D	Industrial and warehouse development
9	A	Repairs to unadopted streets and private ways
10	A	Repairs to services
11	A	Development under local or private Acts or Orders
12	A to B	Development by local authorities
13	A	Development by local highway authorities
14	A	Development by drainage bodies
15	A	Development by the National Rivers Authority
16	A	Development by or on behalf of sewerage undertakers
17	A to J	Development by statutory undertakers
18	A to I	Aviation development
19	A to C	Development ancillary to mining operations
20	A to E	Coal mining development by the Coal Authority Licensed Operators
21	A to B	Waste tipping at a mine
22	A to B	Mineral exploration
23	A to B	Removal of material from mineral-working deposits
24	A	Development by telecommunications code system operators
25	A to B	Other telecommunications development
26	A	Development by the Historic Buildings and Monuments Commission for England
27	A	Use by members of certain recreational organizations
28	A	Development at amusement parks
29	A	Driver information systems
30	A	Toll road facilities
31	A to B	Demolition of buildings
32	A	Schools, Colleges, Universities and Hospitals
33	A	Closed circuit television cameras

Other than permitted development

4.04 If the proposed development does *not* fall within any of the 84 classes of 'permitted development' above mentioned, then a formal application for planning permission will need to be made (TP s. 57). Sections 58 and 62 of the Town and Country Planning Act 1990 require an application for planning permission for development to be made in accordance with provisions 'prescribed by regulations' which means the Town and Country Planning (Applications) Regulations 1988 (S.I. 1988 No. 1812) and the Town and Country Planning (General Development Procedure) Order 1995 to each of which reference must be made. The requisite form on which the application is lodged can be obtained from the local planning authority.

4.05 When making an application for planning permission for development reference must further be made to the Town and Country Planning (Assessment of Environmental Effects) Regulations 1988 (S.I. 1988 No. 1199) as amended in 1990, 1992 and 1994.

4.06 As to what should be the attitude of a local planning authority when faced with an application for planning permission, attention should be paid to Planning Policy Guidance Note 1 (PPG1) dated March 1992, entitled, 'General Policy and Principles' issued by the Department of the Environment. This is a most important document, both for the developer (and those advising him) as well as for the local planning authority.

4.07 PPG1 states the general principles underlying the entire system of control over land development and deals in particular with the important Section 54A of the 1990 Act (inserted by the Planning and Compensation Act 1991) which is in the following terms:

'Where in making any determination under the Planning Acts, regard is to be had to the development plan, the determination shall be made in accordance with the plan unless material considerations indicate otherwise.'

4.08 If the application for planning permission is refused, or is granted subject to conditions unacceptable to the applicant for planning permission, there is a right of appeal to the Secretary of State within six months of the authority's decision (TP Sections 78 and 79). Before deciding the appeal the Secretary of State *must*, if either the applicant for planning permission or the local planning authority so requests, afford each of them an opportunity of being heard by a person appointed by the Secretary of State – an inspector. If the request is granted the hearing will be private to the two parties. Neither party can demand a public local enquiry although the Secretary of State (it is entirely a matter for him) frequently decides to hold such an inquiry. Procedure at such an inquiry is dealt with in the Town and Country Planning (Inquiries Procedure) Rules 1992 (S.I. 1992 No. 2038). The decision of the Secretary of State is final (subject to appeal to the courts within six weeks on matters of law only), the procedure being regarded by the law as an administrative and not a justiciable procedure.

4.09 Even so, the increasing propensity of the judicature to interfere with an administrative decision if it is thought that the Secretary of State has come to a conclusion upon wrong evidence, or upon no evidence at all, is well illustrated in the case of *Coleen Properties Ltd* v *Minister of Housing and Local Government and Another* [1971] 1 All ER 1049.

4.10 Under Section 79 and Schedule 6 of the 1990 Act, it is open to the Secretary of State to empower his inspector holding a local enquiry not only to hold the inquiry but to determine the appeal. The Secretary of State has exercised this power by making the Town and Country Planning (Determination of Appeals by Appointed Persons) (Prescribed Classes) Regulations 1981 (S.I. 1981 No. 804), whereby *all* planning appeals and *all* enforcement appeals (except when affecting a statutory undertaker) are now heard *and determined* by an inspector appointed by the Secretary of State. The procedure at such appeals is found in the Town and

Country Planning Appeals (Determination by Inspectors) (Inquiries Procedure) Rules 1992 (S.I. 1992 No. 2039).

4.11 In addition to appeals to the Secretary of State by private hearing or by public local enquiry (as above described), there is a third method of appeal by what is known as the 'Written Representation Process'. This is dealt with in DoE Circular 18/86 and in the Town and Country Planning (Appeals) (Written Representations Procedure) Regulations 1987 (S.I. 1987 No. 701).

4.12 In any planning appeal the Secretary of State *may* (if he can be persuaded) award costs to the appellant against the local planning authority (see DoE Circular 8/93).

Outline permission

4.13 If the architect knows exactly what he wants to do by way of building operations he will be able to put in a complete detailed application for planning permission. But it may be that he wants in the first place to 'test the temperature of the water', that is to say, to see what are his chances of getting planning permission at all for, say, a block of offices 20 storeys high. If he wishes to do this, then he can save time, trouble, and expense by putting in an application (TP Section 92) for *outline* planning permission so that the principle of having a block of offices 20 storeys high may be tested. If it is approved, then it will be necessary for the architect later on, within the period (if any) specified in the grant of outline planning permission and *before he begins any development*, to put in detailed plans and specifications for the approval of the local planning authority, these being what are called 're-served matters', that is to say, matters reserved, at the stage when the local authority is granting the planning application in outline, for later and further consideration.

4.14 An outline application should make it clear that it *is* an application in outline and nothing more. Thus any plans and drawings which accompany it should be clearly marked as being by way of illustration only. At the stage of applying for outline permission, the architect should not fetter himself as to the *styling* of development. All he wants at the outline stage is to know whether or not he can, under any circumstances at all, have planning permission to do the *sort* of thing he wishes to do. If he gets that permission, then he must return, in due course, to the local planning authority with detailed plans and specifications so that the authority may consider these detailed matters.

4.15 If the outline application for planning permission is refused, there is a right of appeal against that refusal to the Secretary of State within six months. Similarly, if the outline application is granted but, later on, the local authority refuses to approve reserved matters, that is to say, refuses approval of detailed plans and specifications, then again there is an appeal against such refusal to the Secretary of State (see paragraph 4.08).

4.16 It will be seen that for an applicant who does not own land and who wonders how much he ought to pay for it, the making of an outline application to test the position *vis-à-vis* the local planning authority is a useful arrangement. It is not necessary for the applicant to go into details and incur the expense thereby involved. All he wants to know before he makes his bid for the land is whether, if he is able to buy the land, he will then be able to develop it in anything like the manner he has in mind. To get to know this, all that he need do is make an outline planning application.

Notices re planning applications

4.17 Notice of the making of any application for planning permission to develop land *must* be given to the owner of the land and to any tenant of an agricultural holding any part of which is comprised in the land (TP Section 65; T and CP (General Development Procedure) Order 1995 articles 6, 8 and Schedule 2, Parts 1 and 2). Any application for planning permission must be accompanied by a certificate indicating the giving of notice to owners and agricultural tenants. If the appropriate certificate is not included

with the planning application, then the local planning authority 'shall not entertain' the application (TP Section 65 (5)).

General publicity

4.18 In addition to the foregoing personal or private publicity deriving from the notices referred to in the previous paragraph, there must be what can be called *general* publicity by newspaper advertisement for all planning applications (TP Section 65; T and CP (General Development Procedure) Order 1995 article 8). Thus the owners and occupiers of neighbouring land will be informed, provided they keep a sharp eye open for newspaper planning adverisements, of any application to carry out development so that they may give their views and opinions to the local planning authority before a decision is arrived at. Such views and opinions *must* be considered by the local planning authority (TP Section 71).

Site notices

4.19 Moreover, a site notice, exhibited on the site where the development is to take place, may have to be given (T and CP (General Development Procedure) Order 1995 article 8).

Those instances in which a site notice may have to be posted are referred to in the 1990 Act, Section 65 and Article 8 of the (General Development Procedure) Order 1995 and (so far as listed buildings and conservation areas are concerned) in the Planning (Listed Buildings and Conservation Areas) Act 1990 Sections 67 and 73 and the Planning (Listed Buildings and Conservation Areas) Regulations 1990 (S.I. 1990 No. 1519).

Local authority procedure

4.20 On receipt of an application for planning permission, the local planning authority must consider the matter and, generally speaking, give a decision within eight weeks unless an extension of time is agreed (T & CP (General Development Procedure) Order 1995 articles 20 and 21). The authority will probably need to consult the appropriate county council (*ibid.* article 11) and may also have to consult any parish council within whose area the proposed development is going to take place (*ibid.* article 13). The authority may grant the application, may refuse it, or may grant it subject to conditions (TP 1990 Section 70). If the answer is a refusal or conditions are attached to the grant, the reasons for such action must be given (Development Procedure Order 1995 article 22). This is to enable the applicant to challenge the decision of the local planning authority if the applicant decides to appeal to the Secretary of State, as he may do within a period of six months (TP Section 78; Development Procedure Order 1995 articles 22 and 23). If no decision is given within the appropriate period, the applicant may appeal (again, within six months) to the Secretary of State as if he had been faced with a refusal (TP Section 78; Development Procedure Order 1995 article 23).

Conservation areas

4.21 If the site of the development is within a conservation area designated under the Planning (Listed Buildings and Conservation Areas) Act 1990 Sections 69 and 70, then the local planning authority, in considering the application, will have to pay attention to Sections 71, 72, 74 and 75 of that Act and to any directions given to them by the Secretary of State as to the manner in which they should consider applications for development within areas of special architectural or historic interest, the character or appearance of which ought to be preserved or enhanced. In other words, the local planning authority has less of a free hand in connection with development in a conservation area than it has elsewhere.

Conditions

4.22 The local planning authority in granting planning permission may attach such conditions as it thinks fit (TP 1990 Section 70); but this does not mean that it can attach *any* conditions it likes;

not at all. The conditions must be fit, that is to say, fit, meet, and proper from a town planning point of view, because the legislation under which all this control functions is town planning legislation.

4.23 A local planning authority in attaching conditions must ensure that the conditions fairly and reasonably relate to the development. The authority is not at liberty to use its powers for an ulterior object, however desirable that object may seem to be in the public interest. If it mistakes or misuses its power, however bona fide, the court can interfere by declaration of an injunction – per Lord Denning in *Pyx Granite Co Ltd* v *Minstry of Housing and Local Government* [1958] 1 QB 554, CA.

4.24 Suppose one of the conditions attached to a grant is improper and thereby unlawful; does this invalidate the entire planning permission or can the unlawful condition be severed from the rest, leaving the planning permission intact but shorn of the improper condition? There have been several cases on this particularly difficult point, and the last word was spoken in the decision in *Kent County Council* v *Kingsway Investments (Kent) Ltd* [1970] 1 All ER 70. It would appear from the decisions of the courts that the question of whether or not a planning permission is to be held wholly bad and of no effect, by reason of the invalidity of some condition attached to it, is a matter which could be decided on the basis of common sense and with particular inquiry as to whether the valid condition is fundamental or trivial.

4.25 The views of the Secretary of State on attaching conditions to a grant of planning permission are set out at length in the interesting and instructive DoE Circular 1/85 to which reference can be made with advantage (see the Bibliography at the end of the book).

4.26 Local planning authorities seem to be increasingly intent on attaching to a grant of planning permission conditions which seek to recover for the authority something in the nature of a planning gain or benefit which the carrying out of the proposed development itself will bring to the authority in the nature, for example, of increased taxable value for the area of the authority. Some of these conditions are of doubtful validity,* and on certain of these the Secretary of State has made a formal pronouncement. It is dated 1 November 1979 and was made in a decision letter on a planning appeal relating to the proposed creation of 800 houses (DoE reference APP/5231/A/74/6905 and APP/5231/78/06933). The Secretary of State declared that he agreed with the inspector that the local planning authority's only objection of substance related to their wish to obtain a substantial contribution towards the cost of social infrastructure. The Secretary of State went on to say that he 'is of the opinion that, in the absence of any statutory requirement for the developer to contribute financially towards social infrastructure, such payments cannot properly be demanded of the developer even though the need for the infrastructure may have arisen in part from his proposed development. Nor, in the Secretary of State's view, would it be lawful to grant planning permission subject to a requirement that the developer shall enter into an agreement under Section 106 of the Town and Country Planning Act 1990 and other statutory provisions; any such agreement must be entirely voluntary and a matter for negotiation between the relevant parties.'

4.27 The Annex to DoE Circular 1/85 (above mentioned) also refers to this matter of the imposition of planning conditions the object of which is to secure some sort of a planning gain for the local planning authority (see paragraphs 20–21 and 63 of the Annex). The Annex sets out six tests to ascertain whether a planning condition is (as it should be) 'fair, reasonable and practical'. The six tests are (paragraph 11):

1. necessity for the condition;
2. relevance of the condition to planning;
3. relevance of the condition to the development to be permitted;

* See the article 'Planning Bargaining – the Pros and the Cons' (1980) *Journal of Planning Law* p. 631.

4. enforceability of the condition;
5. precision of the condition; and
6. reasonableness of the condition in all other respects.

The Annex puts each of these six tests to close scrutiny which should certainly be read in full in the Annex itself. To take but one example (relating to test (1) about the necessity for a planning condition being imposed at all), the Annex, paragraph 12, declares:

'*Test of need*
12. In considering whether a particular condition is necessary, authorities should ask themselves whether planning permission would have to be refused if that condition were not to be imposed. If it would not, then the condition needs special and precise justification. The argument that a condition will do no harm is no justification for its imposition: as a matter of policy, a condition ought not to be imposed unless there is a definite need for it.'

4.28 It should be remembered that obtaining planning permission for development may not necessarily be the end of the matter. Certain specialized forms of development, e.g. development relating to the display of advertisements (TP 1990 Sections 220–225 and the T and CP Control of Adverisement Regulations 1992 – S.I. 1992 No. 666) or to the creation of caravan sites (Caravan Sites and the Control of Development Act 1960 Part I), are subject to additional control over and above the general run of town planning control.

4.29 Moreover, the architect must never forget that town planning control is a control which functions entirely without prejudice to the long-established control of building operations through the medium of building byelaws created under a code of law relating to public health and dating back to the Public Health Act 1875 and even before. Irrespective of town planning control, such detailed matters as the thickness of walls, the opening of exit doors in public places in an outward and not an inward direction, the provision of means of escape in case of fire – all these are matters which are entirely separate from the sort of control over development which is discussed in this chapter. (For such matters see Chapter 14.)

Duration of permission

4.30 Nowadays, any developer obtaining planning permission must remember that, unless the permission itself specifies otherwise, permission will last for only five years. This is to prevent, among other things, an accumulation in the records of local planning authorities of quantities of planning permissions granted from time to time over a long period of years and never acted upon. This sort of thing had been going on for a long time, but was brought to an end by provisions in the Town and Country Planning Act 1968, now Sections 91 to 96 of the 1990 Act.

4.31 Anybody in possession of a planning permission granted before 1 April 1969 must remember that if he did not begin his development before the beginning of 1968, then he must have begun it not later than five years from 1 April 1969, that is to say, not later than 1 April 1974, after which date the planning permission dissolves.

4.32 In the case of a planning permission granted on or since 1 April 1969, or granted in the future, the limitation is again five years from the date of the grant unless the grant otherwise provides.

4.33 If that which is obtained is an outline planning permission (as discussed in paragraph 4.13) granted on or since 1 April 1969, then it must be remembered that the submission of detailed plans and specifications under the aegis of that outline planning permission must be done not later than *three* years from the grant, while the development itself must be begun within five years of the grant or within two years of the final approval of any reserved matter, whichever of these two periods happens to be the longer.

In the case of an outline planning permission granted before the 1 April 1969, then the aforementioned periods of three and five years respectively run from the 1 April 1969.

Starting development

4.34 When is a project of development to be regarded as having been begun? This is an important question. The 1990 Act provides the complete answer in Section 56 by providing that a project of development is begun on the earliest date on which a material operation in connection with the development is started. A 'material operation' will include, among other things, the digging of a trench which is to contain the foundations of a building. Thus, only a trivial amount of labour needs to be spent in order to ensure that development has been begun and that a town planning permission has been embarked upon.

Abandoning development

4.35 A ticklish question has always been: can a planning permission be lost through non-use? Can it be abandoned? In *Pioneer Aggregates (UK) Ltd* v *Secretary of State for the Environment* (1985) AC 132 a decision of the House of Lords, it was held that there was no legal principle that a planning permission could be abandoned by the act of a party entitled to the benefit of the permission.

Completion notices

4.36 Having begun his development, a developer must remember not to rest unduly upon his oars. If he is dilatory it is open to the local planning authority to serve him with 'a completion notice' requiring the completion of his development within a certain period (TP Act 1990 Sections 94 and 96). A completion notice will declare that the relevant planning permission will cease to have effect on such date as may be specified in the notice but this date may not be earlier than twelve months from the date of the notice. A completion notice will not take effect unless and until it is confirmed by the Secretary of State, who may substitute a longer period for completion. Any person served with a completion notice may demand to be given an opportunity of being heard by an inspector appointed by the Secretary of State. Of course, a local planning authority, having served a completion notice, may for good and sufficient reason be prevailed upon to withdraw it; the law authorizes such withdrawal.

Revoking or modifying planning permission

4.37 It should be remembered that a planning permission once given ensures a right to develop for the benefit of all persons for the time being interested in the land, subject to any limitation of time contained in the grant of planning permission itself or imported into the matter by the 1990 Act, as mentioned in paragraph 4.30. This, however, is subject to the right of a local planning authority to revoke or modify a planning permission by means of an order made by the authority and confirmed by the Secretary of State (TP 1990 Sections 97–100, 102–104). Before confirming the order the Secretary of State must afford the owner and the occupier of the land affected by the order an opportunity of being heard by the Secretary of State's inspector. There are certain revoking or modifying orders which, being unopposed and unlikely to give rise to claims for compensation, can be made by the local planning authority without need for confirmation by the Secretary of State.

4.38 If the local planning authority wish to make a revocation or modifying order they must remember to do so before buildings authorized by the planning permission in question have been started. If they fail to do so, the revocation or modification may not affect so much of the building operations as have already been carried out. Compensation may become payable on the revocation or modification of a previously granted planning permission (TP 1990 Sections 115, 117, 118).

5 Buildings of special architectural or historic interest – listed buildings

Note: In Section 5 of this chapter all references to 'the 1990 Act' refer to the Planning (Listed Buildings and Conservation Areas) Act 1990.

5.01 The British public has tardily come to realize that the quality of life in this country is still worth preserving, but if it is not exceptionally careful, the ambience of the physical environment in which it lives is going to slip away before its very eyes. There is an outcry against pollution of all kinds. We are reminded of our heritage and of the things that interest visitors when they come to this country, and, for sure, they are far more interested in the Cotswolds than nuclear power stations, helpful on a dark night though the latter may be.

5.02 Buildings of special architectural or historic interest are great tourist attractions in this country and, at the moment, tourism is one of the biggest growth industries in our land. Accordingly, the Planning (Listed Buildings and Conservation Areas) Act 1990 (hereafter in this Section 5 referred to as 'the 1990 Act') sets out to give further, better, and more decisive protection to buildings of the sort which are here called 'special buildings'.

Listing

5.03 Lists of special buildings are compiled under Section 1 of the 1990 Act by the Secretary of State or the Historic Buildings and Monuments Commission for England (established under the National Heritage Act 1983). Once a building is listed it is no longer possible for a local authority to make (as hitherto) a building preservation order for it; in lieu the 1990 Act provides a different kind of protection (see further paragraphs 5.09 and 5.10).

5.04 The owner of such a special building need not be consulted before it is listed; he is merely told what has occurred. However, the statutory list of special buildings must be kept open by the Secretary of State for free public inspection. Similarly, a local authority must also keep open for free public inspection any portion of the list which relates to their area.

5.05 To damage a listed building is to commit a criminal offence punishable with a fine of £1 000 and a daily penalty of £100 (1990 Act Section 59; Criminal Justice Act 1991 Section 17 and S.I. 1992 No. 333). (See further paragraph 5.13.)

5.06 A local authority may carry out works urgently necessary for the preservation of an *unoccupied* listed building after giving the owner seven days' notice (1990 Act Sections 54, 55, 60, 76). A local authority may make a loan or a grant towards preserving buildings of special historic interest (whether listed or not) under the provisions of the Local Authorities (Historic Buildings) Act 1962 Section 1 and Town and Country Planning Act 1968 Section 58 which is not replaced by the Town and Country Planning Acts of 1971 or 1990. The Secretary of State may make loans as well as grants (Chapter 9) under the Historic Buildings and Ancient Monuments Act 1953, Section 4, for the preservation of historic buildings not situated in England and the Historic Buildings and Monuments Commission for England may do the like for buildings in England (1953 Act, Section 3A).

5.07 In deciding whether to list a building or not, the Secretary of State may now take into account not only the building itself, but also its relationship to other buildings and the desirability of preserving features associated with the building but not actually forming part of the building. Thus, it is not solely the building which is to be considered but the entire setting of the building (1990 Act Section 1).

5.08 When speaking of a building it must be remembered that the law is so framed as to give protection to any object or structure fixed to a building or forming part of the land on which the building stands and comprised within the curtilage of the building (1990

Act Section 1 and see *Watts* v *the Secretary of State for the Environment* [1991] *Journal of Planning Law*, p. 718).

Listed building consent

5.09 There is no provision for the owner of a special building to appeal against the listing of his building. Once the building is listed, the whole of the protective provisions of Part I of the 1990 Act automatically swing into operation. The consequence of this is that while (as already explained in paragraph 4.04) it is necessary to get planning permission for any kind of development, if the site of the development happens to be occupied in whole or in part by a listed building, then the development simply cannot take place unless an additional form of consent, known as 'listed building consent', is first obtained (the 1990 Act Sections 16, 17, 19).

5.10 Listed building consent must be obtained in order to demolish, alter, or extend a listed building (1990 Act Sections 7, 8, 9). It may be granted (like a planning permission) with or without conditions. The application for listed building consent is made to the local planning authority, and the procedure is given in Sections 10–16 of the 1990 Act and in the Planning (Listed Buildings and Conservation Areas) Regulations 1990 (S.I. 1990 No. 1519). A grant of listed building consent will last for only five years. If planning permission for development has been granted, or if an application for planning permission has been duly made, and if there is a building (unlisted) on the site, the developer may, since 13 November 1980, apply to the Secretary of State for the Environment for a certificate that the Secretary will not list any such building for at least five years (1990 Act Section 3 and see *Amalgamated Investment and Property Co Ltd* v *John Walker and Sons Ltd* [1976] 3 all ER 509 SA). This is a most useful provision when the architect feels that a building standing on the development site is potentially a 'listable' building.

5.11 In deciding whether or not to grant listed building consent with respect to a special building, the local planning authority must pay 'special regard' to the desirability of preserving the building or its setting and of preserving any features of special architectural or historic interest which the building possesses (1990 Act Sections 16, 72). Notwithstanding this, the writer takes the view that the grant of planning permission is one thing and the grant of listed building consent is another. Merely because *planning permission* is granted for development, it does not follow that *listed building consent* will be given to remove some obstructive listed building to allow such development to go forward. The planning permission, once granted, will (as explained in paragraph 4.30) last, generally speaking, for five years. During that time views and opinions about a listed building may change; views and opinions about architecture do tend to fluctuate. During the first years of the planning permission it may be impossible to get the requisite listed building consent to demolish some obstructive listed building. Later on different opinions about preservation may prevail or pressure to carry out development may become stronger. Thus, different considerations in the view of this writer apply when a local planning authority is considering whether it should grant planning permission for development and when it is considering whether it should grant listed building consent for the demolition of a listed building in order to allow planned development to go forward.

5.12 If listed building consent is refused, there is a right of appeal to the Secretary of State after the style of the appeal against refusal of planning permission (the 1990 Act Sections 20, 21 and the Planning (Listed Buildings and Conservation Areas) Regulations 1990 – S.I. 1990 No. 1519).

5.13 It is an offence to demolish, alter, or extend a listed building *so as to affect its character* as a building of special architecural or historic interest, without first getting listed building consent (the 1990 Act Sections 7–9; see also *Britain's Heritage* v *the Secretary of State and Others* (the Peter Palumbo case) [1991] IWLR 153). It is also an offence to fail to comply with any conditions attached

to such consent. The penalty for each of these offences is (on summary conviction) a fine of £20 000 or imprisonment for six months or both, and on conviction on indictment, a fine of unlimited amount or imprisonment for two years or both. It is, however, a defence to prove that any works carried out on a listed building were urgently necessary in the interests of safety or health, or for the preservation of the building and that notice in writing of the need for the works was given to the district planning authority as soon as was reasonably practicable (the 1990 Act Section 9).

5.14 If the owner is faced with a refusal of listed building consent and can demonstrate that in its present state his listed building has become incapable of reasonable beneficial use, then he may serve a listed building purchase notice on the local planning authority requiring the authority to purchase the building (the 1990 Act Sections 32–36 and the Planning (Listed Buildings and Conservation Areas) Regulations 1990 – S.I. 1990 No. 1519).

Listed building enforcement notice

5.15 If unauthorized works to a listed building are carried out, then the local planning authority, in addition to taking proceeding for the commission of a criminal offence, may serve a 'listed building enforcement notice' upon the owner, requiring full reinstatement of the listed building (the 1990 Act Section 38). There is a right of appeal against the notice to the Secretary of State (the 1990 Act Sections 39–41, 64, 65 and T and CP (Enforcement Notices and Appeals) Regulations 1990 – S.I. 1991 No. 2804). Penalties are provided in the case of non-compliance with the terms of the listed building enforcement notice. The guilty person is liable to a fine of £20 000 on summary conviction and of unlimited amount on conviction on indictment (the 1990 Act Section 43). These penalties are recoverable from the owner of the land who is in breach of the notice and this may include a subsequent owner. So the purchaser of a listed building must be careful to ascertain before he buys whether there are any listed building enforcement notices outstanding in respect of the building.

5.16 A local authority is authorized to acquire compulsorily any listed building which is not properly preserved (the 1990 Act Sections 49–50). This power may not be exercised until at least two months after the service on the owner of the building of a repairs notice specifying the work considered necessary for the proper preservation of the building. An owner faced with the possibility of having his listed building compulsorily acquired from him cannot appeal to the Secretary of State, but curiously enough, he can, within 28 days, appeal to the local magistrates' court to stay the proceedings under the compulsory purchase order. If the court is satisfied that reasonable steps have been taken for properly preserving the building then the court may order accordingly. Against the order of the magistrates there is a further appeal to the Crown Court.

5.17 If a listed building is compulsorily acquired, then the compensation to be paid to the owner will, in general, disregard the depressive effect of the fact that the building has been listed. On the other hand, if it is established that the building has been allowed deliberately to fall into disrepair for the purpose of justifying the redevelopment of the site, then the 1990 Act provides for the payment of what is called 'minimum compensation'. This means that the compensation will be assessed at a price which disregards any profit which might have accrued to the owner from the redevelopment of the site. Against any direction in a compulsory purchase order providing for the payment of this minimum compensation there is a right of appeal and, again, this is to the local magistrates' court, with a further appeal to the Crown Court (the 1990 Act Section 50).

Building preservation notices

5.18 Are there any means today of protecting a building which is *not* a listed building, but which appears to the local planning authority to be of special architectural or historic interest? The answer is yes. Although the district planning authority can no longer make a building preservation order, it can serve on the owner of the building a building preservation notice which gives temporary protection for six months, during which time the building is protected just as if it were listed (the 1990 Act Section 3). The object of this is to give time for consideration by the local planning authority and the Secretary of State, or indeed by anybody else, as to whether the building should in fact be listed. If, at the end of six months, the Secretary of State will not make any such listing, then the building preservation notice automatically ceases, and the local planning authority may not serve a further building preservation notice within the next 12 months. Moreover, compensation may become payable to the owner of the building for loss or damage caused by the service of the building preservation notice which failed to be followed by the listing of the building.

5.19 Certain buildings of undoubted architectural and historic interest do not come within the protection of listing at all. These are:

1. Ecclesiastical buildings in use for church purposes (but not the parsonage house, which *is* capable of being listed).
2. A building included in the Schedule of monuments compiled and maintained by the Secretary of State under ancient monuments legislation.

Buildings in conservation areas

5.20 In addition to the special protection given to listed buildings as described above, the 1990 Act Section 74 gives protection to *all* buildings if they happen to be in a conservation area designated under Section 69 of the 1990 Act.

6 Urban Development Corporations; Enterprise Zones; Simplified Planning Zones

Urban Development Areas and Corporations

6.01 The Local Government, Planning and Land Act 1980 Part XVI and Part XVIII (as amended by the Housing and Planning Act 1986 Section 49 and the Leasehold Reform, Housing and Urban Development Act 1993 Section 179) break new ground in the sphere of land development and planning control over such development by providing, respectively, for the establishment of Urban Development Corporations and Enterprise Zones Each of these is briefly dealt with in the following paragraphs.

6.02 The Secretary of State is now empowered to designate an area of land as an 'urban development area' and to establish an Urban Development Corporation to regenerate the area. All this is done by means of an order made by the Secretary of State and approved by affirmative resolution of each House of Parliament. On 14 November 1980 the Minister for Local Government and Environmental Services, Mr Tom King, MP, declared: 'We shall shortly be bringing forward Orders under powers in the [Local Government, Planning and Land] Act to set up Urban Development Corporations as single-minded agencies to spearhead the regeneration of the London and Merseyside docklands and to introduce the bold new experiment of enterprise zones, where business can be freed from such detailed planning control.'

The requisite orders for the London and Merseyside docklands were made in 1981. Further areas have since been made (in 1987) establishing Urban Development Corporations for:

1. Trafford (Manchester)
2. the Black Country
3. Teeside
4. Tyne and Wear
5. Cardiff Bay

and (in 1988) for:

6. Leeds
7. Bristol

8. Sheffield
9. Wolverhampton.

6.03 An Urban Development Corporation (like a New Town Development Corporation) is not an elected body. It is *appointed* by the Secretary of State and comprises a chairman, a deputy chairman, together with not less than five, nor more than eleven, other members as the Secretary of State may see fit to appoint. In making these appointments the Secretary of State must consult such local government authorities as appear to him to be concerned with the regeneration of the urban development area, and he must have regard to the desirability of appointing persons having special knowledge of the locality where the area is situated.

6.04 The Urban Development Corporations will have the duty of regenerating their respective areas by:

1. bringing land and buildings into effective use;
2. encouraging development of industry and commerce;
3. generating an attractive environment; and
4. ensuring that housing and social facilities are available.

The Urban Development Corporations will have powers similar to those of the New Town Development Corporations. They will be empowered to deal with matters of land assembly and disposal, planning, housing, and industrial promotion. They will be able to submit for approval by the Secretary of State their own proposals for the regeneration of their urban development areas. Before approving these proposals, the Secretary of State will need to consult any local planning authority within whose area the urban development area (or any part of it) falls.

6.05 An Urban Development Corporation may by order made by the Secretary of State (and subject to annulment by either House of Parliament) become the local planning authority for its own area (TP Section 7), thereby taking over all the planning control duties of any local government planning authority functioning within the urban development area. If this occurs, a developer of land within an urban development area will find himself more in contact with the appropriate urban development corporation than with the district planning authority when it comes to the matter of obtaining planning permission for development.

6.06 An Urban Development Corporation, once established, must prepare within twelve months a code of practice as to consultation with the relevant local government authorities relating to the manner in which the Corporation proposes to exercise its regeneration powers. This code of practice *must* be prepared (and *may* be revised from time to time) by the Urban Development Corporation acting in consultation with the relevant local government authorities.

6.07 An Urban Development Corporation may, by agreement approved by the Secretary of State with the concurrence of the Treasury, transfer the whole or any part of its undertaking to a local government authority. When all the property and undertakings of an Urban Development Corporation have been transferred, the Corporation may be dissolved by order made by the Secretary of State after consultation with each local authority in whose area all or part of the urban development area is situated.

6.08 It will be observed that, each time an Urban Development Corporation is established, there is bound to be a consequential diminution of the planning control powers of any local government planning authority functioning within the urban development area over whose regeneration it is the responsibility of the Urban Development Corporation to preside. Accordingly, it will not be surprising to find that the establishment of any Urban Development Corporation, and the demarcation of the boundaries of any urban development area, are matters which will be eyed critically by any local government authority out of whose area the urban development area is to be carved. On this it may be mentioned that the London borough of Southwark petitioned the House of Lords to have the boundaries of the London Dockland Development Corporation redrawn. The petition failed.

Enterprise Zones

6.09 Part XVIII of, and Schedule 32 to, the Local Government, Planning and Land Act 1980 deals with the designation of Enterprise Zones within which special provisions relating to planning and rating (i.e. local council tax) will apply.

6.10 The following bodies may be invited by the Secretary of State to prepare a scheme with a view to the designation as an Enterprise Zone of the particular area of land for which the scheme was prepared. Such a scheme may be prepared by a district council, the council of a Welsh county or county borough, a London borough council, a New Town Corporation, or an Urban Development Corporation. If any such scheme is formally adopted by the scheme-making body, then the Secretary of State, if he thinks it expedient to do so, may designate the area to which the scheme relates as an Enterprise Zone. The important point about all this is that any order designating an Enterprise Zone is *of itself* to have the effect of granting planning permission for such development as may be specified in the scheme.

6.11 In the words of the Minister of Local Government and Environment Services (quoted above – paragraph 6.02), 'the bold new experiment of Enterprise Zones will so arrange things that business can be freed from detailed planning control'.

Simplified Planning Zones (SPZs)

6.12 In the White Paper (Cmnd 9571) dated July 1985 and entitled 'Lifting the Burden' – the Burden being that of various forms of government control (including planning and development control) over enterprise in all its manifestations – the Government declared (paragraph 3.5):

'There is therefore always a presumption in favour of development, unless that development would cause demonstrable harm to interests of acknowledged importance.' (This statement must be carefully read in light of the statutory provisions of Section 54A of the Town and Country Planning Act 1990; see paragraphs 4.06 and 4.07 of this chapter.)

The White Paper went on (paragraph 3.6) to declare that:

'3.6 In line with this approach to the control of development, and in support of the general aim of deregulation, a number of other measures are being taken to simplify the planning system and reduce the burden of control:

(i) It is proposed to introduce new legislation to permit the setting up of *Simplified Planning Zones* (SPZ) which will extend to other areas the type of planning regime already established in Enterprise Zones. This will enable the local planning authority to specify the types of development allowed in an area, so that developers can then carry out development that conforms to the scheme without the need for a planning application and the related fee. Planning permission for other types of development can be applied for in the normal way. This type of planning scheme has proved to be effective and successful in Enterprise Zones and can provide a real stimulus to the redevelopment of derelict or unused land and buildings in areas that are badly in need of regeneration. In addition to providing local planning authorities with powers to introduce SPZs, they will also require to consider proposals for the establishment of SPZs initiated by private developers. The Secretaries of State would have reserve powers to direct the preparation of proposals for an SPZ, similar to those that they already have to direct the preparation of alterations to development plans.'

6.13 The Government fulfilled the forgoing promise by the enactment of the Housing and Planning Act 1986, Part II of which related to Simplified Planning Zones. Simplified Planning Zones are now dealt with in the Town and Country Planning Act 1990 Sections 82–87, 94 and Schedule 1, paragraph 9 and Schedule 7, and in the Town and Country Planning (Simplified Planning Zones) Regulations 1992 (S.I. 1992 No. 2414). Simplified Planning Zones

will be established by local planning authorities by means of a new system of Simplified Planning Zone Schemes (it is the word 'Scheme' which is the really important part of this expression) each of which will specify types of development permitted in a zone. A developer will be able to carry out such development without making an application for planning permission and paying the requisite fee.

6.14 The following land may *not* be included in a simplified planning zone:

1. land in a national park;
2. land in a conservation area;
3. land within the Norfolk and Suffolk Broads;
4. land in an area of outstanding natural beauty;
5. land in a greenbelt identified in a development plan; and
6. land notified under the Wildlife and Countryside Act 1981, Sections 28 or 29 as an area of special scientific interest.

If, however, land in a simplified planning zone *becomes* land in any one of the above descriptions, it does not thereby become excluded from the zone.

The Secretary of State may by order provide that no simplified planning zone scheme shall grant automatic planning permission for development:

1. in any area or areas specified in the order; or
2. of any development specified in the order.

But development already begun when the order of the Secretary of State comes into force is not affected.

6.15 Clearly the making of a Simplified Planning Zone Scheme is going to be no simple matter and is going to take time – months rather than weeks (or is it years rather than months?). The local planning authority will need to consider very closely the details of their proposals because the wider or more liberal the development automatically granted by the scheme, the less will the authority, on an *ad hoc*, individual basis, be able to exercise their own policies relating to development control. Control by planning authorities of details about development permitted by the scheme (e.g. the siting of buildings, the materials to be used in their construction, and the dimensions, design and external appearance of buildings) will be beyond control by the local planning authority unless they have been spelt out deliberately and in detail in the scheme itself. Yet if too much detail is put into a scheme there is a chance that more objections to it will be lodged and, accordingly, the more protracted will be any public local inquiry relating to such objections.

On the other hand, a developer will wish to know (by his reading and examination of the scheme) with some certainty whether he may safely go ahead with his development without making any formal application for planning permission and paying the fees currently applicable in such a case, relying on the provisions of the scheme to support his action. After all, if he goes beyond the scope of the scheme (including its conditions, limitations and exceptions) he is in danger of being faced with an enforcement notice on the basis that he has carried out development without planning permission. The developer may decide to take this risk or (if he has time on his hands) he may apply under Section 192 of the 1990 Act for a determination by the local planning authority as to whether or not his development falls within the scope of the scheme.

In short, the drafting of a Simplified Planning Zone Scheme may well be as big a headache to the local planning authority as the construing of the meaning and scope of the scheme will be to a developer eager to press on with development which happens to be of an expensive and substantial nature. In such a case, and in order to be absolutely sure of his ground, will the developer seek an *ad hoc* grant of planning permission from the local planning authority? Will he think it better to be slow but sure rather than rapid and wrong? But if he *does* apply to the local planning authority for an *ad hoc* grant of planning permission, will the authority accept his application and deal with it in the ordinary way or will they refer the developer to the contents of their simplified planning zone scheme? We shall see.

7 Enforcement of planning control

7.01 The enforcement of planning control is dealt with in Sections 171A to 196C of the Town and Country Planning Act 1990.

7.02 The Town and Country Planning Act 1968 made two important alterations to the law relating to enforcement of planning control wherever development is carried out without planning permission. One of these was the abolition of what is commonly called 'the four-year rule' in the case of development comprising a change of use of land (but not a building operation); and the other was the introduction of the 'stop notice' in the case of development comprising a building operation (but not a change of use of land). Today the stop notice procedure applies (since 22 August 1977) also to development involving not operations but only a material change of use (see paragraph 7.12).

7.03 Architects, being associated more with the sort of development that amounts to a building operation rather than a mere change of use, will be affected more by the new stop notice procedure than by the abolition of the four-year rule.

Four-year rule

7.04 The four-year rule derives from the fact that, under the form of town planning control introduced in 1948, if development is carried out without planning permission and if the authorities allow four years to elapse without doing anything about the matter (i.e. without taking action by issuing an enforcement notice), then such development becomes validated automatically for town planning purposes and no enforcement action can be taken thereafter. It may be said at once that nothing in the 1990 Act interferes with this state of affairs so far as building development is concerned.

7.05 However, so far as development involving only a change of use of land is concerned, the four-year rule is abolished, and nowadays it is open to a local planning authority to serve an enforcement notice in respect of a change of use of land which did not carry the appropriate planning permission even though the change of use took place more than four years previously. Indeed, in such circumstances there is now no period of limitation at all. There is one important exception; i.e. the change of use of a building into use as a single dwelling house, in which case the four-year rule still applies.

Certificates of established use

7.06 In the case of a use of land which was instituted before 1 January 1964 (i.e. four years before the Town and Country Planning Act 1968) provision is made in the 1990 Act Sections 191–196 for obtaining a certificate, namely, a 'certificate of established use'. This is obtained from the local planning authority, and there is a right of appeal to the Secretary of State if one is refused. The certificate makes it clear that the use in question, though originally instituted without planning permission, is now immune from enforcement action.

Enforcement notices

7.07 Enforcement action is by way of enforcement notice served by the local planning authority upon the owner and occupier of the land to which it relates (TP Act 1990 Part VII and T and CP (Enforced Notices and Appeals) Regulations 1991 (S.I. 1991 No. 2 804); T and CP (Enforcement) (Inquiries Procedure) Rules 1992 (S.I. 1992 No. 1903 and S.I. 1992 No. 1904). Briefly, the notice requires the doing of all things necessary to amend the breach of planning control which, it is alleged in the notice, has occurred. There is an appeal to the Secretary of State against the notice, and the appeal must now state not only the grounds of the appeal but the facts on which it is based. The penalty for non-compliance with an enforcement notice is, on summary conviction, a fine of £20 000 or on conviction on indictment, a fine of unlimited amount (TP 1990 Section 179).

7.08 Architects should note that a local planning authority is never *obliged* to serve an enforcement notice whenever there has been a breach of planning control. The authority always has a discretion which it must be expected to exercise reasonably, as must any public authority holding discretionary powers. What the authority have to consider is whether, notwithstanding the breach of planning control, it is *expedient* to take enforcement action, and on this the authority must have regard not only to the provisions of the relevant development plan but also to 'any other material considerations'.

7.09 Without doubt, enforcement notices are very tricky things indeed, and the law reports are full of decisions of the courts in which the validity of such notices has been challenged successfully on the ground of some legal flaw in the drafting or the service of the notice. However, all these things are problems for the local authority rather than for the developer and his architect.

Stop notices

7.10 The legal pitfalls associated with an enforcement notice have, in the past, sometimes led a developer to spin out the appeal procedure while getting on in the meantime with his building development. There is an appeal to the High Court on a point of law from the Secretary of State's decision in an enforcement notice appeal, and there are further appeals (on points of law) to the Court of Appeal and to the House of Lords. This is still the position, but the 1990 Act prevents a building developer from continuing his building operations while the protracted appeals procedure is working itself out. There is no longer the possibility of (quite lawfully) finishing the building before the appeal to, and in, the House of Lords is concluded. The stop notice procedure prevents this from happening (TP 1990 Section 187).

7.11 Once an enforcement notice has been served, the local authority may follow it with a stop notice which brings all building operations or changes of use to a halt under a penalty, for breach of the notice, of £20 000 on summary conviction or of a fine of unlimited amount on conviction on indictment (TP p. 187).

7.12 Since 22 August 1977 (when the Town and Country Planning (Amendment) Act 1977 came into operation), a stop notice may also be served following an enforcement notice which relates, not to building or other operations, but to any material change in the use of land (TP 1990 Section 183). If a stop notice is so served, it must be served within twelve months of the change of use occurring. But a stop notice on a change of use can never be served when the change of use is change of use of a building into use as a dwelling house (TP 1990 Section 183(4)).

7.13 There is no appeal against a stop notice. Such a notice is dependent entirely on the enforcement notice with which it is associated. If, on appeal, the enforcement notice fails, so does the stop notice. In this instance, compensation is payable under the 1990 Act in certain (but not all) cases for loss or damage arising from the stop notice (TP 1990 Section 186). Thus a local authority will be inclined to think twice before serving a stop notice.

7.14 Department of the Environment Circular 21/91, dated 16 December 1991, and its six Annexes give much useful guidance on the subject of enforcement notices, stop notices and injunctions to enforce planning control over land development.

8 L'envoi

8.01 The proof of the pudding is in its eating; the proof of planning control may be said to be in its administration. Heaven knows, there is enough planning *law* these days, as the size of the planning Acts of 1990 and 1991 show. After statutory pronouncement on the subject there come voluminous quantities of subordinate legislation in the form of rules and regulations. Then, all this legislation must be read in association with vast quantities of circulars, pronouncements and so forth emanating from the Department of the Environment.

8.02 Notwithstanding all these powers and legal authority, it is said, from time to time, that planning control fails. If it does fail, the failure will have little to do with the powers but with the way they are used or (and this is often the case) *not* used.

8.03 Planning control is not a finite science but an artistic process in which there is, and always will be, room for more than one point of view. Architectural design comes prominently into the arena of planning control, and architectural design, like other types of design, is a matter of taste; e.g. one planning authority will like buildings built one way and another authority will like buildings built another way.

8.04 The important thing about buildings, one would have thought, is to get variety, that is to say, a state of affairs in which the buildings are different but not stridently in opposition to one another. Nobody wants bad manners in civic architecture. Thus, one would not regard it the responsibility of the local planning authority, as a matter of administration, always to turn down an application for planning permission purely because they do not entirely like the design of the building. The authority may not like it but, without doubt, somebody else will. It is not the job of the planning authority constantly to be redesigning buildings so that they conform with some overall corporate taste (established, no doubt, through the processes of a democratic vote) on the part of the authority. If this were to happen, it would lead to a progressive spread of something in the nature of a local government school of architecture. If one wants to know what this could mean, one need only recall the rash of metropolitan borough town halls which sprouted across London after the boroughs had been created in 1899.

202

14

Construction Regulations in England and Wales

LAWRENCE DAVIS*

1 Building Acts and Regulations

1.01 Planning legislation is largely concerned with policy and, in relation to the external appearance of a building, with safeguarding of amenity (Chapter 13). But obtaining planning permission is only the first legal hurdle. The architect is then faced with controls over the construction and design of buildings.

In England and Wales the basic framework of control is found in the Building Act 1984 and in the Regulations made under it. An important feature of the present system of building control is that there are two alternative means of control – one by local authorities operating under the Building Regulations 1991, and the other a system of private certification which relies on 'approved inspectors' operating under the Building (Approved Inspectors, etc.) Regulations 1985.

In practice, most building work will be subject to control by the local authority because at present there is only one approved inspector, namely the National House Building Council Building Control Services Ltd (NHBC): see paragraph 3.03.

Most of the provisions of the 1984 Act have been brought into force. Those which are not yet in force are set out in Checklist 14.1.

The Building Act 1984 is a consolidating statute and draws together most, but not all, of the statutory requirements previously found elsewhere, but notably in the Public Health Acts 1936 and 1961, as amended. The position is complicated by the fact that in more than thirty English counties and boroughs there are local Acts containing additional building control provisions and these must also be complied with. A comprehensive treatment of these controls will be found in *Guide to Building Control by Local Acts 1987* by P. H. Pitt.

Checklist 14.2 sets out the local Acts with building control provisions.

Although the Building Regulations have applied to Inner London since 1986, the London Building Acts 1930 to 1978 remain in force with modifications and the position in Inner London is considered later in this chapter.

2 The Building Regulations 1991

2.01 The Building Regulations 1991 contain the detailed rules and procedures governing building control by local authorities and came into force on 1 June 1992. The Building (Approved Inspectors, etc.) Regulations, 1985 set out the procedures to be adopted by an approved inspector (see Section 3 of this chapter).

2.02 The Building Regulations require that all 'building work' must be carried out in accordance with the requirements of Schedule 1

* This chapter draws on the chapter written for the first edition by Vincent Powell-Smith and subsequently updated by him.

Checklist 14.1: The Building Act 1984

Provisions not yet in force

Section	Content
	Part I
	Type approval of building matter
12.	Power of Secretary of State to approve type of building matter.
13.	Delegation of power to approve.
	Passing of plans
20.	Use of materials unsuitable for permanent building.
	(Sections 26–29 were repealed by the Building Regulations 1985)
	(Section 30 was repealed by the Building Act, 1984 (Appointed Day and Repeal Order) 1985)
	Proposed departure from plans
31.	Proposed departure from plans.
	Tests for conformity with building regulations
33.	Tests for conformity with building regulations.
	Breach of building regulations
38.	Civil liability
	Appeals in certain cases
42.	Appeal and statement of case to High Court in certain cases.
43.	Procedure on appeal to Secretary of State on certain matters.
	Application of building regulations to Crown, etc.
44.	Application to Crown.
45.	Application to United Kingdom Atomic Energy Authority.

---

but there are important limitations on the requirements. Regulation 8 states that nothing need be done other than the necessary works to secure *reasonable standards of health and safety for persons in and about buildings, or matters connected with buildings.* This limitation does not apply to those parts of the Schedule dealing with conservation of fuel and power or access and facilities for disabled people.

Approved documents

2.03 The Building Regulations 1991 contain no technical detail but are supported by a series of 14 approved documents. The status and use of these documents is laid down in Sections 6 and 7 of the Building Act 1984. The purpose of the documents is to give practical guidance with respect to the requirements of any provision of the building regulations. The documents may be approved by the Secretary of State or by some other body designated by him.

The current approved documents all refer to other non-statutory material, including British Standards and certificates issued by the British Board of Agrément. The documents are intended to give designers a considerable amount of flexibility. The details within the documents do not have to be followed if the requirements can be met in some other way.

2.04 Section 7 of the 1984 Act specifies the legal effect of the documents. Failure to comply with their recommendations does not involve civil or criminal liability, but they can be relied on by either party to any proceedings for alleged contravention of the regulation requirements. Thus if an architect proves that he has complied with the requirements of an approved document in any proceedings which are brought against him, he can rely on this as 'tending to negative liability'. Conversely, his failure to so comply may be relied on by the local authority as 'tending to establish liability, and the onus will be on the architect to establish that he has met the functional requirement in some other way.

In *Rickards* v *Kerrier District Council* (1987) CILL 345, in enforcement proceedings under Section 36 of the 1984 Act, the High Court had to consider the application of Section 6. The judge held that the burden of proving non-compliance with the Regulations was on the local authority, but if they established that the works did not comply with an approved document, then the burden shifted. The appellant against a Section 36 notice would then have to show compliance with the regulations in some other way.

2.05 Space does not permit a detailed analysis of the technical content of the approved documents and readers should refer to the *Guide to the Building Regulations, 1991*, a definitive treatment of the subject.

2.06 Checklist 14.3. sets out the requirements of Schedule 1 to the 1991 regulations and there is an approved document for each part of the Schedule. There is a further approved document which supports Regulation 7 – the regulation which states that building work shall be carried out with proper materials and in a workmanlike manner. This document also refers to technical standards originating both in the UK and in Europe.

Subject to specified exemptions (see para. 4) all building work (as defined in the regulations) in England and Wales, must be carried out so that the requirements of Schedule 1 are met. Checklist 14.3 sets out the requirements of Schedule 1.

Checklist 14.2: Principal local Acts with building control provisions

Act	Year	Act	Year
Avon	1982	Kent	1981
Berkshire	1986	Lancashire	1984
Bournemouth	1985	Leicestershire	1985
Cheshire	1980	Merseyside	1980
Cleveland	1987	Mid Glamorgan	1987
Clwyd	1985	Nottinghamshire	1985
Cornwall	1984	Poole	1986
Cumbria	1982	South Glamorgan	1976
Derbyshire	1981	South Yorkshire	1980
Dyfed	1987	Staffordshire	1983
East Sussex	1981	Surrey	1985
Essex	1987	Tyne & Wear	1980
Greater Manchester	1981	West Glamorgan	1987
Hampshire	1983	West Midlands	1980
Humberside	1982	West Yorkshire	1980
Isle of Wight	1980	York City Council	1987

Note: The London Building Acts 1930–1978 apply to Inner London.

2.07 Subject to a number of exemptions which are dealt with later (see paragraph 4.01 ff), the procedural requirements of Part IV of the Building Regulations must be observed where a person proposes to undertake building work covered by the regulations and subject to the control of the local authority. The local authority for this purpose is the district council, a London borough

Checklist 14.3: Technical requirements in Schedule 1 of the Building Regulations 1991 (as amended by the Building (Amendment) Regulations 1994)

SCHEDULE 1 – REQUIREMENTS	Regulations 4 and 6

Requirement	Limits on application

PART A   STRUCTURE

Loading
A1. – (1) The building shall be constructed so that the combined dead, imposed and wind loads are sustained and transmitted by it to the ground –
(a) safely, and
(b) without causing such deflection or deformation of any part of the building, or such movement of the ground, as will impair the stability of any part of another building.
(2) In assessing whether a building complies with sub-paragraph (1) regard shall be had to the imposed and wind loads to which it is likely to be subjected in the ordinary course of its use for the purpose for which it is intended.

Ground movement
A2. The building shall be constructed so that movements caused by –
(a) swelling, shrinkage or freezing of the subsoil, or
(b) land slip or subsidence (other than subsidence arising from shrinkage in so far as the risk can be reasonably foreseen) will not impair the stability of any part of the building

Disproportionate collapse
A3. The building shall be constructed so that in the event of an accident, the structure will not suffer collapse to an extent disproportionate to the cause of the damage.

This requirement applies only to a building having five or more storeys (each basement level being counted as one storey), excluding a storey with a roof space where the slope of the roof does not exceed 70° to the horizontal.

PART B   FIRE

Means of escape
B1. The building shall be designed and constructed so that there are means of escape in case of fire from the building to a place of safety outside the building capable of being safely and effectively used at all material times.

Requirement B1 does not apply to any prison provided under Section 33 of the Prisons Act 1952 (power to provide prisons, etc.).

Internal fire spread (linings)
B2. (1) To inhibit the spread of fire within the building the internal linings shall –
(a) resist the spread of flame over their surfaces; and
(b) have, if ignited, a rate of heat release which is reasonable in the circumstances.
(2) In this paragraph, 'internal linings' means the materials lining any partition, wall, ceiling or other internal structure.

Checklist 14.3 continued

Internal fire spread (structure)
B3. (1) The building shall be designed and constructed so that in the event of fire, its stability will be maintained for a reasonable period.
(2) A wall common to two or more buildings shall be designed and constructed so that it resists the spread of fire between those buildings. For the purposes of this sub-paragraph a house in a terrace and a semi-detached house are each to be treated as a separate building.
(3) To inhibit the spread of fire within the building, it shall be subdivided with fire-resisting construction to an extent appropriate to the size and intended use of the building.
(4) The building shall be designed and constructed so that the unseen spread of fire and smoke within concealed spaces in its structure and fabric is inhibited.

Requirement B3 (3) does not apply to material alterations to any prison provided under Section 33 of the Prisons Act, 1952.

External fire spread
B4. (1) The external walls of the building shall resist the spread of fire over the walls and from one building to another, having regard to the height, use and position of the building.
(2) The roof of the building shall resist the spread of fire over the roof and from one building to another, having regard to the use and position of the building.

PART C   SITE PREPARATION AND RESISTANCE TO MOISTURE

Preparation of site
C1. The ground to be covered by the building shall be reasonably free from vegetable matter.

Dangerous and offensive substances
C2. Precautions shall be taken to avoid danger to health and safety caused by substances found on or in the ground to be covered by the building.

Subsoil drainage
C3. Subsoil drainage shall be provided if it is needed to avoid –
(a) the passage of ground moisture to the interior of the building;
(b) damage to the fabric of the building.

Resistance to weather and ground moisture
C4. The walls, floors and roof of the building shall resist the passage of moisture to the inside of the building.

PART D   TOXIC SUBSTANCES

Cavity insulation
D1. If insulating material is inserted into a cavity in a cavity wall reasonable precautions shall be taken to prevent the subsequent permeation of any toxic fumes from that material into any part of the building occupied by people.

Checklist 14.3 continued

PART E   RESISTANCE TO THE PASSAGE OF SOUND

Airborne sound (walls)
E1. A wall which –
(a) separates a dwelling from another building or from another dwelling, or
(b) separates a habitable room or kitchen within a dwelling from another part of the same building which is not used exclusively as part of the dwelling shall resist the transmission of airborne sound.

Airborne sound (floors)
E2. A floor or a stair which separates a dwelling from another dwelling, or from another part of the same building which is not used exclusively as part of the dwelling, shall resist the transmittance of airborne sound.

Impact sound (floors)
E3. A floor or stair above a dwelling which separates it from another dwelling, or from another part of the same building which is not used exclusively as part of the dwelling, shall resist the transmittance of impact sound.

PART F   VENTILATION

Means of ventilation
F1. There shall be adequate means of ventilation provided for people in the building.

Requirement F1. applies only to –
(a) dwellings;
(b) the spaces within any building containing two or more dwellings which are used solely or principally in connection with those dwellings;
(c) rooms containing sanitary conveniences; and
(d) bathrooms.

Condensation
F2. Adequate provision shall be made to prevent excessive condensation.
(a) in a roof; or
(b) in a roof void above an insulated ceiling.

PART G   HYGIENE

Sanitary conveniences and washing facilities
G1. (1) Adequate sanitary conveniences shall be provided in rooms provided for that purpose, or in bathrooms. Any such room or bathroom shall be separated from places where food is prepared.
(2) Adequate washbasins shall be provided in
(a) rooms containing water closets; or
(b) rooms or spaces adjacent to rooms containing water closets.
Any such room or space shall be separated from places where food is prepared.

Checklist 14.3 continued

Checklist 14.3 continued

(3) There shall be a suitable installation for the provision of hot and cold water to washbasins provided in accordance with paragraph (2).
(4) Sanitary conveniences and washbasins to which this paragraph applies shall be designed and installed so as to allow effective cleaning.

Hot water storage
G3. A hot water storage system that has a hot water storage vessel which does not incorporate a vent pipe to the atmosphere shall be installed by a person competent to do so, and there shall be precautions –
(a) to prevent the temperature of stored water at any time exceeding 100°C; and
(b) to ensure that the hot water discharged from safety devices is safely conveyed to where it is visible but will not cause danger to persons in or about the building.

Part H   Drainage and waste disposal

Sanitary pipework and drainage
H1. – (1) Any system which carries foul water from appliances within the building to a sewer, a cesspool or a septic or settlement tank, shall be adequate.
(2) 'Foul water' in sub-paragraph (1) means waste water which comprises or includes –
(a) waste from a sanitary convenience or other soil appliance;
(b) water which has been used for cooking or washing.

Cesspools, septic tanks and settlement tanks
H2. Any cesspool, septic tank or settlement tank shall be –
(a) of adequate capacity and so constructed that it is impermeable to liquids;
(b) adequately ventilated; and
(c) so sited and constructed that –
  (i) it is not prejudicial to the health of any person,
  (ii) it will not contaminate any underground water or water supply, and
  (iii) there are adequate means of access for emptying.

Rainwater drainage
H3. Any system which carries rainwater from the roof of a building to a sewer, soakaway, watercourse, or some other suitable rainwater outfall shall be adequate.

Solid waste storage
H4. – (1) Adequate means of storing solid waste shall be provided.
(2) Adequate means of access shall be provided –
(a) for people in the building to the place of storage; and
(b) from the place of storage to a street.

Part J   Heat producing appliances

Air supply
J1. Heat producing appliances shall be so installed that there is an adequate supply of air to them for combustion and for the efficient working of any flue-pipe or chimney.

Discharge of products of combustion
J2. Heat producing appliances shall have adequate provision for the discharge of the products of combustion to the outside air.

Protection of building
J3. Heat producing appliances and flue-pipes shall be so installed, and fire-places and chimneys shall be so constructed, as to reduce to a reasonable level the risk of the building catching fire in consequence of their use.

The requirements in this Part apply only to fixed heat producing appliances which –
(a) are designed to burn solid fuel, oil or gas; or
(b) are incinerators.

Part K   Stairways. ramps and guards

Stairways and ramps
K1. Stairs, ladders and ramps shall offer safety to users moving between levels of a building.

Protection from falling
K2. Stairways, ramps, floors and balconies, and any roof to which people normally have access, shall be guarded with barriers where they are necessary to protect users from the risk of falling.

Vehicle barriers
K3. Vehicle ramps, and any floor and roof to which vehicles have access, shall be guarded with barriers where they are necessary to provide protection for people in or about the building.

The requirements of this Part apply to stairs, ladders and ramps which form part of the building.

Requirement K1 does not apply to stairs, ladders and ramps which provide access to levels used only for the purpose of maintenance.

Part L   Conservation of fuel and power

Conservation of fuel and power
L1. Reasonable provision shall be made for the conservation of fuel and power in buildings where appropriate by:
(a) limiting the heat loss through the fabric of the building;
(b) controlling the operation of the space heating and hot water systems;
(c) limiting the heat loss from hot water vessels and hot water service pipework;
(d) limiting the heat loss from hot water pipes and hot air ducts used for space heating;
(e) installing in buildings artificial lighting systems which are designed and constructed to use no more fuel and power than is reasonable in the circumstances and making reasonable provision for controlling such systems;
to the extent necessary to conserve the use of fuel and power in and in relation to the building.

L1 (a), (b), (c) and (d) apply to domestic buildings
L1 (a), (b), (c) and (d) apply to non-domestic buildings whose floor area exceeds 30 m^2.

L1 (e) applies within non-domestic buildings where more than 100 m^2 of floor area is to be provided with artificial lighting.

Checklist 14.3 continued

PART M   ACCESS AND FACILITIES FOR DISABLED PEOPLE

Interpretation
M1. In this Part 'disabled people' means people who have –
(a) an impairment which limits their ability to walk or which requires them to use a wheelchair for mobility, or
(b) impaired hearing or sight.

Access and use
M2. Reasonable provision shall be made for disabled people to gain access to and to use the building.

Sanitary conveniences
M3. If sanitary conveniences are provided in the building reasonable provision shall be made for disabled people.

Audience or spectator seating
M4. If the building contains audience or spectator seating, reasonable provision shall be made to accommodate disabled people.

The requirements of this Part do not apply to –
(a) an extension which does not include a ground storey;
(b) a material alteration;
(c) a dwelling or the common parts of a building which are intended for the exclusive use of two or more dwellings;
(d) any part of a building which is used solely to enable the building or any service or fitting in the building to be inspected, maintained or repaired.

PART N   GLAZING-MATERIALS AND PROTECTION

N1. Glazing, with which people are likely to come into contact while in passage in or about the building, shall –
(a) if broken on impact, break in a way which is unlikely to cause injury; or
(b) resist impact without breaking; or
(c) be shielded or protected from impact.
N2. Transparent glazing, with which people are likely to collide with in passage in or about the building, shall incorporate features which make it apparent.

Requirement N2 does not apply to dwellings.

council, the Common Council of the City of London, the Sub-Treasurer of the Inner Temple, the Under Treasurer of the Middle Temple, and the Council of the Isles of Scilly (1984 Act, Section 126(1)).

Regulation 3 defines 'building work' as meaning the erection or extension of a building, the provision or extension of a controlled service or fitting, the material alteration of a building or of a controlled service or fitting, work required if a material change of use occurs, the insertion of insulating material into a cavity wall and work involving underpinning, hot water supply systems, sanitary conveniences, drainage and waste disposal, certain fixed heat-producing appliances and heating systems.

Two main options are available under the local authority control system, namely the service of a building notice and the deposit and submission of full plans. Either option brings into operation a number of other controls vested in the local authority and commonly called 'the linked powers' (see paragraphs 5.01–5.05). When a building notice is used the plans are not treated as having been deposited under Section 16 of the Building Act 1984 so no approval is issued.

2.08 The Building Regulations 1991 are not a self-sufficient code and other legislation (and non-statutory documents) must be referred to.

Nature of approval

2.09 Before considering the procedural requirements in detail, three important matters must be emphasized: discretion of local authorities, building without approval, and dispensation and relaxation of requirements.

Discretion of local authority

2.10 Local authorities have no discretion when considering plans deposited under the Regulations. The wording of Section 16 of the Building Act 1984 is mandatory. It states that the authority must pass the plans of any proposed work deposited with it under the Regulations unless they are defective or show that the proposed work would contravene any of the regulations or unless some other provision of the Act expressly requires or authorizes them to reject the plans.

Where the plans are defective or show contravention of the Regulations, the local authority does have a discretion since in that case they may either reject the plans or pass them subject to conditions as to modification of the deposited plans and/or that further plans be deposited.

Building control authorities do have a discretion in deciding whether to inspect building work in progress. Section 91(2) of the 1984 Act provides that 'it is the function of local authorities to enforce building regulations in their areas' and it is a matter for their discretion as to whether they inspect or not. They must, of course, give proper consideration to the question of whether they should inspect or not.

'It is for the local authority, a public and elected body, to decide upon the scale of resources which it can make available to carry out its functions ... – how many inspectors, with what expert qualifications, it should recruit, how often inspections are to be made, what tests are to be carried out – must be for its decision' (per Lord Wilberforce in *Anns* v *London Borough of Merton* [1978] AC 728).

Building without approval

2.11 If a building owner fails to serve a building notice or deposit plans or use the option of the approved inspector, he is guilty of an offence, just as he is when work is done contrary to the Regulations: Building Act 1984, Section 35. In *Sunley Homes Ltd* v *Borg* [1969] All ER 332, one of the main points at issue was whether an offence against the Regulations could be complete even though work on the buildings concerned had not been finished, as the buildings were in the course of construction at the time the prosecution was brought.

The builders argued that no offence was committed under Section 4 of the Public Health Act 1961 until the building in question was completed or, alternatively, until the time when the builder could no longer say that he would have remedied the offending work before completion. Lord Parker (then Lord Chief Justice) summarized the problem in this way:

'No one has been able to satisfy me at what stage it might properly be said that a building is complete. If all the workmen have left but the Building Regulations have not been complied with, I should have thought one could say that the building is not complete. However it seems to me that this argument becomes untenable when one looks: (a) at the Regulations; and (b) at the powers given to local authorities to deal with contraventions. ... [The] general tenor of the Regulations is clearly against [the developer's] contentions. They deal throughout with the erection of a building, and while erection might mean the completed building, it might also mean the operation of erecting the building. ... [It] seems to me clear that the erection of a building refers to the operation of erecting and not the completed erection.'

The position appears to be the same under current regulations.

2.12 A related matter is whether breach of any duty imposed by the Building Regulations can give rise to liability in damages.

Although Section 38 of the Building Act 1984 provides that, except where regulations otherwise provide, 'breach of a duty imposed by building regulations, so far as it causes damage, is actionable' it has not yet been brought into force. The section goes on to provide that it does not affect the extent (if any) to which a breach of duty imposed by or arising under Part I of the Act or other relevant legislation or of duties imposed by the regulations generally is actionable at civil law, nor does it 'prejudice a right of action that exists apart from the enactments relating to the building regulations'.

Until Section 38 is activated, the position appears to be that breach of building regulations does not of itself give rise to liability in damages for breach of statutory duty. There are conflicting judicial dicta on the point, but the relevant authorities were fully considered in *Perry* v *Tendring District Council* (1985) 3 Con LR 74 where Judge John Newey QC, a judge of great experience in this field, held that breach of the former building by-laws did not give rise to liability in damages. The liability imposed on the local authority was not an absolute one. His Honour's reasoning was applied by the late Judge David Smout QC in *Kimbell* v *Hart District Council* (1987) 9 ConLR 118 who held that a breach of statutory duty, as set out in Section 64 of the Public Health Act 1936, such as a failure to reject plans, did not of itself give rise to a claim in damages. The statutory duty was not an absolute one, and the plaintiff could only succeed on proof of negligence.

Perry v *Tendring District Council* was also followed in *Kijowski* v *New Capital Properties Ltd* (1988) 15 Con LR 1, where Judge Esyr Lewis QC expressly held that breach of the Building Regulations 1965 did not of itself give rise to liability in damages. It is submitted that this is also the position under the Building Regulations 1991 and that unless and until Section 38 of the 1984 Act is brought into effect, breach of the Regulations without proof of negligence does not of itself give rise to a claim for damages.

2.13 Under the enforcement provisions, the local authority may require the removal or alteration of offending work and/or they may initiate criminal proceedings: Building Act 1984, Sections 35 and 36. Notice to remove, alter, or pull down contravening work may not be given after the expiry of 12 months from the date of completion of the work in question, nor where the local authority have passed the plans and the work has been carried out in accordance with them. The wording of the provision is important; time begins to run against the local authority from the moment when the particular contravention is complete, and not from the date when the building as a whole is completed. However, in a case where the 12 months' time limit had expired, the local authority could apply to the High Court for an injunction, but only with the consent and in the name of the Attorney-General.

Experts' reports

2.14 The person on whom a Section 36 notice is served has a right of appeal to the magistrates' court and an important procedure is provided by Section 37 of the 1984 Act. Under Section 37, the recipient of a Section 36 notice may notify the local authority of his intention to obtain from a 'suitably qualified person' a written report about the matter to which the Section 36 notice relates. The expert's report is then submitted to the local authority and in light of that report the authority may withdraw the notice and pay the expenses reasonably incurred in obtaining the report which will relate to technical matters. If the local authority rejects the report, it can then be used as evidence in any appeal under Section 40 of the Act, and if the appeal is successful the appellant would normally recover the costs of obtaining the report as well as his other costs: 1984 Act, Section 40(6).

Dispensations and relaxations

2.15 An important dispensing power is conferred on the Secretary of State by Section 8 of the Building Act 1984. This enables him to dispense with or relax any regulation requirement 'if he considers that the operation of [that] requirement would be unreasonable in relation to the particular case'. This power has been delegated

to local authorities who may grant a relaxation if, because of special circumstances, the terms of a requirement cannot be fully met: see Regulation 9.

All the requirements of the regulations are now functional i.e. they require that something is provided at an 'adequate', 'satisfactory', or 'reasonable' level. The only course open is one of dispensation. This entails a request to dispense with the whole requirement and this would not normally be acceptable.

Sections 9 and 10 of the 1984 Act lay down the procedure for application; there is no prescribed form. There is a right of appeal to the Secretary of State against a local authority's refusal to dispense or relax with Regulation requirements: 1984 Act, Section 39. If the local authority fails to give a decision on an application for relaxation within two months, it is deemed to be refused and the applicant may appeal forthwith.

Application procedure

2.16 Unless the developer wishes to employ an approved inspector (see Section 3 of this chapter) the general rule is that anyone wishing to erect, extend or materially alter buildings, controlled services or fittings, or to make material changes in the use of buildings, must apply to the local authority for approval under the Building Regulations 1991. All building work must also be carried out so that it complies with the requirements of Schedule 1 of the Regulations. A material alteration is one which would result in the existing building not meeting the requirements regarding structure, fire safety and access facilities for disabled persons, either:

(i) where it had previously, or
(ii) making it more unsatisfactory than it was before in respect of those particular requirements.

The procedure on application is governed by Part IV of the Regulations and there are two main procedures. Prescribed fees are payable.

Building notice procedure

2.17 The first procedure is based on the service of a building notice and is governed by Regulations 11 and 12. This procedure can be used unless the use of the building is designated under the Fire Precautions Act 1971, i.e. hotels and boarding houses factories, offices, shops and railway premises.

There is no prescribed form of building notice, but it must be signed by or on behalf of the person intending to carry out the work. It must contain or be accompanied by the information set out in Checklist 14.4.

Checklist 14.4: Information to be contained in building notice

---

– Name and address of person intending to carry out work.
– Statement that notice is given in accordance with Regulation 11(1) (a).
– Description of the building's location and its use or intended use.
– If it relates to the erection or extension of a building it must be supported by a plan to a scale of not less than 1:1250, showing size and position in relation to streets and adjoining buildings on the same site, number of storeys, drainage details.
– If local legislation applicable, how it will be complied with.
– If cavity wall insulation is involved, information must be given about the proposed insulating material, Agrément Certificate (if appropriate) or conforms to BS and whether or not the installer has a BSI Certificate of Registration or has been approved by the Agrément Board.
– If work includes provision of a hot water storage system with a storage capacity of 16 litres or more (Schedule 1, (G3)) details of the system and its installer are required.

The local authority is not required to approve or reject the notice and have no power to do so. They may ask for any plans necessary to enable them to discharge their building control functions and may specify a time limit for their provision. They may also require information in connection with their linked powers under Sections 18 to 21 of the 1984 Act (see paragraph 7). If the work involves building over a sewer they can lay down conditions. Work can be commenced once a building notice has been given, although there is a further requirement (Regulation 14(1) (a)) that the local authority be notified at least two days before work commences.

Deposit of plans

2.18 Where the building notice procedure is inapplicable, or the developer wishes to adopt this course, full plans may be deposited in accordance with Section 16 of the Building Act 1984 and Regulation 13. The advantage of the full deposit of plans method of control is that if the work is carried out exactly in conformity with the plans as approved by the local authority, they cannot take any action under Section 36 of the Building Act 1984, and the work involved is supervised by the local authority's building control officer.

Under this system, the local authority must give notice of approval or rejection of the plans within five weeks from the date of the deposit of plans. This period does not, however, begin to run unless the applicant pays the prescribed fees at the same time as the plans are deposited. The five week period may be extended by written agreement. The extended period cannot be later than two months from the deposit of plans, and any extension must be agreed before the expiry of the five week period.

Subject to giving the local authority two clear days notice of com-mencement of work (Regulation 14(1) (a)), work may start as soon as plans have been deposited.

If the local authority gives formal notice to that effect, the approval lapses if work is not commenced within three years from the date of deposit of plans: 1984 Act, Section 32.

Applications for determination

2.19 If there is a dispute between a local authority and the person proposing to carry out the work as to whether the plans comply with the requirements of the regulations, that person may apply to the Secretary of State for a determination. A fee of half the plans fee up to a maximum of £500 is payable for this service.

Completion certificates

2.20 Local authorities will issue completion certificates where one is requested at the time of application or where the building is to be used for a designated use under the Fire Precautions Act 1971.

Unauthorized building work

2.21 Where building work has been carried out without approval and notice was not given, the owner may apply for a regularisation certificate. A certificate will be issued if the work complies.

Energy rating

2.22 Notice of the energy rating of a new dwelling must be given to the local authority.

3 Private certification

Approved inspectors

3.01 Part II of the Building Act 1984 deals with 'supervision of building work etc. otherwise than by local authorities', i.e. an alternative system of building control based on private certification. In broad terms, Sections 47 to 58 of the 1984 Act provide that responsibility for ensuring compliance with the Building Regulations may, at the option of the person intending to carry out the work, be given to an approved inspector instead of to the local authority. It also enables approved public bodies to approve their own work. The detailed rules and procedures relating to certification are to be found in the Building (Approved Inspector, etc.) Regulations 1985, which also contain prescribed forms which must be used.

3.02 Section 49 of the 1984 Act defines an 'approved inspector' as being a person approved by the Secretary of State or a body

designated by him for that prupose. Part II of the 1985 Regulations contains the procedures for the grant and withdrawal of approval. Approved inspectors may be corporate bodies, who must be approved by the Secretary of State, or individuals (not firms) approved by a designated body. The designated bodies are eight professional institutions, including the RIBA.

3.03 At the time of writing, the only approved inspector is National House Building Council, Building Control Services Ltd, which is an approved inspector for dwellings. There are difficulties in obtaining adequate insurance cover, and full private certification is a long-term aim.

3.04 Details of the NHBC scheme are to be found in the NHBC booklet *At Your Service* (obtainable from NHBC, 58 Portland Place, London W1N 4BU). This building control service is available to registered house builders, and the fees charged by NHBC compare favourably with those charged by local authorities.

4 Exemptions from control

4.01 Although there is a definition of 'building' in Section 121 of the Building Act 1984 the 1991 Building Regulations contain a much narrower interpretation. One of the main purposes of the regulations was to eliminate controls over the erection of certain small buildings and extensions and these are described in Regulation 9 and Schedule 2.

4.02 Section 4(1) of the Building Act 1984 itself exempts specified buildings from the scope of the regulations. These are:

1. Buildings required for the purposes of any educational establishment erected according to plans which have been approved by the Secretary of State for Education and Science.
2. Buildings of statutory undertakers held and used by them for the purpose of their undertaking, subject to minor exceptions.

4.03 Also exempted from control by Regulation 11(3), is building work which consists only of the installation of a heat-producing gas appliance which is to be installed by, persons approved under the Gas Safety (Installation and Use) Regulations 1984. This exemption covers various sorts of gas-fire heaters but does not apply if any other building work is involved. No building notice or deposit of plans is required.

5 Other controls under the Building Act

5.01 Local authorities exercise a number of statutory public health functions in conjunction with the process of building control. These provisions are commonly called 'the linked powers' because their operation is linked with the authority's building functions, both in checking deposited plans or considering a building notice, and under the private certification scheme. The most important of these linked powers are described below.

Building over sewers and drains

5.02 Section 99 of the Water Industry Act 1991 states that sewerage undertakers must keep a map showing the location of all public sewers and supply a copy to local authorities for public inspection. The map distinguishes among public sewers, those with respect to which a vesting declaration has been made but which has not yet taken effect, and those subject to an agreement as to future declaration. Where separate sewers are reserved for foul and surface water, this must be clearly shown. These four groups of sewers and drains are shown on the map.

5.03 Section 18 of the Building Act 1984 prohibits building over any sewer or drain shown on the map except with the local authority's consent. It provides, where the plans show that the building will be constructed over any sewer or drain, that the authority shall reject the plans unless they are satisfied that in the circumstances of the particular case they may properly consent to its erection. (Local authorities often act as agents for the sewerage undertaker who can give directions to the local authority on how to deal with such matters.)

5.04 The rejection of drawings showing an intended contravention of the Building Regulations, as described in para 2.10, is obligatory because of the wording of Section 16. Section 18 is a provision which expressly authorizes rejection. Any dispute between the applicant and the local authority as to whether the proposed building will be over a sewer and as to the granting of consent can be determined by the magistrates' court.

5.05 What is the position if a local authority simply passes the drawing and says nothing about the sewer or drain over which the building is erected? The point is undecided, but Lumley's *Public Health* suggests that in such circumstances the local authority must 'be taken to have been "satisfied" and to have consented unconditionally and cannot afterwards be heard to say that they had overlooked what was shown on the map'. The editors cite *Attorney General* v *Denby* [1925] Ch 596, in support of this statement, and a reading of the case certainly gives strength to the contention.

New buildings and drains

5.06 Under Section 21 of the 1984 Act new buildings must be provided with drains. This section states that unless the drawings show satisfactory provision for the drainage of the building, or the local authority is satisfied that it may dispense with any provisions for drainage in the particular case, the plans shall be rejected. 'Drainage' in this connection includes roof drainage. The local authority *must* reject plans deposited if no satisfactory provision for drainage is shown on them. Where the local authority is not satisfied with the provision for drainage shown on the drawings, its decision can be challenged by reference to the magistrates' court. In *Chesterton RDC* v *Ralph Thompson, Ltd* [1947] KB 300, the High Court held that the local authority is not entitled to reject plans on the ground that the sewerage system, into which the drains lead, is unsatisfactory. What the local authority must consider is the drainage of the particular building only.

5.07 This statutory provision is badly phrased, particularly in the wording of subsection (3), which does not make it clear whether the authority can pass the drawings subject to conditions instead of rejecting them. The best view is that it may impose any conditions or requirements that can be shown on a drawing, but not other conditions.

5.08 As a result of this provision, the local authority can insist on a separate drain being provided for each building, although in practice, plans showing combined drainage are invariably approved. Moreover, under the next section (Section 22) it may require buildings to be drained in combination into an existing sewer 'where the drains of the building are first laid'. It cannot insist on drainage in combination where it has previously passed the plans, except with the agreement of the owners concerned.

Water supply

5.09 The effect of Section 25 of the 1984 Act is that drawings of a house deposited with the local authority are to be rejected, unless 'there is put before (the local authority) a proposal which appears to it to be satisfactory for providing the occupants with a supply of wholesome water sufficient for their domestic purposes', and if possible the water is to be from a piped supply.

Continuing requirements

5.10 Section 2 of the 1984 Act provides for building regulations to be made imposing continuing requirements on owners and occupiers of buildings. No regulations have yet been made.

Section 24 of the 1984 Act required the local authority to reject plans if the entrances and exits were unsatisfactory. The section

applied to buildings where large numbers of the public were to be admitted. However, it does not apply to buildings where there are building regulations for means of escape. Since 1992 means of escape for all buildings is included in building regulations. Section 71 of the 1984 Act applies to the same buildings but was not linked to the deposit of plans. Section 24 therefore is no longer of effect and Section 71 is limited to existing buildings, means of escape from which is normally controlled under other legislation.

Other matter subject to control

5.11 The preceding cases are examples of the controls which come into play as the result of a deposit of plans or the giving of a building notice under the Building Regulations or the service of an intial notice when using the approved inspector. There are others, e.g. the height of chimneys controlled under Section 16 of the Clean Air Act 1993 (dealt with in paragraph 6.11), but the ones discussed serve to emphasize the importance of the Building Regulations procedure and the local authority's powers.

6 Other national legislation

6.01 More than 200 general statutes contain further provisions affecting the construction of buildings, although this is not apparent from the titles of the Acts concerned. There are also numerous statutory instruments made under powers conferred by many of these Acts. In this section some statutory rules which affect the bulk of building developments will be considered. This list does not claim to be exhaustive, nor does it cover all the relevant sections. (Some provisions of statutes not discussed here are covered in Chapter 16.)

6.02 Certain requirements are dealt with automatically on the deposit of drawings under the Building Regulations or, in some cases, at the same time as the application for planning permission. The following are some of the more important provisions which are relevant at that stage.

The Fire Precautions Act 1971

6.03 The object of this Act is to meet the criticisms that the law relating to fire precautions in certain kinds of residential accommodation and places of public entertainment was inadequate.

6.04 At the time of writing, the Act applies to the following categories of premises:

1. Hotels and boarding houses where sleeping accommodation is provided for six or more guests or staff or any number of guests or staff above the first floor or below the ground floor.
2. Factories, offices, shops and railway premises where more than 20 people are employed, or more than 10 people are employed elsewhere than on the ground floor, or (in factories only) explosive or highly inflammable materials are stored or used in or under the premises.

These are the 'designated' uses under the Act. Single private dwellings are specifically excluded from control.

It should be noted that there is an obligation to provide *reasonable* means of escape in *all* offices, shops and railway premises. Regulations have been made under the 1971 Act which apply to factories, offices, shops and railway premises which do not require a fire certificate relating to the availability of exits and the provision and maintenance of fire appliances. Various sections were added to the Fire Precautions Act by the Fire Safety and Safety of Places of Sport Act 1987. These include the power of fire authorities to grant exemption from a requirement to have a fire certificate. These premises must however have means of escape and means for fighting fire.

6.05 Fire certificates issued by the local fire authority are the main form of control under the Act. The occupier of affected premises must obtain a certificate to the effect that the premises are provided with such means of escape in case of fire as may reasonably be required.

6.06 Under Section 3 the fire authority (in consultation with the local authority) has power to serve a notice which makes a fire certificate compulsory for certain kinds of dwellings, mainly blocks of flats, but this provision is not activated yet.

6.07 If premises fall within the Act, an application for a fire certificate must be made to the fire authority under Section 5. The authority must then inspect the premises and, if they are satisfied as to the means of escape in case of fire and other relevant fire precautions, they must issue the certificate, or inform the applicant of what must be done to bring the premises up to standard.

6.08 Section 13 provides that except in specially defined circumstances, the fire authority cannot require alterations to a building or an extension, if it has already been subject to Building Regulations approval relating to means of escape. The various authorities concerned are also under a duty to consult each other in appropriate circumstances.

The Clean Air Act 1993

6.09 Among other things, this Act controls the height of chimneys on industrial premises, types of installation, and the treatment of offensive fumes from appliances.

6.10 Sections 14 and 15 of the 1993 Act require the approval of the local authority for the height of a chimney serving a furnace, and approval may be granted subject to conditions as to the rate and/or quality of emissions from the chimney. There is a right of appeal to the Minister.

6.11 Similarly Section 16 of the Act provides that in other cases the local authority must reject plans of buildings other than residences, shops, or offices unless the height of the chimney as shown on the drawings will be sufficient to prevent fumes from being a nuisance or a health hazard. The factors to be considered are the purpose of the chimney, the position and description of nearby buildings, level of neighbouring ground, and other relevant matters. These provisions represent an important negative control. See further Chapter 16, paragraph 6.05.

Highways Act 1980

6.12 The Highways Act 1980 consolidated, with amendments, earlier legislation and contains many provisions affecting building work. For example, Sections 73 and 74 deal with improvement and building lines respectively. An improvement line is designed to prevent the erection of buildings on land that may later be required for road widening. Where an improvement line has been prescribed, no new building may be erected nor may a permanent excavation be made nearer to the centre line of the street than the improvement line, except with the highway authority's consent. This may be granted subject to conditions. There is a right of appeal to the Crown Court against the refusal of consent or its grant subject to conditions.

6.13 A building line is a frontage line beyond which a building may not project, irrespective of road widening. A building line may be prescribed by the highway authority under Section 74, and, where it is prescribed, no new building (other than the boundary wall) may be erected in front of the prescribed line except with the authority's consent. This may be granted subject to conditions, or for a limited time. In both cases, a new building includes an addition or extension to an existing building, and hence both provisions are always relevant at the design stage.

6.14 The Highways Act 1980 contains many other prohibitions and rules which affect the architect's work, including Part X (Sections 186 to 196) dealing with new streets. Where new street by-laws have been made, the proposed work must not contravene them, and plans showing any contravention will be rejected (Section 191). Where a new street order has been made under Section 188 and new street by-laws are in force, these will prescribe the centre line of the new street and lines defining its minimum width. Effectively, new buildings will have to be set back in order to leave sufficient land for a street of the necessary width to be formed at that point. Another relevant provision is Section 206, which enables the authority to make a street designation order.

6.15 Even minor works of alteration and extension will not necessarily escape the net of the 1980 Act. For instance, if a building owner wishes to have a garage erected, it will be necessary in many cases for a carriage crossing to be constructed, thus bringing into play the provisions of Section 184. The building owner who wishes to provide new means of access to his premises to be constructed at his expense may initiate proposals for a carriage crossing. In addition, the local authority may, in certain circumstances, construct a crossing on their own initiative, again at the building owner's expense.

6.16 Section 124 of the 1980 Act gives power for a highway authority to be authorized by order of the Secretary of State for the Environment to stop up private access to highways from any premises, if it considers that the access is likely to cause danger to, or interfere unnecessarily with, traffic on the highway. Such an order can be made only where no access to the premises from the highway is reasonably required, or where other reasonably convenient means of access is available or will be provided. There is an objections procedure, and compensation may be payable (1980 Act, Section 126(2)).

6.17 Attention is also drawn to Section 168 of the Act which provides that if, in the course of carrying out building work in or near a street, an accident occurs which gives rise to the risk of serious bodily injury to a person in the street, the owner of the land or building where the work is being carried out is guilty of an offence punishable by a maximum fine of £500.

6.18 Again, Section 177 places restrictions on construction (and subsequent alteration) of buildings over highways maintainable at the public expense, without the licence of the highway authority. Licences may be granted subject to conditions and are registrable as a local land charge (Chapter 5 paragraph 1.08).

6.19 Section 174 prescribes that precautions against accidents must be taken where a person is executing works in a street. These safety measures include, where appropriate, the shoring up of any building adjoining the street. Stringent safety precautions must be observed in relation to builders' skips which may not be deposited on the highway without the highway authority's consent. This may be granted subject to conditions. The provisions relating to skips are found in Sections 139 to 140.

The Workplace (Health, Safety and Welfare) Regulations 1992

6.20 The provisions previously contained in the Factories Act 1961 and the Offices, Shops and Railway Premises Act 1963 relative to health, safety and welfare of persons at work are now within the Workplace (Health, Safety and Welfare) Regulations 1992.

They came into force on 1 January 1993 for all new workplaces and also apply to any modifications, extensions and conversions. The application to existing workplaces is deferred until 1 January 1996. Employers have a general duty under the Health and Safety at Work, etc., Act 1984 to ensure, as far as is reasonably practicable, the health, safety and welfare of their employees at work. The regulations, which expand on these duties, include requirements for ventilation, lighting, sanitary conveniences, washing facilities, drinking water, etc. See Chapter 19 paragraph 2.07.

Special classes of building

6.21 The legislation dealt with so far is, in one sense, of general application. The architect dealing with the design and construction of specialized types of building may find that special controls apply.

All these specialized provisions are extremely complex, and space does not permit any detailed examination of them. As examples, we may refer to the special controls applicable to cinemas and to the keeping and use of radioactive substances.

7 Building control in Inner London

7.01 Inner London consists of the City of London and the 12 London Boroughs of Camden, Greenwich, Hackney, Hammersmith, Islington, Kensington and Chelsea, Lambeth, Lewisham, Southwark, Tower Hamlets, Wandsworth, and Westminister: London Government Act 1963, Section 43.

7.02 Until 1986, the design, construction and use of buildings in this area were regulated by the London Building Acts and By-laws, which formed a code of control different from that which operated elsewhere. The Building (Inner London) Regulations 1985 came into effect on 6 January 1986 and repealed the London Building By-laws, brought most of the national regulations into force in Inner London, and made some amendments to the London Building Acts. The remaining building regulations were applied to Inner London by the Building (Inner London) Regulations 1987, which came into effect on 1 June 1987.

7.03 None the less, Inner London is still subject to many additional controls under the remaining provisions of the London Building Acts 1930 to 1978, and so building control in the area is subject to many special features. The function of building control there is undertaken by 14 District Surveyors/Chief Building Regulation Officers whose former special statutory powers have been emasculated. They supervise the work of approving plans and construction to secure compliance with the regulations, but they also have power to serve Notices of Objection and Notices of Irregularity where the requirements of the London Building Acts are being contravened.

Powers of entry

7.04 The district surveyor and other authorized officers have wide powers of entry, inspection and examination to enable them to carry out their functions: e.g., Section 142 of the London Building Acts (Amendment) Act 1939.

Appeals tribunals

7.05 Provision exists in the London Building Acts for special Tribunals of Appeal (one for each of the building control authorities) which hear appeals referred to them under the London Building Acts: 1939 Act, Section 109. The Tribunals have power to award costs and wide powers to order the production of documents, plans, specifications, and so on. A further appeal lies, by way of case stated, to the High Court: 1939 Act, Section 116.

7.06 Where a notice is given or plans deposited in respect of a building affected by the provisions of the Acts, and it discloses a contravention of the provisions, the district surveyor must serve Notice of Objection on the builder or owner or other person causing or directing the work. In effect this provides a *locus poenitentiae* (an opportunity for repentence).

However, an appeal may be made to the magistrates' court within 14 days after service of the notice: 1939 Act, Section 39.

Notice of irregularity

7.07 The district surveyor also has power to serve a Notice of Irregularity under Section 88 of the 1939 Act. This can be served after the builder has completed the work. It was decided in *Coggin v Duff* (1907) 96 LT 670, that failure to give Notice of Objection is not a bar to proceedings under Notice of Irregularity. This notice will be served where work has been done and it is found that some

contravention exists or that the work is so far advanced that the district surveyor cannot ascertain whether anything has been done in contravention. Its effect is to require the builder within 48 hours to amend any contravention or to open up as much of the work as may be necessary for the district surveyor to ascertain whether or not a contravention exists. The opening-up and rectification is done at the builder's or owner's expense. The notice cannot be served on the builder when he has completed the building, but there is power to serve notice on the owner, occupier, or other person directing the work.

7.08 The sanction behind a Notice of Irregularity is a fine. However, the district surveyor may apply to the magistrates' court for an order requiring the builder to comply within a stated time. Failure to obey an order of the court renders the builder liable to a daily fine: 1939 Act, Section 148.

Specific provisions

7.09 Space does not permit a detailed examination of the provisions of the London Building Acts, but consideration will be given to a number of points of practical importance. For a full treatment of this complex legislation reference should be made to *Guide to Building Control in Inner London 1987*, by P. H. Pitt., which is both up-to-date and authoritative.

Large and high buildings

7.10 Section 20 of the London Building Acts (Amendments) Act 1939, as amended, is important, and gives the borough councils wide control over the following buildings, so far as relates to precautions against fire:

1. Buildings of excess height over 30 metres, or over 25 metres high if the area of the building exceeds 930 square metres.
2. Certain trade buildings of additional cubical extent, i.e. buildings over 7 100 cubic metres in extent used for trade (including warehouses and department stores) or manufacture.

Except where a trade building is properly subdivided into fire divisions of less than 7 100 cubic metres each, all buildings coming within the scope of Section 20 require special consent from the borough council, which will send a copy of the plans, etc., to the London Fire and Civil Defence Authority for comment. When these are received, a consent will be issued, but this is usually conditional upon compliance with a schedule of requirements, e.g. higher standards of fire resistance, automatic sprinklers, hose reels, dry risers, firemen's lifts, emergency lighting on stairs and escape routes.

Full details are required and approval must be obtained of all electrical installations, heating and ventilation systems, sprinkler installations, etc. Additional precautions can be required in 'special fire risk areas' (defined in Section 20(2D)), e.g. where any storey of a garage is located in a basement or is not adequately ventilated.

Readers are advised to obtain the 'Code of Practice for Buildings of Excess Height or Cubical Extent' (Ref 7168 0316X) published by the former GLC, which is essential for those dealing with the design of Section 20 buildings.

Means of escape in case of fire

7.11 Part V of the London Building Acts (Amendment) Act 1939 deals with means of escape in case of fire. An application, accompanied by drawings, must be submitted to the council for approval as to the proposed means of escape for every 'new building' (broadly, those built after 1939) to which Section 34 applies. The notice and drawings must be deposited before or at the same time as any notice is given or plans are deposited in respect of the building. The buildings concerned are:

1. Public buildings.
2. Places of worship or assembly.

3. Every other new building which:
   (a) if single storey, exceeds 600 square feet in area.
   (b) If more than one storey, exceeds 1 000 square feet (excluding basements used only for storage).

The section does not, however, apply to licensed places of entertainment (which have their means of escape dealt with under the licensing procedure) or to a private house in single family occupation which does not have a floor at a height of more than 20 feet or to houses or flats of three or more storeys.

The local authority have two months from the deposit of the plans (or such longer period as may be agreed in writing) in which to approve the proposed means of escape or to refuse it. Approval may be given subject to conditions.

The approved means of escape arrangements from buildings to which Part V of the 1939 Act applies are required by Section 133 to be maintained and fines for contravention are prescribed in Section 148.

Dwelling houses on low-lying land

Part XII of the London Building Act 1930 prohibits the erection or rebuilding of dwelling houses on low-lying land without the consent of the appropriate Inner London borough council.

Party structures

7.12 Part VI of the 1939 Act contains a special statutory code governing party structures and rights of adjoining owners. It does not abrogate common law rules but they are excluded to the extent of these statutory provisions which do not affect the legal title to the structure or any easements or rights in connection with them (Section 54). Negotiations about right of light are separate from awards under Part VI.

Party wall

7.13 Section 44 gives a special definition of 'party wall':

1. A wall which forms part of a building and stands on lands of different owners. Projection of any artificially formed support on which the wall rests on to land of any adjoining owner does not make the wall a party wall.
2. Any part of any other wall as separates buildings belonging to different owners.

Party structure

7.14 Party structure is a party wall, floor, partition, or other structure separating buildings or parts of buildings approached only by separate staircases or entrances from outside the building (Section 4). Tenancy separations in blocks of flats and maisonettes are therefore normally excluded.

Party fence wall

7.15 The legislation also refers to a 'party fence wall'. This is a wall that is not part of a building, but which stands on the lands of different owners and is used or constructed for separating such lands. It does not include a wall constructed on one owner's land, of which only artificially formed supports project on to the adjoining land. Thus rights of adjoining owners do not arise where only the foundations project on to the adjoining land if the wall concerned is a boundary wall, not being part of a building, but they do arise if such a wall separates buildings belonging to different owners.

Procedure

7.16 A special procedure has to be followed if the building owner wishes to invoke his rights under the Act. These are more extensive than the limited rights he has at common law, and as regards existing structures, may be summarized:

1. Where a structure is defective, he may repair, make good, thicken or underpin it, or demolish and rebuild it.
2. If he wishes to build against it and it is of insufficient height or strength, he may rebuild it subject to making good all damage to adjoining property, and raising the height as necessary of chimney and flues.
3. He may carry out all necessary incidental works to connect with the adjoining premises.

A full list of the authorized works is given in Section 46.

Section 50 deals with the underpinning of independent buildings and confers valuable rights on both adjoining owners.

7.17 The first step in the process is for the building owner to serve a *party structure notice* upon adjoining owners, except where their prior written consent had been given or the work is necessary as a result of a dangerous structure notice. The notice contains particulars of the proposed works and is normally accompanied by a party-wall drawing, although a drawing need only be served where it is proposed to use 'special foundations', i.e. foundations in which steel beams or rods are used to spread the load. The notice must be served at least two months before the work is to be commenced in the case of a party structure or one month in the case of special foundations or a party fence wall (Section 47 (2)). The adjoining owner has the right to serve counter-notice requiring carrying out of additional works for his protection. Most party wall surveyors hold that the full 'particulars' of the proposed work (as required by Section 47) must include *plans*. These are also required by Section 48 (2)(c) – counter-notice. The RICS publish a set of Party Structure Notice forms.

7.18 The adjoining owner may, in fact, consent to the proposed works under Section 49. If an owner does not so express his consent in writing to a counter-notice or a notice within 14 days of service, a 'difference' is deemed to have arisen between the parties (Section 49). The special procedure for settlement of differences is in effect an arbitration (Chapter 11) and is contained in Section 55. This enables the parties to agree to the appointment of an agreed surveyor who will make an award upon the difference. This is not usual. In practice, each party appoints his own surveyor, and normally the difference is settled by negotiation between them and they make a joint award. There is provision for the two nominated surveyors to call in a third surveyor who acts as intermediary, but this is very rare.

7.19 When the party wall award has been agreed, it is engrossed (expressed in legal form) and executed in duplicate, each copy being signed and witnessed by the two surveyors. The award will deal with the supervision of the works and the costs. Normally, costs will be borne by the building owner, but this is not necessarily the case. The award can be challenged by an appeal to the County Court within 14 days of issue, or, in certain circumstances, by appeal to the High Court.

7.20 Expenses in respect of party structures are dealt with by Section 56. Where works are for the benefit of both owners (normally when a party structure is in disrepair) the costs are to be shared proportionately. The adjoining owner may also be liable to contribute towards the costs when he makes any use of the works as compared with the use when the works were begun. Such a right of contribution does not exist at common law. Section 56 is not clear as to what can be included in the 'expenses incurred', for which the building and adjoining owners may be severally or jointly liable, and these have been held to include district surveyors', surveyors', and architects' fees in connection with design (see *Fifoot v Applerley* (1985) reported only in *Building News*, 18 September (1985). The costs of the party wall itself are not included, as these will be dealt with specifically in the award itself.

7.21 Any works which are carried out by a building owner under the provisions of the Act are subject to four general conditions under Section 51:

1. The work is not to be carried out in such a way or at such a time as to cause unnecessary inconvenience to the adjoining

owner or occupier. It is submitted that building work carried out at normal times and in a normal manner and taking reasonable precautions to reduce noise and dust to a minimum cannot be said to cause 'unnecessary inconvenience', just as it would not constitute a nuisance at common law (*Andreae* v *Selfridge & Co* [1938] 1 Ch 9).
2. Where any part of the adjoining land or building is laid open, the building owner must erect and maintain at his own expense proper protective hoardings and so on for protection and security of the adjoining occupier.
3. The works must comply with the London Building Acts and By-laws.
4. The works must be in accordance with any plans, sections, and particulars agreed between the owners or approved by their surveyors in the party-wall award.

7.22 It must be be remembered that special foundations cannot be placed under adjoining land without the adjoining owner's written consent.

7.23 Section 53 confers on the building owner, his servants, agents, and workmen a power of entry upon premises, and if the building is closed, he may break open doors to enter, provided he is accompanied by a police officer. Fourteen days must be given, except in emergency.

7.24 In *Gyle-Thompson* v *Wall Street Properties Ltd* [1974] 1 All ER 295, the High Court considered what Mr Justice Brightman described as 'important points of law' arising out of the operation of the 1939 Act. His lordship held that, in the absence of any express right to lower a party fence wall, Sections 46(a) and (k) of the Act (which give a building owner a right to demolish and rebuild) require reconstruction of the wall to its original height. The defendants also contended that under Section 55 the award was conclusive against the plaintiff and could be challenged only by an appeal to the county court. The judge rejected this submission, saying that it is not correct 'in relation to an award which is ultra vires and therefore not a valid award'. 'This case also emphasizes that the steps laid down by the Act as to procedure 'should be scrupulously followed throughout, and short cuts are not desirable'.

8 Local legislation outside London

8.01 Although the Building Act 1984 and Regulations made under it were intended to provide a national code of building control, there are many provisions in local Acts which impose additional controls on the construction of buildings. They supplement the national code, and many of them were enacted quite recently: see Checklist 14.2.

8.02 These local Acts have a special significance in the context of private certification. Regulation 10 of the Building (Approved Inspectors, etc.) Regulations 1985 provides that an approved inspector must ensure that the building regulations are complied with and, inter alia, where a local Act so requires, must consult with the Fire Authority. A local authority can reject an approved inspector's initial notice where the work proposed would 'contravene any local enactment which authorises them to reject plans submitted in accordance with building regulations': 1984 Act, Schedule 3, paragraph 11. However, under private certification the local authority remains responsible for ensuring that the work complies with the requirements of any local Act.

8.03 The provisions of Section 90 of the 1984 Act should be noted. This provides that (outside Inner London) where there is any local Act in force imposing obligations or restrictions as to the construction, nature or situation of buildings, they 'shall keep a copy of those provisions at their offices for inspection by the public at all reasonable times free of charge'.
   The following is not an exhaustive list, but indicates some common local provisions, the content of many local Acts being

similar. Reference should be made to *Guide to Building Control by Local Acts 1987* by P. H. Pitt which is a comprehensive coverage of this local legislation.

Fire precautions for underground parking places

8.04 This is a common provision in many local Acts and applies only to basement garages for more than three vehicles or garages for more than 20 vehicles not belonging to one dwelling. The local authority or approved inspector must consult with the Fire Authority and can impose conditions on the approval of plans, e.g. means of access for the fire brigade, fire-fighting equipment, etc.

Access for the fire brigade

8.05 This is another common requirement. Plans deposited with the local authority must show adequate access for the fire brigade. In some cases, fire tenders must be provided and special fire-fighting stairs and firemen's lifts may be required. The local authority can reject the plans where, after consulting with the Fire Authority, it is satisfied that access is inadequate. An approved inspector must also consult with the Fire Authority.

Multi-storey car parks

8.06 Stringent requirements must be met where there are three or more cars below ground level or more than 20 above. Requirements can include means of escape, cross-ventilation, fire fighting equipment and so on.

External stacks of flammable materials

8.07 A not uncommon provision where flammable material is to be stored. Special fire precautions and fire-fighting requirements can be insisted upon.

Separate drainage system

8.08 In some areas, e.g. Lancashire, Leicestershire, South Yorkshire, Staffordshire, West Glamorgan and West Yorkshire, local legislation requires that each building must have a separate system of drainage for soil and surface water.

High buildings

8.09 Buildings over six storeys may be required to have fire alarms, fire-fighting equipment, sprinklers, etc., with approved internal and external access for the fire brigade. Consultation with the Fire Authority is required.

Large storage buildings

8.10 Where this provision applies, storage buildings exceeding 7 000 m³ may be required by the local authority to have fire alarms, access for the fire brigade, etc. The Fire Authority must be consulted.

Means of escape in case of fire

8.11 Where this provision is in force, it is additional to the requirements of Schedule 1, B i of the Building Regulations 1991, and Section 72 of the 1984 Act (means of escape) is not applicable. After consultation with the Fire Authority, the council may require means of escape.

Other provisions

8.12 This is not an exhaustive catalogue of local legislation. Many other provisions are encountered in different local authority areas. The authorities concerned are of the opinion that they form an essential part of the machinery of control. Indeed, many of these local provisions could well be made applicable to all urban conurbations.

15

Construction Regulations in Scotland

PETER FRANKLIN

1 Introduction

1.01 Building control in Scotland is based on Building Acts. To understand Scottish practice, a knowledge of the Acts is required, as well as of the Regulations made under them. The Building Standards (Scotland) Regulations 1990 are only one part of the whole scene, although admittedly a very important part. Anyone trying to compare Scottish and English building control must bear the above in mind, so that there is a comparison of like with like wherever possible.

1.02 This study is intended to describe the main provisions of the Act and procedures laid down under it, as well as the various Statutory Instruments associated with it. In regard to the Building Standards Regulations themselves, it is obviously impossible to go into minute detail regarding interpretations, etc. The object of each part of the Regulations has, therefore, been stated and reference made to the more important provisions and, where thought applicable, to individual regulations.

Historical background

1.03 Building control is not new, and records of building law go back to the pre-Christian era. The first known are those found in the Mosaic Law of King Hammurabi of Persia c.2000 BC. Fire precautions which have always formed a major part of building codes were an accepted factor of Roman law and of English law from the twelfth century.

Dean of Guild Courts

1.04 In Scotland building control in royal burghs was exercised by Dean of Guild Courts where these existed. Originally, the Dean of Guild was the president of the merchants' guild, which was composed of traders who had acquired the freedom of a royal burgh. The post is an ancient one, e.g. in 1403 one Simon de Schele was appointed Dean of Guild and Keeper of the Kirk Work by Edinburgh Town Council. The Dean of Guild Court's original mercantile jurisdiction fell gradually into disuse to be replaced by a jurisdiction over such areas as markets, streets, and buildings. 'Questions of neighbourhood' were dealt with by Edinburgh Dean of Guild as early as 1584. Gradually the scope and nature of the powers of the Dean of Guild Courts became more precise until during the last 150 years they were subjected to a process of statutory modification.

1.05 Not all burghs had Dean of Guild Courts, and it was not until 1947 that the Local Government (Scotland) Act required burghs without Dean of Guild Courts to appoint one. In other burghs, the functions of the Dean of Guild Courts were either carried out by magistrates or the town council itself. In counties, plans were usually approved by a sub-committee of the public health committee. There was no warrant procedure as in burghs.

By-laws

1.06 During the last 150 years, statutory requirements laid the foundation of specific and more widely applicable standards. The Burgh Police Act 1833 empowered burghs to adopt powers of paving, lighting, cleansing, watching, and supplying water. However, the building legislation content of the nineteenth-century Acts was not large and was related mainly to ruinous property and drainage, attention to the latter being attracted by the large-scale outbreaks of cholera at that time. In 1892 the Burgh Police Act introduced a detailed set of building rules which were repealed by the 1903 Burgh Police Act. This Act gave powers to burghs to make by-laws in respect of building and public health matters. Meanwhile in the counties, the Public Health (Scotland) Act 1897 had already given them the power to make similar by-laws.

1.07 By-laws made under these Acts, although limited in scope, remained the main form of building control until 1932 when the Department of Health for Scotland published model building by-laws for both burghs and countries. Local authorities could, if they wished, adopt these by-laws for application in their own area. However, many did not. The model by-laws were revised in 1934 and 1937, but, apart from a widening of scope, later editions did not differ much from the original 1932 version. A much more comprehensive review was carried out in 1954. Although many local authorities adopted the 1954 model by-laws, adoption was at the discretion of the local authority and many did not. (By 1957, 26 of the 33 counties, 127 of the 173 small burghs, 13 of the 20 large burghs, and none of the cities had adopted the model by-laws.) However, Edinburgh, Aberdeen, and Glasgow had local Acts which combined many of the requirements of old statutes and by-laws with local features.

1.08 The then existing legislation fell short of the requirements of a modern building code able to cope with the rapidly expanding building of post-war Scotland where new techniques and materials were rapidly being introduced. It was decided that the whole concept of building control should be reviewed, and to this end a committee under the chairmanship of C. W. G. Guest QC, later Lord Guest, was appointed by the Secretary of State.

1.09 The committee's terms of reference required that it examine the existing law pertaining to building and jurisdiction of the Dean of Guild Courts and make recommendations on the future form of a building control system for counties and burghs, which was to be flexible enough to take account of new techniques and materials.

1.10 The committee published its report in October 1957. Its main recommendation was that legislation was essential to enable a comprehensive building code to be set up in the form of national regulations to achieve uniformity throughout the country. The basic purpose of building control should be the protection of the public interest as regards health and safety. The law must ensure that occupants, neighbours, and passers-by are protected by preventing the erection of buildings that are liable to collapse or lead to unhealthy or insanitary conditions. It must also prevent individual and collective fire hazards.

1.11 The recommendations were accepted and led to the existing form of control now established in Scotland.

Review of the building control system

1.12 During the period from its introduction until the late 1970s the building control system was kept under constant review. Some of the principles in the original legislation were expanded, and amendments, additions and deletions were made, where necessary to the regulations. This is a continuous process necessary to keep abreast of developments in building practice, technology and materials.

1.13 It is a principle of good management, however, that every so often a detailed analysis and examination be carried out on any system and building control is no exception. It was with this view in mind, together with Government's determination to remove unnecessary restrictions on individual freedoms and minimize the involvement of central Government, that the Secretary of State decided in 1980 that the Scottish Development Department should undertake a comprehensive review of building control.

1.14 In July 1980, in order to gauge the climate of opinion, a wide field of Scottish Interests were invited to give views on the following:

1. the structure and operation of the present system in Scotland with relevance to any major deficiencies and areas of difficulty;
2. changes which might be introduced to make the system more efficient without undermining the protection of public health and safety.

1.15 These consultations revealed that there was wide agreement that the basic framework of building control works satisfactorily, but with scope for improvement. The first priority was seen as rationalizing over-complex building standards regulations. Other areas of concern involved inconsistent interpretation of regulations by enforcing authorities, differences of technical detail within the UK, the effect of liability for latent danger and the scope for private sector involvement. The Secretary of State announced in May 1981 that as a result of the comments received and the parallel review being undertaken in England and Wales proposals for change would be further developed.

Consultative Paper – The Future of Building Control in Scotland

1.16 In 1983, the Scottish Development Department issued for comment a Consultative Paper – The Future of Building Control in Scotland – and invited comment from interested bodies.

The paper was the outcome of the Secretary of State's statement of May 1981 (paragraph 1.15) and the object of the review was stated as:

1. upholding the prime purposes of building control as laid down in the Building Acts;
2. securing simplicity in operation;
3. promoting consistency in interpretation and enforcement;
4. minimizing central Government involvement;
5. providing for increased participation by the private sector within a system of control which continued to be based on enforcement by *local authorities*;
6. making the system self-financing.

1.17 The paper was divided into various headings under which proposals were described in general terms. These headings were as follows:

Simplification of the Building Standards Regulations
Liaison and Co-operation between Building Control
  Authorities
Certification and Type Approvals
Appeals
Liability for Latent Damage
Relaxation of Building Standards Regulations
Exempted Works
Fees for Building Warrants
Other Procedural Refinements.

The paper concluded that earlier consultations endorsed the views that the Scottish building control system was founded on sound principles, but was in need of alterations and improvements rather than demolition and replacement. Many of the proposals could be implemented under existing powers given in the Building Acts with priority being given to the preparation of a more compact and rational set of Building Standards Regulations.

1.18 As a result of the Consultative Paper, a large number of those consulted submitted many and varied comments to the Department. After these comments had been given serious consideration, a statement of intent was issued by the Secretary of State on 29 November 1985.

The statement sums up the results of the consultations and the actions to be followed as a result of the exercise.

Statement of Intent by Secretary of State, 29 November 1985

1.19 The statement by the Secretary of State put forward a series of proposals based on the headings in paragraph 1.15. These can be summarized as follows:

1. *Building Standards Regulations*   Particular attention would be focused upon matters of health, safety and conservation of energy while taking account of welfare and convenience. The revised Regulations would take the form of a functional statement coupled with a qualifying standard and backed up by supporting technical documents. The standards will be prescribed by Statutory Instrument. A revision of the technical content would be carried out at the same time.
2. *Certification*   Powers would be legislated for to give local authorities, within clearly defined limits, the right to accept at their discretion certificates from suitably qualified persons responsible for designing a building.
3. *Liaison/co-ordination between building control authorities*   After listening to various views put forward, the Government proposed to build on its previous liaison meetings with the Scottish Association of Chief Building Control Offices. It will set up a committee chaired and serviced by the Scottish Development Department which will meet at regular intervals to:
   (a) foster common interpretation and administration of the Building Regulations;
   (b) pool and disseminate information for use and reference;
   (c) provide a collective liaison channel between building control authorities and the Scottish Development Department;
   (d) furnish an advisory service for building control authorities on interpretive and other issues.
4. *Appeals*   The present system of appeals to the Sheriff would be retained.
5. *Relaxation of the regulations*   Delegation of the power to relax regulations for all buildings would be delegated in stages to local authorities. The Secretary of State would retain the responsibility for all Class Relaxations and in respect of buildings owned by the local authority in its own area.
6. *Exempted works*   There would be much wider exemption from the Regulations in respect of small buildings including additions to existing buildings. Limited requirements would be retained in certain cases in respect of drainage and structure.
7. *Other procedural matters*   Fees would be kept under constant review.

The removal of Crown exemption was proposed. (This is still under discussion, but an early decision is expected.)

It should be stressed, however, that the Forum is *not* an alternative to the courts and will not consider the content of the Regulations. The latter is the province of the Building Standards Advisory Committee (BSAC). The Forum will take a collective look at the *system* in operation.

Exempted works

1.22 Powers have been taken to extend the scope of exemption from the Regulations to parts of a building.

New powers

1.23 New powers have been taken in the Housing (Scotland) Act 1986 with regard to certification and class warrants. These powers when they are introduced into the system will considerably speed up the process of work starting on site once designs are completed.

The Department will seek an independent assessment from designated bodies as to the building or part of the building's compliance with regulations – thus involving the private sector in the decision-making process.

The class warrant will be binding on all local authority building control departments.

Relaxations

1.24 A further delegation of powers to relax the regulations in respect of building standards regulations was made under the Building Standards (Relaxation by Local Authorities) (Scotland) Regulations 1991 which came into force on 1 April 1991. These regulations complete a circle of delegations which now gives local authorities power to relax regulations in all cases except where the building consists of or contains an enclosed shopping centre or where an application for warrant is referred to the Secretary of State under Section 6A of the Building (Scotland) Act 1959.

There is a right of appeal to the Secretary of State if the applicant is aggrieved by the local authorities' determination of his application.

2 Building (Scotland) Acts 1959 and 1970

2.01 As a direct result of the deliberations of the Guest Committee, the Building (Scotland) Act 1959 was passed. The aim of the Act was to introduce a system which while utilizing some of the then current practice in a more modern form, produced new procedures and standards which were flexible enough to meet rapidly changing building processes. The Act itself was unique in UK legislation and gave Scotland the lead in the field of national building control.

2.02 Certain sections of the Act came into effect on the day the Act was passed, 30 April 1959, but the main provisions did not come into effect until 15 June 1964, a day appointed by the Secretary of State.

2.03 In common with much of our legislation, the Building Acts have in their short history been subject to amendment because of changes in other spheres of Government and in particular the effect of the Local Government (Scotland) Acts 1973 and 1994, the Health and Safety at Work etc. Act 1974 and the Housing (Scotland) Act 1986. While the basic philosophy of the original Building Act and that of 1970 has not changed, details in the enforcement of the requirements and indeed the scope of the Act have been altered. These have been incorporated in the text.

The Act is laid out in four parts, and a brief summary of the content of each is given below.

Local authorities

2.04 The requirement in the 1959 Act for local authorities to appoint building authorities was amended by the Local Government (Scotland) Act 1973, which vested building control in authorities

Progress arising from the Statement of Intent
Simplification of the building standards regulations

1.20 Draft regulations in the form envisaged in the Statement were drawn up and circulated for comment. In the light of these comments a second draft was issued to consultative bodies. As a result a new set of regulations has been drafted and came into force 1 April 1991.

Liaison on harmonizing technical content within the UK has formed an important part of the exercise and joint meetings with DoE and NI form a regular feature of the consultation.

Liaison with local authorities

1.21 A Building Control Forum as envisaged in the Statement of Intent has been set up and met for the first time on 12 September 1985. Its terms of reference were those set out in the Secretary of State's statement and to fulfil these terms the Forum will be required to:

1. identify inconsistencies of interpretation and administration of the regulations;
2. ensure authoritative consideration of ways to eliminate such difficulties;
3. ensure effective communication of the Forum's advice and recommendations to all parties involved with building control (these would include existing professional bodies, trade interests, developers, etc.) and allow then to raise problems, subject to suitable arrangements being worked out, with the Forum.

The Forum meets quarterly with SOEnD who are responsible for issue of any relevant information.

as follows: in the Highland, Borders, and Dumfries and Galloway regions, the regional councils and in other cases, the district councils or island authorities. The Act gave the authorities power to set up their own means of building control, and this has varied from large independent building control departments with directors in charge to combined departments under either planning, environmental health, architectural services, or technical services. It means that powers to deal directly with warrant applications vary with the amount of delegation given to officials. In some instances the chief building control officer deals with and signs warrants for all unopposed applications, in others all applications are put before the appropriate committee, and in others delegation to officials is based on whether or not the application is for work valued above or below a certain financial limit. While the principle of the Local Government Act was to give autonomy to authorities, the lack of central Government guidance or suggested model for a building control department has, therefore, led in turn to anomalies which were not so apparent under the specific legislation of the 1959 Act. From 1 April 1996, the existing local authorities are replaced by new unitary authorities under the Local Government etc. Scotland Act 1994. While procedures will remain basically the same, the new authorities may well differ in the placing and management of building control departments within the new administrative frameworks. (See paragraph 4.13.)

Building Standards

2.05 Part II of the Building (Scotland) Act 1959, as amended by section 75 and Schedule 7 of the Health and Safety at Work Act 1974, deals with building standards and building operations. Section 3 of the Act gives the Secretary of State power to prescribe Building Standards Regulations and details the necessary procedure to be carried out before making regulations (described below in paragraph 2.15). The basis of the Building Standards Regulations is stated as follows: 'they shall be such as in the opinion of the Secretary of State can reasonably be expected to be attained in buildings of the classes to which they relate, having regard to the need for securing the health, safety, welfare and convenience of the persons who inhabit or frequent such buildings and the safety of the public generally and for furthering the conservation of fuel and power'. The standards may make reference to any document published by the Secretary of State or other persons. This means in practice that the Secretary of State can 'deem to satisfy' any document he thinks fit. It is worth noting the fact that the power to make regulations contains two qualifying phrases, i.e. 'in the opinion of' and 'can reasonably', and may well explain the compromise situations which sometimes affect a final regulation as compared with original proposals and indeed technical advice. Certain buildings are exempted from regulations, e.g. Crown buildings and some Atomic Energy Authority Buildings (but see paragraph 1.19 above). The Secretary of State has also been given the power to repeal or modify any enactment in force before or passed in the same session as the Health and Safety at Work Act 1974 if he considers it inconsistent with or unnecessary or requires alteration in consequence of any provision of the Building Standards Regulations.

2.06 The Secretary of State may also make regulations for the conduct of building operations as he thinks necessary to secure the safety of the general public.

2.07 Only the Secretary of State is given power to relax Building Standards Regulations. However, Section 2 of the 1970 Act gives the Secretary of State power to make regulations delegating the power to give relaxation to the local authority.

Class warrants (formerly known as type approvals)

2.08 Under the Health and Safety at Work etc. Act 1974 powers were taken to issue type approvals. The system of type approvals required a designating order to bring it into place. The designating order was never made. When new powers were being taken under the Housing (Scotland) Act 1986 it was decided to redefine the type approval system at the same time. This was done and the term 'type approval' was changed to 'class warrant'.

The basis of a class warrant system is that the Secretary of State would have the power to issue such warrants in respect of buildings which are of a repetitious nature which comply with the relevant building standards. For example, a standard house plan which is built in various areas all over the country might be given a class warrant in respect of its design above damp proof course. The class warrant which is binding on all local authority building control authorities will alleviate the need for separate sets of plans to be prepared for each authority and avoid differences of interpretation. It will speed up the process of commencement of building once plans are completed.

The Scottish Development Department will seek an independent assessment from designated bodies as to the building's compliance with building standards before making a decision on an application for class warrant. This involves the private sector in the decision-making process.

It might also be useful to compare the term 'class warrant' with the term 'class relaxation' in order to avoid confusion. The former would apply where a building, component, etc., met the regulations. The latter would apply where building, etc., does not meet the regulations but is given a waiver of a regulation or regulations either conditionally or unconditionally.

Warrants for construction and demolition

2.09 A warrant for construction is issued subject to the conditions that the building is built in accordance with the description in the warrant, drawings, and specification. The building must also conform to the Building Standards Regulations and any direction from the Secretary of State relaxing any of the Regulations. The local authority cannot impose any other constructional conditions. The warrant is not subject to any requirements for planning permission. The attention of local authorities, regarding the issue of warrants and attempts to impose conditions, was drawn to the relevant statutory instruments by a Building Note* 6/77 issued by the Scottish Development Department.

Local authorities have the power, however, to grant warrant for work to be carried out in stages. This is a discretionary power. Warrant for the demolition of a building must state the length of time the works will take and must include a method statement showing how the applicant intends to demolish the building.

2.10 Section 6(8) as amended by the 1970 Act gives provisions where it would be competent for a buildings authority to refuse warrant. This important section is worthy of careful study, as incorrect interpretation could cause inconvenience and delay. Local authorities can refuse warrant if:

1. The application has not been made in the prescribed manner.
2. The authority considers that application for alterations or extensions to a building would result in either of the following:
   (a) where a building conforms to the Regulations at the time of application, but would fail to conform as a direct result of the proposed works or;
   (b) where a building fails to conform to the Regulations at the time of application and would fail to conform to an even greater degree as a direct result of the proposed works.

2.11 The phrase 'as a direct result' is the important point. The following examples may help to elucidate it:

1. An existing cottage, built pre-Regulation, has a roof which is nearer its boundary than would be permitted by current Regulations. Should an extension to the cottage be built, the roof of which meets the current Regulations, then the existing roof is still acceptable. In other words the new works are not making the existing roof part of the Regulations to any greater degree.

* Building Note 6/77 issued by Scottish Development Department, December 1977.

2. An extension to a factory resulted in the travel distance within the building as a whole being made worse; therefore the travel distance of the whole building, new and existing, was subject to the building standards for a new building.

Travel distance in relation to means of escape from fire is measured from a point on a storey to a protected doorway in accordance with rules laid down in the Regulations.

In regard to the term 'change of use', which plays an important part in determining this area of building control law, particular attention must be paid to the definition of 'change of use'. The meaning is different to that used in England and Wales and failure to appreciate that fact in its context could involve unnecessary extra work. Change of use applies to a component or element of structure as much as to the whole building.

2.12 Section 8 of the Act which allowed the local authority power to issue permission to occupy portions of roads for the deposit of materials was amended by the Road Traffic Act 1984 which transfers the power to the highway authority.

Certificates of completion

2.13 Section 9 relates to the issue of completion certificates by the buildings authority. Where electrical installations are concerned, another certificate is required from the installer certifying that the installations meet the necessary requirements of the Building Standards Regulations. No person may occupy a building erected under warrant unless a certificate of completion has been issued. However, temporary certificates may be issued at the discretion of the buildings authority. The Secretary of State has powers to extend the provision for certification to other than electrical installations, e.g. gas installations.

It should be noted that under an amendment introduced by the Health and Safety at Work Act 1974 and activated by Commencement Order No. 2 under that Act, the wording of Section 9 in respect of completion certificates was modified. The granting of the certificate is now qualified in respect of the building authority's inspection of the building by the words 'so far as they are able to ascertain after taking all reasonable steps in that behalf'.

This phrase recognizes that it is impossible for a building control officer to be continually on site inspecting the construction of a building at all times – indeed, that is not his job. Local authorities were worried that the previous phrasing of the certificate, with its blanket statement that 'the building met both regulations and plans completely', placed an unacceptable and unreasonable liability on their shoulders and represented for the rewording of the certificate in the new terms.

2.14 Powers are given in Section 9 to deal with buildings erected without warrant or in contravention of warrant, and procedures are described. Section 11 of the 1959 Act empowers the authority to enforce certain provisions of the Building Standards Regulations on existing buildings.

2.15 Self certification of design

Following upon the Secretary of State's statement of Intent of November 1984, powers were taken in the Housing (Scotland) Act 1986, Section 19 to introduce a new section to the Building (Scotland) Act 1959 in respect of self certification of design only. The local authority retains final control over the assessment of compliance of a building through its powers to grant or refuse a certificate of Completion Under Section 9 of the 1959 Act.

Benefits of self certification of design are:

1. The speeding up of the processing of applications for warrants by allowing local authorities to accept without further checking certificates of compliance for certain requirements of regulations.
2. The promoting of a degree of self-regulation by the private sector within the framework of local authority building control.
3. The reduction of the workload of local authority building control departments.

4. Recognizing existing good practice by the acceptance of design certificates from, for example, qualified structural and civil engineers.

The introduction of the powers will be by designating order. The parts of the Regulations and who will be entitled to certify have yet to be specified. (See 2.17 below.)

New Regulations

2.16 Section 12 requires the Secretary of State to appoint a Building Standards Advisory Committee, the main purposes of which are to advise him on the making of Building Standards Regulations and keeping the operation of the Regulations under review. The members of the committee are selected as individuals and not as representatives of particular interests. It should be noted, however, that various professional, commercial, research bodies, etc., do nominate representatives for consideration as members. The committee is usually reconstituted at three-year intervals. The present committee includes representatives from building control, architecture, engineering, law, fire services, building, material producers and local government administration.

2.17 The procedure for making regulations is as follows: the Secretary of State consults the Building Standards Advisory Committee and other such bodies which are representative of the interests concerned. In practice, over 200 bodies are asked for their comments regarding proposed amendments to the Building Regulations. The first of these, the Building (Self Certification of Structural Design) (Scotland) Building Regulations 1992 (1992 No. 1911 (S194)) was made on 28 July 1992. This allows certificates to be submitted in respect of structural requirements of Building Standard Regulation 11. The certificate must be issued by chartered, civil or structural engineers meeting the conditions laid down. Consequential amendments to the Procedure Regulations and Forms Regulations are included in this S.I.

Dangerous buildings

2.18 Part III deals with dangerous buildings and goes into detail regarding action to be taken to make them safe, the powers of local authorities with regard to purchasing buildings where owners cannot be found, and the selling of materials from buildings demolished by the local authority.

Civil liability

2.19 The new Section 19A lays down breaches of regulations which may be actionable so far as damage is concerned. Damage includes death or injury of persons.

This section has not yet been brought into operation.

Crown rights

2.20 The Secretary of State has made it clear that Crown buildings should conform to the Building Standards Regulations regarding new buildings and extensions and alterations to other buildings. While Crown buildings do not have to follow the warrant application procedure to local authorities some Crown Bodies, e.g. The Scottish Prison Service, have a full building control system.

Enforcement officers

2.21 Section 21 of the 1959 Act, which laid down a requirement for the appointment of masters of works, was repealed by the Local Government (Scotland) Act 1973 and the enforcement of building control left in the hands of local authorities. There are at present, therefore, no specific qualifications laid down for building control officers.

Schedules

2.22 These relate to matters in regard of which regulations may be made, recovery of expenses, evacuation of dangerous buildings, minor and consequential amendments of enactments.

Commencement Orders

2.23 It should be noted that the extra powers contained in the Health and Safety at Work Act and the Housing (Scotland) Act 1986 have to be activated by Commencement Order, and the first of these was issued as Commencement No. 2 Order 1975 and came into force on 27 March 1975. A further order – Commencement No. 6 Order 1980 – came into force on 17 March 1980 and deals with increased penalties for contravention under certain provisions of the Building (Scotland) Act 1959.

Other provisions

2.24 Part IV is concerned with supplementary provisions and deals with appeals, references to other enactments such as Ancient Monuments Acts, building preservation orders and so on, inspection and tests, penalties, fees, transitional provisions, and general interpretation.

Building (Scotland) Act 1970

2.25 The main purpose of the Building (Scotland) Act 1970 was to amend the 1959 Act as regards making Building Standards Regulations, depositing building materials on roads, and application for warrants. These points have already been mentioned.

2.26 The following additional powers were granted under the Act:

Section 2 gives the Secretary of State powers to delegate to local authorities the power of relaxation, and a new form of relaxation power in respect of certain classes of buildings. This power, which might be described as an 'omnibus relaxation', permits him to direct that a building which may not meet the exact requirements of the Regulations can nevertheless be accepted by local authorities when warrant applications are made. It should be remembered that the term 'building' is defined in both the Act and Standards Regulations and covers both a whole building and its constituent parts. Class relaxations have been issued, e.g. for air supported structures, framed structures, various components in chimney and fire protection. These are situations where individual relaxations would be required in each case.

Section 4 permits the Secretary of State to call in any application for warrant received by a local authority and enables him to determine whether the building concerned will conform to the Building Standards Regulations, to give relaxations, and to impose, after consulting the Building Standards Advisory Committee, requirements additional to or more onerous than those in the Building Standards Regulations. This power is most useful in very large and complex developments where, for instance, the traditional means of protection from fire have to be supplemented by automatic detection systems and sophisticated ventilation schemes.

Building (Procedure) (Scotland) Regulations and subsequent amendments

2.27 The Procedure Regulations were laid before Parliament on 9 November 1981 and came into force on 30 November 1981. They replaced the previous Procedure Regulations, which had been in force since 1975. The Regulations prescribe in detail the procedures to be followed by local authorities. They amend in detail areas of procedure relating to notification of adjoining proprietors and relaxation of regulations by local authorities. The Regulations consolidate amendments since 1975 in the scale of fees, for warrant. The Building (Procedure) (Scotland) Amendment Regulations 1987 amended Regulation 7 of the principal Procedure Regulations in respect of fees. These are not to be charged in respect of building operations consisting solely of the alteration or extension of a building to provide facilities (including in particular means of access to and within the building) for disabled persons who frequent or in the case of dwellings who inhabit or are about to inhabit the building. At the time of writing new revised Procedure Regulations have been issued for consultation.

For note on Building (Procedure) (Scotland) Amendment Regulations 1990, see the end of this chapter.

Interpretation

2.28 Part I of the Regulations deals with interpretation, citation and revocation, definitions, powers of local authorities to charge fees, to issue warrant for the construction of a building in specified stages, and details of certificates of completion. Attention is drawn specifically to the following points:

1. Duration of warrant. A warrant is valid for three years only. This does not mean that a building must be completed within three years of the issue of warrant; it means that construction must be commenced within three years. A warrant is only a permission to construct and is required before the commencement of work to ensure that the building will comply with the Regulations. (See also Section 6 of the 1959 Act.) The interpretation of this section has led to some confusion in the past and draft regulations include a proposal to include both a starting and completion date to clarify the position.
2. Local authorities must either grant or refuse an application for a completion certificate within 14 days, and in the event of a refusal must notify the applicant as to that refusal.
3. The description of the prescribed stages of construction, where work is permitted, under a warrant issued by stages.

Applications for warrant

2.29 Part II of the Regulations deals with applications for warrant. The 1981 Regulations considerably simplify the previous process, particularly in the light of neighbour notification requirements introduced in August 1981 under planning procedures. The following is a précis of the new arrangements. The applicant must lodge his application with the local authority in writing on the appropriate forms. It can be signed by the applicant or by his agent. The application should be accompanied by the principal plan and a duly certified copy. If a direction relaxing any regulation has already been given by the Secretary of State, this should accompany the application. The local authority may ask for additional plans and information and, if necessary, up to two extra copies of the application and plans lodged with it. The form and scale of the plans required are described in Schedule 1, Section H of the Regulations.

2.30 When the application is received, the local authority shall 'forthwith' – the regulation term – consider and determine the application. The local authority shall not refuse an application without giving the applicant notification of the proposed grounds of refusal and an opportunity of being heard and making written representations. Any such oral or written representations must be taken account of in finally determining the application.

Calling in warrants

2.31 Part III deals with the procedure to be followed where the Secretary of State 'calls in' an application for warrant to deal with it partly or wholly by himself. Where the Secretary of State calls in an application for warrant, the local authority must send him the plans, confirmation that the application has been properly made, copies of any previous warrants dealing with temporary buildings and which relate to the application under consideration, and any comments the local authority may wish to make. If on consideration the Secretary of State decides to impose more onerous requirements additional to or more serious than those in the Building Regulations at present, he must consult the applicant, the local authority, the Building Standards Advisory Committee, and any other person he thinks might have an interest. If the Secretary of State thinks fit, he may convene a hearing for the interested parties. It should be stressed that this procedure may also apply only in respect of individual parts of Regulations and in such a case the Secretary of State would then return the application, along with his requirements, for the local authority to process in the normal way. It is for the local authority to notify the applicant of the Secretary of State's decisions and his reasons for those decisions.

Local authority relaxation

2.32 Part IV gives the procedures to be followed by local authorities when dealing with applications for relaxation. These have been considerably simplified from the previous Regulations and give the local authority discretion in relation to who is to be notified as an affected proprietor.

2.33 Part V gives the procedure for appealing to the Secretary of State against the refusal of a local authority to grant relaxation or against a condition of relaxation.

Relaxation by Secretary of State

2.34 Part VI gives the procedure for application to the Secretary of State for a relaxation. The new procedures in Part IV are, in effect, now very closely allied to those which have applied under this part for some years. The applicant must lodge a copy of his plans and application with the local authority when he makes his application to the Secretary of State. The Secretary of State may consult by means of a draft direction with the applicant and other persons he considers to have an interest, and in his final determination shall take into consideration any comments made. The Secretary of State can, however, issue a final direction without consultation, and this has, in fact, been done in certain cases.

Class relaxations

2.35 These are the province of the Secretary of State and relate to a general relaxation, binding on all local authorities, in respect of either a building type or a component of a building. Class relaxations usually refer to individual regulations and parts of the Regulations and may be conditional.

The Secretary of State must consult the Building Standards Advisory Committee and such other bodies as he deems have an interest before making his determination of an application. The relaxations are only granted after a detailed investigation including results of research and testing. It must be stressed that a class relaxation must *not* be confused with a class warrant. With the coming into force of the projected new Regulations, the very nature of the latter should dispense with the need for many of the existing class relaxations although there will be the occasional need for the procedures to be used.

Orders made by local authorities

2.36 Part IX deals with orders relating to buildings constructed without or in contravention of warrant and in respect of dangerous buildings. The part goes into detail regarding notices, appeals, and, where necessary, the convening of hearings.

General

2.37 Part X deals with procedure to be followed at hearings, appointment of assessors (if deemed necessary), maintenance of records, and inspection of records and applications (which must be available for inspection by the public at all reasonable hours). Decisions of the local authority must follow laid-down rules and must be made in writing. Where an application is refused or, for example, where a relaxation is given despite objections, the local authority must state the reasons for their decision.

2.38 Persons carrying out building operations under warrant must give notice to the local authority:

1. of the date on which work commenced within seven days of that date;
2. when a drain has been laid and is ready for inspection and test;
3. when a drain has been infilled and is ready for the second inspection or test;
4. of the date on which operations are completed.

Items (1) and (4) shall be in writing, except in the case of (4) where an application for a certificate of completion has been made in the prescribed form.

Plans to be submitted

2.39 Schedule 1 goes into detail of the particulars of plans required and the minimum scales to which they have to be drawn. The Schedule is divided into sections relating to whether the application for warrant deals with erection, alteration, extension, change of use, or demolition of a building.

2.40 Schedule 2 gives the table of fees applicable for a warrant. The fee scale is based on the estimated cost of the operations and ranges from £5 for small works to figures in excess of £1 000. The fees are a once-only charge – there are no extra fees for inspection, etc. The figures are regularly upgraded to take account of inflation.

Building Operations (Scotland) Regulations 1975

2.41 The Secretary of State had powers conferred on him by Section 5 of the Building (Scotland) Act 1959 to make regulations for the conduct of operations for the construction, repair, maintenance, or demolition of buildings, as he thinks expedient for securing the safety of the public while building operations are in progress.

2.42 The Building Operations (Scotland) Regulations 1975, which came into operation on 16 May 1975, revoke the previous Regulations made in 1963. They lay down requirements for the safety of passers-by and deal with such matters as the erection of hoardings, barricades and fences, footpaths with safe platforms, handrails, steps or ramps, overhead coverings, and so on. In addition, protective works are to be properly lit to the satisfaction of the local authority.

2.43 There are also provisions for clearing footpaths and the securing of partly constructed or demolished buildings. A special regulation deals with additional requirements for demolition operations.

These Regulations are administered by the local authority. At the time of writing these are being revised.

Building (Forms) (Scotland) Regulation 1991

2.44 Section 24 of the Building (Scotland) Act 1959 gave the Secretary of State power to make Regulations prescribing the type of form to be used in the various procedures under the Act.

2.45 The Regulations were completely revised and issued in 1991 coming into force on 1 April 1991. A minor amendment was made in the Building (Self Certification of Structural Design) (Scotland) Regulations 1992. The Regulations prescribe the forms in which applications for warrants, notices, orders, and other documents should be made under the Act. The Regulations are the latest in a series which have been updated in the light of changes to principal legislation and to related regulations. The Regulations provide a common system of forms applicable throughout Scotland for building control purposes.

Building Standards (Relaxation by Local Authorities), (Scotland) Regulations 1991

2.46 These Regulations revoke the previous Regulations of 1985 except for certain transitional provisions. Delegation to relax or dispense with building standards regulations is given to the local authority for all buildings including change of use except in the case of enclosed shopping centres, or where a warrant has been subject to the 'call in' procedure by the Secretary of State.

2.47 The delegation is in respect of individual buildings and must not be confused with class relaxations (paragraph 2.34).

The procedure to be followed both in applying for relaxation and in appealing against a decision of a local authority, should this be sought, is detailed under the Building (Procedure) (Scotland) Regulations 1981 and the Building (Forms) (Scotland) Regulations 1991.

3 Building Standards (Scotland) Regulations 1990

3.01 A completely new and revised set of Regulations in a different format were laid before Parliament on 19 November 1990 coming into force on 1 April 1991. The Regulations take the form of a short statutory instrument which gives the requirements in a functional form under each of the familiar rubics of the older style regulations. As the Scottish Regulations are standards regulations as required under the primary legislation, the statutory instrument requires to be supported by technical standards which have legal status. Published along with the statutory instrument, therefore, was a large and comprehensive set of technical standards in a separate loose-leaf document of A4 size, compliance with which meets the Regulations. The 1990 Regulations were amended by the Building Standards (Scotland) Amendment Regulations 1993 in respect of smoke alarms for buildings. A further change was made by the Building Standards (Scotland) Amendment Regulations 1994.

3.02 Whilst the statutory instrument gives the requirements in functional form, the Technical Standards document is the actual working document. It is laid out in 20 separate sections, 17 of which relate to the relevant clause in the statutory instrument, plus an introductory section, an appendix listing publications used in the Technical Standards and an index.

Each part has basically two sections. The first repeats the regulation and then gives the required standard and the second section gives, on different coloured paper, deemed to satisfy provisions for certain standards. The 'deemed to satisfy' may relate to a code of practice, a detailed specification, etc.

The introduction to the Technical Standards makes it clear that full acceptance is accorded to national standards and technical specifications recognized in other Member States of the European Community which provide equivalent standards of protection or performance, e.g. in Part B: Fitness of Materials.

3.03 It is essential when using the Technical Standards to remember that all definitions are in Part A, and that when a defined term appears in the standard it is printed in italics. When an asterisk appears against a standard it indicates that there is a deemed to satisfy provision in the Part (printed on yellow paper). Ensure you have the latest version which includes amendment No. 2 1994.

3.04 The interpretation of the Regulations is the province of the local authorities that have building control functions. If any dispute arises regarding interpretation, the final decision rests with the Sheriff Court.

The following paragraphs give a brief description of the requirements of the separate parts of the regulations and the appropriate Technical Standard.

Part 1 of the Regulations and Part A of the Technical Standards

3.05 Part I gives the general requirements including citation and interpretation. The latter gives the definitions required for the Regulations. These are repeated in Part A of the Standards together with additional definitions for terms used only in the Technical Standards.

Regulations 3 and 4 are important at the outset of a project as they describe types of buildings which are exempt from the regulations or do not require a warrant. A designer should check the schedules to these Regulations carefully.

Regulation 5 describes limited-life buildings as those 'erected for a period of up to 5 years'. Again it is important to check this requirement at the outset of a design as special provisions for such buildings can be found in the Regulations, e.g. in respect of site preparations. Regulation 6 is extremely important as it clarifies buildings by purpose group (in Schedule 3). The classification affects all areas of the Regulations when applied to building types, particularly in respect of fire safety, ventilation and sanitary requirements.

Regulation 7 as read with Schedule 4 refers to occupant capacity (i.e. the number of persons a room or storey is deemed to accommodate for Regulations purposes). This capacity determines the required standards within the purposes group and is vitally important in respect of means of escape from fire, ventilation and sanitary accommodation. Note that where a room or space is likely to have more than one use the greatest occupant capacity applies.

Regulation 5 as read with Schedule 5 gives the rules of measurement for regulation purposes.

Part A must be carefully applied at the outset of any design as failure to correctly identify its application to the building could cause problems later in the project's life and be expensive and difficult to remedy.

Part 2 of the Regulations and Technical Standards

3.06 This part is the meat of the Regulations and within it are found all the requirements. These are given as functional requirements, with the standards detailed in the Technical Standards; Regulation 9 states that compliance with the Regulations can only be met by the relevant standards. Conformity with the Technical Standards shall be deemed to satisfy compliance.

Fitness of materials (Regulation 10)

3.07 The requirements are given in functional terms and amplified in Part B of the Technical Standards. The use of national codes, Agrément Certificates or equivalent standards recognized by any Member State of the European Community is deemed to satisfy. In addition reference is made to a European technical approval in accordance with Council Directive 89/106/EEC to test evidence from the National Measurement Accreditation Service or similar.

Part B allows material whose suitability depends on suitable maintenance or periodic renewal, provided that replacement is reasonably practicable.

Structure (Regulation 11)

3.08 This regulation requires that every building shall be constructed so that all loads on a building are sustained by the building and safely transmitted to the ground while retaining the stability of the structure. Part C of the Technical Standards give methods of calculations and also lists the relevant criteria to be followed in all cases. In addition rules relating to buildings of five storeys or more (including every basement storey) are given for dealing with disproportionate collapse. This owes its existence to the aftermath of Ronan Point and is intended to give safeguards against progressive collapse. See also the Small Buildings Guide (second edition) published with the Technical Standards and which is deemed to satisfy the regulations.

Structural fire precautions (Regulation 12)

3.08 The theory of fire resistance embodied in the old by-laws, which national regulations replaced, was intended to ensure that each individual building would contain its own fire as far as possible and would be protected from outside. This applied as much to buildings on a plot of land in one occupation as to buildings on separate plots. Two changes were made by Regulations in 1963 and continued in subsequent revisions. These were that it was considered unnecessary that buildings should resist fire from outside if they were capable of containing any fire starting within them and that control should be restricted to safeguarding public interest by preventing general conflagration. By the Building Standards (Scotland) Amendment Regulations 1994 the regulation has been redrafted to refer to 'damage' causing collapse rather than 'failure'. The position in regard to a storey in the roof space when calculating the number of storeys for the purpose of disproportionate collapse has been clarified.

3.09 The Regulation requires that in the event of fire, the building, for a reasonable period, will maintain its stability and inhibit the spread of fire and smoke both within the building and to and from the building.

3.10 Part D of the Technical Standards attempts to achieve its purposes of laying down requirements for fire resistance of the structure. It controls the type of materials used, specifying non-combustibility where necessary as well as surface classification of lining materials. Fire resistance criteria are based on those found in BS fire tests notably BS 476 and its various parts. Roofs do not require fire resistance, not being classified as an element of structure, but they are given a classification in the 'deemed to satisfy' provisions based on the roof's ability to resist penetration by burning brands and the resistance of the surface to spread of flame.

3.11 Large buildings are required to be divided into compartments by means of compartment walls and separating floors and similarly buildings in different occupation have to be separated by such floors and walls. Concessions for certain buildings in respect of non-combustibility requirements are given where there is a low fire load and risk.

There are also strong criteria to prevent the passage of fire via pipes and ducts which penetrate compartments and separating floors and walls. Additionally cavity barriers and fire stops are required to prevent rapid spread of fire along cavities such as certain suspended ceilings and roof voids, etc.

There is, however, an acceptance of the principle that if a building is far enough from its boundary it will not spread fire to buildings on adjoining land in different occupation. Technical Standard D2.6 as read with the 'deemed to satisfy' provision gives various ways of meeting the requirement.

3.12 Technical Standard D3 refers to certain small buildings which may be attached to or within the curtilage of dwellings in Purpose Group 1. These are in the nature of a relaxation of standards applied to buildings of a higher fire risk. It should be noted that with respect to certain small buildings, the exemptions to regulations given in Schedule 1 of the Regulations may already apply.

Means of escape from fire; Facilities of fire-fighting; Means of warning of fire in dwellings (Regulation 13)

3.13 The Regulation merely requires that a building shall be required to be provided with adequate means of escape in the event of fire and adequate fire-fighting facilities. An amendment to the Regulations in 1993* introduced a further requirement for adequate means of warning the occupants of dwellings of the outbreak of fire.

3.14 In meeting the requirements of the Regulations, the Technical Standards, Part E, go into considerable detail, backed up by explanatory diagrams, tables and 'deemed to satisfy' clauses.

The intention is that a person should be able to reach a place of safety or a protected zone within 2½ minutes of becoming aware of fire. Exit widths are calculated using a unit width of 530 mm per person and a discharge rate of 40 persons per minute. (This is a fairly slow rate and is based on a heavily loaded occupancy.) The travel distance from any point to the place of safety or protected zone varies with the purpose group and differential travel distances are given in tabular form.

Every escape route (as defined in Part A) must lead to a place of safety directly or by way of a protected zone. This in turn means the protected zones have to meet specific requirements in the standards, e.g. enclosure of stairs and ramps.

Where, because of the purpose group classification, there is an additional perceived risk, requirements as to the layout of the building within the area between a point and a protected door are specified – for example in high blocks of flats. There is also a requirement in certain residential buildings with only one escape

* The Building Standards (Scotland) Amendment Regulations 1993 No. 1457 (S191)

route to make provision for emergency escape windows which have a specified size and location.

The part also has detailed requirements for assembly buildings, hospitals, certain residential buildings and specified parts of buildings such as stages, mechanical ventilation systems, places of special fire risk, accommodation stairs and escalators, fire doors, fixed seating, emergency lighting. Attention is drawn to the requirements for the disabled, introduced in June 1994.

3.15 The part includes requirements to assist fire-fighters. These range from the provision of fire mains and hydrants to access for fire-fighting vehicles. The latter are differentiated depending on the size and height of a building or whether or not wet or dry fire mains are fitted. In respect of hydrant provision the standards recognize the difficulties faced by buildings in remote areas and accept for fire-fighting purposes, water other than through water mains, for example rivers, lochs, static water tanks, always provided access for a pumping appliance is available.

Heat Producing Appliances (Regulation 14) and Storage of Liquid and Gaseous Fuels (Regulation 15)

3.16 The requirements of Regulation 14 apply to any appliance designed to burn solid fuel (including wood and peat) or gaseous or liquid fuel. The Regulation requires the appliances to operate safely so that their operation does not cause damage to the building, the products of combustion are not a hazard to health and sufficient air for combustion is provided. The storage of fuel oil, supplying appliances providing space and water heating and cooking facilities in any building or liquified petroleum gas for appliances in any building or buildings of Purpose Groups 1 and 2 are covered by Regulation 15. Attention must be paid to the application of the scope of the regulation as other storage facilities may be subject to different legislation, e.g. Health and Safety legislation.

3.17 Part F of the Technical Standards gives details of the required standards. It is divided into six main sub-sections which deal with:

1. The application of Part F.
2. General Requirements for Heat Producing Installations including large installations (as defined).
3. Solid Fuel Burning Installations.
4. Oil-fired Installations.
5. Gas-fired Installations.
6. Storage of liquid and gaseous fuels.

There are also the 'deemed to satisfy' provisions for all sections.

3.18 The division between large and small installations is given as 45 kW output rating, although as is usual with gas installations, small gas installations are quoted as not exceeding 60 kW input rating.

The requirements for large installations are given in functional terms, but those for smaller installations are given in detail with references to codes of practice as acceptable 'deemed to satisfy' provisions.

3.19 The object of Part F is to prevent the ignition of any part of a building or damage to persons from the use of an appliance and its associated flues or chimneys. It also recognizes the need for suitable supplies of combustion air to enable appliances to operate safely. The part, therefore, goes into detail regarding construction, installation and operation of all matters relating to the primary object of safety of persons.

3.20 The requirements for safe fuel storage recognize the considerable increase in the use of such fuels as LPG and the risks associated with improper storage. In the case of oil storage attention is drawn both to the requirements for catchpits and the concession given to very small storage tanks.

Preparation of sites and resistance to moisture (Regulations 16, 17 and 18)

3.21 These Regulations are drafted in functional terms as are the standards in Part G of the Technical Standards. They are, however, backed up by a comprehensive 'deemed to satisfy' set of provisions together with illustrated details.

3.22 Part G contains requirements in respect of site and ground immediately adjoining a site. These must be prepared and treated to protect the building *and its users* from harmful effects caused by harmful and dangerous substances, matter in the surface soil and vegetable matter. Harmful and dangerous substances are defined in Regulation 16(A) and have a very wide application. A site must also be safeguarded from any harmful effects of ground and flood water and existing drains as far as reasonably practicable. **Note:** there are disapplications for certain temporary buildings.

3.23 A building must be so constructed to protect the building and its occupants from the harmful effects of rising damp and the effects of precipitation, e.g. rain and snow. In addition buildings of Purpose Group 1 shall be constructed to protect the building and users, as far as reasonably practicable from the effects of condensation, both surface and interstitial.

Resistance to the transmission of sound (Regulations 19–20)

3.24 The Regulations relate only to dwellings other than wholly detached dwellings and the walls and floors between dwellings and other parts of a building e.g. the floor of a flat over an office or shop. The requirements apply to both airborne and impact sound.

3.25 Part H of the Technical Standards, in its 'deemed to satisfy' provisions goes into great detail in describing methods of meeting the standards and gives examples and illustrations of acceptable constructions. The part draws attention to the fact that the standards required should be achieved by common, economically viable forms of construction which must be allied to good standards of workmanship.

Conservation of fuel and power (Regulation 22)

3.26 The scope of the requirements for conservation of fuel and power were considerably widened when the original plans to make regulations under the Building (Scotland) Act 1959 were changed to include conservation of energy*. The Regulation applies to all buildings other than those listed in Regulation 22(2) which includes limited-life buildings, very small buildings and unheated or lightly heated buildings of Purpose Groups 2–7, air-supported structures, certain greenhouses, conservatories, garages, etc.

3.27 Part J of the Technical Standards gives the requirements under three main headings: Application, conservation of fuel and power: the building fabric and conservation of fuel and power: the building services. There is also a very detailed and extensive 'deemed to satisfy' series of provisions.

3.28 The standards for the building fabric give three different ways of meeting the requirements:

1. The elemental approach which follows closely the previous regulations on the subject.
2. Calculated trade-offs which gives flexibility in relation to window and rooflight openings in calculating total heat loss.
3. Energy targets which gives a very flexible method using not only trade-offs, but useful heat gains.

The methods are described in the Standards with both tables and diagrams.

* Health and Safety at Work etc. Act 1974, Chapter 37, Clause 75, Schedule 7.

3.29 The standards for building services include controls for heating systems, hot water storage vessels and insulation of hot water storage vessels and pipes and ducts. The standards for insulation are backed up by 'deemed to satisfy' provisions.

Ventilation of buildings (Regulation 23)

3.30 The requirements for ventilation are to ensure an adequate supply of air is available for human occupation and can be provided either by natural, mechanical or joint natural/mechanical means. **Note:** the air for combustion appliances is extra and subject to Part F of the Technical Standards. The original regulations have been considerably slimmed down and, with the exception of the requirements for dwellings and the location of ventilation openings, are largely dependent on the use of 'deemed to satisfy' provisions. Part K does not apply to buildings to which certain other legislation applies, e.g. the Factories Act 1961 (1961 C34). It should be noted that the standards now require a trickle ventilator in addition to an opening area of ventilation when natural ventilation is provided in dwellings as well as mechanical extraction for bath and shower rooms.

Drainage and sanitary facilities (Regulations 24 and 25)

3.31 The Regulations require adequate drainage and sanitary facilities to a building. Part M of the Technical Handbook, in its standards for both drainage and pipework give functional requirements which are backed up with extensive use of codes and specifications in the 'deemed to satisfy' provisions. Every building is required to have a drainage system connected to a public sewer or a private sewage works. The latter may be septic tanks in rural areas, but it should be noted that the wording ensures that cesspools are not acceptable. The requirements are very flexible so as to permit a wide variety of different materials both above and below ground. By the 1994 Regulations the regulation is disapplied to certain buildings covered by other specified legislation.

3.32 The standards for sanitary facility provision are divided into general requirements in respect of water closets, specific requirements for Purpose Group 1: Housing, requiring provision of sinks, baths, etc. (**note:** the requirements for and supply of hot and cold water are now in Part M instead of Part Q) and requirements for other buildings. Other buildings may however, be subject to separate legislation, e.g. The Workplace (Health, Safety and Welfare) Regulations 1992 and such legislation takes precedence. While Part M requires a water supply to the fittings of a dwelling, public water supplies are the responsibility of the regional councils (from 1996 the new Regional Water Authorities) and designers should liaise with them at an early stage. There are areas of the country which are not served by a public supply and recourse has to be made to a private supply. Such supplies should be tested for adequacy and potency including chemical and bacteriological testing.

Electrical installations (Regulation 26)

3.33 Both the Regulation and standards are written in functional terms, with exceptions for certain buildings, e.g. buildings to which the Mines and Quarries Act 1954 and the Factories Act 1961 apply. The standards are met by compliance with the relevant conditions of the Regulations for Electrical Engineers published by the Institute of Electrical Engineers.

Miscellaneous hazards (Regulations 27 and 28)

3.34 These Regulations bring together a miscellany of safety requirements to prevent accidents. Part P of the Technical Handbook gives standards relating to collision with projections and glazing, cleaning of windows, safety on escalators and passenger conveyers, and discharge of steam pipes. There is also a standard relating to the danger of malfunction of an unvented hot water storage system. The standard is met by the requirements of a detailed specification in the 'deemed to satisfy' provisions. By the

1994 Regulations, additional requirements are imposed in relation to the positioning of manual controls for the operation of windows and rooflights for means of access to roofs in building other than housing.

Facilities for dwellings (Regulation 29)

3.35 Until 1986, the Building Regulations gave standards in great detail in relation to housing. Since that date the requirements have been reduced to a minimum even to removing minimum ceiling heights. Part Q gives standards in relation to adequate sleeping, kitchen, window space, heating, access between storeys and access from a suitable road. Where available an electricity supply is required.

Solid waste storage, dungsteads and farm effluent tanks (Regulation 30 and 31)

3.36 The requirements for solid waste storage apply to dwellings and require that adequate facilities be provided to facilitate access for storage and removal, minimize health risks and prevent contamination of water supplies and watercourses. Similarly dungsteads and farm effluent tanks must be so constructed, positioned and protected to minimize danger to health and safety and contamination of water supplies and watercourses. Part R of the Technical Standards gives detailed standards backed up by references to relevant British Standards in the 'deemed to satisfy' provisions.

Stairs, ramps and protective barriers (Regulation 32)

3.37 The Regulations require that stairs and ramps must provide a safe means of passage for users of a building. Protective barriers are required as necessary to stairs, ramps, raised floors, balconies, etc. Part S of the Technical Standards gives very detailed standards for the construction of stairs, landings and protective barriers. Certain areas which have limited access, e.g. in industrial and agricultural buildings, may have stairs and fixed ladders complying with the appropriate 'deemed to satisfy' provision.

Facilities for disabled people (Regulation 33)

3.38 The Regulation requires adequate access for disabled persons to storeys of a building (other than dwellings and Purpose Group 7A buildings and 7B and C, other than car parks and parking garages). If an accessible storey contains sanitary facilities these must include adequate facilities for disabled persons. Within stadia and auditoria there is a further requirement relating to a minimum number of spaces for wheelchair users. **Note:** attention is drawn to the definition of 'disabled people' which includes physical, hearing or sight impairment as well as mobility. The standards of Part T are backed up by the 'deemed to satisfy' requirements. Attention is drawn to the exceptions to the standards in Technical Standard T2.2. By the 1994 Regulations there is a major amendment in Part T to the scope and applicability of the requirements for access for the disabled. There is also a reference back to Part E (means of escape from fire) which extends in the Technical Standards to the 'deemed to satisfy' provisions.

1. The requirements are very wide ranging and now require provisions for means of escape from fire in 'every building or part of a building to which the requirements of Part T apply'. The latter part has been extensively expanded in its requirements. The new Regulations are not, however, *retrospective*.
2. Part T applies to all buildings in Purpose Groups 2–6 and to car parks and parking garages of Purpose Sub-groups 7B or 7C.
3. All buildings to which the Regulations apply must be provided with adequate access and *suitable aids* for disabled people. The standards require that car parks should have suitable car parking spaces and suitable access from the car park to the principal entrance to the building, for example level or ramped access.
4. Access within the building must be provided to, and throughout, *each storey* of the building. This access must be ramped,

level or provided with a suitable passenger lift to any storey above or below the principal entrance storey. There are exceptions for small *two-storey* buildings with less than 280 m² in area (of each storey) with stairs suitable for ambulant disabled and for buildings of *more than two-storeys* where the area per storey is less than 200 m² and a suitable stair for ambulant disabled is provided.
5. The means of access *within* a storey must be accessible either by level or ramped access or by a suitable wheelchair stairlift or platform lift.
6. Where sanitary accommodation is provided in an accessible storey (now most storeys), suitable sanitary facilities for wheelchairs must be provided. This is a major change in requirements. There are a series of exclusions on whether lifts are provided, travel distance and numbers of persons in the building.
7. Where there is a changing area associated with sanitary accommodation, at least one changing cubicle must be suitable for disabled people.
8. In a building of Purpose Group 2B containing bedrooms, not less than one in 20 of these bedrooms, or part thereof, must be provided with sanitary accommodation suitable for wheelchair users. This must be en suite if serving one bedroom or if the sanitary accommodation serves more than one bedroom, accessible from a circulation area exclusive to the bedrooms.
9. Areas of audience and spectator fixed seating have to provide adequate suitable and level spaces especially designed for wheelchair users.
10. A new requirement is the provision of suitable aids for people with hearing impairment in auditoria and conference halls with a floor area exceeding 100 m².
11. The new requirements for means of escape from fire require either compliance with the relevant clauses of BS 5588: Part 8 for multi-storey buildings or the provision of wheelchair refuges on every escape stair landing.

Appendix to the Technical Standards

3.39 This includes reference to all British Standards and Codes of Practice and to other publications such as BRE reports referred to in the main text.

3.40 The Regulations are subject to regular scrutiny and, where necessary, alteration in order to take cognizance of new building materials and processes and to take account of new Codes of Practice, etc. The form and presentation of the Regulations is now such that amendments will in the main be made to the Technical Standards handbook rather than to the statutory instruments. At the time of writing comprehensive documents relating to a considerable number of amendments to the Technical Standards have been issued for public consultation.

4 Other national legislation affecting building

4.01 The following list of legislation (although not completely exhaustive) applies in Scotland, and the comments under each heading may give guidance regarding the Scottish scene.

Offices, Shops and Railway Premises Act 1963

4.02 Precise standards for ventilation, means of escape from fire, and occupant load factors are laid down in the Building Standards Regulations. The requirements in the Offices, Shops and Railway Premises Act 1963 are in general framed so that standards of the Building Regulations are *usually* taken by the enforcing authority to meet the requirements of the Act. However, the Building Standards Regulations accept the Sanitary Convenience Regulations 1964 (Regulation D25(2)(C) of the Building Regulations gives exceptions to the provision of sanitary accommodation).

Section 29 of the Offices, Shops and Railway Premises Act previously covered fire and certification, but has been repealed and responsibility passed to the Fire Precautions Act from 1 January 1977. Check also the amendments contained in the Health and Safety at Work etc. Act 1974.

Clean Air Acts 1993

4.03 Sections 14 and 15 of this Act provide a new control for the heights of chimneys serving furnaces. The situation, therefore, is that special application must be made to the local authority for chimney height approval for furnace chimneys. The height of non-furnace chimneys is dealt with under the Building Regulations without need for special application. Constructional details of all chimneys are of course subject to local authority approval. See Chapter 14, paragraphs 6.09–6.11 and Chapter 16 paragraph 6.05.

Factories Act 1961

4.04 Provisions of Part K (ventilation) do not apply to premises subject to the Factories Act 1961, and it is advised that particular ventilation requirements should be discussed with the factory inspectorate at an early stage. However, means of escape for fire requirements are subject to Part F of the Building Standards Regulations. Fire certification previously under this Act is now the responsibility of the Fire Precautions Act as from 1 January 1977 – see the Fire Precautions (Factories, Offices, Shops and Railway Premises) Order 1976. In Scotland, fire authorities are area authorities, eight in number, with their boundaries roughly equivalent to the local authority regional boundaries, but with one brigade covering the Lothian and Borders area. Check carefully the implications of amendment contained in Health and Safety at Work etc. Act 1974.

Fire Precautions Act 1971

4.05 Under this Act, certain premises must obtain a fire certificate from the fire authority as to the suitability of their means of escape. The premises are designated by order, and on 31 January 1972 the Secretary of State designated hotels and boarding houses above a certain size as the first class of premises requiring certificates. The order came into force on 1 June 1972. As the Building Standards Regulations contain requirements for the provision of means of escape, certain sections of the Fire Precautions Act are disapplied to Scotland and certain others apply only to Scotland. Section 14 contains a statutory bar in that where the means of escape meet the Building Regulations requirements, then they must be accepted for fire certificate purposes. This does not mean that all *existing* premises necessarily have to meet Building Regulations standards for new buildings, and many will have reasonable means of escape at present (although not quite up to new building standards). The fire officer has scope to use his judgment in existing premises as far as the statutory bar allows. Attention is also drawn to the definition of 'owner' which differs from that in England. See Chapter 14, paragraph 6.03 ff.

Fire Certificates (Special Premises) Regulations 1976

4.06 These provide that a certificate issued by the Health and Safety Executive shall be required for premises of a kind specified in Schedule 1 of these Regulations and lay down the conditions which may be imposed. The statutory bar for building regulations does not apply to these buildings, but they are of such a specialized nature that close consultation would take place with the relevant authorities at an early stage of design. The Regulations came into force on 1 January 1977.

Sewerage (Scotland) Act 1968

4.07 This Act, which came into force on 1 May 1973, has a bearing on the requirements of the drainage section (Part M) of the Building Standards Regulations. The main effect is to limit the range of the Building Standards Regulations, as many parts of what were termed common drainage will in future become 'public sewer' and will be vested in a local authority.* The term 'drain' is defined as that within the curtilage of a building and for its sole use. Attention is drawn to the definitions in Section 59.

The Act under Section 12 and subject to the conditions of that section gives an owner a right to connect to a local authority sewer or sewage treatment works. The owner of any premises who proposes to connect his drains or sewers to a public sewer or works of a local authority, or who is altering his drain or sewer in such a way as to interfere with those of a local authority, must, however, give 28 days' notice to the *local* authority, who may or may not give permission for the work to proceed. The authority can give conditional approval, and the owner has right of appeal against any decision.

Powers are given in the Act to require defects in drains or sewage treatment works to be remedied. Local authorities have the powers to take over private sewage treatment works, including septic tanks. Other powers include rights to discharge trade effluents into public sewers, emptying of septic tanks, provision of temporary sanitary conveniences, etc.

Health and Safety at Work etc. Act 1974

4.08 The most important effect of this Act is contained in Section 75 as read with Schedule 10. These clauses introduce amendments to the principal Building Acts and extend and alter the powers contained in them. It should be noted that in Part III of the Act only Section 75 is applicable to Scotland. The powers under this section come into force only when the Secretary of State issues a designating order. To date, two such orders have been made: the Health and Safety at Work etc. Act 1974 (Commencement No. 2) Order 1975, and the Health and Safety at Work etc. Act 1974 (Commencement No. 6) Order 1980.

The Act also includes important changes in transferring fire certification carried out under other legislation, e.g. Offices, Shops and Railway Premises Act and Factories Act to the Fire Precautions Act.

Safety of Sports Ground Act 1975

4.09 This Act contains references to buildings authorities in sections 3(3), 4(7), 5(5), 10(5), and 11. Work carried out which requires structural attention is subject to Building Regulations and Procedures. It should also be noted that the only public enquiry in the UK under this Act took place in 1979 in Dundee, with the Secretary of State's decision being issued in 1980.

Fire Safety and Safety of Places of Sport Act 1987

4.10 As well as introducing a number of new requirements, the above Act contains amendments to the Factories Act, and the Offices, Shops and Railway Premises Act 1963. In addition it changes the term stadium in the Safety of Sports Ground Act 1975 to 'sports ground' which has a wider meaning.

In terms of Scots law, attention is drawn to section 7. Note that the references to building regulations in Section 7(3), (4) and (5) relate to England and Wales only and that Section 48 amends the Civic Government (Scotland) Act 1982, Section 98. This section at the moment gives the Secretary of State powers to make regulations for the safe operation of electrical luminous signs exceeding 650 volts. The reference to a limiting size has been replaced by a more functional description.

Licensing (Scotland) Act 1976

4.11 The Act contains references to building control in Section 23(3). Again, structural alterations and change of use are subject to building regulations and procedures.

* The local authority is usually the regional council. From 1 April 1996 power is vested in the new water and sewerage authorities (three in number for Scotland).

Civic Government (Scotland) Act 1982

4.12 This Act covers a wide range of activities and functions controlled by local authorities. It gives power to make and enforce by-laws. Mention should be made of the powers to license various forms of businesses or functions: e.g. places of public entertainment.

Special attention is drawn to Part VIII, Buildings etc. This covers various requirements as to maintenance and repair of buildings, installation of lighting, fire precautions in common stairs. Of particular interest is Section 88 regarding the installation of pipes through a neighbouring property and the procedure to be followed where consent of the neighbouring owner has been withheld or refused.

Local Government etc. Scotland Act 1994

4.13 The act which changes the face of Scottish local authorities to unitary authorities from 1 April 1994 also amends many pieces of legislation including the definition of local authority in the 1959 Building Act. Water and sewerage services pass to three new regional water and sewerage authorities and may have important implications for designers and builders. At the time of writing many of the new authorities have not finalized the detailed plans for 1 April 1996.

5 General

5.01 The following points may be useful to persons wishing to design and build in Scotland for the first time:

1. Scots law differs from that of the rest of the UK (see Scottish articles in this handbook).
2. Building control is exercised by local authorities.
3. Warrant must be obtained from the local authority before any building (including alterations and extensions) can begin, and it is separate from planning permission. A fee related to the total cost of the job is usually payable in accordance with the scale laid down in the table of fees (Schedule 2 of the Procedure Regulations).
4. Ensure that the latest amendments to the Building Standards Regulations are available as well as a copy of the Regulations themselves, the Procedure Regulations, and the correct forms.
5. Relaxation of the Regulations in respect of enclosed shopping, referred warrants and appeals is the responsibility of the Secretary of State for Scotland.
6. If problems occur, consult the building control officer of the appropriate authority, but remember that although he will normally give advice, he is not there to design or redesign, draw or redraw plans.
7. Check carefully the requirements of the sewerage authority where appropriate.
8. Check carefully whether a class relaxation has been issued in respect of a new building product.

EEC

5.02 Legislation produced by the EEC is already having an effect on Building Regulations. The Construction Products Directive of 12/12/88 lays down requirements for all member countries and is very wide in its scope.

Directive 78/170/EEC covers the performance of heat generators and production of hot water in new industrial buildings and insulation of its distribution in new industrial building.

New Health and Safety directives being prepared will also affect Building Regulations. See Section 7 of Chapter 18: European Community law affecting architects and Chapter 19: Health and safety law affecting architects.

Building Notes

5.03 The Scottish Development Department (now the Scottish Office Environment Department) has issued Building Notes to local authorities giving guidance on Building Regulation matters.

As an example, Building Note 6/77 gave advice regarding a number of cases in respect of building control which had come to its notice. The note dealt with technical problems encountered in the actual installation of certain warm air heaters and with procedural aspects under the Building Acts and Procedures Regulations. The latter is particularly interesting to warrant applicants and have been summarized below:

1. A number of cases have been reported where Building Regulations have been wrongly applied to features of existing buildings. The attention of building control authorities is drawn to the extent to which they can apply Regulations to existing buildings, and the appropriate legal references are given. It would appear that some authorities may have erroneously used the application for warrant by a developer to demand that features of a building, not directly involved with the works to be carried out, and which may because they were built pre-Regulations, be brought up to Regulations standard. The Building (Scotland) Act 1959, as amended by the Building (Scotland) Act 1970, is quite specific in its guidelines with regard to existing buildings. If authorities wish to upgrade buildings to current Regulations' standard, Section 11 of the 1959 Act lays down the procedure and limitations which have to be followed and cannot be used in relation to warrant procedures.
2. Reports of authorities attaching conditions to warrants have come to the Department's notice, as well as the practice of withholding warrants until planning permission had been granted. The Department point out that no conditions may be attached to a warrant other than those specified in the Building Act (e.g. in relation to demolition) and that if a warrant is in accordance with the relevant requirements of the Regulations and made in the approved manner, it must be granted.

16

Statutory Authorities in England and Wales

DR A. R. MOWBRAY*

1 Introduction

1.01 Local government in England and Wales, outside London, was completely reorganized on 1 April 1974, when the Local Government Act 1972 came into force. The pattern of local authorities is now simpler than it was before 1974, but Greater London (reorganized in 1965 by the London Government Act 1963) is administered differently, and there are also less important differences between England and Wales. These three parts of the country should therefore now be considered separately.

1.02 In London, the Local Government Act 1985 abolished the Greater London Council and redistributed its functions between the 32 London boroughs, the City of London and new specialized representative bodies (e.g. the London Fire and Civil Defence Authority). Housing is now the responsibility of the boroughs and the City.

1.03 In *England* outside the London area, the country is divided between six metropolitan areas (West Midlands, Merseyside, Greater Manchester, West Yorkshire, South Yorkshire, and Tyne and Wear) and 38 'ordinary' counties. Between 1974 and 1985 in the metropolitan areas there was a metropolitan county for each area, and a varying number of metropolitan districts, each with a council, within each county. Since 1985 the metropolitan counties have been abolished and their functions redistributed to the metropolitan districts and specialized representative bodies. Outside those areas there are 38 counties, each with a county council and a number of districts (approximately 390 in total) each again with a council. In addition, rural parishes which existed before 1974 have been allowed to continue. Further, some of the pre-1974 district councils have been re-formed with parish council status. As an additional complication, district councils have been allowed to apply for a charter giving themselves the status of a borough, although this is solely a ceremonial matter. Some parishes have been allowed to call themselves 'towns' and have appointed 'town mayors', again with no real legal significance. Currently, the Local Government Commission are reviewing the structures of local government in England and their reports may result in the creation of new unitary authorities which will combine the functions of county and district councils.

1.04 In *Wales* there are no metropolitan areas. There are eight counties, each divided into districts with councils at each level. Also each district is divided into a number of 'communities' which have the functions of the English parishes. From April 1996 all local administration will be undertaken by 21 new unitary authorities.

1.05 Outside London county councils are responsible everywhere for the preparation of local plan schemes (for the regulation and

co-ordination of local plans, which regulate development, in their areas) and are concerned with development control involving (only) the mining and working of minerals (Town and Country Planning Act 1990, Section 1). They are also responsible for fire services, main and district highways, refuse disposal, and a few other functions. Outside the metropolitan areas county councils are also responsible for education and welfare services, which in the metropolitan areas are the responsibility of the district councils. All district councils are responsible for housing, refuse collection, drainage, clean air and public health generally (but *not* sewerage and water supply), development control, parks and open spaces, and building controls, etc. A district council may also (by arrangement with the county council) undertake the maintenance of urban roads (other than trunk roads), bridleways, and footpaths within its district. The parishes (communities in Wales) have very few substantial functions, but may provide and maintain recreation grounds, bus shelters, and roadside seats. Part 1 of the Local Government Act 1988 now states that if local authorities wish to provide certain designated services themselves (notably the collection of refuse) they must first subject the service to tender from private contractors.

1.06 From 1974–1989, the provision and maintenance of sewers and sewerage disposal, together with water supply and distribution and the prevention of river pollution, was the responsibility of special authorities, the ten regional water authorities (nine in England, one in Wales). Under the Water Act 1989 the water industry was privatized and as a consequence the sewerage functions of the former water authorities have passed to successor companies, which are in most instances also responsible for water supply, except in those areas where this was formerly the responsibility of statutory water companies which remain in existence. Water and sewerage undertakers are forbidden from causing river pollution, the prevention of which is the responsibility of a new authority (the National Rivers Authority) which operates under the supervision of the Director General of Water Services and the Secretary of State. The successor companies are constituted under the regime of the Companies Acts and are appointed by the Secretary of State to act as water and/or sewerage undertakers. Customers can make complaints to a specially constituted Customer Services Committee who must investigate the matter and may make representations to the Director General, who in turn may issue an order, or suggest that the Secretary of State do so, requiring appropriate action to be taken by the relevant undertaker (Water Industry Act 1991, Sections 28 and 30).

General characteristics of local authorities

1.07 The essential characteristics of every local authority under this complicated system is that it is governed by a council elected on a wide franchise at four-year intervals. In districts, one-third of the councillors retire on three out of four years every year: but a

---

* This chapter draws heavily on the chapter written for the first edition by Professor J. F. Garner.

non-metropolitan district may resolve that all their members shall retire together. In counties all members retire together every fourth year. Since 1974 there have been no aldermen elected by the councillors.

1.08 Local authorities are legal persons, capable of suing and being sued in the courts, entrusted by Parliament with a range of functions over a precisely limited geographical area. Each local authority is subject to the doctrine of *ultra vires*; i.e. it can perform only those functions conferred on it by Parliament, and only in such a manner as Parliament may have laid down. On the other hand, within the powers defined by Parliament, each local authority is its own master. In the two-tier or three-tier system there is no question of an appeal from the lower rank authorities (the district or the parish) to the higher rank (the county council) or from the parish to the district. If the individual authority has acted within its statutory powers, its decision is final, except in cases precisely laid down by Parliament, where (as in many planning situations) there may be a right of appeal to a minister of the central Government (Chapter 13). If, however, a local authority has overstepped the limits of its legal powers, a private citizen who has been aggrieved in consequence may apply to the courts for an order requiring the errant local authority to keep within its powers. Thus, a ratepayer at Fulham successfully obtained an order against the borough council, requiring the council to stop spending ratepayers' money on the provision of a service for washing clothes for members of the public, when the council had statutory powers to provide a service for washing only the bodies of members of the public (*Attorney General* v *Fulham BC* [1921] 1 Ch 440).

Officers

1.09 All local authorities are alike in that they employ officers and other staff to carry out their instructions, while the elected members assembled in council make decisions as to what is to be done. Officers of the authority – chief executive, solicitor, treasurer, surveyor, architect, planning officer, and many others – play

a large part in the decision-making process: they advise the council on the courses of action open to them, and also on the consequences of taking such actions. When a decision has been taken, it is then the duty of appropriate officers of the council to implement it: to notify persons concerned and to take any executive decisions or other action necessary to give effect to the main decision. It is sometimes said that the officers give advice and take action, while the council decides all matters of policy; although basically true (for statutes almost invariably confer the power to exercise discretion on the authority itself) this does not clarify what happens in practice. 'Policy' is incapable of precise definition, for what is policy to some local authorities and in some circumstances may be regarded as routine administration by other authorities or in different circumstances. Thus, every local authority approves its development plan in the final form. Some local authorities like to settle the details of each renovation grant approved under the Local Government and Housing Act 1989 (paragraph 4.02), though most authorities would be content to leave details of such matters to their officers, trusting them to bring before the council (or a committee) particulars of any difficult case.

Committees

1.10 In practice, all local authorities conduct their affairs by the committee system. Committees, consisting of named councillors, are usually considerably smaller in membership than the council as a whole* and are entrusted with specified functions of the council. Thus, every county council has a planning committee and a finance committee, and most district councils will have a parks committee and a housing committee, although details vary from authority to authority. Since 1974, committees have tended to be

---

* There are no general rules, but a council of, say, 48 members may place about 12 councillors on each of its committees. Recently there has been a tendency to streamline committee organization, leaving more routine matters to the discretion of officers.

LAST SITTING of the OLD COURT of SESSION 11 of JULY 1808

wider in scope, and policy or 'general resources' committees are common. Every matter requiring a council decision within the terms of reference of a particular committee is first brought before the committee. The committee then considers the matter and either recommends a certain decision to the council or may itself make the decision. Whether the committee decides on behalf of the council depends on whether the council has delegated to the committee power to take the decision on its behalf, either in that particular matter, or in matters of that kind or falling within a particular class. Section 101 of the Local Government Act 1972 confers on all local authorities power to arrange for any of its functions (except levying a charge or raising a loan) to be discharged by a committee, a sub-committee, or an officer.

1.11 Proceedings in committee are normally held in public and tend to be informal. Officers attend, and volunteer advice and often take part in the discussion, although any decision is taken on the vote or assent of the councillors present. Council meetings and meetings of specified committees such as the education committee are more formal; the press and members of the public are entitled to be present unless they have been excluded by special resolution of the council passed because of the intention to discuss exempted information, such as facts regarding individual council employees (Local Government (Access to Information) Act 1985), and proceedings are conducted in accordance with the council's standing orders. Officers do not speak at a council meeting unless their advice is expressly requested, and as much business consists of receipt of reports from committees, discussion tends to be confined to more controversial topics. Because of the presence of the press and public, party politics tend to be more obvious at council meetings; often in committee, members from opposing political parties will agree, and members of a single party may disagree with one another. In recent years, however, there has been a tendency for authorities to be more closely organized on party political lines. When this occurs, 'group' meetings may be held preceding the committee meetings. Thus on important matters, decisions at committee meetings tend to be 'rubber stamps' of decisions already taken at the group meeting of the political party in power on the council.

1.12 The law requires that councils must meet at least four times a year. Most councils arrange committee meetings in a cycle, monthly or perhaps every six weeks, so that each committee will normally meet at least once between council meetings. The system whereby committees are given delegated powers (as is now customary) provides for a reasonably expeditious dispatch of business, but there may be long delays where the council meets less often than once a month, and there is no adequate provision for delegation to committees and/or to officers.

Officers' powers

1.13 All discretionary powers are in the first instance conferred on a local authority, but under section 101 of the Local Government Act 1972, every local authority has wide powers to delegate any of its discretionary decisions to any of its officers; a power which is often used, especially in planning. But there must in every instance be a clear delegation before an officer can decide on behalf of his authority. Therefore, when an officer of a council who was asked for information as to the planning position in respect of a particular piece of land carelessly gave the wrong information, saying that planning permission was not required, it was held by the courts that the council were not bound by this statement. It could not be taken as the decision of the council, as the officer had in that case no power to act on their behalf (*Southend-on-Sea Corporation* v *Hodgson (Wickford) Ltd* [1961] 2 All ER 46). Similarly, when a public health inspector served a notice on the owner of property requiring certain work to be undertaken, it was declared that the notice was void and of no effect, because the statute required that the local authority should themselves decide to serve such a notice, and under the then existing law they could not delegate such a duty to one of their officers (*Firth* v *Staines* [1897] 2 QB 70). These decisions are still

Table 16.1 Responsibilities of local authority officers

Subject matter	Officer	Local authority
Planning	Planning officer or surveyor	DC
Building regulations	Building inspector or surveyor	DC
Development in a private street	Surveyor	CC
Surface water sewerage	Engineer	SU
Sewer connections	Engineer	SU
Blocked sewers	Engineer	SU
Housing grants; housing generally	Environmental health officer or (sometimes) surveyor	DC
Height of chimneys or other clean air matters	Environmental health officer	DC
Petroleum licensing; most other licensing	Petroleum inspector (often environmental health officer or surveyor)	CC or DC
Music and dancing licences	Local magistrate's clerk	
Liquor licences	Local magistrate's clerk	

Key: CC, county council; DC, district council; SU, sewerage undertaker

Notes
A company operating under the Water Act 1989, whose functions may be exercised by the district council under an arrangement with the sewerage undertaker.
London In Greater London, in all cases (except for liquor licences) the responsible authority is the London borough council or the Common Council of the City.
Planning In planning the authority given above should be contacted in the first instance, although the county council may ultimately make the decision.
Roads In the counties highway functions are commonly administered by district or divisional surveyors, responsible to the county surveyor but stationed locally often at district council offices. In the case of trunk and special roads (motorways) the highway authority is the Secretary of State for Transport, but the local county surveyor acts as his agent at local level. Maintenance of urban roads may be claimed by the DC.
Under the Local Government (Miscellaneous Provisions) Act 1982, several activities are made subject to licensing (e.g. acupuncture, tattooing, take-away food shops, etc.). These provisions are administered by the district council.

good law in circumstances where powers have not been expressly delegated to the officer concerned (see *Western Fish Products Ltd* v *Penwith DC* (1979) 77 LGR 185). As a consequence of local government reorganization there are many more large authorities than there were before 1974. They are also frequently differently organized. In place of the town or county clerk, the principal officer is often known as the 'Chief Executive', and often he has no departmental responsibilities. He may be assisted by a small management team of chief officers such as the Director of Technical Services, the Director of Welfare Services etc., each having broad responsibilities and a number of departments subordinate to him. The committee structure also may be different from the pre-1974 system, being organized rather on a functional basis than one based upon departments.

1.14 A local authority does not stand outside the common law in respect of acts of negligence by its officers and employees. However, the House of Lords has held that a local authority is not generally liable in negligence to owners/occupiers of buildings for failings in the authority's enforcement of the Building Regulations concerning the defective construction of those buildings (see *Murphy* v *Brentwood District Council* [1990] 2 All ER 908).

1.15 An alternative non-judicial method by which an aggrieved individual may seek redress against a local authority's actions or inaction, is to make a complaint to the Local Ombudsman under the Local Government Act 1974 (as amended). If the Local Ombudsman finds that a complainant has suffered injustice as a consequence of maladministration by the local authority he may publish such a finding and recommend a suitable remedy (which can include financial compensation). The local authority are obliged to have regard to the report, but they cannot be compelled in law to implement the Local Ombudsman's recommendations to alleviate the injustice. In recent years approximately 40% of complaints to the Local Ombudsman have been about housing matters and a further 25% have concerned planning functions. The Commission for Local Administration in England can be contacted directly at 21 Queen Anne's Gate, London SW1H 9BU Tel. 0171 915 3210.

Finding the right officer

1.16 Architects in the course of their professional business are obliged to have dealings with numerous local authority officials. Table 16.1 shows the purposes for which a permission, licence, or certificate may have to be obtained from the local authority, giving the officers initially responsible (see Chapters 13 and 14). First, however, it is essential to ascertain the authority in whose area the site lies.

2 Connections to services – statutory undertakers

2.01 When starting to design a building for a client, any architect is obliged at an early stage to consider the availability of mains services and the rights of his client as landowner regarding the various statutory undertakers: sewer and highway authorities, water, gas, and electricity supply undertakings, and possibly the water undertaker if it is proposed to use a water course as a means of disposing of effluent from the building. The legal provisions regulating these matters are discussed below.

Sewers

2.02 Sewers are conduits (artificial or natural) used for conveying effluent (i.e. waste liquids – clear water, surface water from covered surfaces, land or buildings, foul water, or trade effluent) from two or more buildings not within the same curtilage*. A conduit which takes effluent from one building only or from a number of buildings all within the same curtilage is in law a 'drain'. This distinction is important, as a landowner never has any legal right to let his effluent flow into a drain belonging to another person (even if that other person is a local authority) unless he has acquired such a right by at least 20 years' use or as the result of an agreement with the other person (Chapter 2). The same rule applies to a private sewer; but if the conduit to which he proposes to drain his effluent is a *public* sewer, he will have certain valuable rights to use it. All public sewers are vested in (owned by) the sewerage undertakers, and a sewer is a public sewer if it existed as a sewer (regardless of who constructed it) before 1 October 1937, if it was constructed by a local authority after 1 October 1937 and before 1 April 1974, or by a water authority before 1 November 1989, or by a sewerage undertaker after 1 November 1989 and was not designed to serve *only* property belonging to a local authority (e.g. a council housing estate), or if it has been adopted as a public sewer since 1 October 1937.

Rights to connection

2.03 If there is within any distance a public sewer capable of serving his property, any landowner has by Section 106 of the Water Industry Act 1991 a right to cause his own drains or private sewer to communicate with it and to discharge foul and surface water from his premises to it. Connecting sewers or drains from the premises to the public sewer must be constructed at the expense of the landowner concerned. Sometimes – but not often – the sewerage undertaker may itself construct 'laterals', or connecting drains leading from the main sewer to the boundary of the street to which house drains may be connected.

---

* Curtilage: in non-technical terms, the natural boundaries of a particular building; thus the curtilage of an ordinary dwelling house would include the garage, the garden and its appurtenances, and any outbuildings.

2.04 There are a few exceptions to this general rule:

1. No substance likely to injure the sewer or to interfere with the free flow of its contents, no chemical refuse or steam, or any petroleum spirit or calcium carbide, may be caused to flow into a public sewer (Water Industry Act 1991, Section 111).
2. The general rule does not apply to trade effluents.
3. The general rule does not permit a communication directly with a storm-water overflow sewer (Section 106(2)(c) of the Act).
4. Where separate public sewers are provided for foul and for surface water, foul water may not be discharged into a sewer provided for surface water, and surface water may not, without the consent of the sewerage undertaker, be discharged into a sewer provided for foul water (Section 106(2)(b) of the Act). It is particularly important that an architect should know whether the undertaker's sewerage network is designed on the separate system, as he may in turn have to provide a separate drainage for the building he is designing.

Procedure

2.05 A person wishing to connect his sewer or drain to a public sewer must give the sewerage undertaker written notice of his proposal, and the undertaker may within 21 days of notice refuse to permit him to make the communication if the mode of construction or condition of the drain or sewer is such that the making of the communication would be prejudicial to their sewerage system (Section 106(4) of the Act), but they may not so refuse for any other reason. Further, within 14 days of the proposals so served on the undertaker they may give notice that they intend to make the communication to the public sewer (Section 107 of the Act). The private landowner is then obliged to permit the undertaker to do the work of making the house drains or sewer connect with the public sewer, and he has to bear the sewerage undertaker's reasonable expenses so incurred. This may include a reasonable sum extra on the actual cost by way of establishment expenses. When making the communication, the undertaker (or the private owner if he is allowed to do the work himself) has power as necessary to break open any street (Section 107(6) of the Act).

2.06 Any dispute with the undertaker under these provisions may be settled by way of an appeal to the local magistrates, or in some cases by a reference to arbitration. The landowner has a right to this redress if, for example, he is refused permission to make a communication with a public sewer.

Approval

2.07 The arrangements proposed to be made for the 'satisfactory provision' for drainage of a building must be approved by the district council or London borough council at the time when the building plans are considered under the Building Regulations (Building Act 1984, Section 21 and Chapter 14). Disposal of the effluent may be to a public sewer, or to a cesspool or private septic tank, and in the case of surface water to a highway drain or a watercourse or to the sea. In this instance note that the powers remain with the district council and have not been transferred to the sewerage undertaker.

2.08 It remains to deal with discharges to highway drains, to watercourses, and to the sea, and with the special case of trade effluent. If it is desired to drain to a septic tank or similar receptacle on another person's land, this is a matter for private negotiation for an express easement (Chapter 2) with such other landowner.

2.09 If there is no existing main sewer into which the property could be drained, the owner or occupier (usually with the owners, etc., of other premises) may requisition the sewerage undertaker to provide a public sewer, under Section 98 of the Water Industry Act 1991. They must then satisfy conditions specified by the undertaker the most important of which is likely to be that those requisitioning the sewer shall undertake to meet any 'relevant deficit' of the undertaker in consequence of constructing the sewer. But this section applies only to sewers to be used for domestic purposes.

Highway drains

2.10 A landowner has no legal right to cause his drains (or sewers) to be connected with a highway drain, and this applies equally to surface water drains taking effluent from roads and paved surfaces on a private housing estate. Such drains may, in accordance with the statutory provisions outlined above, be connected with a public sewer, but if it is desired to connect with a drain or sewer provided for the drainage of a highway and vested in the highway authority, the consent of the highway authority must first be obtained: the highway authority will normally be the county council. A public sewer may be used to take surface water from a highway, but that does not affect its status as a public sewer, nor does the fact that house drains may in the past have been connected (probably unlawfully) with a highway drain convert such highway drain into a public sewer (*Rickarby* v *New Forest RDC* [1910] 26 TLR 586). It is only to public sewers that drains or sewers may be connected as of right.

Rivers

2.11 If it is desired to discharge effluent into a watercourse the consent of the National Rivers Authority must be obtained for making of a new or altered discharge of trade or sewage effluent under Section 88 of the Water Resources Act 1991. Consents may be granted subject to conditions. If the applicant objects to the conditions or has his application refused he can appeal to the Secretary of State (Water Resources Act 1991 Schedule 10). If a person causes or knowingly permits the discharge of effluent into a watercourse without the permission of the NRA he commits an offence under Section 85 of the Water Resources Act 1991.

The sea

2.12 A private landowner has at common law no legal right to discharge his sewage or other polluting matter to the sea; indeed, as the Crown originally owned the foreshore between high and low tides, he might not have any legal right to take his drain or sewer as far as the water. However, even if such a right can be acquired, and at the present day the Crown's rights have in many cases been sold or leased to local authorities or private landowners, it seems that the discharge of sewage by means of a pipe into the sea is subject to the same control of the NRA (Water Resources Act 1991; see definition of 'controlled waters' in Section 104 thereof). There must also be no nuisance caused as a consequence, and no breach of a local by-law made by a sea fisheries committee prohibiting the discharge of matter detrimental to sea fish or sea fishing (Sea Fisheries Regulations Act 1966, Section 5). If effluent discharging into the sea does cause a nuisance, any person harmed thereby can take proceedings for an injunction and/or damages, as in *Foster* v *Warblington UDC* [1906] 1 KB 648, where guests at a banquet were poisoned from oysters taken from a bed which had been affected by sewage.

Trade effluents

2.13 In the case of a proposed discharge of 'trade effluent', the special controls of the Water Industry Act 1991, Chapter III apply. 'Trade effluent' is defined in the Act of 1991 as meaning 'any liquid, either with or without particles of matter in suspension therein, which is wholly or in part produced by the course of any trade or industry carried on at trade premises, and, in relation to any trade premises, means any such liquid as aforesaid which is so produced in the course of any trade or industry carried on at those premises, but does not include domestic sewage' (1991 Act, Section 141(1)).

'Trade premises' are defined as 'any premises used or intended to be used for carrying on any trade or industry' (including agriculture,

horticulture, fish farming and scientific research) (Sections 141(1) and 141(2) of the Water Industry Act 1991).

2.14 Where it is intended to discharge trade effluent as defined above into a public sewer, consent has first to be obtained from the sewerage undertaker. This is done by the owner or occupier of the premises serving on the undertaker a 'trade effluent notice'. This must specify (in writing) the nature or composition of the proposed effluent, the maximum quantity to be discharged in any one day, and the highest proposed rate of discharge of the effluent. This notice (for which there is no standard form) is then treated by the undertaker as an application for their consent to the proposed discharge. No effluent may then be discharged for a period of two months (or such less time as may be agreed by the undertaker). A decision, when given by the undertaker, may be a refusal to permit the discharge or a consent thereto, and in the latter case a consent may be given subject to conditions as to a number of matters 'including a payment by the occupier of the trade premises of charges for the reception and disposal of the effluent', as specified in Section 121 of the Water Industry Act 1991. These conditions may be varied (not more frequently than once every two years) by direction given by the sewerage undertaker. The owner or occupier of trade premises has a right of appeal to the Director General of Water Services against a refusal of consent to a discharge, against the conditions imposed in such a consent, or against a direction subsequently given varying the conditions (Water Industry Act 1991, Section 122), and such a direction may now be given varying the conditions relating to any discharge (even one made before the passing of the Act; Water Industry Act 1991, Section 122(3)).

2.15 In practice, however, it is frequently desirable for an industrialist's professional advisers to discuss disposal of trade effluent with the officers of the sewerage undertaker, with a view to an agreement being entered into between the owner of the premises and the undertaker under Section 129 of the Water Industry Act 1991. This will avoid the need to serve a trade effluent notice, and better terms can often be obtained by negotiation than by the more formal procedure of the trade effluent notice. The contents of any such agreement becomes public property, as a copy has to be kept at the sewerage undertaker's offices and made available for inspection and copying by any person (Water Industry Act 1991, Section 196).

Water supply

2.16 The water supply authority will be the local water undertaker*, but where before 1989 supply was made by a statutory water company this may remain in existence. The statutory water companies may have their own private Acts of Parliament regulating their affairs. Readers dealing in practice with a particular water undertaking should ascertain whether there are any local statutory variations.

Rights to connection

2.17 If the owner or occupier of premises within the area served by a water undertaker wishes to have a supply for *domestic purposes*, he must give at least 14 days' notice to the undertaker and lay a supply pipe (i.e. a pipe leading from the 'communication pipe' to his premises) at his own expense; if the supply pipe passes through any property belonging to another owner, his consent must be obtained in the form of an express easement or a licence (Chapter 2). The 'communication pipe' (i.e. that part of the pipe serving the premises which leads from the main to the boundary of the street in which the main is laid or to the stopcock) must then be laid by the undertaker, and they must connect the supply pipe with the communication pipe (Water Industry Act 1991, Section 52), and thereupon provide a supply of water. However, the owner will not be entitled to a supply from a trunk

---

* A company appointed for a designated area of England and Wales by the Secretary of State (Water Industry Act 1991, Section 6).

main if his fittings do not comply with the undertaker's by-laws. The undertaker will also have an excuse for not providing a supply if such failure is due to the carrying out of necessary works' (Water Industry Act 1991, Section 60). Any breaking up of streets must be effected by the undertakers and not by the owner requiring the supply.

2.18 This assumes of course that the water main in the nearest street is within a reasonable distance from the house or other premises to be served. Where the main is not readily available, the owner of the premises may serve a requisition on the undertaker requiring them to extend their mains. (Water Industry Act 1991, Section 41). Where such a notice is served the water undertaker may require the owner to undertake to pay an annual sum not exceeding the amount (if any) by which the water charges payable for the use during that year of that main are exceeded by the annual borrowing costs of a loan of the amount required for the provision of that main. Such payments may be levied for a maximum of 12 years following the provision of the main (1991 Act, Section 42). Provided those conditions have been satisfied, the water undertaker must extend their main within a period of three months (1991 Act, Section 44).

Non-domestic premises

2.19 Owners or occupiers of premises requiring a supply of water for industrial or other (non-domestic) purposes must come to terms for a supply with the undertakers or, failing agreement, according to terms determined by the Director General of Water Services (Water Industry Act 1991, Sections 55 and 56).

Gas supply

2.20 The gas industry was privatized in 1986 and gas is now primarily supplied by a single company, British Gas plc (although other companies are gradually offering to supply consumers using above average amounts of gas).

2.21 If the owner or occupier of premises requires a supply of gas for any purpose (not necessarily domestic), he must serve a notice on British Gas at one of their local offices specifying the premises, and the day on which it is desired the service shall begin – and a reasonable time must be given (Gas Act 1986, Section 10). The owner or occupier has to pay the cost of any pipe that may be laid upon the property of the owner or in the possession of the occupier, and for so much of any pipe as may be laid for a greater distribution distance than 30 ft (9.144 m*) from any of the company's pipes. The company must comply with such a request, but only if the premises are within 25 yd (22.680 m) of any of their mains not being a main used for a separate supply for industrial purposes or for conveying gas in bulk.

2.22 Once premises have been so connected to a gas main, the company must give a supply of gas (on the usual charges), unless the failure was due to circumstances not within their control. The company is not obliged to give a supply of gas for any purpose other than lighting or domestic use in any case where the capacity of the main is insufficient for the purpose, unless a special agreement has been entered into (Gas Act 1986, Section 10(7)).

Electricity supply

2.23 The Electricity Act 1989 provided for the privatizing of the generation and supply of electricity. The Secretary of State is authorized to license persons to generate, transmit and supply electricity in designated areas (1989 Act, Section 6).

2.24 Under Section 16 of the 1989 Act, the licensed public electricity supplier for an area is under a duty to give a supply to premises where requested by the owner or occupier (who must

serve a notice specifying the premises, the date supply should commence, the maximum power which may be required and the minimum period for which the supply is required). Where such a request necessitates the provision of electrical lines or plant by the public electricity supplier they may require any expenses reasonably incurred in providing the supply to be paid by the consumer requesting the supply (1989 Act, Section 19). Any dispute arising out of the above obligations may be referred by either the consumer or supplier to the Director General of Electricity Supply for resolution (1989 Act, Section 23).

Telephones

2.25 The Telecommunications Act 1984 provided for the privatization of British Telecommunications. Today consumers can obtain telecommunication services from British Telecommunications plc or other licensed operators (e.g. Mercury Communications) (Telecommunications Act 1984, Section 7). The terms for the provision of telecommunications services depends upon (1) the licence conditions regulating the particular telecommunications company approved by the Secretary of State for Trade and Industry under the Telecommunications Act 1984 and (2) the standard contracts offered by the specific company supplying the service. For example, condition 1 of the licence issued to British Telecommunications plc obliges the company 'to provide every person who requests the provision of such services at any time in the Licensed Area (a) voice telephony services; and (b) other telecommunications services consisting in the conveyance of Messages.' The precise details of British Telecommunications' standard terms for domestic consumers are found in their 'Telephone Service Agreement' (for the provision of a phone line) and their 'Hire Agreement' (for equipment rental) effective from February 1994.

Construction of mains

2.26 All the utility undertakings have inherent powers to negotiate on terms with private landowners for the grant of easements or 'wayleaves' (Chapter 2) to enable them to place mains, cables, wires, apparatus, and so on over or under privately owned land. They also have powers to break open public streets for the purpose of constructing mains. Water and sewerage undertakers (Water Industry Act 1991, Schedule 6), British Gas plc (Gas Act 1986, Schedule 3), electricity suppliers (Electricity Act 1989, Schedule 16) and licensed telecommunications operators (Telecommunications Act 1984, Schedule 2) all have statutory powers enabling them to place such mains and apparatus in private land, without the consent of the landowner or occupier concerned, on payment of proper compensation. Private persons have no such compulsory rights, although rights may be compulsorily acquired for an oil or other pipeline under the Pipelines Act 1962.

2.27 All the utility undertakers can also be authorized, without the consent of the landowner, to place their mains, apparatus, etc., on 'controlled land' (land forming part of a street or highway maintainable or prospectively maintainable at public expense – paragraphs 3.01 ff) or in land between the boundary of such a highway and any improvement line prescribed for the street (New Roads and Street Works Act 1991, Part III).

3 Private streets

3.01 It is not within the scope of this study to describe the whole law governing the making up of a private street by county councils at the expense of the frontagers to such a street, but the special rules that regulate the construction of a building in a 'private street' can be outlined.

Definition

3.02 A private street may or may not be a highway (i.e. any way, footpath, bridlepath, or carriageway over which members of the public have rights to pass and repass), but the word 'private'

---

* The Act says 30 ft exactly. All conversions in this article are therefore to the nearest millimetre.

means, not that it is necessarily closed to the public (although it may be), but that the street has not been adopted by a highway authority, and therefore it is not maintainable by them on behalf of the public. It must also be a 'street', an expresion which has not been precisely defined, but which includes a cul-de-sac, lane, or passage (Highways Act 1980, Section 331(1)). This does not mean, however, that every country road is a street; in a leading case, it was said by Pollock, Master of the Rolls, that

> 'it appears to me that what one has to find before one can determine that the highway in question is a street, is that the highway has become a street in the ordinary acceptation of that word, because by reason of the number of houses, their continuity and their proximity to one another, what would be a road or highway has been converted into a street' (*Attorney General v Laird* [1925] 1 Ch 318 at p. 329).

Advance payments code

3.03 As a general principle, before a new building may be erected in a new street as explained above, the developer must either pay to the local authority or secure to their satisfaction (by means of a bond or mortgage, etc.) a sum equivalent to the estimated cost, apportioned to the extent of the frontage of the proposed building to the private street, of carrying out street works to such an extent that the street would be adopted by the highway authority (the advance payments code – Highways Act 1980 Section 221). 'Street works' means sewering, levelling, paving, metalling, flagging, channelling, making good, and lighting. The standards required are not specified in the legislation, but clearly they must not be unreasonably stringent. In general, the standard prevailing for similar streets in the authority's district is required.

Section 38 of Highways Act 1980

3.04 However, the necessity to pay or give security in advance of the building work being started can be avoided if an agreement has been entered into with the local authority under Section 38 of the Highways Act 1980, pursuant to an exception from the general principle contained in Section 221(4)(a) of the Act.

3.05 Under Section 38, the local authority may enter into an agreement with the developer of land on either side or both sides of a private street; the authority can agree to adopt the street as a highway maintainable at public expense when all the street works have been carried out to their satisfaction, and the developer agrees to carry them out within a stated time. If the works are not so carried out, the local authority can still use their statutory powers to carry out the works (or to complete them), at the expense of the frontagers; it is therefore customary for the developer to enter into a bond for his performance with a bank or an insurance company.

3.06 Such an agreement takes the street, or the part of the street to which the agreement relates, outside the operation of the above general principle. The developer can then sell building plots or completed houses 'free of road charges' to purchasers. Though the street may not have been made up at the time of purchase, the purchaser is protected, as the developer has agreed to make up the street; if he fails to carry out his promise, the local authority will be able to sue on the bond and recover sufficient* to pay for street works expenses without having to charge them to the frontagers. If the authority should proceed against the frontagers, they in turn normally have a remedy against the developer and on the bond, but this may depend on the terms of their purchase.

3.07 The architect is not necessarily professionally concerned in such matters, but it is suggested that it is his duty to be aware of the potential expense to his client of building in an unmade private street, and he should advise his client to consult his solicitor in any difficult case, or where the exact legal position is not clear.

---

* Provided the bond was for a sufficient amount; inflation may cause problems here.

4 Grants

4.01 Below are considered circumstances in which a building owner is able to obtain a grant from the local authority (in this case, the district council) for some alteration or extension of his dwelling. All statutory provisions considered here concern dwelling-houses (or flats and so on), but it may be possible in development areas and enterprise zones (Local Government, Planning and Land Act 1980) to obtain grants for industrial development.

Grants under the Local Government and Housing Act 1989

4.02 There are now four basic kinds of grant under Part VIII of the Act: a *renovation grant* for the improvement or repair of a dwelling, a *common parts grant* for the improvement or repair of the common parts of a building, a *disabled facilities grant* for the provision of amenities for disabled persons, a *house in multiple occupation grant* for the improvement or repair of a house in such occupation (or for the conversion of a building into a house in multiple occupation).

Renovation grants

4.03 These grants can take the form of either mandatory or discretionary grants payable by the local authority (the district council). Owner-occupiers can claim a mandatory grant to bring their property up to the standard of fitness for human habitation, where the local authority considers that renovation is the most suitable course of action (as opposed to, for example, demolition). Landlords can only claim a mandatory grant where they have been served with a repairs notice under the Housing Act 1985 Section 189 (requiring them to make the property fit for human habitation). A dwelling house is unfit for human habitation if it fails to comply with one or more of the following attributes and is thereby not reasonably fit for occupation:

1. it is structurally stable;
2. it is free from serious disrepair;
3. it is free from dampness prejudicial to the health of the occupants (if any);
4. it has adequate provision for lighting, heating and ventilation;
5. it has an adequate piped supply of wholesome water;
6. there are satisfactory facilities in the dwelling-house for the preparation and cooking of food, including a sink with a satisfactory supply of hot and cold water;
7. it has a suitably located water-closet for the exclusive use of the occupants (if any);
8. it has, for the exclusive use of the occupants (if any), a suitably located fixed bath or shower and wash-basin each of which is provided with a satisfactory supply of hot and cold water; and
9. it has an effective system for drainage of foul and waste water.

A 1994 report stated that one home in 13 across Britain is unfit for human habitation ('Papering Over the Cracks', National Housing Forum).

4.04 Discretionary grants are available under Section 115 for the following purposes:

1. to put the dwelling in a state of reasonable repair (it is for the local authority to decide what work is appropriate having regard to, *inter alia*, the age, character and locality of the building);
2. to provide the dwelling by the conversion of a house or other building (Department of the Environment Circular 12/90 encourages local authorities to consider sympathetically proposals to convert unused accommodation above shops or offices);
3. to provide adequate thermal insulation (in determining what forms of insulation are adequate, local authorities may have regard to the Building Regulations and/or the British Standard Code of Practice for Energy Efficient Refurbishment of Housing);
4. to provide adequate facilities for space heating (such works may be either of a minor form, e.g. the installation of a single

room heater, or major, e.g. the installation of a complete central heating system);

5. to provide satisfactory internal arrangements (e.g. the replacement of an unreasonably steep staircase);
6. to ensure that the dwelling complies with particular standards laid down by the Secretary of State (e.g. regarding the 'action level' of radon gas to be found in a dwelling);

4.05 Applications for renovation grants can be made by property owners (i.e. a person owning the fee simple or a term of years with not less than five years unexpired at the time of the application) or tenants (note that the tenant must be under a legal obligation to undertake the relevant works). Applicants must complete a prescribed form available from local authorities.

Amount

4.06 Renovation grants are means tested with the aim of targeting public monies towards those eligible applicants who cannot afford to undertake appropriate works solely through the expenditure of their own resources. The exact amount of a grant will depend upon the estimated expense of the works and the resources of the applicant. The authority determine the estimated expenses by having regard to, *inter alia*, the works that they consider necessary to achieve the purpose of the grant and the appropriate costs involved in those works (normally the applicant will have to submit at least two estimates for the relevant works). Detailed statutory criteria are laid down in Regulations (S.I. 1991 No. 897) for the calculation of the financial resources of applicants (note that different formulas are used for owner-occupiers/tenants and landlords).

4.07 Standard conditions are always imposed on the award of grants. These include the requirement that work is completed within 12 months of the award of the grant and the repayment of grant in the event of sale of the property within a specified period of time (e.g. owner-occupiers are liable to repay the full grant if they sell the property within three years of completion of the works).

4.08 Payment of the grant can be by means of instalments during the progress of the works, provided the local authority are satisfied with the standard of the work (under Section 117, a maximum of 90% of the grant may be paid before completion of the works). Alternatively, the whole grant may be paid after completion of the works. In 1992, local authorities awarded 34 928 mandatory renovation grants.

Common parts grants

4.09 These grants are normally discretionary and applications can be made by landlords or tenants. At least 75% of the flats in the relevant building must be occupied by 'occupying tenants' (e.g. persons having a tenancy of at least five years, or a protected statutory assured or secure tenancy) at the time of application for a grant. Grants are available for repairs and works of improvement to the common parts of eligible buildings. Section 138 defines common parts as including the structure and interior of the building and common facilities provided for occupiers (e.g. lifts). Where a local authority decides to award such a grant it will be subject to a means test analogous to that used for renovation grants.

Disabled facilities grant

4.10 The purposes of this grant are to enable disabled persons to enjoy similar housing conditions to those who are not disabled, and to promote the Government's care in the community programme. Disabled persons are defined as encompassing the blind, deaf, dumb, those suffering from a mental disorder and others who are substantially and permanently handicapped by illness, injury or congenital deformity. Two preconditions for this form of grant are (1) that the works are necessary and appropriate to meet the needs of the disabled applicant and (2) that it is reasonable and practicable to carry out the relevant works having regard to the age and condition of the dwelling (Section 114). In determining if

condition (1) is satisfied in a particular case the local housing authority must consult with the relevant welfare authority (in non-metropolitan areas this will be the county council).

4.11 If one, or more, of the following purposes is satisfied by the grant application, the local authority must make a mandatory award. To:

1. facilitate access to the disabled occupant's dwelling;
2. facilitate the disabled person's access to a room used as the principal family room of the dwelling;
3. facilitate the disabled person's access to a room used for sleeping;
4. facilitate access to toilet and bathroom facilities;
5. facilitate the preparation and cooking of food by the applicant;
6. provide a heating system needed by the applicant;
7. provide access to power, heat or light for the applicant;
8. provide access and movement for the disabled occupant around the dwelling in order to enable him/her to care for another resident.

Mandatory grants will be tailored to the precise needs of the particular applicant (e.g. what special bathroom facilities does applicant X require?). Grants are means tested.

House in multiple occupation (HMO) grant

4.12 HMO grants may be sought by landlords for works to make such a building fit for human habitation or fit for the number of occupants. A HMO is defined as a house or flat occupied by a number of persons who do not form a single household. HMO grants are mandatory where the landlord has been served with a notice under Sections 189, 190 or 352 of the Housing Act 1985. Otherwise, the local authority has a discretion whether to make a payment. HMO grants are subject to the same means test regime as renovation grants.

Agriculture

4.13 Under the Hill Farming and Livestock Rearing Acts 1946 and 1959, a grant may be obtained from the Minister of Agriculture, Fisheries and Food towards the cost of improving a dwelling as part of a scheme prepared with 'a view to the rehabilitation of livestock rearing land'.

Conversion of closets

4.14 A grant not exceeding half the cost may be claimed towards the expenditure incurred by the owners of a dwelling in converting an earth or pail closet to a WC, either pursuant to a notice served by the authority, or where it is proposed to undertake the work voluntarily. In the latter case the grant is payable at the local authority's discretion (Building Act 1984, Section 66).

Clean air

4.15 Where a private dwelling (an expression which includes part of a house) is situated within a smoke control area, a grant may be claimed from the local authority amounting to 70% of the expenditure reasonably incurred in adapting any fireplace or fireplaces in the dwelling to enable them to burn only 'authorized fuels' such as gas, electricity, coke, or specially prepared solid fuels (Clean Air Act 1993, Schedule 2). A similar grant may be obtainable for certain religious buildings (ibid, Section 26).

Historic buildings

4.16 In the case of a building of historic or architectural interest, whether or not it is 'listed' as such (under Section 1 of the Planning (Listed Buildings and Conservation Areas) Act 1990), a grant towards the cost of repair or maintenance may be obtained from the local authority under Section 57 of the 1990 Act, but such grants are entirely discretionary and no amounts are specified in the legislation. Grants and loans are available from the Historic

Buildings and Monuments Commission for England (commonly known as English Heritage) for the maintenance and repair of buildings of outstanding historical or architectural interest. The power to make such payments is found in Section 3A of the Historic Buildings and Ancient Monuments Act 1953. Normally, the Commission only make payments for the maintenance and repair (excluding routine work) of outstanding Grade I or II buildings. The Commission do not normally make payments towards repair schemes costing less than £10 000. Where grants are given they are generally at the rate of 40% of approved expenditure. A similar scheme is administered in Wales by the Secretary of State for the Principality.

Airport noise

4.17 Under the Civil Aviation Act 1982, Section 79, a grant may be obtained from the manager of the aerodrome (a subsidiary company of BAA plc) for a building 'near' an aerodrome towards the cost of insulating it, or any part of it, against noise attributable to the use of the aerodrome. The details of such grants are specified in schemes approved by the Secretary of State for Transport, and further particulars are obtainable from the Secretary of State or BAA plc (130 Wilton Road, London SW1V 1LQ)*.

Water supply

4.18 The local authority has a discretionary power to make a grant towards all or any part of the expenses incurred in the provision of a separate service pipe for the supply of water for any house which has a piped supply from a main, but which does not have a separate service pipe (Housing Act 1985, Section 532).

Home insulation

4.19 Under Section 131 of the Local Government and Housing Act 1989, the local housing authority has a discretion to make grants towards small scale work on properties. Such work includes: loft insulation, insulation of tanks and pipes, and draught proofing. Owner-occupiers and tenants may apply for such grants provided each application is for less than £1 000. Projects necessitating larger sums must be brought under the renovation grant scheme. Local authorities may pay up to 100% of the reasonable costs of the works (or provide suitable materials for applicants wishing to undertake the work themselves).

5 Housing associations and societies

5.01 A housing association may be formed on a charitable basis for provision of houses for those in need, or for special groups of persons, such as elderly or handicapped, in a specified area. Such an association may also be constituted by an industrial firm for housing its employees, or by a group of persons proposing to build its own homes by voluntary (or part voluntary) and co-operative labour. Frequently such associations are strictly housing societies[†] having acquired corporate personality by registration with the Registrar of Friendly Societies. However, a housing association (which may be incorporated as a company under the Companies Acts, or by other means) which complies with the provisions of the Housing Acts (see definition in Section 1 of the Housing Associations Act 1985) and, in particular, does not trade for profit, is entitled to be considered for certain benefits under the Housing Acts. Tenants of a housing association who have occupied their homes for at least five years will have a right to purchase the dwelling under Part V of the Housing Act 1985.

Benefits

5.02 First, the association may be able to obtain 'assistance' from the local housing authority in whose area they propose to build. This may mean making arrangements so that the association can improve existing council-owned houses, or acquisition of land by the local authority, which can then be sold or leased to the association for building houses; or, with the consent of the Secretary of State for the Environment, the authority may make grants or loans on mortgage (at favourable rates of interest – usually 0.25% above the ruling rate charged to local authorities by the Public Works Loan Board) to the association to enable them to build houses. They may be able to obtain a grant from the Housing Corporation (or in Wales a separate organization called Housing for Wales, Part II of the Housing Act 1988) towards the expenses of forming and running the association (Housing Act 1988, Section 50). Registered housing associations may also be able to obtain grants from the Secretary of State where the associations' activities have incurred a liability for income or corporation tax (Housing Act 1988, Section 54).

5.03 When the local authority has agreed to make arrangements of one of these kinds, houses provided as a result will attract annual subsidies from the central Government; these are payable to the local authority in the first instance, but the authority must pass on an equivalent amount to the housing association.

Housing Corporation loans

5.04 These provisions depend on the goodwill of the local authority; a housing association cannot insist on being given assistance. As an alternative, an association may be able to get help by ways of loans for obtaining land and general advice from the Housing Corporation, a public body set up under the Housing Act 1964.

5.05 A loan of money to an association from the Housing Corporation has an additional advantage in that the mortgage given by the association to secure such a loan may be deferred to a mortgage granted by a building society, thereby enabling the association to obtain better terms from the building society (Housing Associations Act 1985, Section 63). However, houses provided by an association with the co-operation in one form or another of the Housing Corporation do not attract government subsidies.

Setting up a housing association

5.06 In practice people proposing to form a housing society would be well advised to obtain advice from the Housing Corporation (Maple House, 149 Tottenham Court Rd, London W1P 0BN), and those proposing to set up an association should get in touch with the National Federation of Housing Associations (175 Gray's Inn Road, London WC1X 8UP).

6 Special premises

6.01 If an architect is designing any kind of building, he must take into account the controls exercised under town and country planning legislation (Chapter 13) and under the Building Regulations (Chapter 14); and he must consider the question of sewerage and mains services and the other matters discussed in this chapter. But if his building is of a specialized kind, or is to be used for some specialized purpose, additional controls may have to be considered; the more usual types of special control are outlined below.

Factories

6.02 The Factories Act 1961 imposes an *a posteriori* control over certain constructional matters in a factory (Factories Act 1961, Section 175, as amended by S.I. 1983/978); there is no special control over plans (other than normal controls of the planning legislation and the Building Regulations), but if the requirements

---

* The only aerodromes to which this provision applies at present are Heathrow and Gatwick (S.I. 1989/247 and S.I. 1989/248).
† The term 'housing association' is the wider one including a housing society which is a special kind of housing association.

of the Act are not met in a particular factory, the occupier or (in a tenement factory) the owner will be liable to be prosecuted for an offence.* Many of these requirements relate to the use and fencing of machinery, keeping walls and floors clean, and so on, and as such they are not of direct concern to the architect.

6.03 A fire certificate[†] will have to be obtained if more than 20 persons are employed or more than 10 persons are employed above (or below) the ground floor (Fire Precautions (Factories, Offices, Shops and Railway Premises) Order 1989, S.I. 1989/76). If a certificate is not required, certain less stringent fire precautions must be observed, including a general duty to provide adequate means of escape in cases of fire (Section 9A of the Fire Precautions Act 1971).

6.04 The effluent from a factory's sewers or drains may well be 'trade effluent' and will then be subject to the special control of the Water Industry Act 1991, Chapter III.

6.05 Under the Clean Air Act 1993 factories are subject to several constructional controls operating quite independently of the Building Regulations, but administered by the same local authorities (district councils). Thus any furnace installed in a building which will be used to burn pulverized fuel, or to burn any other solid matter at a rate of 45.4 kg per hour or more, or any liquid or gaseous matter at a rate of 366.4 kW or more, must be provided with plant for arresting emissions of grit and dust which has been approved by the local authority or has been installed with plans and specifications submitted to and approved by the local authority (Clean Air Act 1993, Section 6). Limits are set by regulations for the rates of emission of grit and dust, and there are certain exemptions from the provisions of Section 5 (see the Clean Air (Emissions of Grit and Dust from Furnaces) Regulations 1971)[‡]. In addition, a furnace of a type to which the section applies (see 1993 Act, Section 14), may not be used in a building unless the height of the chimney serving the furnace has been approved by the local authority (1993 Act, Section 15).

Public houses and restaurants

6.06 A public house or other premises used for the sale of intoxicating liquor either on or off the premises must be licensed by the local magistrates under the Licensing Act 1953. A new 'on-licence' may not be granted unless the premises are in the opinion of the magistrates 'structurally' adapted to the class of licence required (Licensing Act 1964, Section 4(2)). The magistrates themselves are the final judges of what is or is not structurally adapted. In the case of a licence for a restaurant or guest house or the like, an application may be refused by the magistrates on the grounds that the premises are not 'suitable or convenient' for the use contemplated (ibid, Section 98). A restaurant licence may be granted only for premises structurally adapted and bona fide used or intended to be used for the provision of 'the customary main meal for the accommodation of persons frequenting the premises' (ibid, Section 94). Other alterations to licensed premises, e.g. where there will be increased facilities for drinking, must be the subject of a formal consent obtained from the magistrates (ibid, Section 20).

6.07 These controls are operated at the discretion of the magistrates. In practice they will normally not approve an application until they have received a report on the premises (or the proposed premises) from suitably qualified persons, such as an officer of the local firebrigade, an environmental health officer, and often a senior police officer. But such requirements are at their discretion, and details vary among different benches.

6.08 Under Section 20 of the Local Government (Miscellaneous Provisions) Act 1976, as amended by Section 4 of the Disabled

Persons Act 1981, the local authority may by notice require the owner or occupier of any premises used for public entertainment or exhibitions or as a betting office to provide and maintain in suitable positions a specified reasonable number of sanitary appliances for the use of persons frequenting the premises. When complying with such a notice, provision must be made, as far as is practicable and reasonable in the circumstances, for the needs of disabled people (Chronically Sick and Disabled Persons Act 1970, Section 6). If a 'refreshment house' is to be kept open late at night, a special licence will be required from the district council under the Refreshment Houses Acts 1860 to 1967.

Music and dancing

6.09 If a public entertainment is provided at any place there must be a licence issued by the local district council. 'Place' is not defined in the Act but it does not apply to music in the course of religious worship or to any entertainment provided at a pleasure fair or which takes place wholly or mainly in the open air. Public entertainment for this purpose includes 'public dancing or music or any other public entertaining of a like kind'. This was introduced by the Local Government (Miscellaneous Provisions) Act 1982; formerly music and dancing licences were issued by the magistrates.

Hotels

6.10 A fire certificate under the Fire Precautions Act 1971 is required for hotels (see S.I. 1972/236 and 238). An application for a certificate must be made to the fire authority in respect of any new or existing hotel, and this application must be made on the prescribed form (copies of which will be obtainable from the fire authority, i.e. the county council). The authority may ask for plans of the building in support of the application, and they will carry out an inspection. They may then require steps to be taken as to the provision and availability of means of escape in case of fire and as to the means for fighting fire and giving warning in case of fire. If and when they are satisfied as to these matters, a fire certificate will be issued, which may itself impose requirements as to these and related matters. A right of appeal to the local magistrates lies against requirements so imposed by the fire authority. It is a criminal offence under the Act to put premises to a 'designated use' (this includes a hotel) unless there is a valid fire certificate in force or an application is pending, and it is similarly an offence to fail to comply with any requirement imposed by a certificate.

Hotels will, of course, also have to comply with the legal provisions about intoxicating liquor (paragraph 6.06), and possibly in relation to music and dancing (paragraph 6.09).

Petroleum

6.11 Any premises used for keeping petroleum spirit must be licensed by the county council; otherwise the occupier is guilty of an offence (Petroleum Consolidation Act 1928, Section 1). The only exception is when the spirit is kept in separate vessels containing not more than 1 pint (0.57 litre), with the total quantity not exceeding 3 gals (13.64 litres). Detailed conditions are usually imposed when such a licence is granted, and these normally follow the model conditions recommended by the Home Office. Petroleum licences are usually renewable each year at a fee (ibid, Section 2).

Theatres and cinemas

6.12 Theatres are subject to control under the Theatres Act 1968. No premises may be used for the public performance of a play except in accordance with the terms of a licence granted by the local authority,* and in granting such a licence, conditions may

---

* Sometimes by the district council, but more frequently (according to the section under which the proceedings are brought) by HM Inspector of Factories, who is now subject to the supervision of the Health and Safety Executive.
[†] See further under 'Hotels', paragraph 6.10.
[‡] S.I. 1971/162.

* Theatres Act 1968, Section 12 and Schedule 1. The local authorities responsible for administering these provisions are the county councils and in London the city/borough councils (see Section 18).

be imposed as to structure, exits, safety curtains, and so on, but not so as to impose any censorship on the plays given in the theatre.

6.13 Similarly, showing cinematograph films at an exhibition of moving pictures (Cinemas Act 1985, Section 21) must be licensed by the local authority, and structural matters will normally be provided for in the licence (Cinemas Act 1985, Section 1). The local authority is the district council.

Shops and offices

6.14 Shops, offices, and railway premises where persons other than close relatives of the employer (1963 Act, Sections 1 and 2) are employed to work are subject to control by the district council, under the Offices, Shops and Railway Premises Act 1963, provided the time worked at the premises exceeds 21 hours a week (ibid, Section 3). This Act provides for such matters as cleanliness, temperature within rooms, ventilation, lighting, and the provision of WCs (if necessary for both sexes), washing accommodation, and so on. The standards specified are detailed, and the Act and regulations made thereunder should be referred to by architects designing such a building. See the Workplace (Health, Safety and Welfare) Regulations 1992 S.I. 1992/3004. A fire certificate or special fire precautions are required for shops, offices, railway premises, and factories (paragraph 6.03).

Food premises

6.15 In addition, if any part of the premises is used for a business involving food, the more stringent provisions of the Food Safety (General Food Hygiene) Regulations 1995 S.I. 1995/1763 made under the Food Safety Act 1990 must be observed. Premises used as a slaughterhouse or a knacker's yard for the slaughter of animals need to be licensed under the Slaughterhouses Act 1974.

Miscellaneous

6.16 Licences from the district council are also required for the storage or manufacture of rag flock (Rag Flock and Other Filling Materials Act 1951), for the use of premises as a shop for the sale of pet animals (Pet Animals Act 1951), for storage or sale of scrap metal (Scrap Metal Dealers Act 1964), for boarding cats and dogs (Animal Boarding Establishments Act 1963) or for guard dog kennels (Guard Dogs Act 1975), and for keeping a riding establishment (Riding Establishment Acts 1964 and 1970). Nursing homes must now be registered by the Secretary of State (Registered Homes Act 1984, Part II). In all these cases the suitability or otherwise of the premises for the particular purpose may be an issue in the grant or refusal of the licence. Caravan sites used for human habitation also need a licence in addition to planning permission (Caravan Sites and Control of Development Act 1960, Part 1), and detailed conditions as to hygiene and sanitary requirements are customarily imposed. In many districts it will also be necessary to obtain a licence from the council if premises are to be used as a sex shop or for the practice of tattooing or acupuncture or electrolysis or ear-piercing (Local Government (Miscellaneous Provisions) Act 1982). Closing orders may be made restricting the hours for the opening of take-away food shops and late night refreshment houses (1982 Act, Sections 4 and 7).

17

Statutory Authorities in Scotland

ANGUS STEWART QC

1 Introduction: Local government in Scotland

1.01 Local government in Scotland was last radically reorganized by the Local Government (Scotland) Act 1973. Mainland Scotland has a two-tier administrative structure with 9 regions making up the top tier and 53 districts on the lower tier. The Western Isles, Orkney, and Shetland each have all-purpose islands councils exercising all functions which, on the mainland, are allocated between regional and district councils. The Act also provides for the creation, within each district and islands area, of community councils. Their role is mainly representative, and they have no statutory functions in the administration of local government. In terms of the Local Government etc. (Scotland) Act 1994 local government structure will be reorganized again with effect from April 1996. The two-tier structure will be abolished and a new single tier structure instituted.

1.02 All councils – regional, district, and islands – are directly elected. Members of all councils hold office for a four-year term. Elections are staggered so that district councillors are voted in mid-way through the regional term of office.

1.03 As in England local authorities are separate legal persons which perform certain functions laid down by statute, and the doctrine of ultra vires also applies in Scotland (Chapter 16, para 1.08) so that no authority may act outwith its statutory powers.

Officials and committees

1.04 Again, as in England, local authorities appoint officials and staff to enable them to carry out their statutory functions. The 1973 Act requires a regional authority to appoint a director of education, a director of social work and certain other officers. Otherwise it allows authorities a wide discretion in the matter of their internal organization. But in practice all authorities on the same level tend to be organized on broadly similar patterns of departmental responsibility. Each department comes under the jurisdiction of the appropriate committee of the authority. The top official, responsible for co-ordinating the various branches of an authority's activity, is generally styled 'Chief Executive'. 'Director of Finance' is the official in charge of overall financial management. There may be a Director of Administration or Director of Legal Services to supervise internal administration and act as legal adviser to the council in place of the old-style 'town clerk' or 'county clerk'. At district level, from the architect's point of view, the key official will be called something like 'Director of Planning and Building Control', the exact designation of the official and his department being a matter of choice for individual authorities. Certain officials, such as the assessor/council tax registration officer and electoral registration officer, have specific statutory duties which they must perform regardless of any instructions from the authority.

Committees

1.05 Much of the work of the authority is, as in England, delegated to various committees. The implementation of policy is left to the appropriate service committee, such as the planning committee, the highways committee, and the education committee, which have delegated powers in the areas of their responsibility. In addition to standing committees such as these, the authority may also set up special committees from time to time to deal with particular problems as they arise.

1.06 In general all committees are composed of council members only. Officials are present at committee meetings to give advice when required, but without the right to vote.

Functions of local authorities

1.07 The major functions are allocated by statute between regional and district authorities as follows:

Regional	District
Structure plans	Local plans
Highways	Housing (including improvement grants)
Transport, harbours, etc.	Planning permission
Water	Building control
Sewerage	Listed building consent and tree preservation
Valuation	Designation of conservation
Council tax	areas
Police	Improvement grants
Fire	Licensing
Social work	Environmental health
Education	Libraries, museums and galleries
	Recreation and leisure

Lawyers going the Circuit

There are certain exceptions to this scheme. The Borders and Lothian regions combine to form joint fire and police authorities. In the Borders, Highland, and Dumfries and Galloway areas, the regional council is responsible for planning and building control. The same regions are also responsible for all library services in their area. Certain water authorities have jurisdiction over areas which fall within the boundaries of adjoining regions. As has already been mentioned, islands councils exercise *all* local authority functions within their area. Certain areas have been designated as enterprise zones in terms of the Local Government Planning and Land Act 1980.

2 Connection to services

2.01 The 1973 Act is primarily concerned with the structure of local government and does not re-enact or spell out in detail the powers and functions which have been transferred from the old to the new authorities. The main local authority functions for present purposes are to be found in the Building (Scotland) Acts 1959–70, the Sewerage (Scotland) Act 1968, the Town and Country Planning (Scotland) Acts 1972–77. The Water (Scotland) Act 1980, the Civic Government (Scotland) Act 1982 and the Roads (Scotland) Act 1984. Under the Act of 1982 the Sheriff can authorize connections to services through other parts of a building in multiple ownership.

Sewers

2.02 The 1973 Act makes sewerage the responsibility of the regional authorities. The Sewerage (Scotland) Act 1968 details the powers and functions of those authorities in this area. The Act consolidates and simplifies all previous legislation, and introduces a statutory definition of 'drains' and 'sewers' which is the same as that used in England (Chapter 16, paragraph 2.02).

2.03 The Act provides that all public sewers will continue to be vested in local authorities, as will various new sewers. Junctions to public sewers are also vested in local authorities. Thus if a private drain is joined to a sewer, it will be the local authority's responsibility to maintain the junction.

2.04 Sewerage authorities are obliged to provide public sewers as may be necessary for draining their area of domestic sewage, surface water, and trade effluent. The authority has to take public sewers to such a point as will enable owners of premises to connect their drains at reasonable cost. This is subject to the proviso that the authority need itself do nothing which is not practicable at a reasonable cost. Nevertheless, the responsibility for providing sewers is clearly that of the local authority, while the responsibility for installing drains in individual premises is that of the proprietor.

2.05 Local authorities have powers to construct, close, or alter sewers or sewage treatment works. Where they are not under an obligation to provide public sewers (i.e. where they cannot do so at reasonable cost), they may enter into an agreement on construction and taking over of sewers and treatment with any person they are satisfied is about to construct premises in their area. Where authorities are under an obligation to provide sewers, they may not enter into such agreements.

Drains

2.06 Any owner of premises is entitled to connect his drains or private sewer to a public sewer and to allow his drains to empty into a public sewer on giving the authority 28 days' notice. However, the authority may refuse permission or grant it subject to conditions. A proprietor may connect his drains to a sewer in a different local authority area, but he must first serve notice on both authorities. The Secretary of State has powers to require the authority in whose area the premises are situated to pay for the service which the other authority is providing. Previously it was the proprietor who had to make any payment required.

2.07 Where a notice regarding connection of a drain or sewer to a public sewer is served on an authority, the authority has powers to direct the manner in which the junction is to be constructed and to supervise construction. The authority has the same powers in relation to any new drain or private sewer if it appears likely that the drain or sewer will be wanted by it to form part of the general system. Authorities are bound to meet the extra cost arising from implementation of their instructions. To allow supervision, three days' notice of the start of work must be given to the authority.

2.08 A local authority can also require defects in private drains and sewers to be remedied and may itself carry out the work if the proprietor fails to do so. Where the defect represents a health hazard, the authority is empowered to carry out emergency repairs on the basis of a 48-hour notice. The cost of repairs carried out by the authority can be recovered from proprietors.

2.09 Provisions relating to trade effluent, trade effluent notices and agreements, and so on, broadly similar to those contained in English legislation (Chapter 16, paragraph 2.12), are also included in the Act.

2.10 Sewage discharged into a public sewer must not be of such a nature as to cause damage to the sewer or, through mixture with other sewage, to cause a nuisance.

2.11 Where a new development is proposed the responsibility for providing sewers rests with the sewerage authority, although this does not apply in the case of an individual house where all that is necessary is a drain or private sewer to connect with the public system. The situation may arise where a delay by the authority in fulfilling its duty holds up development. If a developer chooses to install sewers at his own expense, he will be able to recover from the authority only if, from the start, he adopts the correct procedure (*Lawrence Building Co* v *Lanarkshire County Council* [1977] SLT 110).

2.12 River Purification Boards have functions in relation to approving discharges of sewage and other effluent, the provision of septic tanks, etc.

Water supply

2.13 Water services in Scotland have not been privatized. Legislation on water supply is consolidated in the Water (Scotland) Act 1980. Regional and islands councils are till 1996 the authorities responsible for water supply. District councils have functions in connection with the supply of water to buildings. In terms of the 1980 Act persons erecting new buildings of any type are obliged to make adequate provisions to the satisfaction of the district authority for a supply of clean water for the domestic purposes of persons occupying or using the building. Local authorities may also require house owners to provide water supplies in, or if that is impracticable, immediately outside their houses.

2.14 Water authorities are under an obligation to provide supplies of wholesome water to every part of their regions where a supply is required for domestic purposes and can be provided at reasonable cost. They are obliged to lay main water pipes so that buildings where domestic supplies are required can be connected at a reasonable cost. When a question arises as to whether water can be supplied in this manner to any area at a reasonable cost, the Secretary of State for Scotland must decide, if requested to do so by ten or more local electors.

2.15 The authorities are also obliged to supply water at reasonable terms for other than domestic purposes, provided that to do so would not prejudice their ability to supply water for domestic purposes.

2.16 The procedure for obtaining a water supply for domestic purposes in Scotland is regulated by the third schedule to the Water (Scotland) Act 1980, and is usually similar to that in England

(Chapter 16, paragraph 2.17). A period of 14 days' notice must be given to the authority of the intention to lay a supply pipe. The supply pipe is laid by the proprietor and then attached to the communication pipe by the authority.

Gas, electricity, and telephones

2.17 On these topics, reference should be made to Chapter 12, paragraph 2.20 ff as what is said there applies also to Scotland. The Gas Act 1986 applies with minor modifications in Scotland as in England. Likewise the Electricity Act 1989 applies with small modifications. Building control covers tanker-supplied gas storage tanks and pipes.

Construction of mains

2.18 Again the remarks on this topic in Chapter 16 (paragraph 2.26) should be referred to. The term for a 'way-leave' in Scotland is 'servitude' (Chapter 6, paragraph 3.08).

3 Private streets and footpaths

3.01 The law on roads, streets and footpaths is consolidated in the Roads (Scotland) Act 1984.

3.02 The Act defines roads as ways over which there is a public right of passage by any means, i.e. roads includes footpaths subject to a public sight of passage. Public roads are roads entered by regional and islands councils in their 'lists of public roads' and are roads which those authorities are bound to maintain. Private roads are roads which the authorities are not bound to maintain. The authorities can require frontagers to make up and maintain a private road. When a road has been properly made up, the council is bound to take it over and add it to the list of public roads if application is made by the requisite number of frontagers.

Footpaths

3.03 The above provisions apply to footpaths as well as vehicular routes. The authorities are also empowered to take over footpaths in new developments.

4 Grants

4.01 As in England various grants are obtainable by a proprietor in Scotland to assist him in alterations or improvements to his property. Discretionary improvement grants and standard grants are payable in Scotland under the Housing (Scotland) Act 1987. Although made under different legislation, these grants are payable

on the same basis as in England, details of which are found in Chapter 16, paragraph 4.01.

4.02 Various grants are available for improvement or rebuilding of agricultural workers' cottages. It is not proposed to examine these in detail, but it should be noted that special grants are available for the Highlands, islands, and crofting areas.

4.03 Many other grants are payable by various authorities, but it should be noted that the Public Health Act 1936 does not apply in Scotland. Grants for installation of WCs are available in the form of standard grants. The Local Authorities (Historic Buildings) Act does not apply in Scotland. The Clean Air Acts and the Airport Authority Act apply, and grants may be obtained under them where appropriate (Chapter 16, paragraphs 4.15 and 4.17). A grant may be obtained as a standard grant for bringing a supply of piped water into a house for the first time. Assistance may be available to install separate service pipes to houses sharing the same supply under Section 233 of the Housing (Scotland) Act 1987.

5 Housing associations

5.01 As in England (Chapter 16, paragraph 5.01 ff) housing associations in Scotland are entitled to various benefits under the Scottish Housing Act. The Secretary of State for Scotland may make advances to them, and they may also borrow money from the Public Works Loan Commissioners. The Scottish Special Housing Association has been reconstituted by the Housing (Scotland) Act 1988 under the name Scottish Homes.

6 Special considerations

6.01 In Scotland as well as in England (Chapter 16, paragraph 6.01 ff) special considerations apply to certain types of building. The Factories Acts, the Offices, Shops and Railway Premises Act, and the Clean Air Acts all apply. Liquor licensing is operated under a separate statutory code, and the structural suitability of any premises is a question which may be considered by the Licensing Board for the district or islands area in which the premises are situated.

6.02 Scottish readers are advised to check all new legislation for applications and/or amendments to Scots law. For example, the Health and Safety at Work Act 1974 applies to Scotland, amending the Building (Scotland) Act 1959. Similarly the Control of Pollution Act 1974 has general application to Scotland (see Section 106) and amends much other Scottish legislation of this kind. (See Chapters 14, 15 and 16.)

18

European Community law affecting architects

HIS HONOUR JUDGE ANDREW GEDDES

1 The European Community and its institutions

Introduction

1.01 The opening up of the Single European Market which it was intended should be completed by the end of 1992, is having a profound effect on every sector of the UK construction industry. Building material producers have easier access to some 320 million people living in the Community (a market which is a third larger than the US, and double the Japanese). Building products and practices are being standardized, building contractors have greater opportunities to tender for public sector projects throughout the Community and architects, surveyors and other professionals are able to practise with greater ease in the EC. In addition, the growing tendency of the Community to insist on higher standards of protection for the consumer and for the environment is placing greater burdens on those working in the building industry who are affected by these matters.

1.02 The Single European Market provides an opportunity for the UK construction industry but it also poses a threat. UK suppliers, contractors and professionals are being exposed to increased competition in the UK from their competitors in the rest of the EC and it is anticipated that this threat will be at its most formidable in respect of the largest and most profitable contracts where economies of scale justify the effort involved in competing away from the home market.

1.03 If the UK construction industry is to compete successfully in this new environment it must have an understanding of those EC measures which affect it and ensure that its interests are taken into account when legislation is being drafted and standards are being agreed. A basic knowledge of the Community institutions and how they work is essential if this is to be achieved.

2 The treaties

2.01 The European Community is founded on three treaties. The European Coal and Steel Community was set up by the treaty of Paris in 1951. The two other European Communities were established by the Treaties of Rome signed on 25 March 1952. The first of these established the European Atomic Energy Community (Euratom), and the second, and by far the most important, is the founding treaty of the European Community (EC).

2.02 The initial objectives of the EC were the establishment of a customs union with free movement of goods between member states, the dismantling of quotas and barriers to trade of all kinds and the free movement of people, services and capital. The original EC Treaty also provided for the adoption of common policies on agriculture, transport and competition. It looked forward to the harmonization of laws and technical standards to facilitate its fundamental objectives and to the creation of a social fund and an Investment Bank.

The Single European Act (SEA) and the Maastricht Treaty

2.03 By 1982 it was recognized that the progress towards the completion of a European Market without physical technical or fiscal barriers had been unacceptably slow and the European Council in that year pledged itself to the completion of this internal market as a high priority. In 1985 the Commission published its White Paper entitled 'Completing the Internal Market' in which it set out proposals for some 300 legislative measures which it considered would have to be adopted in order to achieve this aim. At the same time the member states agreed to amend parts of the Treaty of Rome so as to extend their scope and to facilitate the implementation of the legislative programme. The result was the Single European Act which came into force on 1 July 1987. The principal objective of the SEA was the removal by 31 December 1992 of all the remaining barriers within the EC to the free movement of goods, services, persons and capital. It introduced for the first time a system of qualified majority voting in the Council so that proposed legislation cannot so easily be blocked. The Act also provides for further technological development, the strengthening of economic and social ties and the improvement of the environment and working conditions throughout the Community.

The Treaty was further amended on 1 November 1993 when the Treaty on European Union (the Maastricht Treaty) was ratified. That Treaty marks a further step in the process of European integration and for the first time establishes that the new Community is both an economic and political entity in which its citizens are the possessors of enforceable Community rights.

The member states

2.04 The founding member states were Belgium, France, West Germany, Italy, Luxembourg and the Netherlands. Denmark, Ireland and the UK became members in 1973. Greece entered the Community in 1981 and Portugal and Spain in 1986. Sweden, Finland and Austria joined in January 1995.

The Community institutions and legislation

2.05 Each of the Treaties provides that the tasks entrusted to the ECSC, EC and Euratom should be carried out by four institutions: the Council, the Commission, the European Parliament and the Court of Justice. The Parliament and the Court of Justice have always been common to all three communities and since 1967 this has also been true of the Council and the Commission. Because the three Communities are now managed by common institutions they are increasingly referred to as the European Community (EC). The Council is assisted by a Committee of Permanent Representatives (COREPER) made up of representatives of the various member states and for EC and Euratom matters the Council and the Commission are assisted by an Economic and Social Committee acting in an advisory capacity.

The Commission

2.06 The Commission, whose headquarters is in Brussels, is composed of at least one representative from each member state and at November 1989 consisted of 17 members. Members of the Commission are appointed for four years by mutual agreement of EC governments.

The Commission is supported by a staff of some 12 000 officials, a quarter of whom are involved in translation made necessary by the use of three official languages. The staff are mainly divided between a number of directorates-general, each with a separate share of responsibility. Commission decisions, however, are made on a corporate basis. The Commission is the official guardian of the Treaties and ensures that the EC rules and principles they contain are respected. It is responsible for proposing to the Council measures likely to advance the development of EC policies. Once a measure has been adopted it is the Commission's task to ensure that it is implemented throughout the Community. It has wide investigative powers which it may initiate itself or which it may set into motion as a result of a complaint by a third party. It can impose fines on individuals or companies found to be in breach of EC Rules and these frequently run into millions of pounds. An appeal against a Commission decision lies to the European Court of Justice. In addition the Commission can take a member state before the Court if they fail to respect their obligations.

The members of the Commission act only in the interest of the EC. During their term of office they must remain independent of the governments of the member states and of the Council. They are subject to the supervision of the European Parliament which is the only body that can force them to resign collectively.

The Council

2.07 The Council is made up of representatives of the governments of the member states. Each government normally sends one of its ministers. Its membership thus varies with the subjects proposed for discussion. The Foreign Minister is regarded as his country's main representative in the Council but the other ministers meet frequently for more specialized Council meetings. The Presidency of the Council is held for a term of six months by each member in turn. The Council is the EC's principal legislative body and makes all the main policy decisions. It can act only on a proposal from the Commission.

For some issues (such as taxation, and certain social and environmental matters) the Council must act unanimously if it wishes to alter the text of a proposal from the Commission. Since the passing of the SEA, however, the Council may now act in a wide range of matters by qualified majority. Under this system France, Germany, Italy and the UK have ten votes each, Spain eight votes, Belgium, Greece, the Netherlands and Portugal five, Austria and Sweden four, Denmark, Finland and Ireland three and Luxembourg two votes. Out of the total of 87 votes, 62 are needed to approve a Commission proposal under the qualified majority voting system. The groundwork for the Council's response to Commission proposals is carried out by officials of the member states, coordinated by COREPER.

EC legislation

2.08 Measures adopted by Council and by the Commission where it has decision-making powers have the force of law, which take precedence over the national laws of the member states. In some cases these measures have direct effect throughout the EC. In others the member states must first implement them by way of national legislation.

These measures may be:

1. Regulations, in which case they apply directly.
2. Directives which lay down compulsory objectives to be achieved by a certain date but leave to member states how they are to be implemented into national law. In certain defined circumstances

when a member state has failed to implement a directive in due time a citizen can rely directly on the directive as against the state.

3. Decisions, which are binding only on the member states, companies or individuals to whom they are addressed.

The Council also from time to time adopts resolutions which are declarations of intent and do not have legal force.

Where a national measure implements a directive or even where that measure merely covers the same legislative field as a directive (e.g. because the national measure preceded the coming into force of the directive) the national measure must be construed in so far as possible to give effect to the purpose of the underlying directive as established in the light of the directive's preamble and any relevant decision of the European Court of Justice. In such cases therefore it is almost always necessary to look at both the directive and the relevant national measure before the true legal position can be established.

The European Court of Justice

2.09 The Court, which sits in Luxembourg, consists of thirteen judges assisted by six advocates-general. They are appointed for a period of six years by mutual consent of the member states and are entirely independent. The Court is entrusted with the interpretation of the Treaties and can quash any measures adopted by the Council, the Commission or national governments which are incompatible with it. An application for this purpose may be made by an EC institution government or individual. The Court also gives judgment when requested to do so by a national court on any question of EC law.

Judgments of the Court in the field of EC law are binding on all national courts.

As from September 1989, a Court of First Instance has sat to hear cases principally relating to competition matters. An appeal on a point of law only lies from that court to the ECJ.

The European Parliament

2.10 The Parliament which meets in plenary session in Strasbourg currently consists of 626 members elected from the member states broadly in proportion to their size. Elections take place every five years. Although the Parliament does not have legislative powers like those of national parliaments, it has an important part to play in three areas:

1. *It adopts and controls the EC budget.*
2. *It considers proposals for EC legislation.* In all cases Parliament must be consulted before the Council can adopt an Act. It can by majority vote, confirm, amend, or reject legislation adopted by the Council.
3. *It supervises activities of the EC institutions.* It has the power to question and criticize the Commission's proposals and activities in debate. It can exert influence through its budgetary power and has the power to dismiss the Commission by a two-thirds majority.

3 Public procurement

Introduction

3.01 The opening up of procurement by government bodies and by the utilities to EC-wide competition has been recognized by the member states as a key component in the creation of the internal European market. This huge sector of the economy is estimated by the Commission as representing some 15% (592 billion ECUs at 1989 prices) of Community GDP of which some 7–10% (260–380 billion ECUs) takes the form of contracts falling within the new public procurement regime. Of that total, building and construction represents 28.5%. Although there are a number of directly effective Treaty provisions which must be taken into account in the award of public authority contracts, these are insufficient to ensure that such contracts are opened up to Community-wide tendering. The EC has consequently adopted a number of specific

measures whose purpose is to supplement the Treaty provisions by applying detailed rules to the award of public and utility procurement contracts over a certain value. The two principal measures are the Public Works Directive 71/305/EEC and the Public Supplies Directive 77/62/EEC which have been in force in the UK (by way of ministry circular) since 1973 and 1978 respectively. The Works Directive, which has been substantially amended on a number of occasions has now been consolidated with minor amendments into directive 93/37/EC which was adopted on 14 June 1993. It has been incorporated into UK law by the Public Works Contracts Regulations (as amended) S.I. No. 2680 which came into force on 21 December 1991. The Supplies Directive has also been substantially amended and is now consolidated into directive 93/36/EC which was also adopted on June 14 1993. The opportunity has been taken in the consolidating directive to carry out certain further amendments to the Supplies Directive, primarily in order to bring it into line with the Works Directive with regard to the public authorities affected. The Supplies Directive has been incorporated into law in the UK by the Public Supply Contracts Regulations 1995 which came into force on 21 February 1995.

The contracts covered by the Works and Supplies Directives exclude contracts for works and supplies awarded by certain entities operating in the water, energy, transport and telecommunications sectors because of particular problems in relation to some of those entities being governed by public and some by private law. The award of those contracts is now covered by virtue of a separate Directive 93/38/EEC and known as the 'Excluded Sectors' or 'Utilities' Directive. That Directive has been implemented in the UK by the Utilities Contracts Regulations 1995 which came into force in December 1995 and replaced an earlier set of Regulations.

Despite the introduction of the Works and Supplies Directives, the Commission were dissatisfied with the extent to which member states complied with them (it is estimated, for example that only about 20% of public contracts falling within the provisions of the directives were being properly advertised). This was brought about in part by the inadequacy, or in some cases the total absence, of any remedies available to potential contractors or suppliers for their breach. The Community have therefore introduced two measures designed to overcome this problem. The first, known as the 'Compliance' Directive 89/665/EEC, sets out the remedies which must be made available for breach of the Works and Supplies Directives and relevant Treaty provisions to those injured by such a breach. The relevant provisions of this Directive have been implemented in the UK by their incorporation into the Works and Supplies Regulations. The second measure, known as the 'Remedies' Directive 92/13/EEC, provides similar remedies for breach of the Utilities Directive and has been implemented in the Utilities Regulations referred to above.

The final plank of the Community's public procurement rules was the bringing of public and utility contracts for services within the new regime. This has been achieved in so far as public services contracts are concerned by means of Directive 92/50/EEC which was implemented in the UK on 13 January 1994 by the Public Services Contracts Regulations 1993 (S.I. No. 3228) and which amends the Compliance Directive so as to apply its provisions to contracts for services. Contracts for services in the utilities sector are now covered by the Utilities Regulation referred to above.

The Works Directive and the Public Works Contracts Regulations 1991

3.02 The Directive and therefore the Regulations have three principal aims in respect of the contracts to which they apply:

1. EC-wide advertising of contracts above a certain value threshold so that contractors in every member state have an equal opportunity of expressing their interest in tendering and/or in tendering for them.
2. The prohibition of technical specifications in the contract documents which favour particular contractors.
3. The application of objective criteria in procedures leading to the award, and in the award itself.

In addition, the Regulations make available through the Courts certain remedies (including damages) to contractors who suffer or risk suffering loss as a result of a breach of the Regulations or any related Community obligation.

Contracts to which the Regulations apply

3.03 The Regulations apply whenever a 'contracting authority' whether by itself or through an agent seeks offers in relation to a proposed 'public works contract' other than a public works contract expressly excluded from the operation of the Regulations, regardless of whether a contract is awarded or not. Special rules apply under the Regulations where the public works contract is also a 'public works concession contract', which is defined as 'a public works contract under which the consideration given by the contracting authority consists of or includes the grant of a right to exploit the work or works to be carried out under the contract'.

Meaning of 'contracting authority'

3.04 Contracting authorities under the Regulations include the state and state-controlled bodies, local authorities and certain bodies governed by public law. A list of 'contracting authorities' is set out in Regulation 3(1). The list is not definitive but is 'as exhaustive as possible'.

Meaning of 'public works contract'

3.05 A 'public works contract' is a contract in writing for money or monies worth for the construction or the design and construction of a 'work' or 'works' by a contracting authority, or a management contract under which the contracting authority engages a person to carry out for the contracting authority a 'work' corresponding to specified requirements.

The 'works' referred to are any of the activities listed in a schedule to the Regulations. The schedule sets out a variety of building and civil engineering activities (e.g. 'construction of flats, office blocks, hospitals and other buildings both residential and non-residential') broken down into tasks (e.g. 'erection of and dismantling of scaffolding') carried out in the course of those activities. A 'work' is a larger concept and is defined as the outcome of any works which is sufficient of itself to fulfil an economic and technical function. Thus a 'work' would include the construction of an airport; it would also include the construction of its runways or of a terminal as both these are capable of fulfilling an economic and technical function but it would not include the associated drainage or electrical work as these are merely ancillary and cannot of themselves fulfil an economic and technical function. In some cases a contract may be for both works and services and/or for supplies of goods. Where this arises the contract will be a works contract where the value of the works (including any goods to be used for the purpose of construction) exceeds the value of any goods to be supplied or services to be provided. So for example, a property management contract which incidentally includes a requirement from time to time to carry out some works is a services and not a works contract. A contract specifically for building maintenance or repair is on the other hand a works contract and the higher threshold will apply (see below).

These provisions of the Works Regulations defining what is meant by a public works contract are complemented by similar provisions in the Supply Regulations and the Services Regulations ensuring that each set of Regulations is mutually exclusive as regards the contracts to which they apply. In every case therefore it will be important to establish at the outset whether a public contract is a 'works', 'supply' or 'services' contract.

The public works contracts excluded from the operation of the Regulations

Contracts related to certain utilities

3.06 The Works Regulations do not apply to the seeking of offers in relation to a proposed public works contract by a contracting authority for the purpose of carrying out certain activities in the water, transport, energy or telecommunications sectors. Such contracts will fall to be dealt with, if at all, under the Utilities Contracts Regulations. The activities concerned broadly comprise the operation or provision of public networks or facilities in the sectors referred to and the supply to such networks, together with certain mining activities in relation to gas, oil, coal, and other solid fuels.

Secret contracts, contracts involving state security and contracts carried out pursuant to international ageement

3.07 In addition the Regulations do not apply to a public works contract which is classified by the Government as secret or where the carrying out of the work or works under it must be accompanied by special security measures approved by law or when the protection of the basic interests of the security of the UK require it. Certain contracts carried out pursuant to international agreements are also exempt.

Contracts below certain value thresholds

3.08 Most importantly of all, the Regulations do not apply to the seeking of offers in relation to a proposed public works contract where the 'estimated value' of the contract (net of VAT) at the 'relevant time' is less than 5 000 000 ECUs (£3 743 203). The sterling equivalent is fixed until December 1995 when a recalculated equivalent applying to the following two years will be published in the *Official Journal*.

The 'relevant time' is the date on which the contract notice would be sent to the *Official Journal* if the requirement to send such a notice applied to the contract in accordance with the Regulations (i.e. generally when the contracting authority forms the intention to seek offers in relation to the contract).

The 'estimated value' is the sum which the contracting authority expects to pay under the contract. However, where the public works contract is one of a number of contracts entered into or to be entered into for the carrying out of a 'work' the 'estimated value' is normally the aggregate of the sums which the contracting authority has paid or expects to pay under all the contracts for the carrying out of the work. Exceptionally, where one or more of the contracts is for less than 1 million ECUs (£748 640) such contracts need not be aggregated so long as in total they represent less than 20% of the total cost of the work. Thus for example where a contracting authority seeks offers in relation to site clearance at an estimated cost of 1 million ECUs for the purpose of constructing a hospital at an estimated cost of 20 million ECUs, the Regulations will apply both to the site clearance contract and the construction contract. If the cost of the site clearance was only 900 000 ECUs (and there were no other contracts which together with that one aggregated to 4 million ECUs or more) the contracting authority would not be required to comply with the Regulations in respect of that contract.

Where a contracting authority intends to provide any goods to the person awarded a public works contract for the purpose of carrying out that contract, the value of these must be taken into account when calculating the estimated value of the contract.

In relation to public works concession contracts the 'estimated value' is the payment which the contracting authority would expect to make for the carrying out of the work (taking into account any goods supplied by them) if it did not propose to grant a concession.

A contracting authority must not enter into separate contracts with the intention of avoiding the application of the Regulations to those contracts.

Rules governing technical specifications

3.09 Detailed rules as to the technical specifications which are permitted in public works contracts are set out in the Regulations. The purpose behind these rules is to avoid any discrimination against contractors who might be at a disadvantage if technical specifications were required which could only be met, or met more easily by a national contractor.

Technical specifications (which are defined in the Regulations) whether relating to the works themselves or to the goods to be used in them must be specified in the contract documents and subject to certain exceptions must always be defined by reference to any 'European specifications' which are relevant. 'European specification' means a common technical specification (i.e. one agreed by the member states), a British Standard implementing a European standard or European technical approval. The Commission have issued policy guidelines on what is meant by this obligation to refer to European standards.

Exceptionally technical specifications may be used which are defined other than by reference to a European standard.

Rules governing the procedures leading to the award of a public works contract

3.10 The principal requirement of the Regulations is that in seeking offers in relation to a public works contract from contractors or potential contractors who are nationals of and established in a member state, a contracting authority must use one of the following procedures:

- **the open procedure** whereby any person who is interested may submit a tender;
- **the restricted procedure** whereby only those persons selected by the contracting authority may submit tenders; and
- **the negotiated procedure** whereby the contracting authority negotiates the terms of the contract with one or more persons selected by it.

The Regulations lay down provisions for making the choice of procedure. The negotiated procedure may only be used in certain limited circumstances. Special rules apply in relation to a public housing scheme works contract.

Advertising the intention to seek offers by means of a prior information notice

3.11 The contracting authority must publicize its intention to seek offers in relation to a public works contract in the *Official Journal* as soon as the decision approving the planning of works is taken (the 'prior information notice'). It must do this again at the start of the procedure leading to the award once this has been selected (the 'contract notice'), although the latter requirement is dispensed with in certain circumstances when the negotiated procedure is used. The form of the advertisement and the information which it must contain in relation to the proposed contract is specified in a schedule to the Regulations. If the notice is also to be published in the UK press it must be limited to the information published in the *Official Journal*.

Selection of contract award procedure

3.12 Normally a contracting authority must either use the open procedure or the restricted procedure, at its choice. The negotiated procedure may only be used in the exceptional circumstances specified in the Regulations. These are as follows:

1. Where the use of the open or restricted procedure was discontinued because of 'irregular' tenders or following an evaluation of offers made in accordance with the regulations relating to open or restricted procedures. However, the negotiated procedure may only then be used if the proposed terms of the contract are substantially unaltered from the proposed terms of the contract in relation to which offers were sought using the open or restricted procedure.

   A tender will be 'irregular' if for example the contractor fails to meet the requirements of, or the tender offers variation on, the requirements specified in the contract documents which are not permitted under the terms of the invitation to tender or the work, works, materials or goods do not meet the technical specifications of the contracting authority.

The Regulations (and the directive) do not make clear in what circumstances a contracting authority would be entitled to discontinue the open or restricted procedure in the circumstances defined above. The correct approach is probably that they would be entitled to do so where after excluding irregular tenders and other tenders on grounds permitted by the Regulations (see below) there remained *insufficient* valid tenders for there to be any real competition. It will be noted at (4.) below that absence of tenders is a separate ground for justifying use of the negotiated procedure.

2. When the work or works are to be carried out under the contract purely for the purpose of research experiment or development, but this exception will not apply if the works are to be carried out to establish their commercial viability or to recover their research and development costs.

   Once the experiment or trial has proved successful, this exception will cease to apply and if the contracting authority then decides to go ahead with further works it must comply with the Regulations if the contract is one which falls within their provisions.

3. Exceptionally, when the nature of the work or works to be carried out under the contract is such, or the risks attaching thereto are such, as not to permit overall pricing.

4. In the absence of tenders or of appropriate tenders in response to an invitation to tender by the contracting authority using the open or restricted procedure. However, again this exception may not be relied upon unless the proposed terms of the contract are substantially unaltered from the proposed terms of the contract in relation to which offers were sought using the open or restricted procedure.

5. When for technical or artistic reasons, or for reasons connected with the protection of exclusive rights, the work or works to be carried out under the contract may only be carried out by a particular person.

   It might be argued by a disappointed contractor who had been excluded for technical reasons that given enough time he could have acquired the expertise and/or machinery to qualify technically but the exception can probably be relied upon where for technical reasons only one contractor can carry out the works within the time required by the contracting authority for their completion so long as this is reasonable.

6. When (but only if it is strictly necessary) for reasons of extreme urgency brought about by events unforeseeable by and not attributable to the contracting authority, the time limits specified in the Regulations relating to the various contract award procedures cannot be met.

7. When a contracting authority wants a person who has entered into a public works contract with the contracting authority to carry out additional works which through unforeseen circumstances were not included in the project initially considered or in the original public works contract and,

   (a) such works cannot for technical or economic reasons be carried out separately from the works carried out under the original public works contract without great inconvenience to the contracting authority, or

   (b) such works can be carried out separately from the works carried out under the original public works contract but are strictly necessary to the later stages of the contract. However, this exception may not be relied upon where the aggregate value of the consideration to be given under contracts for the additional works exceeds 50% of the value of the consideration payable under the original contract.

The value of the consideration must be taken to include the estimated value of any goods which the contracting authority provided to the person awarded the contract for the purposes of carrying out the contract

8. When a contracting authority wishes a person who has entered into a public works contract with that contracting authority to carry out new works which are a repetition of works carried out under the original contract and which are in accordance with the project for the purpose of which the first contract was entered into. However, that exception may only be relied upon if the contract notice relating to the original contract stated that

a public works contract for new works which would be a repetition of the works carried out under the original contract may be awarded using the negotiated procedure and unless the procedure for the award of the new contract is commenced within three years of the original contract being entered into.

In accordance with principles of Community law each of the above exceptions must be interpreted strictly.

The open procedure

3.13 As has already been noted the contracting authority must publicize its intention to seek offers in relation to the public works contract by sending to the *Official Journal* a notice (the 'contract notice') inviting tenders and containing specified information in relation to the contract. The form and contents of that notice are set out in a schedule to the Regulations.

The Commission has recommended that contracting authorities use standard notices and standardized nomenclature from 1 January 1992 when advertising public works and public supplies contracts in the *Official Journal*. The standard forms together with an explanatory note as to how they should be used have been published in the *Supplement to the Official Journal* dated 16 November 1991. The UK Government has recommended that all contracting authorities as defined by the Works Regulations and Supply Regulations comply with the recommendations. There are as yet no standard forms for either public works prior information notices or public works concession contract notices. There are strict minimum time limits laid down for the receipt of tenders.

The contracting authority may only exclude a tender from the evaluation of offers if the contractor may be treated as ineligible on grounds specified in the Regulations or if a contractor fails to satisfy minimum standards of economic and financial standing and technical capacity required of contractors by the contracting authority when assessed according to the requirements of the Regulations.

The restricted procedure

Selecting those invited to tender

3.14 When using the restricted procedure the contracting authority must, as with the open procedure, publish a contract notice as soon as possible after forming the intention to seek offers. The contract notice must be in a form and contain the information substantially corresponding to that set out in a schedule to the Regulations inviting requests to be selected to tender. There are strict minimum time limits for receipt of requests to be selected to tender.

The contracting authority may exclude a contractor from those persons from whom it will make the selection of persons to be invited to tender only if the contractor may be treated as ineligible on a ground permitted by the Regulations or if the contractor fails to satisfy the minimum standards of economic and financial standing and technical capacity required of contractors by the contracting authority as assessed according to the requirements of the Regulations.

Having excluded any contractors as above, the contracting authority must select the contractors they intend to invite to tender solely on the basis of the information obtained regarding the contractor's past record, his economic standing and his technical capacity as permitted by the Regulations and in making the selection and in issuing invitations the contracting authority must not discriminate between contractors on the grounds of their nationality or the member state in which they are established. The contracting authority may prescribe the range within which the number of undertakings which they intend to invite will fall. The number invited must be not less than five nor more than twenty. If a range is to be specified it must be specified in the contract notice and in any event the number must be sufficient to ensure genuine competition.

The invitation to tender

3.15 The invitation to tender must be sent in writing simultaneously to each contractor selected to tender, and must be accompanied by the contract documents or contain the address from which they may be requested. The invitation to tender must include the specified information. As before, the Regulations lay down strict minimum time limits for the receipt of tenders.

The negotiated procedure

3.16 In most cases where the negotiated procedure is used contracting authorities are not required to follow any procedural rules other than those relating to the exclusion of contractors on the ground of ineligibility and relating to their selection to negotiate. However, where a contracting authority uses the negotiated procedure:

1. because it has discontinued the open or restricted procedures in the circumstances discussed above, or
2. where the work or works are to be carried out for the purposes of research, experiment or development, or
3. where the nature of the works does not permit overall pricing,

then unless in relation to (1.) above, it has invited to negotiate every contractor who submitted a tender (not being an 'excluded' tender), the following rules apply in addition:

1. The contracting authority must publicize its intention to seek offers in relation to the public works contract by publishing a contract notice in the *Official Journal* in the form prescribed inviting requests to be selected to negotiate and containing the information specified.
2. The date fixed as the last date for the receipt of requests to be selected to negotiate must be specified in the contract notice and must be not less than 37 days (15 days in cases of urgency) from the date of dispatch of the notice.
3. Where there is a sufficient number of persons who are suitable to be selected to negotiate the contract, the number must be not less than three.

Selection of contractors

Criteria for rejection of contractors

3.17 Detailed rules are laid down in the Regulations as to the only criteria on which applicants to tender and tenderers may be excluded as ineligible from the tendering process. These relate to the contractor's financial solvency and business and fiscal probity. In addition a contractor may be excluded as ineligible where he is not registered on the professional or trade register of the member state in which he is established. Special provisions apply in relation to contractors established in the UK, Ireland and Greece (where such registers do not exist) to enable them to satisfy this condition.

The contracting authority may require a contractor to provide such information as it considers it needs to satisfy itself that none of the exclusionary criteria apply, but it must accept as conclusive that the contractor does not fall within any of the grounds relating to financial solvency or fiscal probity, an extract from a judicial record or a certificate issued by a competent authority (whichever is appropriate) to this effect. In member states such as the UK where such documentary evidence is not available, provision is made for the evidence to be provided by binding declaration. Special rules apply to contractors registered on official lists.

Information as to economic and financial standing

3.18 Subject to a similar provision relating to the situation where the contractor is registered on an official list of recognized contractors, under the Regulations the contracting authority, in assessing whether a contractor meets any minimum standards of economic and financial standing, may apparently 'only' take into account any of the certain specified information and it may require a contractor to provide such of that information as it considers it needs to make the assessment or selection.

Where the information specified is not appropriate in a particular case, a contracting authority may require a contractor to provide other information to demonstrate the contractor's economic and financial standing. Where a contractor is unable for a valid reason to provide the information which the contracting authority has required, the contracting authority must accept such other information provided by the contractor as the contracting authority considers appropriate. The information required must be specified in the contract notice.

Information as to technical capacity

3.19 Again subject to a similar provision relating to the situation where the contractor is registered on an official list of recognized contractors, the contracting authority, in assessing whether a contractor meets any minimum standards of technical capacity, may under the Regulations 'only' take into account certain specified information and it may require a contractor to provide such of that information as it considers it needs to make the assessment or selection.

Limits on the information which may be required or taken into account

3.20 The mandatory nature of the Regulations as regards information which may be required and/or taken into account by a contracting authority when assessing a contractor's economic and financial standing and technical capacity is not reflected in the directive. The European Court has held in respect of the provision concerning economic and financial standing that 'it can be seen from the very wording of that Article and in particular the second paragraph thereof that the list of references mentioned therein is not exhaustive' and that consequently a contracting authority is entitled to require a contractor to furnish a statement of the total value of the works he has in hand as a reference within the meaning of that article. The list of references which may be required to establish technical capacity on the other hand *is* exhaustive and a contracting authority may not *require* a contractor to furnish further information on that topic. However there would appear to be nothing to prevent a contracting authority from *taking into account* other information relevant to technical capacity which the contracting authority has acquired by other means. That appears to have been the view taken by the English High Court in *GBM* v *Greenwich BC*, ([1993] 92LG R21) where in relation to a public works contract, it was held that a contracting authority was entitled to take into account when assessing a contractor's technical capacity, any independent knowledge it might have regarding a contractor's compliance with health and safety legislation when carrying out other contracts. Indeed it would seem remarkable if a contracting authority were to be prohibited from taking into account for example, the technical performance of a contractor experienced by it during other dealings with that contractor. A contracting authority may require a contractor to provide information supplementing the information supplied in accordance with the Regulations or to clarify that information, provided that the information required is in respect of matters permitted by the Regulations.

A contracting authority must comply with such requirements as to the confidentiality of information provided to it by a supplier as the supplier may reasonably request.

The award of the public works contract

The basis for the award

3.21 The contracting authority must award the public works contract on the basis either of the tender (including in-house bids) which offers the lowest price or the one which is the most 'economically advantageous' (i.e. best value for money).

The criteria which a contracting authority may use to determine that an offer is the most economically advantageous include price, period for completion, running costs, profitability and technical merit. The list is not exhaustive, but it is clear from the examples given that only objective criteria may be used which are relevant to the particular project, and uniformly applicable to all bidders.

All the criteria the contracting authority intends to apply in determining the most economically advantageous offer must be stated in the contract notice or contract documents preferably in descending order of importance. No criteria not mentioned in the notice or the contract documents may be used. A distinction, however, must be made between a contractual condition requiring the successful contractor to co-operate with some policy objective of the contracting authority and the criteria for the selection of contractors or for the award of the contract. Thus a condition attached to the award of a public works contract, under which the contractor is required to engage a given member of long-term unemployed, is compatible with the directive and therefore the Regulations. It is not relevant to the assessment of the contractor's economic, financial or technical capacity to carry out the work, nor does it form part of the criteria applied by the contracting authority to decide to whom to award the contract. Such conditions must, however, be compatible with the Treaty, particularly with those provisions on freedom to provide services, freedom of establishment and non-discrimination on the grounds of nationality. They must also be mentioned in the contract notice. Thus it would be a breach of the Treaty if it appeared on the facts that the condition could only be fulfilled by national firms or it would be more difficult for tenderers coming from other member states to fulfil that condition. Even a request for information from tenderers (as opposed to the insertion of a contractual term) can in certain circumstances be in breach of the rules if such request would reasonably lead the tenderer to believe that discrimination on local or national grounds is likely to occur. In this context the UK Department of the Environment, basing itself on Treasury guidance, has published a circular to assist local authorities in complying with the rules governing public procurement. The circular clarifies the Commission's view that requiring the tenderer to give information on whether local labour and local experience will be used may imply that a tenderer using local labour would be more likely to win the contract. Local authorities are advised therefore not to put such requirements into contract notices.

When a contracting authority awards a public works contract on the basis of the offer which is most economically advantageous it may take account of offers which offer variations on the requirements specified in the contract documents if the offer meets the minimum requirements of the contracting authority and it has indicated in the contract notice that offers offering variations will be considered, and has stated in the contract documents the minimum requirements which the offer must meet and any specific requirements for the presentation of an offer offering variations.

Post-tender negotiations

3.22 It should also be stressed that in open and restricted procedures all negotiations with candidates or tenderers on fundamental aspects of the contract and in particular on prices are not permitted, although discussion with candidates or tenderers may be held for the purposes of clarifying or supplementing the content of their tenders or the requirements of the contracting authority, provided this does not involve unfairness to their competitors.

Abnormally low tenders

3.23 If an offer for a public works contract is or appears to be abnormally low the contracting authority may reject that offer but only if it has requested in writing an explanation of the offer or of those parts which it considers contribute to the offer being abnormally low and has:

1. if awarding the contract on the basis of lowest price, examined the details of all the offers made taking into account any explanation given to it of the abnormally low tender, before awarding the contract, or
2. if awarding the contract on the basis of the offer which is the most economically advantageous, taken any such explanation into account in assessing which is the most economically advantageous offer.

Thus a contracting authority may not automatically reject a tender because it fails to satisfy some predetermined mathematical criterion adopted in relation to the public works contract concerned. In every case, the contractor must be given an opportunity for explanation and thereafter the examination procedure specified must be followed.

If a contracting authority which rejects an abnormally low tender is awarding the contract on the basis of the offer which offers the lowest price, it must send a report justifying the rejection to the UK Government for onward transmission to the Commission.

The contracting authority's obligations once the contract has been awarded

3.24 It may be a matter of considerable importance to disappointed tenderers to know the outcome of a contract award procedure, not least to establish whether there may be grounds on which to challenge the award. The Regulations impose upon contracting authorities the following obligations in this respect:

1. The authority must not later than 48 days after the award, send to the *Official Journal* a notice substantially corresponding to the form set out in a schedule to the Regulations and containing the information therein specified. The information required may be omitted in a particular case where to publish such information would impede law enforcement, would otherwise be contrary to the public interest, would prejudice the legitimate commercial interests of any person or might prejudice fair competition between contractors.
2. The authority must within 15 days of the date on which it receives a request from any unsuccessful contractor inform that contractor why he was unsuccessful and if the contractor was unsuccessful as a result of the evaluation of offers it must also tell him the name of the person awarded the contract.

A contracting authority must in addition prepare a record in respect of each public works contract awarded containing specified information which must be available for transmission to the Commission if requested. Where a contracting authority decides not to award a public works contract which has been advertised nor to seek offers in relation to another public works contract for the same purpose it must inform the *Official Journal* of that decision and must, if so requested by any contractor who submitted an offer or who applied to be included amongst the persons to be selected to tender for or negotiate the contract, give the reasons for its decision.

Subsidised works contracts

3.25 Where a contracting authority undertakes to contribute more than half of the cost of certain specified public works contracts which will be or have been entered into by another body (other than another contracting authority), the contracting authority must make it a condition of making such contribution that that other body complies with the Regulations in relation to the contract as if it were a contracting authority, and must ensure that that body does so comply, or recover the contribution. The contracts to which this provision applies are those which are for carrying out any of the activities specified in Group 502 of Schedule 1 (civil engineering, construction of roads, bridges, railways, etc.) or for the carrying out of building works for hospitals, facilities intended for sports recreation and leisure, school and university buildings or buildings for administrative purposes.

Public housing scheme works contracts

3.26 A public housing scheme works contract is defined as 'a public works contract relating to the design and construction of a public housing scheme'. For the purpose of seeking offers in relation to a public housing scheme works contract where the size and complexity of the scheme and the estimated duration of the works involved require that the planning of the scheme be based from the outset on a close collaboration of a team comprising representatives of the contracting authority, experts and the contractor,

the contracting authority may, subject as below, depart from the provisions of the Regulations in so far as it is necessary to do so to select the contractor who is most suitable for integration into the team. The contracting authority must in any event comply with the provisions relating to the restricted procedure up to the selection of contractors to be invited to tender. The contracting authority must in addition include in the contract notice a job description which is as accurate as possible so as to enable contractors to form a valid idea of the scheme and of the minimum standards relating to the business or professional status, the economic and financial standing and the technical capacity which the person awarded the contract will be expected to fill.

Public works concession contracts

3.27 The Regulations lay down special rules which apply to public works concession contracts. A public works concession contract is defined in the Regulations as 'a public works contract under which the consideration given by the contracting authority consists of or includes the grant of a right to exploit the work or works to be carried out under the contract'.

Obligations relating to employment protection and working conditions

3.28 A contracting authority which includes in the contract documents relating to a public work, information as to where a contractor may obtain information about obligations relating to employment protection and working conditions which will apply to the works to be carried out under the contract, must ask contractors to indicate that they have taken account of those obligations in preparing their tender, or in negotiating the contract.

The Supplies Directive and the Public Supply Contracts Regulations 1995

3.29 The Supply Regulations apply similar rules to those contained in the Works Regulations to public supply contracts. A public supply contract is defined as a contract in writing for money or monies worth for the purchase of goods (and their siting and installation if any) by a contracting authority or for the hire of goods by a contracting authority irrespective of whether or not the contracting authority becomes the owner of the goods at the end of the period of hire.

As public supply contracts are likely to be of marginal interest to architects it is not proposed to deal with the provisions of the Regulations in detail. The following points should however be noted:

- The definition of a contracting authority is wider than that in the Works Regulations and includes 'GATT authorities' which are public bodies which qualify for inclusion in the Regulations as a result of the EC's obligations under the 1979 GATT agreement. The authorities concerned are listed in a schedule to the Regulations.
- The value threshold for supply contracts (below which the Regulations do not apply) is set at 200 000 ECUs (£149 728 until 31 December 1995) although where the contracting authority is a GATT authority this is reduced to 125 576 ECUs (£94 011).
- When calculating the value of a contract for the purposes of the threshold the value of other contracts of a similar nature may have to be aggregated.
- The circumstances in which the negotiated procedure may be used differ from those set out in the Works Regulations.

The Utilities Directive and the Utilities Contracts Regulations 1995

3.30 The Utilities Regulations apply similar rules to those contained in the Works and Supply Regulations to certain contracts for works supplies or services entered into by entities operating in the water, energy, transport and telecommunications sectors. The entities affected are specified in Schedule 1 and in the Regulations are called utilities.

Certain contracts are excluded from the application of the Regulations principally where the contract is not for the purpose of carrying out an activity specified in the part of Schedule 1 in which the utility concerned is specified but also where the contract is for the purpose of carrying out an activity outside the territory of the Communities, contracts for resale, secret contracts, contracts connected with international agreements, certain contracts awarded by utilities operating in the telecommunications sector and those contracts whose value is beneath the threshold for coverage (the same thresholds apply as in the Works Supplies and Services Regulations). Certain contracts awarded by utilities operating in the energy sector may be exempt from the detailed rules of the Regulations in which case the utility must comply with the principles of non-discrimination and competitive procurement in seeking offers in relation to them.

Like the public procurement Regulations, the principal requirement of the Utilities Regulations is that in seeking offers in relation to a works, supply or services contract, a utility must use either the open procedure, the restricted procedure or the negotiated procedure. However, the Utilities Regulations in accordance with the Utilities Directive has adopted a more flexible approach to the choice of procedure than is contained in the earlier Regulations; so long as the utility makes a 'call for competition' as defined in the Regulations any of the three procedures may be used and in certain specified circumstances no call for competition need be made.

As with the public procurement Regulations, a utility is required to publicize the contracts which it expects to award in the *Official Journal* at least once a year and again when it starts the procedure leading to the award although the latter requirement is dispensed with in certain cases.

Unlike the earlier Regulations, the Utilities Regulations permit the operation of a system of qualification of providers, from which a utility may select suppliers or contractors to tender for or to negotiate a contract without advertisement at the start of the award procedure. In this case the existence of the qualification system must be advertised.

Similar to the public procurement Regulations, the Utilities Regulations lay down minimum time limits in relation to responses by potential providers to invitations to tender, to be selected to tender for or to negotiate the contract, and for obtaining the relevant documents. The Regulations also indicate the matters to which the utility may have regard in excluding tenders from providers who are regarded as ineligible or in selecting providers to tender for or to negotiate the contract, and as before they require that the utility award a contract on the basis either of the offer (including in-house bids) which offers the lowest price or the one which is the most economically advantageous. In addition the Regulations lay down similar rules in relation to technical specifications to publicizing their awards and to the keeping of records and to reporting.

The Regulations introduce a number of innovations into the Community procurement regime. A utility is permitted to advertise an arrangement which establishes the terms under which providers will enter contracts with it over a period of time (called in the Regulations 'framework arrangements') in which case it need not advertise the supply and works contracts made under it. Secondly a utility may, and in other limited circumstances must, reject an offer for a supply contract if more than 50% of the value of the goods are goods which originate in states with which the Communities have not concluded an agreement ensuring comparable and effective access to markets for undertakings in member states.

The Services Directive and the Public Services Contracts Regulations

3.31 Although by virtue of Article 44 of the Services Directive, that directive was required to be implemented into national law by 1 July 1993, the Regulations did not come into effect until 13 January 1994. The directive will nevertheless in almost all cases be directly effective during that period of delay.

As with the Works and Supply Regulations, the Services Regulations apply whenever a contracting authority whether by itself or through an agent, seeks offers in relation to a proposed 'public services contract' other than a public services contract which is excluded under the Regulations. However, unlike the Works and Supply Regulations, the extent of the application of the Services Regulations depends on the type of services contract concerned. The Regulations adopt a two-tier approach. Certain services listed in Part A of Schedule 1 to the Regulations are subject to the Regulations in full, while others listed in Part B of Schedule 1 are subject at present only to the regulations relating to technical specifications in contract documents (Regulation 8), contract award information (Regulation 22), certain reporting responsibilities (Regulations 27(2) and 28), and publication of notices (Regulation 29). Both Part A and Part B services are subject to Part 1 (General) and Part VII (applications to the court) of the Regulations. Part A comprises fourteen separate categories of service of which (j) 'architectural and related services' and (l) 'property management services' are of particular relevance to architects. Other services fall into Part B.

Contracts for both Part A services and Part B services are deemed to be for Part B services only if the value of the Part B services is equal to or greater than the value of the Part A services. Parts A and B of Schedule 1 contain references to the UN Central Products Classification (CPC). In order to establish which services fall into which Part of Schedule 1 it will usually be necessary to check the full CPC reference rather than rely on the abbreviated lists set out in the schedule. For example 'legal services' appear under Category 21 of Part B, but where legal services take the form of 'research and experimental development services on law' they will fall into Category 8 of Part A (research and development services) as provided for in CPC Reference 85203.

The Regulations only apply when a contracting authority 'seeks offers in relation to a proposed public services contract'. They impose obligations only in relation to service providers who are nationals of and established in a member state, but they do not require any preference to be given to offers from them. They do, however, prohibit treating non-EC service providers more favourably than EC service providers. The Regulations only apply when a contracting authority seeks offers from service providers which are not part of the same legal entity as itself, but they do not require a contracting authority to seek outside offers unless it chooses to do so. If it does do so it must treat any in-house offer on the same basis as the outside offers for the purpose of evaluating the bids. If the outside bid is successful the fact that the contract award procedure has been conducted does not mean that a contract has to be awarded. The contracting authority can choose not to accept the outside offer. There could be problems under domestic law however, if the contracting authority does not make it clear from the outset that it reserves the right not to award the contract.

Meaning of 'contracting authority'

3.32 The Regulations apply to the same bodies (contracting authorities) as the Works Directive. These include government, and government controlled bodies, local authorities and certain bodies governed by public law. A list of contracting authorities is set out at Regulation 3(1). Where a contracting authority joins with another person (e.g. a property developer) for the purpose of purchasing services, and both are parties to the contract, the Regulations will apply. The amount of the contracting authority's contribution is not relevant to the application of the threshold: the normal valuation rules apply to the contract as a whole.

Meaning of 'public services contract'

3.33 A public services contract is defined in the Regulations as 'a contract in writing for consideration (whatever the nature of the consideration) under which a contracting authority engages a person to provide services, excluding certain specified contracts for services (e.g. employment contracts and contracts with concessionaires).

In addition certain services contracts although 'public services contracts' for the purpose of the Regulations are excluded from its provisions (see Regulation 6).

Borderline cases

3.34 Where a contract is for both goods and services, or works and services it will only fall within the scope of the Services Regulations if the consideration attributable to the services is greater than that attributable to the goods or to the works. Otherwise it will fall within the Supply or Works Regulations as the case may be. For example where a contracting authority seeks offers in relation to a contract for the provision of computer hardware and bespoke software, the contract will only be a services contract if the cost attributable to the development of the software exceeds the cost of the hardware.

Transitional arrangements

3.35 The directive and therefore the Regulations make no provision for transitional arrangements, however the following matters should be noted. The Regulations will not apply to contracts entered into before 13 January 1994, but as has already been pointed out, the directive will in most cases have direct effect in relation to contracts entered into between 1 July 1993 and that date. Where a public services contract was entered into before 1 July 1993 it may nevertheless be subject to scrutiny by the Commission and possible challenge if it appears to have been entered into with the intention of avoiding the application of the directive. Contracts for services of unusually long duration are likely to attract attention in this respect.

Similarly the directive will not affect contract award procedures which on 1 July 1993 had passed the point at which its application needed to be considered. In the Treasury's view, which it is submitted is correct, that point would have been reached if the date for sending the contract notice to the *Official Journal* in accordance with Regulation 7(12) had passed. From 1 July 1993 the directive will also apply to the seeking of offers for public services contracts, not only if their estimated value exceeds the threshold individually, but also if they do so as one of a series of contracts to which the aggregation rules apply, and for this purpose relevant contracts which were entered into before 1 July 1993, as well as after that date, must be taken into account. In addition the Regulations will require a call for competition for contracts for Part A services entered into after 1 July 1993 to which a framework arrangement entered into before 1 July applies *unless* that framework arrangement has been treated as if it were a contract and awarded in accordance with the Regulations. Contracts entered into before 1 July 1993 and which by their terms are renewable or are for indefinite duration (e.g. banking or auditing contracts) are not caught by the Regulations on renewal.

The public services contracts excluded from the operation of the Regulations

3.36 The Services Regulations do not apply to the seeking of offers in relation to certain specified types of contract.

Contracts below certain value thresholds

3.37 Most importantly the Regulations do not apply to the seeking of offers in relation to a proposed public services contract where the 'estimated value' (net of VAT) at the 'relevant time' is less than 200 000 ECUs (£149 728 until 31 December 1995). The 'estimated value' is normally the sum which the contracting authority expects to pay under the contract and assuming that it exercises any options. Where appropriate these will be the insurance premiums payable in respect of insurance services, the fees, commissions or other remuneration payable for banking and financial services, and the fees or commissions payable for design services.

Aggregation provisions

3.38 Exceptionally the estimated value is to be calculated according to provisions in the Regulations relating to the aggregation of sums paid under a series of similar contracts. These are similar to, but not identical with, the parallel provisions contained in the Supply Regulations.

Rules governing technical specifications

3.39 The rules governing technical specifications are similar to those in the Works and Supply Regulations.

Rules governing the procedures leading to the award of a public services contract

Prior information notices

3.40 One of the fundamental aims of the new EC procurement regime is to ensure that information about prospective contracts should be published throughout the European Community so as to enable potential contractors from all member states to compete on an equal footing.

As soon after the start of each financial year as possible, contracting authorities must publish a prior information notice in the *Official Journal* in the prescribed form setting out contracts for Part A services which it expects to enter into during that financial year and which are above the threshold either individually or because the aggregation provisions apply, and which are expected to total more than 750 000 ECUs (£561 480) for any one of the categories of services in Part A.

Selection of contract award procedure

3.41 As with the Works and Supply Regulations the contracting authority when seeking offers in relation to a proposed public services contract must use the open procedure, the restricted procedure, or the negotiated procedure. The Regulations lay down rules for making the choice of procedure.

Negotiated procedure

3.42 The negotiated procedure may only be used in the exceptional circumstances specified in the Regulations. These are similar to but not identical with those specified in the Supply Regulations. In all other circumstances, the contracting authority must use the open or restricted procedure. Where the negotiated procedure may be used no prior publication of a contract notice in the *Official Journal* (and hence no open competition) is usually required.

A contracting authority may only exclude a services provider from those persons from whom it will make the selection of persons to be invited to negotiate the contract if the services provider may be treated as ineligible on a ground specified in the Regulations or if the services provider fails to satisfy the minimum standards of economic and financial standing, ability and technical capacity, required of services providers by the contracting authority as evaluated in accordance with the Regulations.

Once any services providers have been excluded in the manner described above, the contracting authority must make its selection of the services providers to be invited to negotiate in accordance with the rules laid down in the Regulations.

The open and restricted procedures

3.43 These are similar to those contained in the Works and Supplies Regulations, although it should be noted that under the Services Regulations the *ability* of the services provider is introduced as an additional criterion on which a contracting authority may make its selection of tenderers or those invited to tender.

The award of a public services contract

The basis for the award

3.44 As with the Works and Supply Regulations the contracting authority must award a public services contract on the basis of either the tender (including in-house bids) which offers the lowest price or the one which is 'the most economically advantageous to the contracting authority' (i.e. best value for money).

The criteria which a contracting authority may use to determine that an offer is the most economically advantageous include period of completion or delivery, quality, aesthetic and functional characteristics, technical merit, after-sales service, technical assistance and price. Other economic criteria would include security of supply, avoidance of monopoly and the risk of non-delivery because an offer is known to be based on an unapproved state aid that might have to be repaid. All the criteria which a contracting authority intends to apply in determining the most economically advantageous offer must be stated in the contract notice or contract documents, preferably in descending order of importance. A distinction must however be made between on the one hand a contractual condition requiring the successful services provider to cooperate with some policy objective of the contracting authority (e.g. ensuring that a proportion of its workforce is drawn from the ranks of the unemployed) and the criteria for the selection of services providers or the award of the public services contract on the other.

Where a contracting authority awards a public services contract on the basis of the offer which is most economically advantageous it may take account of offers which offer variations on the requirements specified in the contract documents if:

1. The offer meets the minimum requirements of the contracting authority, and
2. It has stated those minimum requirements and any specific requirements for the presentation of an offer offering variations in the contract documents. If a contracting authority will not accept variations it must state that fact in the contract notice. A contracting authority must not reject an offer offering variations on the contract specification on the ground that it would lead to the award of a public supply contract, nor may it reject an offer on the ground that reference has been made to European specifications or to national specifications which are permitted by the Regulations.

Abnormally low tenders

3.45 The rules relating to abnormally low tenders are similar to those contained in the Works and Supply Regulations.

Post-tender negotiations

3.46 It should be stressed that in open and restricted procedures all negotiations with candidates or tenderers on fundamental aspects of the contract and in particular on prices, are not permitted, although discussions with candidates or tenderers may be held for the purposes of clarifying or supplementing the content of their tenders or the requirements of the contracting authority provided this does not involve unfairness to their competitors.

Contracting authority's obligations once contract has been awarded

3.47 The Regulations impose certain reporting obligations on contracting authorities once the contract has been awarded.

Design contests

3.48 In addition the Regulations lay down rules which must be followed for the holding of certain design contests which may or may not be part of the procedure leading to the award of a public services contract.

A design contest will be caught by the Regulations:

1. If it is organized as part of a procedure leading to the award of a public services contract and the estimated value of the contract (after applying the aggregation provisions) is not less than 200 000 ECUs (£149 728), or
2. Whether or not it is organized as part of a procedure leading to the award of such a contract, if the aggregate of the value of the prizes or payments for the contest is not less than 200 000 ECUs. This regulation only applies to Part A contracts.

Where a design contest is caught by the Regulations the following provisions apply:

- The contracting authority must publicize its intention to hold a contest by sending to the *Official Journal* a notice in a form substantially corresponding to that set out in Part F of Schedule 2 and containing the information there specified.
- The rules of the contest must be made available to all services providers who wish to participate.
- The number of services providers invited to participate may be restricted but the contracting authority must make the selection on the basis of clear and non-discriminatory criteria. The number participating must be sufficient to ensure that there is adequate competition.
- The participants' proposals must be submitted anonymously to a jury who must be individuals who are independent of the participants. Where the participants are required to possess a qualification at least one third of its jury must possess that qualification or its equivalent.
- The jury must make its decision independently and solely on the basis of the criteria set out in the published notice.
- Not later than 48 days after the jury has made its selection the contracting authority must publicize the result in the *Official Journal.*

Subsidized public services contracts

3.49 Regulation 25 imposes an obligation on a contracting authority which undertakes to contribute more than half of the cost of certain public services contracts entered into by a party other than a contracting authority to ensure that that party complies with the Regulations as if it were a contracting authority.

The public services contracts to which this provision applies are contracts which would qualify as public services contracts if the subsidized body were a contracting authority and which are contracts for services in connection with the carrying out of civil engineering projects such as the construction of roads, bridges and railways, etc. (Schedule 1 of the Works Regulations, Group 502), or for the carrying out of building work for hospitals, facilities intended for sports, recreation and leisure, school and university buildings, or buildings for administrative purposes.

Remedies for breach of the Community rules governing procurement

3.50 The Works, Supply, Utilities, and Services, Regulations provide a 'contractor', 'supplier' or 'services provider' (i.e. one who is a national of and established in a member state) and who suffers or risks suffering loss or damage as a result of a breach of the relevant Regulations or the breach of any Community obligation in respect of a contract to which the Regulations apply, with a right to obtain redress by way of court action. A 'services provider' includes one who provides architectural or related services (see paragraph 3.31 above). The remedies available and the procedure by which they may be obtained are very similar in respect of each of the Regulations. In this way the Regulations implement the 'Remedies' Directive and the 'Compliance' Directive already referred to.

The obligation on contracting authorities and utilities to comply with the provisions of the Regulations (other than certain provisions relating to reporting and the supply of information) and with enforceable Community obligations in respect of contracts falling within the Regulations, is conceived under the Regulations as a duty owed to providers the breach whereof gives rise to an action for breach of statutory duty.

A similar duty is placed upon a public works concessionaire to comply with the obligations placed upon it by regulation 26(3) of the Works Regulations and where such a duty is imposed the term 'contractor' includes any person who sought or who seeks or who would have wished to be the person to whom a contract to which regulation 26(3) applies is awarded and who is a national of and established in a member state.

A breach of the duty referred to is not a criminal offence but is actionable by any provider who in consequence 'suffers or risks suffering loss or damage'. Proceedings brought in England and Wales and in Northern Ireland must be brought in the High Court, and in Scotland, before the Court of Session. However, proceedings under the Regulations may not be brought unless:

1. the provider bringing the proceedings has informed the contracting authority (including a concessionaire), or utility of the breach or apprehended breach of the duty referred to and of his intention to bring proceedings under the Regulations in respect of it; and
2. they are brought promptly, and in any event within three months from the date when grounds for the bringing of the proceedings first arose unless the court considers that there is good reason for extending the period within which proceedings may be brought.

In proceedings brought under each of the Regulations the court may, without prejudice to any other powers it may have:

1. by interim order (whether or not the defendant is the Crown) suspend the procedure leading to the award of the relevant contract, or suspend the implementation of any decision or action taken by the contracting authority or utility in the course of following such a procedure; and
2. if satisfied that a decision or action taken by a contracting authority or utility was in breach of the duty referred to,
   (a) order the setting aside of that decision or action or order the contracting authority or utility to amend any document,
   (b) award damages to a contractor or supplier who has suffered loss or damage as a consequence of the breach, or
   (c) do both of those things.

However, in proceedings brought under each of the Regulations, the court can only award damages if the contract in relation to which the breach occurred has been entered into. The court cannot therefore set aside a contract which has been entered into in breach of the Regulations. It is uncertain however whether such a contract in English law is unenforceable as between the parties to it on the grounds of public policy. It is submitted that where both parties are aware of the breach at the time of entering the contract (e.g. where the proposed contract was not advertised) public policy requires that the contract should be unenforceable by both parties. Where only one party is in breach without the other party's knowledge (e.g. where a contracting authority without justification selects a contractor who has not submitted the lowest tender) then the contract should only be unenforceable by the party in breach.

In the English courts any interim order under (1.) above will be by way of interlocutory injunction which it is anticipated will be granted or refused on the familiar principles laid down by the House of Lords in *American Cyanamid Co. v Ethicon Ltd* [1975] AC 396. These principles may be summarized as follows:

1. The plaintiff must establish that he has a good arguable claim to the right he seeks to protect;
2. The court must not attempt to decide the claim on the affidavits; it is enough if the plaintiff shows that there is a serious question to be tried;
3. If the plaintiff satisfies these tests the grant or refusal of an injunction is a matter for the court's discretion on the balance of convenience including that of the public where this is affected.

Although the factors relevant to the exercise of the discretion are many and varied (of which the question whether damages would be a sufficient remedy is arguably the most important) in public

procurement cases the question of the public interest is often likely to be decisive against the grant of the injunction. This fact is expressly recognized by both Remedies directives which provide that:

'The Member States may provide that when considering whether to order interim measures the body responsible may take into account the probable consequences of the measures for all interests likely to be harmed, as well as the public interest, and may decide not to grant such measures where their negative consequences could exceed their benefits. A decision not to grant interim measures shall not prejudice any other claim of the person seeking these measures.' (article 2(4) of both directives)

No such provision appears in the Regulations no doubt because it was considered that the practice of the courts when granting or refusing interlocutory injunctions was entirely consistent with the discretion given by the Remedies directive in this respect.

Even where the public interest element is not decisive the usual requirement that the plaintiff undertake to pay the defendant's damages caused by the injunction should it prove to have been wrongly granted will often dissuade a plaintiff from pursuing this remedy in public procurement cases where such damages are likely to be heavy.

A provider may wish under (2.) above to have set aside a decision to reject his bid made on the basis of criteria not permitted by the Regulations, or a decision to exclude his bid as abnormally low where he has not been given an opportunity to give an explanation. Equally a provider may require that a contract document be amended so as to exclude a specification not permitted by the Regulations.

It will be noted that each of the Regulations while providing providers with a remedy in damages do not specify how those damages are to be assessed. In Community law it is left to national laws to provide the remedies required in order to ensure that Community rights are protected, and until the first cases go through the courts it is uncertain how such damages will be assessed.

In the case of the Utilities Regulations alone the task of recovering certain damage is eased by Regulation 32(7) which provides that:

'Where in proceedings under this regulation the Court is satisfied that a provider would have had a real chance of being awarded a contract if that chance had not been adversely affected by a breach of the duty owed to him by the utility pursuant to [the Regulations] the provider shall be entitled to damages amounting to his costs in preparing his tender and in participating in the procedure leading to the award of the contract.'

Regulation 32(8) makes it clear that that remedy is without prejudice to a claim by a provider that he has suffered other loss or damage or that he is entitled to relief other than damages and further that subsection 7 is without prejudice to the matters on which a provider may be required to satisfy the court in respect of any other such claim.

To what standard the plaintiff will have to prove that he had a 'real chance' (identical words are used in article 2(3) of the directive) of being awarded the contract is as yet unclear but it is submitted that this will be something less than on the balance of probabilities.

The role of the architect in relation to the procurement regulations

3.51 It is to be noted that the obligations imposed by the procurement Regulations are placed on the 'contracting authority' or utility concerned. However an architect employed by such a body may be under a contractual duty to carry out those obligations as its agent and liable to indemnify it where a breach of that duty results in loss. This could occur, for example where the contract award is delayed or where the authority or utility is compelled to pay damages as the result of an infringement.

On the other hand architects who wish to tender for public authority (and utility) contracts for architectural services will be able to take advantage of the provisions of the Services directive to ensure equal treatment with other EC architects. It should be borne in mind that the Services directive applies throughout the Community and that therefore a UK architect can as much take advantage of its provisions in another member state as architects from other member states can take advantage of it in the UK.

Public works contracts and article 30 EEC

3.52 Even where a public procurement contract falls outside the provisions of the relevant directive, architects will still have to take care that they do not specify in such a manner as will render any public authority employer in breach of article 30 EEC.

Article 30 provides that:

'Quantitative restrictions on imports and all measures having equivalent effect shall, without prejudice to the following provisions be prohibited between Member States.'

In Case 45/87 *Commission* v *Ireland*, the Dundalk Urban District Council (a public body for whose acts the Irish Government are responsible), permitted the inclusion in the contract specification for a drinking water supply scheme of a clause providing that certain pipes should be certified as complying with an Irish standard and consequently refusing to consider without adequate justification a tender providing for such pipes manufactured to an alternative standard providing equivalent guarantees of safety, performance and reliability. The contract fell outside the provisions of the Works directive because it concerned the distribution of drinking water. Nevertheless, the Court held that Ireland had acted in breach of article 30. Only one undertaking was capable of producing pipes to the required standard and that undertaking was situated in Ireland. Consequently, the inclusion of that specification had the effect of restricting the supply of the pipes needed to Irish manufacturers alone and was a quantitive restriction on imports or a measure having equivalent effect. The breach of article 30 could have been avoided if the specifier had added the words 'or equivalent' after the specification concerned.

4 Technical harmonization and standards

The Construction Products Directive 89/106 EEC

4.01 A major barrier to the free movement of construction products within the Community has been the differing national requirements relating to such matters as building safety, health, durability, energy economy and protection of the environment, which in turn directly influence national product standards, technical approvals and other technical specifications and provisions.

In order to overcome this problem, the Community has adopted the Construction Products directive whose aim is to provide for the free movement, sale and use of construction products which are fit for their intended use and have such characteristics that structures in which they are incorporated meet certain essential requirements. Products, in so far as these essential requirements relate to them, which do not meet the appropriate standard may not be placed on the market (article 2).

4.02 These essential requirements are similar in style to the functional requirements of the Building Regulations in force in England and Wales, but rather wider in scope. They relate to mechanical resistance and stability, safety in case of fire, hygiene, health and the environment, safety in use, protection against noise, and energy economy and heat retention. These requirements must, subject to normal maintenance, be satisfied for an economically reasonable working life and generally provide protection against events which are foreseeable.

The performance levels of products complying with these essential requirements may, however, vary according to geographical or climatic conditions or in ways of life, as well as different levels of protection that may prevail at national regional or local level and member states may decide which class of performance level they require to be observed within their territory.

4.03 Products will be presumed to be fit for their intended use if they bear an EC conformity mark showing that they comply with a European standard or a European technical approval or (when documents of this sort do not exist) relevant national standards or agreements recognized at Community level as meeting the essential requirements. If a manufacturer chooses to make a product which is not in conformity with these specifications, he has to prove that his product conforms to the essential requirements before he will be permitted to put it on the market. Conformity may be verified by third party certification.

4.04 European standards which will ensure that the essential requirements are met will be drawn up by a European standards body usually CEN or CENELEC. These will be published in the UK as identically worded British standards. European technical approvals will be issued by approved bodies designated for this purpose by the member states in accordance with guidelines prepared by the European body comprising the approved bodies from all the member states.

4.05 Member states are prohibited from interfering with the free movement of goods which satisfy the provisions of the directive and are to ensure that the use of such products is not impeded by any national rule or condition imposed by a public body, or private bodies acting as a public undertaking or acting as a public body on the basis of a monopoly position (article 6). This would appear to include such bodies as the NHBC in their standard setting role.

4.06 The directive has been implemented in the UK by the Construction Products Regulations 1991 (S.I. 1991/1620) which came into force on 27 December 1991.

The implementation of the directive throughout the Community should greatly ease the task of the architect who is designing buildings in more than one member state as it means that he can now be sure that the products he specifies, so long as they comply with the directive, will comply with the regulations and requirements of every member state without his having to carry out a detailed check for that purpose.

5 Right of establishment and freedom to provide services – the Architects Directive 85/384 EEC

The background

5.01 Three of the fundamental principles underlying the Treaty of Rome are the free movement of workers, the freedom to set up business in any member state and the freedom to provide services in a member state, other than that in which the provider of these services is based. In order to ensure that those principles are met so far as architects are concerned the Community has adopted directive 85/384 EEC which has been implemented into UK law by the Architects' Qualifications (EEC Recognition) Order 1987 (S.I. 1987, No. 1824 as amended by S.I. No. 2241).

Mutual recognition of architectural qualifications

5.02 The directive allows architects with appropriate UK qualifications to practise anywhere in the EC and architects from other member states to have the equivalent right to practise in this country. The directive sets out in detail what are the minimum qualifications required for such mutual recognition and how these are to be proved.

Right of establishment and freedom to provide services

5.03 The directive similarly lays down rules for the mutual recognition of an architect's rights to set up in practice in a host member state or to provide architectural services in another member state.

The fundamental principle contained in the directive is that there must be no discrimination against foreign nationals which would make it more difficult for them to establish themselves or provide services in the host state than it would be for nationals of that state.

5.04 Similar provision has been made for the mutual recognition within the Community of those employed in the construction industry by the following measures:

1. **The Certificates of Experience Directive 64/77/EC** This directive aims to ensure that experience of doing a particular job in one member state is recognized in other member states. Certificates are issued by the competent authority in the state where the experience is gained so that a registration body in any other member state can recognize the holder as a suitably experienced person. In some European countries a period of experience and/or training is required before a person can set up as an independent plumber or electrician.
2. **First General Directive on Professional Qualifications 89/48/EC** This directive which has been implemented in the UK by the European Communities (Recognition of Professional Qualifications) Regulations 1991 (S.I. 1991 No. 824) deals with the general system for recognizing professional education and training in regulated professions for which university courses lasting at least three years is required. Courses for engineers, surveyors and other construction industry professionals lasting three years or more are covered by this directive.
3. **Second General Directive on Professional Qualifications 92/51/EC** This directive complements directive 89/48/EC by extending the regime provided by that directive to qualifications obtained on completion of such education and training over a shorter period, whether at secondary level (possibly complemented by professional training and experience), post-secondary level, or even merely through professional experience.

   It applies to any national of a member state who wishes to pursue a 'regulated' profession in a host member state, whether in a self-employed capacity or as an employed person, other than a profession covered by a specific directive establishing arrangements for mutual recognition of professional qualifications (e.g. the Architects directive), or an activity covered by certain specific directives principally concerned with introducing mutual recognition of technical skills based on experience in another member state and listed in an annex to the directive. The directive will only apply in cases where directive 89/48/EEC is inapplicable, i.e. where the training required in the host state is less than three years' higher education at university level. The scheme adopted by the directive is similar to that adopted by directive 89/48/EEC and like directive 89/48/EC it will be reviewed after five years (i.e. in 1999) to determine how effectively it has operated.

   Although the directive is required to be in place by 18 June 1994 it had not been implemented in the UK at the time of writing (October 1995).

6 The Product Liability Directive 85/374 IEEC and the Consumer Protection Act 1987

6.01 The Product Liability directive 85/374 which was adopted on 25 July 1985 was required to be implemented throughout the EC by 30 July 1988. It has been implemented into UK law by the Consumer Protection Act 1987, Part I.

6.02 The directive introduces into every member state a system of strict liability (i.e. without the need to prove negligence) for death, personal injury and damage to private property resulting from defective products put into circulation after the date when the national law came into force (in the UK this is 1 March 1988). A 'product' is very widely defined under the Act (Section 1(2)) as:

'any goods or electricity and . . . includes a product which is comprised in another product, whether by virtue of being a component part or raw material or otherwise'.

Goods are defined (Section 45) as:

'substances, growing crops and things comprised in land by virtue of being attached to it . . .'

It is clear therefore, that building products are covered by the Act and at first sight it might appear that buildings themselves and/or parts of buildings such as roofs or foundations are also covered.

6.03 However, by Section 46(3) of the Act it is provided that:

'subject to subsection (4) below the performance of any contract by the erection of any building or structure on any land or by carrying out of any other building works shall be treated for the purpose of the Act as a supply of goods in so far as it involves the provision of any goods to any person by means of their incorporation into the building, structure or works'.

6.04 Subsection 4 provides in so far as is relevant:

'References in this Act to supplying goods shall not include references to supplying goods comprised in land where the supply is affected by the creation or disposal of an interest in land.'

In the case, therefore, of a builder building under a contract and who does not own the land on which he builds he may be liable as 'supplier' or 'producer' (see below) in respect of defective products supplied or produced by him and incorporated into the building whether by way of construction, alteration or repair and will not be liable as producer of the defective building itself or of its immovable parts such as foundations.

In the case of a speculative builder however, who builds on his own land and then effects the supply of that building by the creation or disposal of an interest in land (e.g. by sale of the freehold or lease) the Act appears to leave him liable as *producer* of the defective building while exempting him from any liability as supplier of any defective product comprised within the building. It is submitted that that is not the case.

6.05 By Section 1(1) of the Act it is provided that the Act must be construed to give effect to the directive.

It is clear from the Recitals and from Article 2 that the directive does not apply to 'immovables' and that buildings and probably parts of buildings fall within that term. It is submitted therefore that when the Act is properly construed to give effect to the directive it must follow that a speculative builder cannot be liable under it as producer of a defective house.

Similarly, neither in article 3(6) (which renders a supplier of a defective product liable if he fails to identify its producer within a reasonable time) nor anywhere else in the directive is any exemption from liability accorded *to the supplier* where the supply is effected by the creation or disposal of an interest in land. It is submitted therefore that no distinction should be made between the liability of a speculative builder and a contract builder under the Act and indeed it is difficult to see in logic why there should be any.

6.06 The Act places primary liability on the 'producer' of the product who will normally be the manufacturer but may also be the product's importer into the EC where it has been manufactured outside the EC. Secondary liability is placed on the supplier of the goods in question where that supplier fails to identify within a reasonable time the person who sold the goods to him.

It may be a matter of importance therefore to know who in a given case is the 'producer' or 'supplier' of a building product for the purpose of the Act. There is as yet no authority on the matter but the following is put forward as a tentative answer:

1. **Where the building is erected by a speculative builder** The builder alone will be the 'supplier' in the first instance of the products incorporated into the building and may therefore be liable as such under the Act (i.e. where he fails to identify his

supplier within a reasonable time). He may also be liable as 'producer' of a product where he has given that product its 'essential characteristics' (see Section 1(2)), an example of such a product would be concrete where this is mixed by the contractor, or where he has imported that product into the EC.

2. **When the building is erected under a contract with the building owner** The contract builder's liability as 'producer' and 'supplier' of the building products he incorporates into the building he erects will normally be no different from that of the speculative builder. However, circumstances may arise, whether by express agreement or otherwise, where the contractor acts as agent for the building owner or his architect in the 'production' or 'supply' of the product in question. In that case the building owner or the architect would be liable as 'producer' or 'supplier' under the Act in the same way as the contractor would have been. Such cases outside express contract are, however, likely to be rare. In *Young & Marten Ltd* v *McManuschilds* ([1986] AC 454, HL), it was held that even where a product was specified that could only be purchased from one source, the contractor purchasing it was liable to the building owner for breach of implied warranty of merchantable quality where the product proved to be defective. It was implicit in that decision that the contractor was not acting as the building owner's agent in making the purchase.

6.07 Even where the builder is not acting as the building owner's agent, he may well wish in future to seek an indemnity from the building owner in respect of any liability he may incur under the Act, particularly in respect of latent defects in products specified by the architect. Similarly, the building owner will no doubt seek an indemnity in respect of such liability from his architect.

6.08 Where the builder has no choice in the product he purchases and where the exercise of reasonable skill and care on his part in the selection of that product is ineffective in ensuring that the product is of merchantable quality (as might well be the case where there is a design defect) it would seem reasonable that ultimate liability under the Act (when this cannot be passed on to the others) should fall on the architect who has chosen the product and who has had the best chance of assessing that product's quality. Such indemnity provisions may well become a common feature of building and architectural service contracts in the future.

7 Safety and health at work

EC legislation on health and safety affects the construction industry's operation on site, in the design of buildings and civil engineering works and in the use of plant. In the UK existing legislation such as the Health and Safety at Work Act 1974 already meets many of the requirements of the European directives. Additional regulations under the 1974 Act have or will be issued to cover the remaining requirements as they come into force.

The fundamental directive is the Safety and Health of Workers at Work Directive 89/391/EC which has been implemented in the UK by the Management of Health and Safety at Work Regulations 1992 (S.I. 1992 No. 2051). The directive sets out the responsibilities of employers and employees for safety and health at work and provides for further directives covering specific areas. Directives made under that framework directive which are of particular relevance to the construction industry are:

1. **Safety and Health for the Workplace Directive 89/654/EC** The directive lays down minimum safety and health requirements relating to the design structure and maintenance of buildings.

2. **Use of Work Equipment Directive 89/655/EC** The directive which has been implemented in the UK by the Provision and Use of Work Equipment Regulations 1992 (S.I. 1992 No. 2932) requires employers to provide for the safe use and maintenance of 'work equipment' (defined as any machine, apparatus, tool or installation at work) and sets out minimum safety and health requirements relating to training and safe operating procedures.

3. **Use of Personal Protective Equipment Directive 89/656/EC and 89/686/EC** These directives have been implemented in the UK by the Personal Protective Equipment at Work Regulations 1992 (S.I. 1992 No. 2966) and the Personal Protective Equipment (EC Directive) Regulations 1992 (S.I. 1992 No. 3139). They set out minimum health and safety requirements for the use by workers of PPE in the workplace and set minimum standards designed to ensure the health and safety of users of PPE.

4. **Mobile Machinery and Lifting Equipment Directive 91/368/EC** The directive which was required to be in force by 1 January 1993 extends the scope of the Machinery Directive 89/392/EC laying down essential safety requirements for mobile machinery and lifting equipment such as dumpers and cranes used on construction sites. Both directives have been implemented in the UK by S.I. 1992 No. 2932 referred to above.

5. **The Construction Sites Directive 92/57/EC** The directive lays down minimum safety and health requirements for temporary or mobile construction sites (defined as any construction site at which building or civil engineering works are carried out). It places particular responsibilities on 'project supervisors' who are 'any person responsible for the design and/or execution and/or supervision of the execution of a project acting on behalf of a client' (article 2(d)) and would therefore include architects. Those responsibilities include:

(a) appointing one or more safety co-ordinators for safety and health matters for any construction site on which more than one contractor is present (article 3(1)). The proper carrying out of the co-ordinators duties is the responsibility of the project supervisor.

(b) ensuring that prior to the setting up of a construction site a 'safety and health plan' is drawn up in accordance with requirements set out in the directive (article 3(2)).

(c) In the case of construction sites on which work is scheduled to last longer than 30 working days and on which more than 20 workers are occupied simultaneously or on which the volume of work is scheduled to exceed 500 person days, communicating a 'prior notice' drawn up in accordance with the directive, to the competent authority (article 3(3)).

(d) taking account of the general principles of prevention concerning safety and health contained in directive 89/391/EC (above) during the various stages of designing and preparing the project, in particular:

(i) when architectural technical and/or organizational aspects are being decided, in order to plan the various items or stages of work which are to take place simultaneously or in succession.

(ii) when estimating the period required for completing such work or work stages. Account must also be taken each time this appears necessary of all safety and health plans drawn up or adjusted in accordance with requirements of the directive (article 4).

The directive has been implemented in the UK by the Construction (Design and Management) Regulations 1994 (S.I. 1994 No. 3140).

The practical ramifications for architects of these directives are discussed in Chapter 19 'Health and Safety Law affecting Architects'.

19

Health and safety law affecting architects

RICHARD DYTON

1 Introduction

At the time of writing, Health and Safety is a major matter of debate between architects, employers and contractors. The most significant health and safety legislation ever to affect the construction industry has been implemented by the Construction (Design and Management) Regulations 1994, which came into effect on the 31 March 1995. The legislation is complex and gives rise to additional costs in compliance.

The degree to which architects are aware of the new health and safety duties is evident in a recent survey[1] in which 96% of respondent firms indicated that they were aware of the new health and safety measures. Relatively high profile cases such as the prosecution of the consulting engineers Kenchington Little (now Kenchington Ford), and the prosecution of Derby City Council as a 'Client' have led to the expression of concern by architects and, indeed, consultants firms in general, that the Health and Safety Executive (which is the enforcement arm of the Health and Safety Commission) is increasingly flexing its legal muscles against consultants as well as contractors, the latter of which have traditionally been responsible for matters concerning safety. Architects are also increasingly aware that the form which any liability can take is not necessarily limited to prosecution by the Health and Safety Executive. Other areas in which liability may attach include civil actions based on the tort of negligence and contractual claims when regulations are incorporated into an appointment or collateral warranty agreement.

The scope of this chapter is to consider the structure of the pre-existing legislation and, more importantly, to provide a practical guide to the obligations of the architect under the new legislation in the context of the various stages within the project plan.

2 Existing health and safety position
The Health and Safety at Work Act 1974

2.01 The Health and Safety at Work Act 1974 (HSW Act) enacted a system to replace progressively the older law which had grown up piecemeal and which addressed only certain types of workplaces or processes (such as under the Factories Act 1961 and the Offices, Shops and Railway Premises Act 1963). The old system had left other workplaces uncovered by the legislation and the HSW Act provided the framework for a system of regulations applying generally to all workplaces, employers and employees. It also extended to many self-employed persons and to others such as manufacturers, designers and importers of articles to be used at work. Examples of the regulations which were brought in under

the new policy were regulations covering the protection of eyes[2], noise[3], the use of lead[4], the use of asbestos[5], the control of industrial major hazards[6], and the control of substances hazardous to health[7].

Structure of the Act

2.02 The structure of the HSW Act is that Sections 2–6 place general duties on employers, the self-employed, persons otherwise in control of premises and designers, manufacturers, importers or suppliers of articles for use at work. The duties are normally qualified by the phrase 'reasonably practicable'. Section 6 refers to the duties of designers together with those who manufacture and import or supply an article for use at work. The general obligation is:

> 'To ensure, so far as is reasonably practicable, that the article is so designed and constructed as to be safe and without risks to health when properly used'.

The structure of the HSW Act is, therefore, divided into general obligations under the Act itself and more specific obligations under the regulations (considered in more detail below).

Buildings and construction sites

2.03 Despite the fact that the CDM Regulations have only recently implemented the general obligation in relation to buildings and construction sites, the Health and Safety Executive have, none the less, already applied the obligation in a number of cases. The most notable of these is the well publicized conviction of Kenchington Little (referred to above) in July 1991 which was overturned in February 1993 on appeal. The conviction was originally for endangering the public and followed the collapse of a factory clock tower in the centre of Nottingham in February 1990. The scheme concentrated on retaining a 1960s facade using a steel frame and resin anchors. In a severe storm the tower toppled over and Kenchington Little were judged to have overstressed the supports. The appeal against the fine of £20 000 with £75 000 of costs was successful. It has been reported, however, that the decision on appeal was based on a technicality as the appeal judges held that the trial judge misdirected the jury in his summing up.

The general policy of the Health and Safety Executive is to increase the level of prosecutions for breaches of health and safety regulations. The prosecution of Derby City Council in 1989 as a 'client' and the prosecution of a company director in 1988 in

[1] Dyton, F. R. R. (1994) EC Legal Developments affecting UK architects and engineers, Centre of Construction Law and Management, Kings College, London.

[2] Protection of Eyes Regulations 1974
[3] Noise at Work Regulations 1989
[4] Control of Lead at Work Regulations 1980
[5] Control of Asbestos at Work Regulations 1987
[6] Control of Industrial Major Accident Hazard Regulations 1984
[7] Control of Substances Hazardous to Health Regulations 1988

which he received a suspended prison sentence for manslaughter following a fatal accident at a factory in Lancashire tends to support the Health and Safety Executive's statement that they will 'have no hesitation against bringing a similar case in future against the consultant'.[8]

Liability under the Act and Regulations

2.04 Breaches of the Act or of the Regulations give rise to criminal liabilities which may lead to sentences of unlimited fines and/or a maximum term of imprisonment not exceeding two years. The policy of the Health and Safety Executive in enforcing the Regulations has been to prosecute and fine an organization rather than an individual, although there is nothing in law to prevent an individual being prosecuted and, ultimately, imprisoned. Codes of practice are regularly issued with the relevant Regulations, and these are used to flesh out the Regulations concerned. Breach of the codes is not, in itself, breach of the Regulations but the codes are admissible in criminal and, indeed, in civil proceedings to determine whether or not there has been a breach of the Regulations.

In the context of civil liability, there are two potential limbs: firstly, the tort of breach of statutory duty which is a 'strict' liability in the sense that it is not qualified by what is reasonable in the context of the profession at large (although the statutory duties in the Regulations themselves are usually qualified by statements such as 'so far as is reasonably practicable') and, secondly, the tort of negligence which arises from common standards becoming established in the profession of which the reasonable architect is deemed to have knowledge and breach of which thereby renders the architect liable.

Breach of the provisions of the Act does not itself give rise to a civil action for breach of statutory duty. However, if there is a breach of the Regulations this may enable a claimant to cite the breach as a basis for a civil claim depending upon whether the specific Regulations allow such a claim and whether the plaintiff's interest is intended to be protected by the Regulations.

Inevitably, the influence of the Regulations will affect the law of negligence in setting specific legal standards in the context of health and safety. A failure to meet those standards may represent a breach of duty in negligence, even if the matter in question is not specifically covered by the Regulations. Therefore, liability is not restricted merely to claims based upon breach of statutory duty but also, indirectly, in the tort of negligence. In addition, the requirement for employers to carry out risk assessments is likely to be of significance when considering questions of foreseeability at common law.

Relevant Regulations

2.05 There are a large number of health and safety Regulations in addition to the CDM Regulations which, whilst not specific to the construction industry, affect the work of architects. Many of these Regulations apply to the duties of employers in the workplace. As such, the architect must have a general knowledge of these when designing such workplaces in order to avoid risks to the health of employees and generally to allow them to be safe. These Regulations are, briefly, as follows:

The Management of Health and Safety at Work Regulations 1992 (implemented 1 January 1993)

2.06 The basic obligation under these regulations is for employers to carry out a risk assessment to consider the risks of the health and safety of all employees arising out of the conduct of the business by the employers.

The Workplace (Health, Safety and Welfare) Regulations 1992

2.07 These Regulations extend the duties of employers into areas not previously the subject of specific statutory provisions such as

[8] *New Civil Engineer*, 25 February 1993, p. 10.

hospitals, schools, universities, hotels and court houses. The Regulations require that the workplace, equipment, devices and system shall be maintained in an efficient state, in efficient working order and in good repair. Specifically, the Regulations specify suitable provision for the ventilation, temperature, lighting, cleanliness and removal of waste materials, sufficient working area and suitable work station provision. There are a number of provisions relating to the condition of floors, windows, skylights, doors, gates, escalators, sanitary conveniences and washing facilities. See Chapter 14 paragraph 6.20.

The Provision and Use of Work Equipment Regulations 1992

2.08 Work equipment is defined broadly to include anything from a pair of scissors to a steel rolling mill. There is an obligation on the employer to ensure that work equipment is used only for the operations for which and under conditions for which it is suitable. If the equipment has a health risk, the employer must restrict its use and maintenance to specific persons.

The Personal Protective Equipment at Work Regulations 1992

2.09 The employer's obligations relate to the suitability of protective clothing to be worn by employees.

The Manual Handling Operations Regulations 1992

2.10 This imposes obligations on an employer to avoid a manual handling operation where there is a risk of injury from that manual handling operation. The employer's duty is to take steps to reduce the risk of injury to the lowest level reasonably practicable.

The Health and Safety (Display Screen Equipment) Regulations 1992

2.11 The employer's duties here apply to all persons who use display screen equipment as part of their normal work. The employer is under an obligation to make an assessment of the relevant risks to health and safety from the operation and reduce the risks to the 'lowest extent reasonably practicable'. It requires employers to plan the activities of their 'users' so that there are periodic interruptions in their work on the display screen equipment. There must be appropriate eye and eyesight tests for the employees.

2.12 The client, who may also be an employer, will rely upon the architect to advise him whether and what assessments are required and the hazards which must be identified in the workplace. He will also rely upon the architect to advise him how to avoid any such hazards and thereby to avoid any potential liability under the Regulations. If the client is a developer who has only a short-term interest in the building, then collateral warranties may be granted to a purchaser or tenant who is to occupy the building or a unit of the building. If the purchaser or tenant is an employer and is found subsequently to be in breach of the regulations it is arguable that unless the architect has, at least, advised on compliance with the regulations and how best to design in order to ensure compliance, then an indemnity and/or damages could be sought. Such an indemnity could be in respect of the defence costs associated with a criminal prosecution or in respect of compensation paid out to employees.

3 Construction (Design and Management) Regulations (CDM)

Background

3.01 The impetus for the CDM Regulations was the increasing high level of fatal and non-fatal injuries to those working in the construction industry. In 1991/92 there were 98 fatal injuries and

3 276 non-fatal injuries in the UK. In 1989 and 1990 the European Council of Ministers agreed to a Framework Directive on health and safety together with five other directives. These are described in Section 7 of Chapter 18. The Temporary or Mobile Construction Sites Directive is a further directive under the Framework Directive and its aim is to limit accidents and injuries to construction workers. Construction sites were specifically excluded from the scope of the Workplace Directive and, hence, this separate measure covers a wide range of construction activities and requires separate implementing legislation in the UK.

Effect of the Regulations

3.02 The implementing legislation takes the form of the CDM Regulations, which became effective on the 31 March 1995. The CDM Regulations were made under the authority of the Health and Safety at Work Act 1974. Subject to very few exceptions, the regulations relate to all aspects of construction and affect all those concerned in the construction process. Projects excluded from the regulations for Planning Supervisors (not designers) are:

1. Projects which are not expected to employ more than 5 persons on site at any one time and not expected to take more than 30 days;
2. Projects for domestic clients, and
3. Minor works in premises normally inspected by a local authority.

The CDM Regulations are hailed as changing dramatically the previous allocations of responsibility for health and safety between contractors, clients and consultants. No longer is the contractor solely responsible for health and safety on site. The Regulations are radical in that they create two new roles within construction projects, namely the planning supervisor and the principal contractor. They also impose specific obligations on designers to consider matters of safety in the execution of their designs and in the subsequent maintenance of the completed structure in subsequent years. The regulations provide for notification of construction projects to the Health and Safety Executive together with a detailed consideration of all variations and financial considerations on safety throughout the duration of the project.

The regulations do have some transitional provisions. For example, if the construction phase of a project started before April 1995, there is no requirement for the client to appoint a planning supervisor or principal contractor until the 1st January 1996. However, a number of these transitional dates have now passed and the Health and Safety Executive (with its increased enforcement staff) has made it clear that the 'softly, softly' approach adopted initially, to enable parties to become used to the legislation, will soon be hardened. Supplementing the regulations is an Approved Code of Practice published by the Health and Safety Executive which, attempts to put flesh on the dry bones of the law, by giving practical examples of how the regulations are intended to bite.

In order to assess the effect upon architects, it is simpler to consider the impact of the Regulations at the various stages in a normal project plan:

Feasibility/outline proposals

3.03 At the feasibility stage the client has an obligation to appoint a planning supervisor who has responsibility for the health and safety aspects of the planning phase. The planning supervisor must prepare a health and safety plan setting out the overall arrangements for the safe operation of the project, monitor the health and safety aspects of the design, advise the client on the adequacy of resource provision for the project, verify that changes to the proposals contained in the tender by the principal contractor take account of health and safety matters and prepare a health and safety file (basically a maintenance manual with health and safety matters specifically noted). It is expected that the lead designer would normally be appointed by the client as the planning supervisor in the majority of projects. He must notify the Health and Safety Executive immediately following his appointment. The effect on the architect at the feasibility stage is therefore twofold: to advise the client of his health and safety responsibilities (and specifically his obligation to appoint a planning supervisor) and to assess and report to the client on the additional costs which the health and safety obligations will involve.

Scheme and Detailed Design

3.04 The CDM Regulations have two broad effects on the architect at this stage: the imposition of specific design obligations in relation to the safety of those who will be building, maintaining or repairing the structure; and the responsibility (if appointed) of the role of planning supervisor for a range of health and safety functions.

Designer

3.05 The designer's obligation is basically to design in such a way as to prevent construction workers being exposed to risks to their health and safety. What this means in practice is not entirely clear, since construction is inherently risky with hazards arising from a large number of potential sources, including feature of design, sequencing, co-ordination, methods of work, weather and lack of operative discipline or training. However, it is clear that designers will be under a duty to design in such a way as to reduce hazards by adhering to good practice (especially that described in the Codes of Practice) taking into account the normal health and safety considerations in relation to hazards identified in current trade literature, and identifying hazards that are exceptional in the circumstances of the particular project and sequencing operations.

Risk analyses and hazard management are already conducted by those responsible for problematic designs (particularly in civil engineering projects) such as large atria, deep excavations or box girder bridges. However, since there are now a large number of construction activities which will be covered ranging from renovations and repair to demolition, and from excavation to maintenance, decoration and cleaning work, the impact on the UK architect is substantial.

Since the designer must integrate his designs with those of specialist sub-contractors, he must give much greater thought to ways of eliminating, reducing or at least controlling hazards, not just in the original design but also if and when variations are instructed during the contract. Specific examples are how heavy loads can be installed (e.g. beams in section) so as to avoid manual handling by construction workers of excessive loads. Other examples which raise obvious problems relate to the duty to design to avoid health and safety problems for those who maintain or clean the structure. Thus, the cleaning of windows or glass atria must be considered at the design stage, as must also the re-pointing of brickwork and the replacement of roof linings in years to come.

Planning supervisor

3.06 Whether or not the architect is appointed as the planning supervisor, he must be aware of this role and, if he is not so appointed, must work closely with the planning supervisor to enable him to carry out his various duties. Briefly, these duties at this stage are as follows:

1. ensuring that designers have complied with their design obligations in relation to health and safety issues. This means a prompting and coordinating duty to ensure that the designs of the entire professional team have considered all the health and safety angles;
2. preparing a health and safety plan to be included in the tender documentation. The Health and Safety Executive have stated their intention to publish a model plan for this purpose and this should enable the contractor to price the procedures to deal with the identified hazards. The plan should specify the approach to the management of health and safety which the contractors should adopt, identify any potential hazards, and require the work to be carried out to recognized standards.
3. compiling a health and safety file similar to but in much greater detail than the Maintenance Manual, and focusing particularly on health and safety aspects of materials used together with

design implications that will affect those who will be maintaining and cleaning the structure.

The impact upon architects has been significant. In a recent survey 40% of respondent firms had already sought advice from the Health and Safety Executive and 30% had taken action to mount training courses within their firms. More significantly, 46% of firms had taken action to review their design management procedures to ensure that health and safety matters are systematically addressed.

Production information and tender action

3.07 The architect will have a duty to check that the health and safety plan is included in the tender documentation. In the event that the architect is also appointed as the planning supervisor for the project, then these duties will be multiplied. Initially the planning supervisor prepares a health and safety plan and makes it available for inclusion in the tender documents. On return of the tender documents the planning supervisor checks that the contract period allows sufficient time for compliance with the health and safety measures. Thereafter, in this role (if he is so appointed), the architect has a duty to assess differences between tenders in relation to the health and safety plan, advise the client on the adequacy of time and money allocated to health and safety aspects, advise the client to appoint a principal contractor, prepare a health and safety file for each structure, and give notice of the project prior to construction to the Health and Safety Executive.

In any tender action, even if not appointed as the planning supervisor, the architect will have a duty to consider a contractor's health and safety record and advise the client accordingly. The architect will be involved in contractor pre-selection with one criterion being health and safety competence. Contractors will be requested to explain and justify their responses to health and safety requirements. A recent case on this particular area has highlighted the potential impact of the regulations. *General Building & Maintenance* v *Greenwich Borough Council* [1993] *The Times* 9 March. This case concerns public sector work where Greenwich Borough Council invited tenders for repair and maintenance work on a stock of 34 000 dwellings. The estimated annual value of the contract was £12 m. The EC Public Procurement Regime therefore applied and when the local housing authority considered the 104 applications from contractors, it took into account their health and safety records as one of the factors used to shortlist those to be invited to tender. One of the contractors who was rejected, General Building and Maintenance, alleged that the housing authority was in breach of the Public Procurement Rules in excluding them since there was no specific wording which allowed the authority to consider and exclude a contractor on the basis of its health and safety record. The judge, however, applied a purposive interpretation to the Rules and held that since the Treaty of Rome expressly stated the need to promote improved working conditions and prevent occupational accidents and diseases, it would be 'incomprehensible' to conclude that consideration of health and safety issues was forbidden by the Rules.

In the light of this case, UK architects should be aware of the high priority given to health and safety issues by public sector clients and, so it appears, by the courts as well.

It is the duty of the client to appoint a *competent* principal contractor. The client will rely largely upon his professional adviser in this respect, and if no enquiries are made as to the health and safety record, it may constitute breach of the Regulations. In addition, the client must ensure that there are adequate resources in terms of time and financial provision to give effect to health and safety measures. Architects must carefully consider these points when assessing tender documents before recommending merely the lowest tender bid. The specific duties of the principal contractor are to prepare the initial execution stage of the health and safety plan and to draw in and coordinate the Health and Safety Plans of sub-contractors. It is also responsible for the execution of the project, controlling access and verifying the compliance of sub-contractors.

Operations on site and completion

3.08 If the roles of planning supervisor and architect are to be performed by the same person or firm (as is likely in the majority

of cases) it is not difficult to conclude that the level of supervision required of the architect will be affected by his knowledge of the level of experience of the contractor and the risks and hazards identified in the health and safety plan. Thus, for instance, even if an experienced contractor is engaged it could be argued that the architect must be present on site to supervise at times of identified hazard. Failure to supervise at these times may constitute breach of appointment or, worse, may bring criminal sanctions following prosecution by the Health and Safety Executive. The Regulations do not, however, require the architect to dictate construction methods or to exercise a health and safety supervisory function over contractors as they carry out construction work. Thus, it is not intended that designers, for instance, should be required to prepare method statements or otherwise intrude into the contractor's domain.

Nevertheless, given that the nature of the architect's supervisory duty and duty to warn of health and safety problems is dependent upon the circumstances of each project, the laying down of specific obligations by the Regulations is bound to have an effect upon that duty.

If a variation is requested, the architect's duty again is affected since, in relation to health and safety, the architect's role as designer means that he must consider the implications of variations and inform the planning supervisor of any impact on health and safety. If the architect is appointed as the planning supervisor for the project then he must discuss with the principal contractor as to how the variation could affect the health and safety plan and he must also advise the client on the adequacy of revised sums and time allowed to give effect to health and safety measures.

4 Summary and practical considerations

As has already been indicated, there are three principal areas of potential liability for the architect in failing to comply with obligations relating to health and safety:

1. criminal prosecution with unlimited fines and/or a maximum of two years' imprisonment;
2. civil action based on the tort of negligence by injured workers, and
3. contractual claims where Regulations are incorporated into the appointment or referred to in a collateral warranty.

The following procedures should be considered by architects in order to take into account the potential liabilities in the following ways:

1. Seek to acquire the necessary information and training by way of professional courses and by absorbing the limited literature on the subject. In this respect the Health and Safety Executive have issued a number of publications, most notably, *Brief for a Designers Handbook* and *Designing for Health and Safety in Construction* written from the designer's standpoint particularly for this purpose. Regular guidance notes are also published.
2. Review design management procedures. At the end of concept and scheme design, during detailed design and immediately before tender documents are prepared, architects are specifically building in 'breaks' to review formally and systematically whether health and safety matters have been considered as part of the design to reduce or control hazards. Those firms who are quality assured have less difficulty in introducing these reviews, since they would normally be part of QA system which would allow them to trace records to confirm that the review has been carried out.
3. Liaise with professional indemnity insurers. Liability both as a designer and planning supervisor (if this role were to be accepted) will be affected by the Regulations and so architects have found it necessary to check with their insurers whether their new potential liability would be covered. Generally, (although every policy is subject to its own terms and conditions) insurers have confirmed that the liability would be insured provided the architect does not accept any general duty above that of reasonable skill and care and diligence. It seems unlikely that any criminal penalty received by an architect would

be covered by insurance, although the defence costs of the architect may be covered in some cases, either in the general wording, or by way of specific endorsement.

4. If the role of planning supervisor is to be adopted by the architect (and it appears that many firms have already conceded this principle since it will bring additional fee income) it is essential that the role be limited to one of *coordinating* all the relevant designers' designs rather than *ensuring* that each design will not expose workers to risks to their health and safety.

5. Architects should avoid incorporating, without qualification, the Regulations or the Codes of Practice into their appointment. The consequence of this would be that any breach of the Regulations or Code would incur contractual claims for damages with the breach forming the ground for the action. If incorporation becomes unavoidable then any duty to comply with the Regulations or Code should be qualified by 'reasonable skill and care'. This is particularly important if collateral warranties are to be issued to funds, tenants or purchasers who may seek to claim an indemnity from the architect if held liable for damages in respect of personal injury to workers. These types of claims may well be limited by the extent to which such damage could have been reasonably foreseeable at the time of entering into the warranty.

6. If architects are to provide indicative designs for temporary works, where they foresee problems, then those designs should only comprise ideas to be adopted, if appropriate, by a contractor who is then responsible for their sufficiency and implementation. In addition, if site visits result in an architect noting serious infringements of the Regulations or Code then any report to the principal contractor or ultimately the Health and Safety Executive must be qualified to the extent that such professional inspections do not attract liability which is properly the responsibility of others. This should be recorded in correspondence at the time.

Part Four

The architect in practice

HONG CONG.

20

Legal organization of architects' offices

GRAHAM BROWN*

1 Managing an architectural business

1.01 Management is a creative activity, the exercise of which is about making and maintaining dynamic cultures within and by which the objectives of people as individuals, teams and organizations are achieved.

The manager of an architectural business is concerned with three types of relationship: between the owners of the business and their clients, between employer and employee, and between the owners of the business themselves. Chapters 8 and 9 deal with the first relationship, Chapter 28 with the second and this chapter with the third.

Successful management of an architectural business is an essential prerequisite of the successful management of architectural projects and, as such, is part of an architect's duty of care.

Critical to the success of any business is its legal form and structure. The choice, therefore, of the form of legal organization is a particularly important part of an architect's duty.

1.02 There are no formal restrictions in the professional codes to the structures under which architects carry on their practices. The Architects (Registration) Acts 1931–1969 permit architects to practise as partnerships or companies, limited or unlimited, provided that the business is under the control and management of a registered architect. The RIBA Code of Professional Conduct states in its Preface that 'A member is at liberty to engage in any activity, whether as proprietor, director, principal, partner, manager, superintendent, controller or salaried employee of/or consultant to, any body corporate or unincorporate, or in any other capacity provided that his conduct complies with the Principles of this Code and the Rules applying to his circumstances'.

1.03 While architects may choose to practise as sole traders, form companies or create larger amalgamations as group practices or consortia, the most common form of architectural business is still the partnership. The main choice for architects setting up business is between partnerships and companies. A partnership provides the breadth of expertise a sole trader cannot provide without the formality of incorporating a registered company. The advantages and disadvantages of each will be considered. (See Checklist 20.4 for a basic outline of the differences between partnerships and companies.)

2 Partnership

2.01 The law of partnership is governed by the Partnership Act 1890. (References to section numbers in the text which follows are references to the Partnership Act 1890.) Unless specified in a

partnership agreement, the provisions of the Partnership Act will apply. Partnership is defined in Section 1 as 'the relation which subsists between persons carrying on a business in common with a view to profit'. 'Business' includes the practice of architecture. A single act, such as designing a house, may not make a business, but if there is a series of such acts, a business will be held to exist. 'A view to profit' requires only the intention to make a profit even if the architects fail to do so. The requirement of acting in common is important. It may be contrasted with barristers, who are in business with a view to profit but do not act in common, merely sharing facilities. Unlike a company, a partnership has no legal personality. Is is nothing more than the sum total of the individuals comprising it.

Formation of partnership

2.02 A partnership is a form of contract (see Chapter 2). Although many architects set up partnerships quite casually it is prudent to create the business formally and expressly by a deed of partnership executed under a seal or written articles of partnership. The existence of a partnership can sometimes be inferred in law, however, from the behaviour of the individuals involved even if no deed of partnership exists, and despite vigorous statements to the contrary.

Importance of clarity

2.03 Considerable importance may be attached to the existence of a partnership. For example, if two architects work together occasionally over several years and then a case of negligence arises, both can be sued if a partnership exists. If there is no partnership, however, one of them may be out of trouble. It can be vital to a client or supplier of a practice to establish whether he is dealing with a partnership or one person. Architects are recommended on all possible occasions to clarify their relationship, particularly when they work as group practices and consortia.

Sharing facilities and profits

2.04 If two or more architects do not intend to practise in partnership, but merely to share facilities, they must take great care to avoid the possibility of third persons with whom any of them has dealings being led to assume that they practise together as partners. Shared ownership of property, even if accompanied by sharing of net profits, is not normally itself evidence of the existence of a partnership. Profit-sharing is, however, prima facie evidence of a partnership, but if it is just one piece of evidence it will be weighed equally with all other available evidence. This is particularly important to architectural practices, since profit-sharing in the form of profit-related bonus payments is quite a common means of remunerating staff. Nevertheless, payment by profit-sharing will not of itself make an employee a partner in the business, nor will

* This chapter draws heavily on material in the chapter in previous editions written by George Young, formerly partner in YRM and deputy chairman of the Institute of Administrative Management.

sharing in gross returns if not accompanied by sharing of property from which those returns are derived of itself create a partnership. It is important to draft any contract of employment including any profit-sharing provision very carefully indeed.

Deed of partnership

2.05 Even though there are ways of determining whether a partnership exists, and the 1890 Act sets out terms which apply if partners have nothing written down, it is more satisfactory if intending partners agree they are going into a business together and set out the terms of their relationship in a deed of partnership. The deed should cover the points set out in Checklist 20.1.

Name of practice

2.06 In naming a firm, there are a number of considerations.

Use of the term 'architect' is restricted by the Architects (Registration) Acts 1931–1969. Only those persons who are on the Register of Architects maintained by the Architects Registration Council of the United Kingdom (ARCUK) are permitted to practise or carry on business under the name, style or title of 'architect'. 'Landscape architects' and 'naval architects' are outside the scope of the Acts. It is advisable for any person wishing to use the term 'architect' in their practice name to check with ARCUK.

The provisions of the Business Names Act 1985 must be complied with if the partnership does not consist of the named partners. Certain names which are set out in statutory regulations or give the impression that the business is connected with HM's Government or a local authority must gain the approval of the Secretary of State for Trade and Industry. The use in the firm's name of a retired, former or deceased partner may be permissible provided there is no intent to mislead; but caution is necessary to avoid the implication that such a person is still involved in the practice. The 1985 Act requires businesses to disclose certain information. The names and addresses of each partner must be prominently displayed at the business premises where the public have access. It is important to comply with the provisions of this Act. Failure to do so is a criminal offence or may render void contracts entered into by the practice. The Business Names Act requires that business documentation must contain the names of each partner. If there are more than 20 partners, however, the names of all partners can be omitted from business documents if they state the address of the principal place of business and also state that a full list of partners' names and relevant addresses may be inspected there.

Size of practice

2.07 There are still restrictions on the size of some partnerships. In the case of architects these have been removed by the Partnerships (Unrestricted Size) No. 4 Regulations 1970 so long as not less than three-quarters are registered under the Architects (Registration) Acts 1931–1969.

Types of partner

2.08 The law is not concerned with distinctions between senior and junior partners. It is up to the partners to decide how to share profits, but they will be shared equally unless special provision is made. The RIBA Practice Note (May 1974) strongly recommended that all persons who are held out to be partners shall be described as such without further distinction. In particular the term 'salaried partner' must be avoided. The purpose of this is to ensure that all persons described as partners share in the decision-making of the business and have access to appropriate information. They are also fully responsible for the professional conduct of their practice and for keeping themselves and their partners properly informed of partnership matters.

Associates

2.09 It is a common practice to recognize the status and contribution of senior staff by describing them as 'associates'. The title

---

Checklist 20.1: Items to be considered when drawing up a deed of partnership

Note: The terms of a partnership agreement, like any other contract, may be widely varied by mutual consent of the parties. Where no provision is made those of the Partnership Act 1890 will apply. The figures in brackets in Checklists 20.1–3 refer to relevant clauses in that Act.

Name of firm

Place of business

Commencement

Duration

Provision of capital
Amount.
Proportion to be contributed by each partner.
Distinctions between what is:

1. not partnership capital – a premium, and
2. capital which is partnership property – contribution to working capital.

Capital should be expressed in money terms.
Any special agreement for interest on capital (24(3), (4)).
Valuation and repayments on death, etc. (42 and 43).
Rules for settlement for accounts after dissolution (44).

Property
What partners bring to the firm including contracts (20, 22, 24).
What:

1. belongs to firm as a whole (21);
2. is co-owned but not partnership property;
3. is individually owned but used in the partnership business (24).

Mutual rights and duties
If these are to be differentiated then specify them – e.g. holiday times, sabbaticals, work brought into firm, etc.

Miscellaneous earnings
For example, lectures, journalistic work, various honoraria . . . whether to be paid into firm.

Profits and losses
Basis for division among partners: if not equally then specify (24(1)).
Any reservations, e.g. about guaranteed minimum share of profits in any individual case.

Banking and accountants
Arrangements for signing cheques, presentation of audited accounts, etc.

Employment of 'locum tenens'
Authority for, circumstances, and terms.

Constitution of firm
Provisions for changes (36).

Retirement at will
Age, fixed term or partnership for life, notice of retirement, etc.
Arrangements for consultants and for payment during retirement.
Repayment of capital and current accounts on death or retirement.

Dissolution
Any special circumstances (see Checklist 20.3).

Restrictions on practice
Any covenant in respect of restraining competition (must be reasonable to interests of parties and public). Areas of operation.

Insurances
Various, including liability of surviving partners for dead partners' share in firm.

Arbitration
Method, number of arbitrators, etc.

'associate' is not referred to in the Partnership Act; it has no meaning in law, and, if it is not intended that associates be partners and share in the liabilities of the partnership, it is extremely unwise to use the term 'associate partner', and would also probably contravene professional codes. If people were misled into thinking associates were partners, associates might find themselves liable as though they were partners, having all the obligations without the rights or benefits.

Rights and liabilities of partners

2.10 Every partner will have the following rights unless there is an agreement to the contrary:

1. The right to take full part in management of the business (Section 24(5)).
2. The right to have an equal share in profits and capital of the business (Section 24(1)).
3. The right not to have new partners added without his consent (Section 24(7)).
4. The right not to have the fundamental nature of the partnership business altered without his consent. The consent of a majority of partners will suffice for changes in all other ordinary matters connected with the business.
5. By Section 24(2) a firm must indemnify every partner in respect of payments made and personal liabilities incurred by him in doing necessary acts or acts in the ordinary and proper conduct of the business of the firm.
6. There is a right to inspect the partnership books, which must be kept at the principal place of business of each firm (Section 24(9)).
7. There is a right not to be expelled without express agreement (Section 25).
8. Any partner has the right to dissolve the partnership at any time by giving notice to the other partners (Section 26(1)).

Assignment

2.11 Assignment will not transfer right to management, accounts, or inspection of partnership books. It will only entitle the assignee to receive a share in the profits (Section 31(1)).

Rights to which partners are not entitled

2.12 By Section 24(4) there is no right to interest on capital subscribed by a partner although by Section 24(3) there is a right to interest on capital subscribed beyond that which was agreed to be subscribed.

2.13 There is no right to remuneration for acting in the partnership business by Section 24(6).

Liabilities

2.14 In English law a partnership is a collection of individuals and not a corporate body. In addition to all his normal individual liabilities, each partner has added responsibilities as a member of a partnership.

2.15 If a partnership is sued, a partner may be proceeded against jointly, or jointly and severally (see Checklist 20.2). By Sections 9 and 10 of the Partnership Act every partner in a firm is personally liable jointly with the other partners for all debts and obligations incurred by the firm when he is a partner as well as jointly and severally for wrongs done by other partners who are acting in the ordinary course of the business of the firm or for wrongs done with the authority of co-partners. If a partnership is sued jointly, one or more partners may be sued at the same time; when judgment is given, even if it is not satisfied, no further action can be taken against any of the other partners. If the action is brought against a firm jointly and severally, the partners may be sued singly or together. When judgment is given against one, further action may be brought against the others one by one or together

until the full amount is paid. If only some of the partners are sued, they may apply to the courts to have their other partners joined with them as co-defendants.

Checklist 20.2: Liability for civil cases under Partnership Act 1890

Debts and obligations to firm
Jointly in absence of agreement to the contrary (5–13 inclusive).

Torts, including negligence
Jointly and severally.

Contract
Jointly and severally – if partners have expressly agreed to be so liable. Note: A deceased partner's estate may be severally liable to the prior payments of his private debts.

2.16 The provisions of the Limitation Act 1980 and the Latent Damage Act 1986 apply to breaches of contract or of duty of care in tort (see Chapter 3).

2.17 Partners are not liable for the criminal actions of other partners, unless they contributed to them or have knowledge of them. The RIBA considers architects liable, however, for breaches of its Code of Professional Conduct by their fellow partners (see Chapter 28).

2.18 A partnership may indemnify one or more of its partners against the consequences of their liability. This device enables members of staff to share the management of a practice without outlaying capital to join the equity partnership.

2.19 A new partner entering the firm does not normally become liable for debts, obligations, or wrongs incurred or committed before his entry (Section 17(1)). However, the position is different for a partner leaving the firm, whether by retirement or death. If a partner retires he will still be liable for debts or obligations incurred before his retirement (Section 17(2)). If he dies his estate will be liable for such debts or obligations. Moreover, a partner will continue to be treated as a member of the firm, attracting the usual liability, until notice of a change in the constitution of the partnership is advertised (Section 36).

2.20 Every partner is an agent of the practice. Any act done by him in carrying out the business of the practice will bind the practice unless it is outside his authority to act for the practice in that particular matter, and the person with whom he is dealing knows that he has no authority or does not believe him to be a partner (Section 5).

2.21 Partners must render true accounts and full information on anything affecting the partnership or the partners (Section 28).

2.22 Partners are accountable to the partnership for any private profits they have received from any partnership transaction or from using the partnership property, names, or connection (Section 29(1)).

2.23 If a partner competes with the practice without the consent of the other partners he must pay all profits made in consequence to the practice (Section 30).

The relationship of partners to one another

2.24 A practice of any size may not discriminate against women partners with regard to the provision of benefits, facilities or services or by expelling her or subjecting her to detriment under the Sex Discrimination Act 1975 as amended by the Sex Discrimination Act 1986. Practices larger than six members may not discriminate in such matters on racial grounds under the Race Relations Act 1976.

Dissolution of partnerships

2.25 A partnership comes to an end:

1. At the end of a fixed term if it has been so set up.
2. At the end of a single specific commission, if it was set up for that commission alone.
3. On the death or bankruptcy of any partner unless the partnership agreement makes provision for continuity of the partnership.
4. If any partner gives notice.

2.26 Prior to the Finance Act 1985 there were tax benefits in cessation and re-formation of a partnership, but those have now been ended.

2.27 If a partner wishes to end the firm but is prevented by his fellow partners, he may apply to the court for a dissolution on one of the grounds shown in Checklist 20.3.

Checklist 20.3: Grounds for dissolution of partnership

---

1 By agreement of parties

a. Agreement per deed

End of fixed term or of single project.

b. By expiration, or notice (32)

If for undefined time – any partner giving notice of intention (32(c)).

c. Illness

Special provisions in deed (to avoid need to apply to courts (35)).

Note: Expulsion. No majority of partners can expel unless express agreement in deed (25). There can be no implied consent to expel.

2 By operation of law and courts

Death and bankruptcy

Subject to express agreement, partnership is dissolved as regards *all* by death or bankruptcy of *any* partner (33).

Illegality

Any event making it unlawful to carry on the business of the practice:

If partner is insane.
If partner is incapable of carrying on their part of agreement.
If partner is guilty of conduct prejudicial to the interests of the firm.
If partner wilfully and persistently breaches the agreement or if their conduct is such that the others can no longer carry on business with them.
If firm can only carry on at a loss.
If, in the opinion of the courts, it is just and equitable that the firm should be dissolved.

---

3 Limited partnerships

3.01 Limited partnerships are governed by the Limited Partnership Act 1907. At first glance these might appear to be an advantageous form of association for architects concerned with protecting themselves from liability. However, there are so many disadvantages that limited partnerships are rarely used. A distinction is made between 'general partners' with unlimited liability and 'limited partners' whose liability is limited.

1. At least one partner must retain unlimited liability.
2. Limited partners' capital must be paid up immediately. They are liable for debts or obligations up to but not beyond the amount contributed.
3. The limited partners may have no role in the management of the business and have no power to bind the firm. If a limited partner takes a management role he will be fully liable as if he were a general partner. Any difference arising as to ordinary matters connected with the partnership business may be decided by a majority of the general partners. A person may be introduced as a partner without the consent of the other limited partners.

4. Limited partners can only dispose of their share in the partnership with the consent of the partner(s) with unlimited liability.
5. Limited partnerships of architects are limited to 20 persons.
6. A limited partnership is not dissolved by the death or bankruptcy of a limited partner and a limited partner has no right to dissolve the partnership by notice.

4 Companies

The view of the professional organizations

4.01 Under the RIBA Code of Professional Conduct the Institute may hold a member acting through a body corporate or unincorporate responsible for the acts of that body. This means that for the purposes of suspension or expulsion from the RIBA an architect who is a director of a company may be held personally liable for the acts of the company. This does not mean, however, that he or she will be held by the courts as personally liable in law for the acts of the company.

A separate legal persona

4.02 The most fundamental principle of company law is that a company is a distinct and separate entity in law from its members or directors. As a separate legal person a company can own and alienate property, sue and be sued, and enter into contracts in its own right. Although the company is owned by its members, or shareholders, and governed by its directors, or managing director, with the supervision of its shareholders, it is distinct in law from all of these. In relation to third parties it is the company which is primarily liable, not the shareholders or directors. This is so however large the percentage of shares or debentures held by one shareholder. A company may be liable in contract, tort, crime and for matters of property. Only in very rare cases such as fraud can the directors or shareholders be held liable for debts and obligations of the company.

Types of company

4.03 A company may be limited (by shares or guarantee) or unlimited. A company limited by shares is one in which the shareholders' liability to contribute to the company's assets is limited to the amount unpaid on their shares. A company limited by guarantee is one where the shareholders are liable as guarantors for an amount set out in the Memorandum (see paragraph 4.04) in the event of the company being wound up. An unlimited company is subject to the same rules as a limited company except that its shareholders are personally liable for all its debts and obligations in the event of the company being wound up.

Formation of companies

4.04 Companies are formed in three ways: by Royal Charter, by special Act of Parliament, and by registration under the Companies Act 1985. The first two methods are archaic and little used, so this chapter will only describe the procedure for registration. Any two people can register a company. The following must be sent to the Company Registrar:

1. A Memorandum of Association setting out the objects of the company. A company may only pursue the objects conferred expressly or impliedly by the Memorandum. All other activity is *ultra vires* and void. For example, a company is not able to borrow money unless provision for this is set out in the Articles. Thus the drafting of a Memorandum of Association requires special care; it must also comply with the relevant ethical codes. The Memorandum should always contain provision for alteration as it can only be changed in certain circumstances as laid down by the Companies Act 1985.
2. Articles of Association containing the regulations of the company (subject to the Memorandum). Companies limited by shares need not register Articles but these will then be in the

form of Table A in the Companies (Tables A–F) Regulations 1985 (S.I. 1985/805). The Articles may be altered by special resolution of a majority of at least three-quarters of its voting members.

3. A statement of initial nominal capital.
4. Particulars of the director(s) and secretary. There must be at least one director and one secretary. Any change in the directors or secretary must be notified to the Registrar of Companies. The Articles may require directors to have qualification shares. Anyone, even a corporation, may be a company director unless they are an undischarged bankrupt (though the court may give them leave to act) or are disqualified by the court under the Company Directors Disqualification Act 1986 or the Articles. The company may remove a director by ordinary resolution before the end of his term. Directors nomally retire in rotation (one-third each year) but may resign by giving such notice as is required in the Articles. Directors are entitled only to such remuneration as is stated in the Articles. Companies may not loan to directors or connected persons except as provided under the 1985 Act.
5. Intended location of the registered office of the company.
6. The prescribed fee.

4.05 The Registrar of Companies will issue a Certificate of Incorporation as evidence that the company is legally registered, and give the company a registered number. Without a Certificate of Incorporation a company does not exist in law and cannot do business.

Public and private companies

4.06 Companies, whether limited or unlimited, may be either public or private. A public company is the only sort of company permitted to offer its shares to the public. Only companies with a nominal share capital of £50 000 may be public limited companies. The Memorandum of Association must state that the company is a public company. Before registering, it is advisable to consider whether the company is to be public or private. An architect's practice will normally incorporate as a private company. The individuals who would otherwise be partners are likely to be the directors and also the shareholders.

Profits

4.07 Profits are distributed among shareholders in accordance with the rights attached to their shares. Although there is a presumption that all shares confer equal rights and equal liabilities, that is normally rebutted by a power in the company's articles to issue different classes of shares. An example of a class of share is a preference share. Holders of preference shares will be entitled to dividends before ordinary shareholders. If there are insufficient funds, preference shareholders will be the only shareholders to receive dividends. Shares are also classed according to whether they have voting rights or not. In most architectural companies profits and dividends are small because directors are remunerated under their service contracts with the company.

Name of company

4.08 Like partnerships, the name of a company is restricted by the Architects (Registration) Acts 1931–1969 and the Business Names Act 1985. Public limited companies must use the word 'limited' after their name. It is an offence for public companies to choose names giving the impression that they are private companies, and vice versa. The use of a name similar to that of another company with the same type of business may constitute an actionable tort.

4.09 A company must state its corporate name on all business documents and on its seal. It must display this name legibly on the outside of its business premises. Other particulars including the place of registration, the registration number and the address of the registered office must be on company business documents.

Size of company

4.10 A company may have an unlimited number of shareholders.

Rights and liabilities of shareholders

Rights

4.11 Shareholders holding shares with voting rights have the right to supervise the management of the company by voting in the annual general meeting, which meetings must be held each year at no greater than a fifteen-month interval, or in such extraordinary general meetings as may be called.

4.12 Shareholders are paid dividends out of the profits of the company, in accordance with the rights belonging to their shares.

Liabilities

4.13 A partnership is bound by contracts made by one of its partners and is liable in tort for the acts or omissions of each partner. In contrast, shareholders cannot make contracts binding on a company, nor are they liable personally for debts or obligations of other shareholders. Shareholders are liable, however, for torts and obligations of a limited company to the amount unpaid on their shares, or, if the company is unlimited for the debts and obligations of the company in the event of its winding-up.

4.14 When a company is dissolved by winding-up, both present members and those who have been members in the 12 months preceding the winding-up are required to contribute towards the assets of the company so that it can meet its liabilities. The liabilities of past company members are not so wide-reaching as those of partners. This is one particular advantage of companies.

Rights and liabilities of directors

4.15 Under the Articles, the directors are normally given the power to manage the company under the ultimate supervision of shareholders. They may often delegate the management to a managing director.

4.16 Directors are not servants or agents of a company and can only bind it if some organ of the company has conferred appropriate authority upon them. Authority for this depends on the Articles or by special resolution of the shareholders. A director may be held to have had usual authority or to have been held out as having authority and thus will bind the company. The third party need not be familiar with the Articles in either case. A managing director can normally be expected to have authority to bind the company.

4.17 The Companies Act 1985 and 1989 and the Insolvency Act 1986 prescribe a large number of duties for directors. The main duties are:

1. Directors must prepare and disclose company accounts in a specified form stating the financial position of the company. They must keep the books at the registered office of the company to be available for inspection by the company officers at any time.
2. Directors must prepare an annual report reviewing the business of the company and recommending the amount of dividends to be paid.
3. The company must be audited yearly.

4. The report, audit, and accounts must be filed with the Registrar of Companies at specified times to be available for inspection by the public.
5. The company must hold an annual general meeting of shareholders in each calendar year at no greater interval than once every 15 months. Two persons can constitute a quorum. Extraordinary general meetings may be convened if there is some business the directors consider to be of special importance.
6. The company must keep a register of directors at its registered office disclosing certain information about directors and their interest in the shares or debentures of the company. These particulars must be notified to the Registrar, who must be informed of any change. A register of members containing similar information must also be kept by the company.
7. Directors have no right to remuneration except that specified in the Articles. Remuneration of directors is normally voted on by the shareholders at their general meetings.
8. Directors owe the company a fiduciary duty of loyalty and good faith. They are considered trustees of company assets under their control. They must account to the company for any profits they make by virtue of their position as directors and cannot use their powers as directors except to benefit the company. They must always devote themselves to promoting the company's interests and act in its best interest. Their duty of loyalty means they cannot enter into engagements where their personal interests might conflict with the company's interest and they must disclose their personal interests in such engagements to the shareholders. This duty can continue even after a director leaves the company.
9. Directors owe a duty to the company to exercise reasonable care in the conduct of the business. Such duties are not unduly onerous. Courts are reluctant to intervene in areas involving business judgment. In some circumstances directors will be expected to seek specialist advice and will be liable if they do

not. Directors will not be liable for anything they have been authorized to do by shareholders. This duty is not owed to shareholders, contractors or creditors (though a director can be liable to the creditor for fraudulent or wrongful trading). Since the duty is owed to the company, the company itself can sue directors who have been negligent or in breach of their fiduciary duties.

Dissolution

4.18 A company may be dissolved in two ways:

1. By winding-up under the Insolvency Act 1986. This may be voluntary or compulsory. Once a company has been wound up no judgment may be enforced against it.
2. By being struck off the Register under the Companies Act 1985. This happens when the Registrar of Companies believes that the company is no longer carrying on business. Companies may seek this form of dissolution themselves. They may do this to save the costs of a formal liquidation.

Companies versus partnerships

4.19 A list of the differences is set out in Checklist 20.4. The relative advantages and disadvantages will differ for individual businesses. Managers need to assess the business priorities when making a decision to form a company or a partnership. The size of the business may be relevant to the decision. Smaller businesses may find the paperwork and administration required for a company too arduous. Taxation is another factor in the decision. This is beyond the scope of this chapter. Managers should seek professional advice from an accountant or from a local tax office.

Checklist 20.4: The differences between companies and partnerships

Partnerships	Companies
1. No separate legal personality (except in Scotland).	Separate legal personality from its shareholders.
2. Partners have unlimited liability.	Shareholders are liable only to the amount unpaid on their shares but may be liable on personal guarantees for some liabilities.
3. Interest of a partner is his partnership which may be difficult to transfer.	Interest of a shareholder is his shares which are usually easy to transfer unless subject to limitations in Articles.
4. It may be difficult for a young architect to join a partnership as he will have to accumulate sufficient capital to buy a share in the partnership or take over a retiring partner's interest.	It is easier to join a company as it does not necessarily involve buying in.
5. The only promotion is to become a partner, so career prospects may be limited.	More kinds of promotion possible.
6. Management through meetings of partners.	Management through Board of Directors supervised by shareholders, meeting annually.
7. Partners share profits equally unless there is an agreement to the contrary.	Company profits are divided according to rights attached to the shares.
8. Can be formed informally by just starting up business with another person.	Must be registered to come into existence. This costs money and it requires time unless an 'off the peg' company is purchased.
9. No restrictions on the powers of a partnership.	A company only has the powers in the objects clause of its Memorandum. Other powers are ultra vires and void.
10. Each partner can bind the partnership.	No shareholder can bind the company.
11. Partnership details cannot be inspected by the public.	Matters filed with the Registrar of Companies are open to public inspection. Such matters include the Memorandum, Articles, details of directors, secretary, and registered office.
12. Partnerships need not publicize their accounts.	Companies must file their accounts with the Registrar of Companies. Unlimited companies are exempt from this requirement only if 50% of their shares are held by a limited company.
13. No audit required.	Annual audit required.
14. A partnership does not require much paperwork or administration.	A company requires more paperwork and administration.
15. A partnership cannot borrow money.	A company can raise money if allowed by its Memorandum by debentures for example, or by fixed and floating charges.
16. Death or departure of a partner causes dissolution of the partnership.	Transfer of shares will not end a company's existence.
17. There are many ways to dissolve a partnership. It can be dissolved instantly by agreement.	A company is dissolved only by liquidation in accordance with the Companies Acts 1985 and 1989 and the Insolvency Act 1986.

Service companies

4.20 Service companies are formed to provide services to a partnership. The company may employ staff and hold the premises. It will also normally provide things such as office equipment, stationery, cars and accountancy services to the practice. The advantages of a service company are related to the balance between income and corporation tax.

Group practices and consortia

4.21 Architects' businesses may come together to work in several forms of association, whether for a single project or on a more permanent basis. This section is not concerned with the operational and management factors for and behind the choice of form, but only with the legal issues. Further guidance is given in the RIBA *Architect's Handbook of Practice Management*. The creation of any association needs to be checked carefully with the professional indemnity insurers of each party.

Loose groups

4.22 These are associations in which practices or individuals pool their knowledge and experience. Such a group does not need to be registered, but some short constitution is desirable which clearly distinguishes it from a partnership. In company law a more formal

'Memorandum and Articles of Association' is necessary and is of far greater significance. It must set out the most important provisions of the company's constitution, including the activities which the company may carry out.

Group practices

4.23 Practices may group together for their mutual benefit and to give better service while each retains some independence:

1. *Association* The degree of association may vary considerably from simply sharing office accommodation, facilities and expense, to a fully comprehensive system of mutual help. Beyond agreeing to a division of overhead expenses each practice retains their profits and their normal responsibility to their respective clients.
2. *Co-ordinated groups* For large development projects it is not unusual for the work to be undertaken by two or more architectural practices with one of them appointed to coordinate the activities of the others. Practices are liable to the coordinating practice for torts committed in their areas of activity. The arrangement may be constructed under head and sub-consultancy agreements.

   Single project partnerships and group partnerships may be entered into on terms which are entirely a matter for individual agreements between the parties and are similar in law to any ordinary partnership.

Consortia

4.24 Consortia are little different in law from group practices. The term normally implies the association of practices with different professional skills acting as one in carrying out projects jointly yet retaining their separate identities and each with their own responsibility to the building owner. A consortium may be formed for the duration of a single project or on a more regular and permanent basis.

Difficulties

4.25 Any association of practices, whether permanent or temporary, must be very carefully planned. If practices are to merge completely, assets should be carefully assessed (including work in progress). Specific agreement is necessary on debts, including liabilities relating to previous contracts. These could be significant if a pre-merger job became the subject of a professional negligence claim.

Agreements

4.26 If practices are to preserve their own identities and to continue to practise in their own right as well as together on common projects, the form of agreement becomes more critical and more complex. A new group or consortium, partnership or company should be created to contract with clients for common projects. Its agreement must resolve how far the assets of member practices are brought in, the extent of liabilities of the group, and the degree of independence retained by each member practice to carry on its own activities. A solicitor should always be consulted.

5 Premises and persons

5.01 Employers are obliged under the general duty of care to protect employees against personal injury in the course of their employment. They are obliged by statute to provide employees with safe and decent working conditions. For office workers these are set out in the Offices, Shops and Railway Premises Act 1963 and the Health and Safety at Work Act 1974 together with regulations made under the two Acts. The Health and Safety at Work Act 1974 shifted the focus from premises to people. This chapter is concerned with its impact on an architect as employer, employee, or occupier of premises.

The Offices, Shops and Railway Premises Act 1963

5.02 Under this Act, architects' offices and the activities normally associated with them count as office premises. Some activities such as modelmaking might fall within the provisions of the Factories Act and factory inspectors should be consulted.

Application of Act

5.03 Office premises are outside the Act if they are occupied only by self-employed people, if the only employees are immediate relatives of the occupier, or if all employees work less than 21 hours on the premises. If the premises are used only temporarily (for less than six weeks) they are not affected.

5.04 The Act and the regulations made under it cover a wide variety of conditions which cannot be dealt with here in detail. They include the maintenance and construction of floors, passages, and stairs, the safety of lifts, the provision of first aid, the amount of space to be provided for each person, cleanliness, heating, ventilation and lighting, provision of washing, sanitary, and eating facilities, drinking water, facilities for storing outdoor clothing and seating.

Accidents

5.05 Employers are required to notify the enforcing authority of accidents on the premises which cause the death, or the disablement for more than three days, of a person employed to work on the premises. A record must be kept of all accidents as they occur. In any case this is useful as a check against the possibility of persons making claims for accidents which did not happen on office premises.

Employees' right to information

5.06 Because the Act is primarily for the benefit of employees and because some employers are forgetful of their duties, the occupier is obliged to give employees information about the Act either by posting up an abstract in a sufficiently prominent place or by giving them an explanatory booklet.

Division of responsibility

5.07 One of the potentially confusing aspects of the Act is the division of responsibility between owner and occupier, particularly in multi-occupied buildings. The employer, if not the occupier, is responsible for notifying the occupier of accidents to his employees and for notifying his own employees of the provision of the Act.

Single occupation

5.08 An employer who occupies a whole building is responsible for ensuring that all provisions of the Act are met.

Multi-occupation

5.09 When a building is in multi-occupation responsibility is divided. The owner is responsible for cleaning, lighting and safety of the common parts, washing and sanitary facilities, fire alarms and signposting, and keeping free from obstruction all exits and means of escape in the building as a whole. Occupiers are responsible for all other provisions of the Act within the parts of the building they occupy.

Occupiers' Liability Acts 1957 and 1984

5.10 Occupiers owe a duty of care to all entrants on their premises. If the entrants are lawful visitors, reasonably practicable steps must be taken to make the premises safe for them and to protect them against all hazards, or give sufficient notice of them. Visiting workpeople such as window cleaners are responsible for their own safe working methods. If it is foreseeable that persons unable to read warnings such as children or blind persons may be likely to get into hazardous areas, then protection must be adequate to keep them out. A duty of care is even owed to trespassers, although this duty is to take such care as is reasonable in all the circumstances of the case to see that they do not suffer injury on the premises by reason of the danger concerned. Sufficient warnings or discouragements will normally discharge the duty.

5.11 Responsibility for injury or damage arising from improper construction or maintenance, is not avoided by the transfer of the premises to another owner (Defective Premises Act 1972).

5.12 If a landlord has a repairing obligation to tenants, then the landlord has a responsibility to anyone who could be affected by the landlord's failure to keep the premises properly maintained.

Health and Safety at Work Act 1974

5.13 The Health and Safety of Work Act is directed at people who work, whether employer, employee, or self-employed persons, and their responsibilities to each other and to third parties who may be affected by the work process or its results. Under the Act employers must maintain safe systems of work and keep plant and premises in safe condition. Adequate instruction, training, and supervision must be given for the purposes of safety. This may extend to guidance or instruction to employees visiting buildings or construction sites in the course of their employment particularly at times when the premises or site may be otherwise unoccupied. RIBA Practice Note (May 1989) provides defiled guidance on safety procedures with particular reference to safety on site. Unless fewer than five people are employed, an employer must prepare a written statement of the business's safety policies, organization and arrangements and make this known and understood by all employees.

5.14 Safety policy should deal with the safety responsibilities of all managers, inspection procedures, supervision, training, research and consultative arrangements regarding safety, fire drill procedure, reminders on keeping stairways and corridors free of obstructions, the marking and guarding of temporary hazards, use of machinery, accidents and first aid. Advice is obtainable from the Health and Safety Commission and Health and Safety Executive. However, employers should ensure that their safety policies are tailored specifically to meet the individual needs of their businesses.

5.15 The employee in his turn has a duty to exercise reasonable care to himself and his fellow employees, to cooperate with his employer in carrying out statutory requirements and not to interfere with safety provisions.

5.16 A number of regulations are important to office environment and organization. Central to these are the Management of Health and Safety at Work Regulations 1992 containing the requirement that employers and the self-employed make and maintain a sufficient and suitable risk assessment for the purposes of identifying the measures required to be taken to comply with health and safety law. Equally important are the Workplace (Health, Safety and Welfare) Regulations 1992. More specific requirements are laid down in the Provision and Use of Work Equipment Regulations 1992, the Health and Safety (Display Screen Equipment) Regulations 1992, the Manual Handling Operations Regulations 1992 and the Personal Protective Equipment at Work Regulations 1992. The Health and Safety (First Aid) Regulations 1981 impose a duty upon employers to provide first aid equipment and facilities, to provide suitable persons with training in first aid, and to inform employees of the arrangements they have made. The British Safety Council Approved Code of Practice, Health and Safety (First Aid) Regulations 1981 is approved by the Health and Safety Commission to provide practical guidance in respect of the regulations. Although failure to comply with the Code's guidance is not in itself an offence, it is prudent to follow it. The Control of Substances Hazardous to Health Regulations 1988 (COSHH) impose a duty upon employers to ensure levels of hazardous substances do not harm employees or others who may be in contact with them. Hazardous substances used in the office include ammonia, solvents (e.g. correction fluid), adhesives, photocopy and laser printer toner, copier emissions, cleaning agents and dusts. The Electricity at Work Regulations 1989 require that electrical systems and equipment be maintained so far as is reasonably practical to prevent danger. Recommendations are provided on the frequency of formal inspection and electrical testing. The Health and Safety Executive publishes guidance enabling the obligations imposed by these, and other relevant regulations, to be met.

Enforcement

5.17 To ensure that the law on health and safety is respected, inspectors appointed by the enforcing authority have the power to enter premises to which the Act applies. They may inspect the premises, question anyone, or ask to see relevant certificates or notices. It is good practice to obtain evidence of their identity and authority before taking anyone round.

5.18 Inspectors have the power to make 'improvement' notices under which the offending practice must cease or the deficiency must be remedied within a certain period. They also have the power to issue a 'prohibition' notice under which the practice must cease or the premises must not be used until their requirements have been met. An appeal against a notice may be made to an industrial tribunal. Offences under the Health and Safety at Work Act are criminal offences, although breaches of the regulations made thereunder can also result in civil liability. It is an offence to contravene requirements imposed by a notice. The offender may be liable to a fine even though damage has not been suffered. It should be borne in mind that, although insurance may be taken out against the possibility of damages being awarded, insurance may not be used to protect against the results of criminal acts, such as fines.

Fire certificate

5.19 The fire provisions of the Offices, Shops and Railway Premises Act 1963 are covered by the Fire Precautions Act 1971 amended by the Fire Safety and Safety of Places of Sport Act 1987 and by various regulations. HM's Government is presently considering ways in which these provisions can be incorporated into regulations implementing EC Directives 89/391/EEC on the introduction of measures to encourage improvements in the safety and health of workers at work and 89/654/EEC concerning the minimum safety and health requirements for the workplace. Whatever principal legislation they eventually come under it is anticipated that risk assessment by employers will be central to the regulations and that all normal requirements covered by existing legislation will be included.

5.20 Under the Fire Precautions Act a fire certificate is compulsory in the case of use as a place of work (amended by the Health and Safety at Work Act 1974) and a use for teaching, training or research, or use for any purpose involving access to the premises by members of the public unless no more than 20 people work in the relevant building at one time with no more than 10 above the ground floor. A fire certificate must be obtained from the enforcing authority. For private practices this is normally the local fire authority. However, the fire authority may exempt premises from the need to have a fire certificate if it thinks fit or in certain specified cases. Even if exemption is granted, premises must still be provided with fire-fighting equipment and means of escape. If this duty is contravened, the fire authority will serve an improvement notice non-compliance with which constitutes an offence. If the fire authority believes that the use of the premises involves a serious fire risk it may serve a notice prohibiting or restricting the use of the premises until the risk is removed.

5.21 For a certificate to be granted, requirements on means of escape, fire-fighting equipment, fire alarm systems and arrangements for fire drills must be satisfied. Failure to have a fire certificate, if not exempted, amounts to an offence.

5.22 Fire alarms must be tested at intervals and occupiers are required to take effective steps to ensure that all occupants are familiar with the means of escape and with the action to be taken in case of fire. Fire drills are the most effective way of doing this.

5.23 If after a certificate has been issued or an exemption has been made, alterations are made to the premises which significantly affect the requirements of that certificate or exemption, the issuing authority must be advised. The authority has continuing powers of inspection to ensure the premises are kept to the original standard and whether changes have been made which render that standard inadequate.

6 Insurance

6.01 A practice protects itself by insurance against financial risks. Some of these are ordinary risks such as fire, some are eventualities which a practice is not obliged to cover but which, as a good employer, it may wish to provide for, such as prolonged sickness of a member of staff. There are cases, however, when a practice is obliged by law to cover damage caused to other persons. Varieties of insurance which cover all these risks are:

Public liability

6.02 An owner or a lessee of premises, or someone carrying on a business in premises, may be legally liable for personal injury or damage to property of third parties caused by their negligence or that of their staff (see Chapter 3).

6.03 Since several people may be involved in a single incident and the level of damages may be very high, it is important for cover to be:

1. Appropriate to status – owner, lessee, or occupier.
2. Extended to cover the actions of employers and employees, not just on the premises, but anywhere while on business.
3. Extended to cover overseas if employers or employees are likely to be overseas on business.

Employers' liability

6.04 An employer is liable for personal injury caused to an employee in the course of employment by the employer's negligence or that of another member of staff. It is important to arrange insurance to cover for injuries sustained:

1. During employment whether on or off the employer's premises.
2. Overseas if employees are likely to be overseas on business.

Employer's Liability (Compulsory Insurance) Act 1969

6.05 Employers are required by statute to take out specific insurance to meet their obligations. The Employer's Liability (Compulsory Insurance) Act 1969 and General Regulations 1971 as amended require that every employer who carries on business in Great Britain shall maintain insurance under approved policies with authorized insurers against liability for bodily injury or disease sustained by employees and arising out of, and in the course of their employment in that business. Cover must extend to an amount of £2 million for any one occurrence. Employers' liability policies are contracts of indemnity. The premium is often based on the amount of wages paid by the insured to employees during the year of insurance. The size of the business is immaterial. The Act also provides for employees not ordinarily resident but who may be temporarily in Great Britain in the course of employment for a continuous period of not less than 14 days. Copies of the insurance certificate must be displayed at the place or places of business for the information of employees.

Motor vehicles

6.06 Third party insurance cover is a legal requirement under the Road Traffic Act 1972 in respect of death or personal injury to third parties or damage to a third party's property. Cover may be invalidated if a car is used for purposes not covered by the policy. Cars owned and operated by a practice must therefore be covered for business use and cars owned by employees and used by them in their duties must be covered for occasional business use.

If staff use their own cars on practice business their cover must be adequate, particularly in respect of fellow employees. Their policies should be checked to ensure that they include a third party indemnity in favour of the employer, otherwise if a claim results from an incident while the car is used on practice business, insurers may repudiate liability.

Professional indemnity

6.07 This is the insurance necessary to cover professional people for negligence. Such policies will normally only cover liabilities to third parties, not loss caused to a person's own business by reason of their negligence. Nor will they cover fraud.

6.08 Every architect in every form of practice should take out professional indemnity insurance. The appropriate scope of the policy, amount of the premium and other details are matters which must be worked out on an individual basis by the architect and an experienced insurance broker. Further information is available from the RIBA Insurance Agency.

6.09 In view of its importance, professional indemnity insurance is dealt with separately in Chapter 23. Incorporated practices also require professional indemnity insurance.

7 Differences between English and Scots law partnerships

7.01 The Partnership Act 1890, the Registration of Business Names Act 1985 and the Limited Partnership Act 1907 apply equally to Scottish partnerships.

7.02 There is, however, an important difference between English and Scottish law regarding the meaning of the word 'firm'. The law uses the word 'firm' to describe those businesses which architects normally refer to as 'practices'. Under English law a partnership is a collection of individuals and not a corporate body, but in Scotland a partnership is a legal persona, distinct in its own right from the partners of which it is composed. In the event of bankruptcy, therefore, the creditors of individual partners do not have a claim on the estate of the firm, although the creditors of the firm qualify for dividends from the estate of individual partners. In England, however, the firm's creditors have a claim only on the firm's estate and the partners' creditors on their private estates, each to the exclusion of the other.

7.03 The differences between English and Scottish law result in the following features in Scotland:

1. A partnership itself owns the funds of the partnership, and the partners are not joint owners of partnership funds. The tax position of a Scottish partnership, however, is exactly the same as for an English one.
2. A firm is the principal debtor in debts owed by the partnership, although the debts must in the first place be constituted against the firm.
3. A partner may sue or be sued by a firm and a firm may be either a debtor or creditor to any of its partners.
4. A firm can be sequestrated* without any of the partners themselves being sequestrated.
5. When a partner retires or a partner joins the firm, the existing partnership comes to an end and a new one is created unless the partnership agreement itself provides otherwise. A new partner is thus not liable for the debts of the firm incurred before his admission, and a retiring partner is liable for the debts of the firm up to the date of his retirement.

7.04 The Limitation Act 1980 does not apply to Scotland, where the distinction between a contract executed under seal and one under hand is not known. The relevant Act is the Prescription and Limitation (Scotland) Act 1973.

Other branches of law

7.05 The Offices, Shops and Railway Premises Act 1963 and the Health and Safety at Work Act 1974 as amended apply also in Scotland as do their effects on architectural practice discussed in this chapter.

* Sequestration: appropriation of income of a property (or firm) to satisfy claims against the owners.

21

Architect's appointment and collateral warranties

A. RODERICK MALES

1 The appointment

1.01 An architect has many factors to consider when considering a commission, and it is important that he should fully appreciate their implications before entering into a legal commitment to undertake the work.

He must be satisfied that the client has the authority and resources to commission the work; he must appreciate the background to the proposal and understand its scope at least in outline; and he must be aware of any other consultants who have been, or are likely to be, associated with the project.

The architect must be satisfied that he has the experience and competence to undertake the work; that the office has the necessary finance, staff, and resources; and that the proposal will not conflict with the RIBA Code of Professional Conduct, the ARCUK statement of Conduct and Discipline, other commissions in the practice, or the policy in the practice.

The preliminary negotiations between the parties may involve the exchange of business references, especially where the architect and the potential client are previously unknown to each other. On occasions, extensive enquiries about the client may be necessary.

It is common for architects to be invited to enter into collateral agreements with funding bodies or other third parties as a condition of the appointment. The possible implications of these agreements needs to be considered by the architect. Collateral agreements are discussed below.

1.02 Any appointment offered to an architect must be considered in relation to the requirements of the ARCUK statement concerning conduct and discipline (Chapter 23), and if the architect is a member of the RIBA or other professional institution, also its code of conduct. The architect must be able to demonstrate that he has acted properly in obtaining the commission and is able to carry out the work properly and in accordance with the codes. An employer may not be conscious of the constraints on the profession, and it is the responsibility of the architect to ensure that he is made aware of them wherever necessary.

The architect must consider his position in relation to other architects who may have been involved with the same scheme. An employer is free to offer the commission to whomever he wishes, to obtain alternative schemes from different architects, and to make whatever arrangements for professional services he considers to be necessary. However, the architect must ensure that he has acted, and continues to act, properly and fairly in his dealings with other architects. In particular he must be able to show that he has not attempted to supplant another architect nor has offered any improper inducements in order to obtain the commission.

An architect who is approached by a potential client in connection with a project with which another architect has already been concerned has a duty to inform the first architect. The first architect has no power to prevent the second architect from proceeding

with the work, but it is ethically desirable and commercially prudent that he should be informed.

1.03 The need to consider the position of other architects is particularly important in large, complex projects involving various consultant architects providing different but related services, especially if the nature of the services changes during the duration of the work.

The scope of services and relations between consultant architects and executive architects are grounds for potential difficulty in developing and changing circumstances. All parties must be very careful to ensure that their terms of reference are fully understood throughout the project.

1.04 Occasionally difficulties may arise where the client wishes to make a single all-in appointment for all the necessary professional consultants. Standard conditions of services and remunerations of various institutions vary in detail and it is necessary for the consultants concerned to agree upon a unified basis before making an offer to a potential client.

2 Agreement of appointment

2.01 Although in law a verbal agreement may be accepted as the basis of a contract of engagement between architect and employer, the risks inherent in such an arrangement are obvious, and a formal procedure of appointment should always be adopted. Such a procedure creates a clearly identifiable legal basis for the commission and establishes a sound business approach to the relationship between architect and employer. The appointment may be made by either an informal exchange of letters or an exchange of a formal memorandum of agreement, in each case supported by appropriate supplementary material such as conditions of engagement.

The exchange of letters is frequently used but is not recommended. Informal letters of appointment are liable to misinterpretation and misunderstanding and are often the source of difficulties and disagreements between the parties.

2.02 Various institutions publish standard forms of agreement and their use is strongly recommended. The format and content of these standard forms varies widely. The forms are generally self-explanatory but it is important that they are carefully read and fully understood by both the architect and the client before signing. The RIBA Standard Form of Agreement for the Appointment of an Architect (SFA92) is discussed below.

2.03 Where a standard form of agreement is not used, it is suggested that the following matters should be clearly identified in any exchange of letters between the parties:

1. The date of the agreement.
2. The name and address of the employer.
3. The name and address of the architect.
4. The title and address of the project.
5. The formal agreement to the appointment of the architect.
6. The basis of remuneration for the architect.
7. The form and scope of services to be provided by the architect.
8. The appointment procedure for a quantity surveyor, other consultants, and the clerk of works as appropriate.
9. The procedure to be followed in the event of the architect's incapacity.
10. The procedure for the termination of the agreement.
11. The procedure for resolving disputes between parties.

The basis of remuneration and the scope of services may be further defined in other documents to which reference should be made in the agreement.

Occasionally, employers may wish to use their own forms of agreement. These should be compared with the standard forms issued by the RIBA and advice sought in the case of serious differences.

2.04 The authority of the architect is strictly limited to the terms of his appointment, that is, as shown in any form of agreement and conditions of engagement. It is in the interests of the employer, the architect, the quantity surveyor, and other independent consultants that these terms should be fully and clearly understood.

2.05 Where a commission arises out of a recognized competition, the competition conditions usually form the conditions of the appointment. Difficulties develop occasionally when the subsequent building is substantially different from that originally envisaged and where there has been a material change in the conditions.

The subsequent appointment of other consultants following a competition may also be a cause of some difficulty.

2.06 The form of appointment agreement should be signed by both parties, witnessed and dated, each keeping a copy. It is a requirement of the ARCUK and RIBA codes that there must be formal agreement on the conditions of the appointment before work commences. Failure to agree and confirm the services to be given and the charges to be made is the most common source of dispute between architects and clients.

2.07 The architect's contract of engagement is usually personal to himself or the partnership. He cannot delegate his duties completely, but he is under no obligation to carry out all the works personally or to go into every detail himself. The extent to which he may be prepared to delegate his duties to an assistant is a matter of competence, confidence, reliability, and experience of the assistant and the principal. The architect is becoming increasingly dependent on the skill and labour of others within his office and elsewhere, but he remains responsible to his client within the terms of his appointment, and continues to be responsible for the acts and defaults of his subordinates. The subordinates in turn are responsible to their principal and could be held liable to their employers for results of their acts.

Where the business is conducted as an unlimited or a limited company, the relationships will depend upon the form of contract involved. However, the ethical responsibilities between the parties remain, and liability in tort continues.

3 Termination

3.01 The contract of engagement between the architect and his employer may be terminated by either party on reasonable notice. Reasons for the termination need not be stated, but in the event of dispute over outstanding fees or payments, the cause of the termination would be of importance to an arbitrator or a court in determining an award.

In the event of the termination of the contract, any outstanding fees for work properly carried out become due to the architect, but it is unlikely that the employer could be held responsible for any loss of anticipated profits on work not yet carried out.

3.02 Difficulties sometimes arise in connection with the use of material prepared before termination of the engagement. The standard form of memoranda of agreement usually defines the rights of the parties in such circumstances. In the absence of any statement concerning the use of material following the termination of an engagement, it is generally assumed that if the work was substantially advanced at the time of termination it would be unreasonable for the employer not to be entitled to complete the project. It is usually accepted that the employer is entitled to a licence to use the drawings to complete the work effectively. The copyright, of course, remains with the architect unless some other agreement is made.

3.03 In the event of the death or the incapacity of the architect, it is usually held that the employer is entitled to the use of the drawings and other documents to complete the work. Provision for the procedure to be adopted in such circumstances should be included in the standard form of agreement. The death of either party to a personal contract generally dissolves the contract, but it is usually possible with agreement, for a third party to assume responsibility for the completion of the contract.

Agreements of appointments between companies and partnerships, rather than between individuals, avoid the occasional embarrassing technical difficulties and delays that occur in the transfer of responsibility to others in the event of death.

3.04 In the event of the bankruptcy of either party, the contract can usually be continued, subject to the agreement of a receiver and assurances about fees and monies which may be due or become due.

4 Ownership

4.01 Ownership of drawings and other documents is often a source of debate. Correspondence and other documents exchanged between the architect and others in connection with the approval of plans, the running of the project, or the administration of the contract by the architect in his role as an agent technically belong to the employer, although it is unusual for all these documents to be transferred to the employer. Other material prepared in the architect's professional capacity belong to the architect, and this accounts for the greater part of the documentation prepared in the course of a project.

5 Standard Form of Agreement for the Appointment of an Architect (SFA92)

5.01 In 1992, partly in response to Government pressure to abandon the publication of recommended fee scales and partly in response to the changing nature of professional appointments, the RIBA produced the Standard Form of Agreement for the Appointment of an Architect (SFA92). The new form of agreement is different in principle and format to its predecessor the Architects Appointment. The recommended fee scales and payment arrangements of the Architects Appointment have been abandoned. The use of the new form is not mandatory and some architects continue to use the Architects Appointment but the adoption of the new form is strongly recommended. The new form is more flexible and more precise in its terms and conditions.

5.02 The Form of Agreement (SFA92) is available in the following versions:

1. the standard form,
2. the form for the Appointment of an Architect Design and Build; Contractor Client version,
3. the form for the Appointment of an Architect Design and Build; Employer Client version,

Memorandum of Agreement

BETWEEN

Parties   (1) _____

of_____('the Client')

(2) _____

of_____('the Architect')

Recitals   **A**   The Client intends to proceed with:

_____

_____

_____('the Project')

The Project relates to the land and/or buildings at:

_____

_____('the Site')

B   The Client wishes to appoint the Architect for the Project and the Architect has agreed to accept such appointment upon and subject to the terms set out in this Agreement.

It is agreed that: 1   The Client hereby appoints the Architect and the Architect hereby accepts appointment for the Project.

2   This Appointment is made and accepted on the Conditions of Appointment and Schedules attached hereto.

3   The Architect shall provide the Services specified in Schedule Two.

4   The Client shall pay the Architect the fees and expenses and disbursements specified in Schedule Three.

5   No action or proceedings for any breach of this Agreement shall be commenced against the Architect after the expiry of _____ years from completion of the Architect's Services, or, where the Services specific to building projects Stages K–L are provided by the Architect, from the date of practical completion of the Project.

6.1   The Architect's liability for loss or damage shall be limited to such sum as the Architect ought reasonably to pay having regard to his responsibility for the same on the basis that all other consultants, Specialists, and the contractor, shall where appointed, be deemed to have provided to the Client contractual undertakings in respect of their services and shall be deemed to have paid to the Client such contribution as may be appropriate having regard to the extent of their responsibility for such loss or damage.

6.2   The liability of the Architect for any loss or damage arising out of any action or proceedings referred to in clause 5 shall, notwithstanding the provisions of clause 6.1, in any event be limited to a sum not exceeding £ _____

6.3   For the avoidance of doubt the Architect's liability shall never exceed the lower of the sum calculated in accordance with clause 6.1 above and the sum provided for in clause 6.2.

Dated _____ 19 _____

AS WITNESS the hands of the parties the day and year first before written

_____   _____
(the Architect)   (the Client)

Definitions

Where the defined terms are used in the SFA documents they are distinguished by an initial capital letter.

Appointment
The agreement between the Client and the Architect for the Project as set out in the Standard Form of Agreement documents.

Architect
The party specified as Architect in the Memorandum of Agreement.

Budget
The sum the Client proposes to spend on the Project inclusive of:

· professional fees and expenses
· disbursements
· statutory charges
· the Construction Budget;

but excluding:

· site acquisition costs
· client's legal and in-house expenses
· and any VAT thereon.

Client
The party specified as Client in the Memorandum of Agreement.

Client's Requirements
The objectives which the Client wishes to achieve in the Project including functional requirements, environmental standards, life span, and levels of quality.

Collateral Agreement
An agreement between the Architect and a third party existing in parallel with the agreement between the Architect and the Client. Sometimes known as a collateral warranty or a duty of care agreement.

Construction Budget
The sum the Client proposes to spend on the construction of the Project.

Contract Documents
The documents forming the building contract between the Client and a contractor, usually comprising conditions of contract, drawings, specifications and bills of quantities or schedules of rates.

Lead Consultant
The consultant given the authority and responsibility by the Client to coordinate and integrate the services of the other consultants.

Procurement Method
The method by which the building project is to be achieved, determining:

· the relations between the Client, the design team and the construction team
· the methods of financing and management, and
· the form of construction contract

Project
As specified in the Memorandum of Agreement.

Services
The Services to be provided by the Architect as specified in Schedule Two.

Site
As specified in the Memorandum of Agreement.

Site Staff
Staff appointed by either Architect or Client to provide inspection of the Works on behalf of the Client.

continued

Definitions *continued*

Specialist

A person or firm, other than the consultants, appointed to provide expertise, skill and care, involving design, in the supply or manufacture of goods, materials or components or in the construction of parts of the Project.

Timetable

The Timetable for the completion of the Services showing *inter alia* any points and/or dates during the course of the carrying out of the Services at which the Architect shall seek the authority of the Client before proceeding further with the Services.

Total Construction Cost

The cost as certified by the Architect of all Works including site works executed under the Architect's direction and control.

It shall include:

· the cost of all works designed by consultants and co-ordinated by the Architect irrespective of whether such work is carried out under separate building contracts for which the Architect may not be responsible. The Architect shall be informed of the cost of any such contract;

· the actual or estimated cost of any work executed which is excluded from the contract and which is otherwise designed by the Architect;

· the cost of built-in furniture and equipment. Where the cost of any special equipment is excluded from the Total Construction Cost the Architect may charge additionally for work in connection with such items;

· the cost estimated by the Architect of any material, labour or carriage supplied by a Client who is not the contractor.

It shall exclude:

· the design fees of any Specialists for work on which otherwise consultants would have been employed. Where such fees are not known the Architect will estimate a reduction from the Total Construction Cost.

Where the Client is the contractor, a statement of the ascertained gross cost of the works may be used in calculating the Total Construction Cost of the Works. In the absence of such a statement the Architect's own estimate shall be used. In both a statement of the ascertained gross cost and an Architect's estimate there shall be included an allowance for the contractor's profit and overheads.

Work Stages

Stages into which the process of designing building projects and administering building contracts may be divided in accordance with the RIBA's model *Plan of Work* for design team operation.

Works

The works to be carried out by the construction contractor as described in the Contract Documents; the place where those works are carried out.

Conditions of Appointment

PART ONE

CONDITIONS COMMON TO ALL COMMISSIONS

1.1 Governing law/interpretation

1.1.1 The application of the Appointment shall be governed by the laws of [England and Wales] [Northern Ireland] [Scotland].
Delete those parts not applicable.

1.1.2 The conditions headings and side notes are for the convenience of the parties to this Agreement only and do not affect its interpretation.

1.1.3 Words denoting the masculine gender include the feminine gender and words denoting natural persons include corporations and firms and shall be construed interchangeably in that manner.

1.2 Architect's obligations

Duty of care
1.2.1 The Architect shall in providing the Services exercise reasonable skill and care in conformity with the normal standards of the Architect's profession.

Architect's authority
1.2.2 The Architect shall act on behalf of the Client in the matters set out or necessarily implied in the Appointment.

1.2.3 The Architect shall at those points and/or dates referred to in the Timetable obtain the authority of the Client before proceeding with the Services.

No alteration to services
1.2.4 The Architect shall make no material alteration to or addition to or omission from the Services without the knowledge and consent of the Client except in case of emergency when the Architect shall inform the Client without delay.

Variations
1.2.5 The Architect shall inform the Client upon its becoming apparent that there is any incompatibility between any of the Client's Requirements; or between the Client's Requirements, the Budget and the Timetable; or any need to vary any part of them.

1.2.6 The Architect shall inform the Client on its becoming apparent that the Services and/or the fees and/or any other part of the Appointment and/or any information or approvals need to be varied. The Architect shall confirm in writing any agreement reached.

1.3 Client's obligations

Client's representative
1.3.1 The Client shall name the person who shall exercise the powers of the Client under the Appointment and through whom all instructions to the Architect shall be given.

Information
1.3.2 The Client shall provide to the Architect the information specified in Schedule One.

1.3.3 The Client shall provide to the Architect such further information as the Architect shall reasonably and necessarily request for the performance of the Services; all such information to be provided free of charge and at such times as shall permit the Architect to comply with the Timetable.

1.3.4 The Client accepts that the Architect will rely on the accuracy, sufficiency and consistency of the information supplied by the Client.

1.3.5 The Client shall advise the Architect of the relative priorities of the Client's Requirements, the Budget and the Timetable and shall inform the Architect of any variations to any of them.

Decisions and approvals
1.3.6 The Client shall give such decisions and approvals as are necessary for the performance of the Services and at such times as to enable the Architect to comply with the Timetable.

Architect does not warrant
1.3.7 The Client acknowledges that the Architect does not warrant the work or products of others nor warrants that the Services will or can be completed in accordance with the Timetable.

1.4 Assignment and sub-contracting

Assignment
1.4.1 Neither the Architect nor the Client shall assign the whole or any part of the benefit or in any way transfer the obligation of the Appointment without the consent in writing of the other.

Sub-contracting
1.4.2 The Architect shall not sub-contract any of the Services without the consent in writing of the Client, which consent shall not be unreasonably withheld.

1.5 Payment

Payment
1.5.1 Payment for the Services shall be calculated, charged and paid as set out in Schedule Three.

Percentage fees
1.5.2 Where it is stated in Schedule Three that fees and/or expenses are payable on a percentage basis, then, unless any other basis has been agreed between the Architect and the Client and confirmed by the Architect to the Client in writing, the fees and/or expenses shall be based on the Total Construction Cost of the Works. On the issue of the final certificate under the building contract the fees and/or expenses shall be recalculated on the actual Total Construction Cost.

1.5.3 The following bases shall be used for the calculation of percentage fees based on the Total Construction Cost until that cost has been ascertained:
· until tenders are obtained – the cost estimate;
· after tenders have been obtained – the lowest acceptable tender;
· after the contract is let – the contract sum.

Revise rates
1.5.4 Unless otherwise stated in Schedule Three, time rates and mileage rates for vehicles shall be revised every twelve months from the date of the Appointment.

Fee variation
1.5.5 Where any change is made to the Architect's Services, the Procurement Method, the Client's Requirements, the Budget, or the Timetable, or where the Architect consents to enter into any Collateral Agreement the form or beneficiary of which had not been agreed by the Architect at the date of the Appointment, the fees specified in Schedule Three shall be varied.

Vary lump sum
1.5.6 Where fees and/or expenses are specified in Schedule Three to be a lump sum, that lump sum shall also be varied in accordance with the provisions of Schedule Three.

Additional fees
1.5.7 Where the Architect is involved in extra work and/or expense for which the Architect is not otherwise remunerated caused by:
· the Clients variations to completed work or services;
· the examination and/or negotiation of notices, applications or claims under a building contract;
· delay or for any other reason beyond the Architect's control;
the Architect shall be entitled to additional fees calculated on a time basis.

1.5.8 Where fees and/or expenses are varied under conditions 1.2.6, 1.5.4, 1.5.5 and/or 1.5.6 or where additional fees are payable under condition 1.5.7, the additional or varied fees and/or expenses shall be stated by the Architect in writing.

Incomplete Services
1.5.9 Where the Architect carries out only part of the Services specified in Schedule Two, fees shall be calculated as described in Schedule Three for:
· completed Work Stage [Schedule Two]
· completed Service [Schedule Two]
· completed part [Timetable, Schedule One]
and for the balance of any of the above the fee shall be on the basis of the Architect's estimate of the percentage of completion.

Expenses and disbursements
1.5.10 The Client shall pay the expenses specified in Schedule Three. Expenses other than those specified shall only be charged with the prior authorisation of the Client.

1.5.11 The Client shall reimburse the Architect as specified in Schedule Three for any disbursements made on the Client's behalf.

As referred to in the Memorandum of Agreement dated   between   and   *(parties to initial)*

Maintain records	1.5.12	The Architect shall maintain records of expenses and of disbursements and shall make these available to the Client on reasonable request.
Instalments	1.5.13	All payments due under the Appointment shall be made by instalments specified in Schedule Three. Where no such basis is specified, payments shall be made monthly on the basis of the Architect's estimate of percentage of completion of the Services.
Payment	1.5.14	Payment shall become due to the Architect on submission of the Architect's account.
No setoff	1.5.15	The Client may not withhold or reduce any sum payable to the Architect under the Appointment by reason of claims or alleged claims against the Architect. All rights of setoff which the Client may otherwise exercise in common law are hereby expressly excluded.
Disputed accounts	1.5.16	If any item or part of an item of any account is disputed or subject to question by the Client, the payment by the Client of the remainder of that account shall not be withheld on those grounds.
Interest on outstanding accounts	1.5.17	Any sums remaining unpaid at the expiry of twenty-eight days from the date of submission of an account shall bear interest thereafter, such interest to accrue from day to day at the rate specified in Schedule Three.
Payment on suspension or termination	1.5.18	On suspension or termination of the Appointment the Architect shall be entitled to, and shall be paid, fees for all Services provided to that time calculated as incomplete Services, and to expenses and disbursements reasonably incurred to that time.
	1.5.19	During any period of suspension the Architect shall be reimbursed by the Client for expenses, disbursements and other costs reasonably incurred as a result of the suspension.
	1.5.20	On the resumption of a suspended Service within six months, fees paid prior to resumption shall be regarded solely as payments on account of the total fee.
	1.5.21	Where the Appointment is suspended or terminated by the Client or suspended or terminated by the Architect on account of a breach of the Appointment by the Client, the Architect shall be paid by the Client for all expenses and other costs necessarily incurred as a result of any suspension and any resumption or termination.
VAT	1.5.22	All fees, expenses and disbursements under the Appointment are exclusive of Value Added Tax. Any Value Added Tax on the Architect's services shall be paid by the Client.
	1.6	**Suspension, resumption and termination**
Services impracticable	1.6.1	The Architect shall give reasonable notice in writing to the Client of any circumstances which make it impracticable for the Architect to carry out any of the Services in accordance with the Timetable.
Suspension	1.6.2	The Client may suspend the performance of any or all of the Services by giving reasonable notice in writing to the Architect.
	1.6.3	In the event of the Client's being in default of payment of any fees, expenses and/or disbursements, the Architect may suspend the performance of any or all of the Services on giving notice in writing to the Client.
Resumption	1.6.4	If the Architect has not been given instructions to resume any suspended Service within six months from the date of suspension, the Architect shall request in writing such instructions. If written instructions have not been received within twenty-eight days of the date of such request the Architect shall have the right to treat the Appointment as terminated.
Termination	1.6.5	The Appointment may be terminated by either party on the expiry of reasonable notice in writing.
Architect's death or incapacity	1.6.6	Should the Architect through death or incapacity be unable to provide the Services, the Appointment shall thereby be terminated.
Accrued rights	1.6.7	Termination of the Appointment shall be without prejudice to the accrued rights and remedies of either party.

	1.7	**Copyright**
Copyright	1.7.1	Copyright in all documents and drawings prepared by the Architect and in any work executed from those documents and drawings shall remain the property of the Architect.
	1.8	**Dispute resolution**
Arbitration	1.8.1	In England and Wales, and subject to the provisions of conditions 1.8.2 and 1.8.3 in Northern Ireland, any difference or dispute arising out of the Appointment shall be referred by either of the parties to arbitration by a person to be agreed between the parties or, failing agreement within fourteen days after either party has given the other a written request to concur in the appointment of an arbitrator, a person to be nominated at the request of either party by the President of the Chartered Institute of Arbitrators provided that in a difference or dispute arising out of the conditions relating to copyright the arbitrator shall, unless otherwise agreed, be an architect.
Scotland	1.8.1S	In Scotland, subject to the provisions of conditions 1.8.2 and 1.8.3, any difference or dispute arising out of the Appointment shall be referred to arbitration by a person to be agreed between the parties or, failing agreement within fourteen days after either party has given the other a written request to concur in the appointment of an arbiter, a person to be nominated at the request of either party by the Dean of the Faculty of Advocates, provided that in a difference or dispute arising out of the conditions relating to copyright the arbiter shall, unless otherwise agreed, be an architect.
Opinion	1.8.2	In Northern Ireland or Scotland, any difference or dispute arising from the Appointment may be referred respectively to the RSUA or the RIAS for an opinion provided that: · the opinion is sought on a joint statement of undisputed facts; · the parties agree to be bound by the opinion.
Negotiation	1.8.3	In Northern Ireland or Scotland, the parties shall attempt to settle any dispute by negotiation and no procedure shall be commenced under condition 1.8.1 or 1.8.1S until the expiry of twenty-eight days after notification has been given in writing by one to the other of a difference or dispute.
	1.8.4	Nothing herein shall prevent the parties agreeing to settle any difference or dispute arising out of the Appointment without recourse to arbitration.

PART TWO		**CONDITIONS SPECIFIC TO DESIGN OF BUILDING PROJECTS, STAGES A–H**
	2.1	**Architect's obligations**
Architect's authority	2.1.1	The Architect shall, where specified in the Timetable, obtain the authority of the Client before initiating any Work Stage and shall confirm that authority in writing.
Procurement Method	2.1.2	The Architect shall advise on the options for the Procurement Method for the Project.
No alteration to design	2.1.3	The Architect shall make no material alteration, addition to or omission from the approved design without the knowledge and consent of the Client and shall confirm such consent in writing.
	2.2	**Client's obligations**
Statutory requirements	2.2.1	The Client shall instruct the making of applications for planning permission and approval under Building Acts, Regulations and other statutory requirements and applications for consents by freeholders and all others having an interest in the Project and shall pay any statutory charges and any fees, expenses and disbursements in respect of such applications.
	2.2.2	The Client shall have informed the Architect prior to the date of the Appointment whether any third party will acquire or is likely to acquire an interest in the whole or any part of the Project.
Collateral Agreements	2.2.3	The Client shall not require the Architect to enter into any Collateral Agreement with a third party which imposes greater obligations or liabilities on the Architect than does the Appointment.
Procurement Method	2.2.4	The Client shall confirm the Procurement Method for the Project.

2.3 Copyright

2.3.1 Notwithstanding the provisions of condition 1.7.1, the Client shall be entitled to reproduce the Architect's design by proceeding to execute the Project provided that:
- the entitlement applies only to the Site or part of the Site to which the design relates, and
- the Architect has completed a scheme design or
- has provided detail design and production information, and
- any fees, expenses and disbursements due to the Architect have been paid.

This entitlement shall also apply to the maintenance repair and/or renewal of the Works.

2.3.2 Where the Architect has not completed a scheme design, the Client shall not reproduce the design by proceeding to execute the Project without the consent of the Architect.

2.3.3 Where the Services are limited to making and negotiating planning applications, the Client may not reproduce the Architect's design without the Architect's consent, which consent shall not be unreasonably withheld, and payment of any additional fees.

2.3.4 The Architect shall not be liable for the consequences of any use of any information or designs prepared by the Architect except for the purposes for which they were provided.

PART THREE CONDITIONS SPECIFIC TO CONTRACT ADMINISTRATION AND INSPECTION OF THE WORKS STAGES J–L

3.1 Architect's obligations

Visits to the Works 3.1.1 The Architect shall in providing the Services specified in stages K and L of Schedule Two make such visits to the Works as the Architect at the date of the Appointment reasonably expected to be necessary. The Architect shall confirm such expectation in writing.

Variations to visits to the Works 3.1.2 The Architect shall, on its becoming apparent that the expectation of the visits to the Works needs to be varied, inform the Client in writing of his recommendations and any consequential variation in fees.

More frequent visits to the Works 3.1.3 The Architect shall, where the Client requires more frequent visits to the Works than that specified by the Architect in condition 3.1.1, inform the Client of any consquential variation in fees. The Architect shall confirm in writing any agreement reached.

Alteration to design only in emergency 3.1.4 The Architect may in an emergency make an alteration, addition or omission without the Client's knowledge and consent but shall inform the Client without delay and shall confirm that in writing. Otherwise the Architect shall make no material alteration or addition to or omission from the approved design during construction without the knowledge and consent of the Client, and the Architect shall confirm such consent in writing.

3.2 Client's obligations

Contractor 3.2.1 The Client shall employ a contractor under a separate agreement to undertake construction or other works relating to the Project.

Responsibilities of contractor 3.2.2 The Client shall hold the contractor and not the Architect responsible for the contractor's management and operational methods and for the proper carrying out and completion of the Works and for health and safety provisions on the Site.

Products and materials 3.2.3 The Client shall hold the contractor and not the Architect responsible for the proper installation and incorporation of all products and materials into the Works.

Collateral Agreements 3.2.4 The Client shall, where the Architect consents to enter into a Collateral Agreement with a third party in respect of the Project, procure that the contractor is equally bound.

Instructions 3.2.5 The Client shall only issue instructions to the contractor through the Architect, and the Client shall not hold the Architect responsible for any instructions issued other than through the Architect.

3.3 Site Staff

3.3.1 The Architect shall recommend the appointment of Site Staff to the Client if in his opinion such appointments are necessary to provide the Services specified in K–L 04–08 of Schedule Two.

3.3.2 The Architect shall confirm in writing to the Client the Site Staff to be appointed, their disciplines, the expected duration of their employment, the party to appoint them and the party to pay, and the method of recovery of payment to them.

3.3.3 All Site Staff shall be under the direction and control of the Architect.

PART FOUR CONDITIONS SPECIFIC TO APPOINTMENT OF CONSULTANTS AND SPECIALISTS WHERE ARCHITECT IS LEAD CONSULTANT

4.1 Consultants

Nomination 4.1.1 The Architect shall identify professional services which require the appointment of consultants. Such consultants may be nominated at any time by either the Client or the Architect subject to acceptance by each party.

Appointment 4.1.2 The Client shall appoint and pay the nominated consultants.

4.1.3 The consultants to be appointed at the date of the Appointment and the services to be provided by them shall be confirmed in writing by the Architect to the Client.

Collateral Agreements 4.1.4 The Client shall, where the Architect consents to enter into a Collateral Agreement with a third party in respect of the Project, procure that all consultants are equally bound.

Lead Consultant 4.1.5 The Client shall appoint and give authority to the Architect as Lead Consultant in relation to all consultants however employed. The Architect shall be the medium of all communication and instruction between the Client and the consultants, coordinate and integrate into the overall design the services of the consultants, require reports from the consultants.

4.1.6 The Client shall procure that the provisions of condition 4.1.5 above are incorporated into the conditions of appointment of all consultants however employed and shall provide a copy of such conditions of appointment to the Architect.

Responsibilities of consultants 4.1.7 The Client shall hold each consultant however appointed and not the Architect responsible for the competence and performance of the services to be performed by the consultant and for the general inspection of the execution of the work designed by the consultant.

Responsibilities of Architect 4.1.8 Nothing in this Part shall affect any responsibility of the Architect for issuing instructions under the building contract or for other functions ascribed to the Architect under the building contract in relation to work designed by a consultant.

4.2 Specialists

Nomination 4.2.1 A Specialist who is to be employed directly by the Client or indirectly through the contractor to design any part of the Works may be nominated by either the Architect or the Client subject to acceptance by each party.

Appointment 4.2.2 The Specialists to be appointed at the date of the Appointment and the services to be provided by them shall be those confirmed in writing by the Architect to the Client.

Collateral Agreements 4.2.3 The Client shall, where the Architect consents to enter into a Collateral Agreement with a third party in respect of the Project, procure that all Specialists are equally bound.

Coordination and integration 4.2.4 The Client shall give the authority to the Architect to coordinate and integrate the services of all Specialists into the overall design and the Architect shall be responsible for such coordination and integration.

Responsibilities of Specialists 4.2.5 The Client shall hold any Specialist and not the Architect responsible for the products and materials supplied by the Specialist and for the competence, proper execution and performance of the work with which such Specialists are entrusted.

Schedule One	Information to be supplied by Client

Part One

All Commissions

The information to be supplied by the Client under Conditions 1.3.2 and 1.3.3 shall specifically include:

Client's Requirements   Budget   Timetable

Other matters:

Part Two

Commissions where Services are specific to the design of Building Projects, Work Stages A–H

Where this Part applies, the further information to be supplied by the Client shall specifically include:

matters relating to the site and any buildings thereon including
- ownership and interests
- boundaries
- easements and restrictive and other covenants
- other legal constraints
- planning consents obtained and applied for
- measured surveys
- explorations
- any requirement to conform to client systems/working methods

Further matters relating to Client's Requirements including
- schedule of accommodation
- general level of quality of specification

Other matters:

Part Three

Commissions where Services are specific to Contract Administration and Inspection of the Works, Work Stages J–L

Where this Part applies, information to be supplied by the Client shall specifically include:

As referred to in the Memorandum of Agreement dated   between   and   *(parties to initial)*

Schedule Two		Services to be provided by Architect					

1 Design Skills	**2 Consultancy Services**	**3 Buildings / Sites**	**4 All Commissions**
1.01 Provide interior design services	2.01 Provide services as a consultant Architect on a regular or intermittent basis	3.01 Advise on the suitability and selection of sites	4.01 Obtain the Client's Requirements, Budget and Timetable
1.02 Advise on the selection of furniture and fittings	2.02 Consult statutory authorities	3.02 Make measured surveys, take levels and prepare plans of sites	4.02 Advise on the need for and the scope of consultants' services and the conditions of their appointment
1.03 Design furniture and fittings	2.03 Provide information in connection with local authority, government and other grants	3.03 Arrange for investigations of soil conditions of sites	4.03 Arrange for and assist in the selection of other consultants
1.04 Inspect the making up of furnishings		3.04 Advise on the suitability and selection of buildings	
1.05 Advise on works of special quality, e.g. shopfittings	2.04 Make applications for local authority, government and other grants	3.05 Make measured surveys and prepare drawings of existing buildings	
1.06 Prepare information for installation of works of special quality	2.05 Conduct negotiations for local authority, government and other grants	3.06 Inspect and prepare report and schedule of condition of existing buildings	
1.07 Inspect installation of works of special quality	2.06 Make submissions to RFAC, UK heritage bodies and/or non-statutory bodies	3.07 Inspect and prepare report and schedule of dilapidations	
1.08 Advise on commissioning or selection of works of art	2.07 Provide information to advisory bodies	3.08 Prepare estimates for the replacement and reinstatement of buildings and plant	
1.09 Prepare information for installation of works of art	2.08 Negotiate with advisory bodies	3.09 Prepare, submit, negotiate claims following damage by fire and other causes	
1.10 Inspect installation of works of art	2.09 Advise on rights including easements and responsibilities of owners and lessees	3.10 Investigate and advise on means of escape in existing buildings	
1.11 Provide industrial design services	2.10 Provide information on rights including easements and responsibilities of owners and lessees	3.11 Investigate and advise on change of use in existing buildings	
1.12 Develop a building system or components for mass production	2.11 Negotiate rights including easements	3.12 Investigate and report on building failures	
1.13 Examine and advise on existing building systems	2.12 Provide services in connection with party wall negotiations	3.13 Arrange for and inspect exploratory work by contractors and specialists in connection with building failures	
1.14 Monitor testing of prototypes, mock-ups or models of building systems	2.13 Provide services in connection with planning appeals and/or inquiries	3.14 Prepare a layout for the development of a site	
1.15 Provide town planning and urban design services	2.14 Advise on the use of energy in new or existing buildings	3.15 Prepare a layout for a greater area than that which is to be developed immediately	
1.16 Provide landscape design services	2.15 Carry out life cycle analyses of proposed or existing buildings to determine their likely cost in use	3.16 Prepare development plans for a site or a large building or a complex of buildings	
1.17 Provide graphic design services	2.16 Provide services in connection with environmental studies	3.17 Prepare drawings and specifications of materials for the construction of estate roads and sewers	
1.18 Provide exhibition design services	2.17 Act as coordinator in health and safety matters		
1.19 Provide presentation material design services	2.18 Prepare, settle proofs, attend conferences and give evidence	3.18 Make structural surveys and report on the structural elements of buildings	3.21 Investigate and advise on fire protection and alarms in existing buildings
1.20 Provide perspective and other illustrations	2.19 Act as witness as to fact	3.19 Investigate and advise on floor loadings in existing buildings	3.22 Investigate and advise on security systems in existing buildings
1.21 Provide model-making services	2.20 Act as expert witness	3.20 Investigate and advise on sound insulation in existing buildings	3.23 Inspect and prepare a valuation report for mortgage or other purpose
1.22 Provide photographic record services	2.21 Act as arbitrator		3.24 ....
1.23	2.22 Provide project management services		
	2.23		

As referred to in the Memorandum of Agreement dated   between   and   *(parties to initial)*

Schedule Two — Services specific to Building Projects

Stages

A–B Inception and Feasibility		C Outline Proposals		D Scheme Design		E Detail Design	
01	Obtain information about the Site from the Client	01	Analyse the Client's Requirements; prepare outline proposals	01	Develop scheme design from approved outline proposals	01	Develop detail design from approved scheme design
02	Visit the Site and carry out an initial appraisal	02	Provide information to discuss proposals with and incorporate input of other consultants	02	Provide information to, discuss proposals with and incorporate input of other consultants into scheme design	02	Provide information to, discuss proposals with and incorporate input of other consultants into detail design
03	Assist the Client in preparation of Client's Requirements	03	Provide information to other consultants for their preparation of an approximation of construction cost	03	Provide information to other consultants for their preparation of cost estimate	03	Provide information to other consultants for their revision of cost estimate
04	Advise the Client on methods of procuring construction	03A	Prepare an approximation of construction cost	03A	Prepare cost estimate	03A	Revise cost estimate
05	Advise on the need for specialist contractors, sub-contractors and suppliers to design and execute parts of the Works	04	Submit outline proposals and approximation of construction cost for the Client's preliminary approval	04	Prepare preliminary timetable for construction	04	Prepare applications for approvals under Building Acts and/or Regulations and other statutory requirements
06	Prepare proposals and make application for outline planning permission	05	Propose a procedure for cost planning and control	05	Consult with planning authorities	04A	Prepare building notice under Building Acts and/or Regulations *
07	Carry out such studies as may be necessary to determine the feasibility of the Client's Requirements	06	Provide information to others for cost planning and control throughout the Project	06	Consult with building control authorities	05	Agree form of building contract and explain the Client's obligations thereunder
08	Review with the Client alternative design and construction approaches and cost implications	06A	Operate the procedure for cost planning and control throughout the Project	07	Consult with fire authorities	06	Obtain the Client's approval of the type of construction, quality of materials and standard of workmanship
09	Advise on the need to obtain planning permission, approvals under Building Acts and/or Regulations and other statutory requirements	07	Prepare and keep updated a Client's running expenditure plan for the Project	08	Consult with environmental authorities	07	Apply for approvals under Building Acts and/or Regulations and other statutory requirements
10	Develop the Client's Requirements	08	Prepare special presentation drawings, brochures, models or technical information for use of the Client or others	09	Consult with licensing authorities	07A	Give building notice under Building Acts and/or Regulations *
11	Advise on environmental impact and prepare report	09	Carry out negotiations with tenants or others identified by the Client	10	Consult with statutory undertakers	08	Negotiate if necessary over Building Acts and/or Regulations and other statutory requirements and revise production information
12	....	10	....	11	Prepare an application for full planning permission	09	Conduct exceptional negotiations for approvals by statutory authorities
				12	Submit scheme design showing spatial arrangements, materials and appearance, together with cost estimate, for the Client's approval	10	Negotiate waivers or relaxations under Building Acts and/or Regulations and other statutory requirements
				13	Consult with tenants or others identified by the Client	11	....
				14	Conduct exceptional negotiations with planning authorities		
				15	Submit an application for full planning permission		
				16	Prepare multiple applications for full planning permission		
				17	Submit multiple applications for full planning permission		
				18	Make revisions to scheme design to deal with requirements of planning authorities		
				19	Revise planning application		
				20	Resubmit planning application		
				21	Carry out special constructional research for the Project including design of prototypes, mock-ups or models		
				22	Monitor testing of prototypes, mock-ups or models etc		
				23			

Work Stages
are specified by circling the stage letters

Basic Services
indicated by the coloured area are specified unless struck out

Additional Services
are specified by circling the relevant numbered items

* Not applicable in Scotland

Schedule Two   Services specific to Building Projects

Stages

F–G Production Information and Bills of Quantities	H Tender Action	J Project Planning	K–L Operations on Site and Completion
01 Prepare production drawings	01 Advise on and obtain the Client's approval to a list of tenderers for the building contract	01 Advise the Client on the appointment of the contractor and on the responsibilities of the parties and the Architect under the building contract	01 Administer the terms of the building contract
02 Prepare specification	02 Invite tenders	02 Prepare the building contract and arrange for it to be signed	02 Conduct meetings with the contractor to review progress
03 Provide information for the preparation of bills of quantities and/or schedules of works	03 Appraise and report on tenders with other consultants	03 Provide production information as required by the building contract	03 Provide information to other consultants for the preparation of financial reports to the Client
03A Prepare schedule of rates and/or quantities and/or schedules of works for tendering purposes	03A Appraise and report on tenders		03A Prepare financial reports for the Client
04 Provide information to, discuss proposals with and incorporate input of other consultants into production information	04 Assist other consultants in negotiating with a tenderer	04 Provide services in connection with demolitions	04 Generally inspect materials delivered to the site
	04A Negotiate with a tenderer	05 Arrange for other contracts to be let subsequent to the commencement of the building contract	05 As appropriate instruct sample taking and carrying out tests of materials, components, techniques and workmanship and examine the conduct and results of such tests whether on or off site
05 Co-ordinate production information	05 Assist other consultants in negotiating a price with a contractor	06	
06 Provide information to other consultants for their revision of cost estimate	05A Negotiate a price with a contractor		06 As appropriate instruct the opening up of completed work to determine that it is generally in accordance with the Contract Documents
06A Revise cost estimate	06 Select a contractor by other means		
07 Review timetable for construction	07 Revise production information to adjust tender sum		07 As appropriate visit the sites of the extraction and fabrication and assembly of materials and components to inspect such materials and workmanship before delivery to site
08 Prepare other production information	08 Arrange for other contracts to be let prior to the main building contract		08 At intervals appropriate to the stage of construction visit the Works to inspect the progress and quality of the Works and to determine that they are being executed generally in accordance with the Contract Documents
09 Submit plans for proposed building works for approval of landlords, funders, free-holders, tenants or others as requested by the Client	09		09 Direct and control the activities of Site Staff
10			10 Provide drawings showing the building and the main lines of drainage
			11 Arrange for drawings of building services installations to be provided
			12 Give general advice on maintenance
			13 Administer the terms of other contracts
			14 Monitor the progress of the Works against the contractor's programme and report to the Client
		19 Incorporate information prepared by others in maintenance manuals	15 Prepare valuations of work carried out and completed
		20 Prepare a programme for the maintenance of a building	16 Provide specially prepared drawings of a building as built
		21 Arrange maintenance contracts	17 Prepare drawings for conveyancing purposes
		22	18 Compile maintenance and operational manuals

Schedule Three   Fees and Expenses

VAT, where applicable, is charged on all fees and expenses

1 Fees

2 Time rates   The rates for Services to be charged on a time basis shall be calculated as follows:

Time rates shall be revised each year on:

3 Expenses   The following expenses shall be charged by the Architect:

- at cost
- cost plus _____ %
- a lump sum of £ _____
- an additional % fee of _____ %

Mileage rates where applicable shall be:
_____
and shall be revised each year on:
_____

4 Disbursements   For disbursements made under Condition 1.5.11 the Architect shall charge:

- at cost plus _____ %
- other _____

5 Instalments   Fees and expenses shall be paid by instalments in accordance with the following programme:

6 Site Staff   For Site Staff (under Conditions 3.3.1 and 3.3.2) appointed and paid by the Architect, the Architect shall be reimbursed as follows:

- on a Time Basis, or
- on Annual Salary Cost plus: _____ % (salaries to be stated, where appropriate)

7 Interest on overdue accounts   The interest rate payable under Condition 1.5.17 shall be:

- either _____ %
- or _____ % over _____   (measure of base rate)

As referred to in the Memorandum of Agreement dated _____ between _____ and _____   *(parties to initial)*

Schedule Four   Appointment of Consultants, Specialists and Site Staff

Consultants   (under Conditions 4.1.2 and 4.1.3)

Services*   Name, address *(where known)*

Specialists   (under Condition 4.2.2)

Services*   Name, address *(where known)*   To be appointed
                                                                          (a) directly by Client
                                                                          (b) indirectly by Contractor

*Extent of services to be defined in appointing letter or other document – to be copied to the Architect.

Site Staff   (under Condition 3.3.2)

Description	Duration	No. of staff	By whom appointed and paid

As referred to in the Memorandum of Agreement dated   between   and   *(parties to initial)*

4. the Historic Building Repairs and Conservation Work; Alternative Schedule of Services, and
5. the Community Architecture: Supplementary Schedule of Services.

5.03 SFA92 comprises:

1. the Memorandum of Agreement which has to be completed to identify parties, their intentions, and the scope and cost of services to be provided,
2. the Conditions, which should only be varied in special circumstances, and
3. the Schedules 1, 2, 3, and 4 which have to be completed. The schedules act as checklists and provide the opportunity for the parties to identify and agree upon the detailed arrangements for the appointment.

5.04 The schedules comprise:

1. **Schedule 1** identifying the information to be supplied by the client covering such matters as the budget, the timetable, site information, and any special information concerning the site and site inspection,
2. **Schedule 2** identifying the services to be provided by the architect – done by means of circling, striking out, or adding to a long 'menu' of possible services,
3. **Schedule 3** setting out the way payments for these services is to be calculated, charged, and paid, and
4. **Schedule 4** dealing with the appointment of other consultants, specialists, and site staff.

The effective operation of SFA92 is dependent upon a careful assessment of the particular needs of any proposed commission and the maintenance and application of good office records.

5.05 Articles 5 and 6 of the Memorandum of Agreement offers the architect the opportunity to propose a limit to the duration of contractual, and a limit to the extent of financial liability. These limits are negotiable and may be taken into account in the determination of fee levels and payment arrangements.

5.06 Prospective clients frequently require an estimate of the anticipated total fees likely to be involved in projects. Difficulties may arise where fees are forecast on the basis of a premature estimate of the likely total cost of the building work. As in all cases of financial forecast, it is important that care should be taken and clients should be advised of the nature of the estimate being made.

Difficulties may also arise where time charges are to be made and the forecast of the likely period of work is given.

5.07 Any value added tax (VAT) chargeable on the services of the architect is chargeable to the client at the appropriate rate current at the time. Clients who are taxable persons under the Finance Act 1972 are able to recover such input tax from the Customs and Excise Department.

5.08 Architects carrying out work overseas in situations where RIBA or other conditions do not apply are advised to uphold any local scales of charges. If there are no locally recognized scales, the architect, of course, would have to devise his own.

5.09 It is by no means uncommon for the client's brief or requirements to change during the course of a commission. Where this has happened, or is likely to happen, it is essential that the architect brings to the attention of the client any implications there may be for the conditions of the architect's appointment. Failure to draw attention to possible changes in the nature or range of service required and the basis of payment can have embarrassing consequences for both the client and the architect.

5.10 Frequently potential clients wish to impose particular conditions on the architect's engagement. The implications of these conditions need to be carefully assessed and where there is a substantial extension to the liability or duties of the architect appropriate additional reimbursement should be negotiated. Extensions

of liability outside those of an existing professional indemnity policy should be discussed with the architect's broker or insurers. Public bodies and large commercial clients may require the architect to undertake to maintain professional indemnity insurance for six years following completion of the works: the architect must insist that the undertaking is subject to the reasonable availability of insurance cover.

5.11 The introduction of the new role of planning supervisor under the Construction (Design and Management) Regulations in March 1995 led to the development of the Form of Agreement for the Appointment of the Architect as Planning Supervisor (see Chapter 19 on health and safety).

5.12 In response to pressure from its members and in an attempt to offer guidance to clients in September 1994 the RIBA published Engaging an Architect: Guidance for Clients on Fees. This included three illustrations from the RIBA's 1982 Architects Appointment which had been withdrawn on Government request as not being in the public interest. However the illustrations which comprise indicative percentage fee scales: new works; work to existing buildings; and a table of the classification of building types and the accompanying explanatory commentary did not provoke any official opposition, although the matter remains subject to possible future action.

5.13 In December 1994 the Institution of Civil Engineers issued its Professional Services Contract form for use in connection with projects let under the New Engineering Contract (NEC). The form differs from conventional forms of engagement for the appointment of architects but its sponsors believe it to be appropriate for the appointments of architects as well as engineers and other consultants. It has yet to gain any significant acceptance.

6 Speculative work and tendering for architects' services

6.01 Two characteristics of the increasingly commercial and competitive environment in which architects now have to operate have had a profound effect on architects' negotiations with their clients, i.e. speculative work and competitive fee tendering. Speculative work in which the architect undertakes work at risk on the basis that payment will only be made in the event of the work proceeding is now widespread, especially in commercial and development work. Competitive fee tendering has become commonplace with official and quasi-official bodies being obliged to obtain competitive tenders for substantial projects, and private clients becoming aware of the possibilities of competitive tendering.

6.02 The extent to which an architect is prepared to undertake speculative work must depend upon many factors such as the policy of the practice, the architect's knowledge of the potential client, the nature of the proposed project, the likelihood of its success, the architect's existing commitments, the capacity of the office now and in the foreseeable future, the possible income and profit from the commission if it proceeds, the extent of competition for the work and so on. But regardless of these conditions and the fact that the architect is not to be paid initially, it is important that there should be a formal agreement between the architect and the client defining the extent of the service to be provided by the architect and the commitment of the client to the architect in the event of the project proceeding. In the event of the project proceeding it is usual for the architect to be reimbursed for the initial work undertaken at risk.

6.03 The cost of speculative work undertaken at risk by an architect may be substantial and it is important that the practice should budget for non-fee earning speculative work, as part of its overheads, fixing a limit to the amount it does, and maintaining strict record of time and costs. Where teams of design and other consultants are involved in joint submissions on a speculative basis it is becoming usual for the costs to be shared.

Form of Agreement for

Collateral Warranty for funding institutions

| CoWa/F |

The forms in this pad are for use where a warranty is to be given to a company providing finance for a proposed development. They must not in any circumstances be provided in favour of prospective purchasers or tenants.

General advice

1. The term "collateral agreement", "duty of care letter" or "collateral warranty" is often used without due regard to the strict legal meaning of the phrase. It is used here for agreements with a funding institution putting up money for construction and development.

2. The purpose of the Agreement is to bind the party giving the warranty in contract where no contract would otherwise exist. This can have implications in terms of professional liability and could cause exposure to claims which might otherwise not have existed under Common Law.

3. The information and guidance contained in this note is designed to assist consultants faced with a request that collateral agreements be entered into.

4. The use of the word "collateral" is not accidental. It is intended to refer to an agreement that is an adjunct to another or principal agreement, namely the conditions of appointment of the consultant. It is imperative therefore that before collateral warranties are executed the consultant's terms and conditions of appointment have been agreed between the client and the consultant and set down in writing.

5. Under English Law the terms and conditions of the consultant's appointment may be "under hand" or executed as a Deed. In the latter case the length of time that claims may be brought under the Agreement is extended from six years to twelve years.

6. Under English Law this Form of Agreement for Collateral Warranty is designed for use under hand or to be executed as a Deed. It should not be signed as a Deed when it is collateral to an appointment which is under hand.

7. The acceptance of a claim under the consultant's professional indemnity policy, brought under the terms of a collateral warranty, will depend upon the terms and conditions of the policy in force at the time when a claim is made.

8. Consultants with a current indemnity insurance policy taken out under the RIBA, RICSIS, ACE or RIASIS schemes will not have a claim refused simply on the basis that it is brought under the terms of a collateral warranty provided that warranty is in this form. In other respects the claim will be treated in accordance with policy terms and conditions in the normal way. **Consultants insured under different policies** must seek the advice of their brokers or insurers.

9. **Amendment to the clauses should be resisted.** Insurers' approval as mentioned above is in respect of the unamended clauses only.

Commentary on Clauses

Recitals A, B and C are self-explanatory and need completion. The Consultant is described in the form as "The Firm". The following notes are to assist in understanding the use of the document:

Clause 1
This confirms the duty of care that will be owed to the Company. The words in square brackets enable the clause to reflect exactly the provisions contained within the terms and conditions of the Appointment.

Paragraphs (a) and (b) qualify and limit in two ways the Firm's liability in the event of a breach of the duty of care.

1 (a)   By this provision the Firm's potential liability is limited. The intention is that the effect of "several" liability at Common Law is negated. When the Firm agrees - probably at the time of appointment - to sign a warranty at a future date, the list should include the names, if known, or otherwise the description or profession, of those responsible for the design of the relevant parts of the Development and the general contractor. When the warranty is signed, the list should be completed with the names of those previously referred to by description or profession.

1 (b)   By this clause, the Company is bound by any limitations on liability that may exist in the conditions of the Appointment. Furthermore, the consultant has the same rights of defence that would have been available had the relevant claim been made by the Client under the Appointment.

Clause 2
As a consultant it is not possible to give assurances beyond those to the effect that materials as listed have not been nor will be specified. Concealed use of such materials by a contractor could possibly occur, hence the very careful restriction in terms of this particular warranty. Further materials may be added.

Clause 4
This obliges the consultant to ensure that all fees due and owing including VAT at the time the warranty is entered into have been paid.

Clause 5
This entitles the funding organisation to take over the consultant's appointment from the client on terms that all fees outstanding will be discharged by the funding authority (see Clause 7).

Clause 6
This affects the consultant's right to determine the appointment with the client in the sense that the funding authority will be given the opportunity of taking over the appointment, again subject to the payment of all fees which is the purpose of **Clause 7**.

Clause 8
Reasonable use by the Company of drawings and associated documents is necessary in most cases. By this clause, the Company is given the rights that might be reasonably expected but it does not allow the reproduction of the designs for any purpose outside the scope of the Development.

Clause 9
This confirms that professional indemnity insurance will be maintained in so far as it is reasonably possible to do so. Professional indemnity insurance is on the basis of annual contracts and the terms and conditions of a policy may change from renewal to renewal.

Clause 11
This clause indicates the right of assignment by the funding institution.

Clause 11S
This is applicable in Scotland in relation to assignations.

Clause 12
This identifies the method of giving Notice under Clauses 5, 6, 11 &11S

Clause 13
This needs completion. The clause makes clear that any liability that the Firm has by virtue of this Warranty ceases on the expiry of the stated period of years after practical completion of the Premises. (Note: the practical completion of the Development may be later).

Under English law the period should not exceed 6 years for agreements under hand, nor 12 years for those executed as a Deed.

In Scotland, the Prescription and Limitations (Scotland) Act 1973 prescribes a 5 year period.

Clause 14 and Attestation below
The appropriate method of execution by the Firm, the Client and the Company should be checked carefully.

Clause 14S and Testing Clause below
This assumes the Firm is a partnership and the Client and the Company are Limited Companies. Otherwise legal advice should be taken.

N.B. The above advice and commentary is not intended to affect the interpretation of this Collateral Warranty. It is based on the terms of insurance current at the date of publication. All parties to the Agreement should ensure the terms of insurance have not changed.

Published by
The British Property Federation Limited
35 Catherine Place. London SW1E 6DY Telephone: 071-828 0111

© The British Property Federation, The Association of Consulting Engineers, The Royal Incorporation of Architects in Scotland, The Royal Institute of British Architects and The Royal Institution of Chartered Surveyors. 1992

ISBN 0 900101 08 6

**MODEL FORM OF COLLATERAL WARRANTY
FOR PURCHASERS AND TENANTS - CoWa/P&T**

<u>**IMPORTANT ADDITIONAL NOTES FOR CLIENTS**</u>

Clients will generally wish to include in their Conditions of Engagement for Consultants, a clause to the effect that the consultant shall be prepared to enter into a stated number of collateral warranties in favour of possible purchasers, a number of tenants in a multi-occupied building and possibly to a funding institution. Model forms of the collateral warranty to be used should be attached to the conditions of engagement, and should be completed so that the consultant is aware of his obligations and liabilities at the time he quotes his fee for the project. CoWa/F should be used for funding institutions as a model.

This model form of collateral warranty for purchasers and tenants, CoWa/P&T, has been agreed by the BPF, the ACE, the RIAS, the RIBA and the RICS after consultation with the Association of British Insurers. It will be acceptable to many purchasers and tenants. It should be noted that in its unamended form it is acceptable to the main insurers of the three professional organisations. However, some purchasers and tenants may demand additional features. These are listed below but it should be remembered that insistence upon them may negate the consultant's professional indemnity insurance.

In this model form for purchasers and tenants, CoWa/P&T, the following points should be noted in addition to the deletions and additions noted in the printed guidance notes.

1.   ECONOMIC AND CONSEQUENTIAL LOSS

Clause 1(a) limits the consultant's liability to the recovery of costs of repair, renewal and/or reinstatement of any part or parts of the Development if the consultant has been in breach of the warranty, i.e. negligent. The clause continues by saying that the consultant shall *not* be liable for any other losses. In other words, if the defect caused by the consultant's negligence causes consequential loss such as loss of profit, loss of production, the cost of removal to, and the renting of, alternative premises etc. then the consultant's liability for them is *excluded.*

Some purchasers and tenants will wish to hold the consultants responsible for "consequential loss". Some consultants may be able to extend their professional indemnity cover to include "consequential loss" and some may be able to obtain additional but separate cover for these losses. In both cases, however, there will almost certainly be a limit to the extent of the consultant's liability. Those clients who wish to extend the consultant's responsibility to cover economic and consequential loss - and who can persuade the consultants to provide adequate insurance cover - should *delete* the last sentence of Clause 1(a) which reads:

> "The Firm shall not be liable for other losses incurred by the Purchaser/the Tenant".

The following sentence should be *inserted* in lieu:

> "The **Firm** shall in addition be liable for other losses incurred by the **Purchaser/the Tenant** provided that such additional liability of the **Firm** shall not exceed £....................
> in respect of each breach of the **Firm's** warranty contained in this Clause 1".

The figure to be inserted as the limit is often the same as the consultant's professional indemnity cover.

2.   **Assignment - Clause 7**

Purchasers and Tenants will wish to have the facility to assign their collateral warranties when selling their property or assigning their leases. On the other hand, insurers will wish to limit the number of assignments because this limits their liability. Clients must give careful consideration to completion of Clause 7.

Consultants who wish to deny any assignment will attempt to insert "not" between "This Agreement may" and "be assigned", in line 1 of Clause 7. This would be *unacceptable* to most purchasers and tenants. Clients are therefore advised to draw a line between "may" and "be assigned".

There is a further space in line 1 of Clause 7 between "be assigned" and "by the Purchaser/the Tenant". This enables the client to insert the number of assignments which may be allowed by the consultant. Ownership of the premises does not change frequently, nor are leases often assigned. A reasonable number inserted in this space would meet most requirements of purchasers or tenants.

3.   **Limitation on Liability**

Clause 9 removes all doubt about the period of liability under the agreement. "6 years" should be inserted for agreements under hand and "12 years" if the original appointment is executed as a Deed and the agreement is also to be executed as a Deed. Requests from consultants to include shorter periods should be resisted.

21st February 1992

British Property Federation
35 Catherine Place
London SW1E 6DY

Telephone: 0171 828 0111
Facsimile: 0171 834 3442

Registration No: 778293 England
Registered Office as above

Warranty Agreement   CoWa/F

Note
This form is to be used where the warranty is to be given to a company providing finance for the proposed development. Where that company is acting as an agent for a syndicate of banks, a recital should be added to refer to this as appropriate.

THIS AGREEMENT

(In Scotland, leave blank. For applicable date see Testing Clause on page 5)

is made the ....day of .... 19 ....

BETWEEN:-

(insert name of the Consultant)

(1) ....

of/whose registered office is situated at ....

.... ("the Firm");

(insert name of the Firm's Client)

(2) ....

whose registered office is situated at ....

.... ("the Client"); and

(insert name of the financier)

(3) ....

whose registered office is situated at ....

("the Company" which term shall include all permitted assignees under this agreement).

SPECIMEN

WHEREAS:-

A. The Company has entered into an agreement ("the Finance Agreement") with the Client for the provision of certain finance in connection with the carrying out of

(insert description of the works)

....

....

(insert address of the development)

at ....

....

....("the Development").

(insert date of appointment) (delete/complete as appropriate)

B. By a contract ("the Appointment") dated ....
the Client has appointed the Firm as [architects/consulting structural engineers/consulting building services engineers/   surveyors] in connection with the Development.

(insert name of building contractor or "a building contractor to be selected by the Client")

C. The Client has entered or may enter into a building contract ("the Building Contract") with

....

....

....

for the construction of the Development.

NOW IN CONSIDERATION OF THE PAYMENT OF ONE POUND (£1) BY THE COMPANY TO THE FIRM (RECEIPT OF WHICH THE FIRM ACKNOWLEDGES) IT IS HEREBY AGREED as follows:-

(delete "and care" or "care and diligence" to reflect terms of the Appointment)

1. The Firm warrants that it has exercised and will continue to exercise reasonable skill [and care] [care and diligence] in the performance of its duties to the Client under the Appointment. In the event of any breach of this warranty:

    (a) the Firm's liability for costs under this Agreement shall be limited to that proportion of the Company's losses which it would be just and equitable to require the Firm to pay having regard to the extent of the Firm's responsibility for the same and on the basis that ......

(insert the names of other intended warrantors)

    ....

    ....

    ....

    ....

    ....shall
    be deemed to have provided contractual undertakings on terms no less onerous than this Clause 1 to the Company in respect of the performance of their services in connection with the Development and shall be deemed to have paid to the Company such proportion which it would be just and equitable for them to pay having regard to the extent of their responsibility;

    (b) the Firm shall be entitled in any action or proceedings by the Company to rely on any limitation in the Appointment and to raise the equivalent rights in defence of liability as it would have against the Client under the Appointment;

(delete where the Firm is the quantity surveyor)

2. [Without prejudice to the generality of Clause 1 the Firm further warrants that it has exercised and will continue to exercise reasonable skill and care to see that, unless authorised by the Client in writing or, where such authorisation is given orally, confirmed by the Firm to the Client in writing, none of the following has been or will be specified by the Firm for use in the construction of those parts of the Development to which the Appointment relates:-

    (a) high alumina cement in structural elements;

    (b) wood wool slabs in permanent formwork to concrete;

    (c) calcium chloride in admixtures for use in reinforced concrete;

    (d) asbestos products;

    (e) naturally occurring aggregates for use in reinforced concrete which do not comply with British Standard 882: 1983 and/or naturally occurring aggregates for use in concrete which do not comply with British Standard 8110: 1985.

(further specific materials may be added by agreement)

    (f)

    ]

3. The Company has no authority to issue any direction or instruction to the Firm in relation to performance of the Firm's services under the Appointment unless and until the Company has given notice under Clauses 5 or 6.

4. The Firm acknowledges that the Client has paid all fees and expenses properly due and owing to the Firm under the Appointment up to the date of this Agreement. The Company has no liability to the Firm in respect of fees and expenses under the Appointment unless and until the Company has given notice under Clauses 5 or 6.

5. The Firm agrees that, in the event of the termination of the Finance Agreement by the Company, the Firm will, if so required by notice in writing given by the Company and subject to Clause 7, accept the instructions of the Company or its appointee to the exclusion of the Client in respect of the Development upon the terms and conditions of the Appointment. The Client acknowledges that the Firm shall be entitled to rely on a notice given to the Firm by the Company under this Clause 5 as conclusive evidence for the purposes of this Agreement of the termination of the Finance Agreement by the Company.

6. The Firm further agrees that it will not without first giving the Company not less than twenty one days' notice in writing exercise any right it may have to terminate the Appointment or to treat the same as having been repudiated by the Client or to discontinue the performance of any services to be performed by the Firm pursuant thereto. Such right to terminate the Appointment with the Client or treat the same as having been repudiated or discontinue performance shall cease if, within such period of notice and subject to Clause 7, the Company shall give notice in writing to the Firm requiring the Firm to accept the instructions of the Company or its appointee to the exclusion of the Client in respect of the Development upon the terms and conditions of the Appointment.

7. It shall be a condition of any notice given by the Company under Clauses 5 or 6 that the Company or its appointee accepts liability for payment of the fees and expenses payable to the Firm under the Appointment and for performance of the Client's obligations including payment of any fees and expenses outstanding at the date of such notice. Upon the issue of any notice by the Company under Clauses 5 or 6, the Appointment shall continue in full force and effect as if no right of termination on the part of the Firm had arisen, and the Firm shall be liable to the Company and its appointee under the Appointment in lieu of its liability to the Client. If any notice given by the Company under Clauses 5 or 6 requires the Firm to accept the instructions of the Company's appointee, the Company shall be liable to the Firm as guarantor for the payment of all sums from time to time due to the Firm from the Company's appointee.

8. The copyright in all drawings, reports, models, specifications, bills of quantities, calculations and other similar documents provided by the Firm in connection with the Development (together referred to in this Clause 8 as "the Documents") shall remain vested in the Firm but, subject to the Firm having received payment of any fees agreed as properly due under the Appointment, the Company and its appointee shall have a licence to copy and use the Documents and to reproduce the designs and content of them for any purpose related to the Premises including, but without limitation, the construction, completion, maintenance, letting, promotion, advertisement, reinstatement, refurbishment and repair of the Development. Such licence shall enable the Company and its appointee to copy and use the Documents for the extension of the Development but such use shall not include a licence to reproduce the designs contained in them for any extension of the Development. The Firm shall not be liable for any such use by the Company or its appointee of any of the Documents for any purpose other than that for which the same were prepared by or on behalf of the Firm.

9. The Firm shall maintain professional indemnity insurance in an amount of not less than

(insert amount)   pounds (£   )

for any one occurrence or series of occurrences arising out of any one event for a period

(insert period)   of   years from the date of practical completion of the Development for the purposes of the Building Contract, provided always that such insurance is available at commercially reasonable rates. The Firm shall immediately inform the Company if such insurance ceases to be available at commercially reasonable rates in order that the Firm and the Company can discuss means of best protecting the respective positions of the Company and the Firm in respect of the Development in the absence of such insurance. As and when it is reasonably requested to do so by the Company or its appointee under the Clauses 5 or 6, the Firm shall produce for inspection documentary evidence that its professional indemnity insurance is being maintained.

10. The Client has agreed to be a party to this Agreement for the purposes of acknowledging that the Firm shall not be in breach of the Appointment by complying with the obligations imposed on it by Clauses 5 and 6.

(delete if under Scots law) [11. This Agreement may be assigned by the Company by way of absolute legal assignment to another company providing finance or re-finance in connection with the carrying out of the Development without the consent of the Client or the Firm being required and such assignment shall be effective upon written notice thereof being given to the Client and to the Firm.]

(delete if under English law) [11S. *The Company shall be entitled to assign or transfer its rights under this Agreement to any other company providing finance or re-finance in connection with the carrying out of the Development without the consent of the Client or the Firm being required subject to written notice of such assignation being given to the Firm in accordance with Clause 12 hereof.*]

12. Any notice to be given by the Firm hereunder shall be deemed to be duly given if it is delivered by hand at or sent by registered post or recorded delivery to the Company at its registered office and any notice given by the Company hereunder shall be deemed to be duly given if it is addressed to "The Senior Partner"/"The Managing Director" and delivered by hand at or sent by registered post or recorded delivery to the above-mentioned address of the Firm or to the principal business address of the Firm for the time being and, in the case of any such notices, the same shall if sent by registered post or recorded delivery be deemed to have been received forty eight hours after being posted.

(complete as appropriate) 13. No action or proceedings for any breach of this Agreement shall be commenced against the Firm after the expiry of   years from the date of practical completion of the Premises under the Building Contract.

(delete if under Scots law) [14. The construction validity and performance of this agreement shall be governed by English Law and the parties agree to submit to the non-exclusive jurisdiction of the English Courts.

(alternatives: delete as appropriate) [**AS WITNESS** the hands of the parties the day and year first before written.

Signed by or on behalf of the Firm ....

(for Agreement executed under hand and NOT as a Deed) in the presence of: ....

Signed by or on behalf of the Client ....

in the presence of: ....

Signed by or on behalf of the Company ....

in the presence of: ....]

(this must only apply if the Appointment is executed as a Deed) [**IN WITNESS WHEREOF** this Agreement was executed as a Deed and delivered the day and year first before written.

by the Firm

....

....

....

by the Client

....

....

....

by the Company

....

....

....]]

<table>
<tr><td>(delete if under
English law)</td><td colspan="2">14S. *This Agreement shall be construed and the rights of the parties and all matters arising hereunder shall be determined in all respects according to the Law of Scotland.*</td></tr>
</table>

IN WITNESS WHEREOF *these presents are executed as follows:-*

SIGNED by the above named Firm at ....

on the .... *day of* .... *Nineteen hundred and* ....

as follows:-

....*(Firm's signature)*

Signature .... *Full Name* ....

Address ....

.... *Occupation* ....

Signature .... *Full Name* ....

Address ....

.... *Occupation* ....

SIGNED by the above named Client at ....

on the .... *day of* .... *Nineteen hundred and* ....

as follows:-

For and on behalf of the Client

.... *Director/Authorised Signatory*

.... *Director/Authorised Signatory*

SIGNED by the above named Company at ....

on the .... *day of* .... *Nineteen hundred and* ....

as follows:-

For and on behalf of the Company

.... *Director/Authorised Signatory*

.... *Director/Authorised Signatory*]

Form of Agreement for

Collateral Warranty
for purchasers & tenants | CoWa/P&T |

The forms in this pad are for use where a warranty is to be given to a purchaser or tenant of a whole building in a commercial and/or industrial development, or a part of such a building. It is essential that the number of warranties to be given to tenants in one building should sensibly be limited.

General advice

1. The term "collateral agreement", "duty of care letter" or "collateral warranty" is often used without due regard to the strict legal meaning of the phrase. It is used here for agreements with tenants or purchasers of the whole or part of a commercial and/or industrial development.

2. The purpose of the Agreement is to bind the party giving the warranty in contract where no contract would otherwise exist. This can have implications in terms of professional liability and could cause exposure to claims which might otherwise not have existed under Common Law.

3. The information and guidance contained in this note is designed to assist consultants faced with a request that collateral agreements be entered into.

4. The use of the word 'collateral' is not accidental. It is intended to refer to an agreement that is an adjunct to another or principal agreement, namely the conditions of appointment of the consultant. It is imperative therefore that before collateral warranties are executed the consultant's terms and conditions of appointment have been agreed between the client and the consultant and set down in writing.

5. Under English Law the terms and conditions of the consultant's appointment may be 'under hand' or executed as a Deed. In the latter case the length of time that claims may be brought under the Agreement is extended from six years to twelve years.

6. Under English Law this Form of Agreement for Collateral Warranty is designed for use under hand or to be executed as a Deed. It should not be signed as a Deed when it is collateral to an appointment which is under hand.

7. The acceptance of a claim under the consultant's professional indemnity policy, brought under the terms of a collateral warranty, will depend upon the terms and conditions of the policy in force at the time when a claim is made.

8. Consultants with a current indemnity insurance policy taken out under the RIBA, RICSIS, ACE or RIASIS schemes will not have a claim refused simply on the basis that it is brought under the terms of a collateral warranty provided that warranty is in this form. In other respects the claim will be treated in accordance with policy terms and conditions in the normal way. **Consultants insured under different policies** must seek the advice of their brokers or insurers.

9. **Amendment to the clauses should be resisted.** Insurers' approval as mentioned above is in respect of the unamended clauses only.

Commentary on Clauses

Recital A.

This needs completion.

When this warranty is to be given in favour of a purchaser or tenant of part of the Development, the following words in square brackets must be deleted.

["The Premises" are also referred to as "the Development" in this Agreement".]

Care must be taken in describing "the Premises" accurately.

When this warranty is to be given in favour of a purchaser or tenant of the entire development, the terms "the Premises" and "the Development" are synonymous.

The following words in square brackets must be deleted

[forming part of. ....

at. .... ("the Development").]

Recitals B & C

These are self explanatory but need completion.

Clause 1

This confirms the duty of care that will be owed to the Purchaser/the Tenant. The words in square brackets enable the clause to reflect exactly the provisions contained within the terms and conditions of the Appointment.

Paragraphs (a),(b) and (c) qualify and limit in three ways the Firm's liability in the event of a breach of the duty of care.

1 (a)   By this provision, the Firm is liable for the reasonable costs of repair renewal and or reinstatement of the Development insofar as the Purchaser/the Tenant has a financial obligation to pay or contribute to the cost of that repair. Other losses are expressly excluded.

1 (b)   By this provision the Firm's potential liability is limited. The intention is that the effect of "several" liability at Common Law is negated. When the Firm agrees - probably at the time of appointment - to sign a warranty at a future date, the list should include the names, if known, or otherwise the description or profession, of those responsible for the design of the relevant parts of the Development and the general contractor. When the warranty is signed, the list should be completed with the names of those previously referred to by description or profession.

1 (c)   By this clause, the Purchaser/ the Tenant is bound by any limitations on liability that may exist in the conditions of the Appointment. Furthermore, the consultant has the same rights of defence that would have been available had the relevant claim been made by the Client under the Appointment.

1 (d)   This states the relationship between the Firm and any consultant employed by the Purchaser/the Tenant to survey the premises.

Clause 2

As a consultant it is not possible to give assurances beyond those to the effect that materials as listed have not been nor will be specified. Concealed use of such materials by a contractor could possibly occur, hence the very careful restriction in terms of this particular warranty. Further materials may be added.

N.B.   The above advice and commentary is not intended to affect the interpretation of this Collateral Warranty. It is based on the terms of insurance current at the date of publication. All parties to the Agreement should ensure the terms of insurance have not changed.

Clause 3

This obliges the consultant to ensure that all fees due and owing including VAT at the time the warranty is entered into have been paid.

Clause 4

This is included to make it clear that the Purchaser/the Tenant has no power or authority to direct or instruct the Firm in its duties to the Client.

Clause 5

Reasonable use by the Purchaser/the Tenant of drawings and associated documents is necessary in most cases. By this clause, the Purchaser/the Tenant is given the rights that might be reasonably expected but it does not allow the reproduction of the designs for any purpose outside the scope of the Development.

Clause 6

This confirms that professional indemnity insurance will be maintained in so far as it is reasonably possible to do so. Professional indemnity insurance is on the basis of annual contracts and the terms and conditions of a policy may change from renewal to renewal.

Clause 7

This allows the Purchaser/the Tenant to assign the benefit of this Warranty provided it is done by formal legal assignment and relates to the entire interest of the original Purchaser/Tenant. By this clause any right of assignment may be limited or extinguished. If it is to be extinguished the word "not" shall be inserted after "may" and all words after "the Purchaser/the Tenant" deleted. If it is agreed that there should be a limited number of assignments, the precise number should be inserted in the space between "assigned" and "by the Purchaser/the Tenant".

Clause 7S

This is applicable in Scotland in relation to assignations. Completion is as for Clause 7.

Clause 8

This identifies the method of giving Notice under Clause 7 & 7S.

Clause 9

This needs completion. The clause makes clear that any liability that the Firm has by virtue of this Warranty ceases on the expiry of the stated period of years after practical completion of the Premises. (Note: the practical completion of the Development may be later).

Under English law the period should not exceed 6 years for agreements under hand, nor 12 years for those executed as a Deed.

In Scotland, the Prescription and Limitations (Scotland) Act 1973 prescribes a 5 year period.

Clause 10 and Attestation below

The appropriate method of execution by the Firm and the Purchaser/the Tenant should be checked carefully.

Clause 10S and Testing Clause below

This assumes the Firm is a partnership and the Purchaser/the Tenant is a Limited Company. Otherwise legal advice should be taken.

Published by
The British Property Federation Limited
35 Catherine Place, London SW1E 6DY. Telephone: 071-828 0111

© The British Property Federation, The Association of Consulting Engineers, The Royal Incorporation of Architects in Scotland, The Royal Institute of British Architects and The Royal Institution of Chartered Surveyors. 1992

ISBN 0 900101 08 7

Warranty Agreement   CoWa/P&T

(In Scotland, leave blank. For applicable date see Testing Clause on page 4)

THIS AGREEMENT

is made the .... day of 199

BETWEEN:-

(insert name of the Consultant)

(1) ....

of/whose registered office is situated at ....

.... ("the Firm"), and

(insert name of the Purchaser/the Tenant)

(2) ....

whose registered office is situated at ....

....

(delete as appropriate)

("the Purchaser"/"the Tenant" which term shall include all permitted assignees under this Agreement).

WHEREAS:-

(delete as appropriate)

A.   The Purchaser/the Tenant has entered into an agreement to purchase/an agreement to lease/a lease with

....

(insert description of the premises)

.... ("the Client") relating to

....

....

....("the Premises")

(delete as appropriate)

[forming part of ....

(insert description of the development)

....

....

(insert address of the development)

at ....

.... ("the Development").]

(delete as appropriate)

["The Premises" are also referred to as "the Development" in this Agreement.]

(insert date of appointment) (delete/complete as appropriate)

B.   By a contract ("the Appointment") dated ....
the Client has appointed the Firm as [architects/consulting structural engineers/consulting building services engineers/   surveyors] in connection with the Development.

C.   The Client has entered or may enter into a contract ("the Building Contract") with

(insert name of building contractor or "a building contractor to be selected by the Client")

....

....

....

for the construction of the Development.

NOW IN CONSIDERATION OF THE PAYMENT OF ONE POUND (£1) BY THE PURCHASER/ THE TENANT TO THE FIRM (RECEIPT OF WHICH THE FIRM ACKNOWLEDGES) IT IS HEREBY AGREED as follows:-

(delete as appropriate to reflect terms of the Appointment)

1. The Firm warrants that it has exercised and will continue to exercise reasonable skill [and care] [care and diligence] in the performance of its services to the Client under the Appointment. In the event of any breach of this warranty:

    (a) subject to paragraphs (b) and (c) of this clause, the Firm shall be liable for the reasonable costs of repair renewal and/or reinstatement of any part or parts of the Development to the extent that

    – the Purchaser/the Tenant incurs such costs and/or
    – the Purchaser/the Tenant is or becomes liable either directly or by way of financial contribution for such costs.

    The Firm shall not be liable for other losses incurred by the Purchaser/the Tenant.

    (b) the Firm's liability for costs under this Agreement shall be limited to that proportion of such costs which it would be just and equitable to require the Firm to pay having regard to the extent of the Firm's responsibility for the same and on the basis that ....

(insert the names of other intended warrantors)

    ....
    ....
    ....
    ....
    .... shall
    be deemed to have provided contractual undertakings on terms no less onerous than this Clause 1 to the Purchaser/the Tenant in respect of the performance of their services in connection with the Development and shall be deemed to have paid to the Purchaser/the Tenant such proportion which it would be just and equitable for them to pay having regard to the extent of their responsibility;

    (c) the Firm shall be entitled in any action or proceedings by the Purchaser/the Tenant to rely on any limitation in the Appointment and to raise the equivalent rights in defence of liability as it would have against the Client under the Appointment;

    (d) the obligations of the Firm under or pursuant to this Clause 1 shall not be released or diminished by the appointment of any person by the Purchaser/the Tenant to carry out any independent enquiry into any relevant matter.

(delete where the Firm is the quantity surveyor)

2. [Without prejudice to the generality of Clause 1, the Firm further warrants that it has exercised and will continue to exercise reasonable skill and care to see that, unless authorised by the Client in writing or, where such authorisation is given orally, confirmed by the Firm to the Client in writing, none of the following has been or will be specified by the Firm for use in the construction of those parts of the Development to which the Appointment relates:-

    (a) high alumina cement in structural elements;

    (b) wood wool slabs in permanent formwork to concrete;

    (c) calcium chloride in admixtures for use in reinforced concrete;

    (d) asbestos products;

    (e) naturally occurring aggregates for use in reinforced concrete which do not comply with British Standard 882: 1983 and/or naturally occurring aggregates for use in concrete which do not comply with British Standard 8110: 1985.

(further specific materials may be added by agreement)

    (f)

    In the event of any breach of this warranty the provisions of Clauses 1a, b, c and d shall apply.]

3. The Firm acknowledges that the Client has paid all fees and expenses properly due and owing to the Firm under the Appointment up to the date of this Agreement.

4. The Purchaser/the Tenant has no authority to issue any direction or instruction to the Firm in relation to the Appointment.

5. The copyright in all drawings, reports, models, specifications, bills of quantities, calculations and other documents and information prepared by or on behalf of the Firm in connection with the Development (together referred to in this Clause 5 as "the Documents") shall remain vested in the Firm but, subject to the Firm having received payment of any fees agreed as properly due under the Appointment, the Purchaser/the Tenant and its appointee shall have a licence to copy and use the Documents and to reproduce the designs and content of them for any purpose related to the Premises including, but without limitation, the construction, completion, maintenance, letting, promotion, advertisement, reinstatement, refurbishment and repair of the Premises. Such licence shall enable the Purchaser/the Tenant and its appointee to copy and use the Documents for the extension of the Premises but such use shall not include a licence to reproduce the designs contained in them for any extension of the Premises. The Firm shall not be liable for any use by the Purchaser/the Tenant or its appointee of any of the Documents for any purpose other than that for which the same were prepared by or on behalf of the Firm.

(insert amount)

(insert period)

6. The Firm shall maintain professional indemnity insurance in an amount of not less than   pounds (£   ) for any one occurrence or series of occurrences arising out of any one event for a period of   years from the date of practical completion of the Premises under the Building Contract, provided always that such insurance is available at commercially reasonable rates. The Firm shall immediately inform the Purchaser/the Tenant if such insurance ceases to be available at commercially reasonable rates in order that the Firm and the Purchaser/the Tenant can discuss means of best protecting the respective positions of the Purchaser/the Tenant and the Firm in the absence of such insurance. As and when it is reasonably requested to do so by the Purchaser/the Tenant or its appointee the Firm shall produce for inspection documentary evidence that its professional indemnity insurance is being maintained.

(insert number of times)

(delete if under Scots law)

[7. This Agreement may   be assigned   by the Purchaser/the Tenant   by way of absolute legal assignment to another person taking an assignment of the Purchaser's/the Tenant's interest in the Premises without the consent of the Client or the Firm being required and such assignment shall be effective upon written notice thereof being given to the Firm. No further assignment shall be permitted.]

(insert number of times)

(delete if under English law)

[7S. *The Purchaser/the Tenant shall   be entitled to assign or transfer his/their rights under this Agreement   to any other person acquiring the Purchaser's/the Tenant's interest in the whole of the Premises without the consent of the Firm subject to written notice of such assignation being given to the Firm in accordance with Clause 8 hereof. Nothing in this clause shall permit any party acquiring such right as assignee or transferee to enter into any further assignation or transfer to anyone acquiring subsequently an interest in the Premises from him.*]

8. Any notice to be given by the Firm hereunder shall be deemed to be duly given if it is delivered by hand at or sent by registered post or recorded delivery to the Purchaser/the Tenant at its registered office and any notice given by the Purchaser/the Tenant hereunder shall be deemed to be duly given if it is addressed to "The Senior Partner"/"The Managing Director" and delivered by hand at or sent by registered post or recorded delivery to the above-mentioned address of the Firm or to the principal business address of the Firm for the time being and, in the case of any such notices, the same shall if sent by registered post or recorded delivery be deemed to have been received forty eight hours after being posted.

(complete as appropriate)

9. No action or proceedings for any breach of this Agreement shall be commenced against the Firm after the expiry of   years from the date of practical completion of the Premises under the Building Contract.

(delete if under Scots law)

10. The construction validity and performance of this Agreement shall be governed by English law and the parties agree to submit to the non-exclusive jurisdiction of the English Courts.

(alternatives: delete as appropriate)

(for Agreement executed under hand and NOT as a Deed)

[**AS WITNESS** the hands of the parties the day and year first before written.

Signed by or on behalf of the Firm ....

in the presence of: ....

Signed by or on behalf of the Purchaser/the Tenant ....

in the presence of: ....]

(this must only apply if the Appointment is executed as a Deed)

[**IN WITNESS WHEREOF** this Agreement was executed as a Deed and delivered the day and year first before written.

by the Firm

....

....

....

....

by the Purchaser/the Tenant

....

....

....

....]]

(delete if under English law)

10S. *This Agreement shall be construed and the rights of the parties and all matters arising hereunder shall be determined in all respects according to the Law of Scotland.*

IN WITNESS WHEREOF these presents are executed as follows:-

SIGNED by the above named Firm at ....

on the .... day of .... Nineteen hundred and ....

as follows:-

..(Firm's signature)

Signature .... Full Name ....

Address ....

.. Occupation ....

Signature .... Full Name ....

Address ....

.. Occupation ....

SIGNED by the above named Purchaser/Tenant at ....

on the .... day of .... Nineteen hundred and ....

as follows:-

For and on behalf of the Purchaser/the Tenant

..Director/Authorised Signatory

..Director/Authorised Signatory]

6.04 Architects should be particularly wary of invitations to prepare design solutions in conjunction with competitive fee tenders often on the basis of scant information – only rarely would such an invitation be acceptable. Architects should also endeavour to discover details of others invited to submit fee tenders and refuse to participate in competitive fee bidding in which the number of tenderers or the form of competition is unreasonable.

6.05 As the range of possible sources of design and procurement routes widens it is understandable that clients should increasingly make detailed enquiries about services and charges before making formal appointments. The basis of comparison is often inadequate and architects should endeavour to ensure that clients appreciate the nature of the service being offered and not make an appointment on the basis of fee alone. Potential clients are often unaware of fundamental differences between, say, conventional design services and design by a contractor's organization; more subtle differences in design services are certain to elude them unless they are carefully explained by the architect. The fee is determined by the service required and the cost of providing that service; unless this is known a fee quotation can be little more than a guess.

6.06 Dissatisfaction with the approach of some large commercial organizations seeking competitive fee bids has resulted in the publication of RIBA's guidance note *Tendering for architects's services*.

7 Collateral warranties

7.01 At the time of appointment the architect may be invited by the client to enter into an agreement with a third party such as a funding institution. These agreements are known as 'collateral warranties' or 'collateral agreement' and occasionally as 'duty of care agreements'. The agreement between the architect and the third party exists in parallel with the agreement between the architect and the client. It makes the architect contractually liable to the third party. In the absence of such an agreement an aggrieved third party can only take an action in tort against the architect; with the agreement in effect an action for breach of contract becomes possible. The use of warranties has become widespread (see Chapter 10 on contractor collateral warranties for a discussion of the principles and application of warranties).

7.02 As a consequence of their increasing use and the proliferation of different forms and conditions the RIBA prepared its model *Form of Agreement for Collateral Warranty (for use where a warranty is to be given to a company providing finance)* in 1988. This form has largely been superseded by the British Property Federation Forms of Agreement for Collateral Warranty (CoWa/F) for use where a warranty is to be given to a company providing finance for a proposed development; and Collateral Warranty (CoWa/P&T) for use where a warranty is to be given to a purchaser or tenant of premises in a commercial and/or industrial development. In a large and complex project there may be several forms of agreement in force; care needs to be taken to ensure that these forms are consistent and compatible.

7.03 The third party is usually seeking the warranty in order to obtain the potential benefits of the architect's professional indemnity insurance policy. The extent to which the underwriters of the architect's professional indemnity policy would be willing to meet a claim brought under the form of warranty would depend upon the conditions of the policy. It is essential that an architect faced with an invitation to enter into a warranty should consult his broker or insurers before signing the agreement.

7.04 The conditions of a proposed form of agreement between an architect and a third party should be very carefully studied and legal advice should be sought before entering into the agreement. The architect should ensure that the conditions of the agreement do not extend the liability of the architect beyond those of the agreement with the client; that the architect's liability to the third party does not exceed that of the client's own liability to the third party; that the architect is not made liable for the acts of commission or omission of the contractor; and that the architect is not expected to assume responsibility for other independent and directly appointed consultants and specialists.

7.05 The conditions of warranties frequently include the architect's assurance that such deleterious materials as high alumina cement and asbestos will not be used. It is important that the conditions state that the architect cannot be held responsible for the inadvertent or concealed use of these materials by the contractor.

7.06 The implications of warranty conditions concerning the rights of third parties to take over the appointment of the architect in the event of the client's default, subject to the payment of fees due, and the use of drawings and documents need to be very carefully assessed.

7.07 The form of collateral warranty may be 'under hand' or in the nature of a deed executed 'under seal', the period of liability being respectively six years or twelve years. It is not essential that the architect's appointment and the collateral warranty should both be either 'under hand' or 'under seal' but the architect must be aware that a warranty 'under seal' would incur a liability of twelve years, regardless of the six year liability of an 'under hand' architect's appointment. The use of warranties by tenants and others may have other implications for liability periods, the point at which liability periods begin to run, and the possible dates at which causes of action may accrue may be significant. (See Chapters 7 and 8.)

CDM Supplement

A supplement to SFA92 to take into account the Health and Safety Construction (Design and Management) Regulations 1994 (CDM) was published in April 1995.

Conditions of Engagement

The Conditions of Engagement for the Appointment of an Architect (CE/95) were devised as a simplified version of SFA92 with which they are compatible. They are appropriate for use on most projects including those where JCT Standard Forms of Contracts IFC'84 and MW80 are being used. These Conditions of Engagement take into account the CDM Regulations. Architects and clients may find it helpful to consult the previously published RIBA guide *Engaging an Architect* when completing the conditions. Provision is made for the use of a Memorandum of Agreement of Appointment but a model form of letter of appointment is offered as an alternative in the guidance notes.

Planning Supervisor

The Form of Appointment as Planning Supervisor (PS/95) under the CDM Regulations follows a similar layout to SFA92. Clients may find it helpful to consider these conditions in parallel with the conditions for the appointment of 'designers' and the 'principal contractor' under the CDM Regulations.

22

Architects' liability

KIM FRANKLIN*

1 Introduction

1.01 This chapter is about liability to pay damages when things go wrong. 'Damages' are sums of money payable to compensate for harm done. The person seeking compensation may set off his claim for damages against the architect's claim for fees, or he may take the architect to court if he owes the architect no fees or if the damages claimed exceed the amount of any fees owing.

Different sources of liability

1.02 It will be necessary to examine the basic principles of liability for breach of contact, the tort of negligence, and the various statutory extensions to both of these.

An architect should have adequate skill and knowledge to enable him to originate, design and plan buildings or other works which require skilled design and arrange for and monitor their construction. Success in these various tasks can not, however, be guaranteed.

The question of professional liability can be approached on three levels:

1. a minimum standard of reasonable care to be exercised in the discharge of professional duties;
2. a higher duty to achieve particular results;
3. a different duty owed when giving advice.

Recent developments in the law of contract and tort also call for the architect's duties owed to his client to be distinguished from those owed to others such as builders or subsequent owners (generally referred to as 'third parties').

Duty of care

1.03 An architect has a duty to use reasonable care and skill in the course of his employment. The extent of this duty was described by McNair J in *Bolam* v *Friern Hospital Management Committee* [1957] 1 WLR 582, at p. 586.

> 'Where you get a situation which involves the use of some special skill or competence, then the test as to whether there has been negligence or not is not the test of the man on the top of a Clapham omnibus, because he has not got this special skill. The test is the standard of the ordinary skilled man exercising and professing to have that special skill. A man need not possess the highest expert skill; it is well established law that it is sufficient if he exercises the ordinary skill of an ordinary competent man exercising that particular art.'

The degree of skill required can be illustrated by two cases, one considerably more recent than the other. In *Lanphier* v *Phipos* (1838) 8 C&P 475 Tindal CJ said:

> 'Every person who enters into a learned profession undertakes to bring to the exercise of it a reasonable degree of care and skill. He does not undertake, if he is an attorney, that at all events you shall gain your case, nor does a surgeon undertake that he will perform a cure; nor does he undertake to use the highest possible degree of skill.'

In *Greaves & Co.* v *Baynham Meikle* [1975] 1 WLR 1095, decided over 100 years later, Lord Denning used the same examples:

> 'The law does not usually imply a warranty that (the professional man) will achieve the desired result, but only a term that he will use reasonable care and skill. The surgeon does not warrant that he will cure the patient. Nor does the solicitor warrant that he will win the case.'

Thus the courts recognize that failure is not conclusive evidence of breach of duty. In this respect the architect differs from the builder and does not guarantee that he will achieve the desired end result.

Duty of result

1.04 An architect can, however, take on the responsibility to ensure that the end product will perform as required. This duty is more onerous than that to take reasonable care and it is less common for it to be required of the professional man. Within the field of construction design such a duty usually arises in design-and-build or 'package deal' contracts. For example in *Greaves* v *Baynham Meikle* the contractors undertook to build a factory complex and warehouse supplying all necessary labour, materials and expertise to produce the finished product. The contracts engaged the defendants, consultant structural engineers, to design the warehouse which was to be built according to a newly introduced method of composite construction and used for storing and moving oil drums loaded on to stacker trucks. Within a few months of completion the first floor began to crack: the floors were not designed with sufficient strength to withstand the vibration which was produced by the stacker trucks. The contractors claimed an indemnity from the engineers on the grounds that they warranted that their design would produce a building fit for its purpose. The Court of Appeal explained that the professional man is not usually under a duty to achieve a specified result but went on to say that when a dentist agrees to make a set of false teeth for a patient, there is an implied warranty that they will fit his gums (*Samuels* v *Davies* [1943] KB 526). Lord Denning said:

> 'What then is the position when an architect or an engineer is employed to design a house or a bridge? Is he under an implied warranty that, if the work is carried out to his design, it will be reasonably fit for the purpose? Or is he only under a duty to use reasonable care and skill? In the present case . . . the evidence shows that both parties were of one mind on the matter. Their common intention was that the engineer should design a

* This chapter in its original form in the third edition was written by John R. Spencer, Fellow of Selwyn College, Cambridge.

warehouse which would be fit for the purpose for which it was required. That common intention gives rise to a term implied in fact.'

He concluded:

'In the light of that evidence it seems to me that there was implied in fact a term that if the work was completed in accordance with the design it would be reasonably fit for the use of loaded stacker trucks. The engineers failed to make such a design and are therefore liable.'

Ordinarily the professional designer does not warrant the ultimate success of his design. If, however, his involvement is either as part of a package deal to design, supply and erect an end product, or to design something to comply with stated performance criteria then he is obliged to ensure that the finished article is fit for its purpose.

Professional advice

1.05 The duty to take reasonable care is a creature of the law of tort. The recent decision of the House of Lords in *Murphy* v *Brentwood District Council* [1990] 3 WLR 414 revolutionized the law of tort and swept away over 15 years of law developed in the wake of an earlier House of Lords decision in *Anns* v *Merton London Borough Council* [1978] AC 728. In *Murphy* the court held that the common law duty in building cases was to take care to avoid personal injury or physical damage to property other than the building in question, only. No duty was owed in tort, to keep building owners or occupiers safe from the cost of repairing defects in their buildings or financial losses incurred whilst remedial works were carried out. This was defined as 'economic loss' and was held to be irrecoverable in an action in tort. In the case of the professional man, however, there is an important exception to this rule.

As a result of the decision of the House of Lords in *Hedley Byrne & Co Ltd* v *Heller & Partners Ltd* [1964] AC 465 the professional man owes a duty, when giving advice in the ordinary course of business, to exercise care in making his reply, if his advice is to be relied upon by the other, to save him from foreseeable loss or damage. Their lordships held that whenever a special relationship came into existence, such as between a professional and his client, there arose a duty to take care when making statements which if made carelessly would cause either physical damage or financial loss.

The architect may be seen to be in a difficult position since he could simply be seen to be providing a service, much as, for example, a builder does, in which case he would be liable only for personal injury or damage to other property as defined in *Murphy* v *Brentwood*, or he could be seen to be giving professional advice as in *Hedley Byrne* v *Heller*, in which case he might owe a duty to keep his client safe from both physical and financial loss. Past cases have suggested that, save in special circumstances, an architect will not owe a duty of care in tort to prevent economic loss. Doubt has been cast on this view by the recent decision of *Wessex Regional Health Authority* v *HLM Design* (1994) 10 Constr LJ 165.

Clients and third parties

1.06 An architect's duties to his client are defined by the contract between them. Third parties, such as builders or subsequent purchasers do not have a contract with the architect. Any remedy they may have against the architect is defined by the common law or statute. The decision in *Murphy* v *Brentwood* has severely limited the remedies available to third parties. As a result, subsequent owners, have been forced to rely upon secondary contractual remedies, such as those given by collateral warranties.

Architects may, however, be vulnerable to claims brought under one of the exceptions to the general rule set out in *Murphy*. If a building has defects that threaten injury to passers-by and adjacent property its owner may be able to claim, in tort, against those involved in its construction, the cost of repairing or demolish-ing the building so as to make it safe. This exception was relied upon in the case of *Morse* v *Barratt (Leeds) Limited* (1992) 9 Constr LJ 158.

Concurrent duties in tort and contract

1.07 For a number of years there has been uncertainty whether an architect owes a duty in tort to a client, with whom there is a contractual relationship. The House of Lords decision *Henderson* v *Merrett Syndicates Limited* [1994] 3 WLR 761 appears to have resolved that question in favour of the existence of a duty in tort concurrent with the contractual duty. This is much more fully discussed in Chapter 3 paragraphs 2.33 to 2.37.

2 Liability for breach of contract

Contractual obligations

2.01 The meaning of 'contract' generally has been explained in Chapter 2. Specific features of contracts between architects and their clients have been discussed in Chapter 21. The contract between an architect and his employer, which is the main concern of this chapter, is an arrangement under which an architect makes various binding promises to his employer in return for the employer's promise to pay his fees. The architect's promises are both express and implied. His *express* promises will be to do any number of a range of things, varying from job to job: to survey the site and the subsoil, to produce drawings, to advise on building regulations and planning, to select a contractor to do the works, to recommend a form of contract for the engagement of the builder, to supervise the works, to issue certificates, and so on. The express promises can be made orally in the course of a telephone or other conversation. Alternatively they can be made in writing, for example in correspondence. Rather than discuss or write down all the express promises made by the architect and his client, the RIBA standard terms of engagement can be incorporated into the contract if they are expressly referred to. If no reference is made to these terms, however, they cannot be implied into the contract (*Re Sidney Kaye, Eric Firmin & Partners* (1973) 4 BLR 1). The courts also deem the architect to make various *implied* promises supplementary to the express ones: first and foremost, an implied promise to use reasonable care in all he does. Thus the architect undertakes to do a careful survey, to draw up competent plans within a reasonable time, to take care in his selection of a builder, and so on.

Breach of contract

2.02 The leading textbook of contract law defines a breach of contract as follows: 'A breach of contract is committed when a party without lawful excuse refuses or fails to perform, performs defectively or incapacitates himself from performing the contract', Treitel (*The Law of Contract* (1987), Steven and Sons, London). So if an architect neglects to do what he undertook to do, or bungles it, he commits a breach of contract which makes him liable to the person who engaged him. His liability may wipe out his claim for fees, but it is not limited to the amount of his fees. Liability for breach of contract includes liability for *consequential loss*, in so far as this is of a reasonably foreseeable type. Consequential loss means loss over and above the money wasted on fees for bad work. For example, if an architect produces incompetent plans which specify inadequate foundations, and the owner of the building later has to spend on underpinning large sums of money greatly in excess of the architect's fees, the cost of underpinning may be recoverable as damages for consequential loss.

The scope of the duty of care owed to the client in contract

2.03 It is, however, a question of law rather than a question of fact what aspects of an architect's work are capable of giving rise to liability if he carries them out without reasonable care as discussed in the last paragraph. Can he be liable for negligent legal

advice? Can he be liable for negligently certifying work which has not been properly done? These are questions of law, and the answer to them is 'yes'. As will appear, there are nowadays few, if any, aspects of an architect's work for which he cannot in principle be held liable, to his client at least, if he fails to take reasonable care. In the examples that follow, it is the architect's contractual liability to his client which is under consideration; how far he is also liable in the tort of negligence to other people as well is discussed later (paragraphs 2.07–12).

Negligent surveys

2.04 An architect can be held liable for failing to make an adequate examination of the site for a building. Particular care should be taken in all matters relating to foundations. Extensive tests may be required, particularly if the ground is made up or gives rise to other difficulties. In *Eames London Estates Ltd v North Hertfordshire DC* (1981) 259 EG 491, the foundations of an industrial building built on made up ground proved inadequate. Extensive repairs were required. The architect was found to be negligent for specifying the loading for piers without ascertaining for himself the ground's bearing capacity and for ignoring a query as to the adequacy of the excavations for foundations raised at the time. If the job of ascertaining the nature of the site is beyond the architect then he should advise the client to engage a specialist to make the necessary investigations.

The architect must take account not only of subsoil but also of other things, such as the effect of planting or felling trees, the rights of neighbours or planning restrictions, which may affect the building. In *Re St Thomas a Becket, Framfield* [1989] 1 WLR 689, architects were blamed for supervising works to the church without ascertaining whether there was ecclesiastical authority for the execution of those works before they were begun. If such enquiries have not been made, the architect would be wise to warn the client.

Incompetent design

2.05 An architect may be liable to the client if errors or omissions are made in the plans, drawings or specification. Liability cannot be escaped on the grounds that the design was delegated to another. If the design is outside of the expertise of the architect he should inform the client. The architect is under a continuing duty to check the design up to completion of the works. Design includes the choice of materials for the building, its 'buildability' and its 'supervisability'.

Inadequate supervision

2.06 The architect is obliged to administer and supervise the works to ensure that the standard is that originally contemplated. Reasonable supervision does not require the architect to stand over the contractor and monitor every detail. He is, however, expected to oversee the principal parts of the works, especially if they are subsequently to be hidden from view, and other aspects sufficient to certify that the works have been executed in accordance with the contract.

Negligent financial advice

2.07 An architect can also be liable if he causes his client damage by negligent advice on likely building costs. In *Nye Saunders & Partners v Bristow* AE (1987) BLR 92 CA the architects were asked to estimate the cost of renovating a country house owned by the successful helicopter millionaire, within a budget of £250 000. In February 1974 the architects gave an estimate of £238 000. In August the estimate was revised and a new figure of £440 000 given. Bristow, saying that he had been misled, terminated the architects' engagement and refused to pay fees totalling £15 000. The architects were found to be negligent for failing to point out that the estimate was based on prices current in February during a time of very high inflation. Similarly in *Aubrey Jacobus & Partners v Gerrard* (1981) 984 BLR 37, the Court held that if an architect bases his estimate on current building costs and makes it plain that he has done so, that ought to be sufficient.

Negligent legal advice

2.08 Architects are expected to have some knowledge of the law as it affects their business, and they can be liable for the consequences to their client if they do not. For example, a surveyor was engaged by a client to negotiate a claim for compensation from the local authority for land belonging to the client which had been compulsorily purchased. A recent decision of the Court of Appeal, which was quite well publicized, had condemned the basis upon which compensation had previously been calculated, and substituted a new basis more favourable to the client. The surveyor was held liable when, in ignorance of the decision, he negotiated a low figure calculated on the old rules (*Weedon v Hindwood Clarke and Esplin* (1974) 234 EG 121). But an architect is not required to have the deep legal knowledge of a QC who is a specialist in planning law, and he is not negligent if he accepts the advice of the planning department of his local authority in so far as this is not obviously wrong. Thus where an architect was told by the local planning department that an Office Development Permit was needed only if the floor area of the office part of the proposed development exceeded the specified size, and that the floor area of ancillary buildings could be disregarded for those purposes – a view of the law which was condemned as incorrect by the judge in the law suit which followed – he was not negligent to act on this advice at the time (*B. L. Holdings Ltd v Robert J. Wood & Partners* (1979) 12 BLR 3).

Negligence in certifying payments

2.09 When an architect certifies that payments are due under a building contract, he often has to judge between the claims of the builder and the complaints of the client. Because of this, it was formerly held that he was, when issuing certificates, in the same position as an arbitrator or a judge – immune from all liability for negligence on grounds of public policy. This view was overturned by the House of Lords in *Sutcliffe v Thackrah* (1974) AC 727, holding that the client can sue the architect if he negligently overcertifies. Before the case reached the House of Lords, Judge Stabb QC considered the proper approach to be adopted by an architect in issuing interim certificates ((1971) 18 BLR 149). Thus, although a prolonged or detailed inspection at an interim stage is impractical, more than a glance round is expected. If the contract provides for certificates to give the valuation of work properly executed, the architect should satisfy himself as to the quality of the work before requiring the employer to make payment in respect of it. Where a quantity surveyor is also engaged, the architect should keep him informed of any defective work so that it can be excluded from interim valuations.

2.10 Architects were also found liable for failing to issue an appropriate certificate under the JCT Standard Form. In *West Faulkner Associates v London Borough of Newham* (1992) 9 Constr LJ p. 232 the plaintiffs were engaged as architects in respect of the refurbishment of a housing estate. The contractors performed very badly and the original programme fell behind. The local authority were unable to determine the contract with the contractors unless the architects issued a certificate under Clause 25 of the building contract stating that the contractors had failed to proceed 'regularly and diligently' with the works. The architects refused to issue a Clause 25 certificate on the basis that although the contractors were behind programme they attended site regularly with plenty of labour. The Judge held that the contractors had failed to proceed regularly and diligently and that the architects were in breach for refusing to issue a clause 25 certificate.

Continuing duty

2.11 In the absence of an express provision to the contrary, an architect is under a duty to review his design as necessary until the works are complete. In *Brickfield Properties Ltd v Newton* (1971) 1 WLR 859, Sachs LJ said:

> 'The architect is under a continuing duty to check that his design will work in practice and to correct any errors which may emerge. It savours of the ridiculous for the architect to be able to say . . . "true my design was faulty, but of course, I saw to it that the contractors followed it faithfully" . . .'

In *University of Glasgow v William Whitfield* (1988) 42 BLR 66 the Court held that an architect's duty to design extended beyond practical completion to the actual completion of the building. Although this duty is not described as arising as an implied term that would appear to be the contemplated basis of the duty.

Liability for negligence

Personal injuries

2.12 There is no doubt that an architect may be liable for negligence which causes foreseeable personal injury to any foreseeable victim. This was established in *Clay v A. J. Crump & Sons Ltd* [1964] 1 QB 533. An architect supervising demolition and rebuilding instructed the demolition contractor to leave temporarily standing a wall which closed off one boundary to the site. He accepted the demolition contractor's word that the wall was safe, and did not check himself, although he visited the site. Had he looked, he would have seen that it was tottering unstably above a 6ft trench cut under its foundations. The architect, together with the demolition contractor and the builder, was held liable when the wall collapsed and injured one of the builder's men. It should be remembered when considering whether an architect was negligent, however, that his main function is to see that his client gets value for money, and that the safety of the builder's employees is mainly a matter for the builder himself. Thus an architect is not negligent if, unlike the architect in *Clay v Crump*, he orders something to be done which involves danger only if it is done the wrong way. Thus an architect was not negligent when he ordered a chase to be cut in a wall, and the builder chose to do it without shoring the wall up, so that it fell and injured a workman (*Clayton v Woodman & Son Ltd* [1962] 1 WLR 585).

Liability to subsequent purchasers for defects in the building

2.13 An architect may owe a duty of care to subsequent purchasers and tenants of a building constructed to his design or under his supervision. The retreat of the law of negligence referred to above culminating in the recent House of Lords decision in *Murphy v Brentwood* has rendered such a duty of so little protection to third parties, should the building prove defective, that the use of collateral or direct warranties, giving the building user a contractual relationship with its designer, has developed. The general view now is that, save in exceptional circumstances, an architect will not owe subsequent purchasers a duty of care to prevent economic loss.

Another restriction to a purchaser's ability to sue for negligence was the courts' insistence that the damage complained of must have occurred during the ownership of the plaintiff. In the case of *Perry v Tendring DC* [1984] 3 Con LR, the judge held that if an owner suffers damage to his property without being aware of it – if, for example, the foundations settle, and the owner sells the property before significant cracks develop – the subsequent owner would be precluded from suing in negligence any person concerned in the building's construction unless the original owner's right to sue were assigned to the new owner. This problem area of the law has been simplified somewhat by the Latent Damage Act 1986 and now in certain circumstances a subsequent purchaser gains the right to sue in respect of any negligence to which the damage to the property is attributable. If the subsequent purchaser had reason to suspect that the foundations were inadequate, and turned down the opportunity to have a survey which would have revealed the troubles to come, he will be regarded by the courts as the author of his own misfortunes and thereby disentitled to sue (*Stewart v East Cambridgeshire District Council* (1979) 252 EG 1105).

In the ordinary course of things, however, if a purchaser fails to have a full structural survey carried out on premises that subsequently prove defective, such omission may be seen to contribute to the purchaser's losses only, and then not to any great degree. Further, the House of Lords in *Smith v Bush* and *Harris Wyre Forest DC* [1989] 2 WLR 790 held that a valuer instructed by, for example, a building society, to carry out a valuation of a modest house for the purpose of deciding whether to grant a mortgage, could be liable to the purchaser if he were negligent in his survey of the house, especially if he knew that the purchaser would rely upon his valuation without an independent survey.

Liability to the builder

2.14 Usually there is no contract between the architect and contractor. Under the terms of most building contracts, however, the acts or omissions of the architect affect the contractor. The question arises as to whether the architect can be liable to the contractor in respect of the exercise of his function under the building contract. In the absence of a contract such liability would be founded in tort. In order to succeed in any claim, therefore, the contractor would have to show that the architect owed him a duty of care. In each case it is necessary to examine the relevant facts, the relationship between the parties and their responsibilities in order to consider whether such a duty arises.

Execution of the works

2.15 In *Oldschool v Gleeson (Construction) Ltd* (1976) 4 BLR 103, Judge Stabb QC held that an architect did not owe a duty to tell the contractor how to carry out the work. He said:

> 'Not only has (the architect) no duty to instruct the builder how to do the work or what safety precautions to take but he has no right to do so, nor is he under any duty to the builder to detect faults during the progress of the work. The architect, in that respect, may be in breach of his duty to his client, but this does not excuse the builder.
>
> I take the view that the duty of care which an architect or a consulting engineer owes to a third party is limited by the assumption that the contractor who creates the work acts at all material times as a competent contractor.'

Thus an architect is generally under no duty to tell the contractor the manner of performance of his work. It was suggested in *University of Manchester v Hugh Wilson* (1984) 2 Constr LR 43, that if an architect knew that the contractors were making a major mistake which would involve them in expense the architect would probably owe a duty to the contractors to warn them. The judge said:

> 'In those circumstances the architect would not be instructing the contractors in how to do their work but merely warning them of the probable consequences of persistence in the particular method which they had adopted.'

Certification

2.16 In *Arenson* v *Arenson* (1977) AC 405, the House of Lords opened the way for contractors to bring a claim against architects for loss resulting from under-certification. Lord Salmon said:

'The architect owed a duty to his client, the building owner, arising out of the contract between them to use reasonable care in issuing his certificates. He also, however, owed a similar duty of care to the contractor arising out of their proximity . . . In *Sutcliffe* v *Thackrah* (1974) AC 727 the architect negligently certified more money was due than was in fact due, and he was successfully sued for the damage which this had caused his client. He might, however, have negligently certified that less money was payable than was in fact due and thereby starved the contractor of money. In a trade in which cash flow is especially important this might have caused the contractor serious damage for which the architect could have been successfully sued.'

Subsequently however there has been no reported case where a contractor succeeded in such a claim. Against this background the decision of the Court of Appeal in *Pacific Associates* v *Baxter and Halcrow* (1988) 44 BLR 33 CA was awaited eagerly. In that case contractors entered into a contract with the Ruler of Dubai for the dredging of a lagoon in the Persian Gulf. The work was delayed and the contractors claimed additional expenses. Their claim was rejected by the engineers. When the contractors referred their claim to arbitration, the Ruler paid them £10 m in settlement. The contractors sued the engineers for £45 m being the unrecovered balance of their claim against the Ruler. The Court of Appeal held that the engineers were not liable to the contractors because the contractors had entered into a contract with the Ruler which excluded liability on the part of the engineers and provided for disputes to be resolved by arbitration. Because of these special factors it is far from clear whether this case resolves the question of the liability of the certifier, be he architect or engineer, to the contractor in all cases.

In fact the decision is not as clear as it might be since it is so heavily dependent upon its particular facts. The basis of the decision was that because of a particular condition of the contract there could be no duty of care imposed or assumed. On the wider point of whether an engineer assumes a duty to a contractor to act with care, the Court gave limited guidance. The different approaches adopted by the three judges in their judgments casts doubt on whether the decision resolves the question of liability of a certifier to a contractor. Until such time as the problem is considered further by the courts, *Pacific Associates* is generally relied upon as authority for the proposition that a certifier does not owe a contractor a duty of care.

3 Liability in contract and in a tort compared and contrasted

3.01 Liability in contract is narrower than liability in tort in one most important respect: it exists only towards the other party to the contract. English law recognizes the doctrine of *privity of contract*, which means that the rights and duties arising under a contract are limited to the contracting parties. Thus where an architect is engaged by a client, only the client can sue the architect for breach of contract; 'strangers to the contract' must base their claim in tort. By way of exception to privity of contract, it is sometimes possible for the benefit of a contract to be *assigned*; that is to say, various legal formalities are performed by which someone other than the original contracting party is substituted as the recipient of the benefits which the other party is bound to confer. Besides the need for appropriate legal formalities to make it effective, there are important limits on assignment. Thus there can be no valid assignment of a right to personal services, which means that the client may not without the architect's consent require him to carry on supervising the site for some other employer. It used to be said that there can be no valid assignment of a right to sue for damages for a breach of contract which has already occurred; thus a client could not, on selling a complete but defective

house, assign to the purchaser his claims for breach of contract against the architect. However, a recent Court of Appeal decision indicates that where property is sold, a right to claim damages in respect of that property may now be assigned with it (*Trendtex Trading Corporation* v *Crèdit Suisse* [1980] 3 All ER 721).

3.02 Contractual liability, although narrower than tort liability in that it lies in favour of fewer persons, is usually more stringent when it does arise. As we have seen, an architect sometimes by contract assumes a duty higher than a duty to take reasonable care: first, he may sometimes guarantee his solution to a problem, and second, in contract he not only undertakes to take reasonable care himself, but also guarantees reasonable care by those to whom he delegates performance of parts of the work. In tort, an employer is vicariously liable as well, but for the negligent acts of a narrower range of people. In tort, he is liable only for the acts of those whom the law quaintly terms his 'servants' – who are, by and large, his full-time salaried employees. In contract, on the other hand, he assumes responsibility not only for the negligence of his employees, but also for that of 'independent contractors' – consultants and suchlike who are independent of his business, whom he calls in at a fee to do part of what he has undertaken to his client to do.

3.03 Contractual liability is also more stringent than liability in tort as economic loss can be recovered in claims in contract whereas claims in tort, with the exception of claims for negligent misrepresentation resulting in economic loss, require actual physical damage to the person or property of the plaintiff.

3.04 There is, however, one respect in which contractual liability is less stringent than liability in tort, which is that the rules about the time within which an action must be brought work more favourably to the defendant in contract claims than in tort.

3.05 From what has been said, it is clear that a claim in contract normally has, from the plaintiff's point of view, a number of advantages over a claim in tort, but there are certain situations in which a claim in tort is stronger. In particular, there is a more favourable limitation period in tort: see Chapter 3 paragraphs 8.01– 7 and paragraph 6.01 of this chapter.

4 Statutory liability

The Defective Premises Act 1972, Section 1

4.01 This provides:

'A person taking on work for or in connection with the provision of a dwelling (whether the dwelling is provided by the erection or by the conversion or enlargement of a building) owes a duty –
(a) If the dwelling is provided to the order of any person, to that person; and
(b) without prejudice to paragraph (a) above, to every person who acquires an interest (whether legal or equitable) in the dwelling:
to see that the work which he takes on is done in a workmanlike or, as the case may be, professional manner, with proper materials and so that as regards that work the dwelling will be fit for habitation when completed.'

The scope of the duty

4.02 Architects undoubtedly count as persons 'taking on work for or in connection with the provision of a dwelling', although builders and their sub-contractors are the persons whom Parliament mainly had in mind. Under this statute, an architect owes a duty not merely to take reasonable care, but also *to see that the work which he takes on is done* in a careful manner. The level of his duty is thus like that of his duty in contract: he must take care himself, and he also must guarantee care is taken by those to whom he delegates parts of his work. The duty is elaborated in

Subsections 2 and 3 in ways more relevant to builders than to architects. These subsections say that when a person takes on work consisting of following instructions furnished by another, he fulfils his duty under the Act in so far as he carries the instructions out; however, a person in this position may incur liability for failure to warn of defects in those instructions, presumably if he spots some obvious defect in the instructions which he realizes no one else has noticed, and says nothing about it. And a person does not escape liability as one who is merely carrying out instructions if it was he who originally suggested what he should be instructed to do. The duty under the Act is owed to the person to whose order the dwelling is provided, and to every other person 'who acquires an interest (whether legal or equitable) in the dwelling'. This means that the duty runs with the land in favour of subsequent owners, landlords, tenants, and mortgagees.

Limitations on the duty – relationship with duties in contract and tort

4.03 In a number of ways, the duty imposed by the Defective Premises Act 1972, section 1 is narrow. It applies only to *dwellings*; thus there is no liability under these provisions for defective work on factories, offices, and warehouses. The duties it creates are owed solely to those to whom the statute says it is owed. Section 2 excludes actions for breach of the duty created by Section 1 in respect of houses covered by an 'approved scheme'. The scheme principally envisaged by this section was the 10 year protection scheme of the National House Building Council. Importantly however, the last NHBC scheme to be approved was their 1979 scheme. The 1985 scheme is not approved. Thus owners of houses covered by this and subsequent schemes can still claim against builders and construction professionals under Section 1.

Until recently the Defective Premises Act was not relied upon by owners of defective homes because the duties imposed by the courts on the builders and construction professionals in contract and tort completely outflanked those created by Parliament by statute. As a result of the retreat of the law of negligence, however, the Defective Premises Act has regained prominence. In the *D & F Estates* case the House of Lords made particular reference to this Act. As a result plaintiffs are likely to seize upon its provisions in an attempt to obtain a remedy now denied them by the law of negligence.

It used to be thought that the Act imposed a two-pronged duty upon designers, namely to see that the work taken on is done in a professional manner with proper materials *and* to design a dwelling which, upon completion, would be fit for human habitation. The recent decision of *Thompson* v *Clive Alexander & Partners* (1992) CILL p. 755 has cast doubt upon this reasoning. Three house owners brought proceedings against the architects and engineers whom they alleged designed and supervised the construction of their house. The action was based exclusively upon the provision of the Section 1(1) of the Act. The designers argued that it was an essential ingredient of the house owners claim that any breach of the Act rendered their homes unfit for habitation. They said that the words 'and so that as regards that work the dwelling would be fit for habitation' did not impose a separate duty on them but was simply part of the standard required in carrying out the duty 'to see that the work which he takes on was done in a workmanlike or professional manner'.

The house owners claimed in respect of many defects which did not make their homes uninhabitable. Thus if the designers were successful in their argument, the home owners' claim would fail in respect of a large number of defects. The judge held that the duty imposed by Section 1(1) of the Act was limited to the kind of defect in the work done and the materials used which makes the dwelling unfit for habitation upon completion. It was not enough for a plaintiff to prove that the defects arose because of the architects' failure to carry out their work in a professional manner with proper materials.

With the demise of the law of tort it is thought that the wording of the Act will be subjected to a lot more judicial scrutiny: the meaning of the term 'fit for habitation' has yet to be considered, for example. House owners are likely to contend for the comparatively generous standard applied in cases under the law relating to landlord and tenant.

Liability for breach of the Building Regulations

4.04 Section 38 of the Building Act 1984 says that a breach of duty imposed by the Building Regulations, shall so far as it causes damage, be actionable except where the regulations say otherwise. The Act elsewhere says that this provision shall come into force when the Secretary of State – meaning in practice the Department of the Environment – shall determine. It has not been brought into force. In fact, it is further from being in force now than when it was first enacted, because it has been brought into force so far as was needed to empower the Minister to make new Building Regulations, for breach of which civil liability will be excluded, and the Department of the Environment says that it has no plans to make the section effective.

Until Section 38 is effective, the relevant case law suggests that breach of the Building Regulations does not of itself give rise to liability in damages for breach of statutory duty. In *Eames London Estates Ltd* v *North Hertfordshire DC* (1980) 18 BLR 23, Judge Edgar Fay QC held that contractors were liable for breach of the relevant building by-laws irrespective of whether they had been negligent. The greater body of subsequent case law is contrary to this finding. In *Worlock* v *Saws* (1981) 20 BLR 94, the Court held that it would be wrong to regard the Building Regulations as giving rise to a statutory duty creating an absolute liability. This view was endorsed by the Court of Appeal in *Taylor Woodrow Construction* v *Charcon Structures Ltd* (1981) 30 BLR 76, where Waller LJ doubted whether breach of a building regulation would by itself give rise to an action for damages without proof of negligence since he was of the view that a regulation of that kind would be difficult to construe as a regulation imposing an absolute duty in an action for damages. Subsequently Judge Newey QC considered a breach of the building by-laws in *Perry* v *Tendring District Council* (1984) 30 BLR 118. He held that a breach did not give rise to liability in damages. More recently Judge Esyr Lewis QC expressly held in *Kijowksi* v *New Capital Properties Ltd* (1988) unreported, that breach of the Building Regulations did not give rise to liability in damages.

It seems therefore that until Section 38 of the 1984 Act is brought into force, a breach of the Building Regulations will not give rise to a claim for damages in the absence of negligence. These cases all concern claims made against contractors or local authorities. Can a claim be brought against a designer or building professional for breach of the Building Regulations?

There is little guidance on this point and the fact that very few claims of this nature have been made suggests that the Building Regulations do not provide fertile ground for claims against construction professionals.

The Supply of Goods and Services Act 1982

4.05 Part II of the Act relates to contracts for the supply of services and this includes services provided by an architect for an employer. Section 13 says that in such a contract there is an implied term that the architect will carry out the service with reasonable skill and care. Section 14 says that if no time has been fixed by the contract in which the service is to be carried out, there is an implied term that the architect will carry it out in a reasonable time.

5 Measure of damages

Principles of calculation

5.01 The basis of calculating damages is theoretically different in contract and in tort. In contract, damages are supposed to put the plaintiff in the position he would have been in if the defendant had kept his promise. In tort, damages are supposed to put the plaintiff in the position he would have been in if the tortious act had never taken place. Looked at another way, the fundamental principle governing the measure of damages is that the plaintiff must be put so far as money can do it in the position he would have occupied if the architect had properly discharged his duty. For some time these different principles made little difference to the damages awarded in the usual sort of case against architects, that is, in which someone complains that because of the architect's lack of reasonable care his building is defective. Whether the claim was brought in contract or tort the damages recovered would be the cost of rectifying the defects in the building.

The recent changes in the law of tort have emphasized the different between the two types of claim. If a client brings a claim against an architect for breach of contract he is entitled to claim the cost of remedying any defects and to recover any commercial losses incurred whilst the works are carried out. A claim for negligence was limited to the cost of repairing damage: economic or financial loss was not recoverable in an action in tort. As the law of negligence went into retreat, the definition of recoverable damage became constricted. Finally in *Murphy* v *Brentwood* the House of Lords decided that the cost of repairing defects in a building was economic loss and not recoverable in an action in tort. As a result of this decision, it is unlikely that any remedy is available to those who do not have a contract with the architect for damages for negligence. The main exception to this rule arises out of the special duty when giving professional advice. If advice is given negligently then as a result of the decision in *Hedley Byrne* v *Heller* the adviser would be liable not only for the cost of repairing any physical damage caused by the advice but also for any financial losses caused. As indicated above, this important point has recently been decided against the professional adviser in *Wessex Regional Health Authority* v *HLM Design Ltd*.

Of course, a plaintiff who can sue a defendant relying on more than one cause of action gets only one set of damages. Damages can also be recovered for inconvenience, distress and annoyance, if for example, the plaintiff has been kept out his house whilst building works take much longer than they should have, or whilst extensive remedial works are executed. Other consequential losses are only recoverable in so far as they were reasonably foreseeable.

Where the damage is too remote

5.02 Two important limitations on the extent of damages should be noted. The first is that the plaintiff is under a *duty to mitigate his loss*. This means that he must behave reasonably to keep the damage as small as possible, and if he fails to do this, he cannot recover for the loss he could have avoided. Thus someone who complains of a defective roof on his house must get it mended as soon as possible. He is not allowed to let the rain wreck his ceilings and his furniture while he sues the architect or builder, and then add the cost of these to the bill. The second is that a defendant is not liable to pay for damage of a kind which is not a reasonably foreseeable consequence of his negligence. Thus if a businessman lost the chance of an enormously profitable contract with an Arab oil sheik as the unforeseeable consequence of the closure of his office on the vital day because of a structural defect, he could not sue for that loss. However, if the general *type* of damage is foreseeable, the defendant is liable even if the *extent* of the damage is not. Thus in one case, an architect negligently failed to take account of the effect of the removal of some fruit trees on the behaviour of the clay subsoil when he calculated the depth of the foundations of a block of flats. Some slight damage from 'heave' was a foreseeable result. Unforeseeably, a row of mature elms was felled nearby as well, and the damage from heave – nearly all of which would have been prevented by adequate foundations – was far worse than could have been anticipated. The architect was held liable to the full extent of the damage (*Acrecrest Ltd* v *W. S. Hattrell & Partners* [1979] 252 EG 1107).

The date of assessment

5.03 Formerly, the plaintiff was awarded the cost of reinstatement at the time when the damage occurred. In times of inflation and rising building costs, this rule was very good for defendants who were builders or architects: the longer they could avoid payment, the less in real terms they had to pay. In *Dodd Properties (Kent) Ltd* v *Canterbury City Council* [1980] 1 All ER 928, this rule was reversed. The defendant damaged the plaintiff's property in 1970; he disputed liability, and was eventually held liable at a trial in 1978. The Court of Appeal held the plaintiff was entitled to the cost of repairs at the time when he could first reasonably have been expected to do them. As it would have caused the plaintiff financial problems to have done the repairs out of his own pocket, and he would not have bothered to do them at all unless the defendant was made to pay for them, the plaintiff was quite reasonable to wait until 1978 before he did the repairs, and was entitled to their cost at that time.

Apportionment

5.04 Large building projects involve many different parties with different functions and skills. Damage or defects in the building may be the result of breaches of duty by more than one participant. Similarly, several parties may be responsible for the same defects but to a different extent. For example, the contractor may be in breach of contract for executing bad workmanship and the architect liable for failing to supervise the works properly and notice the contractor's breach. In such cases responsibility may be apportioned between the various defendants. In *Equitable Debenture Assets Corpn* v *Moss* [1984] 2 Con LR 1 the plaintiff's claim related to defective design of curtain walling and bad workmanship to the parapet walling. The specialist design sub-contractors were held 75% liable for the curtain walling and the architects 25%. The apportionment in respect of the parapet walling was 80% to the subcontractors, 15% to the main contractors and 5% to the architects.

6 When liability is barred by lapse of time
Limitation Act 1980

6.01 Section 2 of this Act provides that certain types of action, of which claims against architects and builders for negligence are one, shall not be brought 'after the expiration of six years from the date on which the cause of action accrued'. The vital question is: When does a cause of action 'accrue?' In general, a cause of action accrues when facts first exist upon which the plaintiff has the right to sue. When this is depends on whether the claim is based on a breach of contract or on tort. A person can first sue for a breach of contract when the breach of contract occurs; he does not have to wait until he suffers damage as a result. In the case of an architect who is sued for a negligent breach of contract, he can be sued from when he acts negligently: if he fails adequately to supervise the laying of drains or foundations, he can be sued then and there. So six years from then, the cause of action against him in contract expires. It matters not that, during those six years, his client was unaware of the negligence because no flooding or cracking had yet occurred – unless, exceptionally, the architect had resorted to fraud to prevent his negligence being discovered. If the flooding or cracking occurs after the six years from the negligent supervision, as far as the law of contract is concerned, that is just the client's bad luck. In tort, on the other hand, no one can be sued until damage is suffered, which means that the cause of action does not accrue until then. Thus in tort, time runs, in the case of a defective building, from when the damage to it occurs. In *Pirelli General Cable Works* v *Oscar Faber* [1983] AC 1 the House of Lords ruled that the limitation period ran from the date when the damage occurred. In that case, a factory chimney had cracked at the top because of negligent design, the cracks not being reasonably discoverable until some two years after they had occurred. The House of Lords ruled that time ran from when the cracks happened, which meant that the defence of limitation succeeded. The time limit within which actions in negligence for defective buildings can be brought have been revised by the Latent Damage Act 1986. Under that Act negligence claims become barred either six years from the date when damage occurred, or three years from the date when the plaintiff discovered the damage, whichever is the later. Actions in either case are subject to a 'long stop' of 15 years from the date of the negligence complained of.

At one stage it was not clear whether the provisions of the Latent Damage Act operated to extend the limitation period in respect of negligent advice rather than a negligent act. In two recent cases, *Horbury* v *Craig Hall & Rutley* (1991) CILL p. 692 and *Campbell* v *Meacocks* (1993) CILL p. 886 the court held that the Latent Damage Act does apply to negligent mis-statements.

6.02 By Section 1(5) of the Defective Premises Act 1972 the limitation period for a claim under that Act is six years from the date when the dwelling was completed, or, if there was later remedial work, from the date when the remedial work was completed.

6.03 The law of limitation in contract is more fully discussed in Chapter 2 paragraphs 13.01–4; and the law of limitation in tort is more fully discussed in Chapter 3 paragraphs 8.01–7.

23

Architects' professional indemnity insurance

PETER MADGE

1 Some basic insurance principles

1.01 The subject matter of an insurance policy may be the property owned by the insured against which he wishes to insure, i.e. the contract works, or the creation of a legal liability against him for which he wants insurance protection, i.e. professional liability.

Good faith

1.02 Like other forms of contract, insurance is subject to the normal contractual rules of offer and acceptance, consideration (the premium), legality, agreement of the parties, contractual capacity of the parties and the intention to create a legal relationship. Insurance contracts, however, differ fundamentally from other commercial contracts in the sense that they are bound by the principle of utmost good faith. There is a duty on the insured to disclose to the insurer all material facts bearing on the risk.

Disclosure of material facts

1.03 A material fact is something which would influence the judgement of a prudent insurer in agreeing to accept the risk or not and in deciding the amount of premium he would charge. The test of whether a fact is material or not is whether it would have influenced the judgement of a prudent insurer, not the particular insurer issuing the policy. Whether or not the insured considered the fact to be material is not relevant. It is the test of the prudent insurer, not the prudent insured.

The insured has a duty to disclose all material facts which have a bearing on the risk proposed and must make no misrepresentation about those facts or the risk. The onus of proving that there

has been a non-disclosure of information or fact is upon the insurers. The insured must disclose all those material facts which are within his knowledge, whether actual or presumed. He must disclose all those facts which he knows, or ought in the ordinary course of business affairs to know or have known about.

1.04 This represents the common law position. Insurers often insist upon a proposal form being completed before insurance is offered. This asks a number of relevant questions which are material to the risk but the important point to note is that even though a question is not asked, if there is something material to the risk then the insured must disclose it. Moreover, most proposal forms contain a declaration and warranty at the foot of the form saying the insured has answered all questions accurately and not withheld material information. The insured has to sign this. The effect of signing this declaration and warranty is that the insured warrants the accuracy of all the answers on the proposal form and further warrants that he has not withheld or failed to disclose all material facts. A warranty in insurance law has a strict interpretation. Thus, any inaccuracy on the proposal form or non-disclosure of material information gives the insurers the right, if they so wish, to treat the policy as void. Hence the importance of making sure that all answers to questions and information shown on proposal forms are correct.

1.05 Over the years many technical and legal rules have been established in relation to non-disclosure. Generally the following will be held to be material and must, therefore, be disclosed:

1. Facts indicating that the subject matter of the insurance is exposed to more than the ordinary degree of risk.
2. Facts indicating that the insured is activated by some special motive as, for example, where he greatly over-insures.
3. Facts showing that the liability of the insurer is greater than he would normally have expected it to be.
4. Facts showing that there is a moral hazard attaching to the insured suggesting that he is not a fit person to whom insurance can be granted, for example a person with a bad criminal history.
5. Facts which to the insured's knowledge are regarded by the insurers as material.

1.06 On the other hand there are facts which, although material, may become immaterial in certain circumstances and there is, therefore, no obligation upon the insured to disclose them. For example:

1. Facts which are already known to the insurers or which they may be reasonably presumed to know.
2. Facts which the insurers could have discovered themselves by making some enquiries.
3. Facts where the insurer has waived further information.
4. Facts tending to lessen the risk – for obvious reasons, since anything that lessens the risk is beneficial to the underwriter.

2 Professional indemnity insurance policy

Purpose

2.01 To protect the insured against his legal liability for claims made against him for breach of professional duty.

The policy

2.02 Policies vary from insurer to insurer. All, however, will make the proposal form, completed by the insured, the basis of the contract. Any inaccuracies on that form or any non-disclosure of material fact may make the policy void.

Most policies agree:

1. To indemnify the insured (the firm or practice including past directors, principals or partners)
2. against any claim made against him during the period of insurance
3. for which he shall become legally liable to pay compensation, together with claimants' costs, fees and expenses
4. in accordance with any judgement, award or settlement made in the United Kingdom (or any order made anywhere in the world to enforce such judgement, award or settlement in whole or in part) in consequence of
5. any breach of professional duty of care by the assured to any claimant or
6. any libel, slander or slander of title, slander of goods or injurious falsehood.

The policy covers *legal* liability not moral liability.

Limit of indemnity

2.03 There is a limit up to which insurers will pay claims but not beyond. It is the insured's responsibility to select an adequate limit. The limit may be an *aggregate* limit covering all claims in every policy year or a limit in respect of each and every *claim* (or series of claims from the same originating cause).

Legal costs

2.04 In addition to the limit of indemnity, insurers will normally pay defence costs incurred with their consent in the investigation, defence or settlement of any claim. However, if a payment is made which is greater than the limit of indemnity insurers' agreement to pay the legal costs is scaled down, e.g. if the limit of indemnity is £1 million and the claim is settled for £2 million then the insurer will only pay 50% of legal costs.

Claims made cover

2.05 It is important to note that the policy is a *claims made* policy. In other words it pays only for claims made against the insured during the period of insurance. It is not a negligence committed policy. *Once the policy lapses so does the cover.* Retired partners should make sure the firm's policy covers them. Sole practitioners need 'run off' cover. Liability continues into retirement.

Exclusions

2.06 These should be read very carefully. Normally the policy will *not* pay for:

1. Any excess or deductible, i.e. the first amount of each and every claim.
2. Any claim arising out of participation in any consortium or joint venture, of which the insured forms part (because the liability of the insured in any consortium or joint venture agreement can be varied or increased by the terms of the joint venture or consortium agreement).
3. Any claim arising out of any circumstance or event which has been disclosed by the insured on the proposal form or renewal declaration form (the previous policy should cover the eventuality – make sure it does by telling the insurers before the policy expires).
4. Claims caused by a dishonest, fraudulent, criminal or malicious act or omission of any partner, director or principal of the insured (but such conduct on the part of *employees* may be covered to the extent it gives rise to legal liability). Where it is the insured's own money or property which has been stolen, it is a fidelity guarantee policy which will apply, not a professional liability policy.
5. Any claim arising out of performance warranties, collateral warranties, penalty clauses or liquidated damages clauses unless the liability of the insured to the claimant would have existed in the absence of such warranties or clauses. Performance warranties or fitness for purpose clauses often extend the insured's duty which is to exercise reasonable care and skill so as to almost guarantee the work performed. Most underwriters take the view that they are only prepared to indemnify the insured against accidental or fortuitous mistakes and not to 'guarantee' the work performed. Collateral warranties may extend the insured's duty to third parties, e.g. subsequent owners of the building or tenants.

Surveys

2.07 Where the insured engages in surveys or valuation reports, there will be a policy condition regulating how such reports should be carried out. Normally such work will only be covered if carried out by a qualified architect or surveyor or ones who have had some years experience. In addition the survey or valuation report must contain a disclaimer to the effect that woodwork or other parts of the structure which are covered, unexposed or inaccessible have not been inspected and the report therefore is unable to comment on whether such property is free from defect.

Where the insured considers that high alumina cement may be present in the building a similar clause must be included in the report to the effect that no detailed investigations have been carried out to determine whether high alumina cement was used during the construction of the building and the report therefore is enabled to say whether the building is free from risk in this respect.

Contract terms must be communicated to the client at the outset and become part of the conditions of engagement. They cannot be introduced after the contract has been concluded.

Territorial limits

2.08 The policy normally covers work performed in the United Kingdom which means England, Wales, Scotland, Northern Ireland, the Isle of Man or the Channel Islands. If work outside these limits is to be performed or you have offices abroad then the insurers must be told and cover agreed.

Fees recovery extension

2.09 Often the insured has to sue his client to recover his fees. The result normally is a counter-claim for breach of professional duty. It may be possible to extend the policy to protect the insured against costs which are necessarily incurred on his behalf in recovering or attempting to recover professional fees.

Policy conditions

2.10 These stipulate certain things that must be done or complied with before insurers pay. They must be read with care since any breach or non-observance of them may result in the insurers refusing to deal with any claim.

1. Once a claim is made against the insured then the insurers must be notified immediately. If the insured becomes aware from any third party that there is an intention to make a claim against him then again the insurers must be notified immediately.
2. If the insured becomes aware of any circumstance or event *which has not yet resulted in a claim* but which is likely to do

so, the insured must give full details of that circumstance or event to the insured. Once he has done so then any claim which subsequently arises from that circumstance or event will be covered under the policy in force at the date the circumstance or event *was notified*, notwithstanding that that policy may not be in force at the time of the claim. Make sure *full details* of the circumstance or event are given. Remember your new or renewal policy will exclude the claim and you will be relying upon your old policy for protection.

3. The insured must not admit liability and make no admission, arrangement, offer, promise or payment without the insurers' written consent.
4. The insured must give all such assistance to the insurers as is necessary for them to handle any claim. However, in the event of a dispute the insured will not be required to contest any legal proceedings unless a Queen's Counsel (or by mutual agreement between the insured and the insurers a similar authority) shall advise that such proceedings could be contested with the probability of success.
5. Insurers will not exercise any right of subrogation against any employee or former employee of the insured unless there is any dishonest, fraudulent, criminal or malicious conduct on the part of that employee.
6. If any claim which is made under the policy for indemnity is false or fraudulent then the policy becomes void.
7. The policy is normally governed by the laws of England and any dispute or difference arising between the insured and his insurers will be referred to a Queen's Counsel to be mutually agreed between the insured and the insurers.

Alleviation of non-disclosure rule

2.11 The non-disclosure rule in insurance law is harsh. Any failure to disclose a material fact or any mistake on the proposal form may make the policy void. Breach of the policy conditions may also invalidate a claim. Some policies contain a clause to the effect that the insurers will not exercise their rights to void the policy or to refuse indemnity to the insured for any breach of non-disclosure of material facts or breach of policy conditions provided always that *the insured* shall establish to the satisfaction of insurers that such non-disclosure or breach was innocent and free of any fraudulent conduct or intent to deceive. *The onus of proof is on the insured*. The words used differ amongst insurers.

3 Risk management

3.01 A sensible approach to the risks that may affect an architect can eliminate some of them and mitigate the effects of others. It is logical to identify and control risk at the outset, rather than to argue about who is responsible for injury, loss or damage after it has taken place.

3.02 Risk management entails a sensible overview of risks and falls into four stages:

1. the identification of those risks which can arise;
2. an analysis and measurement of those risks to see what is involved;
3. treatment of those risks so as to eliminate them or reduce their impact;
4. controlling those risks or transferring them to another party, either by means of clauses in the contract conditions or by insurance.

Some risk management suggestions which may help to prevent claims or put you in better position to defend

3.03

1. Read conditions of *engagement* carefully. Be clear what you have agreed – confirm in writing any variations. Be clear what the *fee* is; disputes trigger off *claims*.
2. Control/supervise the work carefully.
3. Review all office procedures – Control incoming/outgoing post.
4. Have you the experience or knowledge required?
5. Does the fee justify the exposure?
6. Risk/insurance to be put on board meeting agenda.
7. Check agreements with consultants – are they insured?
8. Consider any assignment carefully if it has a US exposure or overseas exposure – take advice. Which law applies?
9. Don't destroy important documents. Have an agreed policy on document retention.
10. Know the work which has problems.
11. Keep an eye on staff with problems (work/domestic/personal).
12. Read collateral agreements, warranties and duty of care agreements carefully. Take advice before signing them.

24

Copyright

MICHAEL FLINT*

1 The basic rules of copyright

1.01 The copyright law of the United Kingdom is contained in the Copyright, Designs and Patents Act 1988 and the subsidiary legislation made under that Act. Copyright exists only in material which comes within one of the categories prescribed as being capable of having copyright protection. These are as follows:

1. Literary works.
2. Dramatic works.
3. Musical works.
4. Artistic works.
5. Sound recordings.
6. Films.
7. Broadcasts.
8. Cable programmes.
9. Typographical arrangements of published editions.

The Act describes all these copyright categories as 'works'.

Material which does not fall within one of the categories will have no copyright protection; it will not be copyright material.

1.02 Copyright subsists for defined periods which differ according to the category of work.

The duration of copyright in each category of work can be summarized as follows:

1. Literary, dramatic, musical and artistic – which includes architectural – works: 50 years from the end of the calender year in which the author died.
2. Sound recordings and films: 50 years from the end of the year in which they were made, or if released before the end of that period, 50 years from the end of the calendar year in which released.
3. Broadcasts and cable programmes: 50 years from the end of the year in which the broadcast was made or cable programme included in a cable programme service.
4. Typographical arrangements: 25 years from the end of the calendar year in which the edition was first published.

The basic rules of copyright

1.03 The European Union Directive entitled 'Harmonizing the Term of Copyright and Certain Related Rights' requires all member states to provide that copyright protection for literary, dramatic, musical and artistic works shall run for the life of the author and for 70 years after his death.

The term of protection for films must be '70 years after the death of the last of the following persons to survive – the principal director, the author of the screenplay, the author of the dialogue and the composer of music specifically created for use in the cinematographic or audiovisual work'.

The term of protection for sound recordings, broadcasts and cable programmes must be 50 years.

The changes in UK copyright law to give effect to the Directive should have been in force no later than 1 July 1995, and the date from which the term of protection for literary, dramatic, musical and artistic works should have been extended to no later than 1 July 1997. However, as this chapter goes to press the implementary legislation has not yet been before Parliament.

1.04 If material is entitled to copyright, the right vested in the copyright owner is that of preventing others from doing certain specified acts, called 'the restricted acts' (paragraph 2.02).

The restricted acts are specified by the Copyright Act in relation to each category of work and differ for each category.

If something is done in relation to copyright material which is not one of the restricted acts specified for that type of work or an act which constitutes 'secondary infringement' and was done by a person who knew, or had reason to believe that the act would be an infringement of copyright, there is no breach of copyright.

1.05 There are certain circumstances in which doing restricted acts without the authority of the copyright owner does not constitute breach of copyright.

The most important of these general exceptions are:

1. Fair dealing (e.g. for purposes of research, private study, criticism, or review).
2. Use of less than a substantial part of a work.
3. Use for certain educational purposes.
4. Use for certain library and archival purposes.
5. Use in parliamentary and judicial proceedings.

There are other important exceptions, differing according to the types of works or subject matters (paragraphs 1.06 to 1.11).

1.06 In most cases the author of a work is its first owner. But there are special rules which can override this general provision.

1.07 There is no copyright in ideas – only in the manner of their expression.

1.08 To acquire copyright protection, works must be reduced to a material form.

1.09 Literary, dramatic, musical and artistic works must be original in order to be entitled to copyright.

1.10 The work must have involved the use of skill and labour by the author.

1.11 The work does not have to be published, nor does it have to be registered, for it to have copyright protection.

1.12 The author or maker of the work must be a 'qualified person'; basically a citizen or resident of the United Kingdom or of

* In the first edition, this chapter was written by George Stringer.

one of the countries which is a signatory to the Berne Copyright Convention or the Universal Copyright Convention (UCC). Alternatively, the work must have been made or published in a qualifying country, which generally speaking (although there are important exceptions for sound recordings, films, broadcasts and cable programmes) are the same countries. There are no significant countries in the copyright context which are not parties to one or the other of these conventions, except China.

The nature of copyright

1.13

'Copyright is a right given to or derived from works, and is not a right in novelty of ideas. It is based on the right of an author, artist or composer to prevent another person copying an original work, whether it be a book, picture or tune, which he himself has created. There is nothing in the notion of copyright to prevent a second person from producing an identical result (and himself enjoying a copyright in that work) provided it is arrived at by an independent process.'

That quotation is from the report of the Gregory Committee on Copyright Law (1952), whose recommendations formed the basis of the Copyright Act 1956.

'A writer writes an article about the making of bread. He puts words on paper. He is not entitled to a monopoly in the writing of articles about the making of bread, but the law has long recognised that he has an interest not merely in the manuscript, the words on paper which he produces, but in the skill and labour involved in the choice of words and the exact way in which he expresses his ideas by the words he chooses. If the author sells copies of his article then again a purchaser of a copy can make such use of that copy as he pleases. He can read it or sell it second-hand, if he can find anyone who will buy it. If a reader of the original article is stimulated into writing another article about bread the original author has no reason to complain. It has long been recognised that only the original author ought to have the right to reproduce the original article and sell the copies thus reproduced. If other people were free to do this they would be making a profit out of the skill and labour of the original author. It is for this reason that the law has long given to authors, for a specified term, certain exclusive rights in relation to so-called literary works. Such rights were recognised at common law at least as early as the fifteenth century.'

The latter quotation is from the report of the Whitford Committee on Copyright and Design Law (1977), upon whose recommendations the Copyright, Designs and Patents Act 1988 is largely based. These two quotations contain as clear an exposé of the nature of copyright as can be found anywhere.

As the word itself implies, 'copyright' is literally a right to prevent other people copying an original work. It should be noted that it must be an original work, *not* an original idea.

Intellectual property and copyright

1.14 The main difficulty in comprehending copyright seems to be the association that is made among copyright, patents, and trade marks. These diverse creatures are, for convenience, usually grouped under the headings of 'industrial property' or 'intellectual property'. It is certainly appropriate to include design copyright – which is registrable, unlike any other form of copyright – under these generic headings, but whilst copyright certainly is a form of property, it is arguable that it would be preferable to group copyright with passing off, breach of confidence, and invasion of privacy.

The sources of copyright law

1.15 Statute copyright law is now entirely contained in the Copyright, Designs and Patents Act 1988 ('the Act').

There are a number of rules and regulations contained in statutory instruments made under the above legislation. In addition, certain Orders in Council extend the provisions of the Act to works originating outside the UK.

The UK is party to a number of conventions dealing with international copyright recognition and other matters of an international nature concerning copyright, of which the most important are the Berne Copyright Convention and the Universal Copyright Convention.

There is a body of case law contained in the law reports consisting of the judgments of copyright cases. Decisions on earlier legislation, the Copyright Acts of 1911 and 1956, are frequently still relevant. They are of particular importance, for example, when determining what constitutes plagiarism and where judgments on matters of degree, rather than pure construction of legislation, must be made.

The history of copyright law

1.16 Copyright effectively came into existence with the invention of printing. The first indications of copyright were the granting of licences by the Crown to printers giving them the right to print (i.e. copy) against the payment of fees to the Crown. In 1662 the Licensing Act was passed, which prohibited the printing of any book which was not licensed and registered at the Stationers Company.

The first Copyright Act was passed in 1709. This Act gave protection for printed works for only 21 years from the date of printing and unprinted works for 14 years. Again, books had to be registered at the Stationers Company.

The Copyright Act 1842 was the next important piece of legislation relating to copyright. Although it accorded copyright protection only to literary works, it laid down as the period of copyright the life of the author plus 7 years after his death, or 42 years from the date of publication, whichever should be the longer.

Architects' plans, provided they had artistic quality, first became entitled to copyright protection as artistic works under the Fine Arts Copyright Act 1862.

The Copyright Act 1911 repealed all previous copyright legislation. This Act extended copyright protection to 'architectural works of art', with the result that, as the courts held in *Meikle* v *Maufe* [1941] 3 All ER 144, both buildings and the plans upon which they were based were entitled to copyright protection. Plans and sketches were protected as 'literary works' and drawings as 'artistic works'. The Copyright Act 1911 was repealed by the Copyright Act 1956.

Protection for works of architecture under the 1956 Act was similar to that accorded by the 1911 Act.

The 1988 Act repealed the 1956 Act. It came into force on 1 August 1989.

2 Protection under the Copyright, Designs and Patents Act 1988

2.01 Works of architecture are included with 'artistic works' for copyright purposes. Section 4 of the Act defines an 'artistic work'. In view of its importance in considering architectural copyright it is worth quoting in full:

S.4 (1) In this Part 'artistic work' means –
    (*a*) a graphic work, photograph, sculpture or collage, irrespective of artistic quality,
    (*b*) a work of architecture being a building or a model for a building, or
    (*c*) a work of artistic craftmanship.
  (2) In this part –
    'building' includes any fixed structure, and a part of a building or fixed structure;
    'graphic work' includes –
      (*a*) any painting, drawing, diagram, map, chart or plan, and
      (*b*) any engraving, etching, lithograph, woodcut or similar work;

'photograph' means a recording of light or other radiation on any medium on which an image is produced or from which an image may by any means be produced, and which is not part of a film;

'sculpture' includes a cast or model made for purposes of sculpture.

Works of architecture include both buildings and models for buildings. The plans, sketches, and drawings upon which works of architecture are based are also artistic works which have their own separate copyright. So also do the notes prepared by the architect, but these are protected not as artistic works but as literary works.

There is no definition of 'fixed structure' although a decision under the 1956 Act held that a garden, in that case a somewhat elaborately laid out garden, was a 'structure' and therefore a work of architecture.

A 'drawing' is not defined by the Act. The definitions of 'artistic work' and 'literary work' are so wide that they cover all the typical output of an architect's office: design sketches, blueprints, descriptive diagrams, working drawings, final drawings, artistic presentations, notes, both alphabetical and numerical and reports.

Restricted acts

2.02 As mentioned in paragraph 1.04 above, there are separate restricted acts specified in the Act in relation to each category of work. The restricted acts applicable to works of architecture are the same as those applicable to artistic works, although there are certain special exceptions (paragraphs 4.03 to 4.06) from these restricted acts in relation to works of architecture.

The acts restricted by the copyright in an artistic work are:

1. Copying the work.
2. Issuing copies of the work to the public.
3. Making an adaptation of the work or doing either of the above in relation to an adaptation.

Originality and artistic content

2.03 Buildings and models require in theory to have an artistic character or design, but in the few reported cases, it would appear that no architect has failed to prove an infringement even though the original building was so ordinary that it might be thought inevitable that someone else would design something substantially similar. In the case of *University of London Press Ltd* v *University Tutorial Press Ltd*, which concerned the copying of examination papers, the judge stated that 'the word "original" does not in this connection mean that the work must be the expression of original or inventive thought . . . but that it should originate from the author'.

2.04 For architectural works, the inclusion of some distinctive design detail will make the architect's task of proving infringement much easier. In the case of *Stovin-Bradford* v *Volpoint Properties Ltd* [1971] Ch 1007, the courts were influenced by the fact that although many details of the architect's drawings were not reproduced in the constructed buildings, 'a distinctive diamond-shaped feature which gave a pleasing appearance to the whole' was reproduced. In *Meikle* v *Maufe* the judge dismissed them as not being of artistic merit.

2.05 Some distinctive design feature may also be important when it could otherwise be proved that the person sued was without any knowledge of the plaintiff's prior design, and that he produced identical solutions because of a similarity in circumstances. In *Muller* v *Triborough Bridge Authority* the United States Supreme Court held that a copyright of the drawing showing a novel bridge approach designed to disentangle traffic congestion was not infringed by copying, because the system of relieving traffic congestion shown embodied an idea which cannot be copyright and was the only obvious solution to the problem.

Duration of copyright

2.07 The protection of copyright in an artistic work extends for the lifetime of the artist/author and a further period of 50 years

from the end of the calendar year in which he died. As explained in paragraph 1.03 above this period will be extended to the lifetime of the artist and a further period of 70 years when legislation changing UK law to implement a European Union Directive comes into force. In the case of architectural works, this period is not affected by the fact that the work was not published during the architect's lifetime.

In the case of joint works, the 50 years begins to run from the end of the calendar year in which the last of the joint authors dies. A joint work is one in which the work is produced by the collaboration of two or more authors in which the contribution of each author is not distinct from that of the other author or authors. Thus if a building is designed by two architects, but one is exclusively responsible only for the design of the doors and windows, so that it is possible to distinguish between the contributions of the two architects it will not be a joint work.

3 Qualification

3.01 In order to qualify for copyright protection in the UK, the qualification requirements of the Act must be satisfied either as regards the author or the country in which the work was first published.

3.02 As regards authors, in the case of unpublished works, copyright will subsist only if the author was a 'qualified person' at the time when the work was made, or, if it was being made over a period, for a substantial part of that period. In the case of a published work, the author must have been qualified at the time when the work was published, or immediately before his death (if earlier).

3.03 For copyright purposes, the expression 'qualified person' does not refer to a professional qualification, but to any British citizen, British Dependent Territories citizen, a British National (overseas), a British Overseas citizen, a British subject, or a British protected person within the meaning of the British Nationality Act 1981, or a person domiciled or resident in the UK or in another country to which the Act extends or is applied, or a body incorporated under the laws of the UK or such another country. The countries to which the Act extends or has been applied are the signatories to the Berne Copyright Convention and the Universal Copyright Convention, which (apart from the People's Republic of China and some Muslim countries) includes all the major and most of the developing countries in the world.

The provision relating to corporations is not important to architects because a corporation cannot be the author of an artistic work.

3.04 As regards the country of publication, the work must have been published first in either the UK or another country to which the Act extends or has been applied, i.e. Berne Convention or UCC countries.

Publication in one country shall not be regarded as other than first publication by reason of the simultaneous publication elsewhere. Publication elsewhere within 30 days shall be regarded as simultaneous.

3.05 The Act now provides that the territorial waters of the UK shall be treated as part of the UK for copyright purposes. In addition, oil rigs and other structures which are present on the UK continental shelf for purposes directly connected with the exploration of the sea bed or the exploration of their natural resources are subject to UK copyright law as if they were in the UK.

4 Publication

4.01 The meaning of the word 'publication' is important as it is relevant to qualification for copyright protection and the duration of copyright.

'Publication' is defined in the Act as meaning the issue of copies to the public. In the case of literary, dramatic, musical and artistic works it includes making it available to the public by means of an electronic retrieval system.

There is a special provision in relation to architectural works. In the case of works of architecture in the form of a building or an artistic work incorporated in a building, construction of the building shall be treated as equivalent to publication of the work.

4.02 However, the issue to the public of copies of a graphic work representing, or of photographs of, a work of architecture in the form of a building, or a model for a building, a sculpture or a work of artistic craftsmanship, does not constitute publication for the purposes of the Act. Nor does the exhibition, issuing to the public of copies of a film including the work, or the broadcasting of an artistic work constitute publication. Thus, the inclusion of a model of a building in a public exhibition such as the Royal Academy Summer Exhibition, would not amount to publication, nor would the inclusion of photographs of the model in a book.

5 Ownership

5.01 Subject to the exception set out in the following paragraph, ownership of copyright resides with the architect who actually drew the plan, drawing, sketch, or diagram, and, being personal property in law, passes to its owner's personal representatives after his death, and thence as directed in his will, or, in the event of intestacy, to his next of kin.

Employees

5.02 There is, however, an important exception to this provision: the copyright in architects' drawings, buildings, or models produced by an employee in the course of his employment automatically vests in his employer, whether the latter is an architect in partnership, a limited company, or a public authority. The copyright in work done by employees in their time and not in the course of employment vests in them. But an employer can discourage employees from accepting private commissions by providing in the contract of service – and a simple letter agreement is a contract of service – that all the copyright in the employee's work, whether produced in the course of employment or not, will vest in the employer. Section 178 of the Act provides that the words 'employed', 'employee', 'employer' and 'employment' refer to employment under a 'contract of service or apprenticeship'. Frequently architects employ independent architects and artists to carry out parts of the drawing service; increasingly persons who would appear to be employees are for a variety of reasons (not unconnected with tax and Social Security payments) engaged as self-employed sub-contractors. Such persons are rarely employed under 'a contract of service' as distinct from 'a contract for services', which is not the same thing (Chapter 2). Employer architects would be well advised to make it an express term of such a sub-contractor's appointment that any copyright arising out of his work should vest in the employing architect.

The old provisions regarding Crown copyright have been changed in the 1988 Act. The position now is that where a work is made by an officer or servant of the Crown in the course of his duties, the Crown will be the first owner of the copyright in the work.

Partners

5.03 Unless the partnership deed (Chapter 20) states anything to the contrary, the copyright in all work produced during the currency of a partnership is a partnership asset, and like other assets is owned and passes in accordance with the general provisions of the partnership deed concerning assets. To avoid dissemination of shares in copyright, it is usually desirable to provide that, upon the death or retirement of a partner, his share in the copyright should vest in the surviving partners. Alternatively, partners could in their wills, leave their shares in the copyright to their surviving partners.

Ownership of drawings

5.04 Ownership of copyright in drawings should be distinguished from ownership of the actual pieces of paper upon which they are drawn. It is settled law that upon payment of the architect's fees the client is entitled to physical possession of all the drawings prepared at his expense. In the absence of agreement to the contrary, copyright remains with the architect who also has a lien on (right to withhold) the drawings until his fees are paid. If all copyright *is* assigned to the client he may make such use of it as he wishes. Architects should note that even if they have assigned the copyright by virtue of the provisions of Section 64 of the Act, they may reproduce in a subsequent work part of their own original design provided that they do not repeat or imitate the main design. This provision enables architects to repeat standard details which would otherwise pass to the client upon prior assignment of copyright.

6 Exceptions from infringement of architects' copyright

Photographs, graphic works

6.01 Frequently photographs of buildings designed by architects appear as part of advertisements by the contractors who constructed the buildings. As a matter of courtesy, the contractor usually makes some acknowledgment of the design, but he is not required to do so. By Section 62 of the Act, the copyright in a work of architecture is not infringed by making a graphic work representing it, making a photograph or film of it, or broadcasting or including a visual representation of it in a cable programme service. Copies of such graphic works, photographs and films can be issued to the public without infringing the copyright in the building and models of it. Making a graphic work in this sense refers to a perspective or even detailed survey of the building as built: it would remain an infringement to copy the drawing or plan from which the building was constructed.

Reconstruction

6.02 Section 65 provides that where copyright exists in a building, it is not infringed by any reconstruction of the building. There will be no infringement of the drawings or plans in accordance with which the building was, by or with the licence of the copyright owner, constructed if subsequent reconstruction of the building or part thereof is carried out by reference to original drawings or plans. This point is of particular importance in connection with the now established 'implied licence' considered in paragraphs 8.05–8.12 below.

Fair dealing

6.03 A general defence to any alleged infringement of copyright in an artistic work is 'fair dealing' for the purpose of criticism or review, provided that there is sufficient acknowledgment. As reproduction by photograph is the most likely method of illustrating a review and as a photograph of a building is specifically exempt from infringement, this defence of 'fair dealing' would appear to be needed only in the case of drawings of buildings. A sufficient acknowledgment is an acknowledgment identifying the building by its name and location, which also identifies the name of the architect who designed it. The name of the copyright owner need not be given if he has previously required that no acknowledgment of his name should be made. As certain self-appointed groups have now taken to awarding prizes for ugliness in design, some architects might find themselves in the unusual position of wishing to have no acknowledgment made of their connection with a design, although perhaps such publicity would hardly be 'fair dealing'.

Fair dealing with an artistic work for the purposes of research and private study, without any acknowledgment, is also a defence to an alleged copyright infringement. However, there are limits on how, and how many copies may be made.

6.04 Special exceptions are contained in the Act for copying for educational purposes and copying by libraries and archives and by public administration. These provisions are too detailed to be included here, and if necessary they should be specifically referred to or professional advice should be obtained.

7 Infringement

7.01 To prove infringement, a plaintiff must show:

1. Copyright subsists in his work.
2. The copyright is vested in him.
3. The alleged infringement is identical to his work in material particulars.
4. The alleged infringement was copied from his work.

7.02 No action for infringement of copyright can succeed if the person who is claimed to have infringed had no knowledge of the existence of the work of the owner. In this respect it differs from patents, which must be registered but which give an absolute protection even if the person infringing a patent had no knowledge of its existence. Copyright restricts the right to copy, which presupposes some knowledge of the original by the copier. Ignorance of the fact that the work copied was the copyright owner's is not, however, a defence. It is in the nature of architects' copyright that the person allegedly infringing must have had access directly or indirectly to the drawings. Infringement can therefore take three forms, as detailed below.

Copying in the form of drawings

7.03 It is rare for drawings to be copied in every detail, and many would-be infringers of an architect's copyright believe that if details are altered, infringement is avoided. This is not so, and Section 16 of the Act makes it clear that references to reproduction include reproduction of a 'substantial part'. The word 'substantial' refers to quality rather than to quantity. Reference has already been made to the distinctive diamond-shaped detail in the *Stovin-Bradford* case. It does not matter that the size of the copy may have been increased or reduced or that only a small detail of an original drawing has been copied.

Copying the drawing in the form of a building

7.04 The leading case on this form of infringement is *Chabot* v *Davies* [1936] 3 All ER. Mr Chabot, who was not an architect but 'a designer and fixer of shop fronts and the like' prepared a drawing for the defendant, who 'was just about to open what is known as a fish and chip shop'. Mr Chabot was lucky enough to be able to prove that the contractor had actually been handed his drawing by the defendant and had made a tracing from it, but the defendant argued that a plan cannot be reproduced by a shop front but only by something in the nature of another plan. The judge held, however, that 'reproduce . . . in any material form whatsoever' must include reproduction of a drawing by the construction of an actual building based on that drawing.

Copying a building by another building

7.05 The leading case on this type of infringement and until recently on architects' copyright generally is *Meikle* v *Maufe* [1941] 3 All ER 144. Most architects have heard of this case, but the facts and argument bear repetition. In 1912 Heal & Son Ltd employed Smith & Brewer as architects for the building of premises on the northern part of the present site of Heal's store in Tottenham Court Road. At that time there were vague discussions about a future extension on the southern part of the site, but because of difficulties over land acquisition nothing could be done. In 1935 Heal's employed Maufe as their architect for the extension of the building. Meikle was by this time the successor in title to Smith & Brewer's copyright, and he claimed that both the extension as erected and the plans for its erection infringed the original

copyright. Maufe admitted that he thought it necessary to reproduce in the southern section of the facade the features which appeared in the original northern section. His object was 'to make the new look like the old throughout nearly the whole of the Tottenham Court Road frontage'. The layout of the interiors was also substantially reproduced. The defendants put forward three arguments:

1. There could not be a separate copyright in a building as distinct from copyright in the plans on which it was based.
2. If there a separate copyright in a building it would belong to the building contractor.
3. It was an implied term of Smith & Brewer's original engagement that Heal's should have the right to reproduce the design of the original in the extension.

7.06 The first argument failed following *Chabot* v *Davies*. The second argument failed because copyright protection in a building is limited to the original character or design, and in the making of such character or design the contractor plays no part. The third argument failed in this particular case as the Copyright Act 1911, under which this case was tried, provided that copyright remained with its original author, unless he had agreed to pass the right to another. Heal's contended that Smith & Brewer had impliedly consented to the reproduction of their design because they had known of the possibility of extension. The judge having heard the facts concerning the discussion about land acquisition held that he could not reasonably imply such a term in this case.

Copying a building in the form of drawings

7.07 As mentioned in paragraph 6.01, copyright in a work of architecture is not infringed by two-dimensional reproductions.

8 Licences

Express licence

8.01 Paragraph 1.7.1 of the Conditions of Appointment which appear as Schedule Two to the RIBA Standard Form of Agreement for the Appointment of an Architect (SFA/92) states that copyright in all documents and drawings prepared by the architect remains the property of the architect. Section 91 of the Act permits prior assignment of future copyright so that client and architect can agree at the beginning of an engagement to vary the Conditions of Engagement so that the copyright which will come into existence during the commission will vest in the client.

8.02 Paragraph 2.3 of the Conditions of Appointment modifies paragraph 1.7.1. to give the client a licence to use the architect's design in certain circumstances. Sub-paragraph 2.3.1. entitles the client to reproduce the architect's design by proceeding to execute the project provided that:

- the entitlement applies only to the site or part of the site to which the design relates;
- the architect has completed a scheme design or provided detail design and production information, and
- any fees, expenses and disbursements due to the architect have been paid.

This entitlement also applies to the maintenance, repair and renewal of the works.

Sub-paragraph 2.3.2 provides that where the architect has not completed a scheme design, the client shall not reproduce the design by proceeding to execute the project without the consent of the architect. It should be noted that earlier versions of the RIBA Standard Form of Agreement provided that in these circumstances the architect's consent must not be unreasonably withheld.

Sub-paragraph 2.3.3 provides that where the services are limited to making and negotiating planning applications, the client may not reproduce that architect's design without the architect's consent, which consent shall not be unreasonably withheld, and payment of any additional fees. The earlier versions of the RIBA

Standard Form of Agreement provided that in these circumstances the architect could withhold his consent in his absolute discretion unless otherwise determined by an arbitrator.

Finally, sub-paragraph 2.3.4 provides that the architect shall not be liable for the consequences of any use of any information or designs prepared by the architect except for the purposes for which they were provided.

The Conditions of Appointment scheduled to the Standard Form of Agreement for the Appointment of an Architect (SFA/92) Design and Build differ slightly. Sub-paragraph 2.3.2 provides that the architect must not unreasonably withhold his consent to the reproduction of the design when he has not completed a scheme design.

Sub-paragraph 2.3.4 introduces a new provision. Where the architect and client have agreed fees on the basis that the employer client will employ a contractor to carry out and complete the works, and for that purpose to complete the designs, the architect's consent is deemed to have been given to permit the reproduction of the design when the architect has not completed the scheme design, or when the services were limited to making and negotiating planning applications.

8.03 Copyright may also be expressly assigned to the client at some later stage, but it is usual to grant a licence authorizing use of copyright subject to conditions rather than an outright assignment of all the architect's rights. An increasing number of public and commercial clients make it a condition of the architect's appointment that all copyright shall vest in the client, but the architect should not consent to this without careful thought. Following *Meikle* v *Maufe* it would seem reasonable that a client should not be prevented from extending a building and incorporating distinctive design features of the original building so that the two together should form one architectural unit. If the time between the original building and the extension were 23 years, as in that case, it would be restrictive to make use of copyright to force the client into employing the original architect or his successor in title. Less scrupulous clients could, however, make use of an architect's design for a small and inexpensive original building with the undisclosed intention of greatly extending the building using the same design but at no extra cost in terms of architect's fees.

8.04 So far as drawings are concerned, it must be remembered that they are the subject of copyright 'irrespective of artistic quality' so that a prior express assignment of copyright to the client could theoretically grant him copyright in respect of even the most simple standard detail contained in the drawings (but see paragraph 5.04).

Implied licence

8.05 Whilst the RIBA Architect's Appointment contains an express licence of the architect's copyright, situations may arise where the RIBA Architect's Appointment does not form part of the contract between the architect and the client or where the terms of the RIBA Architect's Appointment do not cover particular circumstances. Problems may then arise as to what rights the client has to use the architect's drawings. As long ago as 1938, the RIBA took counsel's opinion on the theory that an architect impliedly licenses his client to make use of the architect's drawings for the purposes of construction even when the client does not employ the architect to supervise the building contract. Such an implied consent can be understood when from the beginning of the engagement the client made it clear that all he required of the architect was drawings; for if the client received the drawings and paid for them, they would be valueless unless he could use them for the purpose of construction. The courts would not allow an architect to use his copyright to prevent construction in such circumstances. Counsel advised further that even if it had originally been assumed that the architect would perform the full service and supervise construction but the client subsequently decided that he did not require supervision, an implied licence to use the copyright in the drawings would arise in the client's favour when working drawings had been completed. Counsel did not then believe that

an implied licence could arise at an earlier stage, but since 1938 the extent of architects' work and its stages have increased greatly. Cumulatively detailed drawings required for outline planning consent, detailed planning consent, and Building Regulations consent all create different stages, and an implied licence can now arise earlier than was contemplated in 1938.

8.06 Before any term can be implied into a contract, the courts must consider what the parties would have decided if they had considered the question at the time they negotiated other terms of the engagement. The courts are reluctant to imply a term unless it is necessary to give efficacy to the intention of the parties. Application of these rules to an architect's engagement would suggest that it is reasonable to infer that the architect impliedly consents to the client making use of his drawings for the purpose for which they were intended. If, therefore, the nature of the engagement is not full RIBA service but, for example, obtaining outline planning permission and no more, the architect impliedly consents to the client making use of his copyright to apply for such permission. Again, if an architect is instructed to prepare drawings of a proposed alteration for submission to the client's landlord, the client may use the drawings to obtain a consent under the terms of his lease but not for any other purpose, and certainly not for the purpose of instructing a contractor to carry out the alteration work.

8.07 The whole question of implied licence has been considered by the Court of Appeal in the cases of *Blair* and *Stovin-Bradford*, both of which have been fully reported. The facts in these cases were as follows.

Blair v *Osborne & Tompkins*

8.08 Blair was asked by his clients whether it would be possible to obtain planning consent for development at the end of his clients' garden. Having made inquiries, Blair advised that it should be possible to obtain consent for erection of two semi-detached houses. The clients instructed Blair to proceed to detailed planning consent stage and agreed to pay on the RIBA scale. The application was successful, and Blair sent the planning consent to his clients, with his account for £70 for 'taking instructions, making survey, preparing scheme and obtaining full planning consent'. As was well known to the architect, the clients did not at that stage know whether they were going to develop the land or sell it.

They paid Blair's account which he acknowledged adding 'wishing you all the best on this project' but did not employ him to do any further work because they sold the plot to a contractor/developer. They also handed over Blair's drawings to the contractor, who used his own surveyors to add the detail necessary to obtain Building Regulations consent, and this consent having been obtained the contractor erected the houses. When the architect discovered that his plans were being used he claimed that this was an infringement of his copyright. The Master of the Rolls pointed out that although the RIBA Conditions of Engagement stated that copyright remained with the architect, it was open to him to give a licence for the drawings to be used for a particular site. His Lordship was influenced by the provision in the RIBA Conditions which entitled both architect and client to terminate the engagement 'upon reasonable notice'. To his Lordship it seemed inconceivable that upon the architect withdrawing he could stop any use of the plans on the ground of infringement of copyright. It seemed equally inconceivable that he could stop their use at an earlier stage when he had done his work up to a particular point and had been paid according to the RIBA scale. Lord Justice Widgery approved the defendant's submission that the implied licence was 'to use whatever plans had been prepared at the appropriate stage for all purposes for which they would normally be used, namely, all purposes connected with the erection of the building to which they related'. If this was not right 'the architect' could hold a client to ransom and that would be quite inconsistent with the term that the engagement could be 'put an end to at any time'. In the writer's opinion this was an unfortunate decision and went much further than was required. But it must be lived with.

1 Stovin-Bradford's original design, and warehouses built **2, 3**

Stovin-Bradford v Volpoint Properties Ltd and Another

8.09 The defendant companies, which had their own drawing office, acquired an old factory which they considered had considerable development potential, and applied for planning consent for the erection of seven large warehouses. Permission was refused, and the defendants approached Stovin-Bradford, whose work they had previously admired, explaining that they needed a plan and drawing that 'showed something which was more attractive looking than the existing building'. What they wanted was 'a pretty picture', but because they had their own drawing office, they did not need the full services of an architect. It was accepted by the court that although the then Conditions of Engagement were not incorporated in their contract, both architect and defendants were fully aware that they existed. It was also accepted that both parties were concerned only with obtaining planning permission. As the trial judge held, the agreement reached between the parties was very simple and amounted to this: 'that Stovin-Bradford would suggest architectural improvements to the defendant's existing plan for the modification and extension of the existing building for the purpose of trying to obtain planning permission and that he would receive for this plan the sum of 100 guineas and his out-of-pocket expenses'. The drawing was produced showing an 'effect quite striking to the eye: a unification of two original structures into one with, in particular, a diamond feature in the left hand building caused by the arrangement of the roof line and the windows placed in the top part of the old portal frame building'. The plan was passed to the defendants, who made certain amendments and obtained planning permission. Stovin-Bradford had presented his account for the agreed 'nominal' 100 guineas, headed it 'Statement no. 1' and confirmed that the payment was 'for preparing sketch plans and design drawings in sufficient detail to obtain or apply for planning permission'. With commendable foresight,

at the foot of the bill was typed a note saying: 'The copyright of the design remains with the architect and may not be reproduced in any form without his prior written consent'. The defendants proceeded to erect the buildings, and although many details were changed, the result incorporated the particular features of the Stovin-Bradford design to which the trial judge drew notice **1, 2, 3**. At first instance, the trial judge held that there was an infringement and awarded £500 damages as the amount which would have been reasonably chargeable for a licence to make use of the copyright.

8.10 The Court of Appeal judgment in the *Blair* case having been published shortly afterwards, the defendants appealed on the ground that the *Blair* case was decisive authority for the view that whenever an architect prepared plans for obtaining planning permission, the client could use them for the building as he liked without further payment. This time Lord Denning, the Master of the Rolls, referred to the stages of normal service in the RIBA Conditions (now replaced by Architect's Appointment), which he defined as being: (1) plans up to an application for outline planning permission; (2) plans up to an application for detailed planning permission; (3) working drawings and specification for contractor to tender; (4) all an architect's work to completion of the building. (The author has often thought that this would be the most sensible division of the RIBA stages of normal service, but in fact the stages were not so defined in the then existing Conditions – though the stages in the current Architect's Appointment roughly correspond to this division.) Again the judges referred to the provision for termination upon reasonable notice and commented that the scale charges for 'partial services' seemed to be so fixed that they contained an in-built compensation for the use of designs and drawings right through to completion of the work. Lord Denning pointed out that in the *Blair* case charges had been in accordance with the RIBA scale, i.e. 1/6 of the full fee. But in this case the architect had charged on 'agreed nominal fee' basis, and his fee was far less than the percentage fee (which would have been, at 1/6, some £900). The Court of Appeal confirmed that there was an infringement, that an implied licence had not arisen, and that damages of £500 were reasonable.

Conclusions

8.11 From these two decisions it would appear that charging by the RIBA scales for partial services (whether originally contemplated or brought about by a termination) will give rise to an implied licence, while charging a nominal fee will not. The RIBA Architect's Appointment provides that the client will have an express licence to use the drawings only for the specific purpose for which they were prepared, and in particular that the preparation of drawings for obtaining planning permission does not carry with it the right to use them for construction of the building without the architect's express consent (which ought not to be unreasonably withheld).

8.12 The implied licence probably includes a right to modify the plans, although the law is not settled on this point (*Hunter v Fitzroy Robinson* [1978] FSR 167). If the Architect's Appointment does not apply, the probability is that the implied licence will not be revocable by the architect even if his fees have not been paid (this point is not settled law, but see Laddie, Prescott and Vitoria *The Modern Law of Copyright*).

Alterations to architect's drawings and works of architecture

8.13 If the client alters the plans or the completed building, the probability is that he will not thereby be in breach of the architect's copyright (*Hunter v Fitzroy Robinson*). However, the client may not 'sell or hire' buildings or plans as the unaltered work of the architect (see Section 11 below dealing with moral rights).

9 Remedies for infringement

Injunction

9.01 An injunction can be obtained to prevent the construction of a building that would infringe the copyright in another building, even if that building is part-built. Section 17 of the 1956 act, provided that no injunction could be granted after the construction of a building had started, nor could an injunction be granted to require the building (so far as it has been constructed) to be demolished. This provision was repealed by the 1988 Act and is not re-enacted in any form.

However, there is a general principle of law that an injunction will not be granted if damages are an adequate relief. It is probable that a court would, in most cases, apply this rule in the case of an injunction to prevent the construction of a building when the construction has substantially commenced. The decision of the court will depend upon all the facts and circumstances of the case.

Damages

9.02 In *Chabot* v *Davies* the court held that the measure of damages for infringement of the designer's copyright was the amount which he might reasonably have charged for granting a licence to make use of his copyright. In *Meikle* v *Maufe* the court rejected an argument that the architect might reasonably claim the profit which he would have made if he had been employed to carry out the work which infringed his copyright. 'Such profits do not provide either a mathematical measure for damages or a basis upon which to estimate damages. Copyright is not the sickle which reaps an architect's profit.'

Mr Justice Graham in the *Stovin-Bradford* case confirmed the licence fee basis of the two earlier cases and awarded £500 against the plaintiff's request for £1 000 and the defendant's suggestion of between £10 and £20. Although this point has not been decided with reference to architect's copyright, it would appear that on general principles, exemplary damages could be awarded in addition to the licence fee where the breach was particularly flagrant.

In the case of *Potton Limited* v *Yorkelose Ltd* [1990] 17 FSR, the defendants admitted that they had constructed 14 houses, in infringement of the plantiffs' copyright, on a style of house named 'Grandsen'. The defendants' houses were substantial reproductions of the plantiffs' Grandsen drawings and they had copied the drawings for obtaining outline planning permission and detailed planning permission. It was held that the plantiffs were entitled to the profits realized on the sale of the houses, apportioned to include profits attributable to (i) the purchase, landscaping and sale of the land on which the houses were built; (ii) any increase in value of the houses during the interval between the completion of the houses and their sale; and (iii) the advertising, marketing and selling of the houses.

In the case of *Charles Church Development plc* v *Cronin* [1990] 17 FSR, the defendants admitted that they had had a house built based on plans which were the copyright of the plaintiff. The distinction between this case and *Potton Ltd* v *Yorkelose Ltd* is that in the former case the houses were built for sale and had been sold, whereas in this case the house had not been sold and the plaintiffs had obtained an injunction to prevent its sale. In the former case the plaintiff sued for an account of profits. In the latter case the claim was for compensatory damages for the loss caused by the infringement. The judge held that the measure of damages was a fair fee for a licence to use the drawings, based on what an architect would have charged for the preparation of drawings. The architect's fee should be calculated on the basis that the architect would have provided the whole of the basic services – in that case 8.5% of the building costs.

Rider

9.03 The Court can award additional damages under Section 97(2) of Act in cases of infringement of copyright. In the recent case of *Cala Homes* v *McAlpine Homes* (CH1993 No. 5508) Mr Justice Laddie said that when considering whether to award additional damages, the Court must look at all the circumstances of the case. 'Although the Court must have regard to the flagrancy of the

infringement and the benefit accruing to the defendant, there is no requirement that both or indeed either of these features be present. It is possible to envisage cases where the infringer has gained no benefit from his infringement save for the satisfaction of spite fulfilled. In such a case, if infringement was flagrant it appears that the Court might award additional damages. It is somewhat more difficult to envisage cases where there has been no flagrancy and the Court would be prepared to exercise its discretion to award damages under this Section'. In this case Mr Justice Laddie found that McAlpine Homes had built houses based on plans which they well knew infringed the copyright in Cala Homes plans. For technical reasons which we need not explore here he did not actually award additional damages but he did hold on the facts in that case that the breach of Cala's copyright was committed flagrantly and that it was an appropriate case in which the Court should exercise is discretion to award additional damages under the provisions of Section 92(2) of the 1988 Act. He acknowledged that these damages could be 'of a punitive nature'.

10 Industrial designs

10.01 The law on this subject is complicated and extremely technical. It is not proposed to deal with this matter at length, but merely to warn architects, who may be commissioned to design articles or components capable of mass reproduction, to seek professional advice before entering into any agreement commissioning the design of such articles or components or assigning or licensing the rights therein.

Moreover, any architect who does design such articles or components should seek professional advice as to what steps should be taken to protect them. Industrial design falls mid-way between copyright (not registrable in the UK), which is concerned with 'artistic quality', and patents, which must be registered and are not concerned with artistic quality but with function and method of manufacture. The law on industrial designs was considerably changed by the 1988 Act. The present law is thus contained in the Registered Designs Act 1949 (as amended by the 1988 Act) and the 1988 Act.

Design registration

10.02 Certain designs which are intended for industrial application and which possess an element of eye appeal may be registered at the Patent Office, under the provisions of the Registered Designs Act 1949.

'In this Act, the expression "design" means features of shape, configuration, pattern of ornament applied to an article by any industrial process or means, being features which in the finished article appeal to and are judged by the eye, but does not include; a method or principle of construction, or features of shape or configuration which are dictated solely by the function which the article has to perform, or are dependent upon the appearance of another article of which the article is intended by the author of the design to form an integral part.' (Registered Designs Act 1949, Section 1(1).)

10.03 Unlike copyright, which is negative and entitles the owner to restrain infringements, registration of design is positive and grants to the registered owner the exclusive right to make, sell, hire, etc., any article in respect of which the design is registered. Design registration protects a person who has independently evolved an identical design. For this reason design copyright can subsist, and a registration be valid, only if the design has not previously been used or published in the UK.

Copyright Act 1956

10.04 The Copyright Act 1956 established two sets of rules in respect of artistic designs created before or after 1 June 1957. The basic principle concerning works created *before* this date is that copyright in the original artistic design may be lost if at the time it was created it was capable of being registered as a design under the Design Acts and the author had intended that his design should be used as a model for multiplication by industrial process. After this date, artistic copyright was lost only in respect of designs actually used for industrial reproduction and only in so far as so used. Copyright protection continued for any form of user, and as the date of actual use is what mattered, previous publication of the artistic work did not prevent a subsequent registration of the design for industrial application.

Design Copyright Act 1968

10.05 The policy behind the 1968 Act was simple: the Copyright Acts were concerned with articles of artistic craftsmanship, not mass-productions. The Registered Designs Act 1949 provided all the protection necessary for industrial designs, and those who did not avail themselves of it had only themselves to blame – there was no need for two hammers to hit one nail. Unhappily, design pirates often proved to be so much quicker than the Registrar that they frequently pinched the nail before the hammer fell. This led to the passing of the Design Copyright Act 1968, which amended the relevant section of the 1956 Act so that industrial designs which were also artistic works (and these include design and production drawings) enjoyed artistic copyright for a period of 15 years. Purely functional designs, incapable of registration, enjoyed copyright protection for 50 years plus life.

Protection by registration

10.06 Registered design protection lasts for 5 years, on payment of fees, and is renewable up to 25 years. The owner of the registered design would normally be the original author, and therefore the copyright owner as well, but frequently manufacturers who commission a component insist upon the design being registered in their names.

Definition of industrial use

10.07 A design is taken to have been used industrially for the purpose of the Registered Designs Act if it is applied to more than 50 articles.

Copyright, Designs and Patents Act 1988

10.08 The Act largely abolished copyright protection for most industrial designs and instead introduced a new unregistered right described as 'design right'. 'Design' means the design of any aspect of the shape or configuration (whether internal or external) or the whole or part of an article.

It should be noted that design right does not subsist in a method or principle of construction, nor does it subsist in surface decoration. Moreover, it does not subsist in features of shape or configuration of an article which enables the article to be connected to, or placed in, around or against, another article so that either article may perform its function; nor must it be dependent upon the appearance of another article of which the article is intended by the designer to be an integral part. This means that designs of spare parts are normally excluded from design right protection. Because design right subsists additionally to and does not replace artistic copyright, the exclusions from design right protection do not remove artistic copyright protection from, for example, surface decoration.

Design right does not subsist unless and until the design has been recorded in a design document or an article has been made to the design.

Design right expires 15 years from the end of the calendar year in which the design was first recorded in a design document or an article was made to the design. Alternatively, if articles made to the design are made available for sale or hire within five years from the end of that calendar year, the design right will expire 10 years from the end of the calendar year in which that first occurred.

To qualify for design right protection the requirements set out in Sections 217 to 221 of the Act must be met: these are too detailed to be set out here but have similarity to the qualification requirements described in Section 3 above. However, the differences are such that reference must be made to the actual sections.

Conclusion

10.09 Any architect who designs something which he can foresee might have an industrial application is advised to consult a solicitor or a chartered patent agent before he publishes the design in any way. If he does reveal the design to a manufacturer before registration, his only remaining legal weapon may be an action for misuse of confidential information.

11 Moral rights

11.01 Moral rights of authors have existed in all continental European legal systems for many years, but the 1988 Act introduced them to UK law for the first time.

11.02 There are four basic categories of moral rights contained in the Act:

1. the right to be identified as author;
2. the right to object to derogatory treatment of work;
3. false attribution of work;
4. the right of privacy of certain photographs and films.

11.03 Under Section 77(4)(c) of the Act the author of a work of architecture in the form of a building or a model for a building, has the right to be identified whenever copies of a graphic work representing it, or of a photograph of it, are issued to the public.

Section 77(5) also provides that the author of a work of architecture in the form of a building also has the right to be identified on the building as constructed, or, where more than one building is constructed to the design, on the first to be constructed.

The right must be asserted by the author on any assignment of copyright in the work or by instrument in writing signed by the author. In the case of the public exhibition as an artistic work (for example, the inclusion of a model of a building in an exhibition), the right can be asserted by identifying the author on the original or copy of the work, or on a frame, mount or other thing to which the work is attached. If the author grants a licence to make copies of the work, then the right can be asserted for exhibitions by providing in the licence that the author must be identified on copies which are publicly exhibited.

There are certain exceptions to the right of which the most important is that it does not apply to works originally vested in the author's employer (see paragraph 5.02).

11.04 The author of a literary, dramatic, musical or artistic work has the right to object to his work being subjected to derogatory treatment.

'Treatment' means any addition to, deletion from or alteration to or adaptation of the work. The treatment is derogatory if it amounts to distortion or mutilation of the work or is otherwise prejudicial to the honour or reputation of the author.

The right in an artistic work is infringed by the commercial publication or exhibition in public of a derogatory treatment of the work, or a broadcast or the inclusion in a cable programme service of a visual image of a derogatory treatment of the work.

In the case of a work of architecture in the form of a model of a building the right is infringed by issuing copies of a graphic work representing or of a photograph of a derogatory treatment of the work.

However, and most importantly, the right is not infringed in the case of a work of architecture in the form of a building. But if a building is the subject of a derogatory treatment, the architect is entitled to have his identification on the building as its architect removed.

In the case of works which vested originally in the author's employer the right does not apply.

11.05 In the case of a literary, dramatic, musical or artistic work, a person has the right not to have its authorship falsely attributed to him. Thus an architect can prevent a building which he has not designed being attributed to him as its architect.

11.06 The right to privacy of certain films and photographs applies only to films and photographs commissioned for private and domestic purposes and accordingly is hardly relevant here.

11.07 The rights to be identified as an author of a work and to object to derogatory treatment of a work subsist as long as copyright subsists in the work. The right to prevent false attribution continues to subsist until 20 years after a person's death.

11.08 Moral rights can be waived by an instrument in writing signed by the person entitled to the right. However, moral rights may not be assigned to a third party although they pass on death as part of the author's estate and can be disposed of by his will.

12 Law of copyright in Scotland

12.01 There is no difference between the law of copyright in Scotland and England and the new Copyright, Designs and Patents Act 1988 applies equally to both countries with the exception of Sections 287 and 292, which deal with Patents County Courts and Section 301 which grants the Great Ormond Street Hospital permanent copyright in Peter Pan, all of which apply only to England.

25

Architects and the law of employment

PATRICK ELIAS QC
NICHOLAS VINEALL

1 Sources and institutions

1.01 The law of employment is a mixture of rules developed at common law (see Chapter 1) and those laid down by Parliament. The latter are playing an increasingly important part, sometimes modifying and sometimes supplementing the common law rules.

1.02 A useful basic division can be drawn between individual employment law, which is concerned with the relationship between employers and workers, and collective labour relations law, which regulates the relationship between employers and trade unions.

Individual employment law

1.03 The basic relationship between the employer and the individual worker is defined by the contract of employment. This is the starting point for determining the rights and liabilities of parties. But as we shall see below, the last 20 years have seen the emergence of a whole range of statutory rights relating to such matters as unfair dismissal, redundancy, and maternity rights. Furthermore, it is a fundamental principle that, save in certain very exceptional cases, it is not open to the parties to contract out of these rights. They provide what is sometimes called a 'floor of rights', below which the rights of employees cannot sink. Although these rights originated in different statutes, they are now found consolidated in the Employment Protection (Consolidation) Act 1978, though further amendments have been introduced by the Employment Act 1980.

1.04 An important feature of these rights is that they are not enforced in the courts in the usual way. These new statutory rights are enforced in industrial tribunals which consist of a lawyer-chairman and two other persons, one drawn from a panel nominated by the TUC, and the other from a panel nominated by the CBI and other employers' organizations. All three members of the tribunal should be impartial, and indeed decisions are generally unanimous. The purpose behind the creation of the tribunals is to establish a system for hearing employment disputes which will be cheaper, quicker, more accessible, and generally more informal than the courts. The intention is to enable the worker to represent himself if necessary (and this frequently happens, since there is no legal aid available for cases before tribunals). Furthermore, it does not cost the employee anything to take a case (unless he pays lawyers to represent him) and whichever party loses he will not have to pay costs to the other side unless he was frivolous, vexatious, or otherwise unreasonable in bringing or defending the case.

1.05 Two further points about these tribunal hearings are worth noting. First, in most cases which go to the tribunals (notably unfair dismissals and those where sex or race discrimination is alleged) a conciliation officer seeks to bring about a settlement of the case before it is heard by the tribunal. These officers are employed by the Advisory, Conciliation and Arbitration Service (ACAS), and, like the tribunals themselves, they are to be found throughout the country. They have no power to compel anyone to discuss the case with them. But it is often advisable to do so, because a settlement can save both publicity and the costs of the action.

The second point to note about the tribunals system is that there is an appeal from the industrial tribunal, but only on a point of law, to the Employment Appeal Tribunal (EAT). This is technically a branch of the High Court (see Chapter 1) but is differently constituted, consisting of a judge and two others with experience in industrial relations, rather than a single judge alone. Appeals from the EAT then go to the Court of Appeal, and any final appeal is to the House of Lords.

1.06 An employee who wished to bring a contractual claim, for instance for wrongful dismissal, was until recently obliged to take that type of claim to a court – either the High Court or a County Court. However, since July 1994 industrial tribunals have been empowered to hear claims in contract for damages arising from breach of the contract of employment, or failure to pay sums due under the contract. There is a limit of £25 000 on what the tribunal can award on such a contractual claim.

Collective labour relations law

1.07 The law regulating collective labour relations is still significantly the law of the jungle, being a power relationship. However, the law does regulate this relationship in various ways. First, it sets limits to the industrial sanctions which can lawfully be used by the parties. This area of the law is highly complex, and it is not considered further in this chapter. Second, the state provides conciliation and arbitration services (ACAS) to help promote the peaceful settlement of disputes. Finally, various rights are given to recognized trade unions, i.e. those which have been recognized by employers, and also to the officials and members of recognized trade unions (see Section 4).

2 The contract of employment

2.01 Every worker has a contract with his employer. But a distinction is drawn in law between employees and independent contractors. The former are integrated into the organization of the business, and work under what is termed a contract of service. In contrast, the latter perform a specific function and are usually in business on their own account – e.g. the plumber or window cleaner – and work under a contract for services. In borderline cases the distinction is often very difficult to draw. And the description of the parties as to their status is not decisive, though it will be a factor to consider in a marginal case. The main importance of the distinction in the field of employment law is that only employees working under a contract of service are eligible to benefit from most of the statutory rights, e.g. unfair dismissal, redundancy, and maternity. In addition, an employer may be vicariously liable for the torts committed by his employees, but only rarely for those of independent contractors (see Chapter 3).

Creating the contract: control of recruitment

2.02 The basic principle is that the contract of employment is a voluntary agreement. This means that the employer can choose both with whom he will contract and the terms on which he is willing to contract. However, statute law has curbed this freedom in a number of ways. In relation to recruitment, the employer can choose to employ whomsoever he likes, save that under the Sex Discrimination Act 1975 he cannot discriminate against a person because of his or her sex or marital status, and under the Race Relations Act 1976 he cannot discriminate on grounds of race, colour, ethnic or national origins, or nationality. But other forms of discrimination, such as against trade unionists or non-unionists, or on grounds of age, disability, religion, or politics, are not directly made unlawful.

The anti-discrimination laws

2.03 The scope of sex and race discrimination legislation is quite significant. It covers not merely recruitment to employment but also promotion and any other non-contractual aspects of employment. For example, if the employer gives certain benefits, e.g. cheap loans or mortgages, or training opportunities, he cannot grant these on a discriminatory basis. Also, it is not only direct discrimination that is covered, but also indirect discrimination. This arises where the employer stipulates criteria for a job with which ostensibly both men and women can comply, but in reality a considerably smaller proportion of one sex than the other can meet the criteria, and the complainant has suffered as a result. Unless the employer can justify the criteria, he will be acting unlawfully. A simple example would be an employer who requires applicants for employment to be 6 feet tall and 15 stones. Unless the nature of the job justifies these criteria, it will be discrimination, since obviously a considerably smaller proportion of women than men can meet these conditions. Under this indirect form of discrimination, age discrimination has been held to constitute an indirect form of sex discrimination. The civil service would not accept persons over the age of 28. A woman complained that this in practice operated as a form of discrimination against women because, although in theory both men and women could meet the criteria of being 28 or under, in reality a considerably smaller proportion of women could do so whilst remaining on the labour market because of the responsibility of having and rearing children. The EAT upheld her claim (*Price* v *Civil Service Commission* [1978] 1 All ER 1228).

2.04 Exceptionally, sex discrimination is permitted where it is a genuine occupational qualification, for example on the grounds of physiology or decency. The most relevant permissible discrimination for architects is where a job is given in the UK, but it requires duties to be performed in a country whose laws and customs are such that a woman could not effectively carry out the task. Even then, it must be *necessary* for the employer to discriminate for this reason. So if he already employs a sufficient number of male architects to cater adequately for that particular foreign connection, this exception will not apply. Advertisements for job vacancies also need careful drafting to avoid any suggestion of unlawful discrimination.

2.05 Those who consider they have been discriminated against may complain to an industrial tribunal. If the complaint is successful, the tribunal may award a declaration of the rights of the parties, an order requiring the employer to take such action as is necessary to obviate the adverse effects of the discrimination, or compensation which may include compensation for injured feelings. The legal employer is normally liable, but if the employer

has taken all reasonably practical steps to eliminate the discrimination, e.g. has a clear policy and monitors it, then he can escape liability. In that case, the particular managers who discriminate will be personally liable. There is no longer any upper limit on the compensation which may be awarded.

The interview

2.06 An employee being interviewed is under no obligation gratuitously to disclose details of his past. However, he must not misrepresent it, save that in certain exceptional cases he may lawfully be able to deny that he has committed any criminal offences if his convictions are 'spent convictions' within the meaning of the Rehabilitation of Offenders Act 1974. Whether or not a conviction is spent depends upon the nature of the offence and the period since the conviction.

The terms of the contract

2.07 The basic position, consistent with the notion of freedom of contract, is that it is up to the parties to agree to the terms which will bind them. Exceptionally, terms of the agreement may be struck out as being contrary to public policy, e.g. a term in unreasonable restraint or trade (see paragraph 3.35). But generally the parties will be held to their bargain. From an employer's point of view it is sensible for all the important terms of the contract to be committed to paper and for the job to be conditional on their acceptance. This may eliminate later confusion and disagreements.

2.08 However, in the sphere of employment law the contract is not always expressly stipulated in this way. A number of points need to be noted. First, in many situations there is no real bargaining between individuals at all. The terms of employment are agreed between the employer and a recognized trade union negotiating collective agreements, and variations in those terms occur as the collective agreements are amended from time to time. So the collective agreement operates as the source of the terms of the individual contract of employment.

Secondly, even where terms are expressly agreed between the parties to the contract, they will rarely cover all the matters that will arise in the course of the employment relationship. So the express terms will have to be supplemented by implied terms. These implied terms may be usefully divided into two categories. Some will arise because of the particular relationship between the employer and the employee, and will often depend upon the customs and practices of a particular firm. For example, it may have become the practice of overtime to be worked in certain circumstances, or for employees to be more flexible in the range of tasks they perform than their specific job obligations would suggest. Once practices of this kind become reasonable, well-known, and certain, they will become contractual duties. Other implied terms depend not so much on the particular employment relationship but are imposed as an incident of the general relationship between employers and employees. The judges have said that certain duties will be implied into all employment relationships, e.g. a duty on the employee not to disclose confidential information to third parties, to take reasonable care in the exercise of his duties, and to show good faith in his dealings with the employer. Likewise there are some implied duties imposed on the employer, e.g. a duty to treat the employee with respect, and to take reasonable care for his health and safety.

Equal Pay Act 1970

2.09 Thirdly, it is unlawful for the employer to treat women less favourably because of their sex. This is regulated by the Equal Pay Act 1970, which came into force at the end of 1975. Strictly it is a misnomer, for it covers not merely pay but also all contractual terms and conditions of employment. Broadly it states that if a woman is employed on like work with a man (and this involves looking at what they actually do, and not what they might be required to do under their contracts) or on work which is rated as equivalent on a job evaluation scheme, then she is entitled to have the same terms and conditions applied to her as apply to him. An 'Equality Clause' automatically becomes part of her contract of employment. The main exception to this is where there are differences which stem from a material difference, other than sex, between the situations of the man and the woman. For example, men and women may both be employed doing the same work, but the man may be employed on the night shift and the woman on the day. Here the man could be paid an extra premium for night work, but the basic rates would have to be the same (*Dugdale* v *Kraft Foods Ltd* [1977] 1 All ER 454). Again, if an employee is demoted because of illness, but retains his old wage, this will usually be justified.

2.10 However, if the woman is not employed on like work, she cannot complain under the Act because she considers that the differential between the respective rates of pay is too great. Indeed, in one case a woman who was a leader of a group of adventure playground workers was paid less than one of the men in the group. But the EAT held that since her job was more responsible than the man's, this meant that it was not like work, and consequently she could not claim the same pay (*Waddington* v *Leicester Council for Voluntary Services* [1977] 2 All ER 633)!

2.11 A woman who claims that her employer is infringing the Equal Pay Act may take a case to an industrial tribunal. She may be awarded arrears of pay, but not for a period exceeding two years prior to the date on which the proceedings were instituted.

Race Relations Act 1976

2.12 It is also unlawful, under the Race Relations Act 1976, to discriminate on grounds of race, colour, ethnic or national origins, or nationality in respect of the terms of employment. As with sex discrimination, there is no upper limit on the compensation which may be awarded.

Statement of the main terms of the contract

2.13 The sources of the contract of employment are so diverse that Parliament in 1963 thought it desirable that the employer should give to the employee a written statement of the principal terms. Subsequent legislation has added to these terms. They should be given to all employees working 16 hours or more a week, within 13 weeks of their starting work. Alternatively, the employer can refer the employee to some document, e.g. a collective agreement, which is readily available and wherein all the relevant information can be found. But the written statement is not itself the contract of employment; it is merely the employer's version of the contract and can be challenged by the employee.

2.14 However, if the employer does in fact draw up a proper written contract, this will be binding upon the employee, provided he accepts it as such. If the contract contains all the information that would have to be put in the written particulars, the latter can be dispensed with.

Maternity rights

2.15 There are some important rights conferred on women in addition to the Sex Discrimination and Equal Pay Acts. All women are entitled to 14 weeks' statutory maternity leave under the Trade Union Reform and Employment Rights Act 1993. In order to exercise the right at least 21 days' written notice must be given to the employer. If a woman has 2 years' continuous employment she is entitled to up to a further 26 weeks of maternity leave. Again there are (complex) notice provisions. A woman is generally entitled to return to work after her period of maternity leave, again providing she has given proper notice, and a refusal to accept her will usually be an unfair dismissal. It will be an automatically unfair dismissal if the principal reason is a reason connected with her pregnancy.

2.16 Whilst away from work a woman may be entitled to either statutory maternity pay (SMP) or maternity allowance. The quali-

fying conditions are complicated and the following summary is a simplified version. To qualify for SMP a woman must have had 26 weeks' continuous employment by the time she reaches 15 weeks before the expected week of confinement, and she must have given 21 days' notice to her employer. The rate of SMP is nine-tenths of the normal weekly earnings for the first six weeks, and then it falls to the lower rate of SMP, which is presently £52.50 per week. That sum is paid for up to 12 weeks. The SMP is paid by the employer but most of it, or for small employers all of it, can be recovered by setting it off against employers' National Insurance returns. If a woman is not entitled to SMP she may be able to claim maternity benefit if she has sufficient employment or self employment during which she paid NI contributions. Maternity Benefit is payable for up to 18 weeks at either a lower or higher rate (currently £44.55 or £52.50) dependent on whether she was previously employed or self-employed.

3 Dismissal

Wrongful dismissal at common law

3.01 The most significant intervention of statute law in the area of individual rights has been in relation to dismissal. At common law, provided the employer terminates the contract in accordance with its terms, the employee will have no redress. Generally this means that the employer must give the employee that notice to which he is entitled under his contract of employment. The relevant period of notice will often be specified in the contract, but if it is not, then it will be a reasonable period. However, statute law now lays down a minimum period of notice which must be given, whatever the contract says. This is 1 week's notice for each year of employment up to 12 years, i.e. if 2 years' employment, 2 weeks' notice; 6 years', 6 weeks'; 10 years', 10 weeks'; 14 years', 12 weeks', because this is the maximum minimum period! The contract may stipulate more than this, but not less. Note that this is the notice that the employer must give to the employee. It does not operate the other way. An employee with over 4 weeks' service must give 1 week's notice, but that is the only minimum requirement. Again, though, the contract might specify a longer period.

3.02 If the employer dismisses with no notice or with inadequate notice, then this is termed a 'wrongful dismissal', and the employee will have a remedy in the ordinary courts for breach of contract. The only exception is where the employee has committed an act of gross misconduct; then he may be lawfully summarily dismissed. But the courts do not readily find that misconduct is gross. Such conduct might include dishonesty or physical violence.

Unfair dismissal

3.03 The common law, then, sees a man's job essentially in contractual terms. Provided the contract is complied with, the employee has no grounds of complaint. This means that the reason for a dismissal can rarely be questioned at common law. As long as the employer has given the required notice, it matters not whether it is because the employee is dishonest, or smokes cigarettes, or has blond hair. Managerial prerogative is left untouched. But unfair dismissal does question management's reasons in a much more fundamental way. It requires the employer to have a fair reason for the dismissal, and to be acting reasonably in relying upon it.

The basic law of unfair dismissal can be considered under the following heads.

Eligibility

3.04 The employee must be eligible to take his complaint. This means he must have 2 years' continuous employment, he must be below the normal retiring age for the job or, if there is none, 65 if a man or 60 if a woman; he cannot claim if he ordinarily works abroad (though if he works in various countries but his base is in

Britain, he will not fall into this category); and he must present his claim within 3 months of the dismissal.

Dismissal

3.05 The employee must show that he has been dismissed. Sometimes what in form appears to be a resignation will in law constitute a dismissal (known as constructive dismissal). For example, if the employer unilaterally reduces the wages or alters the hours of work, the employee may leave and claim that he has been dismissed (though the dismissal is not inevitably unfair). Moreover, if the employer takes action which involves destroying the trust and confidence in the employment relationship, this will likewise entitle the employee to leave and claim that he has been dismissed. For instance, such conduct as falsely and without justification accusing an employee of theft, failing to support a supervisor, upbraiding a supervisor in the presence of her subordinates, and a director using intemperate language and criticizing his personal secretary in front of a third party, have all been held to amount to conduct which justifies the employee leaving and claiming that he has been dismissed. In one case a judge even suggested that unwanted amorous advances to a female employee would fall into that category! Technically all these matters constitute a breach of contract, though, of course, it is hardly likely that they would be expressly dealt with in any written document. In addition, a refusal to renew a fixed term contract will amount to a dismissal (see paragraph 3.27).

A fair reason

3.06 Once a dismissal is established, the employer must show that he has a fair reason for the dismissal. A number of reasons are specifically stated to be fair – misconduct, capability, redundancy, the fact that a statutory provision prohibits a person from working, and any other substantial reason.

Capability covers both inherent incompetence and incapability arising from ill health. The latter may include a prolonged absence or perhaps a series of short, intermittent absences. Some other substantial reason is a residual category covering a potentially wide range of reasons. Perhaps the most important is that it may justify dismissals where the employer takes steps to protect his business interests. For example, an employer who was concerned about his employees leaving and setting up in competition decided to require them to enter into a restraint of trade agreement (see paragraph 3.35). Some employees refused to sign the agreement and were dismissed. They claimed that the dismissal was unfair. They had merely kept to the terms of their contract; it was the employer who was seeking to change them. Nevertheless, the dismissal was considered to be fair. The employer was entitled to require this change, under threat of ultimate dismissal, in order to protect his interests (*R S Components Ltd* v *Irwin* [1973] ICR 535). Again, employees who are dismissed because they refuse to accept new hours of work introduced by the employer may well be found to have been fairly dismissed if the changes had been made in order to improve efficiency.

The employer must be acting reasonably

3.07 But it is not enough simply for the employer to have a fair reason. In addition, the tribunal must be satisfied that he is acting reasonably in relying upon that fair reason. Many factors may have to be considered in determining this question. The length of service of the employee, the need for the employer to act consistently, the size and resources of the company or firm will all be relevant factors. For example, a small firm cannot as readily accommodate the lengthy illness of an employee as a large organization.

Procedural factors are often important in these cases. ACAS has produced a code of practice on disciplinary matters – Disciplinary Practice and Procedures in Employment. Like other codes, it is not directly legally binding but should be taken into account in any legal proceedings before a tribunal.

3.08 The code emphasizes the need for warnings, a chance to state a case, and a right of appeal. Usually two warnings will be necessary before the dismissal is carried out. But the code is not sacred: it is advisable for the employer to follow its guidelines in most cases, but a failure to do so will not make a dismissal automatically unfair. For example, there are a number of situations in which the warning procedure can be dispensed with, e.g. where the employee commits gross misconduct, or is negligent in circumstances where the employer cannot afford a repeat performance (e.g. the airline pilot who crashed his plane on landing), or makes it plain that he is at odds with the system of work developed by the employer and intends to do things his own way.

3.09 Employers have got to be especially careful to ensure that the procedure they adopt when deciding to dismiss somebody is fair in itself. The employer cannot say 'I know the procedure I used was unfair, but as it turns out it would not have made any difference to the result even if I had operated a fair procedure'. The view of the courts is that an employee dismissed under an unfair procedure has (in almost all cases) been unfairly dismissed. (See the important case of *Polkey* v *Dayton Services Limited* [1988] ICR 142). Such an employee will probably not recover much compensation if the only thing that made his dismissal unfair was the procedure, but in some circumstances a procedural flaw can make the difference between a large award and no award at all.

3.10 Strictly the ACAS code of practice and procedure applies only to disciplinary cases, but analogous requirements have been required in other dismissals. For example, in illness cases it is hardly apt to talk of warning the employee that he will be dismissed if he does not return. 'Counselling' is a more appropriate term. The employer should consult with the employee and his doctor about the illness, its likely duration, and the chances of the employee being able to do the same work on his return. In the light of this evidence, together with the need of the employer to have the work done and the extent to which he might be expected to be able to cover the absence, the employer must decide at what point it is reasonable to dismiss the employee. Consultation in redundancy cases is also important.

3.11 One general point in these cases is that it is not open to the tribunal to find a dismissal unfair merely because it disagrees with the employer. To put it colloquially, it must not 'second guess' the employer. For example, in a disciplinary case a tribunal might conclude that it would probably have given a further, final warning before dismissing. But that does not necessarily make the dismissal unfair. It is often perfectly possible for there to be a number of reasonable responses to a particular situation. One employer might dismiss, another might give a final warning, yet both may be acting within the range of reasonable responses to particular conduct. Provided the employer acts in a way in which a reasonable employer might have acted, the tribunal should not find the dismissal to be unfair.

Remedies

3.12 There are three remedies envisaged: reinstatement, which means the employee being given the old job back and treated in all respects as though he had never been dismissed; re-engagement, which may involve being taken back in a different job, or perhaps in the same job but without back-pay, or on slightly different terms; and compensation. A tribunal must consider the three remedies in the order just given. In deciding whether to order reinstatement or re-engagement, the tribunal must consider three factors: (1) whether the employee wants his job back – if not, the tribunal must go straight on to consider compensation; (2) whether it is practicable to take the employee back – and in regard to a small firm it is likely that a tribunal will find that it is not because of personality conflicts involved; and (3) whether the employee has caused or contributed to his own dismissal – if he has, at least to any significant degree, he is unlikely to be awarded his job back.

3.13 Usually employees do not want reinstatement or re-engagement, so the tribunal simply assesses compensation. However, even if reinstatement or re-engagement is ordered, the employer is not finally compelled to obey the order, though he will have to pay additional compensation if he refuses to do so.

3.14 The usual compensation is made up of two elements. One is the basic award, which is calculated in essentially the same way as a redundancy payment (see paragraph 3.22). The other is the compensatory award, which is designed to take account of the actual loss suffered by the employee following from the dismissal. This will depend on such factors as when he is likely to obtain new employment, and what he will then earn. Obviously the assessment is very approximate. Furthermore, the amount will be reduced if the employee has caused or contributed to his own dismissal, the tribunal deciding what reduction would be just and equitable in all the circumstances, e.g. the tribunal may find that the employee is 50 per cent to blame and reduce his compensation by half. The compensatory award is subject to a final maximum level of £11 000.

Redundancy

3.15 Sometimes jobs come to an end because there is no more work for the firm or for particular employees employed by it. Usually a dismissal for these reasons will constitute a dismissal for redundancy as defined by the Employment Protection (consolidation) Act 1978, though since the concept of redundancy as defined in that Act is a rather technical one, it should not be assumed that every case where the employee is dismissed for business efficiency reasons and through no fault of his own will be a redundancy.

3.16 The three main situations in which a redundancy arises are (1) where the employer closes down altogether; (2) where the employer moves the place of work (though it should be noted that the place of work is where the employee can be required to work under his contract and not where he normally works, e.g. if the contract stipulates that he can be required to work anywhere in Great Britain and the firm moves from London to Glasgow, but his job is still available in Glasgow, this is not a redundancy); and (3) where the need for employees to do a particular kind of work has ceased or diminished.

Establishing a redundancy claim

3.17 As with unfair dismissal the employee must jump a number of hurdles before he can successfully claim for redundancy.

Eligibility

3.18 He must be eligible to present the claim. In order to do this he must have 2 years' employment over the age of 18, be below 65, and normally work in Great Britain. (Exceptionally, although he normally works abroad, he will be entitled to claim if he is in Great Britain at the employer's request at the time of dismissal.)

Dismissal

3.19 This is defined in the same way as for unfair dismissal. So constructive dismissal applies here also. One point to note, though, is that an advanced warning of redundancy at some time in the future, with no specific date of dismissal being given, is not in law a dismissal. Consequently, an employee who leaves in response to this warning may well be disentitled from claiming under the Act.

Redundancy

3.20 There must be a redundancy situation as outlined above.

Offers of alternative employment

3.21 Once these three hurdles are crossed, the employee is *prima facie* entitled to redundancy pay. But he loses that entitlement if the employer offers him suitable alternative employment which he unreasonably refuses. The job is unlikely to be considered suitable if it means a significant loss of status or pay. Whether any refusal is reasonable will depend upon the employee's personal circumstances. However, the employee does have a trial period of up to four weeks to decide whether a job is suitable, and within that period he is working without prejudice to his redundancy claim. But, of course, if he refuses the job after the trial period, it will still be open to the employer to claim that it was suitable employment and has been unreasonably refused.

Amount

3.22 The employee's compensation depends on his age, wages at the time he was dismissed, and years of service. Broadly speaking it is 1/2 a week's pay for a complete year of service between the ages of 18 and 22, 1 week's pay for each year of service between 24 and 41, and $1^1/_2$ weeks' pay for each complete year of service between 41 and 65. The maximum number of years that can be taken into account is 20. The week's pay is calculated from the gross figure, but is subject to a maximum (at present) of £205 per week. So the most that can be recovered under the statute is for someone with 20 years' service, all over the age of 41, who on dismissal was earning at least £205 per week gross. He will receive £205 × 20 × $1^1/_2$ = £6 150. Of course, employers may voluntarily pay more than the law requires, or they may be bound to pay more than the law requires by a term in the contract of employment.

3.23 Employees in their 64th year when they are dismissed have their redundancy payment reduced by $^1/_{12}$ for each month of their 64th year, so that by the time they reach 65 their redundancy payment has reduced to nil. Of course this makes good sense: employees who retire do not get redundancy payments.

3.24 The redundancy fund, which used to help employers meet redundancy payments, has been abolished.

Redundancy and unfair dismissal

3.25 Generally a redundancy is a fair reason for dismissal. But it might occasionally constitute an unfair dismissal, e.g. if the employer selects trade unionists first, or selects on a wholly unreasonable basis, or perhaps fails to consult with the employees affected. In calculating the unfair dismissal compensation, any redundancy payment already made will be taken into account.

Consultation with recognized trade unions and the D of E

3.26 This is discussed in paragraphs 4.04 to 4.06.

Fixed term contracts

3.27 Special rules apply to fixed term contracts. First, if a fixed term contract is not renewed, this in law amounts to a dismissal. But it is not necessarily unfair. In particular, if the employee is taken on for a fixed period and knows in advance that his contract is likely to be temporary and will not be renewed when the fixed term expires, a refusal to renew the contract is likely to be justified. The employer will still have to show that he is acting reasonably in not renewing the contract, but that should not be too difficult in most situations.

3.28 Second, where a fixed term contract is for a year or more, an employee may sign away his rights to unfair dismissal, i.e. he may agree in writing that he will not claim for unfair dismissal if his contract is not renewed once the fixed term ends. This is one of the exceptional cases where an agreement to sign away statutory rights is binding. But such an agreement is not binding as regards dismissals which take effect during the fixed term, e.g. for misconduct. It applies only to the dismissal arising from the non-renewal of the fixed term. Similarly, rights to redundancy may also be signed away, but curiously only where the fixed term is for two years or more.

3.29 This leaves the crucial question: What is a fixed term contract? The answer is one with an ascertainable date of termination (though it is still fixed term even if the parties can terminate it earlier by giving notice). So if the contract is to last for a particular task, and it is impossible to predict how long the job will last, this is not a fixed term contract. When it comes to an end, it terminates because the task is completed. But this in law will not constitute a dismissal. Consequently, even if the employer is acting unreasonably in not continuing to employ the employee, the latter will have no claim for unfair dismissal.

Reference

3.30 An employer is under no legal duty to provide a reference. If he does so, there are certain legal pitfalls he must take care to avoid. If the statement is untrue, it may be libellous and he could be liable in defamation. However, he will be able to rely upon the defence of qualified privilege, which means that he will not be liable unless it can be shown that the statement was inspired by malice, i.e. was deliberately false and intended to injure the employee.

3.31 An employer who hires an employee on the basis of an untrue reference may bring a legal action against the employer issuing the reference. If it is deliberately false, the liability will be for deceit. If it is negligently written, e.g. claims are made which he could have discovered were false with some inquiries, liability will probably exist for negligence mis-statement under the doctrine of *Hedley Byrne* v *Heller* [1964] AC 465 (see Chapter 3, Section 2).

3.32 Certainly the employer owes a duty to his ex-employee not to prepare a reference negligently. In *Spring* v *Guardian Assurance Plc* [1994] 3 WLR 354, an insurance salesman successfully sued his ex-employers. They had negligently provided a reference to prospective new employers who, relying on the negligent reference, had declined to employ him.

3.33 Finally, if the employer dismisses an employee for misconduct or incompetence, but then proceeds to write him a glowing reference, he may find difficulty in convincing the tribunal that the reason for which he dismissed was, in fact, the true reason.

Duties on ex-employees

3.34 Once the contract is terminated, this does not mean that there are no further duties imposed on the ex-employee. In particular, the employee is not free to divulge confidential information or trade secrets to rivals. However, he can use his own individual skill and experience, e.g. organizational ability, even though that was gained as a result of working for the former employer. But the distinction between the knowledge which can and cannot be imparted is vague.

Restricting competition: restraint of trade

3.35 In addition, the employee may be prevented from setting up in competition with his former employer. But this will be so only if he entered into an express clause in his contract of employment which prohibited such competition. Even then, such clauses will be binding only if they are reasonable and not contrary to the public interest. They must not be drawn wider than is necessary to protect the employer's interests; otherwise they will be considered to be in unreasonable restraint of trade and therefore void. Reasonable restrictions might prevent an architect from soliciting the clients of his former employer, and they may even

encompass restrictions on the employee's right to compete within a certain area for a particular time. But if the area is drawn too widely, or the duration too long, the clause will be void and unenforceable.

4 Collective labour relations law

4.01 As mentioned above, the main provisions in the area of collective labour relations law are concerned with giving certain rights to unions and their officials. However, these are in practice given only to *recognized* trade unions, i.e. those with which the employer is willing to negotiate. There is no legal procedure by which a union can compel an employer to recognize it. The ultimate sanctions for non-recognition are industrial, not legal.

The consequences of recognition

4.02 Once a union is recognized by an employer, the following consequences follow.

Disclosure of information

4.03 The unions have a right to receive information from the employer without which they would be impeded in collective bargaining and which it is good industrial relations practice to disclose. However, there is a wide range of exceptions, e.g. information received in confidence, or information which would damage the employer's undertakings (such as how tender prices are calculated). Some guidance can be given by the Code of Practice on Disclosure of Information produced by ACAS. It should be emphasized, though, that no information need be divulged until the recognized union asks for it.

Consultation over redundancies

4.04 As soon as the decision to dismiss even a single employee for redundancy has crystallized, the employer should consult with any recognized trade union which negotiates for the group from which the redundancy or redundancies are to be made. This consultation is required even if the persons whom it is proposed to make redundant are not union members. The union should be given such information as the numbers to be made redundant, how they have been selected, and how the dismissals will be effected. The union may make representations upon these proposals, and the employer must in turn reply to their points, though he is not obliged to accept them.

4.05 In the case of collective redundancies, certain minimum time limits are specified. Where the employer is proposing to dismiss over 10 workers in a 30-day period he must give at least 30 days' notice, and where over 100 workers in a 90-day period, at least 90 days'. But these periods will not apply if there are special circumstances making it impossible for him to comply with them, e.g. a sudden and unforeseen loss of work.

4.06 In the case of these collective redundancies, it is also necessary to notify the Department of Employment.

Reasonable time off for union officials and members

4.07 Union officials have a right to reasonable time off with pay for industrial relations activities involving the employer, e.g. negotiating, handling grievances, and attending training courses connected with these matters. What is reasonable will depend upon such factors as the size of the firm, the job of the employee, and the number of other officials. Some guidance can be found in the ACAS Code of Practice on Time Off.

4.08 Union members also have a right to reasonable time off, but without pay, for trade union matters, e.g. attending union

The Court of Session Second Division
March 1812   312

conferences. Again the ACAS Code of Practice gives some guidance, though its principal message is that it is for employers and unions themselves to negotiate what is reasonable in all circumstances.

Health and safety representatives

4.09 Recognized unions are entitled to appoint safety representatives, who have an important role to play in helping to maintain health and safety standards. This is further discussed in paragraph 5.04.

Dismissal for union membership or non-membership

4.10 Under the Employment Act 1988 it is automatically unfair to dismiss an employee because he does not belong to a particular trade union, or because he has been refused membership of any particular trade union. The closed shop – and the complicated law relating to it – are now both things of the past.

4.11 The other side of the coin is the same. It is also automatically unfair to dismiss an employee because he does belong to a union.

5 Health and safety

5.01 Two major statutes concerned with health and safety apply to offices in which architects are employed. One is the Health and Safety at Work Act 1974, which is concerned with the general responsibility of employers, employees, and the self-employed, with respect to both each other and third parties. The other is the Offices, Shops and Railway Premises Act 1963, and the regulations made thereunder. This establishes in more detail the obligations of the employer in relation to health and safety. (Technically the duties imposed by the 1963 Act rest on the occupier rather than on the employer, but they will usually be the same person.) The infringement of the provisions of either Act involves the commission of a criminal offence. Offences may be committed by the legal employer, individual managers, and employees, for all have duties imposed upon them by the legislation.

The Health and Safety at Work Act 1974

5.02 This Act imposes a general duty on employers to ensure, so far as is reasonably practicable, the safety, health, and welfare of his employees. More specifically, he must provide and maintain safe plant and equipment, ensure that systems of work are safe, that entrances and exits from the working area are safe, and that such information, training, instruction, and supervision is given as will ensure the health and safety of employees at work. In addition, the general public coming onto the premises must not be exposed to health and safety risks.

5.03 If the employer employs more than five employees, he should draw up a health and safety policy and bring it to the attention of employees. This should include a statement of the employer's organizational arrangements for dealing with health and safety.

Employees are under a duty to take reasonable care of their own health and safety and that of fellow employees, to co-operate with the employer in health and safety matters, and not to misuse safety equipment.

Safety representatives and committees

5.04 Where the employer recognizes a trade union, that union is entitled to appoint safety representatives, who must then be consulted by the employer on health and safety matters. In addition, the safety representatives have a right to formally inspect at least once every three months those parts of the premises for which they are responsible; to investigate any reportable accidents, i.e. those that result in the employee being absent for three days or more; and to examine any documents relating to health and safety, save those for which there are specific exemptions, e.g. personal medical records. Furthermore, provided at least two safety representatives request this, the employer must set up a safety committee within three months of the request. This committee may keep under review health and safety policies and performance.

The Offices, Shops and Railway Premises Act 1963

5.05 This Act applies only to premises where the employer employs someone, other than immediate relatives, for more than 21 hours a week. It covers a very wide range of matters which cannot be considered in detail here. They include the need for adequate heating, lighting, ventilation, sanitary conveniences, washing facilities, and drinking water. In addition, the safety requirements include an obligation to maintain all floors, passages, and stairs properly, and to ensure that they are, so far as is reasonably practicable, free from obstruction and slippery surfaces. Details of the provisions are found in an abstract of the Act, published by HMSO (OSR9), which should, by law, be placed in every office, in a prominent position, for the information of employees.

Enforcement of the legislation

5.06 Inspectors are appointed to enforce legislation. Usually offices belonging to local authorities are inspected by inspectors from the Health and Safety Executive, whilst private offices come under the control of environmental health officers employed by the local authority.

5.07 The powers of inspectors are quite wide, having been extended significantly by the Health and Safety at Work Act. They can enter premises uninvited at any reasonable time, require the production of records or documents which the law requires to be kept, and oblige persons to answer questions. They may prosecute in the criminal courts if they find the laws infringed. But, in addition, they can now take effective action without the need to have recourse to the courts. They may issue 'improvement' or 'prohibition' orders. The former oblige the employer to bring his place or premises up to scratch within a certain specified period. The latter actually compel him to stop using the place or premises until the necessary improvements have been made. But prohibition orders can be issued only if the inspector considers that there is a risk of serious personal injury. The employer can appeal to an industrial tribunal against these orders. An appeal suspends the operation of an improvement order until the appeal is heard, but a prohibition order continues in force pending the appeal unless the employer obtains permission to the contrary from a tribunal. Breach of either order is automatically a criminal offence. Indeed, individual managers who are knowingly parties to a breach of the prohibition order may even be sent to prison.

Reporting accidents

5.08 Every employer should keep a record of accidents at the work place. In addition, some accidents may have to be reported to the enforcing authorities. These include fatalities and accidents involving serious personal injury, including those resulting in hospital in-patient treatment. These accidents have to be reported to the authorities by the quickest practicable means, and a written report must be sent within seven days. For other accidents, involving absences from work of three days or more, notification to the authorities is not necessary provided the employer has reasonable grounds to believe that the employee will claim industrial injury benefit. In this case the relevant information will, in any event, be sent to the Department of Health and Social Security, and they will transfer it to the enforcing authorities.

Compensation for accidents at work

5.09 The legislation discussed above is designed to prevent accidents. It establishes standards that can be enforced irrespective of whether an accident has been caused or not. Where accidents have occurred, though, it is not sufficient for the injured worker to know that criminal proceedings may be instituted. He will wish to recover compensation for the loss he has suffered arising from the accident. This may be claimed in one or more of the following ways:

1. Every employer owes a common law duty to take reasonable care to ensure the safety of his employees. More specifically this requires that he should provide safe plant and appliances, adopt safe systems of work, and employ competent employees. If an accident occurs because of a breach of this duty, the employer will be liable.
2. If an accident arises from a breach of the Offices, Shops and Railway Premises Act, then in some circumstances the employee may be able to claim compensation because of the employer's breach of statutory duty. However, no such claim can be made arising out of breach of the Health and Safety at Work Act.
3. The employer may be liable under the Occupiers Liability Act 1954. This imposes a duty of care on occupiers of premises to all those lawfully entering his premises. The standard of the duty is to take all reasonable practicable steps to make the premises safe. A claim under this Act may be made by someone not employed by the occupier.
4. Where a person, whether a worker or a third party, is injured as a result of the negligence of an employee acting in the course of his employment, the employer will be vicariously liable for the injury caused. Even if he is not personally liable under items 1–3, he may still be held responsible.

6 Employment law in Scotland*

6.01 Employment legislation is UK based and applies to Scotland as to England and Wales. The common law principles derived from Scots law are very similar to their English counterparts. A separate system of industrial tribunals operates in Scotland with appeals to the Employment Appeal Tribunal. Appeals lie thereafter to the Inner House of the Court of Session and to the House of Lords.

* Douglas Tullis of Lindsays Solicitors in Edinburgh has read this chapter and contributed this note on employment law in Scotland.

26

International work by architects

RICHARD DYTON

1 Introduction

1.1 Any international work undertaken by architects is subject to legal complications over and above those in Britain because of the different legal and insurance systems involved. However, increasingly, architects are able to work in a European and, indeed, world market and, providing appropriate advice is taken, the opportunities available outweigh the perceived complications.

1.2 In the following paragraphs brief summaries are given of the legal and insurance requirements of countries in which British architects find themselves involved. There are also references to the very different attitudes and cultures in those other countries which may require an increased sensitivity by UK architects.

Belgium

1.3 Architects are divided into three categories: principals, civil servants and salaried architects. The architect, despite being required to supervise the building work, acts only as adviser to the client and not generally as agent. He provides designs, costings and quantities, technical drawings and supervision. Contractors and architects in Belgium are jointly responsible for major defects in buildings for a period of ten years. Following changes in the law in 1985, professional indemnity insurance is now obligatory for Belgian architects and insurance companies have established a technical inspectorate to reduce the risk of major defects. Approval of a building by the technical inspectorate is usually accepted by insurance companies as evidence of satisfactory construction. The contractual liability of the architect is ten years following the completion of the building, but in tort the normal period of limitation is 30 years. However, with regard to latent minor defects which do not fulfil the statutory 'sufficiently serious' criterion, a client may bring a claim in contract up to 30 years from handover, provided the claim is made promptly on discovery.

Denmark

1.4 The contractual limitation period for claims against the architect is 20 years. However, in principle, under the standard contract conditions, architects' liability may only extend for five years from handover of the building (although in private construction projects this condition may be excluded). The Danish Building Defect Fund is an independent statutory institution which aims both to prevent the occurrence of building faults and to ensure the repair of defects in buildings covered by the Fund (for a period of 20 years). A one-off premium, equivalent to 1% of the building cost, is paid by the building owner to the fund. Half of this sum is used to cover the cost of an inspection which is carried out just before the end of the five year period following handover. If any defects are discovered, the fund has recourse against any consultant found to be liable, including the architect under his professional indemnity

policy, within this five year post-handover period. The remainder of the premium is used to cover the repair of any defects discovered after the five year inspection, for up to 20 years.

France

1.5 In France the architect's profession has traditionally been regarded as artistic rather than technical. By contrast, engineers are highly trained technically and tend to perform the type of technical duties undertaken in Britain by an architect. The architects and engineers in France are assumed to be jointly responsible with the contractor for the completed development. In the event of a claim arising from a defect in the building, all the parties are normally joined in the action and responsibilities will be apportioned between them. The contractual period of liability in France for claims against architects is two years from 'Réception' (approximately equivalent to Practical Completion) for minor repairs and ten years for structural defects. Liability is strict in that any claim against the architect does not need to prove negligence – merely that a building is not fit for its purpose. In addition, full economic and consequential losses are recoverable both in contract and in tort. Insurance is compulsory and 'decennial' liability insurance is taken out by the employer, although any claims paid by the insurance company may be pursued against the architect since subrogation rights are rarely waived.

Germany

1.6 The German construction industry is the largest and fastest growing in Europe. Architects and engineers supervise the construction of a project and the architect's responsibility does not, therefore, end with the design. There is more management and administration work in their job than is the case in many of the other EU member countries. Demarcation between engineers and architects is less clear cut than in the UK. Both professionals have four to six years of technical training before an additional two years of training for each gives them their qualification to practice. For contractual claims the limitation period for an architect is 30 years, but in tort it is three years. The standard German architect's appointment document (the HOAC) sets a statutory minimum fee scale, although clients have devised numerous ways to circumvent the statutory minimum fees. The liability for the architect is, like France, 'strict' in that negligence does not have to be proved, although this is normally only the case for claims of rectification of design or fee disputes. If damages are claimed, then there is a greater onus of proof upon the client. Some loss of profit is normally recoverable but not to the extent of full consequential losses as in France.

Ireland

1.7 The duties of an architect in Ireland are similar to those existing in the UK, so that his terms of engagement will exclude him from liability in respect of work or advice provided by other professional advisers but will make him liable for errors, patent or latent, in the design for which he is responsible. Whereas in England and Wales the position of an architect's liability in negligence towards third parties has been restricted by recent case law, this is not so for Ireland, where anyone affected by the careless act of another, whose interests that other person ought reasonably to have taken into account, would be entitled to recover compensation for negligence unless there was some public policy reason why this should not be permitted.

Italy

1.8 The roles of the architect and engineer overlap considerably. Clients may appoint an architect or an engineer to a project, or alternatively a director of works who takes responsibility not only for the design, but also manages and supervises the construction. Design-and-build contracts have been particularly popular in Italy. As in France the contractual limitation period for actions against architects is ten years. Professional indemnity insurance is not obligatory and is rarely taken out by consultants. Unusually, the construction industry in Italy is not prone to extensive litigation which is largely due to the cost and length of judicial procedures.

Netherlands

1.9 Liability in contract extends for ten years from major defects. However, one important difference in the Netherlands is that the damages awarded to a plaintiff may only amount to half the designer's fees and it is possible to opt out of liability altogether as part of the contract of engagement. Given the nature of the soil in the Netherlands, demolition and piling contractors normally have direct contracts with the employer. For the same reason, many contracts will have an engineering element.

Portugal

1.10 The role of an architect in Portugal is unfortunately ill-defined, but a significant difference is that, for contractors, statutory liability extends only for five years for private works and two years for state works after the commissioning of a building if the contract is silent on the point. Since 1991, professional indemnity insurance is obligatory for 'designers' (including architects) involved in private construction works, such insurance being to provide cover for a five year post construction liability period.

Spain

1.11 In the early 1990s the Spanish construction industry was the fastest growing in Europe, largely due to Government investment in Barcelona (Olympic Games) and Seville (EXPO '92 World Fair). Every building project in Spain must be designed and supervised by a registered architect who is responsible for the aesthetics of the building. He undertakes to design and supervise the building, provide project documentation and prepare sub-contracts for other professionals. Architects' registration is maintained by the 17 colleges of architects, one for each autonomous community. The 'Collegio' has considerable power since each architect must be a member, the level of fees is set by the college and it also provides building permit approval. A separate 'technical architect' is responsible for supervising the technical aspects of the building and his role covers much of the work which would be carried out in the UK by a quantity surveyor. Claims against architects must be made within ten years of the commencement of the project but this is extended to 15 years where there has been a breach of contract.

China

1.12 Most noticeably the culture affecting the industry is, not surprisingly, entirely different. For example, if the client decides to re-design at any stage in the works, then there is no cost implication for the client. A commonly used form of building contract

where British architects or engineers are involved in China is the FIDIC form (see later). However, the concept of an independent consultant acting fairly between the parties is an entirely unknown concept in China and in the event of any disputes involving the architect there is no adversarial system and no lawyers. Any claim, therefore, requires a compromise solution in order to resolve it.

Malaysia

1.13 Like many of the other South East Asian countries experiencing a very rapidly growing construction industry, Malaysia is strictly protectionist. No person can practice or carry on business as an architect unless registered by the governing body: the Architects Registration Board. Foreign architects can secure temporary registration if resident and possessing special expertise or forming the foreign component of a joint venture. Often the best way to proceed in Malaysia is by way of an unincorporated joint venture.

Hong Kong

1.14 Although sometimes described politically as a territory, Hong Kong legally remains a colony of the UK until 1997 when it is handed back to China. English law is, therefore, predominant although English cases are technically only persuasive (and not binding) authorities. Law from other Commonwealth countries is also used to decide the rights and obligations of the parties. Australian cases, in particular, can prove useful as authorities, for example, in relation to the interpretation of 'pay when paid' clauses. Again, cultural differences play a significant role in the legal system and the importance of 'saving face' means that many disputes are referred to arbitration rather than litigation in order to maintain privacy. Consequently, the procedure for arbitration is particularly well established and the prominence of the Hong Kong International Arbitration Centre is an example of its importance. Whilst arbitration procedure is similar to that in the UK, it is regulated by the Hong Kong Arbitration Ordinance and the UNCITRAL United Nations model law on arbitration and procedure is often used. Architects who wish to practise in Hong Kong face a relatively straightforward procedure, although it should, of course, be borne in mind that if work is to continue beyond 1997 a permit will be required from the Chinese Government.

USA

1.15 Apart from Europe, one potential, but as yet largely unrealized, market for British architects is the USA. Whereas in the UK the client normally engages the architect by an appointment separate from those of other consultants, in the USA it is far more common for the architect to be appointed by the client and then for the architect to sub-contract to other consultants the performance of the engineering and mechanical services. Thus the architect will assume vicarious liability for the actions of the consultants employed by him, something which the British architect is best advised to avoid.

In contrast to the UK position, there is much wider use of standard forms produced by the American Institute of Architects (AIA). The AIA produce a whole series of agreements from the 'Owner and Architect Agreement' to the main form of building contract, together with sub-contracts. These are widely accepted within the USA, although there may be slight amendments from state to state.

Although ARCUK is responsible for registration of architects in the UK, in the USA architects must be licensed and individual states and territories regulate entry into, and practice of, the professions within their jurisdiction. State statutes and regulations are based on the principle that practice by one who is not of proven technical and professional competence endangers the 'public's health, safety and welfare'. Licensing laws and regulations often restrict the use of the title 'architect', as well as outlining qualifications and procedures for registration as an architect, addressing any issues of reciprocity of registration with other states and defining the unlawful practice of architecture.

In a similar way, and unlike the UK, each state has its own Building Codes and these are the primary regulatory instruments for the design of buildings and structures on the site. Since local jurisdictions are authorized to adopt and enforce building regulations, Building Codes vary among states and even among cities within the same state. There are an estimated 13 000 Building Codes in the United States. The codes cover, inter alia, specific design and construction requirements, permissible construction types, and egress requirements.

Another important contrast with the UK is that there are no quantity surveyors in the USA. The architect is therefore responsible for the preparation of the contract documents for approval by the client. However, as mentioned above, the standard forms produced by the AIA usually do not require modification since they are widely accepted.

It is the contractor's responsibility to quantify and estimate once the architect has produced plans and specifications. Once again, the AIA produces a guide to tendering or 'bidding' which the client and architect can use to determine to whom the contract is let. The architect's role in producing designs and plans is not greatly different from that in the UK although in the USA 'shop drawings' are produced and a contractor is given somewhat greater scope to decide how to implement those plans.

On the question of liability in general architects tend to be sued slightly more in the USA than in the UK. This may be partly because the nature of US society is more litigious and partly because up to approximately 20% of all claims against the architect are personal injury claims. This latter characteristic is because building workers tend to sue the architect as a way of increasing the amount of compensation received for physical injury (the state-run basis being a no-fault compensation scheme, known as 'Workers' Compensation Insurance'). By accepting the state-run compensation, the worker cannot pursue his employer and may look to the architect to top up his damages.

In relation to insurance, there are general differences between the UK and the USA. Usually, in the latter, there is only one annual aggregate of liability cover whereas in the UK it is usual for each and every claim to be covered (although this may contain a limit in aggregate and other conditions). Also, in the USA there are specific areas of exclusion from cover such as a claim relating to asbestos or pollution. UK insurers will not automatically extend cover for a UK architect to work in the USA and it may be necessary to obtain additional insurance in the USA itself.

1.16 The larger firms of architects in the UK have already been active in seeking appointments abroad and their type of involvement will depend very much upon the role their client gives them. They may be appointed directly by the client as the main architect for the project; they may combine with a local firm of architects and form a kind of joint venture; they may establish a local office in that particular country governed by local laws; or they may simply have an advisory role either to the client or as the job architect in an otherwise uninvolved position. The Architects' Directive which was implemented in the UK in 1987 enabled British architects to practise in any other member country without restriction. In theory this sounds very simple but in practice there are still some restrictions as, for example, in Germany where foreign architects who wish to practise there must satisfy the qualification requirements to show adequate knowledge of German regulations and the language. The European Commission has struggled to force member states to implement the legislation properly. It has brought infringement proceedings against Greece, Italy and Spain and also forced Belgium to amend its legislation to give the Directive proper effect. As the harmonization process continues, the obstacles to British architects working within the European Union shall, likewise, diminish.

1.17 Although these opening paragraphs have concentrated mainly upon Europe, the Far East and the USA, the object of this chapter is to give architects a brief glimpse of some of the legal pitfalls in working abroad together with the areas where architects will need to seek specialist legal advice in relation to their employment worldwide.

The next section deals with the problem of conflicts between different jurisdictions and some examples of the different approaches used to deal with these problems.

2 Conflicts of laws

2.01 The legal problems which the architect encounters when working overseas always involve jurisdiction and proper law: do the courts of the country in which the building is constructed have jurisdiction over him and which law will be applied to resolve a dispute arising from the design and construction of the building? In particular, it is important for the architect to know whether the terms of his appointment will be recognized in another country; whether he will be able to enforce his rights against a foreign party in a foreign jurisdiction; what law will govern the performance of the architect's services; and whether the architect's insurance will cover him for work done overseas.

Jurisdiction and proper law

2.02 It is of the utmost importance that the architect gives early consideration, before the employer has retained other consultants, the Contractor or sub-contractors, to the question of jurisdiction and proper law. Even if the employer has in mind certain contractors/consultants, the architect should attempt to influence the employer in relation to the type of appointment, building contract or sub-contract to be used so that its terms are familiar to the architect and so that the jurisdiction and proper law clauses throughout the contract documents are consistent.

Clearly, the choice of jurisdiction to establish where and in which type of forum disputes will be heard is an important consideration and, in such a clause, consideration should be given to such matters as which law is to be applied, convenience, reliability of the different courts, speed, costs, the location of assets, and whether the resulting judgment will travel. It is possible to provide for exclusive jurisdiction clauses or alternatively, non-exclusive clauses which will allow the parties a choice of forum. In circumstances where there are restrictions on the parties' rights to choose jurisdiction, jurisdiction may be reserved to the local courts. For example, local statutes may prohibit choice of jurisdiction clauses in certain types of contract, or a party may have a constitutional right to be sued in the courts of his State. Furthermore, there may be treaty obligations which regulate the choice, or there may be relevant matters of local public policy. This underlines the importance of taking legal advice so that the position can be confirmed.

There should also be a 'proper' or 'governing' law clause which may be included in the jurisdiction clause but, more usually, is dealt with in a separate clause. Without such provision the English courts, for example, if asked to adjudicate on a dispute between two French parties with the subject matter in France, would apply French law on the basis that this implements the reasonable and legitimate expectations of the parties to a transaction. Although this is the principle adopted by the English courts it is far better to provide expressly in the contract for the proper law. This is because first, local courts in another jurisdiction may adopt other principles and, secondly, it does not leave the parties' intentions open and uncertain to be decided by the court. Most countries with established legal systems will apply the law chosen expressly by the parties to the contract.

Brussels Convention

2.03 The above analysis helps to answer the question, whether the terms of the architect's appointment can be made subject to a familiar jurisdiction and law despite the fact that he is working in a foreign jurisdiction and being subject to foreign laws, provided that care is taken in the drafting of the jurisdiction clause. There is, however, an important qualification to these comments, brought about by the implementation of the Brussels Convention of 1968 (as amended by the Accession Convention) which became law in the UK from 1 January 1987. Currently, the Brussels Convention relates

only to France, Germany, Italy, Belgium, the Netherlands, Luxemburg, Denmark, Ireland, the UK, Greece, Spain and Portugal.

Although the principles extend to other countries, such as Sweden under the Lugano Convention, under the Brussels Convention the general rule is that persons domiciled in a particular member country must be sued in that country. Domicile is a complex concept but can be loosely equated to residence combined with a 'substantial connection' with a chosen country. For corporations domicile is associated with 'seat'. Article 17 of the Convention, however, provides that where parties agree to settle disputes under the jurisdiction of the court in a particular member country, 'that court, or those courts, shall have exclusive jurisdiction'. This overrides any local law prohibiting jurisdiction clauses but it is important that the formalities are complied with in order to give effect to Article 17. These are that the agreement confirming jurisdiction shall be in writing or evidenced in writing unless it relates to a matter involving international trade or commerce, where other rules apply. In addition, there is a strict requirement of evidence of consent by all the relevant parties.

The question of the architect suing for his fees in the context of the rules of the Brussels Convention has been considered by the European Court of Justice in *Hassan Shenavai* v *Klaus Kreischer*. Here a German architect was suing a German national residing in the Netherlands for his fees. According to the Brussels Convention the general criterion for determining jurisdiction is the domicile of the defendant. However, the Court held, that in matters relating to a contract, the defendant may also be sued in 'the courts for the place of performance of the obligation in question'. The principal obligation in question, when the proceedings were for the recovery of architects' fees, was held to be the specific contractual obligation for the defendant to pay out the fee, in the Netherlands, rather than the contractual relationship as a whole. Thus in this case the place of performance was not the place of the architect's practice nor the site of the planned building but the place where the fee was to be treated as being paid, and this was held to be the residence of the client in the Netherlands. Whether that position would apply if the proper law of the contract were English is doubtful. The architect could have safeguarded himself by a jurisdiction clause providing for bare jurisdiction.

2.04 Where there appears to be a conflict between, for example, the obligations of the architect as described in the appointment and governed by English law, and the obligations of the architect as described in the building contract (governed by another law), the appropriate law to be applied would be determined by the particular court having jurisdiction under its domestic law. Thus, for example, if the dispute were to be settled in an English court, that court would be obliged to enquire with which legal system the overall transaction had its closest and most real connection. This would determine the 'proper law' of the contract and the judges would consider a variety of circumstances, such as the nature of the contract, the customs of business, the place where the contract was made or was to be performed, the language and form of the contract, in order to determine which legal system should apply.

2.05 The second question which concerns an architect, once he has gone through the trauma and expense of pursuing, defending or counterclaiming in a dispute against a party from another jurisdiction, is whether he would be able to enforce his successful judgment against that party. Most European Union countries are parties to the Brussels Convention, but outside the European Union the recognition of foreign judgments depends on common law enforcement and/or whether the UK has a treaty with the particular country concerned, which provides for reciprocal enforcement of judgments. If such a treaty exists then, subject to various formalities, the court will enforce the judgment against the defendant's assets in that jurisdiction provided, normally, that the judgment is for money only. Where no mutual recognition treaty exists between the country of judgment and the desired country of execution, the process has to be started afresh in that country unless common law rights can assist. This matter should be dealt with by professional advisers when entering into the appointment.

For enforcement within the European Union, the Brussels Convention is not limited to money judgments nor to final judgments and the court in which enforcement is sought has very limited powers to investigate the jurisdiction of the court which gave the judgment. In other words, it is much easier to enforce a judgment in a country within the European Union than outside it. Enforcement may only be refused on the grounds of public policy, lack of notice of proceedings, the irreconcilability of the judgment with judgments of the other State, and certain cases involving preliminary questions as to status. The foreign court may not question the findings of fact on which the original court based its judgment, nor can a judgment be reviewed as to its substance.

Insurance

2.06 The third question which the architect should always consider in relation to overseas work is the extent to which his insurance will cover him for breaches of duty in the particular country in which he is working. No general answer can be given to this, nor can any statement be guaranteed in the future, since insurers will take different views in relation to various countries and at different times. For example, the type of insurance available on any project carried out in France would be the decennial project insurance towards which all the construction team pay premiums. This would cover the architect for breaches of duty for up to ten years although it may not relieve the architect altogether because there may be subrogation rights to the insurers. However, architects who wish to practise in the USA may (due, perhaps, to the increased prevalence of claims brought against the architect there) have to seek separate professional indemnity insurance with local insurers since many UK-based insurers will not extend their cover to claims arising in the USA. In any event, before undertaking any overseas work the architect should check with his professional indemnity insurers whether or not he will be covered or can obtain cover from them in respect of that work.

An example of the specific problems associated with insurance is the concern caused recently by a law in Belgium (Non-Marine Insurance Law, 24 August 1992) and Supreme Court decisions in Spain and France which have undermined the effectiveness of 'claims made' policies. Underwriters in the UK, concerned that this trend may continue, are attaching UK jurisdiction clauses to the policies of their insureds who have either offices in continental Europe or who undertake work where the end product is constructed on continental Europe.

Contractual duties

2.07 The standard of performance which local law may impose on architects clearly depends exclusively on the law at any particular time in the country concerned, and this can only be determined through personal experience of the architect of work in the jurisdiction and by legal advice. As between the parties who are bound contractually, the architect's duties will normally be defined in the contract documents. If the local law provides that duties are owed by the architect to third parties in tort, or indeed to parties with whom he is already in contract, the standard and scope of such duties can only be determined by reference to local lawyers. The architect will normally have to ensure that there is compliance with the local building regulations, etc., although it will first be necessary to check the architect's role under the building contract to determine if it is simply to check or to ensure compliance.

Copyright

2.08 One important aspect of international work that should be considered by architects is the protection of their copyright in relation to the designs, plans and drawings which they have prepared for the overseas work. Although it may be possible to include provision in the appointment for protection of copyright vis-à-vis the client, the drawings may be used by a number of parties who may be tempted to infringe the copyright of the architect and use the designs elsewhere, without permission. The position in the majority of developed countries roughly approximates

to the provisions of the Berne Convention drawn up in 1886 with the most recent revisions in Paris in 1971. The UK has acceded to these provisions in the Copyright Act 1988. The Berne Convention gives protection for a minimum of the life of the author, and a post-mortem period of 50 years (although amongst EU states this period has now been increased to 70 years) and requires countries bound by it to abandon any rules of deposit or registration as a condition of copyright protection. The Berne Convention also provides for the protection of the author's moral rights, which protects the author's right to have the work attributed to his name and the right to object to derogatory treatment of the work (once the moral right has been asserted). Clearly, if the architect is dealing in a country which is a signatory to the Berne Convention he is fully protected. In other countries there may be a lesser form of protection, as under the Universal Copyright Convention, which gives protection for the life of the author plus 25 years and provides for any condition of registration or deposit to be satisfied when copies bear the symbol © accompanied by the name of the copyright owner and the year of first publication of the document. The USA has ratified the Berne Convention but there are a significant number of countries which belong only to the lesser of the two Conventions, i.e. the UCC (which includes Russia). In many developing countries, such as Thailand, no international treaty obligations subsist whatsoever and the architect will have to rely on local copyright law, if any. Local legal advice should be sought as to the means of protecting copyright and to comply with those local laws.

Commercial considerations

2.09 Finally, the architect should consider practical commercial matters, such as failure of the employer to pay fees, the country's available resource of hard currency, and exchange rate fluctuations, taking advice from persons experienced in international work who may be able to recommend suitable insurance to cover these risks, together with ECGD cover and political credit risk insurance and possibly a performance bond. In addition, if the advice of local lawyers is to be obtained, this might best be channelled through British lawyers since many foreign lawyers, such as those in Germany, are not obliged to advise on the most cost-efficient procedure in any situation.

3 FIDIC

3.01 Although, quite clearly, the FIDIC Conditions of Contract embodied in the 'Conditions of Contract for Works of Civil Engineering Construction' (fourth edition, 1987) apply to duties of the engineer, the role of architect and engineer, particularly in many European countries, becomes indistinguishable, unlike the system in the UK where roles are more clearly defined. It may be helpful to look at some of the problems which British engineers have faced when working with the FIDIC contracts and compare them with corresponding problems which may arise for the British architect if he is appointed under a normal form of RIBA appointment for a development governed by the FIDIC terms, appropriately amended. At least 49 separate national contractors' federations have given their stamp of approval to the FIDIC Conditions. The Conditions are used extensively in building and in industrial and process engineering as well as civil engineering. It is not unreasonable to suppose, therefore, that a British architect may, if he is working abroad, be administering the project under the terms of FIDIC.

3.02 Some of the clauses which require the architect's attention are the following:

Clause 2(1): Engineer's Duties and Authority Where the architect is acting in the role of an engineer, he must check whether this clause is in the contract since it refers to duties for which specific approval is required from the client, and these duties are listed in Part 2 of the Conditions. The items that require approval will generally accord with the legal code of certain countries in which the Conditions are used.

Clause 5(1): Languages and law   Clearly this clause is of major significance since the contract provisions will be construed in accordance with the specified law. The language in which the contract is written is also significant, not only from the point of view of everyday administration but also from the point of view of interpretation. Very often an international contract is written in two languages, one the local tongue and one the language of the engineering consultants who drafted the contract in the first place. In these cases there is an express clause which states that in the event of conflict or ambiguity between the two versions, the language designated the 'Ruling Language' shall prevail.

Once the law of the contract has been established, legal advice should be sought from lawyers experienced in international jurisdictional points and the local law. In addition, a translation of the contract is helpful (if not already in two versions).

Clause 5(2): Ambiguities and discrepancies   The architect should check whether this clause is included since it provides for the conditions of contract to prevail over any other document forming part of the contract. There may be an interpretation problem existing between the general conditions and the conditions of particular application (these are the conditions which would be included in Part 2 of the Conditions) and, according to the order of priority given, the conditions of particular application would take precedence over any standard printed condition since the latter would only appear in 'any other document forming part of the contract' and will be given the lowest priority.

Clause 8: Responsibility for construction and design   This clause is of importance because it sets out very clearly the division of responsibility between the contractor and the engineer or architect. As presently drafted, the engineer or architect has responsibility for the adequacy of the design of permanent works.

Clause 11: Inspection of the site   This is not usually a function of the architect although, under the RIBA appointment, the architect can be employed to advise on the suitability of sites and to make surveys and various other investigations. Under Clause 11 of the FIDIC Conditions there are certain items upon which the contractor is deemed to have obtained information by his own enquiries. Therefore it is important to determine whether such a clause has been amended in any way to require the engineer or architect to provide more information than usual.

There are other clauses of importance in FIDIC but to consider such would be to go beyond the scope of this chapter. The above details some of the main areas for consideration.

4 The future

4.01 As can be seen in other chapters in this book, the liability of architects is not clear-cut and is a point of constant discussion and negotiation, particularly in relation to the architect's appointment and the problems encountered by architects striving to stay within the terms of their insurance cover. In the UK this is due to the change of direction in the law relating to architects' duties. Clearly, when there is such uncertainty in our own country, that confusion can only be compounded when dealing with other jurisdictions, some based on the common law system (which is the basis of our own system) and some based on civil law systems as in many of the European countries.

4.02 The scope for work within Europe has been given a substantial fillip by the potential enlargement of the European Community to the European Union of 16 rather than 12 States. The inclusion of Austria, Sweden, Finland and Norway represents a large potential increase of opportunity in Europe for UK architects. These countries are comparatively wealthy per capita and generally have large public works projects. The European Union is expected to be enlarged further to around 20 States from 1996. Already UK architects have appreciated the significance of the German construction industry, which, in the eastern part of Germany, is expected to grow by around 15% in 1994. Further former Soviet-bloc economies are likely to be included in the expanded European Union and the opportunities for growth are evident. These opportunities are particularly available to the medium or larger sized UK firms because these firms should be able firstly, to analyse effectively the advertisements for work opportunities abroad and, secondly, to establish the necessary local link to enable compliance with local legislation. Those UK architects who most readily adapt to the changing legislation of Europe will eventually reap the rewards in terms of a much greater client base and work experience.

4.03 Elsewhere, architectural practices are increasingly looking towards the high growth economies of Asia, Thailand, Malaysia and Hong Kong in response to the lack of building work and intense competition at home. The main problems experienced in these locations are cultural and financial rather than legal. Increasing experience will, in time, overcome such difficulties and established firms will see the progression into China as the next step. In the USA, UK architects continue to be in demand for their particular style and, although by far the biggest problem is obtaining professional indemnity insurance, careful risk allocation in the appointment documentation increasingly enables UK insurers to extend cover for work in these territories.

27

Direct professional access by architects to barristers

ANTHONY SPEAIGHT QC

1 Introduction

1.01 Architect users of this book have suggested that, in view of the growing importance of legal advice in the work of architects, there should be a chapter discussing the exercise by architects of their recently acquired right directly to instruct barristers.

2 Why architects may need legal advice

2.01 Courts do not expect architects to be proficient legal advisers. But architects are expected to know some law. Mr Justice Gibson said in *B L Holdings* v *Wood* (1978) 10 BLR 48 at 70:

'. . . a professional man, such as an architect, who agrees to act in some field of activity commonly carried on by architects, in which a knowledge and understanding of certain principles of law is required, if the work is to be done properly and the client's interest duly protected, must have sufficient knowledge of those principles of law in order reasonably to protect his client from damage and loss . . .

In many particular cases a professional man engaging in such work will have, and display, a sufficient knowledge of the relevant principles of law by knowing, and by advising his client, that he knows little or nothing of them, and by refusing to incur expense on behalf of his client, or to expose him to risk of financial loss, until his client has obtained legal advice . . .'

The Court of Appeal, whilst disagreeing with the judge's view of the facts in that case, approved his approach on the principle of an architect's duty either to know sufficient law or to advise his client to obtain legal advice.

2.02 One example of a situation in which an architect is expected to know the law is in connection with any demolition or alteration of a building for which a consent is required from a public authority. There has been a recent case in which an architect was convicted of a criminal offence when he interfered with a listed building without the appropriate consent. In *St Thomas a Becket, Framfield* [1989] 1 WLR 689, a judge sitting in an ecclesiastical jurisdiction severely criticized an architect who was responsible for works of repair and redecoration to a sixteenth-century church without the 'faculty' required from the consistory court.

2.03 Another example of an area of law which an architect is expected to know is that of the JCT contract. In *West Faulkner Associates* v *London Borough of Newham* (1994) CILL 988, the Court of Appeal upheld a finding of negligence against an architect who took a mistaken view of the meaning of the phrase 'regularly and diligently' in Clause 25 of JCT 63. The architect took the view that before he would be justified in issuing a notice to the contractor under Clause 25 he must consider the contractor to be proceeding neither regularly nor diligently. The Court took the view that if the contractor was falling down in just one of these respects, that was sufficient to justify a notice by the architect. There had been no previous case on those words and there was no authoritative advice in any textbook. The RIBA urges caution in the matter of the determination of a contractor's employment. Even a solicitor had advised that it was a borderline case and that counsel's opinion should be obtained. One might have thought that the architect's bona fide opinion, even if mistaken, would be pardonable. But the Court of Appeal thought otherwise. The judges regarded the meaning of the phrase as plain, and held the architect negligent. In the course of argument the Court suggested that the architect would have made his position fireproof if he had taken legal advice: whatever the nature of that advice, and whether equivocal or forthright, an architect who obtains and follows legal advice cannot thereafter be held negligent.

2.04 The Court of Appeal approved the statement by the learned editor of Keating (fifth edition) on building contracts (that is Sir Anthony May, now himself a High Court Judge):

'The law of which an architect should know the general rules includes, it is submitted, all statutes and by-laws affecting building, the main principles of town and country planning law, and private rights likely to affect the works. He should also, it is thought, have a general knowledge of the law as applied to the more important clauses, at least, of standard forms of building contract particularly if he is to act as architect under such a contract. If his working drawings, plans or directions result in a building which contravenes the by-laws or building regulations which apply to it, this is, it is submitted, some, but not conclusive, evidence of breach of duty. It would appear to be part of his duty to keep himself informed of recent relevant changes in the law, including important decisions.'

Most architects would regard that as adding up to a pretty tall order. They have two options: master all that law themselves – or take legal advice.

3 Methods by which an architect can take legal advice

3.01 Whenever an architect finds himself in a situation in which a point of law may affect his work for a client, he may be said to have the following options:

1. The architect can tell his client that there is a point of law about which he is not confident to advise himself, and suggest that the client obtains his own legal advice through traditional routes. That course has the merit of safety in avoiding the risk of any allegation of professional negligence against the architect. But legal advice through the traditional route of a solicitor instructing a specialist barrister tends to be expensive. The

architect may not please his client if he sends him off to a solicitor too frequently.

2. The architect can seek his own advice through traditional routes. This course avoids upsetting the client, but involves a cost to the architect's own pocket, which there is probably no good reason why the architect should bear.

3. The architect can suggest to his client that the client authorize the architect to instruct a barrister to advise the client directly. The RIBA has approved the activity of an architect instructing a barrister as a 'Consultancy Service' within Schedule 2 to SFA/92. In this case the architect will not personally bear the cost of the legal advice, and the cost to the client will be likely to be less than under traditional routes to legal advice.

4. If for whatever reason an architect wants legal advice in a situation where a client will not be paying for it, the architect can directly instruct a barrister to advise him (the architect).

4 The Bar of England and Wales and access to its services

4.01 Barristers are those who have been 'called to the Bar' by an Inn of Court after passing the requisite professional examinations and participating to a modest extent in the social life of the professional community by eating a specified number of meals in hall.

4.02 Legal services are provided to the general public by those barristers who are engaged in private practice, or 'independent practice' as it is strictly called. All such barristers must be self-employed sole practitioners. There have been many inquiries into whether barristers ought to be permitted to form partnerships, and all have concluded that there would be no benefit to the public in them doing so. Some barristers take up employment in industry, commerce, local government or the civil service, but they give advice exclusively to their employers.

4.03 The work of a barrister is rather like that of a writer or, say, an architect appearing as an expert witness: the barrister must take responsibility for the advice he gives, and nobody else can recite his lines for him in court. He works as an individual. There is an important difference here between the services offered by, say, the construction Bar and firms of solicitors with strong construction experience: when a client instructs a firm of solicitors to give advice, the client generally does not know precisely who in the firm will handle the work, and after receiving a letter of advice may not know for sure who has contributed to its drafting. The client has the advantages and the disadvantages of dealing with a large organization. With a barrister, on the other hand, the client chooses in advance who is to do the actual work, and whose personal professional reputation is to be at stake.

4.04 The Bar has always been a referral profession. Traditionally, it was solicitors who did the referring. Rather in the same way as a general medical practitioner refers patients to a hospital specialist, so solicitors have over the years referred clients to (hopefully) appropriately specialist counsel. Not only does a barrister's work in practice come by referral, but a barrister is actually prohibited by the Bar's Code of Conduct from accepting instructions direct from a lay client. To some people this appears to be a purposeless, self-inflicted handicap to offering professional services in the modern world. But the prevailing view is that to obtain useful legal advice requires the presentation of reasonably coherent information; and that for the Bar to continue as a low-overhead, cheap-hourly-rate source of legal advice it has to depend on its instructions being prepared competently. However, the Bar no longer considers solicitors the only people capable of competent presentation of instructions.

4.05 In 1989 the Bar Council extended the right to instruct the Bar of England and Wales to a number of other professions, including accountants, chartered surveyors and architects. This followed a recommendation by the Committee on the Future of the Legal Profession chaired by Lady Marre. The Bar calls work from these new professional clients 'direct professional access' or DPA clients.

4.06 The principal purpose of the new arrangement was to save unnecessary costs. For example, accountants who wanted advice on a point of tax law from a leading member of the revenue Bar were obliged to engage a solicitor as little more than a post-box in forwarding on instructions. The change cut out one set of professional fees.

4.07 In the case of architects, the right of access applies to every architect registered with ARCUK. The RIBA and ACA have been accorded the status of recognized professional bodies to deal with the Bar Council on matters relating to the instruction of barristers by architects.

4.08 The Bar operates what is known as the 'cab-rank rule'. That is to say, a barrister cannot pick and choose between clients, or confine his services to only one group. A barrister must accept any work offered to him which is in his usual field of practice and which is remunerated at his usual level of fee. He cannot, for example, act solely for contractors or solely for insurance companies. He can decline to undertake any work at all for non-solicitors; he has to notify his professional indemnity insurers one way or the other about that. But, if he accepts DPA work at all, then he must accept work from any such client.

4.09 All barristers are insured in respect of professional negligence claims. It is a condition of independent practice at the Bar that such insurance is maintained.

5 The types of services which a barrister can perform for an architect

5.01 Broadly speaking a barrister offers two kinds of service:

1. Giving legal advice;
2. Advocacy at a hearing.

5.02 In its 'Direct Access to Barristers Guidance Notes' the RIBA has suggested the following matters on which an architect might seek advice from a barrister:

1. 'All aspects of planning law including consideration of whether planning permission is required for a particular development.' Barristers who specialize in planning work are normally members of the Local Government, Planning and Environmental Bar Association.

2. 'The interpretation of provisions in building or civil engineering contracts and the validity of actions taken by persons concerned with such contracts, e.g. architect's or engineer's instructions, notices of or leading up to determination of a contractor's employment.' Barristers who specialize in construction work are normally members of the Official Referees Bar Association.

3. 'Interpretation of the provisions in leases (such as rent review clauses) or conveyances or other documents affecting the use and enjoyment of land and boundary disputes.' In simple terms such work may be said to be in the field of the members of the Chancery Bar Association.

4. 'The law relating to valuations for statutory purposes, including compensation for compulsory purchase and planning restrictions, rating, taxation and leasehold enfranchisement.' Such advice would best be sought from a barrister with good experience of Land Tribunal work.

5. 'The effect on an occupier of land of any statutory control affecting the way in which land can be used or the products of land disposed of.' In most cases this will be work for the planning Bar.

6. 'Suitable methods by which land transactions can be structured in a tax efficient manner.' Such tax advice is highly specialized work for members of the Revenue Bar Association.

7. 'All aspects of landlord and tenant law.' Many barristers have good landlord and tenant experience.

5.03 Architects are less likely to find themselves instructing a barrister to appear at a hearing than they are to be simply seeking advice. Rules of court require that a solicitor act in High Court and County Court litigation; so in most litigation situations it will not be appropriate for an architect to use a barrister under direct professional access. The most common circumstances where an architect will be instructing a barrister to appear as an advocate are:

1. Arbitrations. For example, arbitrations under JCT contracts.
2. Public inquiries, especially planning inquiries.

Other tribunals before which architects might instruct a barrister to appear include Magistrates Courts, the Lands Tribunal and other statutory tribunals.

5.04 Architect arbitrators are entitled to instruct a barrister direct for the purpose of legal advice to assist them in reaching a decision in an arbitration. They will normally be entitled to pass on the cost as part of the cost of the award to the parties.

6 Method of an architect instructing a barrister

6.01 This involves no more formalities than an architect receiving his own instructions from his client. In an urgent case an architect can simply ring up a barrister and ask for advice over the telephone. But in general the interests of good housekeeping dictate that the arrangement be on a clear footing.

6.02 Almost all barristers use the services of a clerk to administer their practices. With only a very few exceptions, barristers in independent practice are members of organizations called 'chambers'. Chambers will physically be a suite of rooms. It will contain a library and a small administrative unit called the clerk's room. Since chambers are not partnerships, members of the same chambers may, and often do, appear on opposing sides in the same case.

6.03 In general the first step in instructing a barrister is a telephone call to the clerk to check whether the barrister is available, and to make such administrative arrangements as are necessary. So long as an architect bears in mind that the job of a barrister's clerk is, like a theatrical agent, in the ultimate analysis to fix up work for his principals, an architect ought to find the clerk to be a source of good advice on which barrister to instruct on a particular matter. The clerk to a set of chambers will have no reason to suggest other than the most suitable member in the chambers for any particular case; and, if a case is outside the field of work handled by the chambers, will be likely to give sound advice as to a different set of chambers which does handle such work.

6.04 Normally it is the barrister's clerk who discusses fees with solicitor clients. But there is absolutely no reason why a barrister and his professional client should not discuss fees, and in the case of work for professionals such as architects who have not traditionally instructed the Bar it is increasingly common for barristers themselves to talk about fees. There is no set charging pattern for the Bar. Sometimes fees are on a time basis at so much per hour or so much per day. In other cases a lump sum is negotiated in advance for a piece of work. It is always a matter for the parties to agree what suits them. The custom of the profession is that any figure mentioned is exclusive of VAT.

6.05 I recommend architects to make at least an outline fee agreement in advance. If a time basis is to be used, in most circumstances the rate ought not to much more than £100 per hour for an experienced barrister, and from £50 upwards for a young

barrister. Advice should be available from even a well-known QC for £150 per hour. If one barrister or set of chambers asks for too high a fee, try somewhere else. The whole object of DPA is the provision of legal advice at a lower cost to the client.

6.06 The RIBA has published 'Model Terms of Engagement of a Barrister' and recommends their use. It is a comprehensive and well-drafted document. But there is no need to use it, and very frequently architects instruct barristers by a simple letter setting out the problem on which they want advice.

6.07 Since access to the Bar is enjoyed only by members of particular professions, the Bar's rules require that the instructions come from a named individual member of the profession, rather than in the name of a limited company or partnership firm.

6.08 If a barrister considers that it is in the interests of a client that a solicitor should be instructed, he is under a professional duty to say so. This could be because the complexity of the case requires the resources of a solicitor to investigate or collate information; or because the case involves litigation in the High Court or County Court.

6.09 Letters addressed to a barrister personally at chambers will be treated as private correspondence and nobody else will open them. If the barrister is working away from chambers, they will not be opened until he gets back. Letters of an administrative character, such as notifying a date to go in the diary, can be addressed to 'the clerk to Mr X'.

7 Practice matters affecting architects

7.01 The RIBA has pointed out to architects that they are personally responsible for payment of a barrister's fees, and recommended that architects obtain funds in advance from clients; it draws attention to the RIBA members' Rules for Client Accounts. The RIBA states that if a member fails to pay a barrister's fees this would normally amount to professional misconduct under By-law 5. It is understood that architects should notify their own professional indemnity insurers that their range of services includes instructing a barrister to advise where appropriate. In the event of a disagreement between a barrister and a member of either the RIBA or ACA about fees, mediation would be provided by a joint body of the Bar Council and the RIBA or ACA (as the case might be).

8 Attractions for architects of using direct access to the Bar

8.01 Accountants have made considerable use of direct access to the revenue Bar: 75% of the work to some specialist tax chambers now comes from accountants, a remarkable change in the pattern of business activity in just five years. In many cases this is not new work: the same cases would have come to a barrister anyway, but now they are coming by a route which is cheaper for the client. Members of the RICS have also made substantial use of direct access, especially to the planning Bar. For the presentation of a case at most planning inquiries a surveyor and a barrister make up an adequate team.

8.02 Architects were slower than surveyors and accountants to start making use of direct access to the Bar, but such activity is now growing. Planning chambers report that architects who provide town and country planning consultancy services are now making the same use of the Bar as members of the RICS. That is to say, they use the Bar for opinions on such points of planning law as whether permission is necessary, and, if there has to be an appeal, they engage a barrister to appear at the inquiry. One of the attractions here for architects appears to be that they can provide a fuller multi-disciplinary service for their clients, all covered by one fee note.

8.03 Architects are also using the Bar for quick advice on legal points arising during the running of construction contracts. For example, I have been instructed by an architect to attend at a meeting in his office when the employer and design team were to discuss the possible determination of a JCT contract. Often such advice will be required over the telephone, to be, perhaps, confirmed in writing over the fax. Again, part of the attraction for architects seems to be the enhancement of their project management role by their ability to direct the legal consultancy.

8.04 Finally, architects are using the Bar when they themselves want advice, such as when a client seeks to avoid payment of their professional fees. The cheapness of direct advice from the Bar is a major factor here. Barristers' hourly rates are about half those charged by a solicitor sufficiently specialized to offer advice of equivalent worth.

8.05 A lot more thought by an architect would be needed before taking on the running of a major arbitration. Work of that kind requires considerable activity in the preparation of documents, taking of statements and the like, under severe pressure of strict timetables. In a complex case it may not be easy for an architect to combine the roles of expert witness and case administrator.

9 Selecting a barrister

9.01 As with most other professional appointments, the best basis for selection is previous knowledge or personal recommendation. Useful information may be obtained from the directories of their members which are published by the specialist Bar Associations. As each of the specialist Bars is only a few hundred strong, one is in each case talking of quite a small group, within which it should not be too difficult for an architect to locate a suitable set of chambers, if not actually the most suitable individual. Almost every set of chambers today has a brochure, which is available on request: the rules which used to forbid barristers from advertising have recently been progressively relaxed almost to vanishing point. Another source of guidance as to choice of a barrister is the Legal Adviser to the RIBA.

9.02 The specialist bars mentioned above in connection with the fields of work suggested by the RIBA are:

- **The Official Referees' Bar Association**, whose members specialize in construction contracts, professional negligence involving architects, engineers and surveyors, and generally the law of contract and tort as it applies to construction projects. Its secretary is Stephanie Barwise, 1 Atkin Buildings, Gray's Inn, London WC1R 5BQ.
- **The Local Government, Planning and Environmental Bar Association**, whose members specialize in town and country planning, compulsory purchase, and generally the law as it applies to the functions discharged by local authorities. Its secretary is Suzanne Ormsby at 2 Harcourt Buildings, Temple, London EC4Y 9DB.
- **The Revenue Bar Association**, whose members specialize in tax. Its secretary is David Ewart at Pump Court Tax Chambers, 16 Bedford Row, London WC1R 4ER.
- **The Chancery Bar Association**, whose members specialize in land law, trusts, conveyancing, leases, rights of way, boundary disputes, and rights and interests in land generally. Its secretary is Geoffrey Vos QC at 3 Stone Buildings, Lincoln's Inn, London WC2A 3XL.

9.03 Readers will have heard of Inns of Court and Circuits, as bodies to which barristers belong. They are of little significance to architects, or their clients. Knowing to which Inn a barrister belongs tells you nothing about his likely field of expertise. Knowing a barrister's circuit is of assistance only as the roughest of indications of the area of the country in which he may be accustomed to working.

10 The Bar in Scotland

10.01 The Scottish Bar is a separately organized profession, but in most significant respects it is very similar to the profession in England and Wales. Traditionally, the Scottish Bar has been a referral profession receiving instructions from the other branch of the legal profession in Scotland. It, too, has recently extended the right of access to it to additional professions, and amongst those are architects. Fuller information can be obtained from its professional body, the Faculty of Advocates (Tel: 0131 2265071).

28

Architects' registration and professional conduct in England

A. RODERICK MALES

1 The nature of professionalism in architecture

1.01 The concept of a professional person and an institutional profession has been continually evolving since the eighteenth century. Numerous studies of the subject have been made; the most concise appeared in 1970 as the report of the Monopolies Commission (Part 1: *The Report* A report on the general effect on the public interest of certain restrictive practices so far as they prevail in relation to the supply of professional services (Cmnd 4463). Part 2: *The Appendices* (Cmnd 4463–1)). Appendix 5 of the report provides a range of definitions and descriptions which vary considerably. There is general agreement, however, that a professional person offers competence and integrity of service based upon a skilled intellectual technique.

1.02 The history and development of the architectural profession in Britain may be studied in Barrington Kaye, *The Development of the Architectural Profession in Britain* and in Frank Jenkins, *Architect and Patron*.

1.03 The place of professionalism and the role of the professional person in a rapidly changing society is increasingly questioned not only by society in general but also by the members of the professions. The concerns of the architectural profession in a post deregulation period are reflected in the RIBA's on-going Strategic Study of the profession. Society's concerns are reflected in the Government's questioning of the role of the Architects Registration Council of the United Kingdom.

2 Architects Registration Council of the United Kingdom

2.01 In 1899 the first Architects Registration bill was placed before Parliament. It attempted to restrict the practice of architecture to those who were formally qualified. It was rejected as were several others that followed. Thirty-two years later a modified version of a similar bill was successful but the Architects (Registration) Act 1931 did not totally achieve its sponsors intentions. The Act provided for the setting up of a register of architects. The register protected the title 'architect' but it did not prevent others from carrying on the practice of architecture. This remains the position in Great Britain and Northern Ireland. It is an offence for anyone other than those on the register to use the title 'architect' but anyone may design buildings and carry out project administration.

2.02 The Architects (Registration) Act 1931 and the amending Acts of 1938 and 1969 provide for the setting up, maintenance, and annual publication of a Register of Architects; the maintenance of proper standards of professional conduct; and the provision of limited financial assistance for some students. The Registration

Council which administers the register is funded by the annual registration fee of those on the register.

2.03 In the main, admission to the register is by means of passing approved examinations in architecture and professional practice. A list of approved examinations is published by the Registration Council. These examinations are subject to periodic inspections by visiting boards.

2.04 Under the EC Architects Directive, persons who have qualifications accredited by other member states of the Community may be admitted to the register. Special provision is made for other overseas applicants for registration who are subject to interview and possible further study and examination (see Chapter 18 'European Community Law affecting Architects' paragraphs 5.01–5.03).

2.05 A name may be removed from the register permanently or for a stated period if the person concerned has been convicted of a criminal offence or found to be guilty of disgraceful conduct in a professional respect by the Council, following enquiries by the ARCUK Discipline Committee. The ARCUK Standard of Conduct for Architects is discussed below. Failure to pay the annual registration fee may also result in the removal of a person's name from the register.

2.06 The persistent use of the title 'architect' by a non-registered person after a warning invariably results in prosecution by the Registrar in the Magistrates Courts or in the High Court. Action could also be taken by an individual under the Misrepresentation Act 1967.

3 Codes of professional conduct

3.01 The codes of conduct of a professional body are devised to protect the interests of the clients of the profession and to

maintain the status of the profession in the eyes of society. The requirements of the codes develop with changing circumstances and the needs of society. They reflect the attitudes of the membership of the profession and the requirements of statute and public opinion.

3.02 The codes of the architectural profession have been the subject of increasing discussion and negotiation. In particular, the fee scale and the involvement of architects as directors of associated businesses in the construction industry have been subject to heated debate.

3.03 Two codes apply to the profession. The first is that of the Architects' Registration Council of the United Kingdom (ARCUK), to which all architects must subscribe. The second is that of the Royal Institute of British Architects (RIBA), which applies to its members alone. For a period, these two Codes were virtually identical but are now different in concept and content.

3.04 Failure to comply with the ARCUK code could result in the removal of the architect's name from the Register. The person would no longer be entitled to use the title 'architect'. Failure to comply with the code of the RIBA could result in the suspension of the person from membership of the RIBA but he/she would be entitled to retain the title 'architect' as long as his/her name remained on the Register of the ARCUK.

4 ARCUK guidelines

The Standard of Conduct for Architects

A registered person who intends to maintain his integrity so as to deserve the respect and confidence of all those for whom or with whom he may work in his capacity as an architect

Will assure himself that information given in connection with his services is in substance and presentation factual and relevant to the occasion and neither misleading nor unfair to others nor intended to oust another architect from an engagement

Will before making an engagement whether by an agreement for professional services by a contract of employment or by a contract for the supply of services or goods have defined beyond reasonable doubt the terms of the engagement including
    the scope of the service
    the allocation of responsibilities and any limitation of liability
    the method of calculation of remuneration
    the provision for termination

Will have declared to the other parties to the engagement any business interest which might be or appear to be prejudicial to the proper performance of the engagement which he will carry out faithfully and conscientiously
    with proper regard for the interests of those who may be expected to use or enjoy the product of his work
    with fairness in administering the conditions of a building contract
    and without inducements to show favour

Will if at any time he finds that his interests whether professional or personal conflict so as to put his integrity in question inform without delay those who may be concerned and if agreement is not reached to the continuance of any engagement will withdraw from it.

4.01 For many years the code of professional conduct of the ARCUK had been very similar to that of the RIBA. The differences have varied from time to time, but until December 1980 the only difference between the codes was a matter of technical definition. For practical purposes a person registered as an architect was subject to the same restrictions and conditions as a member of the RIBA.

4.02 The code of conduct now takes the form of a simple statement, the *Standard of Conduct for Architects*, based upon an in-

terpretation of the expression 'conduct disgraceful to him in his capacity as an architect' which appears in Section 7 of the Architects Registration Act of 1931. It promulgates the standard of conduct which architects are expected to maintain. The Architects Registration Council reserves to itself the right to deal with specific cases of complaint or comment on merit. The *Standard of Conduct for Architects* is supported by an explanatory memorandum which is revised from time to time in the light of the Council's findings.

Explanatory Memorandum

The Architects Registration Council of the United Kingdom is empowered under Section 7 of the Architects (Registration) Act 1931 to remove the name of an architect from the Register if after enquiry he has been found to be guilty of conduct disgraceful to him in his capacity as an architect.

"This power is not limited by any formal definition of disgraceful conduct and a registered person whose conduct in any circumstances appears to be disgraceful may be called to account for it under the Disciplinary Procedures (See Appendix 2).

Without prejudice to the generality of this power the Standard of Conduct for Architects draws attention in general terms to the more common circumstances of the activities of registered persons. It is published as a guide towards good conduct for the benefit of architects, the Discipline Committee of ARCUK and the public".

Every architect is expected to guard his integrity irrespective of his field of activity or contract of employment or membership of any association whether acting independently or through a corporate body or through any other person.

Subject to this and to Section 17 of the 1931 Act no specific occupation is proscribed nor is any restraint of trade imposed.

Any person who is uncertain about a particular course of action in the context of the Standard may seek advice from the Registrar who will if necessary refer the matter to the Professional Purposes Committee or through that Committee to the Council. Advice given will be within the disciplinary powers of ARCUK.

Where disgraceful conduct is alleged, the Discipline Committee may take into account whether or not the person arraigned sought such advice before carrying out the activity which is the subject of complaint.

Decisions of the Discipline Committee and any advice given during the course of the year will be reviewed by the Professional Purposes Committee and may be published in the Annual Report.

4.03 The standard does not prohibit any specific occupation or activity and it contains no 'rules'. It is devised as a positive guide to good conduct.

4.04 The statement of the ARCUK should be read in conjunction with the Code of Conduct of the RIBA. Certain activities which are permissible under the ARCUK guide Conduct and Discipline are prohibited by the RIBA Code of Conduct. It is important that RIBA members should be aware of the differences between the two Codes.

4.05 The Standard of Conduct for Architects lays down four requirements to which a registered person is subject. The first concerns information being given by the architect concerning his services; the second concerns the engagement of the architect; the third concerns the declaration of interest; and the fourth concerns conflict of interest.

4.06 In addition to the *Standard of Conduct for Architects*, and the *Explanatory Memorandum*, the ARCUK also issues an occasional notice *Advice to Architects*, which offers practical advice on the interpretation of its principles and rules.

5 The RIBA Code of Conduct

5.01 The RIBA Code of Conduct which came into effect in January 1981 made fundamental changes in the Institute's traditional attitude towards professional conduct. It removed the restrictions on carrying on the business of trading in land or buildings, or as property developers, auctioneers, estate agents or contractors, sub-contractors, manufacturers or suppliers in or to the construction industry. It permitted members to negotiate fees with potential clients and abandoned the mandatory minimum fee system. It removed the ban on practising in the form of a limited liability company, it extended the permitted means by which an architect might bring himself to the notice of potential clients and this was further broadened in subsequent revisions. The Rules and Notes concerning the application of the Principles have been frequently amended since the introduction of the Code, most recently: September 1989.

5.02 The Code of Conduct recognizes the needs of current practice and changing circumstances. It establishes three principles as the core of professionalism and a series of rules for their interpretation, supported by a number of guidance notes.

Principle One

The Principle 1.0
A member shall faithfully carry out the duties which he undertakes. He shall also have a proper regard for the interests both of those who commission and those who may be expected to use or enjoy the product of his work.

Note 1.0.1
A member is advised before undertaking or continuing with any work to arrange that his resources are adequate and properly directed to carry it out

Note 1.0.2
A student member who undertakes a commission is advised to seek guidance from an architect

Rule 1.1
A member shall when making an engagement, whether by an agreement for professional services by a contract of employment or by a contract for the supply of services of goods, have defined beyond reasonable doubt and recorded the terms of the engagement including the scope of the service, the allocation of responsibilities and any limitation of liability, the method of calculation of remuneration and the provision for termination.

Note 1.1.1
A member proposing or making an agreement for an engagement as an independent consulting architect should make use of the RIBA Architect's Appointment to define the terms of engagement

Rule 1.2
A member shall arrange that the work of his office and any branch office insofar as it relates to architecture is under the control of an architect.

Rule 1.3
A member shall not sub-commission or sub-let work without the prior agreement of his client nor without defining the changes in the responsibilities of those concerned.

Rule 1.4
A member shall act impartially in all cases in which he is acting between parties. Where he has responsibilities as architect under a building contract; or is similarly acting between the parties, he shall interpret the conditions of such contract with fairness and impartiality.

Principle Two

The Principle 2.0
A member shall avoid actions and situations inconsistent with his professional obligations or likely to raise doubts about his integrity.

Rule 2.1
A member shall declare to any prospective client any business interest the existence of which, if not so declared, would or might be likely to raise doubts about his integrity by reason of an actual or apparent connection with or effect upon his engagement.

Note 2.1.1
This Rule requires the prior disclosure of relevant business interests which could not be inferred from the description of the services offered. If such interests arise during the currency of the engagement Rule 2.8 applies

Rule 2.2
A member shall not simultaneously practise as, or purport to be, an independent consulting architect and engage in or have as a partner or co-director a person who, whether or not in a separate firm, engages in any of the following:

the business of trading in land or buildings; or of property developers, auctioneers, or house or estate agents; or of contractors, sub-contractors, manufacturers or suppliers in or to the building industry

unless he is able to demonstrate that the combination would not prevent his compliance with the Principles of this Code and the Rules that apply to his circumstances.

Rule 2.3
A member shall not and shall not purport to carry out the independent functions of an architect or any similar independent functions in relation to a contract in which he or his employer is the contractor.

Note 2.3.1
Where the client of a member providing a contracting service requires independent advice on quality and budgetary control the member should inform the client of his right to appoint another architect to act as his professional adviser and agent

Rule 2.4
A member shall ensure that whenever he offers or takes part in offering a service combining consulting services with contracting services the consulting component is not represented as independent of the combined service.

Rule 2.5
A member shall not have or take as a partner or co-director in his firm any person who is disqualified for registration by reason of the fact that his name has been removed from the Register under Section 7 of the Architects (Registration) Act 1931; any person disqualified for membership of the RIBA by reason of expulsion under Byelaw 5.1; any person disqualified for membership of another professional institution by reason of expulsion under the relevant disciplinary regulations, unless the RIBA otherwise allows.

Rule 2.6
A member shall not take discounts, commissions or gifts as an inducement to show favour to any person or body; nor shall he recommend or allow his name to be used as recommending any service or product in advertisements.

Note 2.6.1
This Rule does not prevent a member who is a contractor from accepting the trade and cash discounts customarily allowed by manufacturers or suppliers

Rule 2.7
A member shall not improperly influence the granting of planning consents or statutory approvals.

Rule 2.8
A member who in circumstances not specifically covered in these Rules finds that his interests whether professional or personal conflict so as to risk a breach of this Principle shall, as the circumstances may require, either withdraw from the situation or remove the source of conflict or declare it and obtain the agreement of the parties concerned to the continuance of his engagement.

Note 2.8.1
An example of the application of this Rule is that a member who has been appointed assessor for any competition shall not subsequently act in any other capacity for the work except that he may act as arbitrator in any dispute between the promoters and the selected architect or as consultant where that appointment was arranged before his appointment as assessor

Note 2.8.2
A member appointed to give expert advice shall not subsequently allow his terms of reference to be extended into those of an arbitrator

Note 2.8.3
It should be noted that the RIBA may, depending on the circumstances, be one of the parties concerned. For example, where in any case a member is under pressure to act in a way which would bring him into non-compliance with the Code, in addition to any other declarations which it may be appropriate to make, he should declare the facts to the RIBA

Rule 2.9
A member shall have a proper regard for the professional obligations and qualifications of those from whom he receives or to whom he gives authority, responsibility or employment, or with whom he is professionally associated. A member who employs architects shall define their conditions of employment*, authority, responsibility and liability

Note 2.9.11
Upholding this Rule requires that

(a) a member enables the architects he employs to exercise their professional skills and provides them with opportunities to accept progressively greater delegated authority and responsibility in accordance with their ability and experience.

(b) a member acknowledges the contribution and responsibilities of the architects he employs by giving them credit in any publications, exhibitions, etc.

(c) a member permits the architects he employs to engage in sparetime practice and to enter architectural competitions and that the employee does not do so without the knowledge of his employer, and that he acts in accordance with Rule 2.8

* *The RIBA publishes a Guide to Employment Practice which may be of use to employers and to those who are employed*

(d) a member encourages the architects he employs to maintain and advance their competence by participating in continuing professional development and allows them to have reasonable time off to participate in the affairs of the profession;

(e) a member who employs students cooperates with the RIBA and schools of architecture in the practical training scheme; provides as varied experience as possible compatible with his professional responsibilities, and allows student employees to take reasonable time off for academic purposes leading to the qualifying examinations.

Rule 2.10
A member shall conform with the Members' Rules for Clients' Accounts from time-to-time in force.

Note 2 10 1
The Members' Rules for Clients' Accounts are reproduced on pages 13 and 14 hereof.

Principle Three

The Principle 3.0
A member shall rely only on ability and achievement as the basis for his advancement.

Note 3 0 1
Members are encouraged to participate by means of RIBA regional and branch activities, amenity societies and other bodies concerned with the quality of the environment, in local and national affairs concerning the environment and to criticize what they believe to be harmful, shoddy or inappropriate provided that criticism is not malicious or contrary to any Rule under this Principle.

Rule 3.1
A member shall not give discounts, commissions, gifts or other inducements for the introduction of clients or of work.

Note 3 1 1
This Rule does not prevent a member who is a contractor from giving the trade and cash discounts customarily allowed by manufacturers or suppliers.

Rule 3.2
A member who is offering services as an independent consulting architect shall not quote a fee without having received from the prospective client an invitation to do so and sufficient information to enable the member to know the nature and scope of the project and the services required.

Rule 3.3
A member who is offering services as an independent consulting architect shall not revise a fee quotation to take account of the fee quoted by another architect for the same service.

Rule 3.4
A member shall not attempt to oust another architect from an engagement.

Note 3 4 1
(a) Subject to these Rules a member may enter into negotiation with a prospective client on the fee basis for that member's services provided that, in compliance with Rule 1 1 the other terms of engagement are properly defined.

(b) Any member who, in the course of such negotiation, having regard to the objects of the RIBA and Principle 1 of this Code, is unwilling or unable to accept a fee basis proposed by a prospective client, should comply with Rule 2 8 by withdrawing from the negotiation, and declare the facts to the RIBA.

(c) A member who is concerned with the appointment of another as an independent consulting architect should respect the obligations of that member under these Rules.

Rule 3.5
A member on being approached to undertake work upon which he knows, or can ascertain by reasonable inquiry, that another architect has an engagement with the same client shall notify the fact to such architect.

Note 3 5 1
A member who is engaged to give an opinion on the work of another architect should notify the fact to that architect unless it can be shown to be prejudicial to prospective litigation to do so.

Rule 3.6
A member may make his availability and experience known by any means provided that the information given is in substance and in presentation factual, relevant and – neither misleading nor unfair to others – nor otherwise discreditable to the profession.

Note 3 6 1
A member may commission an external public relations consultant or similarly designated person to carry out all or any aspect of his public relations policy provided that he furnishes the RIBA with a written declaration signed by the appointed person that he has received and read Byelaw 5, this Code and the Practice Note entitled 'Members and public relations' In the declaration the appointed person must acknowledge that he will be in breach of contract with his client if any action of his brings the latter into breach of the Byelaws or any Rule of this Code at any time.

Rule 3.7
A member shall not enter any architectural competition which the RIBA has declared to be unacceptable.

Members' Rules for Clients' Accounts

Introduction

Members will see that these Rules require them (a) to keep full books of account recording all money received from and spent for clients, and, (b) in addition to keep clients money in a separate Clients bank account, from which no more may be drawn on the account of a particular client than is held on his behalf.

Handling clients money is an extra service, and consideration should be given to making the agreement in respect of handling and making payments of interest.

The Rules

1   Members shall keep properly written up books of Account

    (a) When a member makes any disbursement on behalf of a client he shall maintain a sufficient record thereof to be able to produce clear and understandable particulars of all disbursements for any client

    (b) When a member receives money belonging to any client the following rules shall also apply

2   In the event that a member receives any money belonging to any client he shall open a ledger account in the name of each such client showing office and client receipts and payments; in the event of a member's having more than one commission from any client it is open to him to deal with each commission on a separate ledger account according with the requirements of these rules.

3   A member receiving money belonging to clients must open a client's account or clients' accounts at a branch of any bank in the United Kingdom in his name or in the name of the relevant practice. The title of such an account must contain the word "client" or "clients". Such accounts may be either current accounts or deposit accounts

4   Members shall pay any money they receive (in whatever form) which belongs to any client into a clients account or clients accounts as soon as is practicable, save that this rule shall not apply

    (a) to money being paid without delay to a third party in the ordinary course of business,

    (b) when the client has authorised the member in writing not to pay the money into the Clients Account, provided that it is dealt with in accordance with the client's instructions

Money received and paid under 4 must be recorded in the member's books of account in conformity with 1

No money other than that specified by this Rule or paid into the account under Rule 8 or 9 below shall be paid into any clients account

5   Money may be withdrawn from a client's account

    (a) if required for a payment to or on behalf of a client

    (b) to make a payment of or to account of a debt due to the member by a client and/or to reimburse a member for money spent on behalf of a client. In the event that money is withdrawn in respect of the member's fees and/or value added tax payable in respect of these fees the member must notify the client in writing of the amount claimed before transferring relevant money from the clients account

    (c) to make a payment on the client's written authority.

Provided that in no case shall more money be withdrawn under this rule than is shown in the members' books of account to be held on behalf of the relevant client

6   Members keeping a clients account or clients accounts shall at intervals of not more than three calendar months (or alternatively on each quarter day) balance the Clients Cash Book and Clients Ledger with the relevant bank statements and shall retain the reconciliation statement prepared at the date of each balance for a period of not less than eighteen months

7   Any member may be required under the Disciplinary Procedures to produce audit certificates in respect of clients accounts forthwith at any time. Such certificates must be signed by a person who is a member of one of the following bodies

    (a) The Institute of Chartered Accountants in England and Wales

    (b) The Institute of Chartered Accountants of Scotland

    (c) The Association of Certified and Corporate Accountants

    (d) The Institute of Chartered Accountants in Ireland

8   If any money is paid into or withdrawn from a clients account erroneously the member shall forthwith withdraw or pay in (as the case may be) such money as is necessary to restore the account to its proper condition and shall make a record in the Journal (i e a book of account) stating the date the mistake was made, the accounts to which the mistake relates and the amount of money involved. An example of an erroneous payment in is a cheque in settlement of a members fees, which belong to the member An example of an erroneous withdrawal is making a payment from the clients account against a cheque which is not paid by bankers

9   In the event that a member receives money which in part belongs to a client and which in part does not belong to a client and who wishes to pay into a single account, he shall pay the money into a clients account and shall immediately thereafter withdraw such part as does not belong to the client from the clients account and pay it into an appropriate account

Additional Points

Members are reminded that in some circumstances there are statutory requirements which relate to the keeping of accounts, for example under *Estate Agents Act 1979*

Members are reminded that there may be a requirement to pay interest on money held as an agent under the rule in *Brown v The Commissioners of Inland Revenue* (1965) AC 244 or otherwise. In these circumstances if they are holding money for any length of time or are holding a substantial amount of money even for a short time, members should consider placing it in a clients deposit account. The accounting implications of the *Brown* case should also be borne in mind, i e that interest earned on a single account may have to be apportioned between several clients

Approved by the Council, March 1986

5.03 Principle 1 concerns the work of the architect in relation to both the client and the users of the buildings. It requires an agreement of service of fees to be made before commencement; it requires the work to be carried out under the control of an architect; it prevents the sub-letting of work without agreement; and it maintains the traditional impartiality of the architect in the carrying out of his work.

5.04 Principle 2 is directed towards the avoidance of inconsistencies or doubts of integrity in the work of the architect. It requires the architect to declare the existence of anything likely to raise doubts about his integrity; it prohibits simultaneous practice as an independent consultant and engagement in one of the previously restricted businesses, unless it can be shown that the two are compatible and that this is so declared. It prohibits simultaneous functions of contracting and the independent practice of architecture; it prohibits partnership with a disqualified person; it prohibits the taking of bribes; it prohibits the improper influencing of statutory approvals; it requires the architect to notify the client of anything likely to breach this principle and if so to either withdraw from the engagement or to obtain the agreement of the client for the continuation of the commission; it requires the member to have proper regard for the status of the architect to whom he gives, or from whom he receives, authority.

5.05 Principle 3 endeavours to ensure that advancement of a member is on the basis of ability and achievement alone. It prohibits the giving of discounts for the introduction of work; it requires fees to be quoted only when the nature of the work is known; it prohibits fee auctions; it prohibits the supplanting of another architect; it requires a member to notify any other architect who may have previously been engaged upon the project; it allows most forms of advertising of services provided that it is not misleading, unfair, or discreditable to the profession; and it restricts competition entries to those approved by RIBA regulations.

29

Professional conduct in Scotland

GEORGE BURNET

1 Introduction

1.01 An architect practising in Scotland can find himself subject to three Codes of Conduct – the RIAS Code, the RIBA Code, and the Code issued by ARCUK – and hopefully a 'super' Code will be published in due course combining the best features of all three. Unfortunately, this has not been found possible so far, but at least there has been some slight improvement inasmuch as, although there are still three Codes, they all now reflect modern attitudes and thinking, and generally speaking permit or forbid the same course of conduct. In particular the RIAS and the RIBA Codes both reflect the abolition, at government insistence, of fee scales – mandatory or otherwise – and recognize the existence of fee competition which is becoming more and more the norm.

1.02 In method of presentation the RIAS and the RIBA Codes are still widely different, and this must tend to confuse the layman and possibly also, at times, members of the architectural profession. It should still be possible for the RIAS and the RIBA to have identical Codes of Conduct, and both bodies must surely work towards this goal. The existence of a separate RIAS Code stems from the fact that the RIAS is rightly proud of the fact that it is a body with its own Royal Charter formed in 1916, at a time when the voice of the RIBA was seldom heard in Scotland and when many architects practising in that country belonged only to the RIAS and not to the RIBA. Times have changed, and although the RIBA has delegated practically all its functions in Scotland to the RIAS, it has tended to retain under its own control the procedure for disciplining its members: this has meant that contrary to the hopes and aspirations voiced in earlier editions, occasions do arise when an architect can be 'tried' twice for the same offence – once under the RIBA disciplinary proceedings and again under the RIAS procedure.

1.03 While at first glance this may well seem contrary to the basic principle of natural justice, it must be pointed out that if an architect chooses to belong to both the RIBA and the RIAS (to neither of which he need belong to practise as an architect), he must be assumed to be agreeing to subject himself to the Codes of both organizations, and if transgressing these Codes, must run the risk of being disciplined separately by both. It must always be remembered that the RIAS can discipline only its own members and cannot, therefore, take action against a member of the RIBA practising in Scotland, unless such a member also belongs to the RIAS; nor, of course, can it proceed against a member under any provision of the RIBA Code. At the present time the majority of architects practising in Scotland belong to both organizations, although there is a growing tendency among newly qualified architects to seek membership of the RIAS.

2 The RIAS Code

2.01 The current RIAS Code of Conduct was approved by the members of the Royal Incorporation at a general meeting held in March 1982, and took effect on 1 July 1982. It is, in effect, not so much a Code as a Statement of Professional Conduct that consists solely of one paragraph: 'A Member shall be mindful of the Declaration signed by him upon his election, and in particular of his responsibility for upholding the repute of the Royal Incorporation as a professional body and of his fellow Members as individuals. Dishonouring of the Declaration shall be held to constitute unprofessional conduct, and as such will be dealt with by Council.'

2.02 The Declaration referred to in the Statement is in the following terms: 'I declare that I have read the Charter and By-Law of the said Incorporation and the By-Laws of my Chapter, and will be governed and bound thereby, and will submit myself to every part thereof and to any alterations thereof which may hereafter be made until I have ceased to be a member; and that by every lawful means in my power I will advance the interests and objects of the said Incorporation.'

2.03 The preamble to the Statement makes it clear that an architect who contravenes the declaration renders himself liable in terms of the by-laws to reprimand, suspension, or expulsion. The same by-laws also authorize the Council of the RIAS to issue from time to time intimations defining action to be taken on current matters of professional conduct, and these intimations, in practical terms, point an architect in the direction in which he should be going.

3 Intimations

3.01 The following are the intimations published by the Council simultaneously with the adoption of the Statement of Professional Conduct:

1. 'A Member in practice shall observe the provisions for Conduct and Discipline adopted by ARCUK on 17 June 1981.'

While there is no similar Principle or Rule (as they are called) in the RIBA Code, it may be compared with Rule 2.5 interpreting Principle 2 of that Code. Membership of ARCUK is one of the qualifications required for election to Associate or Fellowship of the RIAS.

2. 'If a Member engages in any activity concurrent or otherwise with that as architect, he shall at all times act in compliance with the spirit of the Declaration.'

This intimation may be compared with Rule 2.2 of the RIBA Code. Although not specific in its terms, it is presumably intended to achieve the same result as the RIBA Rule – to ensure that if an architect is in fact acting as a house agent or a property developer, for example, this role is subordinate to his professions as an architect and in the spirit of the overriding Declaration.

3. 'A Member shall not in his capacity as an architect accept any trade or other discounts. However, this does not prohibit receipt by a member of the discounts which are customary and normal when engaged in commercial activities otherwise than as an architect.'

This is similar to Rule 3.1 to Principle 3 of the RIBA Code and recognizes the accepted custom in the contracting industry that trade and cash discounts are frequently allowed by manufacturers or suppliers.

4. 'If a Member wishes to make approaches to individuals and organizations or make public display of his work or advertise his services in any other way, he should have care to observe the spirit of the Declaration signed by each member upon election.'

This intimation corresponds to Rule 3.6 of Principle 3 of the RIBA Code and reflects the freedom to advertise now permitted to the profession. In the last few years all professions – not least the architectural profession – have begun to advertise their services and the boundary between an acceptable and an unacceptable advertisement is often difficult to define.

5. 'If a Member at any stage attempts to supplant another architect by any means, he may be found by Council to have contravened the Declaration.'

This intimation is directly comparable to Rule 3.14 to Principle 3 of the RIBA Code, and the prohibition against an attempt to supplant another architect remains as adamant as ever.

6. 'A Member having any matter of complaint or protest against another member of the profession must in the first instance bring the matter before the Council of the Incorporation through his own Chapter, and must on no account make any other protest.'

Strangely enough, there is no comparable principle to this intimation in the RIBA Code, although it has always found a place in Codes of Conduct issued by the RIAS. Its absence from the RIBA Code is surprising, as it provides a dignified way of resolving disputes between architects, and its value has been proved on many occasions in the history of the RIAS.

7. 'If a Member undertakes any architectural commission he shall arrange for the architectural work on that commission to be under the control of an architect.'

This intimation is the equivalent of Rule 1.2 to Principle 1 of the RIBA Code. It is, however, more widely expressed, although clearly covering the limited situations envisaged by the RIBA rule.

8. 'If a Member is invited or instructed to proceed with work upon which he knows or which he can ascertain by reasonable enquiry that another architect has been engaged by the same client, he shall notify the fact to such artefact.'

Rule 3.5 to Principle 3 of the RIBA Code is identical to this intimation. Until recently it was fairly generally understood that an architect approached by a client who had previously employed another architect should not accept that client's instructions until satisfied that fees due to the first architect had been paid in full. It seems clear, in fact, that there is no such duty and that all the second architect is required to do is to send a simple notification to the original architect informing him of his appointment, and thereafter no further action is required.

9. 'A Member shall have regard to the RIAS Architect's Appointment.'

This intimation is similar to Rule 1.1.1 to Principle 1 of the RIBA Code.

10. 'A Member offering services as an independent consulting architect shall not quote a fee without having received from the prospective client an invitation to do so, and sufficient information to enable the member to know the nature and scope of the project and the services required.'

11. 'A Member offering services as an independent consulting architect shall not revise a fee quotation to take account of the fee quoted by another architect for the same service.'

These two intimations which can conveniently be considered together are in similar terms to Rules 3.2 and 3.3 to Principle 3 of the RIBA Code. They mark the end of the mandatory fee scales which were abolished by both the RIAS and the RIBA in 1982. Both organizations still publish *recommended* fee scales and while in practice these may be used as 'a bench mark' in many sectors fees are frequently negotiated down from these levels. The clear instruction contained in Intimation 11 ensures that in no circumstances may any form of 'auction' take place after an architect has submitted his quotation to his potential client.

12. 'A Member handling money belonging to a client shall be required to comply with the Client Account Rules approved by the Council on 29 November 1989 and any amendments thereto which may be subsequently approved by the Council.'

This important intimation corresponds with Rule 2.10 of Principle 2 of the RIBA Code. Both the RIAS and the RIBA (whose Client Account Rules were issued in 1986) have now come to grips with the fact that there are occasions when architects have to handle clients' money (although both organizations advise members to avoid this if possible) and their failure to do this in a business-like and efficient way is undoubtedly a major source of complaint by clients. While the RIAS and the RIBA Client Account Rules are not identical they each lay down a clearly defined Code for dealing with clients' money which must be complied with. The RIBA Rules contain a statement making it clear that a member of the RIBA who is also obliged to follow the Client Account Rules of the RIAS, will be deemed to have satisfied the RIBA Rules if he complies with the Rules of the RIAS.

4 Conclusion

4.01 Whatever merits there may be in a single paragraph statement – and from the point of view of the RIAS Council they are considerable – it does place a firm duty on that Council to ensure that members of the RIAS are kept fully aware of how the Council interprets the Statement and the Declaration by issuing further intimations as and when they are necessary. The recent publication of Intimation 12 and of the Client Account Rules is a clear indication of the Council's determination to do this.

Bibliography

General construction law

Bickford Smith, S. *et al.* (1993) *Butterworths Construction Law Manual*, Butterworths, London
Holyoak, J. (1992) *Negligence in Building Law, Cases and Materials*, Blackwells, Oxford
James, M. (1994) *Construction Law*, Macmillans, Basingstoke
Latham, M. (1994) Constructing the Team: Joint Review of Procurement and Contractual Arrangements in the U.K. Construction Industry Final Report, HMSO, London
O'Reilly, M. (1993) *Principles of Construction Law*, Longmans, Harlow
Uff, J. (1991) *Construction Law* (5th edn), Sweet and Maxwell, London
Wallace, I. N. D. (1994) *Hudson's Building and Engineering Contracts* (11th edn), Sweet and Maxwell, London

General liability: contract and tort

Burns, A. (1994) *The Legal Obligations of the Architect*, Butterworths, London
Dias, R. W. M. (1989) *Clerk and Lindsell on the Law of Torts* (16th edn) (4th Cumulative Supplement 1994), Sweet and Maxwell, London
Guest, A. G. (1989) *Chitty on Contracts* (Supplement 1990), Sweet and Maxwell, London
Jackson, R. and Powell, J. (1992) *Professional Negligence* (3rd edn), Sweet and Maxwell, London
James, R. (1993) *Limitation of Actions*, Tolley, London
Percy, R. A. (1990) *Charlesworth and Percy on Negligence* (8th edn), Sweet and Maxwell, London
Treitel, G. H. (1989) *An Outline of the Law of Contract* (4th edn), Butterworths, London

Architects' professional liability

Burns, A. (1994) *The Legal Obligations of the Architect*, Butterworths, London
Cornes, D. (1994) *Design Liability in the Construction Industry* (4th edn), BSP, Oxford
Cecil, R. (1991) *Professional Liability* (93rd edn), Legal Studies and Services, London
Coombes Davies, M. (1989) *Avoiding Claims*, E. and F. N. Spon, London
Cox, S. and Hamilton, A. (eds) (1991) *Architects' Handbook of Practice Management*, RIBA, London
Hay, S. (1987) *Starting up in Practice*, RIBA, London
Lavers, A. (1992) *A Legal Guide to the Professional Liability of Architects* (2nd edn), RIBA, London
Manjoni, C. and Constructor Legal Services Ltd (1991) *The Legal Responsibilities of Architectural Practices*. Package 2/7 of Professional Studies in British Architectural Practice, RIBA, London
May, S. (1987) *Starting up in Practice*, RIBA, London
Paterson, F. (1991) *Collateral Warranties Explained*, (Supplement 1993) RIBA, London
Sharp, D. (1991) *The Business of Architectural Practice* (2nd edn), BSP, Oxford

Arbitration and dispute resolution

Bernstein, R. (1993) *Handbook of Arbitration Practice* (2nd edn), Sweet and Maxwell, London
Fenn, P. and Gameson, R. (1992) *Construction Conflict, Management and Resolution*, E. and F. N. Spon, London
Stephenson, D. (1993) *Arbitration Practice in Construction Law* (3rd edn), E. and F. N. Spon, London
Timpson, J. (1994) *The Architect in Dispute Resolution*, RIBA, London
Uff, J. and Jones, E. (1990) *International and ICC Arbitration*, Centre of Construction Law, London

Building contract law and contract administration

Birkby, G. and Brough, P. (1993) *Extensions of Time Explained*, RIBA, London
Chappell, D. (1993) *Understanding JCT Standard Building Contracts* (3rd edn), E. and F. N. Spon, London
Chappell, D. and Greenstreet, R. (1989) *Legal and Contractual Procedures for Architects* (3rd edn), Butterworths, London
Chappell, D. and Powell-Smith, V. (1994), *Building Sub-contract Documentation*, BSP, Oxford
Chappell, D. and Powell-Smith, V. (1993) *The JCT Design and Build Contract*, BSP, Oxford
Clamp, H. (1993) *The Shorter Forms of Building Contract* (3rd edn), RIBA, London
Cooke, B. (1992) *Contract Planning and Contractual Procedures* (3rd edn), Macmillan, Basingstoke
Eggleston, B. (1992) *Liquidated Damages and Extensions of Time in Construction Contracts*, BSP, Oxford
Fellows, R. (1995) *1980 JCT Standard Form of Building Contract: Commentary for Students and Practitioners* (3rd edn), Macmillan, Basingstoke
Green, R. (1995) *The Architect's Guide to Running a Job* (5th edn), Butterworths, London
Keating, D. (1995) *Building Contracts* (6th edn), Sweet and Maxwell, London
Lord-Smith, P. (1994) *Avoiding Claims in Building Contracts*, Butterworth-Heinemann, Oxford
Murdoch, J. and Hughes, W. (1992) *Building Contract Law*, Longmans, London

Murdoch, J. and Hughes, W. (1992) *Construction Contracts: Law and Management*, E. and F. N. Spon, London

Potts, K. (1994) *Major Construction Works: Contractual and Financial Management*, Longman, Harlow

Price, J. (1994) *Sub-contracting Under the JCT Standard Format Building Contract*, Macmillan, Basingstoke

Thomas, R. W. (1993) *Construction Contract Claims*, Macmillan, Basingstoke

Turner, D. (1995) *Design and Build Contract Practice* (2nd edn). Longman, Harlow

Copyright

Flint, M. F. (1990) *A User's Guide to Copyright* (3rd edn), Butterworths, London

Laddie, H. L. *et al.* (1991) *The Modern Law of Copyright* (2nd edn), Butterworths, London

Skone James, E. *et al.* (1990) *Copinger and Skone James on Copyright* (13th edn), (Supplement No. 1 1994) Sweet and Maxwell, London

Employment law

Bowers, J. (1994) *Employment Law* (4th edn), Blackstone Press, London

Jefferson, M. (1994) *Employment Law*, Cavendish Publishing, London

Selwyn, N. (1993) *Law of Employment* (8th edn), Butterworths, London

European and EU law

Burr, A. (1993) *European Construction Contracts*, Chancery Wiley, London

Charlesworth, A. and Cullen, H. (1994), *European Community Law*, Pitman, London

Cox, A. (1993) *The Single Market Rules and the Enforcement Regime after 1992*, Earlsgate Press, Birmingham

Geddes, A. (1993) *Public Procurement: A Practical Guide to the UK Regulations and Associated Community Rules*, Sweet and Maxwell, London

Marsh, P. (1994) *Comparative Contract Law: England, Germany, France*, Gower, Aldershot

Land law

Burn, E. H. (1994) *Cheshire and Burn's Modern Law of Real Property* (15th edn), Butterworths, London

Gray, K. J. (1993) *Elements of Land Law* (2nd edn), Butterworths, London

Kenny, P. and Hewitson, R. (1994) *Property Law*, Butterworths, London

Megarry, R. and Thompson, M. (1993) *Megarry's Manual of the Law of Real Property* (7th edn), Sweet and Maxwell, London

Partnership and company law

Abbott, K. (1993) *Company Law* (5th edn), DP Publishing, London

Gower, L. C. B. (1992) *Gower's Principles of Modern Company Law* (5th edn), Sweet and Maxwell, London

Morse, G. (1991) *Partnership Law* (2nd edn), Blackstone Press, London

Morse, G. *et al.* (1995) *Charlesworth's Company Law* (15th edn), Sweet and Maxwell, London

Oliver, M. C. (1994) *Company Law* (12th edn), Pitman, London

Scammell, E. H. and l'Anson Banks, R. C. (1995) *Lindley on Partnership* (17th edn), Sweet and Maxwell, London

Planning and local government law

Bailey, S. (1992) *Cross on Principles of Local Government Law*, Sweet and Maxwell, London

Garner, J. F. (1990) *Law of Sewers and Drains* (2nd edn), Shaw and Sons, London

Greenwood, B. (1992) *Butterworths Planning Law Handbook* (3rd edn), Butterworths, London

Heap, D. (1991) *An Outline of Planning Law* (10th edn), Sweet and Maxwell, London

Moore, V. (1994) *A Practical Approach to Planning Law* (4th edn), Pitman, London

Powell-Smith, V. and Billington, M. J. (1992) *The Building Regulations* (9th edn), BSP, Oxford

Roberts, M. (1995) *Index to the Building Regulations*, HMSO, London

Sauvain, S. (1989) *Highway Law and Practice*, Sweet and Maxwell, London

Stephenson, J. (1993) *Building Regulations Explained* (4th edn), E. and F. N. Spon, London

Telling, A. E. and Duxbury, R. M. C. (1993) *Planning Law and Procedure* (9th edn), Butterworths, London

Table of Statutes and Statutory Instruments

Table of Cases

Index